"A persuasive case for protonarratives in Paul's letters that provides a new framework for reading the letters. I recommend the work enthusiastically."
— GREGORY E. STERLING, Yale Divinity School

"The important controversies concerning 'narrative substructures' in Paul's theology have lacked methodological rigor—until now! Heilig uses his expertise in narratology and text grammar to set this scholarly discussion on a firm footing."
— JOHN M. G. BARCLAY, Durham University

"Christoph Heilig masterfully shows how in the apostle Paul's letters, the Word has become a story; in other words, how Paul's theology is deeply embedded in episodic and grand narratives. . . . A terrific resource for studying Paul and the storied nature of Paul's theology."
— MICHAEL F. BIRD, Ridley College, Melbourne, Australia

"Narrative study in Paul takes a giant step forward with *Paul the Storyteller*. Heilig delivers a brilliant, comprehensive analysis of both explicit and implicit narratives in Paul's letters, providing in-depth research, clear definitions, and numerous examples of the importance of narrative structures for interpreting Paul."
— LYNN H. COHICK, Houston Theological Seminary

"Stories are everywhere, if we have eyes to see and ears to hear. Christoph Heilig's book helps us attune our senses to notice both explicit and implicit storytelling in Paul's letters."
— JAMES MCGRATH, Butler University

"Few Pauline scholars have considered narrative as closely as Christoph Heilig, and those who have will need to reconsider in light of this book. Monumental, penetrating, and utterly compelling, this book is a game-changer."
— CONSTANTINE R. CAMPBELL, Sydney College of Divinity

"Proposing a fresh narratological approach to the question of whether Paul can be considered a storyteller, Heilig points a way forward in an area of study that has been at something of a standstill. This book might well be the start of the second quest for the narratological Paul."
— BRUCE LONGENECKER, Baylor University

"Christoph Heilig masterfully examines the linguistic and metalinguistic factors by which the narrative side of the *Corpus Paulinum* can be meaningfully interpreted. I am particularly pleased with his consistent inclusion of text-grammatical factors."
— HEINRICH VON SIEBENTHAL, Staatsunabhängige Theologische Hochschule Basel

"Christoph Heilig takes the narrative approaches of Richard B. Hays and N. T. Wright and shifts them onto a foundation in narrativity, correcting some missteps and grounding his own exegesis more solidly in linguistics and, thus, in the text. The readings that emerge from Paul's letters, both narratives and implicit narratives, will provide much fuel for future discussion and debate."
— LAURA J. HUNT, University of Wales, Trinity St. David

"Proceeding on a grammatical-narratological methodological footing considerably more meticulous than those in prior narrative approaches to Paul's letters, Christoph Heilig shows that Paul not only refers to implicit stories but also constructs explicit narratives in his epistolary corpus."

—PAUL D. WHEATLEY, University of Notre Dame

"*Paul the Storyteller* not only offers valuable insights into Pauline thought but also abandons the old prejudice that Paul does not tell stories. In so doing, Heilig contributes greatly to Pauline scholarship and also provides biblical scholars with a profound introduction to narratology."

—NILS NEUMANN, Leibniz Universität Hannover

"Even readers who do not share all Heilig's assumptions or conclusions will have much to learn from his sophisticated and cutting-edge engagement with narratological and text-linguistic theory and the new insights into Paul's stories it affords."

—SIMON DÜRR, Pontifical University of St. Thomas Aquinas

"While narrativity in the Gospels has been researched extensively and with a high degree of methodological specialization in recent decades, Paul's letters have received less attention. Christoph Heilig's new book is now devoted to the apostle's explicit and implicit narratives with great expertise."

—UTA POPLUTZ, Bergische Universität Wuppertal

"Heilig has made a significant contribution to the narratological analysis of Pauline epistles through his incorporation of text linguistics, text grammar, and cognitive linguistics. The clarity of his writing and his command of the relevant scholarly discussions make *Paul the Storyteller* a commendable entry point for newcomers or those desiring to keep abreast of new developments."

—STEVEN E. RUNGE, *Biblica*

"I recommend this book as a milestone in narratological research on Paul's letters. It offers profound methodological insights into storytelling and new perspectives on Paul's communicative strategies."

—UTE E. EISEN, Institut für Evangelische Theologie, Justus Liebig Universität Gießen

"Heilig articulates a way forward for analyzing Pauline stories with unmatched rigor, excavating at once both the grammar of narrative and higher-level concepts that drove Paul's storied approach."

—JUSTIN WINZENBURG, Crown College

"This well-argued and accessible monograph is a must-read for everyone wanting to gain a deeper understanding of Paul's letters and theology."

—VOLKER RABENS, Friedrich Schiller Universität Jena

Paul

THE STORYTELLER

A NARRATOLOGICAL APPROACH

CHRISTOPH HEILIG

William B. Eerdmans Publishing Company
Grand Rapids, Michigan

Wm. B. Eerdmans Publishing Co.
4035 Park East Court SE, Grand Rapids, Michigan 49546
www.eerdmans.com

© 2024 Christoph Heilig
All rights reserved
Published 2024

Book design by Leah Luyk

Printed in the United States of America

30 29 28 27 26 25 24   1 2 3 4 5 6 7

ISBN 978-0-8028-7895-3

Library of Congress Cataloging-in-Publication Data

A catalog record for this book is available from the Library of Congress.

*To Prof. Dr. Jörg Frey,
my Doktorvater*

Contents

Preface	ix
List of Abbreviations	xvii
1. Introducing Narrative	1
2. The Grammar of Narration	55
3. Stories in Context	145
4. Fragments of Implicit Protonarratives	200
5. Of Narrative Substructures and Worldview Narratives	310
Bibliography	361
Index of Authors	373
Index of Subjects	376
Index of Scripture and Other Ancient Sources	382

Preface

My research into Paul as a storyteller commenced in 2013, following my master's degree studies at the University of St. Andrews. There, during a New Testament research seminar, we had read N. T. Wright's manuscript for *Paul and the Faithfulness of God* in advance of its publication. While I explored different opportunities for doctoral studies, Prof. Jörg Frey from the University of Zurich showed interest in my work, much to my delight. This culminated in a successful application for funding from the Swiss National Science Foundation. From 2014 onward, I was employed at the University of Zurich to study narrative structures in the letters of Paul. I finished my dissertation in 2018, and it was published in 2020 as *Paulus als Erzähler? Eine narratologische Perspektive auf die Paulusbriefe*, BZNW 237 (Berlin: de Gruyter). It won the Manfred Lautenschlaeger Award for Theological Promise in 2022. During my time in Zurich, Prof. Frey provided me with countless opportunities to establish myself as a researcher and teacher of the New Testament, and I profited immensely from the trust he placed in me and the freedoms I enjoyed as a result. For this reason, the present book is dedicated to him, my *Doktorvater*. Since he was always nudging me to ensure that my theoretical and methodological interests still led me back to interaction with the source text, I hope that this most recent presentation of my thinking on the issue of narratives in Paul will meet with his approval, as it aims to shed light on a great many Pauline texts.

I should say a few words about how the present book relates to my dissertation. At over one thousand pages, my German book is quite an extensive study of the phenomenon of narrativity in Paul's letters. It ended up being so voluminous because I soon recognized that I could not successfully reach my original goal of evaluating the proposals of the "narrative approach" to Paul—associated mainly with Richard B. Hays and N. T. Wright—without first laying a solid theoretical and methodological basis. That then led me to

Preface

shift focus from implicit stories to explicit narratives as a first step, which in turn required extensive analyses of a huge number of Pauline text passages before I could ultimately sketch how this might all affect the larger questions surrounding supposed narrative substructures and worldview narratives. In some sense, my dissertation thus consists of several books: one on the relationship between narratology, text linguistics, and biblical exegesis; another on explicit narratives in Paul; and a third on implicit stories in the apostle's letters and the implications of these findings for the "narrative approach." The fact that my results appeared as a single, bulky study was due to my university's requirement that the doctoral thesis be published in this form for the title to be awarded. However, it was always my intention to eventually present my findings in a more accessible way.

I must emphasize that the book you are currently holding in your hands is not simply a translation of my German dissertation. This can already be seen from the fact that the word count of this English version is a mere 40 percent of the German book. My goal was to offer a more concise presentation of my argument, and I therefore tried to steer away from the goal of exhaustiveness that was important for my dissertation. The aim for this book was to write something that would highlight the main steps of my argument and present what I find to be the most impressive exegetical findings. Still, I wanted to cover the whole thought process that I went through in my German book, which is why the structure of *Paul the Storyteller* follows the outline of my dissertation quite closely. The idea was to concentrate on the most telling examples and to make extensive use of references to my German book for those who want a fuller picture of each phenomenon, including all the messy details and fuzzy borders of categories. When illustrating a certain aspect of Paul's narration, I aimed to provide in footnotes most of the other attestations that I could not discuss in detail in the main text. However, those using this book for research purposes are still encouraged to consult the index of the German version if a passage they are interested in is not included under a heading that would normally seem relevant. Note that I generally tried to distinguish two kinds of references to *Paulus als Erzähler*: if a certain passage is discussed on only one or two pages in the German book, I often reference these pages directly. However, at many points I also refer to whole sections of that earlier publication. In these cases, either the discussion here follows the argument there quite closely over an extended portion of the text, or it was important to me to highlight that the Pauline passage in question had been analyzed by me in a very specific context. My hope is that these repeated references to important chapters and sections of the German book

Preface

will be of help to those who primarily want to use this book as a key to my more extensive German publication. It seemed to me that they would be served better with such references to the relevant sections and subsections than with page ranges to isolated portions of that book. Note that my BZNW volume was published in Open Access and can be downloaded without any costs from the de Gruyter website. In times when competency in German as a research language in biblical studies is becoming less and less a matter of course, I hope that the present book will help many to more easily access my more extensive German research on the topic.

    That being said, I also want to emphasize that *Paul the Storyteller* is not simply a shortened or watered-down English version of *Paulus als Erzähler*. Admittedly, there is at least some truth to the latter (mis)understanding in that I indeed aimed at avoiding unnecessarily technical language. In my opinion, the apostle Paul is one of the most successful storytellers in human history. I thus hope that this book will also be informative for scholars and even laypeople who are interested in narrativity but who do not know Koine Greek. For this reason, I usually give translations for both Greek texts that I quote (at least in the main body of the text) and quotations from non-English secondary literature. While my book should not be used as an introduction to narratology (something that unfortunately has happened to some other books that deal with the intersection between narratology and biblical exegesis), I have tried to introduce the key narratological concepts that I am working with in chapter 1. Note that I did not deem it helpful to add cross-references every time I reference one of those concepts. Therefore, if, for example, you come across the statement that Paul narrates "unreliably" in a certain passage and you are uncertain about what this means, I suggest you consult chapter 1 for definitions and the subject index to find other relevant passages. By contrast, I did make extensive use of cross-references to help readers navigate between different portions of this book whenever a Pauline passage is discussed at different places because more than one narratological category seemed relevant. Despite all these attempts to make the book as accessible as possible, I am aware that it remains very dense. And at times, fully grasping the nuances of my arguments may require deeper familiarity with discourses that space constraints allow me to only touch upon here. In this sense, while I strive to present my case as clearly and accessibly as possible in this volume, I recognize that some readers may find it helpful to turn to my more detailed German-language publication for additional context and elaboration on certain points. I am aware that this is a compromise that may leave some readers unsatisfied. However, I still think it is a valuable

Preface

experiment in that we need to explore different ways in which we can ensure that research output becomes distributed effectively in a rapidly changing academic landscape.

Similarly, I must nuance the conception that this book is "merely" a summary of my German book. While I am confident that all the main points from my dissertation also appear in this book, the reverse is not true. I did not set out to simply abbreviate my German book. Rather, I returned to the subject anew, revisiting all the twists and turns of my argument, scrutinizing more closely those Pauline passages that seemed particularly important with respect to my thesis, and taking into account much more secondary literature while evaluating my initial results in the process of writing this English book. I point this out because this may not be evident from the surface of the text, given that I generally tried to keep references to the secondary literature to a minimum in order to not further clutter the pages with footnotes. This means that in many cases I was able to add much more nuance to my initial analyses, and sometimes I even felt a need to revise the assessment in my dissertation more substantially (in which case I tried to indicate that). If you want to know my thoughts on a Pauline passage, you may find more details (such as discussions of syntactical problems or references to ancient parallels) in the German book, but the interpretation that I offer here more closely represents my definitive thinking (so far) about the text in question. Hence, I trust that even the very few people who have read the whole of my German book will find a lot of new material in this book.

All this being said, I also want to address those readers who do not care about the relationship between the present book and my earlier German work, who simply come to this book because they find the topic interesting and would like to learn more about it. To you I apologize for the lengthy remarks so far, and I want to broadly indicate why I am confident that I have made an important argument in this book. If you are interested in a Pauline passage that involves events of any kind—which, let's be honest, covers a pretty wide territory—you will find the discussions in this book highly relevant to those specific verses. For as I try to demonstrate, explicit miniature stories and closely associated phenomena—something like implicit "almost stories"—are indeed ubiquitous in Paul's letters. Note that this does not imply that, in all these cases, the narratological categories that I employ will turn out to be vital for you to interpret these textual units correctly. This is because, as I will emphasize repeatedly, narratology offers a set of descriptive tools that have a heuristic function and that, as such, only point to aspects of the text that are merely potentially, not necessarily, relevant with respect to establishing the text's meaning. However, I am hopeful that the examples I discuss in more detail do demonstrate that at countless points Paul's talk about events of all kinds is indeed significantly illuminated if we analyze it through a narratological lens, shedding new light on common and fundamental discourses within Pauline studies. Despite the fact that this book makes use of some technical jargon, I hope that Pauline exegetes in general will use it to see whether they can learn something for their own work, including on passages that might at first not seem to be prototypical narratives. I hope that awareness will grow in the discipline regarding what narratives actually are, how omnipresent they are in early Christian texts, and how immensely we will profit when we describe these phenomena within the conceptual (and terminological) framework established in narratology. So far, narratology seems to be regarded by too many biblical exegetes as an obscure structuralist aberration at worst or a tool of "synchronic exegesis" at best.

I want to emphasize for interested readers of all kinds that this book is meant not simply to collect various observations but to advance a very specific thesis, namely, that the so-called narrative approach to Paul does in fact deserve our full attention. Discussion of narrative structures in Paul's letters is not simply a passing fad, one that may already seem somewhat outdated given the many new contexts within which we supposedly must approach Paul to be able to understand what he truly meant. Explicit stories are a vital part of his communication strategy and, given everything we know about narrativity and human interaction, this finding thus deserves our careful attention if indeed our goal is to understand the texts that have been handed down to us under the apostle's name. Moreover, it is exactly this focus on strictly defined phenomena, which can be identified and described in a very empirical way, that leads us into the territory of implicit narratives—including what Richard B. Hays has termed narrative substructures and the worldview narratives that N. T. Wright has proposed. While I am not convinced by the way these scholars justify their focus on these implicit narrative elements, and while I remain skeptical about some of their theses, I have come to the conviction that from a narratological and text linguistic perspective it can be shown that they have indeed identified fundamental dynamics at play in Paul's letter writing. In a certain sense, this whole book can thus be read as replacing what appear as mere proposals in the writings of these authors with a detailed case that justifies their general approach to the Pauline texts. As I see it, this argument is structured in a way that is very strict, which makes the result all the more convincing. Moreover, in my view

Preface

the evidence that I encountered along the way is unusually comprehensive. I am very much looking forward to seeing this book's thesis scrutinized—especially by those who so far have not been convinced by proponents of the narrative approach to Paul.

When I was writing the preface for my last book—*The Apostle and the Empire*, published by Eerdmans in 2022—I did so in a situation of great uncertainty with respect to my own future in academia, and I used the opportunity to draw attention to the insecurities (and injustices) that most early career researchers face. I was heartened by the positive feedback that I received in that regard, though I must also confess that I can see few signs of systemic changes pointing in the right direction. With respect to myself, at least, I am happy to report that I have found an opportunity to continue my research—including my research on early Christian narratives—for the next couple of years. I received funding from the (modestly named) Elite Bavaria Network to establish a research group at the University of Munich, integrated into the Faculty of Protestant Theology and associated with the International Doctoral Program in Philology, that will study the topic of narrative perspective (or focalization) in early Christian texts. I am incredibly grateful for this opportunity. My Habilitation thesis—which would not have been possible without Prof. Moisés Mayordomo—sketches how this parameter of narrative perspective is significant for interpreting various canonical and noncanonical texts from that milieu. It was submitted to the Faculty of Theology at the University of Basel in the spring of 2024, and I am currently preparing it for publication. You will find some foreshadowings of the chapter on Paul in this current book. But I do not just want to preview my own forthcoming work here. I am also particularly happy to be able to report that as a consequence of this research funding two more early career researchers are currently applying narratological tools to early Christian narratives. Triantafillos Kantartzis is focusing on apocryphal literature (especially the Gospel of Nicodemus) and Dr. Ellen Howard is scrutinizing Christ narratives—in Paul! I can thus announce here that very exciting research on Paul as a storyteller is already in the works. You can find more details about our project on our webpage (http://www.early-christian-narratives.com) and follow us on Twitter/X for updates (@EarlyNarratives).

Last, I want to close by creating another link to my last Eerdmans book. In its last chapter, I discussed advancements in the digital humanities as holding promise for our discipline as well as challenging some prevailing assumptions, methods, and results. How much has changed in these two years given the progress in the realm of large language models (LLMs), known

Preface

to the public especially due to ChatGPT becoming available in November 2022, just one month after my comments on the digital humanities were published! Whole books can (and should!) be written on the new challenges for biblical studies in particular but also for the humanities in general that have become manifest or at least foreseeable since then. Any attempt to address this complex issue here would inevitably not do justice to the matter. Yet, it seems important to at least mention the elephant in the room, especially because I drew attention to the digital humanities in my last book. Thus, I want to at least invite you to keep the nagging questions that the advent of powerful LLMs have raised in the back of your mind while you read this book. What does this book contain that an LLM cannot or has not yet come up with? How might such a book look in a couple of years? Would it be a book? What can we still learn from Paul's stories? What must we still know about them? And how do we still need to approach them to benefit from them in the present age?

Ulm/Munich
May 1, 2024

Abbreviations

AGG	Siebenthal, Heinrich von. *Ancient Greek Grammar for the Study of the New Testament*. Oxford: Lang, 2019
BDAG	Danker, Frederick W., Walter Bauer, William F. Arndt, and F. Wilbur Gingrich. *Greek-English Lexicon of the New Testament and Other Early Christian Literature*. 3rd ed. Chicago: University of Chicago Press, 2000. (Numbers refer to the entries of the digital version of BibleWorks.)
BDF	Blass, Friedrich, Albert Debrunner, and Robert W. Funk. *A Greek Grammar of the New Testament and Other Early Christian Literature*. Chicago: University of Chicago Press, 1961
BECNT	Baker Exegetical Commentary on the New Testament
BGU	*Aegyptische Urkunden aus den Königlichen Staatlichen Museen zu Berlin, Griechische Urkunden*. 15 vols. Berlin: Weidmann, 1895–1937
BNTC	Black's New Testament Commentaries
BTS	Biblical Tools and Studies
BZNW	Beihefte zur Zeitschrift für die neutestamentliche Wissenschaft
CEV	Contemporary English Version
CGCG	Emde Boas, Evert van, Albert Rijksbaron, Luuk Huitink, and Mathieu de Bakker. *The Cambridge Grammar of Classical Greek*. Cambridge: Cambridge University Press, 2019
Duden	*Duden, die Grammatik: Unentbehrlich für richtiges Deutsch*. Edited by Angelika Wöllstein with Kathrin Kunkel-Razum, Franziska Münzberg, and Saskia Ripp. 9th ed. Berlin: Dudenverlag, 2016
EC	*Early Christianity*
EKKNT	Evangelisch-katholischer Kommentar zum Neuen Testament
FRLANT	Forschungen zur Religion und Literatur des Alten und Neuen Testaments

Abbreviations

GGNT	Siebenthal, Heinrich von. *Griechische Grammatik zum Neuen Testament: Neubearbeitung und Erweiterung der Grammatik Hoffmann / von Siebenthal.* Gießen: Brunnen, 2011
HThKNT	Herders Theologischer Kommentar zum Neuen Testament
JSNTSup	Journal for the Study of the New Testament Supplement Series
JTS	*Journal of Theological Studies*
KJV	King James Version
L&N	Louw, Johannes P., and Eugene A. Nida, eds. *Greek-English Lexicon of the New Testament: Based on Semantic Domains.* 2nd ed. New York: United Bible Societies, 1989
LNTS	The Library of New Testament Studies
LSJ	Liddell, Henry G., and Robert Scott. *A Greek-English Lexicon.* Revised and supplemented by H. S. Jones with the help of von R. McKenzie. 9th rev. ed. Oxford: Clarendon, 1996. (Numbers refer to the entries of the online version: http://stephanus.tlg.uci.edu/lsj/.)
Menge	Bibelübersetzung Hermann Menge
MSG	The Message
NA[28]	*Novum Testamentum Graece,* Nestle-Aland, 28th ed.
Neot	*Neotestamentica*
NET	New English Translation
NGÜ	Neue Genfer Übersetzung
NICNT	New International Commentary on the New Testament
NIV	New International Version
NPNF[1]	*The Nicene and Post-Nicene Fathers,* Series 1. Edited by Philip Schaff. 1886–1889. 14 vols. Repr., Peabody, MA: Hendrickson, 1994
NTOA	Novum Testamentum et Orbis Antiquus
NTS	*New Testament Studies*
SBLDS	Society of Biblical Literature Dissertation Series
SBS	Stuttgarter Bibelstudien
SCS	Septuagint and Cognate Studies
SJT	*Scottish Journal of Theology*
SUNT	Studien zur Umwelt des Neuen Testaments
TGV	Today's Greek Version
TWNT	*Theologisches Wörterbuch zum Neuen Testament.* Edited by Gerhard Kittel and Gerhard Friedrich. Stuttgart, 1932–1979
VF	*Verkündigung und Forschung*
WUNT	Wissenschaftliche Untersuchungen zum Neuen Testament

1. Introducing Narrative

Narrativity in the "Narrative Approach"

One of the major controversies that have divided recent academic study of the letters of the apostle Paul pertains to the concept of narrative. On the one hand, some argue it is not meaningful to speak of "narratives" in connection with Paul's writings, as he *never specifically recounts stories*. These scholars emphasize that Paul was primarily engaged in composing letters, not gospels, and that his main concern was to present arguments for his theological ideas. On the other hand, another group of scholars acknowledges that explicit narratives are not prominent in Paul's works yet still emphasizes the significance of *implicit stories* for comprehending his writings.

Even though the disagreement is strong and the potential consequences for interpretation enormous, for a long time no detailed research addressed the conflict itself. This book summarizes my findings of several years of research on exactly this issue. I will argue that a careful theoretical, methodological, and empirical analysis confirms the heuristic value of the concept of implicit narratives. However, while I agree with the narrative approach concerning its affirmations, I also strongly disagree with the presupposition that it shares with its critics. Contrary to this consensus, I believe that it can be demonstrated that Paul does indeed convey a multitude of *explicit stories* in his letters.

Moreover, I believe that only by fully engaging with these narratives can we venture into more disputed territories and consider the potential of uncovering implicit stories as well. The scholarly debate, in my observation, has reached a deadlock largely due to overlooking stories that Paul undeniably told. Without this foundational bedrock, the discourse seems to resemble trench warfare: researchers on opposing fronts consistently exchanging the same citations, advancing little toward a mutual understanding. Both

Chapter 1

factions are deeply dug into their positions, showing scant willingness to negotiate or bridge gaps. I attribute this stagnation mainly to an absence of substantive material for dialogue. However, I am hopeful that this book, commencing with an examination of Paul's clear-cut narratives, will herald a shift toward more fruitful discussions.

This introductory chapter will begin by examining what proponents of the narrative approach have in mind when they invoke the notion of stories in relation to Paul. It will show that, up to this point, their understanding lacks the required theoretical depth. In the latter part of the chapter, I will shift the focus to my own approach. Primarily, this involves employing narratology to refine our perspective on stories in Paul's letters—a shift that necessitates defining explicit stories as the first priority. Based on this foundation, in subsequent chapters we will critically engage with the narratives of Paul, and only then can we cautiously venture into more speculative terrains.

Back to the Roots

This book is dedicated to a narrowly defined discussion surrounding the merit of considering Paul as a narrator. Admittedly, there are scholarly contributions addressing this general topic that extend beyond the purview of our analysis. For instance, there are works that focus on the methodological query of whether it is appropriate to apply tools designed for narratives to *nonnarrative* material.[1] However, generally speaking, when people apply terms like "story" and "narrative" in the context of Paul's writings, they do so under the conviction that there is indeed a component that warrants precisely this designation, even if this narrative essence may be somewhat latent. It is widely acknowledged in academic circles that this trend, which henceforth will simply be termed the "narrative approach," originates from the work of Richard B. Hays and N. T. Wright. Their "methodological rigour" is seen as the unifying factor that differentiates them from those who subsequently have adapted and modified their insights.[2]

Regrettably, this methodological foundation is somewhat unstable. Even

---

1. Cf. Christoph Heilig, *Paulus als Erzähler? Eine narratologische Perspektive auf die Paulusbriefe*, BZNW 237 (Berlin: de Gruyter, 2020), 39–42.
2. Bruce Longenecker, "Narrative Interest in the Study of Paul: Retrospective and Prospective," in *Narrative Dynamics in Paul: A Critical Assessment*, ed. Bruce W. Longenecker (Louisville: Westminster John Knox, 2002), 10. On the larger point, cf. Heilig, *Paulus*, 42–43.

Introducing Narrative

more concerning, the issue at hand turns out to be not merely a problem of optimizing methodology (i.e., "How do we most reliably reach goal X?"). Instead, upon closer examination, it becomes evident that the problem is fundamentally deep-seated, with a troubling lack of consideration at the theoretical level (i.e., "What—and, therefore, where—is the X that we aim to reach?").[3] If this assessment is accurate, it indicates that the narrative approach is fundamentally flawed. After all, one must first establish a solid understanding of what stories are before debating whether stories might be implicitly present or considering the most suitable tools for identifying and describing them. In the paragraphs that follow, I will substantiate my admittedly severe evaluation of the theoretical underpinning of the narrative approach.

Richard B. Hays and "Narrative Substructures"

Let us begin with Richard B. Hays, whose groundbreaking 1983 work, *The Faith of Jesus Christ: The Narrative Substructure of Gal 3:1–4:11*, is arguably the most influential publication for the narrative approach.[4] Despite the fact that Hays's dissertation contributed significantly to many other exegetical discourses—most notably the debate concerning the proper understanding of πίστις Χριστοῦ—his goal was also to challenge contemporary assumptions about the essence of the apostle's gospel and the ideal categories for interpreting it. He was especially critical of the focus on abstract theological concepts.[5]

There is much to be said about Hays's specific understanding of implicit narratives—his "narrative substructures"—but this will be discussed later in chapter 5 along with his focus on the relationship between these narrative substructures and discourse primarily based on argumentation. For the time being, our interest lies solely in how Hays defines the narrative

---

3. Cf. Heilig, *Paulus*, chapter 1, section 6.3, on the relationship of theory and method. Cf. also Theresa Heilig and Christoph Heilig, "Historical Methodology," in *God and the Faithfulness of Paul: A Critical Examination of the Pauline Theology of N. T. Wright*, ed. Christoph Heilig, J. Thomas Hewitt, and Michael F. Bird, WUNT 2.413 (Tübingen: Mohr Siebeck, 2016), 115–50.

4. Richard B. Hays, *The Faith of Jesus Christ: The Narrative Substructure of Galatians 3:1–4:11*, 2nd ed., SBLDS 56 (Atlanta: Society of Biblical Literature, 1983; repr., Grand Rapids: Eerdmans, 2002).

5. Regarding the relevant evidence from Hays, *Faith*, and Hays's introduction to the 2002 second edition, see Heilig, *Paulus*, 859–68.

Chapter 1

concepts themselves. It is intriguing that while Hays devotes considerable attention to identifying the subtle dynamics between supposed narrative substructures and the argumentative appearance of the text, he elucidates the category of narrativity itself only cursorily. As a matter of fact, Hays is content to reference a definition from the *Oxford English Dictionary* for the term "story": 'A recital of events that have or are alleged to have happened; a series of events that are or might be narrated.'[6] Hays seizes on this second part, arguing that "it points fundamentally to the sequence of events which underlies the recital."[7] Therefore, he differentiates between the nouns "story" and "narrative," with the former not being necessarily verbally told: "Paul's gospel *is* a story, and it *has* a narrative structure, but it is not *a* narrative except when it is actually narrated, as in Phil 2:6–11."[8]

Through this definition, Hays omits the aspect of *textuality* as a necessary condition in our understanding of what constitutes a story, reserving this aspect for 'narrative' as a distinct concept. In doing so, he also automatically deals with the more particular issue of the correlation between story on the one side and *argument* as a certain type of discourse on the other. After all, if story is independent of the text, the specific configuration of the text does not impact the question of whether some story elements exist or not.

As neat as this preemptive justification might be, it is not particularly helpful for the analysis of Pauline texts. These definitions do not give us much insight into the features of the text we should actually be examining. It is worth noting that in this view explicit narratives are simply defined as speech acts that articulate a story, which in turn is characterized by its "narrative structure." But what exactly does this structure entail? The definition merely offers the concept of "a series of events."[9] This raises numerous questions.

For instance, the definition might suggest that any event sequence occurring in the natural world could constitute a story. If an apple falls unnoticed from a tree and hits the ground—without anyone acknowledging or talking

---

6. Hays, *Faith*, 18.

7. Hays, *Faith*, 18–19.

8. Hays, *Faith*, 19. Since there is no adjective from "story," he uses "narrative" in such cases too.

9. Hays is not alone in being unclear about this issue. See, for example, Edward Adams, "Paul's Story of God and Creation: The Story of How God Fulfils His Purposes in Creation," in Longenecker, *Narrative Dynamics*, 23: "A story/narrative is a series of events that can be perceived as sequentially and consequentially connected." For a critical discussion, see Heilig, *Paulus*, 59–61.

Introducing Narrative

about the incident—does this already qualify as a story? This implication seems counterintuitive. Consequently, it seems that the definition may be too inclusive, recognizing too many phenomena as stories.

This lack of precision in Hays's definition also affects the handling of explicit stories. While Hays does not primarily concern himself with this category, he acknowledges its existence precisely by arguing for the significance of implicit stories. However, in attempting to dissociate story from narrative in order to focus on the former without dealing with the latter, Hays unintentionally dilutes the concept of narrative. If narrative is defined in relation to story, and story is not defined through its inherent association with the act of narration (the production of narratives), then narrative (the explicit verbalization of a story) itself becomes somewhat elusive.

Considering this, a rather surprising question arises: How can we even determine if Paul does *not* frequently tell narratives if they are defined only relative to a category (i.e., story) loosely associated with "events"? Ironically, it is by forcing a separation between narrative and story—out of an assumed fear of backlash for his argument—that Hays implicitly questions the very necessity of this separation. He inadvertently convolutes the categories he seeks to clarify, creating a paradox. So, while Hays's dissolving of story from narrative may serve his argument for implicit narratives, it inadvertently weakens the distinguishability of explicit narratives and thus practically undermines the narrative approach's desired distinctiveness.

N. T. Wright and "Implicit Worldview Narratives"

Assessing the theoretical basis of the narrative approach as presented by N. T. Wright, who is often recognized as the second pivotal figure in this field, proves more challenging than with Hays. We must take into account a multitude of Wright's works, each providing incremental insights into his understanding of narrativity.[10] It is clear that for Wright, too, stories have to do with events and, more particularly, with the relationship between them: "For a story, a narrative, something has to challenge the equilibrium of the original statement."[11] So while he does not think "the cat sat on the mat" is a story (it is merely "a statement"), such a statement can become a story

---

10. For a detailed assessment, see Heilig, *Paulus*, 45–50.
11. N. T. Wright, *Paul and the Faithfulness of God*, vol. 4 of *Christian Origins and the Question of God* (London: SPCK, 2013), 475.

Chapter 1

when additional events are added, such as "the mat caught fire" or "up came a mouse and tweaked its tail."

Despite the sporadic insights into Wright's understanding of what constitutes a story, like Hays he appears to be more invested in advocating for 'story' as a category somehow *dissociated* from explicit narratives than in providing a comprehensive explanation of either concept. While Hays uses a diverse array of scholars to bolster his thesis, Wright has a rather straightforward solution.[12] Following Norman E. Peterson's *Rediscovering Paul*, he argues that it is possible to use the sequence of events mentioned or implied in a letter, "the poetic sequence," in order to construct a "referential sequence" of events in the "narrative world" of the text[13]—and, by extension, even of Paul's narrative world in general.[14]

On the surface, this solution appears to elegantly sidestep potential criticism that story terminology is inappropriate in relation to Paul, given that he is not an explicit storyteller. After all, if we presume that every letter intrinsically "has" a story, there is no need to prove the existence of explicit narratives in the text to assume the existence of said story within the letter. Furthermore, if the story concept primarily resides within an individual's worldview, it seems that, as with Hays's argument, we do not even require a *text* for the use of story terminology to be justified.[15]

Despite these arguments, numerous questions about this approach remain unanswered. Most fundamentally, it is not clear what in this framework actually constitutes the story of the letter. Asserting that the story can be reconstructed based on the "poetic sequence" (borrowing Peterson's terminology) suggests that we are already operating with some notion of narrativity in the background. Only with this context can we effectively scrutinize the text and make judgments regarding its conformity to the pattern that Peterson has envisaged. In essence, while Wright may have identified a

---

12. Hays, *Faith*, 33–71, builds in particular on the work of biblical scholars Oscar Cullmann, Ernst Käsemann, C. H. Dodd, and Dan Via. He also takes up "intimations" by Amos Wilder, Stephen Crites, James A. Sanders, William Beardslee (9–14), and refers to Northrop Frye, Paul Ricoeur, and Robert Funk for the theoretical underpinning of his approach (21–29).

13. Norman R. Petersen, *Rediscovering Paul: Philemon and the Sociology of Paul's Narrative World* (Philadelphia: Fortress, 1985).

14. N. T. Wright, *The New Testament and the People of God*, vol. 1 of *Christian Origins and the Question of God* (Minneapolis: Fortress, 1992), 404.

15. Note that Wright, *Faithfulness*, xvii, continues to reserve the term "worldview" for an entire community and prefers "mindset" for individuals. I do not follow this differentiation in this book.

method for recognizing worldview stories (a point to which we will return in chapter 5), like Hays he provides limited clarity regarding the *theoretical* question of what a story actually is.

Further Developments

We could simply take note of this lack of interest in explicit narratives and the corresponding absence of well-developed categories for engaging with them in the works of Hays and Wright. On that basis, we could then progress to their specific proposals of implicit stories—the narrative substructures and the worldview narratives. Indeed, this is often how scholarship on the narrative approach has progressed. This methodology, however, leads to two different outcomes, both of which I find problematic and attribute to the stalled advancement in the discussion of narratives in Paul's letters.

First, we can observe a shift in theoretical and methodological discussions from narrativity toward *intertextuality*.[16] Rather than probing the Pauline text in question for indications of a narrative—or grappling with the even more elementary issue of what that concept of narrativity involves—scholars shift their focus to potential sources for Paul's stories, which are believed to underlie nonnarrative sections in his letters. Much of this is catalyzed by another pioneering work of Richard B. Hays, *Echoes of Scripture in the Letters of Paul*, in which he asserted that Paul's allusions to the Septuagint do not merely serve as supportive "proof texts."[17] According to Hays, Paul refers to these texts through subtle "echoes," thus invoking their original—often *narrative*—contexts in the new utterance. While it may be the case that understanding both explicit and implicit narratives in Paul's letters is made easier through intertextual considerations, it ultimately does not assist us in forming a clearer conception of what stories really are.

Second, some of the scholars who have attempted to refine the original framework by Hays and Wright proceed promptly to the *what* and *where* of the stories in question, instead of investing significant effort in grappling with the concept of narrativity itself.[18] Do these stories concern the world?

---

16. For more details, see Heilig, *Paulus*, 51–53.
17. Richard B. Hays, *Echoes of Scripture in the Letters of Paul* (New Haven: Yale University Press: 1989).
18. We observe such a focus on the question of content in particular among those voices that challenge the idea that Paul's stories are all just reconfigurations of scriptural

Chapter 1

Israel? Jesus's faithfulness? And what exactly do we mean when we propose that these stories are solely implicit? In my perspective, while these questions may hold theological interest, they are simply premature. After all, it seems rather complicated to evaluate the content of something whose characteristics (i.e., the attributes by which we recognize it) are unknown. Likewise, it does not appear particularly productive to debate the most fitting spatial metaphor (in? behind? underneath? etc.) for the relationship between these stories and the text of Paul's letters if we have not first comprehended how the feature of textuality itself relates precisely to the realm of narrativity—a question that must remain unresolved as long as we have not agreed upon a definition of narrativity to begin with.

Indeed, a narrative approach that builds upon discussions in these two areas might yield many insightful observations. However, it should not come as a surprise if contributions to this debate continue to be marked by a certain confusion regarding the fundamental parameters of the issue at hand. It strikes me as rather symptomatic that in a collection of essays on the narrative approach we encounter the surprising situation where only one author, Edward Adams, makes an attempt to provide a definition of what a story is, while another, Douglas A. Campbell, explicitly dismisses the importance of such a definition.[19] Further, when a third person, John M. G. Barclay, opts to focus on explicit narratives in his contribution, he is rebuked by a fourth contributor, David G. Horrell, for his interest in the "story on the surface of Paul's text."[20] I find it revealing that Barclay is accused of "some ambivalence" regarding his story terminology because it does not align with usage in the narrative approach (i.e., for implicit narrative structures): "Barclay positions himself in opposition to the thrust of the narrative approach, while his frequent use of story terminology seems implicitly to embrace it."[21]

I respectfully disagree. Instead, it appears to me that an interest in narrative features in Paul's letters that might have the capacity to advance the scholarly discussion should start with the following observation: *Hays and Wright* situate themselves in continuity with *narratology*, while their fre-

---

material. Cf. Ben Witherington III, *Paul's Narrative Thought World: The Tapestry of Tragedy and Triumph* (Louisville: Westminster John Knox, 1994), 2–3.

19. See Adams, "Paul's Story" and Campbell, "The Story of Jesus in Romans and Galatians," in Longenecker, *Narrative Dynamics*, 99.

20. John M. G. Barclay, "Paul's Story," in Longenecker, *Narrative*, 136; David G. Horrell, "Paul's Narratives or Narrative Substructure? The Significance of 'Paul's Story,'" in Longenecker, *Narrative Dynamics*, 158.

21. Horrell, "Paul's Narrative," 158–59.

quent use of story terminology seems to *go beyond* the common usage in this discipline. Rather than holding Barclay accountable for adhering to standard narratological concepts in his search for potential stories in Paul's letters, it would seem more appropriate to demand that this narrative approach take into account the discipline devoted to defining and describing the very category it constantly invokes.

Countering the Dismissal of Explicit Narratives

As demonstrated in this brief overview, it is not advisable to merely observe the lack of interest in explicit narratives demonstrated by the pioneers of the narrative approach to Paul and then immediately delve into the specifics of the implicit stories they propose. I am not suggesting that we should neglect this topic. On the contrary, later we will delve into this subject in great detail. Rather, what I am attempting to convey is that, if we bypass these foundational issues now, they will eventually come back to haunt us. Consequently, I will first provide a narratological definition of the category of 'story' and an empirical evaluation of text portions that align with this pattern in Paul's letters. Afterward, we will broaden the purview of this investigation.

Before proceeding, however, we will address the predilection Hays and Wright demonstrate for implicit stories. After all, my work expressly aims at reforming the narrative approach, claiming a certain level of continuity with these scholars. Insisting that they do not truly define narrativity might seem like quibbling over details. And indeed it could be the case that, fortuitously, their notion of implicit stories does not necessitate a clear concept of story. Yet my thesis is that favoring explicit narratives is highly *advantageous* for the narrative approach. So even if readers remain unconvinced that the gap that I have attempted to outline above with respect to defining narrativity is ultimately problematic for characterizing and then identifying implicit stories, I hope it should at least be indisputable that the pursuit of explicit stories demands that we first define the textual attributes that allow such a classification. Ultimately, I hope that the entirety of this book will persuade proponents of the narrative approach that explicit narratives warrant our attention—and that they do so precisely *in preparation* for addressing the undoubtedly fascinating question of implicit stories. The proof, as the saying goes, will be in the pudding. Concurrently, I wish to briefly address the critique that Hays and Wright level with respect to the kind of dessert that I envision. I hope this will at least compel those who are primarily interested in implicit narratives to sample what I have to present in the upcoming sections.

Chapter 1

In Hays's case, the disinterest in explicit narratives serves a very distinct rhetorical purpose. Approaching his work, one would perhaps expect that he analyzes Gal 3:13–14 and 4:3–6 with reference to narrative structures precisely because they can reasonably be classified as explicit stories. By contrast, Hays prefers to call them "argumentative recapitulation[s]" that contain "traces of Paul's foundational story."[22] In my perspective, this tact artificially amplifies the divergence from supposedly authentic, "briefly recapitulated christological" stories like Phil 2:6–11 in order to *minimize* the distance to Gal 3–4 as a whole.[23] This is certainly a savvy maneuver on Hays's part. If it is feasible to apply narrative categories to Gal 3:13–14 and 4:3–6, *and* if these passages are predominantly argumentative, it paves the way for analyzing the broader literary context, containing a significant amount of argumentation, through the lens of a "narrative logic."

Temporarily setting aside the problematic classification of the given passages as ultimately nonnarrative, we can also observe that, in elevating the category of narrative substructures, Hays very broadly, and unnecessarily, downplays explicit stories:

> We all know that people sometimes tell stories in order to illustrate ideas: the preacher or lecturer, in order to make a point, uses an anecdote that ornaments or emphasizes the intended message. In this case, the story belongs not to the "substructure" of the discourse, but to its "superstructure"; it could be replaced by a different illustrative story without materially altering the "meaning" of the discourse.[24]

It appears rather arbitrary to me to consider Paul's explicit stories as mere replaceable illustrations, accepting only implied versions as genuinely significant for the discourse. Hays's language seems to do a considerable amount of work here. Can an explicit story be a "superstructure" because it is merely a "superficial" element of the text while the "substructure" occupies the unshakeable foundation? Why not refer to it, in a more neutral manner, as an "intrastructure," which would acknowledge that these stories are organically integrated into the broader literary context of the letters?

Moreover, one might also suggest that it is possible in many cases to replace specific *arguments* (not only explicit narratives) in the text with

22. Hays, *Faith*, 28.
23. Hays, *Faith*, 28.
24. Hays, *Faith*, 22.

Introducing Narrative

others without altering the conclusions and, consequently, the meaning of the discourse. In fact, if we assume that Paul frequently employs argumentation not just to arrive at a logical conclusion but to elicit a certain type of response, then the interchangeability of arguments becomes even more apparent—and is sometimes even corroborated by the fact that exegetes propose that Paul stacks a variety of distinct arguments to induce a certain kind of behavior.[25] This is exemplified by Betz, who discerns six "proofs" in Gal 3:1–4:31: namely, an argument from experience in Gal 3:1–5; one from Scripture, namely, God's promise to Abraham, in Gal 3:6–14; one that builds on common human practice of law in 3:15–18; one from Christian tradition in 3:26–4:11; one relating to friendship in 4:12–20; and a last one that makes use of allegory in 4:21–31.[26]

Ultimately, it appears to me that Hays may be culpable of precisely the same predilection for argumentative versus narrative structures that he accuses his colleagues of exhibiting. I want to note that I am not denying the possibility that thorough interpretation might lead to the conclusion that some illustrative narratives are of lesser importance for the discourse, but this should not be assumed from the start of the investigation. Indeed, I would argue that there are innumerable instances of human utterances—both from antiquity and our contemporary era—where "illustrations" play a significant role in aiding the speaker to attain their communicative goals. In any case, the decision on whether a specific explicit story is dispensable for the discourse to effectively deliver its message must be made individually. The same applies when determining the assumed significance of arguments or potential narrative substructures. I do not see why we should treat explicit stories any differently.

In Wright's case as well, the dismissal of explicit stories seems somewhat inconsistent with his general approach to narrativity. After all, even in his earlier 1991 book, *The Climax of the Covenant*, he applies Hays's (and, consequently, Greimas's) methodology to an explicit story in Rom 8:3–4 (he calls it a "dense passage" but does not question its narrative nature).[27]

---

25. For example, we will see in our discussion of conditional constructions in chapter 4 that Paul sometimes adduces arguments that are not controversial in the context of utterance. But they allow him to transition to something that is indeed of importance to him—and sometimes that is a *narrative*.

26. Hans Dieter Betz, *Galatians: A Commentary on Paul's Letter to the Churches in Galatia*, Hermeneia (Philadelphia: Fortress, 1979).

27. N. T. Wright, *The Climax of the Covenant: Christ and the Law in Pauline Theology* (London: T&T Clark, 1991), 206.

Chapter 1

Considering this, it seems rather curious that by the time of writing *Paul and the Faithfulness of God*, Wright's inclination to emphasize implicit worldview narratives (as he had also done in the interim in *The New Testament and the People of God*) has made room for an outright denial of the relevance of explicit stories.

What transpired? It appears to me that Wright's primary stimulus in downplaying the significance of explicit stories for Pauline exegesis is apologetic rather than based on actual problems that he identifies in the application of this category. It is clear that he is significantly irritated by the criticism of Francis C. Watson, who asserts that "Paul is simply not a storyteller" and "in his extant writings never actually tells a story" (with Gal 1–2 being the only exception).[28] In response to this critique of the narrative approach, Wright reasserts his interest, which he maintains is shared by "most narrative theorists," in a story that is "underlying what [Paul] is doing, rather than a story he is retelling."[29]

Wright does not really dispute Watson's basic assumption, contributing only a few more "exceptions," such as Phil 2:6–11 and 3:2–11.[30] Instead, he emphasizes implicit stories and advocates for this preference (for a category seemingly immune to Watson's critique) by basing it on the purported *superiority* of implicit stories over explicit ones, with the former appearing to be "deeper and more powerful."[31] Even in instances of literature and drama, asserts Wright, it is "highly unlikely" that the "underlying narrative" that encompasses the writer's implicit worldview "coincides with the narrative on the page."[32] In other words, focusing on explicit narratives might even be quite misleading in our pursuit of "Paul's stories"!

However, upon closer inspection, Wright's entire line of reasoning appears to contain a rather conspicuous category error. The reason why we cannot leap from a fictional work, such as *Pride and Prejudice*, to the worldview of its author is explicitly due to its character *as fiction*.[33] In contrast, if we are dealing with factual narration (cf. below, p. 30, on this distinction), we

---

28. Francis C. Watson, "Is There a Story in These Texts?," in Longenecker, *Narrative Dynamics*, 232 and 239.

29. Wright, *Faithfulness*, 463.

30. Wright, *Faithfulness*, 462. He also refers to Rom 7:1–8:11 and 9:6–10:21 one page later as "actual stories."

31. Wright, *Faithfulness*, 463.

32. Wright, *Faithfulness*, 463.

33. Wright, *Faithfulness*, 463. We will discuss the concept of 'fictionality' later in this chapter.

Introducing Narrative

have every reason to believe that "the narrative on the page" should provide some insight into the storyteller's mindset, that is, what their "underlying narrative" encompasses.

Indeed, Wright is so intent on refuting what he perceives as a caricature of his object of research that, in the heat of the moment, he commits yet another category mistake, ironically while making such an allegation against his critics:

> To point out Paul's lack of actual stories . . . looks, at least to begin with, like a sort of category mistake: as though one were to declare that the singer could not be singing a song because she was not singing the word "a song." To object that, because worldview-narratives do not lie on the surface of a text, one must assume that they do not exist, is like objecting that, because I have not up to this point written the words "I am sitting at a desk writing a book," I cannot therefore be sitting at a desk writing a book. Indeed, normally, if I were to write those words, it would mean that I was *not* writing a book, but something else—a letter, perhaps. Thus it is no objection to observe that Paul never says "Once upon a time," and hardly ever lays out his material in an explicit narrative sequence with a beginning, a middle and an end. To observe this fact ought not to lead to the conclusion that Paul did not have a narratable gospel.[34]

Let us attempt to bring some order to the various entities mentioned by Wright. On one level, Wright references different *products of verbal acts*, such as a song, book, or story. Naturally, their existence does not require the *utterance of a metalinguistic expression* that describes their nature. Had Wright kept these two parameters separate, a sentence analogous to "I sing a song" or "I write a book" would, of course, be "I tell a story." Indeed, individuals can tell stories without stating that they are doing so.[35]

However, Wright does not complete his reflection in this manner. Instead, when he transitions to stories, he suddenly introduces a third aspect, namely, an *element that is characteristic of this kind of text*. Note that he does not do anything similar with reference to books and songs, and had he done so, his mistake would have immediately become evident. Of course, we do

---

34. Wright, *Faithfulness*, 463.
35. Though sometimes they may introduce their storytelling in such a manner; see below, in our discussion of narration-specific tasks, p. 183.

Chapter 1

not need to talk about our verbal acts for them to be occurring. No one has claimed that. But, yes, certainly we would demand there to be some characteristic features of, for instance, vocal qualities if we were judging whether or not something that is verbally expressed by a person is deserving of being classified as a song. Likewise, we would expect the object called a "book" to fulfill the defined criteria of such an object.

Therefore, ironically, Wright makes a compelling case for the demand that we ought to point to *characteristics of narrativity* in the text if we wish to use the term "story." Admittedly, the elements in question do not need to be something like "once upon a time," which indicates not narrativity in general but a specific genre. This, indeed, is another rhetorical device wherein Wright veils his mistake by suggesting that those requesting demonstrable examples of actual stories in Paul's writing are asking for something absurd. No one is asking for Paul's text to display a phrase typical of modern fairy tales as a criterion for the application of narrative terminology—just as we do not require there to be a rhythm unique to country songs for the claim that we hear a song to be justified.

Given this, it is reasonable to conclude that the caution demonstrated by Hays and Wright when engaging with explicit narratives stems from the concern that acknowledging the significance of such narratives might undermine their arguments. Beginning with the assumption that Paul ostensibly does not frequently employ explicit narratives, they feel forced to clarify that this has nothing to do with their understanding of story terminology. They seem to suppose that if they do not go down this route, their approach could potentially be dismissed by critics, who may highlight this seeming absence of explicit narratives.

As will be discussed in chapter 2, the initial assumption regarding the supposed absence of explicit narratives in Paul's letters is incorrect. Therefore, there is no underlying reason for someone who aligns with the larger claims of the narrative approach, concerning the importance of implicit narratives, to avoid the concept of explicit stories. Admitting the existence and potential significance of explicit narratives does not necessarily eliminate the concept of the story from the discourse. Moreover, the specific arguments that Hays and Wright present to justify their disinterest in explicit narratives ultimately appear quite thin. Given the eloquence with which these researchers argue the relevance of implicit narratives, their case against explicit narratives seems to be more of a veneer hiding the fundamental concern about the scarcity of genuine narratives within Paul's letters. Readers who broadly agree with Hays's and Wright's ideas should recognize that their particular arguments against explicit

Introducing Narrative

narratives are weak enough that they should not feel obligated to adhere to them. The narrative approach may have bitten the hand that could have nourished it, which would have allowed it to flourish more rapidly and evenly. Yet, it seems it has done so with rather dull teeth, leading to little real consequence.

Admittedly, there is some vulnerability associated with shifting our emphasis, at least for now, to explicit narratives. I do not want to dismiss this. If my conclusions concerning the presence of explicit narratives in Paul's letters are deemed unpersuasive, this could potentially cast doubt on the pursuit of implicit narratives as well, given that I have framed the latter quest as reliant on the former. Nonetheless, I see no other viable route—at least not if we aim to advance the discourse beyond a pretheoretical stage and transition from a "narrative" to a "narratological" approach.[36]

36. Unfortunately, the dialogue between biblical studies, especially New Testament studies, and literary criticism, specifically narratology, remains very superficial for the most part. Cf. the disappointing evaluation by Moisés Mayordomo, "Exegese zwischen Geschichte, Text und Rezeption: Literaturwissenschaftliche Zugänge zum Neuen Testament," *VF* 55 (2010): 36. However, the broad acknowledgment that narratology offers significant potential for exegesis seems uncontested. Therefore, it is unsurprising that I have not yet encountered anyone from the Hays and Wright camp advancing the argument that the study of narrative dynamics in Paul's letters should deliberately avoid explicit engagement with narratology. This likely reflects a consensus that such an approach would amount to admitting a lack of substantial connection to the concept of narrativity. However, cf. Joel R. White, review of *Paulus als Erzähler?* by Christoph Heilig, *Jahrbuch für evangelikale Theologie*, April 25, 2021, https://rezensionen.afet.de/?p=1208, who, in his review of my German monograph, seems to come close to such a surprising demand: "Wright primarily aims to investigate to what extent Paul's discussions in his letters fit into an overarching early Jewish metanarrative and thus become more understandable. This poses a methodological problem for Heilig when it comes to evaluating Wright's framework from a narratological perspective. After all, a metanarrative cannot be derived (at least not solely) from an analysis of individual Pauline texts, and Wright does not even attempt to do so. Instead, he conducts—quite understandably, in my opinion, given his research subject and objectives—a comparative literary study of early Jewish sources of impressive scope. That Heilig shows no interest in this—at least there is no single reference to an early Jewish source in his bibliography—is also understandable. For narratological approaches are effective only at the text level and are less suitable for the analysis of metanarratives, which by definition lie 'behind' the text. Here, Heilig allows himself to be led by Wright, who himself repeatedly loses sight of this methodological limitation and continually mixes ideological and narrative categories, down a laborious path into a dead end." The German original reads: "Wright will vor allem untersuchen, inwiefern sich die Ausführungen des Paulus in seinen Briefen in ein übergreifendes frühjüdisches Metanarrativ einklinken und aufgrund dessen verständlicher werden. Das stellt Heilig vor ein methodisches Problem, wenn es darum gehen soll, Wrights Entwurf aus narratologischer Perspektive zu beurteilen. Denn ein Metanarrativ kann man nicht (jedenfalls nicht ausschließlich) aus einer Analyse einzelner paulinischer Texte erheben, und Wright versucht es gar nicht.

Chapter 1

It is also important to distinguish between critiquing the coherence of the arguments that Hays and Wright present against explicit narratives and laying blame on them for such a stance. Their proposals are abductive in the best sense. Both scholars identified shortcomings in the established paradigms of their time and offered novel explanations for the data. It is quite common for these types of proposals to require subsequent modification and bolstering. This is a task that is, in my view, long overdue. It appears to me that scholars who have followed in the footsteps of Hays and Wright have

---

Stattdessen führt er—meines Erachtens völlig nachvollziehbar, weil seinem Forschungsobjekt und -ziel angemessen—eine vergleichende literaturwissenschaftliche Untersuchung frühjüdischer Quellen von beeindruckendem Umfang durch. Dass Heilig dafür überhaupt kein Interesse aufbringt—jedenfalls gibt es in seinem Quellenverzeichnis keinen einzigen Verweis auf eine frühjüdische Quelle—, ist auch nachvollziehbar. Denn narratologische Ansätze greifen nur auf der Ebene des Textes und eignen sich weniger für die Analyse von Metanarrativen, die per definitionem 'hinter' dem Text liegen. Hier lässt sich Heilig von Wright, der selbst diese methodische Einschränkung immer wieder aus den Augen verliert und weltanschauliche und narrative Kategorien miteinander immer wieder vermischt, auf einen mühsamen Weg in eine Sackgasse verleiten."

It is unfortunate that White makes these far-reaching claims in a book review rather than in a research article, in which the format would have forced him to substantiate these claims. First, it is of course not true that I do not cite early Jewish sources; I simply, and very intentionally, decided to list them either under Greco-Roman authors or with papyrological sources. Second, despite this quibble, it must be noted that the general perception is, of course, correct that I do not interact with Wright's general reconstruction of an early Jewish worldview narrative. However, the reason for that is that this supposed Jewish worldview narrative presupposes a narratological analysis that is as rigorous as the one of Paul's letters. Even just ascertaining the worldview narrative of Paul—*a single Jew*—comes with many problems, which we will discuss below in chapter 5. Venturing a synthesis of a Jewish worldview narrative in general seems exponentially more daunting, especially because here, too, Wright does not rely on explicit narratives alone but likewise uses many narrative fragments to synthesize a narrative whole. It is beyond me why White thinks that for such a task one could adopt an approach of "literary studies" that, as implied, would be devoid of narratological concerns. This presupposed dichotomy between literary criticism and narratology does not make sense to me. Since literary criticism goes hand in hand with narratology, there is absolutely no reason for supposing that an analysis from this perspective would point us toward a phenomenon that should be inaccessible to narratological categories. Ultimately, White's claim boils down to the admission that the narrative approach to Paul's letters is unsubstantiated at the moment if scrutinized from a narratological perspective. By rejecting such a framework itself, he, however, marginalizes his own approach by admitting that the reference to narrativity lacks substance. The only solution to this dilemma is to build on the promising findings by Hays, Wright, and others and to finally address the shortcomings of the narrative approach by taking narratology seriously.

incorporated various considerations concerning the source, content, and location of the supposed implicit narrative into the framework established by the founding fathers of the narrative approach. However, its theoretical basis is still shaky.

In the latter part of this chapter, we will delve into the interdisciplinary theory of narrative, known as "narratology." This will provide us with an opportunity to reexamine the theoretical foundations of the quest for narratives in Paul's letters. Consequently, this will equip us to refine the methods that we might deploy in subsequent chapters in our pursuit of narratives, both explicit and implicit, in Paul's letters.

Toward a Narratological Approach

To ensure the success of this project, we must first lay down clear definitions—a task that, as we have noted, has not been prioritized by proponents of the narrative approach. We begin with defining what a definition is in the first place.[37]

Defining Definitions

First, we need to clarify what type of *things* we are referring to that need definition. For instance, we can define words (or phrases, in short: expressions), as I did in the closing paragraph of the previous section, where I specified how I would use the term "narratology." While lexicographers simply note descriptively how words are used within a language community and attempt to encapsulate their entire semantic range, definitions in scholarly publications are somewhat different. In this context, we typically concentrate on one of these meanings and aim to provide a detailed account of it. The objective is to facilitate clear communication of ideas and prevent misinterpretation. So, for instance, I could expand my definition of the term "narratology" to note that, within the confines of this book, its use generally does not intend to reference a specific school of thought or its unique position on handling narrative texts, such as, for example, the structuralist analysis advanced by Greimas and others.[38]

37. For more details on what follows, see Heilig, *Paulus*, 83–89.
38. Which is also why I will not use the plural "narratologies."

Chapter 1

Definitions like these assume that we already have some specific concepts in mind, and we are simply clarifying the relationship between certain expressions and these mental constructs. For instance, as you might have already noticed, I use the nouns "story" and "narrative" interchangeably, that is, for the same concept. Therefore, we could say that "story" means "narrative," or it means "Erzählung" in German. Although such formulations can often be clear enough, especially if the context already provides some indication of the author's intent, they can be misleading in other situations. After all, the interchangeable use of certain terms is mediated by a shared meaning as a mental construct. One word does not "mean" another word. It would therefore be more accurate to say that these terms mean the same thing, that they express the same semantic concept. In actual language use, the concepts associated with certain synonymous terms usually overlap and are not entirely identical, particularly when crossing language barriers. A deviation would only occur if I stipulate such synonymity—as I do for this book with "story" and "narrative." Given this premise, it seems prudent to avoid reliance solely on *glosses*.

Take the following example:

Διήγησις, "story," never occurs in Paul's letters.

Here, "story" is used as a translation equivalent for διήγησις, but the usage of the two terms in English and Greek is not entirely identical.[39] Therefore, it would be beneficial to provide more detailed *definitions* that aim to translate the concept into the code of language.[40] To highlight the distinction between expression and content levels, I will employ single quotation marks ('...') for such definitions, which are usually called "nominal" or "stipulative" definitions. For example:

Διήγησις can be defined as 'discourse consisting of an orderly exposition of narration' according to L&N.

Until now, we have discussed the correct way to define *words*. However, merely discussing terminology alone does not ensure successful

---

39. On this general issue, cf. also Heilig, *Paulus*, 4–5 n. 12.

40. Structuralist semantics did not really recognize the difference between these definitions and the mental constructs. For structuralists, definitions *are* meanings. On the problems with this, see Michael G. Aubrey, "Linguistic Issues in Biblical Greek," in *Linguistic and Biblical Exegesis*, ed. Douglas Mangum and Josh Westbury, Lexham Methods Series 2 (Bellingham, WA: Lexham, 2017), 173–86.

communication. After all, if participants do not share the same assumptions regarding underlying concepts—what constitutes them and how they are distinguished from one another—misunderstanding naturally ensues. Overreliance on dictionary entries (note that Hays's definition is taken from the *Oxford English Dictionary*) can be particularly problematic in this respect, as they usually attempt to be as concise as possible because of their objective of providing the user with sufficient information to differentiate between suitable contexts for words from the same semantic domain.[41] By contrast, our aim is not merely to determine if an English speaker—especially in a casual context—would use the term "story" rather than, for instance, "novel," "poem," or "instruction."[42] Rather, we want to grasp the exact boundaries of the *concept* triggered by the term "story" itself—and we need to do so with the understanding that scholarly debate may have necessitated distinctions that are not necessary in our normal daily routines. To differentiate between statements about words and statements about concepts (so-called real definitions), I will continue to use single quotation marks, as here too the focus is on the semantic level vis-à-vis the expression level. For example:

> I use both "story" and "narrative" (and likewise the German "Geschichte" and "Erzählung") for the concept 'story,' as it will be defined in this section.

Additionally, it is worth noting that definitions can manifest in various *forms*.[43] Traditionally, a well-structured definition (called an "equivalence definition") outlines all the necessary conditions that a real-world object must meet to be accurately categorized. Not only should these conditions be necessary, but when combined they should also be sufficient. This means that when these conditions are met, we can confidently classify an object into the category without mistakenly excluding objects that rightfully belong or including those that do not.

---

41. Another function is to differentiate within the semantic spectrum of a verb so as to state the different meanings in case of polysemy.

42. This is not to say that this is an unimportant task. With the exception of L&N, dictionaries on Koine Greek pay far too little attention to these paradigmatic relationships. See Christoph Heilig, *Paul's Triumph: Reassessing 2 Corinthians 2:14 in Its Literary and Historical Context*, BTS 27 (Leuven: Peeters, 2017), 82–95, for an example of how such an analysis can guide lexicographers in coming up with appropriate definitions.

43. On what follows, cf. Heilig, *Paulus*, 90–92.

Chapter 1

There are alternative forms of definitions as well. One prominent example is the "prototypical" definition. Here, concepts are thought to revolve around specific core features displayed by all members of a category. Simultaneously, there's a spectrum of additional properties that become increasingly less prevalent. Some prototypes of the category might encompass all these properties, while more peripheral examples might only display the central features. In contrast, the "cluster definition" extends this notion, positing that it might not even be possible to identify a consistent core. Instead, elements are categorized together due to a web of overlapping features, distinguishing them from other items.[44]

Depending on the task at hand, one of these forms might be more suitable than another, which does not mean that one of them is inherently "better." For our purposes, I intend to follow a relatively traditional definition of narrativity in both form and content. Both decisions are linked to my intention to make the argument for the thesis in this book as robust as possible.

Certainly, we could simply employ a prototypical definition of narrativity. At its core, it would probably include elements that likely would not apply to Paul's letters. This approach might seem like an easy path forward that avoids a lot of complications. We could discuss varying "degrees" of narrativity in relation to Paul's letters and, for instance, the Gospels. This approach seems to adequately address the critique of the narrative approach while still maintaining the applicable narrative terminology to Paul's letters to some extent. Indeed, one could argue that the features that Paul's alleged implicit stories lack compared to their explicit equivalents are not necessarily located near the core of a prototypical definition but rather on its fringes.[45] This would suggest that we can discuss implicit stories as comfortably as we do explicit stories.[46]

However, skeptics would quickly draw attention to the issues inherent in such an apparently streamlined procedure. Advocates of the narrative approach would likely be accused of jumping to a conclusion by picking a very specific center for their definition (i.e., a target easily achieved by

---

44. Ironically, Campbell, "Story," 99, who, as we have seen, does not like the idea of using definitions, continues right after that comment with a description of narrativity that he explicitly links to the concept of 'family resemblance' and that might justifiably be classified as a prototypical definition. Cf. Heilig, *Paulus*, 90.

45. For a detailed assessment of the proposal by Marie-Laure Ryan, "Toward a Definition of Narrative," in *The Cambridge Companion to Narrative*, ed. David Herman (Cambridge: Cambridge University Press, 2007), 22–35; see also Heilig, *Paulus*, 92–98.

46. Cf. Heilig, *Paulus*, 529–47.

Introducing Narrative

both explicit and implicit stories). Moreover, this approach would present practical challenges for the discourse within the narrative approach because for each use of terms like "narrative" and "story," we (as readers or writers) would need to discern or specify which part of the narrativity spectrum is meant in each instance.

Against this backdrop, I prefer to start with a rather conservative definition that, through its necessary conditions, specifically *excludes* the types of objects Hays and Wright are considering from the realm of narrativity. If, in analyzing the textual units that are selected by this fairly rigid procedure, we still repeatedly encounter items that *almost* qualify to be called "stories" or "narratives" in this broader sense, we could then still consider—and be in a very strong position to do so, far above any potential accusation of being overly speculative—using an additional, broader definition. This means that in subsequent steps we might apply fewer necessary conditions, allowing us to include a larger number of objects under the umbrella of this wider concept of narrativity. Thus, we can still benefit from the advantages of a prototypical approach, being able to discuss narrativity in a graded way, while avoiding some potential difficulties.

Up until now, I have explained why my attempt to define narrativity follows a relatively conservative path in terms of the form of definition that I use. I also mentioned that my definition is rather conservative in terms of content, indicating that I am stringent regarding which elements merit labels such as "stories" and "narratives." The traits that these entities must exhibit in order to qualify for such a classification will be elaborated in the upcoming section.

Defining the Concept of Narrativity

We are now prepared to tackle the question of what is meant by "stories" and "narratives" in the subsequent chapters. In other words, we will now define the concept of 'story' that we reference with these terms. Which features must we examine to determine if the quality of narrativity is present in a given object? Let us begin with a fairly traditional yet precise definition provided by two leading German narratologists, Tom Kindt and Tilmann Köppe: "A text is a narrative if and only if it deals with at least two events that are ordered temporally and connected in at least one further meaningful way."[47]

47. Tilmann Köppe and Tom Kindt, *Erzähltheorie: Eine Einführung*, Reclams

Chapter 1

In the following section, we will delve deeper into what this concise definition entails. First, we can observe that the two scholars commence their definition with a focus on texts. In other words, this presumes that every narrative is associated with an *act of narration*. The relationship between the two is causal in one direction (the narration produces the narrative) and logical in the other direction (every narrative, therefore, implies a prior act of narration).

We will outline shortly what this implies for our undertaking. For now, I want us to consider the features that, according to these scholars, said texts need to exhibit in order to qualify as narratives. The connection between the narrative and the aspect under consideration here is one of semantics, meaning the *content* of the narrative/story is in focus. So, what are these semantic traits that distinguish narrative texts from other kinds of texts and consequently, acts of narration from other kinds of discourse? According to the aforementioned definition, the key is whether we are dealing with the assertion of (at least two) events that are connected both temporally and meaningfully.

Regarding the concept of 'event,' Köppe and Kindt employ a rather "intuitive" understanding of it. An event encompasses three elements: a point in time, an object or circumstance, and something that is predicated with respect to that object or circumstance. Admittedly, this leaves a degree of ambiguity, as demonstrated in their example:

Peter sneezes.

Does this represent just one event, or could this sentence be categorized as a story based on the fact that it communicates a somewhat complex biological process? The authors argue, however, that in practice we can easily identify the events that any given narrative "deals with" or "is about" because when making such claims about stories, we typically focus on the events that are truly significant for the plot of the story. In any case, the authors contend that "merely possible" events do not qualify as events in their view. This means that only events that are asserted to have occurred can fulfill this aspect of the definition.[48]

Universal-Bibliothek 17683 (Stuttgart: Reclam, 2014), 43: "Ein Text ist genau dann eine Erzählung, wenn er von mindestens zwei Ereignissen handelt, die temporal geordnet sowie in mindestens einer weiteren sinnhaften Weise miteinander verknüpft sind." The following elaborations on this definition are based on the discussion in Heilig, *Paulus*, 98–109.

48. Cf. Köppe and Kindt, *Erzähltheorie*, 110: "Da nach unserer Definition *bloß mögliche* Ereignse keine Ereignisse darstellen."

Introducing Narrative

As for "temporal order," Köppe and Kindt clarify this aspect of the definition as including both "sequentially" and "simultaneity," providing one example of each:[49]

> First, the apple hung on the tree. Then it fell.[50]

> While the police were still searching for him, Peter fled the country.[51]

The requirement of an additional *"meaningful" connection* between events essentially demands that a substantial relationship between the two must be discernible, with causal relationships being the most evident. This criterion is added to exclude texts like the following:

> The police were searching for Peter, and at the University of Chicago, the curricula for the winter semester were being created.[52]

If we are uncertain whether two events are connected in a meaningful way, one option is to simply leave the question of whether or not we are dealing with a story unresolved. Since the authors in this case explicitly tell us there is no such connection between the two events in this example, we would not categorize this short text as a narrative—at least not if we understand our task of interpreting the text as involving authorial intention (see below, p. 51). Of course, we could also try to devise something that would provide coherence to these events, thus creating our own narrative.

Much could be said about each of these requirements. Even though I will not delve into the specifics for the purpose of this book, it will be necessary

---

49. It is actually helpful to distinguish a third category, "inclusion," from these two. It is different from sequentiality in that the events do not need to overlap but can still be recognized as belonging together temporally by being connected to the same time period. For example: "In 2020, we experienced the COVID-19 pandemic, but the FC Liverpool won the Premier League." Notice that the "but" introduces a meaningful connection here. In many other examples, an understanding of the text as a description rather than a narrative might be more natural.

50. Köppe and Kindt, *Erzähltheorie*, 50: "Erst hing der Apfel am Baum und dann fiel er herunter." I simplified the temporal connector in the English translation.

51. Köppe and Kindt, *Erzähltheorie*, 50: "Während die Polizei noch nach ihm fahndete, setzte sich Peter ins Ausland ab."

52. Köppe and Kindt, *Erzähltheorie*, 51: "Die Polizei fahndete nach Peter, und an der Universität von Chicago wurden die Lehrpläne für das Wintersemester erstellt."

Chapter 1

to examine and adjust some aspects in order to have more refined tools at our disposal when approaching the Pauline letters. Nonetheless, for the remainder of this section, my focus will be on the initial part of the definition, specifying that Köppe and Kindt regard the task of spotting narratives as tantamount to *categorizing texts*. The inherent emphasis on texts within this definition carries two significant implications that must be analyzed prior to exploring the other conditions, which are associated with the content of the utterance under discussion.

First, the definition presupposes that the only *medium* that can be considered a narrative is text. If something is not a text—like a picture, a movie, a dream, or a thought—it cannot be termed a "story" in this particular sense due to its inability to fulfill this definition of narrativity.[53] Although it is entirely feasible to watch a movie and later recount it to friends, it is only through this actual act of narration that a real narrative emerges. Some narratologists do not prescribe such a narrow focus on oral or written texts and are amenable to incorporating visual media as well. However, we will adhere to this stringent requirement for our purposes. It has the upshot that critics of the narrative approach cannot accuse us of opting for an easy way out. After all, discussions about "nonnarrative narratives," "stories behind the text," and "narrativity in nonnarrative sections," among others, become self-contradictory within this framework.[54] If our analysis of such strictly defined narratives *still* indicates the presence of what can be considered "almost narratives," implicit in the text, then this fact indeed bolsters the argument for the narrative approach to Paul.

Second, it is crucial to note that the definition is deliberately structured in a way that positions the recognition of narratives as a textual *classification* task. In simpler terms, it distinguishes between *entire texts* that are either narrative or nonnarrative. I am of the opinion that this definition faces a certain dilemma that we must address, even though it might initially seem like an exercise in splitting hairs.

As previously mentioned, it is possible to replicate the benefits of a prototypical definition (which allows for discussing varying degrees of narrativity) in the more traditional approach that posits necessary conditions. This could be done by using a multitude of definitions of this sort with a rising quantity

---

53. Köppe and Kindt, *Erzähltheorie*, 45–46. Contrary to how they explicate their own definition, it does not actually exclude the possibility that non-texts might be narratives as well. What they apparently mean is "an item is a narrative if and only if it is a text and . . ."

54. Köppe and Kindt, *Erzähltheorie*, 44.

of necessary conditions to provide a progressively restrictive view on what is considered a narrative. In doing so, we could create a highly minimalistic definition, which would categorize many texts as stories, and a more exacting one, which would assign this label (in a stricter sense) to fewer texts.

Köppe and Kindt attempt to do exactly this by defining, in a second phase, *"more meaningful" narratives*.[55] According to them, these more significant narratives are characterized by the additional criteria of demonstrating a full arc of suspense, "tellability" (i.e., suitability as an interactional element), and a more profound interpretation of eventfulness. For the final point, they furnish this example:

> First, the apple still clung to the tree. Then, abandoned by its strength, it plunged toward the ground.[56]

The apple here is presented as an entity with intentions and aspirations. Consequently, the narrated events assume importance, with the story evolving into a "small personal drama."

I question whether the two definitions can be aptly employed as I have just described, to provide a broader, minimalistic definition for all narratives and a more stringent one for meaningful narratives. My skepticism arises from doubting that every meaningful story also meets the criteria of the "minimalistic" definition. Put simply, I am not convinced that all meaningful narratives fall within the scope of the initial definition. To illustrate this, let us examine the following embellished version of the apple story:

> He heard the wind whistling through the leaves before it reached him. Would it hit him hard? He did not think so. As a result, he did not muster all his strength, reserving some for the afternoon when the farmer's boy might come to shake the tree again. Oh, foolish apple, you had no idea this gust would seal your fate! Indeed, before he could even grasp what was happening, he found himself plummeting toward the ground.

The extent of eventfulness is greatly amplified, which makes it abundantly clear that we are handling a story that is meaningful or, in other words, a text

---

55. Original: "gehaltvoller." Cf. Heilig, *Paulus*, 109–13, for their additional criteria.
56. Köppe and Kindt, *Erzähltheorie*, 65: "Erst hielt sich der Apfel noch am Baum, dann stürzte er, von seinen Kräften verlassen, ab."

Chapter 1

that far surpasses the basic criteria required to be considered a narrative. However, does this imply that it also meets the "minimalistic" definition?

Keep in mind again that the definition not only assumes that the narrative is somehow "connected" to the category of text but proposes that the narrative *is* a text. Now, when it comes to defining this category of textuality, Köppe and Kindt simply allude to the criteria set forth in the field of text linguistics.[57] We will delve into this issue more thoroughly later (pp. 45–46), but it is worth mentioning here that one rather clear defining feature of texts is that they are *self-contained units of communication*.

However, this poses a problem for treating this example as a narrative according to the first definition. After all, many parts of this text do not assert that something has occurred. Indeed, we learn about what the apple did *not* think, which can thus be considered an outright nonevent. Besides, we have a question, not a claim. Furthermore, we are told about the intention of the apple, which at that point is future oriented, which means this event cannot be recounted in retrospect in this text. Finally, the narrator's announcement also refers to an event that, at that point in the story, has neither transpired nor been narrated. Of course, we could note that there is at least an explicit mention of the actual happening of the wind making a noise and the apple falling toward the ground. But the definition compels us to consider whole texts, not isolated sentences here and there. In other words, this text, viewed as a complete unit, would *not* be classified as a narrative according to the supposedly minimalistic definition.

One method of addressing this issue could involve interpreting the section of the definition stating that we are searching for texts that "deal with" temporally and semantically connected assertions of events in a specific manner. One could contend that this merely requires the text to "contain" two meaningfully asserted and temporally related events.

However, this approach also has a significant disadvantage. This modified version of the definition would categorize all texts containing the relevant components as "narratives," even if these temporally and meaningfully connected events were not pivotal to the structure and function of the text. If this adjusted minimalistic definition of Köppe and Kindt were consistently applied, then all of Paul's letters would be characterized *as* narratives, since they all incorporate at least one connection of two events—a claim that stretches far beyond asserting that these letters somehow "possess" their own stories. Furthermore, in the prior examples with the apple, it would

---

57. Köppe and Kindt, *Erzähltheorie*, 43–44.

Introducing Narrative

seem somewhat problematic to state that the text "deals with" or "is about" the two events—the blowing of the wind and the subsequent fall of the apple. Rather, the text appears to be largely engaged with the internal viewpoint of the apple.

I therefore propose a straightforward modification of the definition to ensure its utility for our purposes, specifically that we are examining both *entire texts* and *sections of texts*. In simpler terms, we maintain that the objects in question indeed consist purely of representations of asserted events that are temporally and meaningfully connected. However, we do not mandate that the textual objects in question be whole texts. On this basis, one could then argue that more intricate narratives are texts that contain numerous such miniature stories and also meet additional criteria.[58] In other words, the definition of miniature narratives could be perceived as delineating a *pattern that is implemented to varying degrees in more elaborate narratives*. This is analogous to how Köppe and Kindt perceive the relationship between their more "meaningful" stories on the one hand and literary works of narration, such as novels, on the other hand. For the latter occasionally transcend the former pattern, in that these literary works of narration usually also exhibit narrative pauses and similar elements, where no narration occurs at all.[59]

In terms of Paul, this definitional foundation allows us to accept that while his letters (as complete texts) might not normally be classified as narratives, they may still display uninterrupted stretches of text that adhere to Köppe and Kindt's definition and therefore constitute "miniature narratives"

---

58. Cf. Noël Carroll, *Beyond Aesthetics: Philosophical Essays* (Cambridge: Cambridge University Press, 2001), 118–19: "I suspect that when we call more large scale discourses, such as histories or novels, narratives, we do so because they possess a large number of narrative connections or because the narrative connections they contain have special salience or a combination of both." Köppe and Kindt in the new edition of their introduction have apparently noticed the problem with their definition and no longer speak of their definition as identifying "minimalistic" narratives but rather "narrative connections" ("Ereignisverknüpfungen"). See Tilmann Köppe and Tom Kindt, *Erzähltheorie: Eine Einführung*, 2nd ed., Reclams Studienbuch: Germanistik (Stuttgart: Reclam, 2022), 25. When writing this book, I still worked with the first edition, from which all other citations come. As it is the very nature of art, there have been writers who have attempted, implicitly, to write literature that breaks free from the boundaries of these definitions. For example, Padgett Powell in *The Interrogative Mood* makes (naturally tiresome) use of questions to write what the subtitle characterizes as a "novel," though there too with a question mark. Similarly, Alain Robbe-Grillet's *Jealousy* maximizes description at the expense of there not being any real action.

59. Köppe and Kindt, *Erzähltheorie*, 101–2.

Chapter 1

embedded within the larger discourse. In my view, it makes good sense to call these passages "narratives," and we should reiterate that the criteria are not as minimalistic as they seem, given that they assume textuality and assertiveness. In other words, if we can identify text sections that fulfill these criteria, and someone still insists that Paul "never tells stories," this would suggest that they are presupposing an understanding of narrativity that is so strict that, if they apply it consistently, they would also be forced to say that our example with the falling apple is not a story. Hence, I believe that the fairly strict requirements we implement (for now) for the applicability of narrative terminology will prove to be vital in building a persuasive case for the narrative turned narratological approach to Paul.

This is not just about making the argument rhetorically appealing but also about respecting the time investment of those who remain skeptical about such theses and about giving these counterclaims room in the debate. For example, perhaps we can agree that Paul tells many miniature stories but only a few elaborate ones. Although, I must add immediately, we should tread carefully before dismissing the possibility that dense narration can result in narratives that fulfill additional criteria. The entire art of crafting "one-liners" is based on the assumption that it is possible to create stories comprising only a few propositions that remain engaging, surprising, and satisfying. A classic example comes from Woody Allen: "I once stole a pornographic book that was printed in Braille; I used to rub the dirty parts."[60]

Content and Presentation of Narratives

As we have observed, narratives come into being when a speaker or writer crafts a text (or a part of a text) in an act of narration, that is, a text (part) with a specific semantic structure. Among narratologists, there is a well-established convention to denominate this aspect of a narrative as a "story" and use the term "discourse" to describe the varied decisions a storyteller can make concerning how they desire to present that content. Hays fundamentally latches onto this aspect, which—in our definition, at least—presupposes the existence of an actual text produced through narrative discourse,

---

60. Fielding Mellish in Woody Allen's 1971 movie *Bananas*. If "one-liners" of that kind appear as standalone texts, they are often referred to as "flash fiction." The most famous example is the following tragic "very short story," which is often attributed to Ernest Hemingway even though it predates his literary work: "For sale: baby shoes, never worn."

Introducing Narrative

a text from which this story can then be extracted. Precisely to prevent such maneuvers that easily introduce story terminology, I do not utilize the terminological distinction between story and narrative in this book.

In German, we can speak of "die Erzählung," which is produced through the act of "das Erzählen" and whose content can be termed "das Erzählte." Analogously naming the content of a story/narrative "that which is told" might best reflect the relationship with both the act of narration and the produced narrative, but it is slightly cumbersome. Therefore, I will typically use the terms "content" and "presentation" to label these respective aspects of the narrative.

Regardless, the conceptual differentiation is quite clear. It is immediately evident that the same *subject matter* can be narrated in an astounding variety of ways.[61] For instance, in his *Exercises in Style*, Raymond Queneau provides a great variety of texts (ranging from a blurb to a haiku), each capturing the experience of meeting a certain man twice in one day in Paris (although the narrativity of some of these texts is admittedly debatable).[62]

When discussing the occurrences within a narrative in the broadest sense, I favor the term "action." Simultaneously, it proves handy to also utilize a term for a narrower conception of a narrative's action. For this notion, I will use the word "plot." Contrary to the action of the story as a whole, the plot includes only its pivotal elements. Selecting these events and determining both their temporal sequence and their significant interconnection require a substantial degree of interpretation. Thus, the plot is not, strictly speaking, an "element" of the narrative that can be easily isolated in a mechanistic fashion.

When we speak of more than one "plotline" or "storyline" within a single complex narrative, such as a novel, this seldom coincides with a presentation that diligently follows different characters in alternating chapters or even entire subsequent sections of a book. Rather, we employ this language to communicate our belief that the most suitable interpretation of the work enables us to explain its action in a rather abstract manner, essentially identifying *multiple*

---

61. If in everyday talk we speak about "the same story" being told in different ways, we are either thinking about variations to an original utterance or are actually presupposing the technical understanding of "story" that I just mentioned. "Subject matter" can be the source material for a creative narrative act and does not have to align easily with the "topic" of the narrative. We will unpack that latter concept later in this chapter.

62. For example, this transformation into "interjections" such as these: Psst! h'm! ah! oh! hem! ah! ha! hey! well! oh! pooh! poof! ow! oo! ouch! hey! eh! h'm! pffft! Well! hey! pooh! oh! h'm! right!

self-contained plots within the same text. The labels "subplot" or "secondary plotline" express the additional evaluative aspect that there is a "main" plot that is central to the work.

Please note that this disclaimer about the extent of interpretation required to make justified claims is even more applicable concerning the "topic" of the narrative, which is sometimes distinguished from the theme, with the latter making a statement about the former, such as "love" (topic) versus "love cannot be a sin" (theme).

Note that even with a rather wide definition of action, it is possible that we might encounter other semantic elements that are connected with the text but do not fall under this rubric. Every reader approaches narratives with their beliefs about the real world and applies them to the text to the extent that the text does not make other stipulations, for example, concerning certain physical laws. As readers, we thus automatically imagine a "story world" or "narrative world," which offers a context for the events that are actually told. Storytellers rely on their audience to draw upon such principles and form conclusions about figures and connections that are not addressed explicitly in their narrative.

In terms of the relationship between what is narrated and implied on the one hand and the real world on the other, narratives can be either *fictional* or *factual*. Factual narratives are created with the intention of directly discussing the real world. Conversely, the writing and reading of fiction occur within a mutually agreed framework, where the storyteller invites the audience to engage in an act of imagination. During this process, making inferences from the imagined story world to the real world is not accepted.

It is important to note a terminological differentiation that, unfortunately, is not as well-established in English literature as in counterparts in German: the elements of the narrative world created in a *fictional* narrative are *fictive*. Consequently, letters that bear the apostle's name but are judged to stem from other individuals should not be termed "fictive letters of Paul." After all, these writings are not merely elements of our imaginative activity or fictive items of a fictional text. However, if Colossians were judged to be pseudepigraphic (i.e., fictional), one might consider applying that label (i.e., fictive) to the letter to Laodicea mentioned in Col 4:16.[63] All this presumes that pseudepigraphic works are not produced with the intent to

---

63. This presupposes that the letter writer did not make intentional use of an actual early Christian letter, in which the situation is a little bit different. Cf. Köppe and Kindt, *Erzähltheorie*, 154–60.

deceive. If deception was the intention, they would not be considered fictional because they would not have been created within a framework that presupposes that readers are aware of the inappropriateness of projecting their imaginings onto the real world. In such a case, referring to it as a "fictitious" work would be more accurate.

Every narrative has at least one narrator: the author. In the case of Paul, he is thus both the "storyteller" (the actual originator of the text in question) and the "narrator" (the narrative voice) of the narratives in his letters. However, it is essential to note that the previous section makes it clear that a "fictive narrator" can only be assumed if we are dealing with a fictional text *and* this fictional text prompts us to conjure a fictive figure that narrates. In such an instance, we are dealing with a primary narrative about a fictive narrator and another narrative level (a secondary narrative) that they produce. If we do not have such indications, it is only the author himself or herself who tells the overarching narrative, even in fictional stories. (I am emphasizing this due to the widespread assumption that every fictional narrative is associated with a fictive narrator.) Factual narratives, too, can feature multiple *levels of narration*, where narratives (and corresponding acts of narration) are *embedded* into the primary (or frame) narrative.[64]

The narratives of Paul are typically factual, except when he clearly states that he encourages his readers to envision events that did not actually occur. While in such cases the category of fictionality might apply, these cases are of no interest to us at the moment, because it is then generally also implied that we are dealing with nonevents. However, if we understand the Pastoral Letters as belonging to the ancient genre of the epistolary novel, this indeed raises the question whether they encourage readers to picture a fictive Paul composing these letters. This would imply that the letter-writing activity

---

64. Take, for example, the book of Acts. Assuming the literary unity of Luke-Acts, we encounter the primary narrator, the author, in Luke 1:1–4. He then largely fades away. But in the story that he tells, we encounter many other narrators that tell their stories (embedded narratives of first rank). Sometimes, their stories in turn contain speech acts, uttered by their former selves or by other narrative figures that feature in these speeches, that could be classified as narratives (thus making them embedded narratives of second rank, etc.). While in Acts 10 the primary narrator tells the story of Corenlius's conversion, the narrative figure Peter does so in an embedded narrative in 11:4–17 (cf. the introduction ἐξετίθετο αὐτοῖς καθεξῆς in verse 4). Within that embedded narrative we even find references to other speech acts, such as the report by Cornelius (verse 13), which again quotes the angel (verse 13–14). Note, however, that in the first case we only have reported speech, and in the second case we have a command, not a narrative.

Chapter 1

constitutes the frame narrative, with every miniature narrative within the letter serving as an embedded narrative by that fictive narrator.

In my perspective, not everything currently discussed regarding the dichotomy of fictionality versus factuality truly pertains to this contrast. It would therefore be prudent to bear the following alternative differentiations in mind.

First, *unreliable narration* (a feature of narration, the presentation of narrative) involves the narrator making claims that are fundamentally untrue. The veracity of these claims must be evaluated within the confines of the particular narrative world in question. This means an unreliable narrator could potentially make a statement in a fictional work that, while accurate in the real world, remains untrue within the context of the narrative. Unreliable narrators can be forthcoming about potential discrepancies between their portrayal and the reality of their respective narrative world. For example, they may announce in advance that their recall of events might be hazy. Alternatively, they can be sly, offering no initial indication that they might be misleading the reader. The New Testament authors are generally believed to never narrate unreliably.[65] However, as we will discuss later, there is a clear instance of unreliable narration in 2 Cor 12 (see below, pp. 222–23).

Second, much of the discussion regarding narrative works and fictionality in the New Testament centers on the question of how to tackle "signals" of fictionality in these otherwise distinctly factual texts. Scholars should remember that in everyday life, our standards for accepting an utterance as a case of "reliable factual narration" are somewhat flexible.

Third, in this context, we must also consider that the same events occurring in the real world can be narrated in very different manners without necessarily impacting the conditions of truth applicable to the respective statements. In this scenario, the difference lies only in *conceptualization*; that is, the same situation is communicated but it is construed differently. If we revisit the earlier German example involving the falling apple, we can see that even the choice of verb—"herunterfallen," which stands behind my use of "to fall down" in the translation—is significant with respect to the construal. For in German, we also have the option "hinunterfallen." Both verbs would be acceptable for the actual (narrative/real-world) event, but the former implies that the event is being observed from the ground, whereas the latter suggests the perspective of someone observing

---

65. Sönke Finnern and Jan Rüggemeier, *Methoden der neutestamentlichen Exegese: Ein Lehr- und Arbeitsbuch*, Uni-Taschenbücher 4212 (Tübingen: Francke, 2016), 178.

these events from above (e.g., in the tree). In English, "to come" and "to go" similarly imply different vantage points from which a movement is observed.

The mention of "perspective" leads us to an important point in the portrayal of narrative: *focalization* (or simply "narrative perspective"). While the narrator is the one "speaking," focalization deals with the question "Who sees?" In other words, narrators can adopt the viewpoint of characters within the narrative world, allowing their perception of the (narrated) reality to shape the way situations are expressed. If a text aligns with the perception of one of its characters—a "focalizer"—in such a manner, we consider the narrative to be "internally" focalized. Note that the point is not about whether we can "look into the head" of a character (indicated by phrases such as "he thought," etc.). Rather, the crucial question is whether the narration is constrained by what is mentally accessible to a certain narrative character (due to their spatio-temporal location, their cognitive abilities, etc.). "External" focalization is different in that here the criterion is precisely whether we look at characters merely from the outside. If we get any direct insights into the thoughts of a character, the text is not externally focalized. However, it is not, as just indicated, automatically internally focalized. Rather, texts can also be non-focalized, namely, if we are unable to assign either internal or external focalization to them. Note that perspectives can shift within a text and can also blend.

The category of focalization becomes particularly relevant in relation to Paul because we are dealing both with a "narrating I" and a "narrated I." It is often challenging yet rewarding to discern whether a portrayal of a past situation is part of a perception that is exclusive to a former self or, alternatively, whether the presentation aligns with a perspective that he, the narrator, still shares in the present. Additionally, a portrayal might even be the result of later reflection and, therefore, differ from his original perception.

For instance, in 2 Cor 1:8–9, Paul begins by signaling that he will recount a story about afflictions in the province of Asia (Οὐ γὰρ θέλομεν ὑμᾶς ἀγνοεῖν, ἀδελφοί, ὑπὲρ τῆς θλίψεως ἡμῶν τῆς γενομένης ἐν τῇ Ἀσίᾳ). The way he characterizes these events seems to mirror his and his coworkers' perspective at that earlier time, especially when stating that it went "beyond our strength" (ὑπὲρ δύναμιν). This does not seem to be his present assessment of the situation. After all, their fear that they would die (see verse 9) ultimately did not materialize; it apparently was not *too* much. By contrast, in verse 9 Paul reflects on the entire episode by attributing a purpose to it, which presupposes the perspective of someone who, in fact, survived. It is

Chapter 1

only in retrospect that he recognizes that their despair had the goal of making them trust in God, the one who raises the dead (ἵνα μὴ πεποιθότες ὦμεν ἐφ' ἑαυτοῖς ἀλλ' ἐπὶ τῷ θεῷ τῷ ἐγείροντι τοὺς νεκρούς).[66]

This phenomenon of the intermingling of focalization signals from the narrating and narrated "I" is rooted in what, following Genette, is often discussed under the heading of various *types of narration* differentiated by the temporal relation of the narrator to the events narrated. "Subsequent" narration, where the narration follows the events narrated, is arguably the most common type. For some narratologists, it aligns closely with the prototypical center of narrativity, since from this temporal stance it is most apparent why someone might be able to make affirmative statements about events, namely, because these events have already transpired, allowing the narrator to look back on them.[67] However, this condition can also be met in "simultaneous" narration (i.e., "narrative in the present contemporaneous with the action"), for instance, if I say that I am "currently writing a book." And then there is "interpolated" narration, where "the story and the narrating can become entangled in such a way that the latter has an effect on the former."[68] This type of narration is particularly prominent in diaries, where the author records past events often while still being emotionally impacted by them. This can lead to quick shifts—and sometimes even confusions—of focalization and also other text features, such as the grammatical tenses used.[69]

This classification of stories according to different narration types assumes that the "deictic center" (i.e., the chronological point from which one refers to specific events) coincides with the time of the act of narration. However, there are instances where an actual shift of this deictic center toward the past or future can be observed. Contrary to some other recent voices, I insist that Greek tenses (i.e., the indicative verb forms) express "absolute temporality" (not "relative temporality," meaning the various past tenses differ only in aspect and do not imply a sequence). Note though that even this statement, seemingly absolute at first glance, presupposes the presence of a time interval that provides a stable point for temporal orientation. This fixed point is typically the time of utterance. However, in the "historic present," the speaker

---

66. On the "we-narrator" as a matter of focalization, see Heilig, *Paulus*, 124.

67. Cf. Gerald Prince, *Narratology: The Form and Function of Narrative*, Janua Linguarum: Series Maior 108 (Berlin: Mouton, 1982), 150.

68. Gérard Genette, *Narrative Discourse: An Essay in Method*, trans. Jane E. Lewin (Ithaca: Cornell University Press, 1980), 217.

69. See below, pp. 159–60, on the unusual use of the indicative perfect tense in Paul's letters.

or author, so to speak, travels into the past, allowing the present tense to become a tense of *subsequent* narration.[70] Similarly, an author can employ the position of the recipients of his message (which in ancient letter writing could be quite distantly future) and discuss events from that perspective—a perspective from which the act of writing itself is already in the past. In the New Testament, such a shift of the deictic center results in the use of the indicative perfect tense in one instance (see below, p. 241 on Acts 15:27, but probably not in 2 Cor 12:17) and, quite frequently in Paul's letters, the indicative aorist tense.[71] These tenses are thus used for *simultaneous* narration (narration about events that occur at the same time as the act of writing).[72]

Similar dynamics can be identified in English, particularly in sports commentary. Often, these statements are not strictly "live," due to many of the events having such a short duration—that is, the time of the event is shorter than the time required to narrate the events truly concurrently. As such, we may actually be dealing with subsequent narration (regarding things that have just transpired), even though the narration is articulated in the present tense.[73] Conversely, commentators sometimes anticipate something and employ the present tense for actions that will occur only a moment later. In such cases, we are, in the strictest sense, dealing with *prior* narration, where the act of narration (portrayed as simultaneous to the event in this instance) takes place before the actual situation unfolds.

There is considerable debate surrounding whether these "predictive narratives" produced by this fourth type of narration should even be classified as narratives.[74] As previously explained, in this book we follow Köppe and Kindt who argue that "merely possible events are not events at all."[75] In other words, when we say a narrative "deals with" events, we are

---

70. On this debate, cf. Heilig, *Paulus*, 316–19.

71. Cf. Heilig, *Paulus*, 307–13.

72. Heilig, *Paulus*, 348–49. It can also be used for events in the future of the letter writer (i.e., as part of predictive narration, see Phil 2:28; Phlm 12; cf. in the disputed letters Eph 6:22; Col 4:8). See also Heilig, *Paulus*, 579–80.

73. On the use of the Greek present indicative, see Heilig, *Paulus*, 349–51.

74. Note that Robert E. Longacre and Shin Ja J. Hwang, *Holistic Discourse Analysis*, 2nd ed. (Dallas: SIL International, 2012), 37, in a work quite influential for the linguistic analysis of New Testament texts, propose several "discourse types," differentiating within the category of "narrative" between "prophecy" on the one hand and "story" on the other hand, depending on whether it involves "projection."

75. Köppe and Kindt, *Erzähltheorie*, 110: "Nach unserer Definition [sind] *bloß mögliche Ereignisse keine Ereignisse*." Note that in their discussion of what events are, they adduce one that relates to the future (49).

Chapter 1

specifying that the text *asserts that events either happened or are currently happening*. This seems to exclude all statements of "predictive narration" as acts of actual narration. This highlights the complexity of distinguishing between narrative and nonnarrative. *Paul* would likely have disagreed with the modern notion, underlying narratological classification systems, that it is impossible to have highly confident insights into the future. Therefore, while for now we exclude all statements that cast any doubt on the actual occurrence of a (potential) event in the past and present, as well as all statements referring to the future, we can also observe that it might be appealing to work with a prototypical definition that emphasizes the *certainty* of the event assertion (regardless of narration types) and regards texts about only potential events (in the past, present, and future) as having a lower degree of narrativity. However, to avoid any criticism of making the verification of the existence of "narratives" in Paul's letters too easy, we will take the former route here, considering only past and present events as building blocks of stories, while still keeping an eye open for phenomena associated with the future that closely mirror the stories that we will uncover.

Genette's influential work on narrative focalization—covered under the heading "perspective"—is included under the broader domain of "mood" alongside what Genette refers to as "distance." Both focalization and distance concern the regulation of narrative information: "just as my view of a picture depends for precision on the distance between me and it, and for breadth on my position relative to any partial obstruction that is more or less blocking it."[76] Most phenomena explored in New Testament exegesis categorized as "vivid" actually fall under this category. In this book, for lack of better words in English, we will mostly use "vividness," even though this term can potentially be misunderstood.[77] It would be a mistake to think that vividness in this sense can only refer to accounts of very dynamic processes. But with "distance," the problem might be more significant. After all, a text could provide a highly graphic portrayal without necessarily encouraging readers to imagine themselves in any specific, let alone particularly close, location to the narrated events.[78] Ultimately, the vividness of any text (or part of a text) is determined by how much it constrains our imagination of aspects perceptible to the senses in the fictive world.

---

76. Genette, *Narrative Discourse*, 162.

77. In German, I prefer "Anschaulichkeit." In English, "concreteness" might be an option, but it is not widely used.

78. Köppe and Kindt, *Erzähltheorie*, 197.

Introducing Narrative

There is another aspect of narrative portrayal often associated with greater vividness (that is, lesser "distance")—particularly slow narration, which "stretches" the narrated time and naturally provides more opportunities for the narrator to include details.[79] The *speed* of narration is generally determined by considering how the actual reading duration of the text relates to the time that passes in the narrative world (presuming, for now, comparable mechanics of time). If the two durations are roughly equal, we often speak of a "scenic" tempo of narration. However, the speed of narration can also exceed the pace of events in the narrated world, resulting in an "accelerated" narration. At times, it can be challenging to differentiate between a *summary* of events in the narrated world compressed into a single text statement and an *ellipsis*, where we progress faster than the events in the narrated world but without even alluding to them.[80]

Thus far, we have assumed that there exists a distinct correlation between the events depicted in the narrative and actual narrated events. However, it is certainly possible for the same situation to be recounted at different speeds in various portions of the same text, particularly if it appears at different levels of the narrative. In such instances, where the narration's *frequency* is concerned, we refer to it as "repetitive" narration—a concept that can sometimes be challenging to differentiate from a series of independent narrations that discuss the same subject matter (i.e., instances of *renarration*). This is especially true in our context, as we are working with texts that are not entirely narrative in nature but merely contain narrative passages interspersed throughout. Consequently, establishing whether Paul is simply resuming a narrative thread following a pause—as is fairly evident, for instance, in 2 Cor 7:5, where the arc of suspense introduced in 2:13 finally finds its closure, so that the subsequent passage truly continues the narrative with only slight overlap (see below, pp. 314–16)—or dealing with two entirely separate narrations (that might have certain variances, like focalization, etc.) can prove to be a challenge. Hays's example of Gal 4:3–6 following 3:13–14 may very well represent such an instance.[81]

In pinpointing a conceptual counterpoint to "repetitive narration," one might propose "singulative narration," characterized by a one-to-one correspondence between narration and narrated events. Another candidate for a

---

79. It is not a "canonical" form in Genette, *Narrative Discourse*, 95. Note also that he further includes the "narrative pause" here, which, however, often lacks the hallmarks of narrativity. Cf. Köppe and Kindt, *Erzähltheorie*, 184.

80. On Gal 1:21 as an example, see Heilig, *Paulus*, 464–65.

81. Cf. Heilig, *Paulus*, 123–26.

Chapter 1

corresponding strategy of narration might be one that involves segmenting a broader narrated event into finer subevents. In contrast, the category of frequency that one usually comes across in tandem with repetitive narration is "iterative" narration. Even though it is at times framed as antithetical to repetitive narration, its nature is fundamentally distinct, making it an incongruent counterpoint.[82] Indeed, delineating "multiple instances of the same event" within a singular narrative act is unfeasible given the unique temporal distinction of each event. Instead, in iterative narration a variety of events are lumped together based on shared characteristics, so that they are subsequently aggregated into an "event bundle" and presented as a unified entity. Notably, in Greek the use of the imperfective aspect for verbs that express brief events produces a portrayal of a series of events. This sheds light on the somewhat ambiguous prerequisite of "at least two" events highlighted earlier. Due to the specific grammatical nuances of this aspect in Greek, there are instances where a single verb form can represent a multitude of events. Consequently, such a verb form alone can result in a stand-alone narrative.[83]

Finally, we must discuss the aspect of *order*. This is likely the area where the divide between the presentation of a narrative and its content is most apparent. Although events in most narrative realms unfold chronologically, mirroring our everyday experiences and how we interpret them, the narrator has the liberty to alter this order during their narration. Essentially, there are two options: the "analepsis" or "flashback," which inserts into the text a segment that reverts to an earlier point in the narrated time than what has just been detailed, and the "prolepsis," which briefly advances into the narrated future.

It is worth noting that to apply these categories, we must establish what forms the "base narrative." Sometimes, it can be debatable whether we are dealing, for example, with a base narrative and a subsequent analepsis or a prolepsis followed by the base narrative. Take, for instance, Rom 15, where Paul twice refers to "now" (νυνί) in verses 23 and 25 within a section that clearly provides simultaneous narration about the current state of his mission in the eastern Roman Empire and his present journey to Jerusalem.[84] In verses 26–27, Paul discusses what occurred earlier in Macedonia and Achaia, establishing some connections to the present in the latter verse. Is this an

---

82. On the relation to accelarated narration, see Heilig, *Paulus*, 116.
83. Heilig, *Paulus*, 282–83.
84. For a detailed analysis of Rom 15:18–32, see below, pp. 245–53.

analepsis? My contention is that it indeed is. If, after that section, Paul had returned to the subject of verses 18–22, the even earlier phase of his eastern mission, one could argue convincingly that this time interval ought to be regarded as the base narrative, meaning that verses 26–27 and everything relating to an even later time (i.e., the time of writing) should be classified as a prolepsis. However, in the existing text Paul's narrative merges into predictive narration in verse 28 (cf. also the hint in verse 24) discussing Paul's further travel plans. This constructs a timeline in which verses 26–27 appear as a deviation from the sequential progression of events, thus qualifying as a flashback.

It is crucial to note that some individuals interpret the term "prolepsis" differently. They might argue that Paul's statements about his own future are merely "foreshadowings." The reasoning behind this differentiation is the notion that prolepses assume that the events actually take place within the narrative world, whereas Paul's travel plans extend beyond the temporal horizon available to him at the time in which he is writing. However, it is debatable if the term "foreshadowing" is beneficial in such instances, since there is also the subcategory of *certain* foreshadowings.

Further examination of the specific case of references to a future time from the narrator's perspective (i.e., true predictive narration) will be conducted later (pp. 240–309). For now, we will only consider events that occur in the narrator's past or present but are sequentially later than the surrounding text events. Here, we can differentiate between a phenomenon of narrative order on the one hand (that is, if an ellipsis is present in the appropriate location later in the narrative) and a phenomenon of narrative frequency on the other hand (if no corresponding ellipsis is found later in the text; we are then dealing with a special case of repetitive narration).[85]

We are now well equipped with narratological categories and the corresponding terminology that we can apply in our analysis of Paul's narratives. In introducing these tools, we have also briefly explored some Pauline narratives, which served as illustrations for these concepts. However, before we can delve deeper into a more detailed examination of the Pauline texts, one additional task remains. We need to clarify how the application of these narratological labels to specific textual phenomena aligns with *exegesis*—both broadly in terms of the respective goals of narratological analyses and biblical interpretation, and specifically in terms of how we might need to adapt these concepts to make them suitable to texts written in Koine Greek.

---

85. Cf. Heilig, *Paulus*, 584–87.

Chapter 1

Narratology and Interpretation

Earlier in this chapter, I expressed criticism of the narrative approach for its lack of due consideration for narratology as a suitable framework for exploring Paul's narrations. However, it is insufficient to merely "incorporate" narratological concepts into our exegetical practice. The theoretical correlation between narratology and exegesis is not inherently clear. Therefore, before moving ahead, I wish to briefly elaborate on how I personally associate narratology with interpretation and, by extension, exegesis (assuming that the ultimate aim of exegesis is to extract the meaning of texts in a rule-driven manner, "interpretation"). The discussions in this book are guided by a collection of fairly specific assumptions on this matter, which I will briefly sketch out here in broad outlines.[86]

First, it is widely accepted that it is feasible in principle to differentiate between *descriptive* and *interpretive* operations on texts. While the details are debated, there seems to be broad consensus that the former approach is aimed at the classification of textual phenomena, while the latter seeks to ascertain meaning. Second, the prevailing opinion posits that narratological concepts are fundamentally descriptive. It is worth noting that narratological—and consequently descriptive—categories can indeed be applied to semantic features, as evidenced, for example, in the category of 'plot.' However, what renders a narratological category like plot descriptive is, third, the fact that the category remains *neutral with regard to any specific interpretation theory* one might choose to adopt. This may initially seem like an obscure distinction but proves significantly coherent when we acknowledge that interpretation theories differ in how they conceptualize what constitutes meaning (e.g., authorial intention) and the methodologies they employ to uncover this meaning. The 'plot' category can be applied to the semantics

---

86. Throughout this section I will rely on the more detailed discussion in Heilig, *Paulus*, 134–52. See also Theresa Heilig and Christoph Heilig, "Teaching Biblical Exegesis: The Distinction between Methods of Description and Interpretation," *Didaktikos* (forthcoming). The argumentation is based mostly on Tom Kindt and Hans-Harald Müller, "Wieviel Interpretation enthalten Beschreibungen? Überlegungen zu einer umstrittenen Unterscheidung am Beispiel der Narratologie," in *Regeln der Bedeutung: Zur Theorie der Bedeutung literarischer Texte*, ed. Fotis Jannidis, Gerhard Lauer, Matías Martínez, and Simone Winko, Revisionen 1 (Berlin: de Gruyter, 2003), 286–304, and (in English!) Tom Kindt and Hans-Harald Müller, "Narrative Theory and/or/as Theory of Interpretation," in *What Is Narratology? Questions and Answers Regarding the Status of a Theory*, ed. Tom Kindt and Hans-Harald Müller, Narratologia 1 (Berlin: de Gruyter, 2003), 205–19. See also for a succinct presentation Köppe and Kindt, *Erzähltheorie*, 34–36.

of stories irrespective of our opinion on the first aspect, that is, regardless of which conception of meaning we choose, regardless of where we locate this "content" of the text, whether in the mind of the author, the readers, or elsewhere. This argument has two significant implications.

Initially, it emerges that we must dispute the notion that presents narratology *as* an interpretive approach. This persuasion takes various forms. Some academics perceive narratology as presenting a synchronic interpretive technique that they deem *supplemental* to more traditional diachronic methods. Such assessments, however, often miss the crux of the matter. What these authors call "narratology" is frequently just a collection of very specific tools constructed on structuralist assumptions, which implicitly suggest that meaning is inherent in the text. Thus, these methods are far from neutral when it comes to the selected interpretation theory. Concurrently, numerous diachronic methods, which are utilized in crafting, for example, biblical commentaries, are not actually interpretive steps but are merely descriptive in themselves. This ambiguity translates into a generally inconsistent approach to biblical texts where a variety of actions are enacted upon them without a discernible system.

We observe more cohesive models among scholars who aim to reform their interpretive methodologies via the *incorporation* of narratological categories. The most basic strategy of this kind is the application of narratological categories as tools for a *close reading*, as Irene de Jong (pioneer with respect to narratological commentaries on ancient narrative texts) envisions the function of narratology in her work.[87] Nevertheless, what is needed for a complete theory of interpretation (besides a well-defined conception of meaning) is a methodology of interpretation that applies to all texts, not simply narrative ones. Therefore, there emerges a risk of narratology furnishing our commentary on the biblical text with such a technical lexicon that it can seem as though we have expressly exercised considerable contemplation regarding the issue of methodology. However, if we articulate our interpretations in sophisticated manners but lack guiding categories for establishing these meanings in the first place, narratology does little more than mask our deficiency of a coherent methodology of interpretation overall.

For similar reasons, I maintain some skepticism toward what has gained traction in biblical studies known as "cognitive narratology."[88] With respect

---

87. Irene J. F. de Jong, *Narratology and Classics: A Practical Guide* (Oxford: Oxford University Press, 2014), v.

88. For erudite presentations see, in particular, Sönke Finnern, *Narratologie und*

Chapter 1

to the cognitive turn, these authors, justifiably, accentuate mental processes in both text generation and reception.[89] In my opinion, they are also correct to underline the reductionism inherent in structuralism, which concentrated solely on the text's internal dynamics.

However, we must not overlook the fact that this emphasis on text production and text reception suggests that these cognitive categories have a specific relationship to the task of interpretation, mainly as components of the methodology of very particular interpretation theories. Some of these cognitive categories align with a pursuit of authorial intention (text production), while others might enhance the existing tools of an approach mostly known as "reader-response criticism" in biblical studies (text reception).[90]

It is crucial to note that these two interpretation theories presuppose drastically contrasting concepts of what constitutes 'meaning.' Of course, it is entirely acceptable if a single scholar becomes interested in various kinds of meanings.[91] Ultimately, the choice of the conception of meaning depends on the presumption of norms that cannot be justified solely based on analysis of the text but necessitate reasoning beyond the text, in other words "hermeneutics." Simply put, it is impossible to argue that only a single interpretation theory is suitable for Paul's letters based on these interpretations' results alone.

Nonetheless, this observation should indeed sensitize us to the fact that the nature of cognitive linguistics is misunderstood if it is employed as a unified interpretation theory. It will be more beneficial in refining exist-

---

biblische Exegese: Eine integrative Methode der Erzählanalyse und ihr Ertrag am Beispiel von Matthäus 28, WUNT 2.285 (Tübingen: Mohr Siebeck, 2010); and Jan Rüggemeier, *Poetik der markinischen Christologie: Eine kognitiv-narratologische Exegese*, WUNT 2.458 (Tübingen: Mohr Siebeck, 2017). Through Finnern and Rüggemeier, *Methoden*, many of these assumptions have entered exegetical pedagogy. To be sure, there are also many other movements that aim at remodeling classical narratology into interpretive frameworks of a specific kind. I focus on this one because it usually builds its claim on the universal importance of cognition and not on the relevance of specific contexts (such as feminist, postcolonial, etc., approaches), which one might simply "choose" to be interested in or not.

89. Cf. Finnern and Rüggemeier, *Methoden*, 174.

90. For a broad sketch of what a methodology within such an interpretation theory might look like, see Moisés Mayordomo, "Rezeptionsästhetische Analyse," in *Das Studium des Neuen Testaments*, ed. Heinz-Werner Neudorfer and Eckhard J. Schnabel, rev. ed. (Wuppertal: Brockhaus, 2006), 417–39. For a masterful analysis along these lines, see Moisés Mayordomo, *Den Anfang hören: Leseorientierte Evangelienexegese am Beispiel von Matthäus 1–2*, FRLANT 180 (Göttingen: Vandenhoeck & Ruprecht, 1998).

91. Cf. Mayordomo, "Exegese," 36–37.

ing methodologies within separate interpretive approaches. Against this backdrop, the problematic nature of merely reformulating narratological categories in cognitive-linguistic terms should become apparent. In this process, we will usually have to decide whether to conform them to the mental processes of the speaker/author or the audience. If we do not clearly state our choice, we might inadvertently mix differing interpretation theories.

But even if we are remarkably consistent in stipulating how these reshaped narratological categories relate to the meaning that we seek, we face a twofold issue. First, we strip narratological categories of their broader use in alternative interpretive approaches, because we will not be able to utilize them in this altered form in those contexts (since they will no longer be neutral with respect to interpretation theories). In essence, we would require different introductions to narratology (or, rather, narratologies) contingent on the interpretive framework that is assumed. In the more traditional understanding of narratology, everyone can use the same introduction, and the distinctive work pertains to determining the best methodology for interpreting texts within each interpretation theory.

Second and, in my opinion, much more concerning, we might also damage the methodologies of the respective interpretive approaches. Since narratological categories were not developed for the purpose of interpretation, we will almost undoubtedly overlook aspects of meaning if we limit our methodological repertoire to these cognitively enhanced narratological concepts. We overtask these categories if we expect them to shoulder the burden of interpretation, with the unfortunate consequence, I fear, that we will be compelled to supply the meaning that we desire them to uncover covertly (and therefore outside of methodological control). Concurrently, we are also in danger of neglecting crucial elements of cognitive-linguistic research if traditional narratology does not already hold a place for them.

To be fair, the foundational works on this matter generally avoid this issue by focusing on large-scale narrative elements such as narrative characters, where substantial machinery has typically been utilized, and cognitive-linguistic considerations certainly offer many enhancements.[92] "Quick and dirty" methods are not automatically bad. In some contexts, such as the emergency room, they can be lifesaving and superior to detailed analyses,

---

92. See, e.g., the insightful contributions in Jan Rüggemeier and Elizabeth E. Shively, eds., "Cognitive Linguistics and New Testament Narrative: Investigating Methodology through Characterization," special issue, *BibInt* 29 (2021).

Chapter 1

which are prone to many mistakes.[93] However, there is the potential for a misunderstanding, especially for novices who are just encountering this ostensibly very "technical" language and, hence, assume that the approach as a whole has been worked out in detail, even though it is a rather young attempt to build on eclectic insights from an ever-developing interdisciplinary discussion. The fact that "cognitive narratology" in biblical studies thus far does not appear to be concerned with the fundamental parts of narratives—events and their conceptualization—suggests to me that we are not yet dealing with a fully formulated methodology, supposedly enriched by cognitive linguistics insights, for interpreting narrative texts.

Thus far, we have discussed the negative implications of merging narratology and interpretation, which led to a rejection of combining the tasks into "cognitive narratology." The next crucial consequence of upholding the descriptive nature of narratological categories is the imperative to posit also in a positive way how we intend to proceed with our analysis of narrative texts. The initial step requires clarity about the meaning we aim to uncover in the interpretation process. Subsequently, we must develop a methodology within this framework (or multiple methodologies for various frameworks if we are intrigued by different types of meaning). In doing this, we might find it beneficial to incorporate cognitive-linguistic insights, but only if the searched-for meaning necessitates this and only in conjunction with other tools that may likewise be pertinent to our approach. Then, we can interpret specific texts and employ traditional narratological categories (if the texts in question are narrative) with primarily two objectives.

First, these descriptive categories might serve a *heuristic* function by aiding in identifying elements of the text that could be relevant for our interpretation. Essentially, understanding that we are dealing with a narrative and discerning how narrators can alter their narration may assist us in discovering features that are significant in determining its meaning. However, it is essential to note that narratological categories, as heuristic tools, aid in uncovering text elements that have only potential relevance for text interpretation. It is entirely possible that a narratological category can be applied easily but that this observation is not particularly relevant for determining the narrative's meaning (or that the observation is relevant only for a specific interpretation theory).

Second, these categories might provide descriptive clarity to the *outcomes* of our interpretations by rendering them more comparable to the

---

93. I am grateful to Matthew B. Joss for discussing this issue with me.

interpretations suggested by others. For instance, categories related to the notion of plot might aid us in communicating different ideas we have about a story's action, enabling a comparison of alternative interpretations even when different interpreters employ various interpretation theories.

Given this context, I am now in a position to provide a concise overview of my approach in this book. I will interpret the Pauline texts aiming specifically to discern the *author's intent*. I chose this particular conception of meaning because it remains prevalent in historical-critical research. (Indeed, the "historical-critical method" extends beyond a mere method; it is an interpretation theory!) Moreover, it is indisputable that Paul's letters are artifacts of communication, regardless of whatever else they may be and apart from the validity of alternative approaches that view them as literature, that is, as pieces of art.[94] As the backbone of the methodology leading to this goal, I will use Heinrich von Siebenthal's text grammar.[95] The narratological categories, as defined in this chapter, will guide my interpretation (scrutinizing, for example, how "temporal order" is expressed in the text) and help describe the outcomes of my interpretation. This approach may provide those who are familiar with other narrators with an understanding of how Paul, as a storyteller, relates to them.

Textuality and Text Grammar

Before the emergence of text linguistics as a field of study in the 1960s, texts were commonly viewed simply as an accumulation of sentences, which were deemed the largest unit of linguistic interest. Even with the evolution of a "transphrastic" understanding of text—that is, the recognition that texts contain phenomena that cannot be adequately explained by looking at sentences in isolation—this did not significantly change in practice.[96]

---

94. On literariness, see Heilig, *Paulus*, 17–18. See now also the excellent introduction to literary theory and New Testament scholarship by Michal Beth Dinkler, *Literary Theory and the New Testament*, Anchor Bible Resource Library (New Haven: Yale University Press, 2019).

95. *AGG* 297–354. (Unless otherwise noted, all citations from von Siebenthal are paragraph numbers.) I will introduce its basic tenets only very briefly here, given that von Siebenthal's grammar is now available in English too. I am working on a more detailed introduction to his text grammar for Eerdmans.

96. Cf. Christina Gansel and Frank Jürgens, *Textlinguistik und Textgrammatik*, 3rd ed., Uni-Taschenbücher 3265 (Göttingen: Vandenhoeck & Ruprecht, 2009), 35–39.

Chapter 1

It was only through the insight that the coherence of the text at a semantic level was critical for differentiating texts from other sentence structures that new categories needed to be introduced into the discourse.[97] However, even this broadened understanding of text is ultimately inadequate. After all, the same propositional structures can be used very differently depending on the context.[98] As such, it is essential to also incorporate pragmatic features into our definition of textuality.

In his text grammar, von Siebenthal thus aligns with the proposal set forth by German text linguists Christina Gansel and Frank Jürgens, who define the text as a 'self-coherent unit of linguistic communication with a recognizable communicative function and a structure organized in a specific way.'[99] These scholars characterize this understanding of textuality as "integrative" because it strives to blend both text structure and text function or, in other words, semantics and pragmatics.[100] It is important to note that the aspect of "structure" comprises the interaction between sentences and propositions; that is, it can be defined in reference to both the expression and the content side of texts.[101]

Von Siebenthal primarily concentrates on this intersection between expression (i.e., "grammar") and content dimensions of the text.[102] Indeed, the process of conveying meaning through texts can largely be described in terms of the creation and, subsequently, the reconstruction of propositional structures.[103] Thus, paying attention to this dynamic of propositional structure is an important aspect of the specific task of text linguistics in creating a text grammar (the rules that govern the creation of whole texts) within any given language.

On the content side of the text, propositions are the fundamental building blocks roughly corresponding to sentences on the expression side. I use

---

97. Cf. Gansel and Jürgens, *Textlinguistik*, 39–49.

98. Gansel and Jürgens, *Textlinguistik*, 49–51.

99. Gansel and Jürgens, *Textlinguistik*, 51: "Ein Text ist eine in sich kohärente Einheit der sprachlichen Kommunikation mit einer erkennbaren kommunikativen Funktion und einer in spezifischer Weise organisierten Struktur." Cf. *AGG* 297.

100. Gansel and Jürgens, *Textlinguistik and Textgrammatik*, 52.

101. See already Klaus Brinker, *Linguistische Textanalyse: Eine Einführung in die Grundbegriffe und Methoden*, 3rd ed., Grundlagen der Germanistik 29 (Berlin: Schmidt, 1992), 21.

102. But see *AGG* 302–14.

103. Cf. Gansel and Jürgens, *Textlinguistik*, 166–69.

"roughly" because participle phrases, infinitive phrases, and even some constructions with adjectives or nouns can take the place of sentences and are subsequently considered to express propositions.[104] It is often feasible to identify a close relationship in content between two consecutive propositions that thus form a distinct "connection" (German "Konnexion"), a construction, in which the two connecting parts are called "connects."[105] These connections can be classified by generalizing the roles the two propositions assume within these liaisons—for example, reason-result, means-purpose, condition-consequence—and subsequently grouping them according to their semantic qualities into various connection types (causal, telic, conditional, etc.).

Take note that sentences displaying variations in mood, aspect, tense, and negation can still express the same "propositional value." For example, the sentences "Paul tells a story," "Paul does not tell a story," "Does Paul tell a story?," and "Paul, tell a story" all communicate the same proposition, which can be symbolized as {<Paul> [tell a story]}.[106] Von Siebenthal emphasizes that a proposition is a "content entity," suggesting that it can include corresponding sentences from other languages, such as the German "Paulus erzählt eine Geschichte."[107]

Von Siebenthal's "content entities" more closely align with paraphrases of the entirety of what is communicated, that is, the "utterance meaning."[108] This is why von Siebenthal distinguishes between "reason-result" and "reason-exhortation" relationships.[109] In essence, in his endeavor to incorporate pragmatics into his analysis, his paraphrase for the "meaning" of each sentence (or sentence-like structures) also includes additional elements (specifically, epistemic mode and communicative function).[110] I propose that it may be more beneficial to initially focus on propositions proper and stress that texts with identical propositional structures can still

---

104. *AGG* 311.
105. *AGG* 312b.
106. On different ways of displaying verb constellations and propositions, cf. Heilig, *Paulus*, 265. This builds on Carlota S. Smith, *The Parameter of Aspect*, 2nd ed., Studies in Linguistics and Philosophy 43 (Dordrecht: Kluwer Academic, 1997).
107. *AGG* 312a.
108. On speech acts, cf. below, pp. 166–68.
109. Cf. *AGG* 333.
110. Cf. Heilig, *Paulus*, 161–63.

Chapter 1

differ significantly due to pragmatic factors, which aligns with the above understanding of textuality.

Here is an example taken from Acts 20:7 that demonstrates the points made so far, with reference to a connection that arguably constructs a miniature story and, interestingly enough, features Paul as a character who narrates stories (figure 1).[111]

Figure 1. The semantic structure of a miniature story in Acts 20:7

Semantic roles of the propositions	Propositions	Communicated content	Greek connector construction
result	{<Paul>[intend to leave next day]}	'Because he intended to leave the next day.'	μέλλων ἐξιέναι τῇ ἐπαύριον
reason	{<Paul>[talk to them]}	'Paul began talking to them.'	ὁ Παῦλος διελέγετο αὐτοῖς

Observe that the semantic roles that the two propositions occupy in relation to each other are linked to the semantics of a "connector" in the Greek text, usually a conjunction, an adverb, or a preposition. However, in the instance of the miniature story in Acts 20:7, we merely have an adverbial participle that is used with a causal force. In this book, we also treat participial constructions and even main clauses that follow asyndetically as "connector structures."[112] The connect that carries the connector is called the "internal connect," the other one the "external connect."

The type of connection we identify on the content level often matches the semantic class of the connector in the connector construction on the expression level of the text. For instance, an adversative nucleus-contrast relationship is typically marked by an adversative connector such as ἀλλά. However, the two matters are not entirely identical. For instance, καί, an additive connector, in certain scenarios can be used in connections with

---

111. It could be argued that μέλλων and ἐξιέναι each have propositional value and we could further split this part up into an introduction-content connection (*AGG* 323b).

112. Heilig, *Paulus*, 163–64.

Introducing Narrative

more specific semantics, such as a temporal sequence (e.g., "and then").[113] Von Siebenthal's grammar does not provide a dictionary for Greek connectors, as has been made for German with considerable effort.[114] Rather, it presents an overview of different connection types with a list of connectors that can be employed within them. The fact that we will discuss the same connectors in a variety of connector types might suggest either a high degree of polysemy or, more likely, that the classification of the communicated connections does not correspond neatly to the semantic demarcations of the connectors that are used.

Even though connections have a two-part structure, they can still be applied to texts longer than just two sentences. Typically, one of the propositions is "communicationally more prominent," and it serves as a junction point within the entire propositional nexus to establish yet another connection with another proposition (or another propositional nexus).[115] We will delve further into this issue of "information structure" below (pp. 62–65). For now, we can observe that this method of depicting the semantic structure of a text is a plausible model for how text production and comprehension operate. Two propositions, which together form a connection, can be envisioned as creating a new macroproposition, in which certain parts hold greater communicative prominence. These macropropositions can then engage in their own semantic relationships on a higher "level" of the text's semantic structure.[116] Figure 2 provides such an analysis of the propositional structure of Acts 20:7 in its entirety, which presents Paul as a storyteller.[117]

---

113. Heilig, *Paulus*, 195–97.

114. Leibniz-Institut für Deutsche Sprache, *Wörterbuch der Konnektoren*, https://grammis.ids-mannheim.de/konnektoren. This site is the result of the mammoth project by Renate Pasch, Ursula Brauße, Eva Breindl, and Ulrich Hermann Waßner, eds., *Linguistische Grundlagen der Beschreibung und syntaktische Merkmale der deutschen Satzverknüpfer (Konjunktionen, Satzadverbien und Partikeln)*, vol. 1 of *Handbuch der deutschen Konnektoren*, Schriften des Instituts für Deutsche Sprache 9 (Berlin: de Gruyter, 2003); and Eva Breindl, Anna Volodina, and Ulrich Hermann Waßner, eds., *Semantik der deutschen Satzverknüpfer*, vol. 2 of *Handbuch der deutschen Konnektoren*, Schriften des Instituts für Deutsche Sprache 13 (Berlin: de Gruyter, 2014).

115. *AGG* 312d.

116. At the moment, the best tool for creating such depictions of macropropositional structures is the free program HermeneutiX (https://sourceforge.net/projects/hermeneutix/).

117. The example is taken from Heilig, *Paulus*, 173.

Chapter 1

Figure 2. The propositional structure of Acts 20:7

The expression side of the text	Connections	The content side of the text (utterance meaning), reproduced in English
Ἐν δὲ τῇ μιᾷ τῶν σαββάτων συνηγμένων ἡμῶν	────── means ──────	'When we were gathered on the first day of the week
κλάσαι ἄρτον,	temporal specification ── PURPOSE ──	to break the bread,
ὁ Παῦλος διελέγετο αὐτοῖς	NUCLEUS ── NUCLEUS ── RESULT ──	Paul was talking to them,
μέλλων ἐξιέναι τῇ ἐπαύριον,	────── reason ──────	because he intended to leave the next day.
παρέτεινέν τε τὸν λόγον μέχρι μεσονυκτίου.	Amplification ────────────────	And he extended his message until midnight.'

According to this analysis, Acts 20:7 can be fundamentally interpreted as a nucleus enhanced by an amplification.[118] The nucleus, in turn, is a sort of "macroproposition" that the reader constructs on the basis of a nucleus and a time specification (which is of lesser importance). This time specification can be further dissected as an instrumental relationship while the nucleus comprises a causal connection.

It should be evident why this text-grammatical approach is so pivotal for our project. Most fundamentally, it empowers us to accurately delineate what a text that satisfies our definition of narrativity would resemble, both on its expression and its content level, and how both aspects could be varied by the narrator without transcending these confines. Upon applying this to specific texts, we can easily (and unequivocally!) identify parts that align

---

118. It is not without alternative. It could be argued that contextually it should rather be MEANS-purpose instead of means-PURPOSE (i.e., with the chronologically earlier element being more important). Cf. Heilig, *Paulus*, 174.

Introducing Narrative

with this broader pattern, thereby *classifying them as narratives*. Simultaneously, we will also be able to perceive how precisely Paul utilizes this pattern or, in other words, be able to provide a detailed description of his narratives and, thus, determine what *kind of narrator* he is.

At the very least, to me, it appears that this argument is structured in a highly transparent manner. Granted, not everyone will concur with my evaluation. It is essential to remember that I am utilizing these text-grammatical categories as part of an interpretation methodology that presupposes a specific concept of meaning. In other words, if I strive to uncover "*meaningful* connections" between events, I am solely interested in the relations that Paul might have perceived between them. However, even readers of Paul's letters who are not concerned with authorial intent might find some merit in my analysis because the propositional structures of texts will likely feature in their own framework. Granted, they will inevitably base their decision of whether or not to assume a certain connection between propositions on other factors and not on whether it most convincingly reflects Paul's intention.[119]

As I conclude this section, it is important to note that while I believe grammar contributes a significant element to discerning an author's intent in a text, it does not guarantee full consensus among interpreters, not even when they share the same interpretive framework or theory. First, dispute may arise over the propositional structure of the text dependent on the evaluation of certain syntactical phenomena. Second, and more crucially, contextual assumptions play a significant role in the interpretive process. They shape the reconstruction of the propositional macrostructure by influencing the decision of which of the two propositional elements is more crucial for communication.[120] Moreover, the actual topic of the story may be deeply embedded within the text's propositional structure (and not simply visible on the outer layer of the propositional structure), especially if a subtle narration strategy is assumed and/or there is an extensive shared understanding between the narrator and the recipients.

Furthermore, "interpretations" of texts in a broad sense can vary even more widely regarding the same text if we also consider the function of the text. The very same textual structure can serve vastly different purposes

---

119. Cf. Heilig, *Paulus*, 150–52.
120. For example, David I. Yoon, "Prominence and Markedness in New Testament Discourse: Galatians 1,11–2,10 as a Test Case," *Filología Neotestamentaria* 26 (2013): 3–26, thinks that the subjunctive verb form εὐαγγελίζωμαι in Gal 1:16 marks this proposition as central to the narrative. For that reason, he gets the topic of the story completely wrong, in my opinion. See Heilig, *Paulus*, 185.

Chapter 1

depending on how the author/speaker positions themselves with respect to the content of that text and with respect to the recipients. Von Siebenthal's text-grammatical approach, while valuable, carries the risk of misinterpreting the reconstruction of propositional structures in isolation as a complete process of interpretation. To counter such misunderstanding, I will discuss the pragmatics of Paul's stories in a separate chapter (chapter 3) after we have addressed the propositional structure of these texts (chapter 2).

Having been rather critical of "cognitive narratology" in biblical studies above, I deem it appropriate to add a self-critical note to these observations. While I am confident that my approach allows me to keep the descriptive narratological categories untainted by the assumptions of my particular interpretation theory, and while I firmly believe that the text-grammatical framework offers a robust guideline for establishing the meaning of a text, at least in its general structure, I acknowledge that my analysis would likely have benefited in numerous areas from a more comprehensive understanding and integration of cognitive linguistics. As I have mentioned, my goal is to supplement von Siebenthal's approach, which places significant emphasis on propositional structures, with pragmatic considerations (see chapter 3), but I am cognizant of the fact that further advancements could be made in this direction.

Let us now shift our attention to the Pauline narratives themselves.[121] Specifically, I aim to concentrate on their propositional structure as a means of illuminating the elements of (a) temporal order and (b) meaningful re-

---

121. There are several different ways to present the results of the analysis of the two sides of the structure of narrative text parts in Paul's letters and their function. In the German work underlying this book, I spend a chapter each—and over three hundred pages in total (Heilig, *Paulus*, 213–525)—on (a) the content side of narratives; (b) the expression side of narratives; (c) temporal order and how it is realized on both sides; and (d) the pragmatics of Pauline stories. Here, to save space, I will choose a different route. We will, for the moment, not go into the details of how narrative text parts are characterized on the surface level of the text. Rather, I will jump directly to the first question of how Paul realizes "meaningful connections" and "temporal order" in the propositional structure of his texts (chapter 2). To be sure, since connections reflect connector constructions, we will touch on the syntax of these texts too. But we will not explicitly discuss the criteria pertaining to the surface structure of the text that eliminate some potential examples. We will learn more about these assumptions when we turn to the pragmatics of Paul's narration. In other words, I will discuss the former area of interest (b) in the section "The Pragmatics of Paul's Stories" in chapter 3. It is in this context that I will come back to the expression side of narratives, because we will see that pragmatics influence the lexical and grammatical shape of narratives immensely.

lationships, which we have identified as crucial for narrativity. It is notably convenient that it is possible to classify the myriad of propositional relationships into two primary categories, depending on whether they are (a) predominantly temporal or (b) rooted in propositional logic, that is, the study of how simple statements can be combined to form complex statements and how their truth values relate.[122] It is apparent that each of these two groups corresponds closely to those two criteria of narrativity. We will observe how both these classes of connection types are evident in Paul's letters, thereby contradicting the notion that Paul seldom narrates stories.

As conditional and causal connections contribute significantly to argumentation and, equally, "argumentation is found frequently inter alia in the letters of Paul," we will only briefly comment on the nonchronological connections.[123] The real crux of the matter regarding the debate about whether or not there are narratives in Paul's letters undoubtedly lies with temporal connections, making it advisable to focus on this issue. Of course, given that narrativity requires *both* temporal order and meaningful relationships, we will also explore how temporal connections might communicate additional meaningful aspects and how nonchronological connections might yet imply a temporal relationship.

If you have been diligently following this discussion thus far, one concern that might need to be addressed at this juncture pertains to the expression side of Paul's stories. To be sure our definition of narrativity comes with implications for both the content and the expression side of the text. Thus, we need to take both spheres into account in order to classify a Pauline text (part) as a story. In other words, before we can talk about miniature narratives in Paul's letters, we must not just identify specific connections on the content level but also consider the *impact of our definition on the grammatical structure of the text*.

I chose to focus on the content level initially because the semantic perspective is frequently neglected in the exegetical realm, and it facilitates our progression beyond syntax-focused discussions, which can sometimes obfuscate the actual subject matter at hand. That is not to say we will disregard the expression facet of Pauline narratives entirely. For now, however, our primary interest lies in *whether* Paul actually conveys stories rather than in the specific style of his narration. We will embark on our exploration by looking for the relevant connections, while also specifying when specific

---

122. See Heilig, *Paulus*, 171. Cf. *AGG* 352b.
123. *AGG* 304e.

Chapter 1

grammatical constellations are necessary in addition for the fulfillment of our definition and while also, as we go, making some cursory notes regarding Paul's portrayal of certain relationships among events at a grammatical level, thus adding some nuance to our picture of *how* he narrates.

We will then later address the expression dimension of Pauline narratives in more detail when we analyze these stories in their respective contexts (chapter 3). Our reason for this sequence is that the context in which a story is told significantly shapes its presentation—the narrative discourse.[124] Given that texts can always be examined from both content and expression perspectives, a linear discussion, as is inherent in a book format, invariably involves decisions about how to present the material accompanied by certain unavoidable limitations. However, it appears to me that this is the optimal approach. We have delineated a definition of narrativity with a strong emphasis on semantics. Therefore, it seems logical to analyze, in the next step, whether these content features can be detected in Paul's writing. Subsequently, we can delve into how this content is given form on the grammatical level in Paul's writings and how the communicative circumstances of these writings might have influenced his choices in the storytelling process.

---

124. Admittedly, this influence on the presentation of the narrative, the "discourse" (see above, p. 28), goes beyond grammatical aspects. After all, the very same two events in the real world can be connected in different ways in the narrative portrayal, depending on the communicative needs. This will also affect parameters such as the choice of connection types. An event that Paul characterizes as a result (in a causal connection) in one case might feature as an intention (role: goal in a purpose-oriented connection) in another case, depending on what effect he wants to create among his readers.

2. The Grammar of Narration

Temporal Order

It is a widely observed crosslinguistic phenomenon that humans utilize spatial metaphors when discussing time. In doing so, they condense three-dimensional space into a one-dimensional "timeline." When dealing with temporal connections, we grapple with structures that articulate a pair of propositions. Each of these propositions occupies a more or less precise position on that timeline, hence relating to each other in terms of either sequence or overlap. One of the two propositions provides a "reference situation" that delineates a temporal interval in relation to which the event in the second proposition is "situated."

While this might appear quite straightforward initially, it is in fact quite intricate. We will pare down this complexity by largely neglecting the specifics of the syntactical structures that underpin the corresponding temporal connections. Undoubtedly, these too are integral to an author's unique style, given that identical propositional structures can be crafted through various methods, thereby offering insights into the question of "how Paul narrates." However, at this juncture in our argument, our foremost interest lies in establishing whether temporal order even exists in Paul's letters. Hence, we will concentrate on that content level. We will remark only on striking departures from the norm in Paul's style compared to other New Testament storytellers in terms of syntax.

Sequence

As we have seen above, sequential or simultaneous relationships between events are the two basic possibilities for establishing "temporal order," one

Chapter 2

of the two prerequisites for a text to constitute a narrative. We will discuss sequentiality first.

Adverbs as Connectors

Let us first examine sequence, where we can differentiate between *anteriority and posteriority*. The meaning of these terms can be clarified using two main clauses as an example, as is the case in our miniature story from the previous chapter:

First, the apple hung on the tree. Then it fell.

Here, "first" functions not as a connector but rather as a *correlative* supporting the interpretation of the connection.[1] From the first word, we get a signal of what is to follow. However, the semantic roles of the two propositions corresponding to the main clauses are not determined by this word. That responsibility belongs to the adverb "then." Thus, our example can be simplified to:

The apple hung on the tree. Then it fell.

The internal connect (the second main clause) expresses an event that is situated on a timeline. It is situated in relation to an earlier event, which is not marked by a connector, meaning the first main clause serves as the reference situation for the event marked by the adverb.

Iconicity

It is vital to note that in this case, the textual order mirrors the chronological timeline: what happened first is also conveyed first. This means the sequence of clauses is "iconic"—the text is constructed in analogy to the real (or narrated) world. As a result, we will classify such an example as falling under the *anterior connection type*. The first element in the text communicates the earlier, or anterior, situation. It is important to observe that the rather

1. *AGG* 381c.

The Grammar of Narration

specific adverbial connector is not required to signal this connection type. An anterior connection with the same propositions can also be expressed simply by utilizing an additive connector like "and," or even an asyndetical construction.[2] For instance, we could say:

The apple hung on the tree. And it fell.

The apple hung on the tree. [. . .] It fell.

Opposite to temporal-anterior connections are temporal-*posterior* connections. In these, the situated situation, which contains the connector, is positioned in reference to a chronologically subsequent situation. Note that we cannot simply switch the order of the two main clauses to establish posterior connections, as their textual order in this specific connector construction is fixed. We cannot say:

*Then it fell. The apple hung on the tree.

Rather, for a posterior connection, we need a different connector, such as the adverb "before" (or "first," which can also function as a connector):

The apple fell. Before, it had hung on the tree.

Here too, it is possible to use an additive connector or forgo a connector altogether to represent the same sequence. However, in posterior connections this method is less acceptable because it requires additional interpretation. This is due to the order of the main clauses being "anti-iconic." Therefore, when we read, "The apple fell. It had hung on the tree," we encounter more challenges in reconstructing the underlying sequence of the real events, even though in English it is somewhat manageable since English tenses can express relative temporality. Note that in narratological terms, within a single connection, posterior propositional relationships involve an analepsis.

The terminology can indeed be a tad perplexing. In narratological lit-

---

2. See above, p. 48. I do not claim that the semantics of "and" is temporal, but the connection is, and in the right context it can be built with a connector that is only additive in meaning.

erature, Genette's subsequent narration type is sometimes referred to as "anterior narration," and his prior narration type as "posterior narration." While in that context (see above, pp. 34–36), the focus is on the temporal relationship between the narrator and the narrated events, our concern here pertains to the depiction of the temporal relationship among the narrated events themselves. To prevent confusion, I will use the adjectives "anterior" and "posterior" solely in reference to connection types and use "subsequent" and "prior/predictive" for narration types.

"Then" and "Before" Narration in Paul's Letters

How are these two patterns represented in Paul's letters? Let us examine the latter category first, since it does not need a long discussion. None of the adverbial *posterior* connectors listed by Heinrich von Siebenthal ever function as a connector in Paul's letters, despite the adverbs being well attested for other uses (see below, pp. 104–11).[3]

Interestingly, this observation aligns well with what we also encounter in the narrative works of the New Testament.

In contrast, adverbial connectors of *anterior*-temporal connections frequently appear in the Gospels and Acts. Matthew, in particular, is recognized for his liberal usage of τότε, which culminates in a somewhat monotonous "then"-oriented narration style in literal translations. Compared to this, Paul's usage of such adverbial connectors appears significantly more restrained.[4] He *never* employs τότε as part of an actual narrative, although the adverb appears fourteen times in his letters.

Here, we encounter our first indication that the concept of narrativity may extend in usefulness in Paul's letters beyond our definition's rather strict confines; in 2 Thess 2:8 τότε indeed appears (along with καί) as a connector of two successive events, although these events are situated in the future (... καὶ τότε ἀποκαλυφθήσεται ὁ ἄνομος).[5]

---

3. *AGG* 328a; Cf. Christoph Heilig, *Paulus als Erzähler? Eine narratologische Perspektive auf die Paulusbriefe*, BZNW 237 (Berlin: de Gruyter, 2020), 403–7.

4. Heilig, *Paulus*, 389–94 and 453–54.

5. This presupposes that καὶ τότε is not (also) a connector of simultaneity (i.e., as in "and at that time"). See Heilig, *Paulus*, 438. Cf. Eva Breindl, "Temporale Konnektoren," in *Semantik der deutschen Satzverknüpfer*, ed. Eva Breindl, Anna Volodina, and Ulrich Hermann Waßner, vol. 2 of *Handbuch der deutschen Konnektoren*, Schriften des Instituts

Against this backdrop, the relatively frequent employment by Paul of the adverbs εἶτα and ἔπειτα, which are uncommon in other New Testament works, is worth noting. Yet, they are seldom used as connectors. The repeated appearances of ἔπειτα in a mere handful of verses, particularly within Paul's detailed narrative in Gal 1:13–2:21 (specifically in 1:18, 21, and 2:1), thus stand out all the more. Additionally, 1 Cor 15 illustrates once more how closely Paul's statements about the eschatological *future* in verses 23–24 mirror his narration of past events in verses 5–7, where we find an actual narrative about the appearances of the risen Jesus.

Indeed, this passage highlights another observation: conventional anterior narration by means of adverbial connectors is evidently not typical for Paul. However, when he does utilize this anterior pattern, he tends to do so chiefly through the additive connector καί. Multiple times within his letters, this narration style appears within contexts that make it abundantly clear that he is drawing upon larger narrative traditions. This is particularly evident in 1 Cor 11:24, where he renarrates the institution of the Last Supper, and in 1 Cor 10:8–10, where he discusses the demise of the generation of the wilderness, under the discernible influence of the Septuagint.[6] Paul also uses καί interchangeably with the adverbial connector in his extensive narrative in Gal 1:17–2:21 (on which we just commented). Here the context is similar, as it involves a larger story where the general flow of events is rather clear. Against this backdrop, Paul's use of the coordinating conjunction as a connector in 2 Cor 12:4 appears to be almost ironic. There, he signals an extensive narration of visions and revelations (verse 1), yet he conspicuously refrains from divulging the tantalizing details (verses 2–3)! He is clearly playing with his readers' expectations, which he himself helped to raise to great heights! We will later (pp. 222–24) delve into his motives for doing so.

Based on our analysis thus far, a certain pattern begins to emerge. While Paul evidently utilized classic anterior narration on occasions—and seemingly quite intentionally—the overall impression is indeed a negative one. Paul is not a storyteller in the same vein as Matthew, for instance. This intu-

---

für Deutsche Sprache 13 (Berlin: de Gruyter, 2014), 315, on "da" (which can indicate simultaneity) and "dann" (which cannot have this role).

6. There, however, probably with an additional consequential nuance. But see also 2 Cor 11:33 for a narrative with different material.

Chapter 2

itive impression, shared by many scholars, can be thoroughly substantiated by our text-grammatical analysis.

However, we must be extremely cautious about the implications of this conclusion. It should not be construed to mean that Paul cannot reasonably be characterized as a creator of narratives. Rather, we could more appropriately describe him as a *different kind* of storyteller, one whose narratives adhere to different patterns than those of other early Christian storytellers. As we proceed to explore other propositional relationships—still within the sphere of sequence—our understanding of Paul as a skilled teller of numerous stories will be reinforced, and our perception of his narrative style will gain greater precision.

Subordinating Conjunctions as Connectors

Text Order

Until now, we have only discussed connections in which both the "internal connect" (the one with the connector) and the "external connect" are main clauses. As previously noted, a connect can be a main clause, but it may also take the form of a subordinate clause, an infinitive or participle phrase, or even an adjective or a prepositional construction with an action noun. Let us observe what occurs when we convert our examples of adverbially marked anterior and posterior connections using a subordinate connector:

> Anterior connection: "The apple hung on the tree. Then it fell." > "After the apple had hung on the tree, it fell."

> Posterior connection: "The apple fell. Before [adverb], it had hung on the tree." > "Before [subordinating conjunction] the apple fell, it had hung on the tree."

At first glance, these changes might not seem to bring about much alteration. In the rephrased anterior connection, the earlier event still precedes the later one. Similarly, in the newly formulated posterior connection, the later event is still introduced first. The only difference is that the connector is now integrated into the reference situation rather than the situated situation.

However, this is where the intuitive logic of this classification system ceases. With subordinate constructions, text order typically becomes variable. For instance:

Anterior connection but anti-iconic: "The apple fell after it had hung on the tree."

Posterior connection but iconic: "The apple had hung on the tree before it fell."

In other words, a posterior connection with a subordinate connector can starkly resemble an anterior connection with an adverbial connector:

Iconic anterior connection with adverb as connector: "The apple hung on the tree. Then it fell."

Iconic posterior connection with subordinate conjunction as connector: "The apple had hung on the tree before it fell."

For this reason, some scholars have dispensed with the distinction between anteriority and posteriority in their classification of temporal connectors entirely. An alternative is to categorize connectors based on whether they mark the earlier situation ("before" [adverb], "after") or the later situation ("then," "before" [subordinating conjunction]).[7] However, we will adhere to the categorization that is now most widely recognized in New Testament studies due to von Siebenthal's grammar. This approach has the advantage of retaining the parameter of iconicity. That is quite relevant from a narratological perspective as it is tied to the matter of the order of narration.

In fact, from a narratological viewpoint, it might be appealing to use iconicity as the primary criterion, that is, to classify the latter two examples together as cases where the narrator presents the earlier situation first. But for now, our primary focus is not as much on the analysis of Paul's narration as it is on demonstrating its existence. Thus, we will maintain von Siebenthal's classification system, providing comments when we observe noticeable patterns concerning iconicity in sequential connections with subordinate constructions.

7. See Breindl, "Temporale Konnektoren," 288–94.

Chapter 2

Communicative Weight

Before proceeding to examine sequential connections in Paul's letters that involve subordinate constructions, we must first revisit the issue of *information structure*—a topic we have already mentioned above (p. 49). In communication, not all aspects of a given text hold equal significance. This is underscored by von Siebenthal, who capitalizes one of the two roles (e.g., "RESULT-reason") to indicate its greater importance. It appears that, according to his perspective, the structure of information within the connection is closely linked to the *connection type* itself.[8] For instance, in the case of causal and consequential connections (which we will explore later in this chapter), he attributes the greater communicative emphasis consistently to the event occurring later chronologically and never to its cause.[9] Similarly, with respect to temporal connections, von Siebenthal seems to make distinctions *within* these categories based on syntactical grounds. He presumes that adverbial connectors suggest equal communicative emphasis ($NUCLEUS_1$–$NUCLEUS_2$), while subordinate constructions infer a greater attention to the main clause as opposed to the temporal specification. However, if scrutinized more closely, it becomes clear that both of these considerations—the connection type and syntactical subordination—can only serve as rules of thumb.[10]

That the matter is more complicated becomes clear if we consider in greater detail what "communicative weight" even means. In simplest terms, this phrase implies that within a given context, one element of a statement holds more importance for communication due to the existence of *alternative options* that could, in theory, have been chosen. By selecting a specific option, these potential alternatives are dismissed, resulting in a greater volume of information being conveyed. In contrast, if a point is mentioned that is already assumed within the context—either through mutual world knowledge or because it has been affirmed in a previous statement (having been the communicatively important piece *there*)—it could be repeated to provide context for the new statement. However, this point could be seen as less vital for the overall discourse due to its already established status. We designate the more dominant portion as "focal," while the remaining component is termed the "background."

In spoken English, the sentence accent signals the focal part within a

---

8. Cf. *AGG* 312d with some further references.
9. Cf. *AGG* 333 and 334.
10. See Heilig, *Paulus*, 172–91, for details.

The Grammar of Narration

sentence. Generally, if there is doubt about the information structure of an utterance, a simple question test serves as the most effective method to determine the focal component. The objective is to unveil the answer to an underlying question addressed by the statement. This question is often implicit, although it can sometimes be explicit.

For example, imagine a context in which we have a conversation between two people and one of them asks the other: "What happened after the apple was hanging on the tree?" The question already presupposes the initial situation of the apple on the tree. But there are, apparently, several options for what happened next. The apple might have fallen. But perhaps the speaker is also considering the option that it was picked by someone. Or that it remained up there. Each of the six configurations of our miniature narrative about the apple seem possible as a response. (Capitalization indicates the sentence accent.)

With adverbial connectors:

The apple hung on the tree. Then it FELL.

The apple FELL. Before, it had hung on the tree.

With subordinate connectors, with fronted subordinate clauses:

After the apple had hung on the tree, it FELL.

Before the apple FELL, it had hung on the tree.

With subordinate connectors, with postponed subordinate clauses:

The apple FELL after it had hung on the tree.

The apple had hung on the tree before it FELL.

Some of these options might potentially feel more natural to you. Numerous context-dependent factors exist, notably the register, which discerns whether the conversation is, among other things, formal or informal. However, there are general principles at work in such cases. For instance, a common tendency transcending language borders is for people to first present the background information before concluding with the focal situation. Therefore, "After the apple had hung on the tree, it FELL" may seem

Chapter 2

more natural than "The apple FELL, after it had hung on the tree." In other words, we tend to reiterate the shared background knowledge before introducing new information into the conversation. Additionally, the order of the text is iconic in the first example, reflecting the chronology in the real or narrated world, which is another significant factor when it comes to ordering connects (i.e., the factor of "linearization") in human storytelling.

However, these principles can sometimes be at odds with each other. Let us picture a different context in which the question "What did the apple do before it fell?" is posed. In this scenario, the apple's fall is taken as a given. The point under discussion is what transpired leading up to this event. Was the apple hanging on the tree? Or perhaps someone was holding it in their hand? In this instance, the fronted subordinate clause in "Before the apple fell, it had HUNG on the tree" is advantageous in that the focal point comes last. Nonetheless, the inverse order—"The apple had HUNG on the tree before it fell"—offers the benefit of adhering to an iconic structure, which for some speakers might render it the more natural choice.

Note that not all connectors introducing subordinate structures offer these varied possibilities with respect to linearization. Examine the following two instances where the subordinate conjunctions are substituted with prepositional phrases:

Prior to falling, the apple had hung on the tree.

Following the apple's hanging on the tree, it fell.

The postponed placement of these subordinate structures—"The apple had hung on the tree prior to falling" and "The apple fell, following the apple's hanging on the tree"—is considerably less acceptable in these instances.

Consequently, in most cases, both in English and in Greek, determining the focal proposition within a connection is not straightforward and requires a careful examination of minimal pairs, where only one element is varied and the effect on the information structure scrutinized. What we thus ultimately need is a comprehensive analysis of Greek connectors that dissects the semantic differences of connectors within the same semantic class, taking into account information structure and possible linearization.

For the time being, the most effective approach in our analysis of Pauline miniature narratives involves utilizing sentence accent in English translations to intuitively discern which stress placement feels accurate and, in conjunction with this, considering the question to which the connection likely provides an answer. In most instances, this question will not be explicitly articulated in the text. Instead, we must ponder the context, discern its presupposed elements, and understand which aspects are at play. We must identify which elements may be disputed, that is, may be in competition with other possibilities that the miniature narrative subsequently dismisses.[11]

Given the complexity and relative lack of research regarding this situation, in the subsequent sections I will primarily use lowercase letters to designate both the semantic roles of the two connectors. In these instances, I am not asserting any particular claims about the information structure within these connections. This approach, in other words, does not rule out the possibility of identifying a focal and a background element. However, when I do make use of uppercase letters, this is intended to provide a clear indication of how I interpret the communicative weight that the different propositions hold within a miniature narrative.

"When" and "After" Narration

Having articulated these important preliminary points, we will now turn our attention to anterior connections that contain subordinate constructions, that is, those *marked by a connector in the connect that expresses the earlier situation*.[12] A notably significant connector for Paul in this regard is ὅτε. Regrettably, lexicons are somewhat confounded when it comes to this subordinating conjunction, and we thus first need to address the issue of how to define this temporal connector.

BDAG seems to suggest that ὅτε primarily serves as a connector for simultaneous occurrences, distinguishing between its usage with the aorist in the sense of a 'marker of a point in time that aligns with another point in

---

11. Sometimes, the question is indeed formulated in the text. And given that there are no native speakers of Koine Greek, such examples are actually very valuable in reconstructing which information structures are possible with specific connectors. Take, for example, the causal connector ὅτι. In Matt 13:10, Jesus's disciples ask him: "Why do you speak in parables to them?" (διὰ τί ἐν παραβολαῖς λαλεῖς αὐτοῖς;). Jesus answers in verse 11: "Because the knowledge of the secrets of the kingdom of heaven has been given to you but not to them" (ὅτι ὑμῖν δέδοται γνῶναι τὰ μυστήρια τῆς βασιλείας τῶν οὐρανῶν, ἐκείνοις δὲ οὐ δέδοται). Note that the background—the fact that Jesus speaks in parables to the other people—is not even repeated in the response, a rather typical phenomenon in spoken language. Cf. Heilig, *Paulus*, 190.

12. See Heilig, *Paulus*, 394–402, on what follows.

time' and the usage as a 'marker of a period of time running parallel with another period of time,' when followed by an imperfect.[13]

I am uncertain how one could reach such a conclusion. It is as if a peculiar understanding of aspectuality might have influenced this interpretation (the "punctiliar" aorist?). Adding to the confusion, the editors of BDAG appear to have been misled by the German gloss "als" in the original edition. They correctly recognized that in English "als" can often be translated as "when." However, they seem to have overlooked the fact that both the German and the English subordinate conjunction are not confined to simultaneity but can also signify sequence. The editors then approached the Greek connector with this faulty frame of reference, attempting to bifurcate according to verbal aspect *within* the category of simultaneity.

However, ὅτε clearly possesses a broader semantic spectrum. Upon examining how aspect influences the meaning of the temporal connection that emerges, we find precisely what one would expect based on the standard function of Greek aspects (see below, pp. 157–59, for more). The imperfect presents the situation of the temporal clause from an internal perspective, thereby making such temporal clauses conducive to *simultaneous* connections, where the temporal clause specifies a reference situation that envelops the situated situation. Conversely, the aorist indicative, due to its perfective aspect, portrays the situation in the temporal clause as having reached its inherent endpoint. Hence, unsurprisingly, we can observe a correlation between this aspect and *sequential* connections, where the situation in the main clause follows the completed situation expressed in the temporal clause.

This, of course, bears striking similarity to the situation with the English connector "when" (and the German connector "als"). BDAG cites Matt 9:25 (ὅτε δὲ ἐξεβλήθη ὁ ὄχλος . . . ἐκράτησεν τῆς χειρὸς αὐτῆς) as an instance of the presumed simultaneous usage. However, the majority of English Bible translations appear to clearly envision a sequence. The NIV articulates this unmistakably by using the unambiguous connector "after." Yet, even with "when" as a gloss, the situation remains quite clear because English (and German) past tenses, unlike Greek ones, express relative temporality. Therefore, translations such as "When the crowd *had been put* outside . . ." render the intended meaning quite apparent. Simi-

---

13. BDAG 5412. For a more detailed analysis, cf. also Christoph Heilig, "Zeit im Verhältnis: Narratologische und linguistische Perspektiven," in *Zeit und Ewigkeit: Ein Lehrbuch*, ed. Benjamin Schliesser, Jan Rüggemeier, and Michael Jost, Uni-Taschenbücher (Tübingen: Mohr Siebeck, forthcoming).

larly, in German the constellation can also be clarified in such a way: "Als die Menge hinausgetrieben *worden war* . . ."

In this context, one might pose the question of whether English "when," German "als," *and* Greek ὅτε should perhaps be considered as connectors whose meaning is not adequately characterized by the presumption of polysemy (indicating simultaneity with one meaning and sequence with another). From a lexicographical standpoint, it might be more expedient to postulate the existence of a class of *unspecifically situating* temporal connectors, which can be employed in conjunction with earlier, simultaneous, and even subsequent events, depending on aspectual and contextual factors. However, for the question surrounding the connection that is ultimately communicated, this distinction is negligible.[14]

Against this backdrop, we can now shift our focus to Paul's letters. What we discern there aligns well with this outline I have just drawn, and it does not coincide at all with the portrayal in BDAG. A majority of temporal clauses with ὅτε and the aorist indicative in Paul's letters (cf., for example, Gal 4:4; Titus 3:4) can easily be categorized as anterior connections.[15] Two instances exist where concurrent interpretations may seem compelling (Phil 1:15; 4:15), but even these can be interpreted within a sequential framework relatively effortlessly. Once again, we can observe a conspicuous cluster of this temporal connector in Paul's narration in Gal 1:13–2:21, especially in the part discussing the Antioch incident (2:11, 12, 14). This further accentuates the impression that Paul adheres to a more typical narration style in this passage.

We can briefly touch on the aspect of linearization. In German, there is only a slight inclination toward placing the sequence connector "nachdem" ("after") in the fronted position, resulting in an iconic order of the connects.[16] Contrarily, in Paul's letters we find a strong preference for the temporal clause with ὅτε to be in the fronted position and, thus, for an iconic linearization.[17] Adverbial participles also seem to follow this trend both in

---

14. Cf. Breindl, "Temporale Konnektoren," 297–327. I could not find a Greek example for the last category. It is also quite rare in German and English (e.g., "I had already left when he arrived").

15. I am wondering whether ὅτε might semantically be quite similar to English "when" (or German "als"). It seems worthy of further investigation whether perhaps it remains quite unspecific with respect to the precise temporal relationship *even* in combination with the aorist indicative.

16. Breindl, "Temporale Konnektoren," 328.

17. Rom 13:11 is an exception, but the syntax is different there for other reasons any-

Chapter 2

traditional material (1 Cor 11:24: "and, after he had given thanks, he broke [it] and said"; καὶ εὐχαριστήσας ἔκλασεν καὶ εἶπεν) and original narratives (2 Cor 2:13: "After I had bid them farewell, I set out for Macedonia"; ἀποταξάμενος αὐτοῖς ἐξῆλθον εἰς Μακεδονίαν). Similarly, a fronted genitive absolute is found in Gal 3:25.[18]

This particular case warrants special attention, as it carries implications for our pursuit of implicit narratives, a goal that remains in the back of our minds while we are looking for explicit narratives. Although the participle construction in Gal 3:25 refers to a concrete historical event, that is, the "coming of faith" (ἐλθούσης . . . τῆς πίστεως), the situated situation is expressed in a negative manner: "we are *no longer* under a guardian" (οὐκέτι ὑπὸ παιδαγωγόν ἐσμεν). Interestingly, Paul does not recount the event that actually did occur. Thus, we could say that in this verse Paul "tells a non-story." In essence, he discounts the likelihood of someone narrating a story in which "we" came to faith yet continue under a guardian's oversight. Or rather, were anyone to narrate such a story (an activity Paul implies his opponents are engaged in), these narrators would be deemed unreliable.

Therefore, it can be inferred that Gal 3:25, while not representing a miniature narrative within our conceptual framework, *points toward actual narratives*, thus making them implicit elements of this text. Additionally, since the verse presupposes that there was a period when "we" were indeed under a guardian, it also alludes to another story, a *potential* one—that is, a story that a reliable narrator might have relayed at an earlier point in time, or could relay presently if they ensure it is framed as an instance of subsequent narration, not of the simultaneous narration type. In summary, we can observe that phenomena which could aptly be termed "implicit narratives" appear to naturally show up at the periphery of our focus on explicit narratives.

In contrast to Paul's use of ὅτε, it is notable that the subordinating conjunction ὅταν appears just once with an overt sequential meaning—ironically, in a "predictive narrative." In 1 Cor 16:5, Paul announces his plan to visit the Corinthians (Ἐλεύσομαι δὲ πρὸς ὑμᾶς) after having traversed Macedonia (ὅταν Μακεδονίαν διέλθω). Intriguingly, the linearization here is anti-iconic. A comparison of ὅτε and ὅταν concerning their lineariza-

---

way. Note that the preference for a fronted placement also holds true for the use of ὅτε in simultaneous connections, with Col 3:7 being an exception (cf. below, p. 87).

18. In Heilig, *Paulus*, 402, I also adduce Rom 9:11–12 for a case of a negated participle. But μήπω is probably better classified as a connector of posterior connections ("not yet" = "before").

tion potential in Koine Greek texts could prove insightful. Perhaps ὅταν is a more logical choice for a postponed placement? While the evidence is scant, I think a case can be made that Paul's letters exhibit minimal post-dictation editing. If both these assumptions hold true, it follows plausibly that 1 Cor 16:5 lends insight into Paul's dictation process, where he realizes the need to include a temporal specification, adds a temporal clause (even though it results in a less common anti-iconic order), and opts for ὅταν over the more ubiquitous ὅτε as it is more fitting in this instance. However, at this stage, this suggestion remains speculative.

The use of prepositions is likewise rather limited. Only in the traditional material of 1 Cor 11:25—which agrees with Luke 22:20 verbatim—do we find an example ("after the meal"; μετὰ τὸ δειπνῆσαι; the main verb is to be supplied from the context). We never encounter an action noun in the accusative after μετά in connection with an asserted subsequent event. However, in Titus 3:10 we at least get a glimpse at what such a miniature narrative might look like. There, we find indeed talk of something "after" another event, namely, the (if necessary repeated) act of warning. But this later situation is expressed by means of an imperative and, thus, refers to the future (". . . reject!"; παραιτοῦ). Again, this is not an actual miniature story. However, if Titus adheres to what Paul wants him to do, he *will* be able to tell a story—either one in which he first warned a divisive person and in which that person then changed their behavior or one in which he warned them twice and then rejected them. Note also that the entire situation—and, hence, the potential story—is hypothetical in another respect as well. What is in view is "a divisive person" (αἱρετικὸν ἄνθρωπον). If no such person shows up in the congregation, Titus will not have to act in the stipulated manner and will never be in a position where he can tell such a story in retrospect. To be sure, the letter indicates there is indeed a need for such a procedure, but in isolation Titus 3:10 only hints at a potential situation.

Differentiating between Subordinating Posterior Connectors

Having completed our overview of anterior connections in Paul's letters, we now turn to posterior connections that incorporate a subordinate construction, that is, those marked by a *connector in the connect that specifies the subsequent event*. Given the absence of the adverbial "event B. Before, event A" pattern in Paul's letters, one might not anticipate many instances of the reformulated version employing subordinate constructions. However, contrary to this expectation, we discover that this form of narration is quite a prominent feature in Paul's letters.

To evaluate these instances, we first need to consider a distinction *within* this category that Heinrich von Siebenthal proposes in his grammar. While all these connectors share the characteristic of being integrated into the event they mark as subsequent to the situated situation, von Siebenthal distinguishes between connectors that (a) emphasize a "preceding period of time" and those that (b) highlight a "preceding point in time."[19]

The typical English translation for connectors of the first category, (a), would be "until." This word introduces an event that marks the end of something, and von Siebenthal posits that this "something" should be a situation that endures for some period. Consider, for example, the sentence "He smoked." One possible interpretation of this statement is that it expresses a singular act—the consumption of a cigarette—with the transformation of the cigarette into ash constituting the intrinsic endpoint of this action. If we take this main clause and augment it with the temporal specification, "He smoked . . . until his mother came," it narrows the scope of possible interpretations for "He smoked." Typically, in this context, we would reinterpret the main clause to refer to a regular activity or a certain habit that does not reach an inherent endpoint after smoking a specific amount of cigarettes, making it atelic.[20] In other words, the cigarette-smoking activity was ongoing for a certain period, with the mother's arrival demarcating a limit, although it does not necessarily imply an immediate or permanent cessation of the activity! It is worth noting that explicitly adding "one cigarette" renders the sentence less acceptable: ?"He smoked one cigarette until his mother came." Most readers would likely find this sentence ungrammatical or interpret the main clause narrowly so that the situation can be considered atelic. This would entail understanding "smoking one cigarette" as a series of inhalations, that is, an activity. Conversely, a sentence like *"He finished his first cigarette until his mother came" seems entirely unacceptable.

Up to this point, von Siebenthal's distinction within subordinating posterior connectors seems cogent. Furthermore, this dichotomy initially appears to be upheld when we consider (b), the sentence "He smoked before his mother came," in light of our preceding discussion. For one might argue that the event of the main clause is somewhat "punctiliar," if we understand

---

19. *AGG* 329a. For what follows cf. Heilig, *Paulus*, 408–9.
20. See below, pp. 154–56, for details on the differentiation among situation types.

The Grammar of Narration

this to mean the smoking of a *single* cigarette as opposed to the continuous action of smoking cigarettes in general.

However, although von Siebenthal draws his distinction from a leading German grammar, it ultimately appears to be problematic and requires some modifications.[21] This can be observed even on the basis of the English example. The act of smoking a cigarette is telic—it encapsulates a goal or endpoint—but it is not instantaneous; it consumes time. In Greek too, it quickly becomes evident that subordinating conjunctions such as πρίν ("before") are not exclusively paired with "achievements," that is, telic situations void of duration (cf. below, p. 155).

For instance, consider Mark 14:30, where the event that Jesus foretells to transpire "before the rooster crows twice" (πρὶν ἢ δὶς ἀλέκτορα φωνῆσαι) encompasses a sequence of events, specifically Peter's *repeated* denial of Jesus (σὺ σήμερον ταύτῃ τῇ νυκτὶ ... *τρίς* με ἀπαρνήσῃ). Hence, the situated situation is not restricted to punctual achievements but can also be a telic situation that demands duration (i.e., an "accomplishment").

Additionally, there seem to be numerous examples of situated situations that are even atelic altogether.[22] So, in contrast to what we see in (a), where the main clause seems to be restricted to durative and atelic situations (states and activities), with respect to (b) there do not appear to be any requirements concerning the situation type of the situated situation.[23]

For this reason, I believe von Siebenthal's differentiation is misleading. It is possible that the connectors he lists under category (b) may have spe-

---

21. *Duden* 1767.

22. John 8:58, as eccentric as it might seem in other respects, does not rank as an exception in this aspect. Cf., for instance, Isa 23:8: αὕτη ἦν ὑμῶν ἡ ὕβρις ἡ ἀπ' ἀρχῆς πρὶν ἢ παραδοθῆναι αὐτήν.

23. Similarly, the English phrase: "A wind came. The apple bounced once before it fell" is grammatically sound (unlike: *"A wind came. The apple bounced once until it fell"). Note that in the case of an atelic situated situation, it is only the commencement of this activity or state that is marked as occurring prior to the reference situation. In simpler terms, situation A is presented as having been the case "even before" situation B. While telic situations must reach their inherent end before the occurrence of the event in the temporal clause, the absence of such an inherent endpoint in atelic situations allows these actions or states to continue even after the reference situation. For instance, when John 17:5 speaks of the glory that Jesus possessed "before the world existed" (πρὸ τοῦ τὸν κόσμον εἶναι παρὰ σοί), it does not insinuate that during the period between the world's creation and his incarnation (i.e., between John 1:3 and 1:14), he did not maintain this glory. Similarly, during that time span Jesus existed before Abraham, but that does not mean he ceased to exist upon Abraham's birth (cf. John 8:58).

Chapter 2

cific restrictions regarding the types of situations that are possible in the temporal clause. Namely, I suspect that the reference situation must be telic (something that also seems to apply to the other subtype though). In any case, concerning the *situated* situation in the main clause, I do not observe such restrictions. Therefore, it seems inaccurate to me to claim that these "before" connections emphasize a "preceding point in time."[24]

Based on these observations, we are led to the conclusion that the definitive divide between connectors—such as (a) ἕως, etc. ("until"), on the one hand, and (b) πρίν, etc. ("before"), on the other hand—*does not pertain to the type of the situation that is highlighted in the main clause* but appears to rest elsewhere entirely. In my opinion, the most striking distinguishing characteristic pertains to the *degree of neutrality these connectors exhibit regarding the temporal boundaries of the situated situation*.

Connectors of the first type, (a), introduce temporal clauses that not only position the situated situation on a timeline (specifically, somewhere before the reference situation), but they also delineate the "right border" of the situation from the matrix clause. In many contexts, this suggests that the situation—such as the act of smoking or the condition of hanging on a tree—actually *ended* at that designated point in time. Nonetheless, it is important to remember that this is simply an implicature derived from the context. The purpose of the connector is to specify a point in time up to which a certain situation is considered. The situation may still continue later, which is particularly common in statements about the future.[25]

In contrast, connectors of the second type (b) appear to be neutral concerning how closely the time under consideration approaches the point in

---

24. In any case, it is notable that in German, the reference situation in analogous construction must be telic (Breindl, "Temporale Konnektoren," 336, on "bevor" and "ehe"). In English too, it seems that an ingressive reinterpretation occurs. If we say, "The apple was hanging on the tree before it lay on the ground," the temporal clause seems to imply "before it *began* to lie there." This requirement seems to also apply to the constructions with the Greek connectors that von Siebenthal lists. So, for example, a verb like ἔρχομαι ("to come") in such contexts does not mean 'to be on one's way' but 'to arrive.' But I have to stress that I have done only very preliminary research on this so far. In any case, it seems rather conspicuous to me that the imperfective infinitive is scarcely used after πρίν (cf. however John 17:5: καὶ νῦν δόξασόν με σύ, πάτερ, παρὰ σεαυτῷ τῇ δόξῃ ᾗ εἶχον πρὸ τοῦ τὸν κόσμον εἶναι παρὰ σοί; and Ps 57:10 LXX: πρὸ τοῦ συνιέναι τὰς ἀκάνθας ὑμῶν τὴν ῥάμνον ὡσεὶ ζῶντας ὡσεὶ ἐν ὀργῇ καταπίεται ὑμᾶς). Yet this restriction is not specific to (b). Connectors of type (a) also require telic situations in the temporal clause. Cf. Breindl, "Temporale Konnektoren," 384, on the situation in German.

25. Breindl, "Temporale Konnektoren," 384.

The Grammar of Narration

time specified by the temporal clause. It is possible that the situated situation occurred right before the event of the temporal clause, but it is equally plausible that there was an interim period.

Adopting *border neutrality* as the guiding principle, we can categorize connectors of the first type (a), such as ἕως ("until"), to be in the same class as connectors for which von Siebenthal uses the gloss "since" and that he discusses under the rubric of simultaneous connectors (see below, pp. 98–101). Conversely, the second type of connectors (b), like πρίν ("before"), are seemingly more related to subordinating anterior connectors (like ὅτε with aorist, "after"), since they also express a sequence without defining the duration of the matrix clause's situation.

For the purposes of this book, we will adhere to von Siebenthal's classification, which offers the benefit of concentrating on chronology. Both types of connectors indicate sequences, and sequence is one of the primary concepts of temporal order in the realm of narratological discussions. This distinction thus makes sense for our text-grammatical analysis. However, it must be stressed that our acceptance of this fundamental classification system does not mean that we consider category (a) ("until" connections) and category (b) ("before" connections) as mirror images of each other in the way that von Siebenthal seems to assume. Instead, the former gives information about the right border of the preceding situation, and it therefore comes with restrictions regarding potential situation types for that prior event. The latter, by contrast, does not possess implications for either of these parameters. We cannot, for instance, say *"The apple was hit once by a beam of sunshine three hours until it fell." Conversely, it is entirely correct to say, "The apple was hit once by a beam of sunshine three hours before it fell." Bearing all this in mind, we now turn our attention to the Greek connectors.

"Until" Narration

First, we examine subordinate constructions that define the right border of a preceding event. This version of the posterior connection, unlike the one with the adverbial connector, is well attested in Paul's letters.[26] There is a notable frequency of such connections; however, they do not quite form miniature narratives.

For instance, in the construction with ἕως in 2 Thess 2:7, the situated sit-

---

26. For details, see Heilig, *Paulus*, 409–14.

Chapter 2

uation is something that is presently in place at the time of writing (with details subject to the understanding of the syntax), and it might hence spark the expectation for a story of the simultaneous narration type. Yet, the temporal clause clearly projects toward the *future* (the removal of the "restrainer"). Similarly, in 1 Cor 4:5 the situated situation is merely a commanded event and thus an event projected into the future. Indeed, this is an event that Paul does *not* want to happen. The Corinthians are instructed *not* to "judge anything before the time" (μὴ πρὸ καιροῦ τι κρίνετε), which is explicated in the temporal clause as the point in time when the Lord comes (ἕως ἂν ἔλθῃ ὁ κύριος). In other words, no one should be able, at any point in time, to accurately narrate a story about them behaving in such a way.

We can observe similar dynamics with ἄχρι[ς] οὗ. Both in 1 Cor 11:26 and 15:25, there is a focus on future events in the temporal clauses—the second coming of the Lord (ἄχρι οὗ ἔλθῃ) and the gathering of all enemies beneath his feet (ἄχρι οὗ θῇ πάντας τοὺς ἐχθροὺς ὑπὸ τοὺς πόδας αὐτοῦ). These events mark the ultimate boundaries of the time periods of the respective situated situations: the Lord's death proclamation in the Eucharist in one instance, and Christ's rule in the other. It is evident from the context that both periods have already commenced (though this inference is clearer from contextual clues in 1 Cor 15, especially verses 4 and 20). However, we are not yet able to narrate the events immediately succeeding these situations.

Note that with respect to 1 Cor 15:25, the question arises as to whether the current situation might continue uninterrupted, even after the point in time when the reference situation occurs. Yet, verse 24 suggests that "reigning" in verse 25 signifies a unique (exclusive) kind of authority, which Christ will no longer possess after "he has handed over the kingdom to God the Father" (ὅταν παραδιδῷ τὴν βασιλείαν τῷ θεῷ καὶ πατρι; cf. pp. 98–101). The cessation of Christ's reign, in this specific sense, is thus implied by the temporal construction in verse 25.

In Rom 11:25, we find a similar focus on the present time in the situated situation (though most translations do not reflect the perfect tense accurately) and an upcoming event that signifies its end. Structures with μέχρι[ς] as a subordinating conjunction align perfectly with this pattern (see Gal 4:19; Eph 4:13).

This observation about the underlying temporal pattern also holds for the use of μέχρι[ς] as a preposition with an action noun in 1 Tim 6:14: "until the appearing of our Lord Jesus Christ" (μέχρι τῆς ἐπιφανείας τοῦ κυρίου ἡμῶν Ἰησοῦ Χριστοῦ). Just as in 1 Cor 4:5, the situated situation here is something that Paul commands (cf. παραγγέλλω in verse 13; cf. below, pp. 282–86, on

The Grammar of Narration

constructions with this verb). The preposition εἰς in 1 Thess 4:15 in a similar vein introduces a future situation: the return of Christ (εἰς τὴν παρουσίαν τοῦ κυρίου). In Col 3:10, there is also a glimpse into the future, namely, the enriched knowledge of God (εἰς ἐπίγνωσιν κατ' εἰκόνα τοῦ κτίσαντος αὐτόν). Interestingly, however, in this instance this event is tightly linked to a past event (putting on the new self; καὶ ἐνδυσάμενοι τὸν νέον) and a present process (its ongoing renewal; τὸν ἀνακαινούμενον).

The potentially temporal meaning of the preposition in Gal 3:24 has been the subject of considerable debate. Here, a temporal understanding of εἰς Χριστόν is critical for Jimmy Dunn's version of the New Perspective on Paul. In his interpretation, the law as the παιδαγωγός does not have the Lutheran function of "bring[ing] us unto Christ" (KJV), but rather plays a positive protective role that is no longer necessary following Christ's arrival (ὥστε ὁ νόμος παιδαγωγὸς ἡμῶν γέγονεν).[27]

The temporal meaning of the same preposition in the previous verse, Gal 3:23, appears more evident. "Until the (coming of the) faith that would be revealed" (εἰς τὴν μέλλουσαν πίστιν ἀποκαλυφθῆναι) also points to the future. Yet, this is a "future in the past," an event that has indeed occurred prior to the time of the author's writing. The phase of being under the law (ὑπὸ νόμον ἐφρουρούμεθα) ends at this juncture. While the preceding examples resemble "almost stories," this contrastingly might be seen as an "almost nonstory." The past situation, which concluded with the revealing of the faith, is lucidly stated (ὑπὸ νόμον ἐφρουρούμεθα). However, the actual pivotal moment—which has undoubtedly transpired, in Paul's view—seems to be assumed within this context, and thus does not demand detailed affirmation (cf. below, pp. 175-81).

Against the backdrop of these extensive uses of subordinate constructions for indicating subsequent events in posterior connections—which, however, all diverge to some degree from strict expectations one might have of miniature narratives—the use of the connector ἄχρις οὗ in Gal 3:19 appears even more relevant. Here, a past event—the addition of the law due to transgressions (τῶν παραβάσεων χάριν προσετέθη)—is situated with reference to an event that, from the speaker's perspective, has already occurred. The arrival of "the descendant to whom the promise was made" (ἄχρις οὗ ἔλθῃ τὸ σπέρμα ᾧ ἐπήγγελται) clearly lies in Paul's past, given that in verse 16 he explicitly states that this descendant is Christ. Here, at last, we have a

---

27. James D. G. Dunn, *A Commentary on the Epistle to the Galatians*, BNTC (London: Continuum, 1993), 197-98.

Chapter 2

posterior connection—and even a third event, the promise (cf. also the following διαταγεὶς δι' ἀγγέλων ἐν χειρὶ μεσίτου)—that fulfills our rather strict definition of narrativity. Nonetheless, even here it is significant that only the immediate literary context allows us to definitively conclude that the verse is intended as a miniature narrative.

It cannot be overstated that this exploration of "until" posterior narration has once again primarily raised elements that narrowly fail our definition of narrativity, mostly because they orient toward the future, exemplifying what Genette referred to as prior or predictive narration. Even at this stage of the discussion, it seems unavoidable to acknowledge that maintaining our limited focus on explicit narratives alone may inadvertently prevent us from fully exploiting the potential of narratological categories in the exegesis of Paul's letters.

We can make another observation before moving on. The frequent use of subordinating constructions by Paul to create posterior connections is remarkable. The fact that the vast majority of these instances do not constitute miniature narratives, as per our strict definition, does not diminish the significance of this observation. Conversely, the situation is different with regard to Paul's use of adverbial connectors. Not only does he abstain from using them to relate explicit stories (aligning with our observation concerning subordinating constructions), but he does not use them at all to establish posterior connections. Therefore, the pattern of Paul's use of posterior connectors necessitates elucidation.

It might be that, when discussing sequences of events, Paul favors an *iconic* text order. All the examples we just examined are cases where the subsequent situation is introduced after the prior situation in the text—something unachievable with adverbial posterior connectors. However, the phenomenon seems odd considering that adverbial *anterior* connectors likewise allow for (indeed, necessitate) this order of connects. And Paul's use of subordinating posterior connectors is at least commensurate with his use of these adverbial anterior connectors.

In this respect, Paul's preference for the former connectors might be elucidated by the fact that "until" connections are *marked* in contrast to "then" connections when it comes to the right border of the situated situation. Consequently, we can hypothesize that in the instances of "almost stories" that we just discussed, it was likely insufficient for Paul to merely express a sequence of an earlier event A followed by a later event B. Instead, Paul presumably intended to communicate the added element that the situation time of event A extends right up to the point in time of situation B (possibly

The Grammar of Narration

implying that situation A ceased at that point in time). In simpler terms, *his focus seems not to be solely on the question "when?" but, more specifically, on the question "how long?"* (or, barring the implication of cessation, "how long, at least?"). This already gives us important clues concerning the issues that are at stake in these sections, which Paul tries to resolve by means of connections that are at least very reminiscent of actual narratives.

"Before" Narration

Now, let us examine subordinate constructions that make use of genuine posterior sequence connectors, that is, those that mark the earlier reference situation in order to situate the subsequent situation, the one in the matrix clause, but without explicitly emphasizing the right border of that event. The subordinate conjunction πρίν is present in all of the Gospels and in Acts, but it does not appear in any of the other New Testament writings. By contrast, with respect to the construction πρό + infinitive we have some overlap in narration style between Paul and the other New Testament storytellers. It occurs, even though less frequently, in the aforementioned narrative works, and it is also attested twice in Galatians. In both Gal 2:12 and 3:23, the preposition is used with ἐλθεῖν ("to come"). In the first scenario, those who come are "certain individuals from James" (τινας ἀπὸ Ἰακώβου), while in the second instance it is "the faith" (τὴν πίστιν).

To revisit von Siebenthal's characterization of these connectors, we notice that there is no "punctiliar" situated situation. In Gal 2:12 we have a recurring practice (note the imperfect) of eating with gentiles (μετὰ τῶν ἐθνῶν συνήσθιεν), and in Gal 3:23 the durative situation (implied again by the imperfect) of being kept under the law is under discussion (ὑπὸ νόμον ἐφρουρούμεθα). We can only observe that, unlike in the case of the "until" connectors, it is *possible* to have a telic (and nondurative) situated situation. This is demonstrated by the action noun in Eph 1:4. There, the creation of the world (πρὸ καταβολῆς κόσμου) situates the act of our prior election (ἐξελέξατο ἡμᾶς ἐν αὐτῷ). As previously mentioned, the actual distinguishing characteristic between "until" connectors and "before" connectors is that the latter remain neutral concerning the right border of the situated situation.

Consequently, it is only from the context that we can infer that Paul implies in Gal 2:12 and 3:23 that the situated situation held true also *"immediately* before" the event of the reference situation. In these specific instances, it does seem as though Paul could have utilized the "until" version with

Chapter 2

essentially the same outcome, stating that Peter was eating with the gentiles "until" those from James arrived or that the state of being under the law extended "until" the arrival of the faith. Additionally, context makes it clear in both cases that this behavior or state continued until the specified point in time but *ceased* thereafter (Gal 2:12: ὅτε δὲ ἦλθον, ὑπέστελλεν καὶ ἀφώριζεν ἑαυτόν φοβούμενος τοὺς ἐκ περιτομῆς; Gal 3:25: ἐλθούσης δὲ τῆς πίστεως οὐκέτι ὑπὸ παιδαγωγόν ἐσμεν).[28] The requisites concerning situation types for "until" narration are also satisfied here. Note that in the latter case, he even combines the two: "before" the arrival of the faith (Πρὸ τοῦ δὲ ἐλθεῖν τὴν πίστιν) "we" were in a particular state that lasted "until" the revelation of the faith (εἰς τὴν μέλλουσαν πίστιν ἀποκαλυφθῆναι).[29]

Therefore, one might question why an author would opt for the less-marked version in such circumstances. Examining Gal 2:12 in its entirety (see figure 3), we can observe how Paul's choice of a "before" connector allows him to *decelerate* the pace of the narration, making it more vivid and granting his audience more opportunities to immerse themselves within the narrative world.

Figure 3. Propositional structure of Gal 2:12. Only the temporal connectors are highlighted.

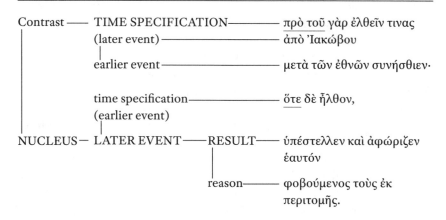

28. Interestingly, in both cases the future development is also something of interest for the discourse. In Gal 2, Paul seems to imply that Peter took up his activity of eating with the other believers after Paul confronted him. And reentering the state of 3:25 is of course precisely what he blames the Galatians for doing at the moment when he is writing the letter.

29. See above, p. 75, on the preposition.

Under this proposal, this miniature narrative, which is part of a larger story, fundamentally conveys—as evidenced on the "highest" level of the text, in the left column—Peter's startling behavior. This behavior is chronologically anchored to a prior event and explained as an action that Peter undertook for a specific reason. This entire propositional nexus stands in stark contrast with the fact that he had exhibited a very different behavior until a certain point.

Note the event of the "arrival" is the turning point and is referenced twice, thus constituting an instance of *repetitive* narration. I would argue that in the second case, the time specification (in an anterior connection) contributes *background information*, as the event itself has already been mentioned and does not represent new information and the temporal clause does not further elucidate any details. In the preceding posterior connection, it seems, by contrast, apt to interpret the time specification as *focal*, meaning it carries greater communicative weight. After all, the bare fact that Peter ate with gentiles could hardly be startling news.[30] If anything, a temporal connection like "After Peter met Cornelius, he began eating with gentiles" would lend meaningful emphasis to this practice.

Thus, for these very broad contextual reasons, it seems plausible that Paul highlights the fact that *before* situation B, situation A was (of course) true. By creating this contrast foil, he naturally raises the question of what transpired *after* B. Ascertaining whether or not the fronted position of the πρό phrase itself marks this information structure would necessitate further investigation into the use of this preposition.[31] In any case, we witness here a typical progression in terms of information structure, where the formerly focal element becomes the background for a new focal element as the discourse develops.

Thus far, we have extensively examined sequential connections in Paul's writings. It appears evident that Paul employs them rather sparingly, par-

---

30. Cf. Christoph Heilig, "The New Perspective (on Paul) on Peter: How the Philosophy of Historiography Can Help in Understanding Earliest Christianity," in *Christian Origins and the Establishment of the Early Jesus Movement*, ed. Stanley E. Porter and Andrew W. Pitts, Christian Origins and Greco-Roman Culture 4 (Leiden: Brill, 2018), 459–595.

31. The postponed πρό + infinitive construction in Matt 6:8 seems focal too. While πρίν occurs, at least in the New Testament, with a clear preference for anti-iconicity (with John 4:49 being an exception), the distribution is more even with respect to πρό + infinitive (cf. Matt 6:8; Luke 2:21; 22:15; John 17:5 for an iconic order, i.e., the later event in the internal connect appearing later also in the text).

tially validating the initial impression that "Paul never tells stories." However, on closer inspection this broad claim does not withstand scrutiny. While sequential connections are quite uncommon, often appearing in discernable clusters, they surface at various junctures throughout the Pauline corpus. Moreover, Paul utilizes a broad palette of different types and subtypes of sequential connections—although sometimes the distribution deviates from that which we are accustomed to in the New Testament's narrative works, both as an entirety and occasionally individually (e.g., with τότε appearing primarily in Matthew). These findings reveal that a distinctly Pauline style of narration can be discerned despite the rather sparse data. Finally, it is clear that Paul's use of sequential connections extends well beyond cases that conform to our definition of narrativity—particularly since they, at least in part, pertain to future events. The fact that our focus on a critical feature of real narratives (i.e., sequence) has uncovered so many "almost stories" as a side effect of our investigation provides credibility to the category of implicit narratives. It is not simply a phantom phenomenon arising from loosely defined concepts of narrativity, which are designed to discover such ambiguous phenomena at all costs.

Simultaneity

We are now prepared to delve into the second major category of temporal relationships in narratives—simultaneity. At first glance, we may assume that we have a relatively firm, intuitive grasp of simultaneity, viewing it as a rather homogeneous concept akin to 'existing or occurring at the same time.'[32] However, even a cursory glance at our initial example of this temporal connection shows that the situation is more complex.

> While the police were still searching for him, Peter fled the country.

The qualifier "still" implies that situation A commenced before the onset of situation B. Moreover, since escaping the country is unambiguously goal oriented, we would usually interpret the main clause with the simple past to mean that the "accomplishment" indeed achieved its inherent goal—that is to say, event B comes to fruition within the timeframe of situation A. To illus-

---

32. *Merriam-Webster*, s.v. "simultaneous," accessed August 31, 2023, https://www.merriam-webster.com/dictionary/simultaneous.

trate, contrast the above with the subsequent reworking of the example that is equally "simultaneous" but conveys a completely different meaning:

As long as the police were hunting for him, Peter was on the run.

In the subsequent sections, we will systematically tackle this intricate issue by adhering to the subcategories that von Siebenthal assumes in his grammar.[33]

"As Soon As" Connectors

Rather than delving immediately into the prototypical "while" simultaneity, I propose that we initially consider the "as soon as" subtype. This category can be particularly challenging given its striking resemblance to sequentiality. Considering our recent discussion of anterior and posterior connections, it might be most practical to first grapple with this problematic subcategory. Some observers have characterized it as signifying "immediate anteriority," that is, an intensified "after" construction, expressing the fact that the later event B followed upon the earlier event A without any pause. However, it seems more precise to say that in the case of "as soon as," the reference situation is marked specifically with respect to delineating the left boundary of the situated situation. It specifies the commencement of a period during which the situation of the external connect unfolds. Sometimes, this left boundary of the situated situation aligns with the left boundary of the reference situation. For instance:

As soon as it dawned, the apple began to rejoice.

Alternatively, the left boundary of the situated situation occasionally coincides with the right boundary of the reference situation, further reinforcing the impression of the connector falling within the domain of sequences.[34] An example of this would be:

After/as soon as the stalk broke, the apple began to fall.

33. *AGG* 330.
34. Cf. Breindl, "Temporale Konnektoren," 358–59, for cases where it is the *right* border of the reference situation that coincides with the situated situation's left border.

Chapter 2

In Paul's writings, the majority of instances where ὅταν is used with aorist subjunctive can be categorized as belonging to this "as soon as" connector group.³⁵ Notably, there is a suspicious accrual of this in 1 Corinthians involving a range of future events. Both 1 Cor 13:10 and 15:24 express nexuses of eschatological events. It is "as soon as" that which is perfect arrives (ὅταν δὲ ἔλθῃ τὸ τέλειον) that the incomplete will be abolished (τὸ ἐκ μέρους καταργηθήσεται), and it is "as soon as" the final victory is achieved (ὅταν καταργήσῃ πᾶσαν ἀρχὴν καὶ πᾶσαν ἐξουσίαν καὶ δύναμιν) that the end will come (εἶτα τὸ τέλος).³⁶ While 1 Cor 15:27 is somewhat atypical, both the subsequent verse 28 and verse 54 clearly demarcate the "starting point" (as von Siebenthal classifies it) of eschatological situations.³⁷

In chapter 16, Paul remains consistent in his utilization of this connector, maintaining the future perspective but now moving away from eschatology. In 1 Cor 16:3, Paul states that he does not want the Corinthians to hurriedly begin amassing funds only "as soon as" he arrives (ὅταν ἔλθω). Counterintuitively, Paul refrains from using an undeniably sequential construct here, which would have established more distance between the two situations. This deviates from the misleading implication of the NET translation, "Then, when I arrive . . ." In 16:5, we seem to encounter an anterior usage (see above, pp. 68–69). Arguably, Paul cannot traverse through Macedonia and set foot in Corinth simultaneously—he must first journey through Thessaly, which at the time was part of Achaea. (An "as soon as" interpretation might be applicable if we postulate that πρὸς ὑμᾶς encompasses the people living north of Corinth in Achaea.) Following this, 16:12 seems to revert to "as soon as" simultaneity: Apollos will arrive (ἐλεύσεται) "as soon as" he finds an opportunity (ὅταν εὐκαιρήσῃ).

The same juxtaposition of different future references can also be found in Colossians, where an eschatological perspective is evident in Col 3:4, and a relatively brief temporal gap is apparent in 4:16. The latter verse refers to the time of reading the letter (ὅταν ἀναγνωσθῇ παρ᾽ ὑμῖν ἡ ἐπιστολή). The situated situation here is a command, the execution of which is meant to occur precisely at that point in time. This pattern of using the construction in discussions of both eschatological scenarios (1 Thess 1:10) and urgent

---

35. For what follows, see Heilig, *Paulus*, 435–40.
36. If the variant παραδῷ in the first temporal clause ὅταν παραδιδῷ τὴν βασιλείαν τῷ θεῷ καὶ πατρί were original, the implication would be that both the handing over and the victory must coincide because they would specify together the same point in time, the left border of the beginning of the end.
37. Here, τότε in the situated situation *might* point to a sequential interpretation.

The Grammar of Narration

travel concerns (Titus 3:12) can also be observed in other Pauline letters, both disputed and undisputed ones.

Interestingly, each of these instances (see also 2 Cor 10:6) is oriented toward the *future*.[38] Once more, we are left with the impression that Paul employs an element intrinsic to narrative in situations that defy our tight definition of what forms a story. Evidently, the precise dating of a situation by denoting its left boundary was especially significant in relation to future events. It was insufficient to merely know that something would happen "after" something else at an unspecified time. Instead, Paul's "almost-narration" reveals a particular interest in defining the initiation of future situations.

"While" and "When" Connectors

Having addressed the "as soon as" subtype, we can now turn to what most will consider the prototypical case of simultaneous connections. According to Heinrich von Siebenthal, who mentions this subcategory in first position, these connections express a kind of simultaneity that comes with a straightforward emphasis on them being simply "in progress" at the same time.[39]

Speaking of "at the same time," it should be noted that this is indeed a typical English phrase for connecting two propositions in this manner, with "meanwhile" likely being the most common adverbial connector. Of course, in both English and Greek, main clauses linked with additive connectors can likewise suggest simultaneity. However, in Paul's writings, such constructions predominantly appear to signify sequence.[40]

I begin the discussion of this subset of simultaneous connectors in the tar-

---

38. In some sense, 1 Tim 5:11 is an exception. Here, we find the general wish of the "younger widows" who want to marry (γαμεῖν θέλουσιν) "as soon as" their desires direct them into that direction (ὅταν γὰρ καταστρηνιάσωσιν τοῦ Χριστοῦ). Here, it seems a present subjunctive for repeated simultaneity would also have been possible. See below, pp. 91–98.

39. *AGG* 330b.

40. But cf. 2 Tim 4:17 (ὁ δὲ κύριός μοι παρέστη καὶ ἐνεδυνάμωσέν με). There are many factors that help the reader in that interpretation. For example, with some geographical knowledge, Gal 1:17 cannot be misunderstood as indicating simultaneity (ἀλλὰ ἀπῆλθον εἰς Ἀραβίαν καὶ πάλιν ὑπέστρεψα εἰς Δαμασκόν). Generally, if both situations are atelic, this facilitates a simultaneous interpretation. But cf. below, p. 155, for a transformation of our sequential apple example with two states: "First, the apple hung on the tree. Then it lay on the ground." Continuity of the subject by contrast suggests sequence, because human agents have a natural limit of things they can do at the same time.

Chapter 2

get language(s) due to a noteworthy phenomenon observable in both English and German—the fact that a single subordinating conjunction is prevalent in this category, namely, "while" in English and "während" in German. (English is a bit more variegated because it also has the preposition "during.") These subordinating conjunctions come with a distinct semantic constraint. The reference situation of these temporal clauses *contains* the situated situation (either having the same situation time or wider left and/or right borders).[41] Indeed, von Siebenthal also acknowledges that the situated situation is regularly "rather brief."[42] In other words, we can frequently observe in von Siebenthal's first category of simultaneity an *iconicity relating to syntactical dependency*, where the atelic (and durative) situation in the main clause provides a kind of "(back)ground" for the smaller "figure" of the dependent clause.[43] Given that this phenomenon is characteristic of "while" and "während," I propose we utilize the (improper or proper) inclusion as a defining criterion for this subcategory of Greek simultaneous connections as well.

This stricter formulation of the category carries a beneficial side effect. Consider how other frequent connectors used with such temporal relationships between situations—especially "when" in English and "als" in German—appear to have a rather *unspecific* meaning, since they can appear in propositions that express events prior to, simultaneous with, or later than the event in the matrix clause, and they can be integrated not only into the ground but also into the figure (i.e., into the situation with the smaller time interval). One cannot say, *"I was preparing the dinner while I glanced for a second at the watch," but it is possible to say, "I was preparing the dinner when I glanced at the watch for a second." Depending on the situations expressed by the connects, such connectors with unspecific meanings might still produce connections that fit our tight category of "while" simultaneity. However, the connectors themselves do not come with such requirements

41. Breindl, "Temporale Konnektoren," 465.
42. *AGG* 330b.
43. See Heilig, *Paulus*, 186–87. Cf. Eva Breindl, "Das Zusammenspiel von syntaktischer und semantischer Struktur in Konnektorkonstruktionen," in *Semantik der deutschen Satzverknüpfer*, ed. Eva Breindl, Anna Volodina, and Ulrich Hermann Waßner, vol. 2 of *Handbuch der deutschen Konnektoren*, Schriften des Instituts für Deutsche Sprache 13 (Berlin: de Gruyter, 2014), 65. In this work the question must remain open whether this also affects *linearization*, with a preference for the temporally larger event being adduced first and the other order being marked. We will also not address the issue of *information structure*, specifically the question of whether the ground itself can be focal as in the following example: "When did you eat the apple?"—"I ate the apple while I was still standing in the garden."

concerning the situation types. Therefore, it will be interesting to observe, in the analysis that follows, whether some of the cases within von Siebenthal's broad category of "focus on progress" might deviate from the "while" simultaneity and constitute a *separate subcategory* due to the more unspecific semantics of the connectors involved. (Note that for ὅταν, ὅτε, ὡς, von Siebenthal provides the dual gloss "when/while"!)[44]

Now let us proceed to an examination of connectoral constructions in Paul's letters that include a connector that Heinrich von Siebenthal adduces for this subcategory.[45] First, we can observe that there are a few instances of ἅμα ("at the same time") in a temporal sense, that is, an adverb marking the situated situation. In 1 Tim 5:13, it is stated that the widows learn to be idle (ἅμα δὲ καὶ ἀργαὶ μανθάνουσιν) as a side effect of the dynamic outlined in verses 10–11—whether we choose to label this a "description" or a narration of "event bundles" is debatable (cf. the ὅταν clause in verse 11).[46]

Colossians 4:3 is even farther away from classical narration since the reference situation is a command to pray and give thanks (and thus not an event in the past). The connector is integrated into a participle construction, which thus adds the command to simultaneously also pray for "us" to the general encouragement for prayer in verse 2.

Philemon 22 is remarkably similar in that we are also dealing with a situated situation that is a command, this time expressed via the imperative: "At the same time, also prepare a guest room for me" (ἅμα ... καὶ ἑτοίμαζέ μοι ξενίαν). Intriguingly, however, this action is not supposed to occur simultaneously with a reference situation that is also a command, nor are we dealing with an announcement. Instead, in verse 21 Paul conveys his confidence that Philemon will do even more than what he is instructed to do (ὑπὲρ ἃ λέγω ποιήσεις). Note that this "more" must be the wish from verse 13, namely, that Paul might keep Onesimus. So, while Paul explicitly refrains from directly dictating this action in verse 8, the assumption that Philemon will do precisely this action is ultimately implied in the temporal connection. Once again, it seems that Paul has devoted considerable thought to future events under various circumstances, making his decisions (concerning communication and beyond) with a precise objective in mind. It almost compels one to conclude that he is desiring that he might soon

---

44. *AGG* 330a.
45. See Heilig, *Paulus*, 415–22, for more details.
46. On the distinction between description and narration in such cases, cf. above, pp. 37–38.

Chapter 2

be in a position to recount a certain story as he reflects on events that will have transpired.

When examining connectoral marking of the reference situation in subordinate construction, it is evident that Paul rarely uses prepositions. In the New Testament, the deployment of the infinitive following ἐν to create temporal connections primarily occurs in the Gospel of Luke but, intriguingly, only occasionally in Acts. In Luke, we frequently see (καὶ) ἐγένετο, "(and) it came to pass," succeeded by the prepositional construction and, subsequently the main clause, which is often also introduced by καί, a construction indeed identifiable as a Hebraism.[47] It also appears without γίνομαι as a temporal phrase (Luke 2:27: καὶ ἐν τῷ εἰσαγαγεῖν τοὺς γονεῖς τὸ παιδίον Ἰησοῦν . . . ; "And when the parents brought in the child Jesus . . ."). And it can also be found embedded into a construction with γίνομαι and a dependent accusative with infinitive, which is the standard Greek construction (Luke 3:21: Ἐγένετο δὲ ἐν τῷ βαπτισθῆναι ἅπαντα τὸν λαὸν . . . ἀνεῳχθῆναι τὸν οὐρανόν; "But it happened, when the whole people were being baptized . . . that the heaven was opened"). It would be intriguing to ascertain whether a more extensive sample could confirm the impression that the New Testament occurrences provoke concerning the linearization of components, namely that, with ἐν as a temporal connector, we generally encounter the situating background first and then the temporally smaller figure.[48]

Be that as it may, Paul's usage does not conform to the typical New Testament pattern. In Gal 4:18, the preposition ἐν introduces a temporal specification, namely, "when I am present with you" (ἐν τῷ παρεῖναί με πρὸς ὑμᾶς). Nevertheless, the connection ultimately fails to constitute a miniature narrative because the situated situation does not declaratively posit an actual event but rather descriptively illuminates what would be "good." By contrast, 1 Cor 11:21 adheres more closely to our definition. The meaning of προλαμβάνω in the main clause is disputed. Some suggest that ἕκαστος . . . τὸ ἴδιον δεῖπνον προλαμβάνει envisages a situation where, during a shared meal, everyone enjoys their private meal. Others argue that Paul envisions eating "in advance" of the gathering. If we accept that ἐν τῷ φαγεῖν does not merely indicate "with respect to meals," it must be that "during" a single meal there is a sequence of eating acts

---

47. *AGG* 217e and 226a.
48. Cf. also Matt 27:12; there are exceptions, such as Luke 9:34: ἐφοβήθησαν δὲ ἐν τῷ εἰσελθεῖν αὐτοὺς εἰς τὴν νεφέλην.

that Paul disapproves of—the wealthy eating before the less fortunate can partake.⁴⁹

Set against the previous analysis of the preposition ἐν, our first observation when transitioning to ὅτε is that this subordinating conjunction is primarily used with respect to past situations. Romans 2:16 and 2 Tim 4:3 are exceptions to this tendency. There are two instances where two states are correlated, Rom 6:20 ("For <u>when</u> you were slaves of sin, you were free in regard to righteousness"; ὅτε γὰρ δοῦλοι ἦτε τῆς ἁμαρτίας, ἐλεύθεροι ἦτε τῇ δικαιοσύνῃ) and Gal 4:3 ("<u>When</u> we were minors, we were enslaved under the elements of the world"; ὅτε ἦμεν νήπιοι, ὑπὸ τὰ στοιχεῖα τοῦ κόσμου ἤμεθα δεδουλωμένοι).⁵⁰ In other places (Rom 7:5 and likely also 1 Cor 12:2; Col 3:7), we draw nearer to the figure-ground conception with a dynamic activity being presented against a state's backdrop. Colossians 3:7 deviates with respect to linearization because this is the sole example where we encounter the background following the figure in the text. It would be enlightening to scrutinize to what degree the preposition ἐν may provide varying flexibility in that regard. While in the aforementioned cases Paul looks well into the past—to a period preceding the recipients' conversion—he refers to his more recent stay with the recipients in 1 Thess 3:4 (cf. 2 Thess 3:10) in order to situate his apparently repeated pronouncements of afflictions, which, at that particular time, lie in the future but have since come to pass (καθὼς καὶ ἐγένετο).

We have already encountered the connector ὅταν with an aorist subjunctive in two contexts, primarily for an "as soon as" simultaneity but also, in one instance, for forming an "after" clause. In contrast, with the *imperfective* subjunctive we would generally anticipate a reference to repetitive event constellations in the present. Indeed, we will turn to this shortly. At first

---

49. In this case, Paul could also mean that when it comes to meals, the Corinthians always eat at home first. It seems notable that the aorist infinitive is used in the construction ἐν τῷ φαγεῖν (cf. Lev 22:16; 2 Kgs 4:40 for ἐσθίειν). But it cannot mean "after the eating" (cf. *AGG* 226a) here. One might translate it as "when the meal happens."

50. Just as in Gal 4:3, Paul also points to the time of being a "minor" in 1 Cor 13:11, but this time it does not seem to be directly metaphorical, and he uses the first-person singular verb form. Obviously, there is supposed to be a contrast between that time and the corresponding childish behavior with the temporal connection that immediately follows. But interestingly, Paul does not use the aorist indicative to express the change of becoming an adult and the corresponding transformation of behavior but instead uses the perfect indicative (ὅτε γέγονα ἀνήρ, κατήργηκα τὰ τοῦ νηπίου). The change to simultaneous narration only makes sense if we assume that Paul uses the first-person singular verb form here in a representative way, expressing a general principle.

Chapter 2

glance, 1 Thess 5:3 might also appear to fit well into that category. It would be plausible to envision the slogan "peace and security" (ὅταν λέγωσιν· εἰρήνη καὶ ἀσφάλεια) being recited repeatedly while destruction already casts its shadow over these speakers as an ever-present threat (αὐτοῖς ἐφίσταται ὄλεθρος ὥσπερ ἡ ὠδὶν τῇ ἐν γαστρὶ ἐχούσῃ). However, note that in the situated situation the correlate τότε αἰφνίδιος clearly indicates that we are not dealing with a state but rather a punctiliar event that will "then, suddenly" occur. Furthermore, the potential event of the cited speakers being able to escape is denied strongly (καὶ οὐ μὴ ἐκφύγωσιν). Thus, at least with respect to the situated situation, we are apparently dealing with a reference to a specific event in the future. This raises the question of whether the temporal clause also takes into consideration a specific, perhaps also future, event and juxtaposes the scenario of repeated assurance with a sudden disruption that terminates such claims, which would mean that the entire connection constitutes a case of "prior" narration.

Upon initial observation, 1 Cor 15:24 appears to be quite similar. Here, the arrival of the end (εἶτα τὸ τέλος) is indicated with two temporal clauses. The latter one is in the aorist subjunctive and poses no complications (see above, p. 82). However, the former is quite puzzling. What exactly makes "When he hands over the kingdom to the father" (ὅταν παραδιδῷ τὴν βασιλείαν τῷ θεῷ καὶ πατρί) so perplexing? English Bible translations usually interpret the situated situation as "then comes the end," that is, as a telic situation—a change of state, an arrival. Indeed, it is beneficial not merely to translate it as "and then there will be the period 'the end,'" because the second temporal clause seems to be a clear instance of an achievement that takes place before the event of the matrix clause (the annihilation of all authority and power). Accordingly, we would not anticipate an atelic situation to succeed it. Hence, it is most fitting to interpret the clause without the verb εἶτα τὸ τέλος ingressively, as expressing the initiation of that final state.[51] But how does the act of "handing over" (παραδίδωμι) relate to this temporal configuration? When examined in isolation, we could likely assume that the situation it represents is also telic and of relatively brief duration—an accomplishment that does not require much time, even though it is possibly not a punctiliar achievement. Nevertheless, the scenario seems to greatly differ from, for instance, 1 Thess 5:3, as it is uncertain how the situation of the first ὅταν clause in 1 Cor 15:24 could constitute something akin to a larger

---

51. Cf. Breindl, "Temporale Konnektoren," 355–56, on the constellation with similar German connectors.

context into which the assumed figure of the main clause, the initiation of the final state, could be incorporated. In other words, it does not seem that here the external connect can be embedded into the situation time of the internal connect.

There are several possibilities to consider as potential explanations for this unusual construction. First, and least probable, is the hypothesis that the variant with the aorist subjunctive might have been the original choice. For then it would be inexplicable why anyone would alter a perfectly logical choice of aspect.

Second, we must consider the possibility that Paul intended a sequence in spite of his aspectual choice. In actuality, it seems plausible that Paul, while dictating his letter, may have identified his sentence as not being acceptable but did not see a need to revise it (potentially due to the verbless clause, which might have lessened the sense of unacceptability). Instead, he may have opted to include an elucidating remark—a second and (more acceptable) ὅταν clause. If this was the case, the function of this second clause would be to provide retrospectively a date for the event of the handover, which in and of itself lacks a specific temporal connection to the expressed timeline as something that will transpire between the destruction of evil powers and the transition into the final state. If this explanation holds true, it would provide another compelling insight into the dynamics of Paul's use of secretaries.

Third, I believe consideration should be given to the possibility that, during Paul's time, ὅταν may have been closer in meaning to English "when" (or German "als") than to English "while."[52] Indeed, the issues we encounter—specifically here, but also to a lesser extent in other passages—with differentiating between simultaneous and sequential connections could hint at how the Greek connector remains somewhat vague within the context of the temporal relation existing between the two scenarios. As we pointed out previously, there is reason to consider that von Siebenthal's category of "while" simultaneity might in fact require a distinction between connectors that remain ambiguous in relation to specific temporal relationships (like the English "when") and those that convey the concept of temporal inclusion

---

52. Cf. *Wörterbuch der Konnektoren*, "als," last modified July 8, 2016, https://grammis.ids-mannheim.de/konnektoren/407056: 'Markiert den Bezugspunkt auf Grund dessen zwei Sachverhalte in ihrer zeitlichen Relation zueinander in Bezug gesetzt werden; nicht auf eine bestimmte Zeitrelation festgelegt. Diese ergibt sich in Abhängigkeit vom Tempus der Konnekte.'

Chapter 2

of the situated situation (such as "while"). The second ὅταν clause of 1 Cor 15:24 might, indeed, support this notion.

After all, if we use the events of that verse as our starting point and momentarily disregard aspect, the most intuitive interpretation probably would not posit the ὅταν clause as contributing either the larger ground or an event preceding the event of the matrix clause. Instead, it would be quite reasonable to view the act of handing over as part of a longer process leading up to the end. In such a case, the connector ὅταν would mark the figure, not the ground.

Note that in Modern Greek, όταν can indeed express both the larger time interval (Το λεωφορείο αναχώρησε όταν έτρωγα; "The bus departed when I was eating") as well as the shorter event (Έτρωγα όταν αναχώρησε το λεωφορείο; "I was eating when the bus departed"). Perhaps a similar idea underlies the first two clauses in 1 Cor 15:24, and perhaps it is made intuitively accessible through the linearization we encounter here. I find it noteworthy that in English, the similarly ambiguous "when" can only have the latter function of marking the shorter event if it follows the main clause (i.e., "I was eating when the bus left," but not *"When the bus left, I was eating.").[53] Similarly, in German "als" constructions the ground usually precedes the figure (regardless of which element carries the connector).[54] Therefore, it might have been more natural for Paul than von Siebenthal's grammar suggests to use ὅταν in a postponed position to situate the figure of "handing over" within the ground of an "approaching" end. Still, this explanation admittedly does not resolve all issues, as it would necessitate the assumption that, upon adding the second clause, Paul reconceptualized the verbless clause as a telic situation (the "arrival" of the end versus the process of its "approaching").

Of course, it is also possible Paul was indeed anticipating the transition into the final phase from the onset. The role of the first ὅταν clause would simply be to approximate it to the time of Jesus's act of handing over the realm to God the Father. In this scenario, the imperfective aspect remains puzzling as it precludes the actual reception of the rule by God the Father. It could be that Paul's intention was to indicate that, when signs of this process become perceptible, it implies that the end is near. He then adds another ὅταν clause in the aorist subjunctive to underscore that this process only commences after the event of the enemies' destruction. One might para-

---

53. Leonard Talmy, *Concept Structuring Systems*, vol. 1 of *Toward a Cognitive Semantics* (Cambridge: MIT Press, 2000), 398.

54. Breindl, "Zusammenspiel," 65.

phrase this as follows: "Then, the end will arrive. This will transpire around the time when Jesus will be transferring the kingdom to God the Father, a process that will start after he has concluded the eradication of every dominion, authority, and power."

"Whenever" Connectors

In our exploration of the subcategories of simultaneous connections that von Siebenthal puts forth in his grammar, we started with instances that are marked by connectors that can be translated as "as soon as." While von Siebenthal mentions this scenario only in the fourth column of his overview table of possible meanings, we started with this phenomenon because it is essentially on the border of sequentiality, and it, therefore, naturally segues from our prior examination of sequential connections. Only thereafter did we pivot to what von Siebenthal seems to perceive as a sort of unmarked constellation of concurrent situations, which are simply "in progress" at the same time. However, as we have seen, upon closer scrutiny this seemingly prototypical and straightforward subcategory may actually need even further differentiation. While some of the connections we surveyed contain a connector in the temporal clause that conveys the occurrence of a longer situation that includes the shorter situation of the main clause, other connections seem to express the inverse setup or ultimately unspecified relationships of some form of overlap.

We could now advance our discussion with simultaneous connections that place emphasis on either the beginning or the end of simultaneity, two further subcategories that von Siebenthal cites. But, as will soon become evident, this distinction is also not precise enough for our needs and will require further elaboration.

For this reason, I wish to proceed with the subcategory of simultaneity that von Siebenthal presents as the fifth option. This subcategory is marked by an emphasis on "iterativeness," that is, it takes into account the *repeated* coincidence of situations. It should be noted that it is possible to specify the frequency of a situation in an absolute manner—from "never" (e.g., οὐδέποτε) to "always" (e.g., πάντοτε)—using adverbs. However, in this case, frequency is specified by means of a reference situation (while the absolute frequency remains open in principle). In other words, in every "instance" of the reference situation, a co-occurrence of the situated situation will be present.

Chapter 2

Note that this definition presupposes a series of events with clear intermissions. The interaction between durative aspect and the verb's situation type determines whether such a constellation is communicated. However, it is not always readily apparent whether we are dealing with a merely "linear" or an "iterative" aspectual nuance.

For instance, how should we approach Rom 8:23?[55] There, Paul states in the indicative present: "We ourselves [not just creation, verse 22] groan inwardly" (ἡμεῖς καὶ αὐτοὶ ἐν ἑαυτοῖς στενάζομεν). The act of producing a στεναγμός, a groan, can be classified as a "semelfactive," which means that the combination of aspect and verbal semantics conjure the scenario of a series of multiple groans (not a single, extended groan).

However, it seems as if Paul is representing these repetitious groans as a sort of interconnected habit, not a repeated action. After all, he aligns the groaning with the situation of "us" anticipating the event of adoption (υἱοθεσίαν ἀπεκδεχόμενοι). This suggests a state "we" are presently in, which began in the past and will persist until Jesus returns (cf. also 2 Cor 5:2, where the groaning is linked with the state verb "longing": στενάζομεν . . . ἐπιποθοῦντες).

Paul can assert such *continuous* groaning, even though in reality this habit indeed carries intervals, so that the communicated situation is essentially *interruptive*. Take note that in real-life scenarios, too, the claim "I've done nothing for the past hour except read this damn book" does not necessitate modifications such as "Well, actually that's not true, there's the two and a half minutes that I went to the bathroom, and the two thirty-second periods I spent looking out the window, and all those fractions of seconds I was blinking . . ."[56] Similarly, Paul's miniature narrative can be viewed as being reliably narrated, even though one might observe the "us" of Rom 8:23 at times breathing normally.

These considerations could lead one to classify the temporal connection in Rom 8:23 as a case of two durative situations with equal temporal extension (much akin to "while" connections). However, it is likewise possible to interpret this miniature narrative as the unfolding of iterative simultaneity, with bursts of deep-felt yearning that each time results in a sigh. For if we

---

55. For a narrative reading of Rom 8:19–23, Cherryl Hunt, David G. Horrell, and Christopher Southgate, "An Environmental Mantra? Ecological Interest in Romans 8:19–23 and a Modest Proposal for Its Narrative Interpretation," *JTS* 59 (2008): 546–79.

56. The example is from Carl Bache, "Aspect and Aktionsart: Towards a Semantic Distinction," *Journal of Linguistics* 18 (1982): 65–66. On the whole issue, cf. Heilig, *Paulus*, 343–44.

take into account the wiggle room when it comes to portraying behavior in everyday narration, it also follows concerning the psychological state of "eagerly waiting" (ἀπεκδέχομαι) that it cannot be constantly experienced with the same intensity. To sum up, the distinction between iterative and noniterative simultaneity can be contentious at times, as this example demonstrates.

The first observation to note with respect to Paul's iterative-simultaneous narration is that we can dismiss *adverbial* connectors altogether.[57] My analysis of πάντοτε, which von Siebenthal cites as an adverbial connector, shows that its use always follows the manner I have previously discussed—namely, to express something as occurring "all the time" in an absolute sense, rather than binding a situation connectorally to a series of events mentioned immediately prior.[58]

Admittedly, in some instances, we can still discern a temporal relationship between what is occurring "all the time" and another event mentioned in the same context. After all, if something takes place "all the time" (such as the act of thanking God in Phlm 4) and another repeated action is also mentioned (like remembering Philemon in prayer in the same verse), the latter will naturally always coincide with the former. However, this is simply a temporal implication and not an instance of a temporal connection.

This leaves us with *subordinate constructions*, that is, with the connectoral marking of the reference situation, for which it is true that every single time "it" (i.e., one instance of that event bundle) takes place, it is linked with the simultaneous occurrence of the situated situation. There is a range of potential syntactical constructions to articulate this notion, depending in part on the type of narration utilized.

In regard to (a) the *subsequent narration type*, the evidence for repeated simultaneity in Paul's letters is limited. Theoretically, ὅτε combined with the imperfect tense should be able to convey this idea (as seen in Hag 2:16), but it appears to only be used for individual situations in the New Testament (predominantly activities and states). Similarly, the iterative optative that would have been utilized in classical times for such instances does not appear in the New Testament. Instead, this construction is entirely replaced by augmented indicatives with ἄν, also known as the "Hellenistic preterite

---

57. On what follows, cf. Heilig, *Paulus*, 422–28.
58. Note that von Siebenthal has already made a change with respect to his example Phlm 4 in *AGG* 330c in comparison to the original (*GGNT* 330c).

Chapter 2

iterative of the subordinate clause."[59] Given that ὅταν is a merger of ὅτε and ἄν, it can indicate iterative simultaneity when used with the aorist indicative (see the comparison of the imperfect in Mark 3:11 with the aorist indicative in Mark 11:19). There appears to be only one relevant case of this in Paul's letters, paired with ὡς, in 1 Cor 12:2.[60]

The subordinating conjunction ὅταν with a present subjunctive offers deeper insights. This is surprising because even within narrative works like the Gospels, this construction typically appears in combination with the *prior "narration" type*. For instance, this occurs when a speaker outlines when or how often a command should be followed. Take Matt 6:16 for example: "When(ever) you fast, do not be like . . ." (Ὅταν δὲ νηστεύητε, μὴ γίνεσθε ὡς . . .). This is understandable given that most cases of what could be termed "prototypical" narratives concentrate on singular events rather than bundles of events in the past. And regarding the present, repeated coincidences are even more difficult to imagine, being possible only if we allow for a relatively broad conception of the time interval that constitutes the "now," and even then we might still not be dealing with narration because it might be more straightforward to label such cases "descriptions" of recurring processes.

Against that backdrop and in light of our earlier observations on other connectors, it may thus be slightly surprising that within Paul's writings, ὅταν with a present subjunctive is generally part of an act of narration that belongs to (b) the *simultaneous narration type*.[61] The main clause typically employs the present indicative. At times, the temporal clauses appear to closely resemble general-prospective conditional clauses.[62] This resemblance is due to either the unknown absolute frequency of the reference situation or its

---

59. Cf. *AGG* 211i.
60. There, Paul reminds the Corinthians of something they know (Οἴδατε ὅτι . . .). The situation is first dated generally to the time "when you were pagans" (ὅτε ἔθνη ἦτε). The syntax of what follows (πρὸς τὰ εἴδωλα τὰ ἄφωνα ὡς ἂν ἤγεσθε ἀπαγόμενοι) is a little unclear. Either ὡς picks up the ὅτι and explicates what was happening at said time, with the prepositional phrase having moved before the subjunction. Then the situated situation would be: "(you know that, how) you were repeatedly led to the mute idols, being led astray." Or the phrase forms a unity with the participle that needs to be supplemented periphrastically with ἦτε. In that case, the situated situation would be: "you were led astray repeatedly to the mute idols" and we would have *another* reference situation: "whenever you were led."
61. On 1 Thess 5:3 as a potential exception, see above, p. 88.
62. Cf. *AGG* 282.

The Grammar of Narration

relative unimportance, with the focus instead lying on the regularity of the coincidence itself (see Rom 2:14; 1 Cor 3:4; 2 Cor 12:10; 13:9).[63]

However, in certain cases, the absolute frequency of the reference situation is more evident, and the categorization of the text sections as products of simultaneous narration seems clear-cut. Perhaps the most compelling case can be made for 1 Cor 14:26, where the repeated "coming together" (ὅταν συνέρχησθε) provides the backdrop for various activities specified in a series of main clauses (ἕκαστος ψαλμὸν ἔχει, διδαχὴν ἔχει, ἀποκάλυψιν ἔχει, γλῶσσαν ἔχει, ἑρμηνείαν ἔχει·πάντα πρὸς οἰκοδομὴν γινέσθω).

Intriguingly, when read in context, this brief narrative about early Christian church gatherings, which so wonderfully fits our definition of narrativity, must be understand as a "*corrective* word."[64] In the very verse where Paul most clearly iteratively narrates with ὅταν, he is *not* informing the Corinthians about any practices—a scenario that would be quite odd, considering he is referencing their own gatherings—but is actually attempting to promote certain behavior. Despite this, the text segment remains a story, but its communicative function diverges from what we typically associate with most narratives. This provides an informative suggestion: when examining Paul's stories, it is crucial to pay particular attention to their *pragmatics*, that is, to what Paul is trying to achieve by telling them (see chapter 3).

The prominence of the simultaneous narration type when it comes to iterative simultaneity within Paul's writings can also be seen from his considerable use of relevant connectors, which stands out remarkably when contrasted with other New Testament narrators' choices. One can refer to a somewhat abnormal instance of ὡς with the present indicative in 2 Tim 1:3.[65] Additionally, the construction ὁσάκις ἐάν is found within the New Testament only in Paul's depiction of Jesus's instructions at the Last Supper (1 Cor 11:25 and 26) and in Rev 11:6. Paul also employs the term ἡνίκα in 2 Cor 3:15–16, a term that while frequently seen in the Septuagint is not present in other New Testament texts.

This final passage, 2 Cor 3:15–16, provides valuable insights as it clarifies the relation between "whenever" connectors and narration. The two verses draw our attention to a specific time frame, which began in the past and endures "until today" (ἕως σήμερον), as specified in verse 15. From verse 16,

---

63. Cf. *AGG* 276d.
64. Gordon D. Fee, *The First Epistle to the Corinthians*, NICNT (Grand Rapids: Eerdmans, 1987), 690. Emphasis added.
65. It seems that ὡς with ἄν belongs to the "as soon as" type in Paul. Cf. 1 Cor 11:34.

we learn that this situation will only cease in the future. Verse 15 narrates a story about the repeated coinciding of two situations during that period. The veil lies on "their" hearts (κάλυμμα ἐπὶ τὴν καρδίαν αὐτῶν κεῖται)—namely, "whenever Moses is read" (ἡνίκα ἂν ἀναγινώσκηται Μωϋσῆς). This is a prime example of a miniature story that narrates repeated simultaneity in the simultaneous narration type (with a broad interpretation of what constitutes the "now").

In verse 16, the situation alters slightly. Now, Paul peers into the future to a time when this repeated co-occurrence will cease, when the reading of Moses can transpire without a veil on "their" hearts. Thus, many Bible versions interpret the connection of verse 16 as a case of "as soon as" simultaneity. The removal of the veil (περιαιρεῖται τὸ κάλυμμα) will occur at a certain point in the future, specifically when Israel (?) turns back to the Lord (ἡνίκα δὲ ἐὰν ἐπιστρέψῃ πρὸς κύριον). This construct would represent an example of the predictive narration of a distinct future event constellation with ἐάν reinforcing this specific-prospective outlook. However, others add the subject τις, "anyone," interpreting this in harmony with verse 15, as another case of repeated simultaneity, only this time of the prior narration type.

It is, in fact, even possible to question the extent to which this miniature story of concurrent events is even confined to the future. Surely, Paul has been preaching for some time; the "now" has already started in the past. According to Paul, Jewish individuals have already turned to the Lord with the veil being lifted from their hearts. This instance shows how closely this temporal construction aligns with a *conditional* connection. Instead of categorizing this as a miniature story, one could argue with equal justification that Paul is rather detailing the plot of various stories that he deems narratable under certain conditions. In other words, the distinction between an actual narrative on the one hand and a summary of these stories into a potentially narratable plot—and, thus, many implicit stories—on the other hand becomes blurry.

In my opinion, this complexity of distinguishing a clear pattern of asserted, narrated events rather than merely conditional constellations in 2 Cor 3:16 may point to a more intrinsic issue. It may suggest that the semantics of the connector ἡνίκα are not clearly defined in terms of temporal parameters. This suggestion finds some support in the fact that verse 16 can be easily (mis)interpreted as an "as soon as" constellation.

With this in mind, it proves illuminating to explore the text to which Paul alludes in this passage, for here too we can discern a degree of temporal ambiguity. In Exod 34:34, the act of removing the veil (περιαιρέω here as well) is associated with Moses repeatedly approaching God for conversation (cf. εἰσπορεύομαι). The verb περιαιρέω appears to be telic, suggesting the separation of something from something else as its final outcome (cf. Acts 27:40 regarding anchors being slipped: καὶ τὰς ἀγκύρας περιελόντες). When employed in the imperfective aspect, we are either confronted with an internal perspective on a single process that may culminate in this eventual separation (such as the process of losing hope in Acts 27:20: περιῃρεῖτο ἐλπίς) or with an iterative reinterpretation, which is evidently the case in Exod 34:34 where περιῃρεῖτο is used. However, it is curious how in that passage there is a temporal link between the act of removing the veil and an "until" phrase (ἕως τοῦ ἐκπορεύεσθαι).[66] The main idea is certainly not that Moses was engaged in the act of removing his veil throughout the entirety of his encounter with the Lord, but that the implied state of having removed the veil spanned the duration of their conversation. The subsequent event of replacing the veil is left unmentioned, and it falls upon the reader to pinpoint exactly when in the process of departing (ἐκπορεύομαι) it occurs (verse 35 implies there was a short period during which he was outside without the veil on his head). What remains even more unanswered is the question of whether Moses took any other preparatory steps before entering the presence of the Lord and how they might have related temporally to the removal of the veil. To sum up, this verse presents a lack of temporal specificity, and it seems possible that there could be an interval between the earlier and the later events that are linked by ἡνίκα.

Therefore, it is not too surprising to find in other passages even a reversal of this order. For instance, in Lev 10:9 the act of approaching the Lord (ἡνίκα ἂν εἰσπορεύησθε εἰς τὴν σκηνὴν τοῦ μαρτυρίου ἢ προσπορευομένων ὑμῶν πρὸς τὸ θυσιαστήριον) is paired with a command to abstain from alcohol (οἶνον καὶ σικερα οὐ πίεσθε σὺ καὶ οἱ υἱοί σου μετὰ σοῦ), an admonition which most certainly not only applies to the priests' time on duty but also is clearly intended to prevent alcohol consumption before these ritual activities, to avoid any potential intoxication during these *later* duties (cf. also Exod 34:24).

Similarly, we can assume that in 2 Cor 3:15–16 we must allow for some degree of ambiguity as to how "turning" toward the Lord (ἐπιστρέφω) combines with the event of the veil's removal. Against the backdrop of these other passages, it seems entirely realistic to suggest that, in Paul's mind, turning to the Lord and the lifting of the veil were *two interconnected pro-*

---

66. For the use with the infinitive in the New Testament, cf. Acts 8:40 ("until he came to Caesarea"; ἕως τοῦ ἐλθεῖν αὐτὸν εἰς Καισάρειαν).

Chapter 2

cesses, two dynamics conceivable as separate situations yet reinforcing each other simultaneously with individual phases of these situations influencing each other. Therefore, when commentators claim that Paul demonstrates confused logic—in which the veil is only removed after conversion to Christ, an event that is in turn rendered impossible due to the presence of the veil— this might, in fact, arise from attributing an overly precise temporal meaning to the connector ἡνίκα.[67]

This ambiguity regarding the temporal positioning of the situated situation prompts the more fundamental question of whether we should categorize "connectors of frequency," as they are sometimes termed, as temporal connectors at all, or whether they might more appropriately be considered *conditional* connectors.[68] We can at least note that our discussion of 2 Cor 3:15–16 coheres well with the notion that "temporal order" all too easily blends into conditional constellations. Therefore, we can note that in our pursuit of explicit narratives in Paul's letters, we are once again led to the unexpected finding that precisely when we believe we have identified clear-cut instances of miniature narratives within Paul's writing, the language employed by the apostle in his narrations directs us beyond this relatively narrow range of textual phenomena and places the potential, implicit story squarely in our field of attention.

"Since" Connectors

We can now wrap up this discussion by examining simultaneous connections that, per von Siebenthal, encapsulate either a concentration on the onset or conclusion of simultaneity. Initially, we will delve into connectors presumed to focus on the *inception* of simultaneity, the third subclass that von Siebenthal examines.[69] Von Siebenthal's choice of an English equivalent for these connectors is "since" (German: "seit"), which he contrasts with

---

67. Note that Thomas Schmeller, *Der zweite Brief an die Korinther*, 2 vols., EKKNT 8 (Neukirchen-Vluyn: Neukirchener, 2010, 2015), 1:221, presupposes that the veil is removed only after the completed turn to the Lord: "Durch diese [christologische] Deutung entsteht die Schwierigkeit, dass Paulus offenbar zirkulär argumentiert. Die Hülle wird erst weggenommen, wenn die Bekehrung zu Christus erfolgt ist, die aber von der Hülle gerade verhindert wird. Verhüllung und Verstockung sind theologische Deutungsversuche, den Unglauben Israels zu erklären, die eine gewisse Hilflosigkeit nicht verbergen können."
68. Cf. the discussion in Breindl, "Temporale Konnektoren," 387–89.
69. On what follows, see Heilig, *Paulus*, 431–35.

connectors such as "as long as" (German: "solange") for the termination of simultaneity.

However, if we concentrate on the role that the reference situation serves with respect to the situated situation, we can see that the "since" connectors bear a closer resemblance to the "until" connectors, which von Siebenthal categorizes as posterior and, thus, sequential (cf. above, pp. 69–73). Both "until" and "since" constructs pinpoint the *duration* of the situated situation by indicating its right border in the first instance and its left border in the second instance. In other words, they address the question "how long?" and not "when?"

Just as it can be debated whether "until" connectors are genuinely sequential (since they do not rule out possible overlap with the reference situation), we can also question whether "since" connectors are indeed simultaneous. After all, while it is often the case that the reference situation is durative and presents a situation time that is entirely consumed by the situated situation (unlike the case of "while," wherein the situated situation may in some cases be only applicable for smaller fragments of the period), there are instances where the left boundary of the situated situation is defined by punctiliar events.

Romans 1:20 (cf. below, p. 100) might serve as a Pauline case in point. It is not entirely equivalent to say that God's attributes can be perceived "since" the world exists and "since" the world was created. Note that in the latter scenario, it is, technically speaking, the phase immediately *following* the reference situation, not the reference situation itself, that sets the left boundary of the situated situation, thus pushing the phenomenon toward the realm of sequential order. Nonetheless, even if the categorization of connectors that von Siebenthal proposes as "simultaneous" might present problems, it is undoubtedly true that these connectors can produce connections where there is overlap between the (prolonged) reference situation and the situated situation—which is ultimately what our narratological examination seeks to probe.

Note that the situated situation is invariably atelic and that its left boundary, specified by the reference situation, is always associated with a change of state. You cannot, in other words, say: *"Since Peter was sixteen, he has had asthma. But he had also already had it before." The right border of the situated situation often aligns with the time of speech (e.g., "Since he was elected in 2016, Donald Trump has been President of the United States," spoken, for example, in 2018). However, this is not always the case (e.g., "In 2016, it had been twelve years since a Republican president was last elected"). Although

Chapter 2

the simultaneous narration type is, thus, customary, and subsequent narration is at least possible, the concept of "prior narration" does not apply to this subtype of simultaneous connection.[70] This observation may lead us to anticipate the discovery of a larger proportion of actual miniature narratives in our subsequent analysis, given that Paul's tendency to talk in narrative-like fashion about the future should not intervene here.

Nonetheless, in Paul's letters the construction with a preposition is relatively uncommon. There are a few potential instances with ἐκ (most prominently in Gal 1:15 and Rom 1:4), but these are not unmistakably temporal. With ἀπό, at least in Rom 1:20, the case seems quite clear. It is "since the creation of the world" (ἀπὸ κτίσεως κόσμου) that God's invisible attributes are perceived (καθορᾶται). However, as mentioned earlier, the telic nature of the reference situation eventually establishes what is arguably a sequential connection. Furthermore, if we interpret this case as an example of a "tolerative passive," we will not even categorize this as a narrative at all, since the statement would only denote potential occurrences (i.e., "perceivable") if interpreted in this way, with the participle νοούμενα then assuming a conditional function (i.e., "if they are understood").

The typical Greek subordinating conjunctions (ἀφ' οὗ, ἐξ οὗ, and ἀφ' ἧς) yield but a few attestations, namely, only ἀφ' ἧς in Col 1:6 and 1:9—and these only in the original form with ἡμέρας, leading to debatable perspectives on whether we are dealing with a fully grammaticalized conjunction here. Nevertheless, this usage in Col 1 is indeed significant and warrants closer examination.

In the initial occurrence, verse 6, the temporal clause outlines the duration of the gospel's fruit-bearing "activity" among the Colossians, namely, "since the day you heard and understood the grace of God in truth" (ἀφ' ἧς ἡμέρας ἠκούσατε καὶ ἐπέγνωτε τὴν χάριν τοῦ θεοῦ ἐν ἀληθείᾳ). Verses 7–8 reveal that Epaphras was the one who communicated the gospel to the Colossians and relayed their affection for Paul and Timothy. Here, we receive both an analepsis into the propagation of the gospel and learn about an event that transpired later, during the ongoing growth of the gospel in Colossae. In verse 9, the event of hearing from Epaphras is revisited with ἀφ' ἧς ἡμέρας and signals the commencement of a new situation that is still current at the time of writing: "we have not stopped praying for you . . ." (οὐ παυόμεθα ὑπὲρ ὑμῶν προσευχόμενοι . . .).

---

70. If the left border of a situation in the future were to be marked, we would use an anterior connector: *"Since A, B will be the case" versus "After A, B will be the case."

Despite the presence of this construction twice within a short span of verses and its apparently similar functionality, closer scrutiny reveals key differences. Most notable among these is how the reference situations, utilized to specify the duration of the situated situations, are introduced in the text. Before its employment as a reference situation, the event of informing Paul and Timothy about the Colossians' love for them is explicitly mentioned already in verse 8, accompanied by a relatively specific and uncommon verb of communication (δηλόω). Conversely, it is not until the temporal clause in verse 6b that we learn about the element of "understanding" God's grace (ἐπιγινώσκω). Preceding this, in verses 5–6a it had simply been noted that the gospel had "come" to the Colossians and they had "heard" it.

The probable explanation for this configuration is that the recipients, of course, already have knowledge of their conversion. This event can be summoned as a chronological reference point without the need for preestablishment. By contrast, the interaction between Paul and Timothy, on the one hand, and Epaphras, on the other hand, is something the Colossians would only hear about upon receiving the letter. Certainly, these observations primarily pertain to the narrative world of the letter, which may still be fictional. Yet, it undeniably illustrates that when handling the disputed letters of the Pauline corpus, it is vital to realize that they do not simply "rehash" other Pauline material (an approach assumed by many commentators). Rather, they invite us to envisage a context of unique interactions between Paul and the recipients, evident in the specific pragmatics of his narratives.

"As Long As" Connectors

At last, we can address the subcategory of simultaneity that, according to von Siebenthal, is focused on the "end" of co-occurrence. In English, "as long as" serves as a standard subordinating conjunction that can function as a gloss in such instances (in German "solange" has this function).[71] This subcategory may initially seem to parallel "since" connector cases. However, as previously explained, "since" connectors primarily characterize duration rather than simultaneity. In contrast, "as long as" connectors always indicate simultaneity. Within that broader context of simultaneity, they contrast with "while" connectors. In the former case, the reference situation specifies an uninterrupted time interval during which the situated situation was true. In

---

71. Breindl, "Temporale Konnektoren," 374–77.

Chapter 2

the latter case, it is possible for the situated situation to hold true for only a partial interval of the reference situation.[72] Consider the following examples for clarification:

> <u>While</u> Paul was in Galatia, he was ill. But not for the entire time.

> *<u>As long as</u> Paul was in Galatia, he was ill. But not for the entire time.

Observe that "as long as" connectors only denote the *minimal* duration of a situated situation. This situation may well have been present even before:

> Paul was ill <u>as long as</u> he was in Galatia. However, he had also been ill before.

> *Paul was ill <u>since</u> he had arrived in Galatia. However, he had also been ill before.

In a similar vein, it is permissible for the situated situation to extend *beyond* the reference situation:

> <u>As long as</u> Paul was in Galatia, he was ill. However, he had also been sick before *and he continued to be sick after he had left.*

However, in certain contexts, the end of simultaneity is at least implied, lending some justification to von Siebenthal's assertion about the kind of connection that such connectors can relay. The last example works seamlessly if it is an answer to the question, "How was Paul doing in Galatia?" Conversely, if the question were "How long was Paul sick?" the example would likely be an unacceptable response. In essence, the information structure appears to determine whether or not "as long as" connectors imply an actual end to the situated situation.

When considering the evidence within Pauline letters, we can largely dismiss the subordinating conjunctions ἕως and ἄχρι(ς).[73] By contrast, ἐφ᾽

---

72. Cf. Breindl, "Temporale Konnektoren," 374.
73. Cf. Heilig, *Paulus*, 428–31. Strictly speaking, these are "until" connectors defining the right boundary of a situated situation. As outlined above, in some contexts, this situation might extend beyond the reference situation, ultimately communicating

The Grammar of Narration

ὅσον (χρόνον) appears to be genuinely analogous to "as long as." Further, it holds significant intrigue for our analysis. Although it is somewhat uncommon in the New Testament and is not found in the LXX at all, there are multiple attestations in Paul's letters.

In Rom 7:1, the lifespan of a human being (ἐφ᾽ ὅσον χρόνον ζῇ) determines the minimal duration of the law's sovereignty over them (ὁ νόμος κυριεύει τοῦ ἀνθρώπου). In the specific context, it is evident that the end of life also signifies the maximal timeframe for the law's rule, a point further elaborated in verse 2, where Paul uses the analogy of a woman who is legally bound to her husband "as long as" he lives. The attributive participle that specifies the husband as "alive" (ἡ γὰρ ὕπανδρος γυνὴ τῷ ζῶντι ἀνδρὶ δέδεται νόμῳ) serves to determine the maximal time frame (with the implicit event of marriage acting as the left boundary; cf. ὕπανδρος). This is further substantiated by the ensuing conditional construction, which directly communicates what transpires upon the man's death: "But if the husband dies, she is released from the law of the husband" (ἐὰν δὲ ἀποθάνῃ ὁ ἀνήρ, κατήργηται ἀπὸ τοῦ νόμου τοῦ ἀνδρός).

At first sight, this appears to be a fairly unambiguous instance of a simultaneous connection employed for a miniature narrative of the simultaneous narration type. Still, one could argue that this entire connection is not asserted outright but is actually part of a question: "(Or) don't you know, brothers and sisters . . . that . . ." (Ἢ ἀγνοεῖτε, ἀδελφοί . . . ὅτι . . .). Consequently, Paul is not "narrating" these simultaneous situations in the strictest sense. Yet, we might view such concerns as overrestrictive. We could counter by pointing out that Paul, though he poses it as a question, seems convinced that the answer must be: "Yes, of course, we know that!" This is particularly apparent considering his parenthetical comment: ". . . for I speak to those who know the law . . ." (γινώσκουσιν γὰρ νόμον λαλῶ). Therefore, even if we insist on not categorizing this as a miniature narrative, it nevertheless underscores the presence in Paul's letters of structures that, while not strictly narratives, still warrant narratological examination. Paul is, in essence, *compelling his readers to tell that story* in their affirmative—if only implied, mental—response.

---

a constellation of simultaneity. Nonetheless, the majority of Pauline instances clearly belong to the category of posterior connections. One could argue that 1 Tim 4:13 serves as a potential exception. However, therein the situated situation is not a recounted event but a command to Timothy, signifying that we are not dealing with a miniature narrative in this case. Cf. also Gal 6:10 for a potentially relevant construction with ὡς and an adhortative subjunctive in the matrix clause.

Chapter 2

In 1 Cor 7:39 ("A wife is bound as long as her husband is living"; Γυνὴ δέδεται ἐφ᾽ ὅσον χρόνον ζῇ ὁ ἀνὴρ αὐτῆς), Paul combines the form of Rom 7:1 (absent the interrogative element), that is, the use of ἐφ᾽ ὅσον χρόνον as a connector, with the content of Rom 7:2, which discusses a woman being bound to her husband. Here too, a conditional construction immediately clarifies that the end of the man's life also marks the end of the woman's period of being bound to him (ἐὰν δὲ κοιμηθῇ ὁ ἀνήρ, ἐλευθέρα ἐστὶν ᾧ θέλει γαμηθῆναι, μόνον ἐν κυρίῳ). The fact that Paul articulates this point so explicitly should caution us against assuming that ἐφ᾽ ὅσον χρόνον *itself* implies the termination of the situated situation.

Indeed, it seems to me that the interpretation of Gal 4:1–7 is severely muddled as it presumes that ἐφ᾽ ὅσον χρόνον ("as long as") in verse 1 must effectively mirror ἄχρι ("until") in verse 2. It is by no means evidently the case that the period during which "an heir is no different than an enslaved person, though he is lord of all" (Gal 4:1b: οὐδὲν διαφέρει δούλου κύριος πάντων ὤν) terminates when the heir reaches adulthood (verse 1a: ἐφ᾽ ὅσον χρόνον ὁ κληρονόμος νήπιός ἐστιν). It is entirely conceivable that Paul in verse 1 simply introduces adulthood as a prerequisite to receiving one's inheritance and yet continues in verse 2 to elaborate that, even after reaching that stage, heirs might remain under guardians and stewards until a predetermined time, namely, the divinely ordained death of the father (ἄχρι τῆς προθεσμίας τοῦ πατρός).[74]

Temporal Order and Logic-Based Connections

We have already seen that Paul's style of narration can be incredibly compact at times. There is yet another observation that underscores this point. When examining his use of adverbs that can, under certain conditions, function as temporal connectors, what is noteworthy is how often they are used differently—serving as *additional temporal markers in logic-based connections*.[75]

In this context, I will exemplarily discuss the combination of νῦν/νυνί

---

74. For an interpretation of this passage as a potential anti-imperial counternarrative, see Christoph Heilig, "Counter-Narratives in Galatians," in *Scripture, Texts, and Tracings in Galatians and 1 Thessalonians*, ed. A. Andrew Das and B. J. Oropeza (Lanham, MD: Lexington, 2023), 171–90.

75. On everything that follows, cf. Heilig, *Paulus*, chapter 7, section 5.

("now") and ποτέ ("formerly"). Theoretically, each of these adverbs could connectorally mark a connection as chronologically focused, with the respective other adverb potentially functioning as an additional correlate (see figure 4).

Figure 4. νῦν/νυνί and ποτέ as connectors and correlates

	External connect: reference situation	Internal connect: situated situation
Anterior connection (iconic)	Earlier situation. (With or without ποτέ as correlative.)	νῦν/νυνί: Later situation.
Posterior connection (anti-iconic)	Later situation. (If referring to the time of utterance: with or without νῦν/νυνί as correlative)	ποτέ: Earlier situation.

Indeed, in Paul's letters, these adverbs appear as pairs in both iconic (ποτέ ... νῦν/νυνί) and anti-iconic (νῦν/νυνί ... ποτέ) order. However, it is significant to note that these instances do not serve as examples of anterior or posterior connections. Instead, Paul incorporates these pairs into other types of connections, which do not primarily concentrate on temporality. By doing this, Paul is able to both vividly express the meaningful relationship between the two relevant events, without overly extending his text, and also reinforce the temporal order.

Iconic Order

We will commence with occurrences of the iconic pattern, that is, connections where the text's order mirrors the sequence of the narrated events. In Rom 7:9 and Titus 3:3–5 we encounter adversative connections in which a prior situation is initially established and then compared to something occurring later, though this later occurrence takes place before the moment of utterance, which explains the absence of the correlating adverb νῦν/νυνί. In the former example, the prior situation is classified as having been, once, "alive apart from the law" (Rom 7:9: ἐγὼ δὲ ἔζων χωρὶς νόμου ποτέ). In the latter, the former state is characterized as having been, once, "foolish, dis-

Chapter 2

obedient, misled, enslaved to various passions and desires, living our lives in evil and envy, hateful and hating one another" (Tit 3:3: Ἦμεν γάρ ποτε καὶ ἡμεῖς ἀνόητοι, ἀπειθεῖς, πλανώμενοι, δουλεύοντες ἐπιθυμίαις καὶ ἡδοναῖς ποικίλαις, ἐν κακίᾳ καὶ φθόνῳ διάγοντες, στυγητοί, μισοῦντες ἀλλήλους). What occurred in the more recent past that evidently altered this state of affairs—alluded to by the adversative connector δέ—is that "sin came alive" (Rom 7:9: ἡ ἁμαρτία ἀνέζησεν) in one instance and "salvation" (Titus 3:5) in the other.

Even though the content of these two narratives markedly differs—they concentrate, after all, on distinct timeframes for the later situation, plus it is arguable whether both are "autobiographical" in the same sense (i.e., have the same referent)—their structure bears a striking similarity. Indeed, the parallels extend even further. In both cases, the later situation that stands in contrast with the prior situation is itself composed of two propositions that connect temporally. In other words, a temporal clarification is offered, explaining precisely when the "prior" times ended.

This is demonstrated in Rom 7:9 by a perfective participle: "as soon as [?] the commandment had arrived" (ἐλθούσης ... τῆς ἐντολῆς). In Titus 3:4, the earlier period is situated by means of ὅτε with aorist indicative: "when [?] the kindness and love of God our Savior had appeared" (ὅτε ... ἡ χρηστότης καὶ ἡ φιλανθρωπία ἐπεφάνη τοῦ σωτῆρος ἡμῶν θεοῦ). Parallels like these in narration style between undisputed and disputed letters of the *Corpus Paulinum* are ubiquitous.

Before examining cases where νῦν/νυνί signals a shift to the present of the narration, it is necessary to pay attention to Rom 11:30 and Col 1:21–22. In these cases, the adverb also appears, but we are still dealing with the recent past. In the latter passage, the connection is concessive.[76] "Even though" the recipients of the letter were, once, estranged from God, their hostile behavior evidencing their enmity (verse 21: ποτε ὄντας ἀπηλλοτριωμένους καὶ ἐχθροὺς τῇ διανοίᾳ ἐν τοῖς ἔργοις τοῖς πονηροῖς), they have "now," that is, recently, undergone reconciliation (verse 22: νυνὶ δὲ ἀποκατήλλαξεν) through the event of Christ's death.[77] Interestingly, the death of Christ is

---

76. There is no reason to translate, as most versions and commentators do, the participle as an attribute to the personal pronoun, which would make the whole verse 21 an afterthought to verse 20 at best ("... —including you, who once ...") and an outright anacoluthon at worst. Cf. Heilig, *Paulus*, 442. Ephesians 2:11–13 seems to implicitly, and unjustifiably, inform such an understanding.

77. On δέ: The macroproposition Col 1:21–22 is part of an adversative connection with what precedes. The idea is that reconciliation exists "not only" for everyone (verse 20)

not narrated in the indicative but rather supplied in a nominal phrase (ἐν τῷ σώματι τῆς σαρκὸς αὐτοῦ διὰ τοῦ θανάτου), which is further elaborated by a telic infinitive. The goal of a presentation before God in a "holy, blameless, and irreproachable" state (παραστῆσαι ὑμᾶς ἁγίους καὶ ἀμώμους καὶ ἀνεγκλήτους κατενώπιον αὐτοῦ) does not hark back to the past act of reconciliation from verse 21 but looks forward to the eschaton. This is made clear by verse 23, which introduces a stipulation signaling that the sequence of events will only truly become a "success story" if the Colossians adhere to certain behaviors (εἴ γε . . .).

In Rom 11:30, we once again encounter an adversative connection. The complexive aorist initially presents the former act of disobedience toward God (ὑμεῖς ποτε ἠπειθήσατε τῷ θεῷ). Subsequently, δέ introduces another main clause that narrates a subsequent event, the granting of mercy (νῦν δὲ ἠλεήθητε). Here, νῦν refers to the immediate past. This time, the moment of change is not presented as a temporal subconnection but is expressed in a causal adjunct, "due to their [i.e., Israel's] disobedience" (τῇ τούτων ἀπειθείᾳ).

While we are at it, it is worth pointing out that this passage is an excellent example of how such a compressed miniature story fits into its broader context. The macroconnection of Rom 11:30—which could be viewed as the "salvation history" of the gentile believers in Rome—serves as a comparison. Here, ὥσπερ is the connector in verse 30, and οὕτως is the correlate in verse 31. The story that Paul primarily wants to focus on is marked by the fact that it features different protagonists—not "you" as in verse 30 but "they" in verse 31 (cf. καὶ οὗτοι). In this plot, what has taken place "now" (νῦν) with respect to "them" parallels the recipients' own past behavior (ἠπειθήσατε . . . ἠπείθησαν).[78] However, the second event—the reception of mercy—is not explicitly narrated but primarily introduced as a potential event, a goal: "so that they too would [now] receive mercy" (ἵνα καὶ αὐτοὶ [νῦν] ἐλεηθῶσιν).[79] In other words, we witness here how Paul tells an explicit story solely

---

and as a mere intention (verse 21) but also as an actually implemented situation that is narratable with respect to the recipients of the letter in particular.

78. One might consider whether the aorist of ἀπειθέω in this case, though identical in form, has something else in view, namely, the "punctiliar" rejection of the gospel. Cf. τῇ τούτων ἀπειθείᾳ in verse 30.

79. The phrase "through your mercy" (τῷ ὑμετέρῳ ἐλέει) before the telic clause is a bit ambiguous. It clearly picks up the event introduced in the indicative in verse 30 with ἠλεήθητε. Now that it has been recounted it can simply be referred to by a noun. It is clear that what is meant is "the mercy that you have experienced." It might mimic τῇ

Chapter 2

to articulate something that arguably *cannot* yet be related in retrospect, something that for now is only a potential story, one that Paul confidently anticipates to become "tellable" in the future.[80]

Moreover, since we have ventured down this path, a quick diversion to verse 32 may be permissible. Here, a causal connection is established by γάρ with what has been previously "narrated": "For God has consigned all to disobedience so that he may have mercy on them all" (συνέκλεισεν γὰρ ὁ θεὸς τοὺς πάντας εἰς ἀπείθειαν, ἵνα τοὺς πάντας ἐλεήσῃ).[81] At this point, we arguably leave the mode of (pseudo)narration entirely. The declaration does not add another episode to the storyline but recapitulates the chronological structure from a bird's-eye perspective. Paul seizes the plot of actual and potential events and scrutinizes it. Then he presents an interpretation of the events that have transpired or, more accurately, of the events as he has shaped them into a specific narrative structure conducive to such interpretation. The ultimate communicative goal is clear: to facilitate a reinterpretation of the ongoing circumstances.

Our brief exploration of Rom 11:30 has indeed taken us somewhat off course, directing us toward other pertinent questions regarding the presence of *implicit* (potential) narratives and *communicative goals*. I have inserted these observations here to exemplify how the analysis of even the smallest Pauline miniature narratives can generate numerous profound implications. In many cases currently under consideration, we overlook these potential

---

τούτων ἀπειθείᾳ in verse 30 with the idea being that both causes are actually two sides of the same coin. The gentiles received mercy "because" the primarily intended recipients were not interested (verse 30), and this act of rejection was in some way orchestrated by God "because" he knew that this would allow him to show mercy to the gentiles. If this interpretation is correct, this would imply that within verse 31 God would be introduced as a focalizer. The formulation would take the perspective of the past, when at the time of the Jewish rejection of the gospel the showing of mercy to the gentiles is still future. An alternative understanding of the text might build on the assumption that the phrase simply comes proleptically before the subordinate clause. In this case, the present state of the gentiles having received mercy (verse 30) would be introduced as a means of implementing the goal of having that mercy also reach the Jews. While the means is already in place, the result still has to materialize. Cf. Rom 11:11 for precisely this thought process.

80. Note that the νῦν, if original, this time simply refers to the "present" in a very general sense, namely, to the time period that has begun in verse 30 with ἠλεήθητε and resulted in a state that is still in place.

81. Paul could also have used a consequential connector. The causal connector picks up the level of the communicative act: The whole "story" can be "told" because of this underlying motivation of God.

The Grammar of Narration

further insights that the discussed miniature narratives might afford, simply because we cannot concentrate on all these aspects simultaneously.

Let us now pivot back to the ποτέ and νῦν/νυνί pattern in Paul's letters, focusing on cases where the latter adverb refers more strictly to the present time of letter writing. In Eph 5:8, former conduct is juxtaposed with the current situation in a compact manner in an adversative connection: "For once you were darkness, but now [you are] light in the Lord" (ἦτε γάρ ποτε σκότος, νῦν δὲ φῶς ἐν κυρίῳ). The same is true for Phlm 11: ". . . who was once useless to you but now is useful to [both] you and me" (τόν ποτέ σοι ἄχρηστον νυνὶ δὲ [καὶ] σοὶ καὶ ἐμοὶ εὔχρηστον).

Concluding this discussion by looking at Col 3:7, we once again find support for what appears to be a constant rule in our quest for actual narration in Paul's letters—that for every clear explicit miniature story we identify, we also, as a by-product, find at least one passage that shares its structure but transgresses the boundaries of narrativity. Colossians 3:7 presents past behavior in a rather detailed way, supplementing the adverb ποτέ with an additional temporal clause. This verse could be paraphrased as: "You, too, once walked in these sins when you were living among the disobedient."[82] Contrary to expectation, verse 8 does not follow with a statement about the current state of affairs. Instead, the contrast is articulated as a *command*, implying that the cited act of abandoning anger, wrath, malice, slander, and abusive language is, at the time of writing, only a potential development (νυνὶ δὲ ἀπόθεσθε καὶ ὑμεῖς τὰ πάντα, ὀργήν, θυμόν, κακίαν, βλασφημίαν, αἰσχρολογίαν ἐκ τοῦ στόματος ὑμῶν).[83]

Anti-iconic Order

The anti-iconic order ("now . . . once"; νῦν . . . νυνί, ποτέ) appears less frequently in Paul's letters and seemingly never in isolation. Instead, in every identifiable instance, preceding this is an instance of iconic (anterior) narration. Only against this backdrop does the earlier situation reemerge in an act of *repetitive narration* presented anew as an *analepsis*.

---

82. Cf. Heilig, *Paulus*, chapter 7, section 4.2.2, for more details. I think that the text-critically debatable phrase ἐπὶ τοὺς υἱοὺς τῆς ἀπειθείας in Col 3:6 must be considered original for Col 3:7 to be adequately resolvable.

83. Ephesians 2:1–5 differs significantly from Col 3:7–8. For a detailed discussion that would take us too far afield here, see Heilig, *Paulus*, 446–47.

Chapter 2

Such a construction can be found in Gal 1:23. Here, the "now" applies to the perspective of the churches of Judea mentioned in verse 22, during a time when Paul was actively engaged elsewhere (verse 21). In other words, in verse 22 there is a switch of storylines, and we witness simultaneous events tied to other narrative characters. As the introduction to verse 23 makes clear (μόνον δὲ ἀκούοντες ἦσαν ὅτι...), we are dealing with an embedded narrative—specifically, a case of embedded *repetitive* narration, as what follows is an account of what the Christians in Judea had heard more than once. These narratives concern the character of the "former" persecutor (ὁ διώκων ἡμᾶς ποτε). He "now"—that is, at the previously present time when the focalizers heard these stories—proclaims the faith (νῦν εὐαγγελίζεται τὴν πίστιν).

A concept from this main clause (i.e., the subject) is here elaborated by means of a nominalized participle, which mentions past actions. Note that these previous acts of persecution do not need an initial recounting in the indicative because in the original context of the embedded narrative(s), this is already a known fact. Furthermore, within the secondary context of the letter, the mention of this persecuting activity has been likewise established already, namely, by the indicatives of the same verbs in Gal 1:13.

But the embedded narrative does not stop here, making this a rather sophisticated example. We can see how contextual factors and Paul's choice to follow an iconic order of events, which is easier to process, establish a backdrop. Against that, Paul then adds a relative clause, which further characterizes the Christian faith (i.e., the direct object) as having been "formerly" subject to Paul's destructive intentions (ἥν ποτε ἐπόρθει).[84]

We thus find a chiasm—a concept that, while overused in exegesis, still applies here. In the frame, there is mention about "us" at the start and "the faith" at the end of the sentence, but it is clear that the same activity of persecution is being referenced. What is the heart of this complex narrative arrangement? At the center, we encounter the surprising revelation that Paul is preaching the gospel.

Within Eph 2:13, we also discover an analepsis, and once again it is introduced via an explication of a narrative character. Mirroring the previous example, this is done through a nominalized participle, added in this instance as an apposition to the pronoun. "Now"—that is, recently—the event of drawing near to God, which was made possible by Christ's death (νυνὶ δὲ ἐν Χριστῷ Ἰησοῦ ... ἐγενήθητε ἐγγὺς ἐν τῷ αἵματι τοῦ Χριστοῦ), is related

---

84. On the issue of description/identification, cf. below, pp. 133–35, in the context of explanatory "connections."

The Grammar of Narration

against the background information that the participle contributes concerning the subject: "... you who were formerly far away" (ὑμεῖς οἵ ποτε ὄντες μακράν). In the broader context, this reference to the past picks up the more explicit narration of verses 11–12, which, therefore, form the backdrop of verse 13 as an "implicit" story pulled from (most recent) memory, enabling the terse reference to evoke the relevant details.

Meaningful Relationships

It is easy to see that in the above cases the criterion of temporal order is fulfilled. In fact, we even get rather detailed insight into how Paul plays with this parameter of *sequentiality* in these nonchronological connections in a nuanced way. We will continue to focus on this main category of connector types, which is not characterized by a chronological relationship of the underlying situations in the real and/or narrated world, but which rather builds on logical relationships among the two propositions in question.

Now, however, I will provide a brief overview of the possible sense relations with a particular emphasis on whether or not they have the potential to make a text (or a part of it) into a narrative by establishing *meaningful relationships among events*.[85]

Not all of these logic-based connections are equally suitable for constructing stories. The issue does not lie in the lack of "meaningfulness" in some of these sense relations. Rather, we must pay close attention to whether or not they indeed involve the fundamental elements of stories, namely, *actual events*. This caution is necessary because the relationship of these propositions to reality, and thus their capacity to function as assertions about the occurrence of certain events, is a significant parameter in differentiating between different types of connectors.[86]

Conditional Connections

First, we must address *conditional* connections, where the construction analogous to the English "if" clause introduces a condition, while the main

---

85. For all that follows, cf. Heilig, *Paulus*, 222–37.
86. Siehe Ulrich Hermann Waßner, "Faktivität," in Breindl, Volodina, and Waßner, *Semantik der deutschen Satzverknüpfer*, 137–48.

Chapter 2

"then" clause specifies a consequence.[87] In Greek, the most relevant connectors for this type of connections are εἰ and ἐάν.

Initially, εἰ seems relevant for our purposes since many grammars present it as the so-called "real" conditional clause. If this characterization were accurate, the protasis (the "if" clause) would correspond to an assertion of an event, and the apodosis (the "then" clause)—since it necessarily follows from the protasis—would likewise express that something did (or is/will) happen.

However, this reasoning is based on the erroneous assumption that these constructions grammatically encode a grounding in reality. However, as von Siebenthal rightly stresses, "the relationship to reality is principally left open" in these constructions. Therefore, the fulfillment of the condition can only be assumed based on contextual grounds and is not encoded grammatically.[88] The mere fact that in Paul's letters it can often be assumed that both the apostle and his audience agreed on the factuality of the event expressed in the protasis does not alter the conclusion that in these cases Paul is *not*, strictly speaking, narrating stories.

Nonetheless, the observation that in many of these examples we are inclined to treat these connections as miniature narratives demonstrates, once again, that the concept of *implicit* narratives may have significant heuristic value. There is a sense in which the conditional relationship is also significant for *explicit* narratives because its logical structure also underlies the "causal connections in the widest sense" that we will now discuss.[89]

Causal Connections

For instance, the *causal connections in a narrower sense* build upon this conditional relationship but now explicitly present the situation of the "if" clause as being real.[90] The most common connectors for this are ὅτι (subordinating) and γάρ (coordinating). It is evident that this type of connection is highly relevant for our purposes, as causality represents "the most important type of meaningful relationships amongst events."[91]

---

87. *AGG* 331.
88. *AGG* 381a.
89. On this, cf. *AGG* 332.
90. *AGG* 333. Cf. on the whole section Heilig, *Paulus*, 224–27.
91. Tilmann Köppe and Tom Kindt, *Erzähltheorie: Eine Einführung*, Reclams

The Grammar of Narration

Furthermore, since it is always the preceding event that causes the subsequent one, this connection inherently exhibits a *temporal structure*, with the element that contains the connector representing the cause and, thus, the earlier event. Therefore, in most cases, causal connections can indeed be treated as concise narratives. However, there are two critical caveats that need consideration.

First, there are times when the connector does not serve to connect propositions. Instead, it introduces a *rationale for the speech act* that produced the initial proposition. This indicates an occurrence of "utterance relatedness."[92] This particular phenomenon often arises in conjunction with commands, as a justification for the utterance of the command. Hence, in many instances, when a causal clause follows a command, it does not necessarily provide a reason for the commanded event's occurrence, as would be the case in: "Eat something. For you are hungry." Contrarily, in the scenarios I am referring to, the causal clause justifies why the speaker feels entitled to issue that command: "Eat something. For I am your father."[93] Further discussion of these instances is not required, as we are intentionally excluding commands as representations of narrative events.

Second, the category of a "symptom-oriented perspective" is more pertinent to our analysis of explicit stories.[94] In these instances, the connection occurs on an *epistemic level* (i.e., neither on the level of content nor on the level of the speech act). That is, the situation in the main clause is portrayed as a conclusion drawn from the evidence provided in the causal clause. There are two main implications for our narratological analysis.

Most fundamentally, we must keep in mind that the reason why certain elements can function as an "epistemic cause" at all is that they are symptoms of the "physical cause" that is deduced.[95] Thus, the chronology of events is

---

Universal-Bibliothek 17683 (Stuttgart: Reclam, 2014), 51: "Der wichtigste Typ einer sinnhaften Ereignisverknüpfung ist die Kausalität."

92. So *AGG* 333d.

93. I have already criticized the fact that von Siebenthal differentiates between exhortation-reason and result-reason-connections (cf. above, pp. 47–48). The reason for my critique is that these phenomena are distinguished not on a propositional level but only with respect to the parameter of *communicative function*. This differentiation within causal connections on the level of pragmatics correlates well with utterance relatedness, that is, with the connector connecting the two text parts not on the level of their contents but on the level of the speech act.

94. *AGG* 333d.

95. Often, such inferences are not conclusive because there are several explanations for the symptoms.

turned on its head. The subsequent event, which is caused, is presented as the "cause" not in a physical sense but in the sense of inspiring the thought process that reconstructs the earlier physical conditions. It should be apparent that a misclassification of such a causal connection could potentially have significant exegetical implications. However, most cooperative readers would not be prone to such misunderstandings. For instance, when reading 1 Cor 10:5, did you ever interpret it as saying that God first looked at the Israelites who were scattered in the wilderness and that this sight then caused him to be not pleased with them? (Ἀλλ' οὐκ ἐν τοῖς πλείοσιν αὐτῶν εὐδόκησεν ὁ θεός, κατεστρώθησαν γὰρ ἐν τῇ ἐρήμῳ.) Clearly, Paul provides epistemic grounds for his conclusion about God's attitude toward that generation. The fact that they suffered said fate demonstrates that God was not disposed favorably to them in the first place. Nevertheless, there are instances where the determination of the kind of cause that we are dealing with is more challenging. For example, this classificatory question significantly affects the interpretation of the scene narrated in Luke 7:47. Did Jesus forgive the woman after he noticed the love she had shown him? Or did he infer that God must have forgiven her, as evidenced by her capacity to love in the manner she did?

Moreover, the symptom-oriented perspective in causal connections is pertinent to our analysis in yet another respect. Observe that in these instances, the speaker becomes prominent because the focus shifts from the events of the narrated world and their interrelationships to the act of narration itself. Despite the fact that we are still dealing with the assertion of both events, the earlier event (the physical cause) is specifically identified as an *inference* by someone, thereby drawing attention to that person's mental activity. This suggests that a symptom-oriented perspective can be treated as a *signal of focalization* either indicating the perspective of one of the narrated characters, who just encountered the symptoms, or (much more frequently) revealing the narrator's own epistemic limitations.

Consequential Connections

The conditional relationship is also crucial for connections that are *causal in a broader* sense.[96] In consequential connections, for example, the connector is not incorporated into the "if" element of the underlying conditional struc-

---

96. *AGG* 332.

The Grammar of Narration

ture but into the "then" element. Hence, they are essentially mirror images of the causal connections.[97] However, consequential connections carry a significant constraint. While there appears to be some flexibility with the placement of the causative element with the connector before or after the portion expressing the result, at least with subordinate causal constructions (i.e., not with γάρ), consequential connections always seem to be iconic. In other words, if a narrator wishes to present the later of two causally connected elements first, they cannot make use of a consequential connection. This is a clear indication of the inherent temporal structure of consequential connections.

Considering this, it is all the more remarkable to observe that not all these connections build narratives. Rather, in the case of Greek consequential connectors, the decision on whether or not the situation of the result proposition is communicated as having actually happened or as being in the process of occurring at the time of utterance must be made individually. This is more complicated in Koine than in Classical Greek because the differentiation between the use of ὥστε with the indicative for actual results and the use of this connector with the infinitive for potential results is no longer clear.[98]

We see the classic construction in Gal 2:13, where "hypocrisy" leads even Barnabas to participate in the action (ὥστε καὶ Βαρναβᾶς συναπήχθη αὐτῶν τῇ ὑποκρίσει; note the indicative). However, we should consider 2 Cor 1:8 as a narrative as well, in spite of the resulting event of not being narrated in the indicative: "We were under immense pressure so that we despaired of life itself" (καθ' ὑπερβολὴν ὑπὲρ δύναμιν ἐβαρήθημεν ὥστε ἐξαπορηθῆναι ἡμᾶς καὶ τοῦ ζῆν; note the infinitive).[99]

Modal-Instrumental Connections

Heinrich von Siebenthal introduces another relatively expansive category that is causal in the broadest sense, termed as "modal-instrumental" connections.[100] In these cases, one situation is represented "as the means (instrument or manner)" by which the other situation is realized.[101] From a

---

97. Cf. Heilig, *Paulus*, 227 and 229.
98. Cf. *AGG* 221b with *CGCG* 46.9.
99. Cf. Heilig, *Paulus*, 377.
100. *AGG* 335. Cf. Heilig, *Paulus*, 228–30.
101. *AGG* 335b.

Chapter 2

narratological viewpoint, several comments regarding this proposed category are in order.

First, in numerous instances it remains uncertain whether we are encountering two *distinct* situations. It should be noted that von Siebenthal unpacks the somewhat vague notion of 'means' using two concepts: 'instrument' and 'manner.' Particularly with respect to the adverbial participle expressing manner, that which is under consideration does not always appear to constitute "specific concomitant circumstances" but can simply specify the way in which the exact same situation unfolds.[102] In such cases, the situation times of the two situations are necessarily *identical*. In English, we sometimes translate these participles as adverbs to elaborate on how the main situation is taking place. From a narratological perspective, these instances do not provide a complete story in themselves, as we are dealing with one single event. Within the context of a larger narrative, such a connection can be considered a case of repetitive (specifying) narration of the same event as part of a more extensive plot.

Second, grammarians utilizing the modal-instrumental category often encounter difficulties in distinguishing this connection type from *consequential* connections. These difficulties arise when consequential connections not only specify the result but also emphasize the characteristics of the cause.[103] This issue, alongside others, has led some scholars to entirely discard the notion of the *modal* part of this large group of connections.[104] The resulting system offers the advantage of presenting a clear pair, much like the causal or consequential opposition: "instrumental" (connector in the earlier element) and "purpose-oriented" (connector in the later element) constructions. The cases categorized as "modal" in the more traditional system are relocated into a separate category of "comitative" constructions, residing within the broader class of additive relationships (to which we will turn shortly). This suggested sense relationship is rather unspecific, indicating merely that situation A is "accompanied" by another circumstance B. Different connectors express a wide variety of degrees of involvement with situation A: for example, means, concurrent occurrence, material, partner, and so on. While this study will largely refer to these cases as "modal" connections, it should be

---

102. *AGG* 231e. The whole matter is quite messy. Cf. Heilig, *Paulus*, 238 and 629, in critical interaction with Daniel B. Wallace, *Greek Grammar beyond the Basics: An Exegetical Syntax of the New Testament* (Grand Rapids: Zondervan, 1996), 627–30.

103. *Duden* 1790.

104. Eva Breindl, "Die semantische Klassifikation der Konnektoren des Deutschen," in Breindl, Volodina, and Waßner, *Semantik der deutschen Satzverknüpfer*, 252 and 263.

kept in mind that this category might semantically be not as close to other connectors that von Siebenthal classifies as "causal in the widest sense."[105]

The *instrumental* subcategory within the broader modal-instrumental connections appears relatively easier to define at first glance. Unlike the modal participles that merely reiterate the same situation with a different verb, instrumental connections usually presume a sequence because they closely emulate the conditional base. However, for this very reason, we can sometimes encounter challenges in setting boundaries between instrumental connections and other types, namely, *causal* connections. Yes, there seems to be a distinguishing factor, namely, that instrumental connections are more specific. While I believe they do not always imply intentionality, as is the case with purpose-oriented connections (to which we will turn in the next section), the causal element must at least be *suitable for intentional use* to be considered a "means."[106]

This criterion appears to be a fairly reliable indicator for distinguishing between participles expressing merely that one event preceded another and those further characterizing this preceding event as a means. For instance, although "plucking out" one's eyes may be a prerequisite for giving them to others, it does not inherently constitute a suitable means for this transaction (see Gal 4:15: . . . τοὺς ὀφθαλμοὺς ὑμῶν ἐξορύξαντες ἐδώκατέ μοι).[107] In contrast, Paul's assumption in Rom 1:27 seems to be that if a man truly wished to be consumed with lust for other men, initially forsaking, in his view, natural intimacy with a female partner would indeed be an effective method to achieve this objective (ὁμοίως τε καὶ οἱ ἄρσενες ἀφέντες τὴν φυσικὴν χρῆσιν τῆς θηλείας ἐξεκαύθησαν ἐν τῇ ὀρέξει αὐτῶν εἰς ἀλλήλους).

A further instance of an instrumental participle seems to be found in 2 Thess 3:8 (cf. 1 Thess 2:9). There, an implied situation of "eating bread" is being negotiated. The act of working, expressed by the participle ἐργαζόμενοι, is the tool by which to get to the point where someone is in the position to have a meal. However, this example also illustrates that identifying instrumental participles can indeed be tricky. For we are not dealing with

---

105. *AGG* 332.

106. Cf. Ulrich Hermann Waßner, "Finale und instrumentale Konnektoren," in Breindl, Volodina, and Waßner, *Semantik der Deutschen Satzverknüpfer*, 1054.

107. Sometimes, the lexical semantics of the participle do not allow for an instrumental interpretation. While running a ship onto a reef might be a good method for getting your ship intentionally stuck, Luke in Acts 27:41 uses the verb περιπίπτω, which seems to exclude the possibility of intentionality so that a reformulation of the sentence with ἵνα does not seem to be acceptable (not just in this context, but generally).

Chapter 2

a single instance but instead with bundles of events. After all, it is expressly stated that the labor occurs "night and day" (νυκτὸς καὶ ἡμέρας). This, of course, must be interpreted intermittently (i.e., "interruptatively")—otherwise, there would have been no time left for either preaching the gospel or partaking in meals.

But there are open questions that persist. Are we encouraged to visualize a scene of work followed by a subsequent period of meal-taking, upon which the hard-earned money is spent? In other words, are we dealing with a sequence of events? Or is the relationship between the two activities more intricate, to the degree that we eventually find ourselves grappling with a nexus of events that interlock unsystematically, thereby obfuscating any clear sequence—possibly leading us to a somewhat simultaneous, intermingled, contextualization of the situations?

In the end, our decision on this matter will hinge on the accuracy of our reconstruction of the economic profile of the implied labor—the duration and effort each work session demands, and the corresponding financial returns. This verse, therefore, serves as a captivating example of how the semantic level of reference (cf. pp. 145–52)—can determine our interpretations of the stories Paul narrates. It reinforces my argument that Paul's accounts cannot be fully comprehended on a purely propositional plane. Rather, these narratives are formed in the context of lived experience—and *earlier stories* about labor, which constitute the backdrop against which the meaning of Paul's stories can be understood more precisely.

The uncertainties of the last paragraph are emblematic of the disputed status of instrumentality as an "adverbial nuance" of adverbial participles. Nonetheless, as a semantic category of propositional relationships, it appears well-defined, and I see no reason why adverbial participles should not function in this manner.[108] An issue warranting further exploration is the use of

---

108. *CGCG* 52.42 lists "manner or means" as one option for interpreting circumstantial participles. However, I would question the assumption that the sequential participles (52.36) in context always solely express a temporal relationship without including the aspect of instrumentality. In his discussion of adverbial participles, von Siebenthal (*AAG* 231e) chooses "manner" as the main label for modal participles—the same designation that in his text grammar he uses to cover both modal and instrumental meanings. In the case of adverbial participles, he distinguishes along similar, though not identical, lines within this manner category, namely, between "the way in which the 'action'/'situation' is meant to unfold (is sometimes best translated as an adverb phrase)" on the one hand and "specific concomitant circumstances" on the other hand. It seems to me that the latter *includes* the means nuance and that the large category is not modal but modal-instrumental. Note also that when he discusses adjuncts in general (*AGG* 259l), he indeed

The Grammar of Narration

instrumental participles (as perhaps exemplified in 2 Thess 3:8) that seem to express simultaneity. A phenomenon that is relevant in that regard and that seems to be relatively well demonstrated is that an instrumental participle can indeed offer a type of redescription of a situation. However, in contrast to the renarrating modal participle, this supplementary depiction of circumstances still appears to maintain a result-centered perspective.[109] For instance, in Luke 7:29–30 being baptized (βαπτισθέντες) is characterized as an act that reveals one's attitude toward God and that, thus, has consequences beyond the limited scope of the event of the baptism itself (ἐδικαίωσαν τὸν θεόν). Similarly, in Luke 15:13, each step in the journey marked by "wild living" (ζῶν ἀσώτως) can be perceived as an activity progressively depleting wealth with a pronounced focus remaining on the ultimate outcome of poverty (διεσκόρπισεν τὴν οὐσίαν αὐτοῦ).

Notably, there are no instrumental *clauses* in Koine Greek, so it is often debatable whether an instrumental adjunct is actually expressing a proposition (cf. in English the nonpropositional "with a hammer" versus the propositional "by hammering it").[110] Despite this fact, instrumental connections strike me as quite significant for analyzing Paul's miniature narratives. Often, Paul does not use the causal or consequential connections, which would clearly delineate the temporal structure of the situations mentioned, but he opts instead for instrumental connections. These provide us a sort

---

distinguishes instrumental adjuncts from modal ones. However, when he returns to the syntactical level to discuss clauses, a focus on "means" pops up again as a subcategory of "manner" (*AGG* 287), with there this time being no room for modality in a narrower sense as a separate subcategory. To me, it makes most sense to keep the distinction between "comitative" (i.e., modal) constructions of any kind on the one hand and—semantically richer—instrumental connections on the other hand. I cannot see the advantages of the proposal of Wallace, *Grammar*, 629, who indeed differentiates between participles of (modal?) "manner" on the one hand and (instrumental?) "means" on the other hand but argues that the first case is restricted to expressing emotion or attitude and that the second "is almost always contemporaneous with the time of the main verb" and basically only allows for exceptions when the sense of the participle seems to blend with a causal nuance (Wallace, *Grammar*, 629). That seems to restrict both subcategories in the wrong way. If we approach the issue from a text-grammatical perspective, I suggest that a focus on the contrast with purpose-oriented constructions emphasizes the need for instrumentality as a rather broad category.

109. On the similar situation in German, cf. Waßner, "Finale und instrumentale Konnektoren," 1057.

110. Cf. *AGG* 287b. German has "indem" as a subordinating conjunction with instrumental meaning. Still, nonpropositional instrumental adjuncts are the rule. Cf. Waßner, "Finale und instrumentale Konnektoren," 1045.

Chapter 2

of birds-eye view, focusing more on the means-result dynamic and less on the specific temporal relationship. In doing so, he frequently relies on the assumption that the events in question are already familiar to his readers, and we sometimes even find their more explicit narration within the immediate context. This aligns well with the relatively limited syntactical options that Paul does have for instrumental connections. For even if we are only dealing with a noun, it is within a specific context that it can be clear that it refers to a specific event that is conceptualized as an instrument. In other words, the lack of subordinating conjunctions, which would permit the narration of the instrumentalized event in the indicative, does not deter effective communication.

An intriguing example can be found in 1 Cor 8:10–11.[111] It begins, in verse 10, with a prospective conditional clause containing an event of "seeing" and the seen event (as an "accusative with participle"). The issue that is at stake is that "someone sees you dining in an idol's temple" (ἐὰν γάρ τις ἴδῃ σὲ τὸν ἔχοντα γνῶσιν ἐν εἰδωλείῳ κατακείμενον). The person dining is identified as someone who "has knowledge." Given that not everyone has this knowledge (verse 7), we can infer a third event, namely, the moment of insight. Then, another two events are referenced in a question. In the aforementioned scenario, "will not his conscience, he being weak after all, be encouraged toward eating idol meat?" (οὐχὶ ἡ συνείδησις αὐτοῦ ἀσθενοῦς ὄντος οἰκοδομηθήσεται εἰς τὸ τὰ εἰδωλόθυτα ἐσθίειν;). Here, a state of the narrative character being weak and a resulting development are depicted. Note that, thus far, the entire scenario is hypothetical. However, the temporal structure of this nexus of events is readily apparent.

In the context of our current discussion, the following verse (verse 11) presents an intriguing turn. Here, an instrumental connection is made: "your knowledge" serves as the means (ἐν τῇ σῇ γνώσει) by which "the brother, for whom Christ died" (ὁ ἀδελφὸς δι᾽ ὃν Χριστὸς ἀπέθανεν) is ruined (ἀπόλλυται). We remain within the hypothetical scenario sketched in verse 10, yet the indicative is utilized, presupposing the situation as if it were real for rhetorical purposes, immersing us further into the narrative world. Christ's death introduces a flashback into earlier times that have so far been absent, while the rest of the verse is strikingly devoid of temporality compared to verse 10.

Taken out of context, understanding verse 11 would be quite challenging. Yet within context, it becomes clear that when Paul selects the point of departure—the state of having attained knowledge—he also considers ev-

---

111. On what follows, cf. Heilig, *Paulus*, 238–40.

erything that ensues, as outlined in the preceding verse. Equally, in context there is a chance of understanding what "perishing" entails—it could refer to the same act as "eating idol meat" or even look beyond the time frame of verse 10, into the future to the eventual loss of faith (and potentially subsequent judgment).

Consequently, we can infer that when reading verse 11, we interpret it with the temporal structure of verse 10 serving as background knowledge. This enables us to understand how Paul can come up with his characterization of the *relationship between the two agents.* It is the hypothetical sequence of events that explains why one party can be considered the "antagonist" of the person who, rather surprisingly, turns out to be the tragic hero of the story. Note that in turn this means that while in verse 10 we are largely presented with a temporal constellation without many evaluations, as cooperative readers we are still able to reconstruct the meaningful connections among them and thus a whole "plot." Verse 11 fleshes out this plot structure at its most basic level again for nobody to miss. Thus, in some sense, verse 11 is a case of *repetitive narration* of verse 10—or, viewed from another perspective, Paul's *interpretation of the story* presented in verse 10, a rather descriptive account that summarizes what, in his view, is the proper understanding of the sequence of verse 10, drawing attention to what it actually would mean to tell a story that contains such a sequence of events.

It is also important to note how, from a *rhetorical* standpoint, the choice of an instrumental connection is considerably less aggressive than a purpose-oriented connection would have been in this context. It does not claim that the means are employed with a specific goal in mind. Rather, it posits merely that it is a cause that naturally leads to such an endpoint. In Paul's view, the "almost story" in 1 Cor 8:10–11 needs to be "told" expressly because the individuals who may potentially commit acts leading to said result are oblivious to the consequences of their actions. They would act without the "goal" of ruining their brothers and sisters in Christ. Paul counts on the inherently good intentions of these individuals and wants to make them realize that their knowledge—and the behavior that is, from their perspective, naturally associated with it—could result in the destruction of their fellow Christians. He wishes to alert them to the discord between their explicit intentions and the implicit way their actions could function as instruments toward such a destructive end. We are, thus, encountering here a remarkably subtle form of rebuke—one that refrains from imputing ill motives, thus likely making it more rhetorically persuasive. Compare this with Paul's repeated use of θέλω, "want," in Galatians when attributing intentions to his opponents (1:7;

Chapter 2

4:17; 6:12–13; cf. also 4:9 and 4:21 with respect to the Galatians themselves), sometimes even explicitly combined with a bad motive portrayed in an ἵνα clause (4:17 and 6:13).

To round off our discussion, let me pose a question: Did the use of narratological terminology in the last section concerning 1 Cor 8:10–11 strike you as objectionable? In a sense, it should have. After all, if we adhere strictly to our definition of narrativity, we certainly cannot say we have a "narrative" in verse 10. Yes, the event of having acquired knowledge is not called into question. But this is merely the backdrop for the other events. Even the initial event, which sets everything in motion—the participation in a meal at an idol's temple—is merely a hypothetical one expressed in a prospective conditional clause.

Nonetheless, it is indeed hard to discuss this verse without invoking narratological terms. Even within this single verse, we encounter a series of events interlinked in such a way that allows us to easily *imagine* the scene unfolding. In fact, one might even come away from reading these words with the impression that we are dealing not just with an ordinary miniature narrative but potentially with a "more meaningful" story—especially if we interpret verse 10 in light of the evaluations made explicit in verse 11, which Paul likely already anticipated when crafting verse 10. At any rate, one must acknowledge that it is indeed feasible to construct a much lengthier story in the indicative that might prove less engaging and, considering the pragmatic dimension, less relevant to this particular audience. This seeming inevitability of deploying narratological terms for text that does not constitute miniature stories suggests anew that a narratological perspective not exclusively focused on explicit narratives may indeed hold potential.

Purpose-Oriented Connection

Purpose-oriented connections bear close resemblance to instrumental connections. At first glance, they seem to be merely their mirror image. The preceding situation is associated with a conscious agent and can be dubbed a "means" with respect to the later situation. Additionally, as far as I can ascertain, in Greek we seem to encounter a situation not unlike the causal/consequential pair, where connectors are used for one of the two parts in each of the two connections. In other words, while instrumental connections mark the preceding situation with a connector (akin to causal connections),

The Grammar of Narration

purpose-oriented connections assign the connector to the later situation (similar to consequential connections).[112]

However, there are two significant semantic differences between instrumental and purpose-oriented connections. First, purpose-oriented connections involve a semantic element that is not compulsory for instrumental connections. While the result in the former cases is not necessarily intended (although the agent may often find it desirable), intentionality is a *prerequisite* for purpose-oriented connections.

Second, purpose-oriented connections lack a semantic element typical for instrumental connections. Whereas in the latter instance, the "result" is actually occurring or has occurred, nothing is asserted about this in constructions of the former type, where the subsequent event is consistently considered as *nothing but* a "goal." It may be evident from the context that the goal is achieved, but the connector does not convey this itself.

For instance, the grammar alone—the telic infinitive—in Gal 1:18 does not provide any information about whether Paul successfully got to know Peter in the intimate manner he intended (ἱστορῆσαι Κηφᾶν). However, one could argue that, first, we would anticipate an explicit indication if that attempt were unsuccessful, particularly since, second, Paul later mentions in the same verse that he remained two weeks with Peter, which seems to imply an ideal circumstance for the realization of the stated goal.

Note that, at times, an author can utilize this ambiguity to prompt their readers to consider whether the designated goal has been reached. In my opinion, this is likely the case in Gal 1:4, where the Galatians must deeply reflect upon Paul's opening statement that Jesus gave himself for "our sins in order to rescue us from the present evil age" (τοῦ δόντος ἑαυτὸν ὑπὲρ τῶν ἁμαρτιῶν ἡμῶν, ὅπως ἐξέληται ἡμᾶς ἐκ τοῦ αἰῶνος τοῦ ἐνεστῶτος πονηροῦ). Has this event already occurred, or is it yet to be seen? And if the latter, what might potentially undermine it?[113]

Purpose-oriented connections invariably raise a question. They do not constitute miniature narratives in themselves—instead, they highlight the

---

112. In German and English, the situation is different because there are adverbial connectors that are integrated in the later situation in instrumental connections. *AGG* 335 does not list analogous connectors. A search for typical English/German connectors (e.g., "hierdurch," "hereby") in translations shows that ἐν τούτῳ might be a candidate, though it is mostly understood as a consequential connector. Cf. John 16:30 (NET): "Now we know that you know everything and do not need anyone to ask you anything. Because of this we believe that you have come from God."

113. For a detailed analysis, see Heilig, *Paulus*, 840–50.

Chapter 2

act of storytelling itself by prompting the audience to ponder whether the sequence of events *could* be narrated or whether it *could have been told* under counterfactual circumstances. Hence, these connections might point toward potential narratives, or, in the case of foiled plans, impossible narratives (or stories that could only be recounted unreliably). Once again, the text-grammatical approach directs us to a collection of phenomena that cannot be classified as miniature narratives in a strict sense but nonetheless imply something like implicit narratives that warrant our attention. This calls for an expansion of our analytical framework.

Concessive Connections

Before we proceed, I will once again outline in a table (see figure 5; note that modal connections are excluded) the various connections that are causal in the broadest sense, exhibiting a shared connection to a conditional base.[114]

Figure 5. Examples of connections that are causal in a broad sense and their common conditional base

Conditional basis	If we save money today,	[then] we will have more left tomorrow.
Causal connection	Because we save money today,	we will have more left tomorrow.
Consequential connection	We save money today,	so we will have more left tomorrow.
Instrumental connection	By saving money today,	we will have more left tomorrow.
Purpose-oriented connection	We save money today	in order to have more left tomorrow.

The next two types of connections—concessive and adversative—are frequently explicated on the basis of a conditional premise as well. However, in

---

114. Cf. the German examples for modal-instrumental and purpose-oriented connections in *Duden* 1789 and 1791.

this instance, the juxtaposition is "contradirectional," that is, it runs counter to the presupposed conditional relationship.[115]

At the very least, such a conditional foundation is largely acknowledged with respect to *concessive* connections. Here, the event of the "if" part is assumed, but concurrently the "then" part is declared *not* to follow, despite expectations to the contrary. In Koine Greek, the connectors εἰ καί and ἐὰν καί often mark the concession.

Do these connections offer miniature "narratives"? It depends. More often than not, the "contraexpectation"—that which is stated despite not corresponding with the anticipation—is simply the negated "then" clause. For example, in 2 Cor 10:3 the conditional foundation appears to be "If one walks in the flesh, then they will also fight according to the flesh." Paul accepts the protasis "For even though we walk in the flesh . . ." (Ἐν σαρκὶ γὰρ περιπατοῦντες . . .) but negates the expected conclusion: ". . . we do *not* fight according to the flesh." Galatians 2:3 might serve as another example: not even Titus, even though he is a gentile, is compelled to be circumcised (οὐδὲ Τίτος ὁ σὺν ἐμοί, Ἕλλην ὤν, ἠναγκάσθη περιτμηθῆναι).

These two instances cannot be counted as complete narratives. An event is expressed, but then the ensuing statement categorically contradicts the occurrence of another event. Essentially, concessive connections revolve around the fact that certain stories *cannot* be recounted (truthfully). Nevertheless, many of us would inevitably perceive that somehow, somewhere, the above cases still involve stories. While they are not recounted, they are discussed. To comprehend the importance of the circumstance expressed via the external connect, we need to grasp the background expectations. The concessive connections are meaningful "anti-narratives" as they contrast with somewhat dull, actual (but only implicit) narratives.

That being said, under certain circumstances concessive connections not only invoke actual stories but also satisfy the definition of narrativity themselves. This is true when the apodosis is negated already in the underlying conditional basis. In other words, there is an expectation that event B will not follow from event A—and yet it does. For instance, in Rom 1:32 we seem to encounter the following assumption: "If someone knows that a specific action is deserving of death, they will *not* engage in it." The "contraexpectation" in this case is the affirmation that the negated apodosis is, shockingly, nevertheless enacted in reality. Even though "they" have such knowledge (οἵτινες τὸ δικαίωμα τοῦ θεοῦ ἐπιγνόντες ὅτι οἱ τὰ τοιαῦτα πράσσοντες ἄξιοι

---

115. *AGG* 337.

Chapter 2

θανάτου εἰσίν), they *still* continue to practice it, and, heightening astonishment by even more strongly contradicting expectations, they even promote it (οὐ μόνον αὐτὰ ποιοῦσιν ἀλλὰ καὶ συνευδοκοῦσιν τοῖς πράσσουσιν).

Regrettably, the issue needs further complication. Even if the apodosis in the underlying conditional basis is an affirmative statement, the concessive connection can still sometimes be classified as a story—namely, when the element contradicting the expectations is explained by a pair of propositions with a "negative-positive" adversative structure (see below, pp. 210–14). Despite event A occurring, event B did not happen, *but* event C did. The assumption is that if A, then B (an expectation that is disappointed), but also that if B, then not-C. So, what is eventually asserted in the concessive connection is not only the protasis (A) but also another (unexpected) event (C). The fact that A happens but that then B unexpectedly does not occur suddenly paves way for C to transpire. This pattern can be observed, for instance, in 1 Thess 2:5–7. Although the apostle and his coworkers could have exerted their authority based on their position (7a: δυνάμενοι ἐν βάρει εἶναι ὡς Χριστοῦ ἀπόστολοι), they (unexpectedly) did not act in such a way (verses 5–6) *but instead demonstrated a completely different behavior* (verse 7b: ἀλλὰ ἐγενήθημεν νήπιοι ἐν μέσῳ ὑμῶν).

Further contributing to the complexity, it is worth noting that sometimes the "not-B" element is omitted, leaving out the explicit mention that something expected did not, indeed, happen. In such cases, we transition directly from the concession (i.e., "even though A") to another actual event (C). The implication that event B was expected and that, in this case, event C would not have occurred, is merely presupposed. Such a case is found in 1 Cor 9:19. The conditional basis seems to be: "If someone is free from all, they will endeavor to maintain that status." Paul adopts the protasis with a concessive participle: "Even though I am free from all" (Ἐλεύθερος . . . ὢν ἐκ πάντων). Then, he proceeds directly to discuss an action which is unexpected given this context: "I have made myself an enslaved person to all" (πᾶσιν ἐμαυτὸν ἐδούλωσα). In an unabbreviated form, it would read: ". . . I did *not* (as one might expect) remain free from all, *but* . . ."

The pattern found in 1 Cor 9:19 seems to fulfill the condition of narrativity, as it presents an uninterrupted series of propositions that affirm ongoing events. Yet, the case could be made that even 1 Thess 2:7 approximates this status of an explicit narrative, given that the concessive clause (with its affirmed event) follows the negated matrix clause, thereby allowing the two actual situations to be presented next to each other within the text. Although verse 7 is not syntactically independent, we nonetheless observe a kind of shift from the denial of events to the explicit narration of actual events.

To sum up, we need to examine concessive connections with a keen eye when looking for narratives. But it is not only the question of whether or not we are dealing with narratives at all that should provoke our narratological interest. Rather, the expectations presupposed in these relationships also warrant attention. For a proper understanding of a concessive narrative within its broader communicative context, it is essential to clarify the nature of these expectations. *Whose* expectations are involved? Is the author building on a rule that is part of his era's general world knowledge, or are the expectations uniquely theirs? Or is the narrator endeavoring to rectify the assumptions of the readers or a third group?[116]

Consider, for example, 2 Cor 10:3, which I cited earlier. The fact that in verse 2 Paul has just introduced narrative characters as potential focalizers might suggest that it is their expectations that are scrutinized. These characters might construe a "fleshly fight" by Paul and his coworkers as the anticipated continuation. After all, they think that they "walk *according* to the flesh" (... τινας τοὺς λογιζομένους ἡμᾶς ὡς κατὰ σάρκα περιπατοῦντας; λογίζομαι introduces their perspective). People with such a perception might anticipate that, just as Paul and his associates walk according to the flesh, they would fight in the same manner. The conditional basis itself, which is presupposed in the background, does not seem to be controversial for Paul. Rather, in verse 3 he points out that such a perception fails to differentiate between walking *according* to the flesh and simply walking *in* the flesh ('Ἐν σαρκὶ γὰρ περιπατοῦντες ...). To Paul, it is clear that merely walking in the flesh does not necessarily lead to a predisposition toward fighting according to the flesh. However, he understands that those who fail to make said distinction could attach the expectation of a fleshly fight to either behavior.

---

116. Wolfgang Schrage, *Der erste Brief an die Korinther*, 4 vols., EKKNT 7 (Neukirchen-Vluyn: Neukirchener, 1995), 2:338, argues that the participle in 1 Cor 9:19 is causal: "Freedom itself is always also the freedom for servitude, the freedom for Agape, and thus the freedom from oneself.... [It is] the underlying basis and starting point of servitude." (German: "Die Freiheit selbst ist immer auch die Freiheit zur Knechtschaft, die Freiheit zur Agape und damit die Freiheit von sich selbst.... [Sie ist] der tragende Grund und Ausgangspunkt der Knechtschaft.") One could construe this difference in interpretation in terms of different assumptions concerning focalization. Schrage here takes on the perspective of Paul. By contrast, I think Paul builds on generally shared assumptions to then make his point. Ultimately, these different readings are rooted in different assumptions concerning the pragmatics of Paul's text: Is he merely aiming at self-expression? Or is he not rather, more likely in my view, trying to persuade his readers?

Chapter 2

While 2 Cor 10:3 may not constitute a story per se, it thus qualifies as a form of "metanarrative commentary" by Paul. It is important to note that the story upon which Paul comments does not fully materialize within the text. Indeed, verse 2 does not state, "They think: 'They walk according to the flesh and, thus, also fight according to the flesh.'" Perhaps these individuals from verse 2 narrated such stories (unreliably, from Paul's point of view). Possibly Paul is referencing a story that he predicts such individuals might fabricate. The circumstance that the story that is commented upon remains implicit makes verse 3 all the more remarkable. Rather than offering a straightforward counternarrative—"We walk in the flesh, and we fight according to the Spirit!"—Paul acknowledges the perspective of the (potential) narrators in verse 2, allowing it to influence his anti-narrative in verse 3, even though from his standpoint the protasis of the underlying conditional basis (i.e., "Merely *in*, not *according to*!") remains unfulfilled.

Additive and Adversative Connections

Adversative connections are also very often explained with reference to a conditional basis. However, if there indeed is one, it must at least be admitted that it is often much less transparent. Moreover, there is general acceptance that an additive component does exist within adversative connections, even if this aspect is considered subordinate to the adversative element.[117]

Moving forward, I will broaden this scope and work with a larger category termed "additive-based" connectors. These are recognized by their ability to link propositions that, however, remain independent of each other to a larger degree and that lack the specific relationships we have discussed thus far. Against this backdrop, we will then delve into a discussion on adversative connectors.[118]

The most fundamental subcategory of connections formed by additive-based connectors are those that von Siebenthal, too, simply calls *additive* connections.[119] Here, the prototypical καί in Greek combines two elements of propositional value, just like English "and" or German "und." The semantics of this *connector* is generally unspecific as it "primarily signifies an

---

117. Cf. *Duden* 1793–99.
118. For details, see Eva Breindl, "Additiv basierte Konnektoren," in Breindl, Volodina, and Waßner, *Semantik der deutschen Satzverknüpfer*, 393–588.
119. *AGG* 325.

addition."[120] However, it can appear in *connections* that convey a more nuanced relationship, owing to what are referred to as "implicatures," elements communicated rather implicitly in concrete utterances within their specific contexts.

Hence, the *additive connector* καί frequently appears within *temporal connections*, encompassing both sequential ones, in the sense of "and (then)," and simultaneous ones, meaning "and (at the same time)."[121] We typically infer these implied temporal relationships instinctively. For instance, when Paul states in Gal 1:17 that he "went up to Arabia and returned again to Damascus" (ἀπῆλθον εἰς Ἀραβίαν καὶ πάλιν ὑπέστρεψα εἰς Δαμασκόν), our geographical comprehension automatically leads us to perceive a sequence. Suppose, by contrast, I were to say, "I flew to Rome and ate an unpalatable chicken breast because I wasn't fond of the vegetarian option." Even without the causal clause, everyone would comprehend that I am referring to a meal consumed *during* the flight. This deductive reasoning operates based on our collective background knowledge about the poor quality of in-flight catering and deliciousness of Italian food. Note that this knowledge is not necessarily rooted in personal experience. Stories that we have heard can also enable us to draw the right conclusions when we are presented with additive connectors. Once again, the concept of "stories behind the text" does not seem so far-fetched after all.

Adversative connections hold a similarity with von Siebenthal's additive connections in that they pair two situations that are potentially comparable in certain aspects.[122] Yet, their "sameness" is explicitly negated by the connector, leading instead to a contrast between the two situations. In Greek, the prototypical connector for this relationship is ἀλλά, which aligns well with "but" in English and "aber" in German. Frequently, it is incorporated into the proposition that carries more communicative weight, termed "NUCLEUS" by von Siebenthal, than the other proposition, primarily serving as a "contrast." In cases where both propositions carry equal weight, von Siebenthal simply denominates them as "NUCLEUS$_1$" and "NUCLEUS$_2$."

Significant portions of recent work on δέ operate under the assumption that it is not an adversative connector but rather a "discourse marker," signifying a form of discontinuity on higher text levels. Counter to that perspec-

---

120. So in the important footnote 23 in *AGG* 312c.
121. On Paul's use of this additive connector to express miniature narratives, see above, p. 59.
122. On what follows, cf. Heilig, *Paulus*, 233–34.

tive, I assert that, first, δέ meets the criteria of a *connector*, not a discourse marker. It serves as a conjunction, capable of linking a variety of elements (akin to, e.g., καί), but what is of relevance is that it also binds constructions expressing propositions. It is crucial to acknowledge that in some instances δέ establishes connections at the level of speech acts, a phenomenon that can also occur with other connectors (cf. the earlier notes on causal connectors). This is primarily observed when there is a shift to a new topic.

This distinct utilization guides us, second, toward the *semantics of the connector*. It is important to note that even in cases where δέ connects at the level of speech acts, it maintains its adversative character. It *contrasts* the decision to transition to a different topic with the alternative of continuing with the existing topic. Further research is warranted, and von Siebenthal's citation of the connector for a rather broad array of connection types might suggest that it more closely aligns with καί—an additive connector entailing a variety of different implicatures.[123] However, for the majority of cases, the assumption of a (mildly) adversative profile seems perfectly suitable.

Overlooking this aspect could result in misinterpretations. For instance, we will later (pp. 142–44) delve in more detail into Gal 1:13–14. The δέ in verse 15 is often either glazed over or associated with incorrect elements in the text, constructing a contrast between Paul's former progress in Judaism (verses 13–14) and the Damascus experience (verses 15–16a), thus portraying the entire passage as a story about revelation. Taking δέ seriously as a connector and understanding its functionality helps us recognize that, first, a contrast does indeed exist and, second, that Paul's previous life in Judaism serves as a negative backdrop for the actions narrated in verses 16c–17.

Von Siebenthal also categorizes the "negative-positive" pairs, typically linked with ἀλλά, as having an adversative meaning. Proceeding under the assumption of "additive-based" connectors as an overarching category, we can recognize a subcategory within it where the connector necessitates at least one of the two propositions to be counterfactual. In this framework, ἀλλά serving as a connector for a negative-positive pair would occupy a more specific subcategory within this broader category, often labeled as *corrective*. There is a prevalent presumption that event A occurred. However, the connection communicates that event A, in reality, did *not* transpire *but rather* event B did. For English speakers, it may come as a surprise to consider this as a distinct category, given that they—like the Greeks—use the same default connector for adversative and corrective connections. Lexi-

---

123. *AGG* 354.

cons that merely gloss ἀλλά with "but" subsequently mislead students. It almost inevitably hinders them from understanding this crucial differentiation, which is relatively nonintuitive. It is so difficult to grasp this distinction because the logical structure is entirely identical here as it is in the case of adversative connections where the external connect is negated ($\neg\, p \cap q$).

For instance:

Adversative: "Hans isn't stupid, but he is lazy."

Corrective: "Hans isn't stupid, but lazy/but he's lazy."

Even though both sentences might seem identical at first glance, they must be distinguished semantically. In the adversative connection, a certain inference that seems plausible based on the first proposition is rejected. The sentence refutes an unspoken assumption that if Hans is lazy, he must also be stupid. The statement disassociates these two traits, affirming that the two characteristics—laziness and intelligence—can coexist in the same individual. "Although" Hans is intelligent, he is "still" lazy.

By contrast, in the corrective connection, the entire proposition is denied. The issue does not lie with an assumed correlation between intelligence and laziness. Instead, the speaker points out that attributing stupidity to Hans is the problem. This judgment needs to be replaced by a different characterization.

Many native speakers are often unaware of the nuances, but most languages lacking a specific corrective connector (unlike, e.g., German, which uses "sondern" in these instances) often mark the difference through other syntactical means. In the above English examples, the "normal" adversative "but" necessitates the repetition of the subject and verb, while in the corrective version a reduction is required. Therefore, these two connection types are also differentiated on a syntactical level in English. I am not aware of analogous differentiating syntactical features in Koine Greek.

Negative-positive pairs, much like their analogous adversative connections with a negated element, typically do not constitute stories on their own. This is because, most of the time, they report only a single specific event, with a sequence of events in the affirmative proposition being the exception. This single event is further characterized by highlighting the non-occurrence of a negative foil.

Occasionally, what has not transpired is described quite vividly and that can, in turn, point to rather elaborate "implicit" stories in the background.

Chapter 2

Galatians 4:14 provides an example where Paul, within a more detailed narration, also mentions the event of the Galatians accepting him "like an angel of God, like the Messiah Jesus" (ἀλλὰ ὡς ἄγγελον θεοῦ ἐδέξασθέ με, ὡς Χριστὸν Ἰησοῦν). Note that this in itself raises the question about what stories about the reception of angels of God or the Messiah might be circulating. For the purpose of our present discussion, it is important to note that this is the positive element of a corrective construction, a single event. What actually transpired shines more brightly as it contrasts with the culturally expected rejection referenced earlier in verse 12 ("you did me no wrong"; οὐδέν με ἠδικήσατε) and expounded in greater detail in verse 14 in the negative element ("you did not despise or reject the trial that my condition posed to you"; καὶ τὸν πειρασμὸν ὑμῶν ἐν τῇ σαρκί μου οὐκ ἐξουθενήσατε οὐδὲ ἐξεπτύσατε).

What lies behind the account of Paul's past interaction with the Galatians is what *might* have been narratable had things turned out differently. The corrective connection does not tell a story per se, but it intimates a *myriad of potential stories* that are rejected as nonnarratable—at least not reliably—namely, all the narratives that would incorporate the negated event as part of their plot. Here yet again, we encounter a textual phenomenon that, while not a narrative in itself, directs us to the stories somehow underpinning the text (more details to follow, pp. 210–14).

Restrictive Connections

Restrictive connections are significant from a narratological perspective chiefly because they serve as a valuable reservoir of *metanarrative* comments from the narrator because they exhibit "utterance relatedness."[124] An illustrative example within the New Testament is found in John 4:1–3. Here, in verse 1, an embedded narrative is presented, something that the Pharisees learned about: Jesus was baptizing more than John. Verse 2 then inserts the qualifying remark: ". . . although, in fact, it was not Jesus who baptized, but his disciples" (καίτοιγε Ἰησοῦς αὐτὸς οὐκ ἐβάπτιζεν ἀλλ' οἱ μαθηταὶ αὐτοῦ).

Paul sometimes utilizes this particular conjunction to make remarks on his earlier narrations. For instance, in Gal 1:7 he initially asserts that there is nothing else equivalent to his prior proclamation deserving the title "gospel" (. . . ὃ οὐκ ἔστιν ἄλλο). Following this, though, he narrows down this claim of nonexistence to permit for something that, at least nominally, is "gospel-

---

124. *AGG* 342.

associated"—specifically, "certain individuals" who stir trouble (εἰ μή τινές εἰσιν οἱ ταράσσοντες ὑμᾶς) and who, in reality, undermine the objectives of the gospel (καὶ θέλοντες μεταστρέψαι τὸ εὐαγγέλιον τοῦ Χριστοῦ).

What is also narratologically noteworthy about the corrective connection in Gal 1:7 is that the nucleus of the nucleus-amplification pair is negated. Note that in the Gospel of John, an assertion is made and then its relationship to reality is qualified. By contrast, in Galatians, a claim is refuted and only afterward is some existence acknowledged. First, it is worth noting that this acknowledgement is anything but insignificant, precisely because it is cloaked in the seemingly benign rhetorical attire of a partial revocation of the apostolic pronouncement. The narrator admits to a "mistake," only to parlay this concession into an assault. Second, this structure also affects how we interpret the narrated events. In the former case in John, as the reading process continues, we start questioning whether there "actually is a story," whereas in the Pauline instance we are drawn deeper into the real happenings. These happenings, far from being as innocuous as their initially subdued rendition may imply, emerge as constituting a "shocking" narrative (cf. verse 6).

Explanatory Connections

Explanatory conjunctions have a shared attribute with restrictive conjunctions in that they "qualify" previous statements.[125] A common connector is the additive καί in its "epexegetical" usage. For instance, in 1 Cor 15:37 Paul discusses the sowing process, noting that you do not plant the eventual harvest but "the bare grain," be it wheat or from another kind of plant. In verse 38, he continues this story about regular processes: "But God gives it a body as he has determined." Having just spoken in the singular, he then provides further elucidation: ". . . namely, to each of the seeds its own body" (. . . καὶ ἑκάστῳ τῶν σπερμάτων ἴδιον σῶμα).

Particularly within those explanatory relationships that von Siebenthal refers to as nucleus-parenthesis types and nucleus-comment types, it is apparent that we are presented once more with "utterance relatedness," thereby dealing with metanarrative commentary (if the text in consideration is a narrative). In Paul's letters, an exemplary case is found in a textual unit universally acknowledged as a narrative. In Gal 1:19, Paul details his visit to Jerusalem. He then moves forward in verse 21 to his travels to Syria

---

125. *AGG* 340.

Chapter 2

and Cilicia. Tucked between these two accounts, we discover a remark by the narrating "I," which provides commentary on the assertions of verse 20: "I swear before God that what I've written is not a lie" (ἃ δὲ γράφω ὑμῖν, ἰδοὺ ἐνώπιον τοῦ θεοῦ ὅτι οὐ ψεύδομαι).

Frequently, the terms that Heinrich von Siebenthal labels as "connectors" of that sort do not actually connect two propositions. Instead, they work to explicate a "particular item" within the first proposition.[126] Relative pronouns are emblematic in such instances.[127] It is feasible to distinguish between item-identification relationships and item-description relationships, which align well with restrictive and nonrestrictive relative clauses, respectively, in English translation.[128] Both can be significant in ensuring the coherence of a narrative text.[129]

In *item-description* relationships, an already established concept is further elucidated. In terms of narratology, what is grammatically an attribute to a noun in the main clause often serves as a flashback. However, the supplementary information need not be chronological; it can also detail other facets such as, for instance, the agent of the action in the main clause. Occasionally, as in Gal 1:23, the contrast between the main action and the additional details can create a similar effect to a concessive conjunction: "He is proclaiming the faith, which he had tried to destroy/even though he had tried to destroy it!" (νῦν εὐαγγελίζεται τὴν πίστιν ἥν ποτε ἐπόρθει; cf. above, p. 110, on the temporal structure of this verse).

This interpretation, of course, presumes that the relative clause is a nonrestrictive attribute and, in turn, πίστις on its own already represents the specifically Christian faith (cf. Gal 3:23). Otherwise, if it simply referred to 'religious orientation' in a broad sense, the relative clause might also serve a restrictive function, clarifying the type of faith being discussed—perhaps distinguishing it from the Ἰουδαϊσμός in Gal 1:13, 14 ("He is preaching the very faith that he had previously tried to annihilate!").[130] However, it is highly unlikely that we are encountering an *item-identification* relationship in this particular case. The fact that our English usage of "faith" differs significantly from πίστις, risking the projection of interpretative options from the former realm into the latter, is revealed by the remarkable facts that πίστις

---

126. *AGG* 341c.
127. Cf. *AGG* 319.
128. Cf. *AGG* 289b.
129. Cf. *AGG* 316.
130. The translation ". . . the faith he once tried to destroy . . ." (NIV, for example) is ambiguous.

The Grammar of Narration

in the New Testament is neither found in the plural form nor accompanied by a demonstrative pronoun.

In general, item-description relationships appear more relevant for a narratological analysis, mainly because in these instances the concepts of the main clause are already known, and the narrator has the latitude to add as much supplemental information as they deem necessary. Conversely, item-identification relationships are crucial for the narrative principally because, akin to phoric and deictic words, they can amplify the coherence of the text.[131] For instance, when Paul tells the Philippians in Phil 1:30 that they "have the same fight" (τὸν αὐτὸν ἀγῶνα ἔχοντες) which they also saw him confront (οἷον εἴδετε ἐν ἐμοὶ καὶ νῦν ἀκούετε ἐν ἐμοί), this creates a link back to Phil 1:7—and even further back, beyond the text, into the experience preceding the letter writing (and into the realm of implicit stories that are inaccessible to us).

Comparative Connections

Comparative connections convey similarities between the circumstances expressed in two propositions.[132] Within the context of narration, these relationships typically involve "utterance relatedness" as well. Essentially, an event that is narrated as part of the story receives particular characterization from the narrator through comparison with other situations. However, these comparative situations are often not the central focus of the communication but are brought forth to enhance and give more depth to the actual narrative.

The background upon which the narrator builds is often marked by conjunctions like καθώς ("just as"). Given that this background story is usually already *known*, it tends to be summoned very economically, allowing the narrator to concentrate more effort on adding color to the situation of primary interest. In this main clause, we often encounter an adverb such as οὕτως ("so"), which functions as a correlate to the connector.

Let us take a look at 2 Tim 3:8 as an example. There, further details are

---

131. Cf. *AGG* 316.
132. On what follows, cf. Heilig, *Paulus*, 237, and *AGG* 344. For a critique of the category, see Breindl, "Semantische Klassifikation," 252–53. The subtype of "proportional connections" (*AGG* 345) does not seem to be attested in Paul's letters. For an occurrence in other NT writings, see Mark 7:36.

Chapter 2

provided about how "people" will conduct themselves in the last days (cf. verse 1: ἐν ἐσχάταις ἡμέραις). "Just as Jannes and Jambres opposed Moses" (ὃν τρόπον δὲ Ἰάννης καὶ Ἰαμβρῆς ἀντέστησαν Μωϋσεῖ), these individuals, corrupted in mind and disqualified in the faith, "oppose the truth" (οὕτως καὶ οὗτοι ἀνθίστανται τῇ ἀληθείᾳ). While we are typically accustomed to viewing the past as the usual subject of narration, here we encounter a brief reference to a story from the Old Testament (Exod 7:11), which is notably enriched by additional traditions, including the names of the magicians who remain anonymous in the LXX. The narrator presumes familiarity with this story, subtly alludes to it, but focuses chiefly on the main concern—something that lies ahead in the future. It could be argued that the more detailed declaration about future bad behavior could reasonably be classified as "predictive narration."

Using narratological terminology to describe this passage seems almost unavoidable if we assume the letter to be pseudepigraphic. For in this case, the narrator of the frame narrative has the narrative character of Paul making certain assertions about his future as a means to discuss the already existing situation in the real world that prompted the author to pen this work.[133] This strategy allows the narrator to use an embedded "almost story" to communicate their message more effectively.

Similarly, the connection in Eph 5:2 preconditions readers to conceptualize the situations depicted therein as if they were components of actual narratives—even though one of them is not (yet). In this case, καθώς leads, unlike in 2 Tim 3:8, to a fairly detailed account, a recapitulation of what Jesus did for "us" (καθὼς καὶ ὁ Χριστὸς ἠγάπησεν ἡμᾶς καὶ παρέδωκεν ἑαυτὸν ὑπὲρ ἡμῶν προσφορὰν καὶ θυσίαν τῷ θεῷ εἰς ὀσμὴν εὐωδίας). Here, the narrator is not relying on the readers' memory. Rather, he is eager to ensure the readers grasp how the already familiar story of Jesus's passion applies to the quasi-narrative wherein they emerge as narrative characters. Nevertheless, there is also a similarity to 2 Tim 2:8 in that, here too, the negative foil is not juxtaposed with a somewhat similar account of the recipients' past acts of love, possibly framed in sacrificial terms as one might expect. Instead, the verse commences with the injunction "walk in love!" (περιπατεῖτε ἐν ἀγάπῃ).

The focus, thus, is on a situation that is yet to occur and therefore cannot yet be narrated retrospectively. The events under consideration here are

---

133. Cf. Alfons Weiser, *Der zweite Brief an Timotheus*, EKKNT 16.1 (Zurich: Benziger, 2003), 246.

not only in the future but are also uncertain and wholly contingent on the readers' cooperation. Once more, it is not coincidental that this desirable behavior presents itself in the text in conjunction with an explicit story. The comparative element not only adds depth to what "walking" implies here but also bolsters the hortative dimension itself, hinting at the possibility that the commanded situation may likewise *evolve into* a narratable story in the future.

In a way, Gal 3:6 represents an intensification of the structure of Eph 5:2 and a contrasting case to 2 Tim 2:8. Here, the "actual" story—the one seeming to carry the most weight from a communicative perspective, and the topic that is at stake (as indicated by the context)—appears to completely vanish from the text. Paul introduces the story of Abraham (quoting Gen 15:6) with καθώς, yet without a clear narrative in the text that would match the story's plot. As you might anticipate at this stage, in my view this gap does not indicate that Paul is uninterested in his audience contemplating the larger narrative shape of the implied situations. In fact, precisely because comparative conjunctions usually serve as a sign that the narrator is momentarily stepping away from the act of narration itself to connect what has been narrated thus far to a different narrative, the absence of one of these narratives in the text naturally prompts readers to look for the corresponding component themselves.

In my opinion, Paul provides what he believes to be the obvious answer to the rhetorical questions of Gal 3:1–5 by initiating a comparative connection, which he then, however, leaves incomplete because the Galatians already know the story, and the contrasting foil he has put forth provides them with all the necessary elements to end the sentence in their minds with, ". . . so too in our case, it is through faith that . . ." Frustratingly for us, the "real story"—the nucleus—remains entirely implicit, obliging us to speculate about what exactly faith accomplishes or has accomplished among the Galatians. However, we can possibly infer from how Paul himself singles out the question in verse 2 that this is what he has in mind. For there he asserts that, despite the numerous questions bursting forth from him, there is only "one thing" he wishes to learn from the Galatians (τοῦτο μόνον θέλω μαθεῖν ἀφ' ὑμῶν)—that is, how they received the Spirit.[134]

---

134. I assume here that the questions in verses 3–5 are not simply reformulations that deal with the same matter.

Chapter 2

Meaningful Relationships and Temporal Connections

As we previously explored in chapter 1, the subsequent two sentences do not constitute a narrative following the definition of narrativity that we have chosen to employ: "The police were searching for Peter, and at the University of Chicago the curricula for the winter semester were being created." Indisputably, one could posit that the coordinating conjunction "and" is incorporated here to signify a temporal relationship, likely denoting simultaneity rather than sequence, as suggested by the change of location. This would mean that the connection could satisfy at least one criterion of narrativity. Nevertheless, we should refrain from categorizing this as a narrative since the scenarios outlined by the two clauses do not appear to harbor a substantial correlation with each other—at least not in the perception of the authors who deliberately crafted this example to be devoid of meaning. By contrast, in many communicative contexts we rightly assume that when speakers present us with temporally connected events, they want us to process them as narratives and, thus, reconstruct meaningful relationships among propositions even if they make use only of additive or temporal connectors.

Hence, we must confront the question of how meaningful relationships may be established in connections with a purely *temporal* focus.[135] This assists us in understanding the difference between the example involving the police and the University of Chicago and, let's say, the text that von Siebenthal selects in his text grammar to introduce the concept of macropropositional structures: the parable from Matt 13:45–46. In verse 46, we read: "He sold everything . . . and bought it" (πέπρακεν πάντα ὅσα εἶχεν καὶ ἠγόρασεν αὐτόν), referring to the previously mentioned pearl of great value (πολύτιμον μαργαρίτην).

Cooperative readers can understand how these two propositions relate to each other even in the absence of context. They are capable of not only identifying the sequence but also understanding how both propositions work together to advance the plot. After all, both propositions concern the same agent, and it is immediately comprehensible, even in the modern world, that pearls are often items of desire, that notable examples may possess significant value, and that their purchase could necessitate considerable financial assets. Thus, readers can effortlessly

---

135. On everything that follows, cf. Heilig, *Paulus*, chapter 5, section 5.

interpret the agent's intention as the cohesive element linking both actions and comprehend that the first event acts as a precondition for the second to occur.

The situation would differ completely with a text such as "Bill Gates was looking for fine watches. He saw a particularly beautiful Rolex in a store window. Instantly, he sold everything he possessed and bought the watch." Only under very specific circumstances—for instance, if one were engaging with a story about watches possessing magical powers that drive collectors into madness upon seeing them—can we reconstruct meaningful connections among these events and, thus, interpret the text as a narrative.

When we encounter temporally connected events within a text, we generally anticipate—unless we are engaged in a conversation with, for example, a drunk individual—that the speaker or writer intends to convey a narrative, and that the chosen events adhere to established principles. Hence, we expect the presence of a plot, potentially a moral, and a salient point the communicator seeks to emphasize within the given context. Consequently, we engage our background knowledge of the world, focusing particularly on human behavior, to invest the events presented to us with a cohesive structure. If the narrator is competent, they will avoid using additive connectors, which do not provide explicit detail regarding the relationships among the events, except in circumstances where their temporal and substantial connection is apparent. Generally, ambiguities that one might encounter at the level of a single nexus of two propositions are addressed higher up in the propositional hierarchy.

In the context of the mentioned parable, for instance, figure 6 elucidates that the two coordinated propositions (in conjunction with an accompanying movement) embody the "result" of a "reason" that is stated in verse 45. The latter consists of the combined circumstances whereby our protagonist exhibits interest in fine pearls and stumbles upon a particularly enticing specimen. Therefore, the sale of his assets and the ensuing purchase of the pearl must be perceived as interconnected stepping stones triggered by the discovery of this particular pearl. Consequently, it is evident that the protagonist's disposal of his possessions is not a random act but rather a direct consequence of his desire to acquire the pearl.

Chapter 2

Figure 6. Propositional structure of Matt 13:45–46 according to Heinrich von Siebenthal

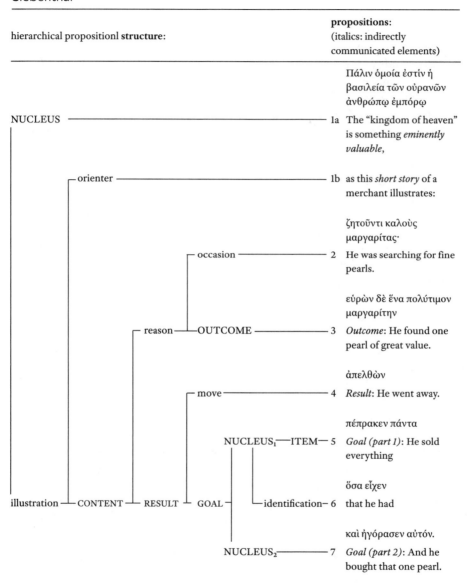

From *AGG* 312e.

It should be pointed out that in this specific case, world knowledge does most of the heavy lifting. Indeed, even at the higher propositional levels, we do not come across logic-based connectors. In fact, I have numerous reservations concerning von Siebenthal's reconstruction of the propositional structure of this brief text. Had he chosen an example with a greater number of logic-based connectors, chances would have been that we had more agreement.

First and foremost, von Siebenthal overlooks the one obvious connector besides καί, namely δέ, which he appears to interpret as a discourse marker, saying that the "weak adversative δέ 'but' functions as a connective, often indicating some development in a text."[136] By contrast, I believe it clearly serves as a connector linking the main clause (proposition 5) with the nexus consisting of propositions 1a and 1b. Proposition 1b merely offers a characterization of the individual introduced in proposition 1a, but the act of searching seems to be what is picked up as a negative foil. The contrast lies in the initial search and a subsequent complete alteration in behavior. The coordinating conjunction δέ occupies the second position of the sentence, but it has a syntactical connection to the main clause (πέπρακεν πάντα). Initially, the man is in search of something to purchase. *However*, later, he is offloading his possessions.

Two intervening events explain this dramatic shift in behavior. The discovery of a valuable pearl is first narrated through the use of a participle. Immediately following this, another participle, ἀπελθών, introduces a temporal intermediate step—an apparent prerequisite for the merchant to be able to dispose of his belongings. Perhaps we are led to imagine him leaving the marketplace where he was shopping in order to gather and sell his possessions? Or is the merchant an international traveler compelled to return home from a distant locale such as the Persian Gulf? These are open questions concerning the meaning of the parable on the level of reference.

By contrast, the only real question concerning the semantic structure of this story that warrants debate, in my opinion, is whether proposition 7 enters into a connection with proposition 5 (plus proposition 6) or whether it belongs to a higher level of the semantic structure. Essentially, the query

---

136. In *GGNT* 212e, von Siebenthal was still clearer about this being a normal connector, even though he already used language reminiscent of discourse markers. There he wrote: "*Als Konnektor* steht das schwach adversative δέ 'aber.' Hier dient es offenbar dazu, den Beginn der eigentlichen Erzählung, Pp2–7, zu *signalisieren*." Emphasis not in the original.

Chapter 2

is whether the entirety of verse 46 contrasts with the setting established in verse 45 (i.e., the merchant searching for something to buy). Is the crux of the narrative that the merchant, after a prolonged and unsuccessful search, finally strikes a beneficial deal? Alternatively, we might consider the contrast to be of a more restricted purview. Initially, the merchant is on a quest for something to purchase. However, he himself ends up selling something to bring his search to its conclusion. The actual purchase could then be seen as an addendum, an epilogue that, after the foreshadowing in the nexus of propositions 5 and 6—who would liquidate all of their possessions if in the end they are still unable to secure the object of their desire?—almost feels like a foregone conclusion.

To summarize, it is often beneficial to *consider logic-based connections at higher levels of the propositional structure* to better understand the relationships among situations that share only temporal connections at the microlevel. Occasionally, this can impact exegesis significantly.

For example, in Gal 1:17b–c we find a statement that initially mimics the structure of the non-story on page 138 involving Peter and curricula at the University of Chicago: "I went to Arabia and came back to Damascus" (ἀπῆλθον εἰς Ἀραβίαν καὶ πάλιν ὑπέστρεψα εἰς Δαμασκόν).[137] The reason we swiftly attribute an overall intention to Paul's movements in this case is because we understand they occur within a broader narrative context in his letter to the Galatians. When we consider this miniature narrative, this little sequence, in the wider context of the sentence that begins in verse 15, it becomes instantly clear that this temporal connection is part of a macroproposition bound together by the adversative connector ἀλλά.

In other words, this scene contrasts with an alternative storyline that Paul opts not to pursue (verses 16c–17a). At this level of the propositional structure, there are still multiple interpretations of how precisely "not immediately consulting flesh and blood" (verse 16c) and "not going to those already apostles in Jerusalem" (verse 17a), taken together, provide an *alternative* to Paul's actual travel movements in verses 17b–c. However, this ambiguity is resolved once it is recognized that the entire sequence of verses 16c–17c recounts what Paul chose not to do, and instead did do, as part of a sequence of two events, with God's decision to reveal his Son to Paul (and, implied, Paul's reaction to that) being the earlier event (cf. verses 15a–16b). Note that at the start of verse 15, we see δέ, another adversative connector, marking Paul's subsequent interactions and movements as a *deviation* from an expec-

---

137. For a detailed discussion of what follows, cf. Heilig, *Paulus*, 246–60.

tation set by the narrative in Gal 1:13–14, which portrays Paul as orienting himself toward human standards. Therefore, the point of Gal 1:15–17 must be that when Paul's "pattern of religion" changed, he did not continue to behave in the same manner, orienting himself toward the authorities within this new framework. Instead, a transformation of his personality occurred. This changed narrative character is no longer dependent on human approval.

To sum this up, we can see that the top-down analysis of the propositional structure illustrates that the ambiguous talk in verses 16c and 17a probably pertains to local Christian authorities in Damascus on the one hand and the Jerusalem apostles on the other hand. Furthermore, the two movements connected solely by καί in verse 17b–c are recounted by Paul because they are both examples of *independent* traveling and evangelizing. Hence, in this passage Paul's use of logic-based connectors facilitates the straightforward reconstruction of the propositional structure—a structure that is not at all easily compatible with many of the proposals concerning what this story is supposedly "about" (Paul's conversion, his call, an apocalypse, or whatever).

Another critical factor that assists readers in reconstructing meaningful relationships amid temporally ordered events relates to the concept of "narration-specific tasks." We will delve into this subject in greater depth in chapter 3 (pp. 182–97). Hence, we will only briefly touch upon its implications for plot reconstruction here. The underlying principle behind this notion is that a narrator must complete a series of communicative tasks to successfully tell a story, one of which is to introduce the act of narration. These preliminary segments often provide a preview of the topic or even a glimpse into the overall theme of the narrative, thereby encapsulating the message that is to be conveyed. If the reader who approaches a story already possesses an abstract overview of its content, decoding the plot becomes markedly easier.

For this reason, *indications from the immediate context*, including any conclusions drawn or morals derived from the narrative, are sometimes crucial for interpretation. In particular instances, this might be the only available interpretive tool, given that a story may lack *any* logic-based connectors at higher propositional levels.

Consider the previously discussed passage Gal 1:13–17 again. At a higher propositional level, this passage forms one macroproposition followed by three more blocks of propositions, each introduced by ἔπειτα ("then"). So, how is this sequence of four episodes to be interpreted? Much of the debate surrounding this narrative of Gal 1:13–2:21 in the secondary literature likely

Chapter 2

stems from the atomized approach often taken in exegetical studies—isolating half-verses and single words without concurrently considering the macropropositional structure and the embedding of individual text parts within the whole of the communicative act. Any valid interpretation of Gal 1:13–17 must elucidate its role within the broader narrative. And, conversely, any hypothesis regarding the meaning and function of the story must be able to explain why Paul chose precisely these four sequential blocks to create his narrative.

Upon examining how Paul transitions into the narrative mode (Gal 1:10–12) and progresses afterward (especially the actual conclusion of the narrative, Gal 2:1–10, and then, after the transition in 2:11–21, the next distinct part of the discourse, Gal 3:1–5), it becomes evident that Paul selects precisely this sequence of evidence because he thinks it supports the thesis that he had put forward in Gal 1:12—that his gospel is of divine origin and that it remains untouched by human interference.[138] This forms the overall theme that provides coherence to the nexus of sequential episodes. It, likewise, confirms our analysis of the internal structure of the first of these temporal blocks in Gal 1:15–17.

Therefore, comprehending the immediate context of the story in Gal 1:13–2:21 not only further clarifies why Paul effortlessly "transitions" in the text between Arabia and Damascus but also helps illuminate, at a fundamental level, the narrative's true focus and Paul's reasons for sharing it with the Galatians. Here, we are already touching on the question of why Paul tells a story to make exactly this point, what he wants to achieve with this within the context of the wider communication, leading us into the realm of *pragmatics*—and, thus, giving us a segue into the next chapter.

---

138. For a detailed analysis along these lines, cf. Heilig, *Paulus*, 492–511.

3. Stories in Context

Beyond Macropropositional Structures

Transposing the narratological definition of narrativity into a textgrammatical framework has proven to be heuristically fruitful. This approach has enabled us to scrutinize Paul's letters and to distinguish miniature narratives (many of them components of larger stories) on the content level by seeking temporal and meaningful relationships that are marked by connectors signaling chronological and logical connections, pairs of propositions. As is evident even from this preliminary overview, Paul indeed tells stories. He does so in many places and by employing many different tools to vary his narration.

As has become apparent in our analysis of temporal order in Paul's letters in the first half of chapter 2, the apostle's storytelling style differs from, say, Matthew's narration in his Gospel. Nonetheless, this does not negate that Paul can indeed be rightfully designated as a storyteller. However, our work does not end with merely having successfully categorized Paul as a narrator. It is paramount that we delve deeper into the motivations that prompted Paul to utilize such a *compact style of narration*. At times, we already caught a glimpse into the dynamics that gave rise to the specific configuration of Paul's narratives. We regularly encountered "implicit" narratives lurking in the backdrop, as Paul built upon prior acts of narration. In such instances, it becomes clear from the outset that the *function* of Paul's stories cannot simply be to "inform" his letter recipients about past events. Thus, these phenomena have already pointed us toward the *pragmatics* side of Paul's narratives. To fully comprehend not only that Paul narrates but also how he narrates and what this means for the role of narration within his broader literary (and real-life) activity, we must consider how Paul utilizes narrative textual units as part of his wider communicative strategy.

Chapter 3

Similarly, our evaluation of meaningful relationships among propositions in the second half of chapter 2 has not only enhanced our understanding of how events interconnect in Paul's stories, but it has also consistently prompted us to look beyond these overt narratives. We specifically noted how certain types of connections naturally invite us to depart from the narrative world and instead concentrate on the act of narration itself. These connections do so by introducing the dimension of utterance relatedness. In these instances, Paul is not merely recounting a story about something, but is "commenting," in the broadest sense, on existing narratives. Thus, these phenomena further underscore that Paul's stories do not exist in a vacuum. They are the products of specific acts of narration—acts intricately interwoven with other communicative strategies.

While I am confident in having demonstrated that miniature stories are far from infrequent or nonexistent in Paul's letters, it remains crucial to emphasize that these writings do not constitute continuous narratives. We are not dealing here with an uninterrupted implementation of the pattern of narration. Therefore, it is imperative that we evaluate how these separate acts of narration connect with each other and how they nest within textual segments composed also according to *different textualization strategies*.

This same line of inquiry is also suggested as a prudent next step by additional observations we have made in relation to logic-based connections, particularly those that due to the semantics of their connectors seem to constitute something akin to a "borderline narrative." We must ask ourselves why we naturally perceive some connections, such as many cases of purpose-oriented or conditional proposition pairs, *as* miniature stories even though the connectors assign a semantic role to at least one of the propositions that does not explicitly confirm the occurrence of the event in a narrative world. In this respect, too, it appears necessary for us to consider contextual aspects that frame such instances of "near narration" and lead us to assume the occurrence of some of these events, despite this aspect not being settled at the grammatical level. As clearly demonstrated, context significantly matters in numerous ways.

Against the backdrop of these observations, this chapter will concentrate on some of the most fundamental ways in which *contextual factors* shape Paul's narration. By doing so, we highlight critical elements that need consideration in our analysis of the apostle's narratives. This particular chapter serves as a compendium of observations that I deem vital for the analysis of Pauline narratives, exceeding what can be captured through a text-grammatical focus on the propositional structure of texts. For this reason, this section amalgamates a broad range of observations, even though they may seem only loosely connected at times. What unites them is that they all *augment* a perspective on Paul's stories that centers on the propositional structure of these texts (or text parts). Indeed, they all transcend the "meaning" of Paul's stories in such a restricted sense.

Whenever we discuss "meaning," it is vital that we clarify exactly what we actually, well, mean with this term. This necessitates transparency about which conception of meaning is selected, whether we hold interest in, for example, the author's intention or the text's reception by subsequent readers (see above, pp. 40–45). Nevertheless, even when our pursuit is distinctly defined, another facet calls for our close scrutiny. Meaning can be characterized on different *levels*, which vary according to their *degree of abstraction*.

At the most concrete level (a), we grapple with utterances. These are distinct acts of speaking or writing—unique events occurring at a specific time. Next (b), we encounter sentences. Note that the same sentence can manifest in a variety of utterances, differentiated by time and context. When we describe sentences, we are primarily interested in their grammatical dimension. (By contrast, utterances do not necessarily conform to the grammatical form of a sentence—consider, for example, "Ouch!"). Progressing further along the spectrum of abstraction, we then (c) encounter propositions. At this level, we are fundamentally focused on the situations that are expressed—the grammatical structure of the sentence becomes irrelevant. To illustrate, the sentences "The apple fell," "May the apple fall," and "Did the apple fall?" all share the same proposition, namely, {<Apple> [fall]}.

We have already alluded to this above (p. 47), but it is worth revisiting because of its significant implications for our analysis of Pauline narratives. In propositions, we eliminate grammatical specifics from verbs (mode, tense, aspect) in order to extract "situations proper." Therefore, when we analyze the propositional structure of a narrative, we must remember that we are operating at a highly abstract level. For instance, the propositions behind the following two texts are identical:

Give me the apple! For I am hungry.

You gave me the apple. For I was hungry.

Indeed, the manner in which we represent the relationship among these propositions is even more abstract. The label "cause-effect" is assigned to

147

Chapter 3

both of these brief texts as well as to all other texts showing the same semantic structure. For instance,

> Give me your bicycle. Because my car is broken.

On this most abstract level, we are examining a fundamental semantic structure of the text, the semantic roles that propositions play in relation to each other, primarily mediated through the lexical semantics of the connectors being employed.

In essence, the propositional structure of a text provides us with a sort of summary of its content—and, if it is a narrative, an abstract approximation of its plot. It is, metaphorically speaking, the "skeleton" of the text. However, interpretation requires more than just assembling these bones. When we consider syntax (the meaning on the level of the sentences) and pragmatics (the meaning on the level of the utterances), we are adding—staying within the metaphor—flesh, skin, hair, and so forth to that skeleton.

Don't misunderstand me; determining the propositional structure of a narrative is a significant stride toward competently comprehending the meaning of the text. I wish *every* exegete would integrate this step into their methodology. Nevertheless, we must be frank about the limitations of such an approach. The substance of a story extends far beyond its basic propositional skeleton.

First, we must acknowledge that beyond its propositional value, every sentence (note that we are now transitioning to a less abstract level of semantic analysis) possesses its own more specific *expression meaning*.[1] Here, we consider the sentence with its grammatical form but still determine what it means "in and of itself," that is, independent of context.[2] For example, the sentence "For I was hungry" includes the pronoun "I." This English

---

1. Sebastian Löbner, *Understanding Semantics*, 2nd ed., Understanding Language Series (New York: Routledge, 2013), 1. It can cause some confusion that others call precisely this entity "proposition."

2. We do not have space here to discuss the extent to which this is actually possible. Cognitive linguistics and construction grammar are becoming more and more usage-based and question the assumption that meaning devoid of context even exists, arguing that this notion is a relic from generative grammar. Accordingly, one might argue that in all these supposedly abstract examples of sentences we always presuppose an implicit context. However, so far, the contours of this supposed context likewise remain very vague. I thus think that it remains valid to differentiate between expression meaning and utterance meaning, even if we might be forced in the future to explicate this difference merely in terms of different degrees of imagining specific scenes.

Stories in Context

pronoun conveys that the individual being referred to is the same as the speaker—whomever that might be in any specific utterance. The verb's tense situates the scenario in the past relative to the moment of utterance—whenever that might be in any particular usage of the sentence. In other words, when building on our analysis of the propositional structure of narratives, our interpretive efforts will also take into account the specific *grammatical configuration* of each sentence.

Second, transitioning from the sentence level to an even less abstract level of meaning—the utterance level—we can recognize semantic aspects unique to this level of *utterance meaning*. The features under consideration here include all those contributed by the sentence's use in a specific "context of utterance," consisting in the constellation of speaker(s) or producer(s), addressee(s), time, place, and other circumstances.[3]

For example, when *Paul* uses a sentence with a first-person singular pronoun, the meaning is not merely a general directive to the reader: "Look for the speaker—they are the referent of the pronoun." Rather, the apostle Paul employs this pronoun with its grammatical meaning to refer to himself among all the individuals in human history who could have used such a pronoun (in their respective language, if indeed that language possesses such a pronoun). Succinctly put, we must also consider *referents* at this level of analysis. We are moving beyond the realm of the text itself here as we correlate it with realities *outside* the text—into the context in which it is created.

Third, it is important to acknowledge that there are features tied to the context of utterance that are classically considered external to the field of semantics and more closely associated with pragmatics. We not only infer from Paul's use of a first-person pronoun that he is referring to himself, but we also make a myriad of other inferences about his situation based on what he writes. For instance, if we observe the sentence "Give me the apple!" being uttered by a small child toward an adult female, we might deduce—among other possibilities and with limited certainty—that this person is their mother and that the child might be hungry. These kinds of conversational *implicatures* are also tremendously important in interpreting stories.

Take, for example, the depiction of Paul as a storyteller in Acts 20:7 (see above, pp. 48–50). To understand how it can be that the fact that "Paul wanted to depart the next day" caused him to speak the night before, we need to make a series of inferences, processes that for us as co-

---

3. Löbner, *Understanding Semantics*, 4–6.

149

Chapter 3

operative readers happen instinctively. For example, we would infer that Paul had the general desire to have such a dialogue in Troas, and after his departure this would no longer be possible. We would also understand that the prior seven days apparently did not provide him with an opportunity to do what he wished.

Fourth, we pivot directly to the heart of pragmatics, as we finally embark on a discussion of what is occasionally referred to as *communicative meaning*.[4] Here, we are interested in the way a speaker interacts with their intended audience through their discourse, what they "do" with their text. A proposition, in essence, expresses a particular situation. But merely by identifying a proposition, we have not articulated (1) how the speaker's utterance relates the situation to the real world or (2) how the recipient fits into all of this.

Let me unpack that quickly in what follows. If, in addition to recognizing the proposition, we can also point out an *epistemic mode*, which is the speaker's attitude toward the situation, then we encounter a novel, more complex form of propositional structure, the *"epistemic minimal unit."* Crucial markers permitting us to discover an epistemic mode include adverbs, as, for instance, in this sentence: "Hopefully, it will rain soon."

At first glance, this brief detour on "epistemic minimal units" might seem like an unnecessary deviation. However, it proves to be quite essential to our present concern. Epistemic minimal units are potential candidates for propositional structures that express not only situations (and their connection to the world) but also possess an additional layer of expressing how the speaker relates the epistemic unit to the recipients of the utterance. We call these types of propositional structures "illocutions" (or "communicative minimal units"). To repeat, they comprise a standard proposition (propositional content = situation) coupled with an epistemic mode as well as what we call *communicative function*. In summary, if we can identify a communicative function for an epistemic minimal unit (and the underlying proposition), we shift our focus from the attitude of the speaker toward the situation to their intent with regard to the recipients.

This may initially seem complex, but I am hopeful that the forthcoming example will clarify these distinctions regarding the pragmatic layer of meaning. The sentence, "Hopefully, you'll come back soon," shares its propositional content with an array of other sentences that are centered

---

4. Löbner, *Understanding Semantics*, 6–7. On what follows, cf. Christoph Heilig, *Paulus als Erzähler? Eine narratologische Perspektive auf die Paulusbriefe*, BZNW 237 (Berlin: de Gruyter, 2020), 162–63.

around the situation of returning. In common with these other sentences, the phrase can also employ a wide assortment of referents, contingent on the context in which it is uttered. Within these contexts, with varying speakers and listeners, we can also explore the pragmatic dimension of the utterance. In this particular instance, searching for a communicative function makes considerable sense because it is evident that the sentence includes an epistemic mode. After all, the expressed situation is plainly specified as a hope. It thus constitutes an epistemic minimal unit. As such a type of propositional structure, it can have different kinds of functions. For instance, in a given utterance, a speaker may wish to utilize the sentence with a *directive* force—an attempt to persuade someone to return promptly.

It is crucial to acknowledge that the grammatical form of sentences and the communicative function correlate only to a limited degree.[5] Not all declarative sentences genuinely constitute assertions. Conversely, even questions can serve an assertive function.[6] Traditionally, following Searle, one differentiates between assertives (speaker's commitments regarding the truth of the proposition), directives (intended to prompt the addressee[s] to act), commissives (commitments to a future action), expressives (expressions of the speaker's attitudes and emotions toward the proposition), and declarations (speech acts that change the reality in accord with the proposition).

Distinguishing varying types of propositional structures—mere propositional content, epistemic minimal units, and illocutions—is instrumental in clarifying the distinctive ways in which connectors can link two connects. While connectors customarily connect at the level of the propositional content (i.e., between the situations themselves), they are capable as well of *linking at the level of the epistemic mode*. Contrast the subsequent two complex sentences:

Jim is going to the movie theater this evening, <u>because</u> they will be showing his favorite film.

Hopefully, I'll secure tickets for this evening, <u>because</u> I am eager to see that movie.

---

5. Cf. *CGCG* 38.2, examples 12 and 13.
6. Cf. *CGCG* 38. On "wishes" as clause types and/or communicative functions, cf. Heilig, *Paulus*, 751–52 and 763–64.

Chapter 3

In the first example, the proposition involving the causal connector provides the rationale for the situation in the first clause. In the second instance, the clause marked by the connector does not furnish a cause for "securing tickets." Rather, it elucidates the speaker's attitude toward this situation and, specifically, the hope therein. Von Siebenthal's analysis of the "symptom perspective" with causal ὅτι is indeed a unique iteration of this phenomenon of a connection at the epistemic level: The rationale for making an assertion about a specific situation is presented.[7]

Similarly, it is feasible for connectors to *bind two elements at the level of the communicative function*. We have previously encountered this phenomenon in relation to causal connectors, where such "utterance relatedness" is quite common. The cause gives the reason why a certain instruction, for instance, is provided. Note that certain connectors exist *solely* to connect illocutions. Von Siebenthal's classification of "restrictive connections" is birthed from collecting such cases into one category (see above, pp. 132–33). These connectors can be labeled "metacommunicative connectors." For this phenomenon—for connectors that do not ever engage on the level of propositional content—it seems well founded to use the term "discourse markers." This is in contrast to the prevalent usage of this nomenclature for instances in which we are actually handling, arguably, lexemes that are connectors functioning perfectly "ordinarily" (i.e., that have the ability to connect clauses on the level of propositional content; cf. above, pp. 129–30, on δέ).[8]

The Expression Side of Paul's Stories

At first glance, the distinction between the different levels of meaning in the preceding section might appear tedious. However, I believe that it serves as a vital foundation for progressing to an analysis of Paul's letters that expands beyond a reconstruction of their propositional macrostructure, their semantic "skeleton." I would like to stress that this by no means implies that the arrangement of these propositional bones is a futile task. On the contrary, it is of the

---

7. Cf. *AGG* 277a.

8. For a much more detailed discussion, cf. Heilig, *Paulus*, chapter 4, section 8. My main sparring partner there is Christopher J. Fresch, "Discourse Markers in the Septuagint and Early Koine Greek with Special Reference to The Twelve" (PhD diss., University of Cambridge, 2015). In the meantime, this work has been published as Christopher J. Fresch, *Discourse Markers in Early Koine Greek: Cognitive-Functional Analysis and LXX Translation Technique*, Septuagint and Cognate Studies 77 (Atlanta: SBL Press, 2023).

essence! From my perspective, many exegetical propositions in the secondary literature radiates reconstructions that, upon closer examination—especially at the joints (the connectors)—are highly improbable. Regrettably, standard exegetical methods seldom provide a way to probe the reconstruction presupposed by declarations about "what Paul really said." More often than not, we are presented with a reconstruction that conceals its backbone under numerous layers of purportedly relevant aspects of meaning. To even begin to assess the merit of such interpretations, one is required first to peel back these layers oneself. Consequently, I am optimistic that the analysis of Paul's narratives conducted so far is valuable to the discussion because it strives to establish macropropositional structures at the outset. Doing so ensures that this fundamental layer of their meaning can be adequately appraised. With that said, it is now time to move forward and probe what more can be conveyed about Paul's narratives if we widen our lens and introduce less abstract layers of meaning into the fold.

First, in light of the preceding section, we are now in a position to delve deeper into the meaning of Paul's narratives at the *sentence* level, focusing specifically on the *syntactical* dimension. Adopting von Siebenthal's terminology, we are now shifting our attention to the "expression side" of the text, having spent most of our time examining its "content side." Utilizing classic narratological terms, we could say that thus far we have centered our attention on the "story"—that which is narrated (cf. above, pp. 28–29). Certainly, the "narrative discourse," the manner in which the "story" is recounted (i.e., the narration), includes facets such as the relationship of the sequential presentation of events and their natural order in the narrated world. This is something we have meticulously scrutinized in our analysis of connections. Nonetheless, the dimension of narrative discourse (narration) extends significantly beyond these aspects. If multiple individuals narrate stories about the same events, their narration will vary not only in relation to the situations they choose to portray and the order in which they present them, but also in numerous details regarding *how they structure the sentences* that constitute the entirety of the text.

Much could be said about these different choices that narrators can make during their acts of narration. It is important to note that what follows is grounded in a detailed analysis of the expression side of Pauline narratives, spanning over one hundred pages.[9] The length of this discussion is due to, among other factors, the fact that some of the grammatical parameters that need consideration are still subjects of intense debate. I will merely hint at

---

9. See Heilig, *Paulus*, chapter 6.

Chapter 3

such debates here and refer readers to the more comprehensive treatment in my German monograph.

Also, while it is often possible to make very fine distinctions regarding the surface level of narratives written in Koine Greek in general, it is pivotal to remember that this spectrum is only partially realized in Paul's letters. While his narration is indeed diversified and diverse points of the total spectrum of possibilities emerge at various places, it is not necessary for our current purpose to constantly consider the totality of these options. I therefore want to underline that while a careful consideration of the different grammatical choices in the process of narration in Koine Greek is the backdrop of my analysis of all Paul's narratives, for the purpose of this work I will not continually draw connections and point out how a specific narrative move fits into the larger picture of potential choices regarding the sentences that Paul crafts during his narration.

Having provided that background, let us now shift our focus to the expression side of Paul's narratives. Most fundamentally, we first need to identify a structure that corresponds to a proposition, which acts as the fundamental building block of the content side of the narrative text structure. What follows will describe, on the one hand, the basic options Paul had for configuring the expression level to form structures that express propositions. This will also, on the other hand, retrospectively provide you with insights into the filters that I employed when scanning the Pauline letters for miniature narratives. In other words, you might have questioned why certain verses were not included in our discussion in the previous chapter, for instance, as examples of sequential connections. The upcoming discussion will offer detailed insights into the grammatical parameters I deemed crucial for identifying propositions and, thus, potential building blocks of narratives.

Situation Type Potential

Typically, the conceptual core of a proposition is supplied by the predicate and, consequently, by a verb.[10] The lexical semantics of the verb, its "situation type potential" (German: "Aktionsartpotenzial"), should therefore be our first point of examination with respect to the expression side of the text.[11]

10. Cf. *AGG* 22f.
11. For a detailed discussion, see Heilig, *Paulus*, 263–74. I am only scratching the surface of this issue here.

The most prevalent classification among "verb constellations" (i.e., verbs with their arguments) initially differentiates between (1) states and all other situations, with only the former being positively marked for the criterion of stativity. Among the remaining situations, (2) activities are noteworthy due to their absence of telicity, that is, their lack of an inherent goal point (a feature they naturally share with states). Among telic verb constellations, one can further differentiate between those that carry some degree of durativity, termed (3) "accomplishments" (of course, they share this feature of durativity with both states and activities) and (telic) situations that are punctiliar, which are referred to as (4) "achievements."

The implications are numerous. For example, we can note that in our apple narrative ("First, the apple hung on the tree. Then it fell."), the initial sentence expresses a state. It also seems feasible to rephrase this miniature story with two consecutive states: "First, the apple hung on the tree. Then it lay on the ground." (Of course, there now exists the possibility that it reached the ground through means other than "falling.") Moreover, and quite relevant for our endeavor, we can now also see how a single verb—and thus a single sentence, without a propositional pair at the content level—might constitute a narrative by fulfilling the condition of "dealing with at least two events." After all, accomplishments and achievements are telic and thus imply some *change of state*—just as the combination of the two state verbs did.[12] For all other verb constellations (i.e., those that are *atelic*) it appears that we require a connector construction on the syntactical level—that is, two constructions of propositional value—for a story to materialize. To be sure, most often the original and/or resulting state will also be explicitly mentioned in the text, even when dealing with a telic verb. Nevertheless, given that we are dealing with very small text segments, it is crucial to emphasize that the situation type of the verb determines if a single verb can independently constitute a story.

It is also possible to establish a correlation between the distinction between "minimalistic" and more meaningful narratives (see above, p. 25) by considering the lexical semantics of the chosen verbs. However, in order to do so, a slightly different classification system is needed, one that incorporates the criterion of agentivity. When we utilize an "action verb," which involves an agent, such as "to cling" in our example, it greatly enhances the

---

12. For more differentiation, see Heilig, *Paulus*, 275–76.

Chapter 3

level of eventfulness in the narrative, as it automatically anthropomorphizes the apple.[13]

Finally, it is worth noting that languages also have a conventionalized way of conceptualizing real-world events. For instance, the sentences "The ship moved" and "The ship was in motion" convey the same situation. In most cases, both sentences would be acceptable to native speakers. However, the latter construction is a less conventional—and therefore more significant—choice for describing this real-world event, as it "freezes the motion" for the readers.[14] In this way, these lexical choices can modulate the narrative *distance* or the *pace* of narration.

Voice

One parameter that the narrator can manipulate to influence the conceptualization of a situation, beyond the choice of lexeme, is *voice*.[15] It is important to recognize that for a narrative to be constituted as such, the verb form on the expression side of the text underlying the proposition does not necessarily have to be in the active voice.

When interpreting Pauline narratives, it is crucial to consider the peculiarities of the Greek voice system, which differs significantly from English, where the passive voice is simply derived from the active voice. In Koine Greek, on the other hand, active and middle forms coexist without being reducible to one another. Therefore, it is worth noting that forms with -(θ)η-, typically referred to as the "aorist passive," are actually middle forms alongside those with (-σ-). They cover a certain spectrum of the semantics of the middle voice.[16] The "passive" meaning is *part* of that—and forms without a passive meaning should, thus, not be mistakenly

---

13. However, action verbs do not seem to be necessary for a story to reach that status. See Heilig, *Paulus*, 274.

14. Carlota S. Smith, *The Parameter of Aspect*, 2nd ed., Studies in Linguistics and Philosophy 43 (Dordrecht: Kluwer Academic, 1997), 7. Cf. Heilig, *Paulus*, 276–78.

15. On what follows, see Heilig, *Paulus*, 368–70. The discussion is largely based on Rachel Aubrey, "Motivated Categories, Middle Voice, and Passive Morphology," in *The Greek Verb Revisited: A Fresh Approach for Biblical Exegesis*, ed. Steven E. Runge and Christopher J. Fresch (Bellingham, WA: Lexham, 2016), 563–625.

16. On the possibility of a "tolerative passive" as part of that semantic spectrum and on the potential implications for the quest for narratives, cf. above, p. 100, in relation to Rom 1:20.

categorized as "passive forms without passive meaning," as commonly described.

The distinction between middle verbs and active verbs reveals fundamental differences in how situations are conceptualized. First, in middle verbs the energy involved in the action remains within the same entity without transferring energy from one entity to another. Second, this results in a narrowing of focus from two entities to just one (specifically, the endpoint of the energy). Finally, this shift in focus directs attention to that particular entity.

When analyzing narratives in Koine Greek, it is often fruitful to inquire why a narrator chose a specific conceptualization of a situation that arises from the middle voice. In other words, it is important to explore why they opt to limit the focus in this way. Since focalization has to do with the regulation of information, such an exclusion of the agent might at times be indicative of a vantage point from which only a limited perspective on the unfolding events is possible and, thus, of internal focalization.

The reverse, the choice of the active voice, can also sometimes be of significance. Note, for instance, that in 1 Cor 2:8, Paul describes Jesus's crucifixion using the active voice (τὸν κύριον τῆς δόξης ἐσταύρωσαν) rather than choosing the more anonymous alternative, which would have been "safer." By doing so, Paul creates a confrontational counternarrative that explicitly involves the agents of crucifixion, the Romans.[17]

Aspect and Tense

Taking a detailed look at grammatical *aspect* and (in combination with the indicative mood) the *tenses* in Koine Greek would be highly valuable for our analysis.[18] However, due to space limitations, I will only mention the most significant implications for our study, focusing solely on Paul.

We can organize this overview based on the various *types of narration*

---

17. Cf. Christoph Heilig, *Hidden Criticism? The Methodology and Plausibility of the Search for a Counter-Imperial Subtext in Paul*, 2nd ed. (Minneapolis: Fortress, 2017), 127–29; and Christoph Heilig, *The Apostle and the Empire: Paul's Implicit and Explicit Criticism of Rome* (Grand Rapids: Eerdmans, 2022), 37–39. On the Roman nature of crucifixion and Pauline counternarratives to Roman ideology, cf. Christoph Heilig, "Counter-Narratives in Galatians," in *Scripture, Texts, and Tracings in Galatians and 1 Thessalonians*, ed. A. Andrew Das and B. J. Oropeza (Lanham, MD: Lexington, 2023), 171–90.

18. On aspect, see Heilig, *Paulus*, 278–305. On tenses, see Heilig, *Paulus*, 305–68.

Chapter 3

(as discussed above, pp. 34–36), which involve different relationships between the temporal standpoint of the speaker and the situations they are describing.

In the *subsequent* narration type (a), the choice often lies between the indicative aorist and the imperfect.[19] However, it is important to note that this "choice" is not always completely unrestricted. For instance, the indicative aorist, due to its perfective aspectual nature and, thus, its focus on endpoints, typically transforms state situations into telic situation types, also known as the "ingressive aorist." By contrast, especially when dealing with activities, we do encounter straightforward aspectual contrast.[20] In other words, both verbs express the same situation, with identical truth conditions in both cases, but there is a difference in conceptualization. The imperfect offers a close-up view that can create a sense of *vividness* and serve as an important *signal of focalization*.[21] It may fulfill this function by suggesting that a character that is closely involved in the events of the narrated world is acting as the focalizer, offering us perceptual access to the unfolding scene through their perspective.

In the case of (b) the *simultaneous* narration type, the indicative present does not have a direct aspectual counterpart in the perfective aspect.[22] Hence, for the most part, the narrator of a simultaneous narrative does not have much aspectual choice between imperfective and perfective aspect. This choice only arises in specific contexts, such as when discussing "general truths" (although their relevance to narratives is questionable anyway) or when employing the "epistolary aorist."[23]

It is worth noting that Greek often uses the indicative present in cases

---

19. The historical present seems to be an interesting option only in Gal 2:14 (Heilig, *Paulus*, 316–19); the categories of the "historical" and the "aoristic" perfect are both not without problems.

20. The aorist can also "summarize" series of individual acts. But note that achievements in the imperfect will automatically be reinterpreted as a multitude of events (because the imperfective aspect requires an internal perspective on the event, which is not possible if it is very short). By contrast, the aorist indicative could also focus on the individual occasion, which is why there is often adverbial specification in the case of the aorist indicative.

21. There is also a tendency for propositions of lesser communicative weight in a connection to appear in the imperfect. But that is just a natural secondary phenomenon of the aspect, which lends itself to being used for situations that are ongoing in relation to, e.g., the event that occurs in a corresponding main clause. Cf. Heilig, *Paulus*, 332–42.

22. Heilig, *Paulus*, 342–48.

23. Heilig, *Paulus*, 348–59.

where English would prefer the present perfect tense (e.g., 2 Cor 12:19: Πάλαι δοκεῖτε ὅτι ὑμῖν ἀπολογούμεθα ... = "For a long time, you *have been* thinking..."). Thus, the choice of the imperfect instead of the more natural indicative present can be significant. Note, however, that this does not constitute a choice of aspectual nuance but rather a choice of narration type! It may indicate that the narrator intentionally overlooks the ongoing truth of the statement, perhaps to create a signal of focalization, namely, by suggesting that a character in the narrated past contributes the perspective that is used to portray the event in question.

That being said, there is also a choice between tenses *within* the simultaneous narration type, specifically between the indicative present and indicative perfect.[24] However, to discuss the same events *different verbs* must be used.[25] For instance, in the longer ending of Mark, Jesus "lives" (Mark 16:11: ζῇ). This is akin to him "having been raised (with the result that he now lives)" (cf. the resultative participle ἐγηγερμένον in Mark 16:14). Paul too employs the resultative aspect several times in 1 Cor 15 in the indicative (ἐγήγερται). It is important to note that when he uses the *same* verb in the indicative aorist in Rom 6:4 (ἠγέρθη), this decision, by contrast, constitutes the choice of a different narration type, namely, subsequent narration (cf. also Mark 16:6).

Regarding (c) the *interpolated* narration type, we can anticipate a pattern of frequent shifts between past and present tenses, and even some confusion with regard to reference. I put forward that a unique use of the perfect indicative especially in 2 Corinthians may be explained in this way. The perfect forms in 1:9, 2:13, 7:5, 11:25, and 12:9 have typically been interpreted as replacing a standard aorist verb. This interpretation, however, is problematic due to debatable assumptions about the timeframe when such overlap between these two tenses developed.[26]

Alternatively, these instances have occasionally been characterized as "historical perfects" analogous to the historical present.[27] Notably, Robertson points out in reference to 2 Cor 1:9 that the experience was still present to Paul at the time of writing as "a dreadful memory."[28] In other words, the

24. Heilig, *Paulus*, 361–63.
25. It is only in the case of state verbs that there is no difference in situation time. Rather, we encounter an intensification of the situation.
26. Cf. Heilig, *Paulus*, 319–20.
27. For a discussion that also offers details on potential problems of this categorization, see Heilig, *Paulus*, 320–24.
28. Archibald T. Robertson, *A Grammar of the Greek New Testament in the Light of Historical Research*, 3rd ed. (London: Hodder & Stoughton, 1919), 896.

Chapter 3

memory is so potent that despite the rescue, the feelings remain tangible in some way. Therefore, it seems worthwhile to me to at least consider further exploration of the possibility that we may not see a shift of the "deictic center" into the experienced past (as would be the case with a "historical perfect"), but we might actually be dealing with the standard meaning of the perfect indicative.

This would therefore represent a notable shift in narration type, interweaving simultaneous into subsequent narration, as is typical for the composite type, interpolated narration.[29] On the one hand, the situation is in the past and has culminated there, so Paul uses the indicative aorist in verses 8 and 10. However, because he is still emotionally engaged in the situation, as if it were ongoing, he selects the indicative perfect in verse 9.[30]

Mood

Discussing "tenses" in Greek presupposes we are dealing with the indicative—setting aside for a moment the future verb forms since we have excluded "predictive narration" from the realm of proper narration. But what about the other *moods*?[31] Genette is quite definitive on this subject in his masterful work on narratives, disregarding all nonindicative verb forms:

> Since the function of narrative is not to give an order, express a wish, state a condition, etc., but simply to tell a story and therefore to "report" facts (real or fictive), its one mood, or at least its characteristic mood, strictly speaking can be only the indicative—and at that point we have said everything there is to say on this subject, unless we stretch the linguistic metaphor a little more than is fitting.[32]

---

29. For details, see Heilig, *Paulus*, 363–68.
30. If, in fact, the situation of being under this "sentence of death" is indeed over. I cautiously questioned this universally held assumption. This line of reasoning is now considered in greater detail by Jonathan B. Ensor, *Paul and the Corinthians: Leadership, Ordeals, and the Politics of Displacement*, LNTS 652 (London: Bloomsbury, 2022), 176–80.
31. For details, see Heilig, *Paulus*, 371–75.
32. Gérard Genette, *Narrative Discourse: An Essay in Method*, trans. Jane E. Lewin (Ithaca: Cornell University Press, 1980), 167. He admits that there are "differences between degrees of affirmation" and connects that with "modal variations," but he obviously has a very limited phenomenon in mind. This is demonstrated by the continuation: "... be they the infinitive and subjunctive of indirect discourse in Latin, or, in French, the con-

Since our aim is to identify indisputable instances of narratives in Paul, we generally adhere to this rather rigorous requirement. As such, we will not regard the situations expressed by verb forms in the subjunctive, imperative, and optative as representations of "events" in the sense of our definition, because they are merely potential events (cf. above, p. 23).

However, there are a few exceptions of the subjunctive in subordinate clauses, where Genette's dismissal of nonindicative verb forms appears unjustified. For in these instances, the depiction of the situation's relation to reality appears to be equivalent to alternative indicative verb forms. This includes some temporal clauses (e.g., ἄχρις οὗ ἔλθῃ in Gal 3:19; cf. above, p. 75), potentially the consecutive clause in Gal 5:17, and the highly debatable thesis, resulting in a radically different interpretation, that the ἵνα clause in Rom 5:20 is causal (and not telic).[33]

Clause Types

Take note that this decision regarding moods—to consider primarily indicative verb forms—also affects the clause types that might qualify as representations of "events" in the sense that we are investigating. As already indicated, the following question, command, and assertion all share the same propositional content: "Does the apple hang on the tree?"; "Let the apple hang on the tree!"; and "The apple hangs on the tree." Our decision about the indicative mood as a (generally applicable) requirement for narrative clauses dictates that we only accept the last sentence as contributing (potentially, as part of a connectoral construction) to a narrative. Thus, it seems logical that we will not consider *desiderative* clauses in our current analysis of Paul's letters.

Moreover, in Greek there is no "interrogative mood" for *interrogative* clauses, and we likewise exclude these clauses from our analysis—despite them being in the indicative mood—because they typically do not affirm that something indeed occurred. For the same reason, we will exclude *negated* declarative sentences. This implies that in seeking narratives in Paul, we cannot automatically consider every declarative clause as asserting that something in the actual or narrated world indeed occurred or is occurring. As a general rule, we can conclude that if we come across a clause in Paul's

---

ditional that indicates information not confirmed." On actual differences in "degrees of affirmation," see the discussion on "disnarration" in chapter 4 (pp. 208–39).

33. On these issues, see Heilig, *Paulus*, 372–74.

Chapter 3

letters and are pondering whether it might express a situation that could count as a narrative event, we need only consider it if it is an *affirmative, declarative clause*.

However, it is worth noting (as has already been suggested above, p. 151) that clause types only correlate loosely with communicative functions, which mildly complicates matters. We might, in particular, *overlook* phenomena that closely resemble affirmative declarative clauses.[34] For instance, some rhetorical questions actually perform the communicative function (the "illocutionary role," as it is called in speech act theory) of asserting something.[35] In the discussion thus far, I have disregarded these exceptions. At the worst, this rather strict approach might result in false negatives, potentially making the task of proving that there are abundant narratives in Paul's letters more challenging, rendering the success of this endeavor that I hope is evident even more meaningful.

The Pragmatics of Paul's Stories

So much on clauses. As seen with respect to clause types, explicating the definition of narrativity at a grammatical level is associated with difficulties in certain areas. Now, we venture into even trickier territory. Bear in mind that in Koine Greek dependent clauses can frequently be replaced by *infinitive or participle phrases*.[36] We must therefore consider their role as well.[37] While these nonfinite, or "nominal," verb forms undoubtedly express situations, they do so without encoding mood or temporality (outside of the future). Hence, unlike indicative verb forms—and the clauses they create—these nonfinite verb forms *cannot narrate in isolation*.[38] This observation presents a conundrum. Although these nominal verb forms lack parameters

---

34. Note that in speech act theory "declarations" are illocutionary acts that affect a change of reality, such as pronouncing someone husband and wife. We follow here the terminology of *AGG* 266.

35. Cf. *CGCG* 38.2 for an example.

36. *AGG* 270f.

37. For what follows see Heilig, *Paulus*, 376–86.

38. There are some cases in Paul where a participle occurs without any obvious syntactical subordination, thus being used like a finite verb form. Cf. 2 Cor 7:5: "For when we came into Macedonia, our flesh had no rest, but *we were troubled* in every way" (Καὶ γὰρ ἐλθόντων ἡμῶν εἰς Μακεδονίαν οὐδεμίαν ἔσχηκεν ἄνεσιν ἡ σὰρξ ἡμῶν ἀλλ᾽ ἐν παντὶ θλιβόμενοι).

of grammatical meaning seemingly vital to narrativity, they repeatedly surface in contexts where they clearly designate actual occurrences, the reality of which is beyond question. How should we navigate such a perplexing situation in our attempt to comprehend "narratives" at a grammatical level? This dilemma naturally leads us to the issue of the pragmatics of Paul's stories.

Pragmatic Relief of the Expression Side of the Text

In order to address the issue that nonfinite verb forms do not, by means of the grammatical information they encode, specify the occurrence of events, yet frequently appear in texts universally considered as narratives, I propose a distinction between two styles of narration going forward. For "contextually unaffected" narrative, we need to adhere to very strict syntactic requirements. This means only considering those connects that grammatically communicate the defining features of narrative events, thereby excluding all nonindicative verb forms.

Simultaneously, we must acknowledge that nominal verb forms—even verbal nouns—are often employed to refer to events whose occurrence is beyond question *in their specific contexts*. This is valid, for example, in many instances of purpose-oriented clauses in the subjunctive, where the audience can assume the goal has been achieved, or in temporal relationships with infinitive constructs, where the event at stake is understood to have already taken place. In some constellations, nonfinite verb forms can even express the factuality of a situation in the intratextual context, that is, in combination with the construction on which they are dependent. This is true for adverbial participles whose modality depends on the modality of the governing verb.[39]

In other words, it would not be acceptable for a narrator to deny an event that they brought into the story through a participle dependent on a verb in an affirmative declarative sentence. For example, the Corinthians would have objected if Paul had continued the narrative in 2 Cor 2:13, "Having bid them goodbye [note the participle ἀποταξάμενος], I journeyed [note the indicative ἐξῆλθον] to Macedonia," by subsequently denying the initial situation, "But I did not actually bid them goodbye" (cf. above, p. 68). Therefore, we can conclude that contextual factors play a part in enabling nonfinite verb

---

39. Cf. *CGCG* 52.6 and 52.8.

Chapter 3

forms to create narrative connections, too, if these exhibit the same propositional structure as the finite equivalents of these connectors.

In line with this (see figure 7), we could recast the example stories from Köppe and Kindt in several ways, with only the initial one meeting the added condition of "contextually unaffected" narration.

Figure 7. Different ways of expressing narrative events without finite verb forms

Indicative default case	First, the apple hung on the tree. Then it fell.	While the police were still searching for him, Peter fled the country.
With nominalized infinitive	After the hanging on the tree, the apple fell.	During the ongoing police search, Peter fled the country.
With participle phrase[40]	Having been hanging on the tree, the apple fell.	Still sought by the police, Peter fled the country.
With action noun	Before its fall, the apple was hanging on the tree.	During the still ongoing police search, Peter fled the country.

In a way, we can liken the proposal of a contextually unaffected, grammatically comprehensive version of narration as a separate category to the effort by Köppe and Kindt to present a stricter definition of more "meaningful" narratives, in addition to their minimalist definition of all kinds of narratives (cf. above, p. 25). While they incorporate additional *pragmatic* criteria, this definition imposes an extra *syntactical* requirement.

The key difference is that in this instance we indeed restrict the texts deemed as "stories." As discussed earlier, the issue with Köppe and Kindt's approach is that while some miniature narratives may indeed also meet the

---

40. Note that Tilmann Köppe and Tom Kindt, *Erzähltheorie: Eine Einführung*, Reclams Universal-Bibliothek 17683 (Stuttgart: Reclam, 2014), 65, use this option of a nonfinite verb form in their attempt to link the events of the narrative to the mental inner life of the apple: ". . . von seinen Kräften verlassen . . ."

more demanding definition, most complex stories typically contain sections that are not miniature narratives. Hence, fulfilling the "minimalistic" definition is not a necessary condition for being a more substantial narrative—and being a pragmatically more elaborate narrative is likewise not a sufficient condition for there being a story that meets the ostensibly "minimalistic" definition. It is thus more appropriate to perceive the two definitions by Köppe and Kindt as merely intersecting—there are "miniature narratives" that do not qualify as "elaborate narratives" and vice versa. This is parallel to the relationship between elaborate narratives on the one hand and narrative works on the other hand, such as novels. In contrast, in the case of our syntactically stricter definition of contextually unaffected narration, the scenario is different. Every case that meets these stringent conditions will also fulfill the requirement that the resulting text is purely composed of temporally and semantically connected propositions. Hence, if something is a product of contextually unaffected narration, it automatically follows that it is also a "miniature narrative." Simultaneously, it is clear that not all miniature stories adhere to this grammatically explicit pattern. This holds true, to an even greater degree, for the "more meaningful" narratives. It could perhaps be feasible to expand the length of a "miniature" story even to that of a typical novel (e.g., by using only affirmative declarative sentences), but it is likely to result in a rather monotonous piece of literary work or, if not, it would indeed be a truly remarkable accomplishment!

Why does narration often, if not almost always, diverge from the strict pattern in practice? I would contend that it is for the same reason that we frequently encounter the more elaborate, meaningful narrative pattern that exceeds the basic structural requirements of miniature narratives. To put it plainly: just as pragmatic necessities sometimes demand *better* stories, pragmatic factors often call for a *syntactically leaner* pattern of narration. Similar to how influencing (or entertaining, etc.) people with *poor* stories is not a simple task, achieving the desired communicative impact can be more challenging if processing the narrative demands *significant effort* from the audience.

Syntactically streamlining a narrative not only reduces the workload for the storyteller but also improves the chances of the story being well received by the audience, who have limited time and attention resources. And nonfinite verb forms are an effective tool for streamlining narratives.[41] Like all

---

41. See Randall Buth, "Participles as a Pragmatic Choice: Where Semantics Meets Pragmatics," in Runge and Fresch, *Greek Verb Revisited*, 273–306. Cf. Heilig, *Paulus*, 382–83.

Chapter 3

human activities, communication requires energy, and if situations allow for the delivery of a specific message with less effort, humans tend to take advantage of these circumstances—constantly working to find the right balance, where the narration is not yet so concise that it might rebound into a communication failure. This perspective is perfectly articulated by text linguists Gansel and Jürgens: "Both oral and written text production and reception are largely determined by pragmatic factors. This results in *pragmatic considerations relieving the demands on syntax.* The aim of text production is not only to generate grammatically well-formed and complete sentences; it can also count on the fact that constituents and sentences with fewer cohesive means can be comprehended when they are contextually embedded."[42]

Put differently, one could argue that if pragmatic factors have no influence, a narrator would be compelled to steer clear of nominal verb forms. However, it is important to note that this does *not* imply that such syntactically rigid narration is in any way "prototypical." Quite the contrary, such narration is actually a rarity. This is because narration always presupposes a certain degree of extratextual familiarity between the author and the recipients (even if it is only through the medium of conventionalized genres), leading to some form of *pragmatic alleviation* of syntax as the norm.

As such, it should come as no surprise that we witness Paul diverge from the strict narrative pattern continually. It stands to reason that his stories are fundamentally shaped by the contexts of utterance in which they emerged. The actual question, then, becomes *which specific pragmatic factors* permitted such a syntactically lighter structuring of his narratives. To delve deeper into this matter, we now shift our attention to the complex topic of the *function* of texts.

Text Function

Analyzing the propositional structure of texts can greatly aid in interpreting their meaning in an intersubjectively comprehensible and contestable

---

42. Christina Gansel and Frank Jürgens, *Textlinguistik und Textgrammatik*, 3rd ed., Uni-Taschenbücher 3265 (Göttingen: Vandenhoeck & Ruprecht, 2009), 174. Italics added. German original: "Mündliche und schriftliche Textproduktion und -rezeption sind in starkem Maße durch pragmatische Faktoren determiniert. Dies hat zur Folge, dass Pragmatisches die Anforderungen an die Syntax entlastet. Die Textproduktion hat nicht nur grammatisch wohlgeformte und vollständige Sätze zum Ziel, sondern kann darauf bauen, dass auch Konstituenten und Sätze mit weniger kohäsiven Mitteln verstanden werden, wenn diese situativ eingebettet sind."

manner. Given the extent to which exegetical literature often wrestles with this very task, we should by no means devalue the utility of propositional analysis. However, as we have established in this chapter, texts' meanings extend beyond this relatively abstract skeleton. On the grammatical level, these texts present precise configurations that contribute information surpassing the generalized roles that connectors assign to individual propositions. These choices, in turn, mirror specific circumstances—the particular contexts of utterance in which a story originates. Notably, narratives are shaped by the relationship between the speaker or writer and the addressees. This introduces the *textual function*—the communicative intention of the text's author.[43]

As previously mentioned, propositions can occur with a pragmatic dimension (assuming that they also, more basically, display epistemic mode). Utterances are not confined to individual sentences but can also encompass more complex texts. Hence, it is possible to refer to entire texts as "macro-illocutions," that is, to determine a prevailing function of the text within its context of utterance.

One approach to identifying the overarching text function is by diligently examining the individual illocutions that constitute the utterance as a whole. For instance, the title "Patient Information Leaflet" might initially suggest that we are dealing with a text primarily intended to inform. However, upon analysis, it becomes clear that such a text consists of directive speech acts supported by assertions.[44] Texts with such a title constitute a text type that has a warning character, and they are thus decisively directive.

Specifically for narrative texts, we can also consider how the act of narration is incorporated into the broader discourse context, such as the complete letter. We will turn to these considerations shortly. However, at this juncture, it is important that we first elaborate on the various possible text functions.

Text linguists usually orient their classification of text functions around illocutions. For example, Heinrich von Siebenthal differentiates between the following six options:[45]

1. Information
2. Appeal
3. Commitment

---

43. For everything that follows, cf. the detailed discussion in Heilig, *Paulus*, chapter 8, section 4.
44. Gansel and Jürgens, *Textlinguistik*, 84.
45. *AGG* 302.

Chapter 3

4. Contact
5. Declaration
6. Poetry/Entertainment

In the following analysis, I will presume the analysis by Wolfgang Motsch, which as its point of departure addresses the question of what *kind of change in the recipients' consciousness* the text's creator intends.[46] Whether or not this communicative intent is successful is an entirely separate issue. "Effective function" and "text function"—or perlocution and illocution in the parlance of speech act theory—are distinct concepts.[47]

At the base level, Motsch suggests, a text can be crafted with the intention either to alter (1) the recipients' *volition* related to something or (2) their *beliefs* held on this matter. In the first case, the speaker gives a *direction*. In the second case, we can distinguish between three different types of informing acts. An informative text can be (a) an *assertion*, (b) a *stipulation*, or (c) an *evaluation*. Texts can exhibit a dominant function and contain text parts with various functions that bolster the overarching communicative objective.[48]

In my view, the expression side of Paul's narratives can be satisfactorily explained at many junctures when analyzed from this perspective. As we will discuss in more detail in what follows, Paul's letters are, in general terms, characterized by a directive communicative intent. To accomplish this communicative goal, Paul utilizes narratives, among other things. However, these are *not* primarily informing-assertive but mostly meant to prompt reevaluations. In fact, I believe that the prevalent view that "Paul does not tell stories" is intrinsically connected to the fact that Paul seldom merely informs the recipients of his letters about the occurrence of certain events. It is not his aim "to convey knowledge," to borrow the phrase that Heinrich von Siebenthal uses to characterize the text function "information."[49]

---

46. Wolfgang Motsch, "Handlungsstrukturen von Texten," in *Text- und Gesprächslinguistik / Linguistics of Text and Conversation*, ed. Gerd Antos, Klaus Bringer, Wolfgang Heinemann, and Sven F. Sager, Handbücher zur Sprach und Kommunikationswissenschaft / Handbooks of Linguistics and Communication Science 16 (Berlin: de Gruyter, 2000–2001), 1:414–21. Followed by Gansel and Jürgens, *Textlinguistik*, 83.
47. Cf. Heilig, *Paulus*, 556, on "Bewirkungsfunktion," following Gansel and Jürgens, *Textlinguistik*, 82–83.
48. Correctly recognized by *AGG* 302h.
49. *AGG* 302b.

The Supposed Incompatibility of Letters and Exhortation with Stories

In secondary literature that challenges the narrative approach to Paul, the assumption that the categories of "narrative" and "exhortation" are mutually exclusive is frequently encountered. Alongside the presupposition that "letter" and "narrative" are in conflict with each other, this viewpoint often precludes any constructive evaluation of the narrative approach from the outset. Given the foundational nature of these assumptions, it would be prudent to take a moment here and address this broader issue of how the categories of narrativity, letter writing, and exhortation actually interrelate.[50]

First, let us examine why some people think that letters and narratives are incompatible. To comprehend the perceived dichotomy between these categories, it is necessary to identify the counterparts associated with both. In New Testament scholarship, the category of "letters" is often posited as a genre alongside others, including "gospels." Because within the canon gospels and letters seem to form distinct corpuses, and because the former category consists of clearly narrative works, there arises an assumption that the latter must be somewhat "nonnarrative."[51] This dichotomy is sometimes explicitly invoked to explain why Paul ostensibly "does not tell stories"—after all, he "writes letters."[52]

This leads us directly to the presumed incompatibility of narrative and exhortation. Occasionally, the notion of a divide between "letters" and "narrativity" is reinforced by highlighting that Paul's letters serve a specific "purpose," namely, to encourage their readers to *act* in a certain way. Typically, "argumentation" is associated with a directive intention and is then contrasted with "narration," a subject for which the issue of communicative intent is, interestingly, far less frequently addressed. To compound matters, this bifurcation between supposedly argumentative-directive letters and the (informing?) narrative Gospels manifests itself in a methodological partitioning: while narratology (or "narrative analysis") is said to be the right tool for analyzing the Gospels, the letters in the New Testament are left to be interpreted through the lens of "rhetorical criticism." And if someone, by chance,

---

50. For everything that follows, cf. the much more detailed discussion in Heilig, *Paulus*, chapter 1, section 3.

51. For a detailed discussion, cf. Heilig, *Paulus*, chapter 1, section 2.

52. Cf., e.g., Eric Kun Chun Wong, *Evangelien im Dialog mit Paulus: Eine intertextuelle Studie zu den Synoptikern*, SUNT 89 (Göttingen: Vandenhoeck & Ruprecht, 2012), 44: "Lukas erzählt, Paulus schreibt Briefe" (i.e., "Luke narrates, Paul writes letters").

Chapter 3

grows skeptical about this entire system, it can always be pointed out that potential narrative portions in Paul's letters are covered within the framework of rhetorical criticism due to this paradigm also focusing on *narrationes*.

Hence, the perceived indissoluble bond between the elements of a letter, argument, and exhortation excludes the possibility of considering that Paul might indeed recount evaluative and directive stories in his letters. From a text-linguistic standpoint, this evaluation—both in its entirety and in each of its details—is seriously flawed.

Text Sorts

The problems begin with the fact that the literary category of 'genre' has quite limited applicability in the context of this discussion. Not only do most New Testament scholars often disregard how the term 'genre' is used in (current) literary studies, but they also regularly overlook the fundamental fact that this concept is only relevant when New Testament texts are discussed *as literature*, that is, as pieces of art. While a solid argument can be made for such a perspective (see above, p. 45, on the interpretation of literature), this is certainly not the exclusive approach for examining biblical writings. Indeed, Paul's letters can—and, I believe, should—be analyzed as *artifacts of communication within their historical context*. The same consideration also applies to the Gospels, which in their unique ways contribute to the social system that we now call "early Christianity." In fact, many who discuss 'genre' in relation to these texts are, despite the invoked terminology, primarily concerned with the role of these texts within their original social contexts. In that case, however, the appropriate term would be "text sort," and, much more importantly, the corresponding theoretical framework should be text linguistics, not literary studies!

Text sorts play distinct roles within certain "areas of communication," such as early Christianity. I call the role that each text sort plays for the respective area of communication the "systemic function" (German: "Bereichsfunktion").[53] Individual text specimens can be attributed to text sorts, and these text sorts, in turn, can be organized in a hierarchical structure. On the highest level lies the "text class" of "early Christian texts." At a level below this, all the text sorts pertaining to this class can be divided into different "orders." As an example, one such order could be "texts associated with

---

53. Gansel and Jürgens, *Textlinguistik*, 81, call it the "Bereichsfunktion."

apostolic proclamation." These associated texts can undergo further subdivision into various "text families," depending on fundamental distinctions in systemic function. For instance, we could differentiate between a text family that aids in establishing or extending the system and another text family that aims at maintaining it.

Though this is a quick overview, I believe it provides a robust framework for categorizing Paul's letters. I propose that within the latter family of texts—early Christian texts that aim at maintaining the social system—we could distinguish a text sort identified as "apostolic letter," which is attested primarily through the canonical letters of the apostle Paul. The differentiation between letters to individuals and letters to congregations might then be considered as variations of the basic pattern of this text sort, termed "text sort variants."

Text Types

It is important to note that in this entire hierarchical system, "Paul's letters" do not emerge as a standalone text sort (let alone a "genre"). In fact, "letters" *in general* have no place in this system. For a piece of writing to be classified as a letter, it merely indicates something about the *medium* of the text and how it is delivered to the recipient. I am not discrediting the validity of classifying texts based on this criterion, but rather pointing out that by utilizing this classifying method we are *not creating a text sort*. Instead, the grouping that emerges should be deemed a "text type," that is to say, a cohort of texts that cuts *horizontally* across our hierarchical system of text sorts and aligns all text sorts—potentially even those belonging to text classes that might be far removed from each other—that fulfill this single criterion according to which we filter all the available text sorts.

Please note that "narrativity" is an entirely separate parameter. From a text-linguistic perspective, narration is one of several ways in which a theme (what is said about a topic in a text; cf. chapter 1) gets developed in a text—the other methods being description, explication, and argumentation. Therefore, it is one of the *core strategies for translating thoughts into text*, a unique approach of "textualization" or "text production" if you will. It is indeed feasible to establish a separate typology of text sorts according to the dominant text production strategy that brought them forth. This process would certainly distance the canonical Gospels from Pauline letters despite their proximity in the hierarchical system. Medium and textualization strat-

Chapter 3

egy are, thus, simply two distinct features of text sorts that allow for *alternative* typologies of them.

If anything, we will detect a *positive correlation* between the "letter text type" and the "narrative text type." After all, many letter text sorts are indeed predominantly narrative. Those that do not primarily employ a narrative textualization strategy are actually the exceptions. An instance of this would be the text sort "love letter" (taking its place in the "interaction system" of love). Here, we find a concentration on internal emotions rather than external events, resulting in a descriptive textualization strategy. Against this backdrop, we can infer that if we were to define any expectations from the fact that Paul's texts are classified as belonging to the text type "letter," it would be the assumption that his writings would most likely be *dominated* by narration. So, what truly requires explanation is not the idea that there might be narratives in Paul's letters, but rather the contrary claim that there allegedly are not any. What is categorically impossible, in any case, is to jump to the conclusion that Paul's letters cannot be (not even contain!) narrative "because they are letters."

Text Function and Text Production Strategy

The same applies when dismissing a narratological approach to Paul's letters based on the premise that the apostle wants to "convince" his audience or "encourage" a specific behavior, which is often implicitly associated with the supposition that only argumentation could serve these purposes. Note that *text function* is yet another facet based on which text types can be constructed.

Klaus Berger's influential work on classifying the "genres" of the New Testament essentially culminates in a typology grounded on the intended communication purpose.[54] Although Berger's approach is not flawless, it reveals that when we consider the intended effect as the foundational criterion for creating different text types, we indeed find "argumentation" in service of a variety of text functions. In simpler terms, while some scholars contend that argumentation is the unique feature of the "genre" of letters and that therefore there is a considerable difference between letters and gospels regarding their function, Berger's perspective on the classification of New

---

54. See, e.g., Klaus Berger, *Formen und Gattungen im Neuen Testament*, UniTaschenbücher 2532 (Tübingen: Francke, 2005). On this, cf. Heilig, *Paulus*, chapter 1, section 3.5.4.

Testament texts highlights that different textualization strategies can work toward the same communicative goals.[55]

To be sure, there is a significant overlap between text sorts that aim to encourage certain behavior and those which extensively utilize the text production strategy of argumentation, but that does not negate the existence of purely narrative or descriptive texts in this text type. Furthermore, in many of these predominantly argumentative directive text sorts, narrative text sections play a critical role in supporting the communicative function.[56]

Contrast this depiction of how text functions, text production strategies, and mediums interact with each other as distinct parameters of text sorts with the tangled critique that Lee presents against Richard B. Hays's approach:

> The obvious fact is that the primary purpose of Paul in writing his letters is not to retell the so-called fundamental narrative. If his intention were

---

55. Michal Beth Dinkler, "New Testament Rhetorical Narratology: An Invitation Toward Integration," *BibInt* 24 (2016): 203–28, has made a similar point in arguing against the divide between "New Testament rhetoric" and "New Testament narrative." Her thesis is that narrative can be seen "as a mode of persuasion in and of itself." One of the advantages of "rhetorical narratology" is that it puts the pragmatics of the narrative text center stage and thus avoids the dichotomy between narrative and argument that is so typical of New Testament scholarship. Moreover, it prevents a structuralist analysis that at times is prone to adduce narrative aspects without explicating their significance. Still, I appreciate more classical narratological approaches that do take into account the pragmatic dimension of the text, though perhaps not as the guiding question and by also allowing for persuasion to be one among other pragmatic effects. Cf. also Michal Beth Dinkler, "Influence: On Rhetoric and Biblical Interpretation," *Brill Research Perspectives in Biblical Interpretation* 4 (2019): 1–105.

56. The only inevitable connection between text production strategy and text function lies in the fact that the different strategies I have mentioned above are indeed reserved for texts that imply some form of assertion. For further discussion on this point, see Matthias Aumüller, "Text Types," The Living Handbook of Narratology, March 6, 2014, https://www-archiv.fdm.uni-hamburg.de/lhn/node/121.html. In other words, these text production strategies do not seem to encompass the totality of texts but rather only a subset of them. It should be noted, however, that even if a narrative text serves a directive communicative function, it also necessarily (see above, p. 150) exhibits an epistemic mode. More specifically, it makes claims about the reality within the narrated world. The text production strategy—termed "text type" in Aumüller's terminology, not to be confused with our notion of 'text types'—of narration thus presupposes a specific, assertive epistemic mode at its foundation. It is on this foundation that it often becomes possible to identify an additional layer of a specific communicative function, referred to as "mode of discourse" in Aumüller's terminology (e.g., "persuasion").

Chapter 3

to reveal the fundamental narrative, he would have sent a short story such as a condensed Gospel. Rather, most of Paul's letters appear to be composed of logical structures using various rhetorical argumentative devices, such as comparison, analogy, example and so on. Even when he mentions the story of the Old Testament or Jesus, the story itself is not his main concern. Rather, the story tends to be used as a way to pursue his argumentative goal.[57]

While Lee offers some insightful points regarding Paul's use of narration, he fails to distinguish between text function ("purpose") and textualization strategy ("to retell," "argumentative devices," etc.). This significant oversight causes him to neglect the fact that he is *not* really arguing against narration (and for argumentation), but rather against an informing-assertive text function of these narratives (and for a directive one).

For instance, he refers to an "argumentative goal" in relation to Gal 4:21–31.[58] However, he actually seems to be considering the pragmatic dimension of this (narrative!) text passage, as becomes evident from his remark that Paul's "intention is not to tell the narrative itself but to convince his readers to embrace their liberation from slavery to the law."

Regrettably, such statements are abundant in biblical studies. By comparison, from a text-linguistic perspective, the task of classifying Paul's writings is quite straightforward. Rather than fixating on "genres" and creating a dichotomy between "nonnarrative letters" and "narrative Gospels," the objective should be to categorize early Christian texts into distinct text sorts that played unique roles in the social system of early Christianity.

For each of these text sorts, one can then establish the "text sort pattern" according to which these texts were produced (and which might have been modified according to circumstances).[59] An essential aspect of describing this

---

57. Jae Hyun Lee, "Richard B. Hays and a Narrative Approach to the Pauline Letters," in *Pillars in the History of Biblical Interpretation*, ed. Stanley E. Porter and Sean A. Adams, 2 vols., McMaster Biblical Studies Series 2 (Eugene, OR: Wipf & Stock, 2016), 437.

58. Lee, "Narrative Approach," 437 n. 51. My emphasis.

59. Gansel and Jürgens, *Textlinguistik*, 92–93. Cf. Heilig, *Paulus*, 22–23. Scholars have long tried to recognize a diachronic development in the "epistolary formula" that underlies the letters of the New Testament. For a recent example, see Karl Matthias Schmidt, "Ein Anklang wohnt dem Anfang inne: Die relative Datierung neutestamentlicher Pseudepigraphen im Lichte eines dynamisch veränderten Briefformulars," in *Die Datierung neutestamentlicher Pseudepigraphen: Herausforderungen und neuere Lösungsansätze*, ed. Wolfgang Grünstäudl and Karl Matthias Schmidt, WUNT 470 (Tübingen: Mohr Siebeck, 2021). It seems to me that it would be valuable to supplement such analyses with

text sort pattern is recognizing *how the various strategies of text production intertwine and how this coordination works to achieve the communication goal.*

To sum up the discussion hitherto, concerning Paul's letters we can first note that they belong to a text sort that utilizes the *medium* of letter writing. Second, I believe it is reasonable to suggest that at least the majority of these letters are characterized by a communicative intent to alter the readers' will, indicating that their *function*, at a global level, leans toward being directive. It is also quite noticeable that to achieve that goal, Paul frequently employs the *text production strategy* of argumentation in many cases.[60] Simultaneously, as our previous analysis indicates, narrative segments also seem to be a critical feature of the text production pattern underlying Paul's letter writing. It appears that Paul thought that storytelling would aid in accomplishing his communicative objectives.

Uninformative Stories

In light of this context, we can now revisit the intuitive impression that Paul "does not tell stories." It is accurate to say that Paul *almost never narrates stories with an informing-assertive intention*. At times, his stories might be aimed directly at influencing the recipients' volition. In other instances, he may have targeted the domain of their beliefs about a specific subject, but with an emphasis on altering their perspective of certain situations, triggering a *reevaluation* of particular events.[61]

This observation provides a satisfactory explanation for the "pragmatic relief" of the syntax noted above in relation to Paul's narration. If Paul's ob-

---

a text-linguistic perspective. Pseudepigraphic Pauline letters might belong to a text sort that differs markedly in terms of the pragmatic dimension from authentic letters of Paul, even if they follow the same pattern. Conversely, it might be possible to discern a diversification in a multitude of patterns within a single text sort over time. On this, cf. Heilig, *Paulus*, 27–28.

60. Cf. Moisés Mayordomo, *Argumentiert Paulus logisch? Eine Analyse vor dem Hintergrund antiker Logik*, WUNT 188 (Tübingen: Mohr Siebeck, 2005).

61. Paul is not alone in this among ancient storytellers. As Claus-Jürgen Thornton, *Der Zeuge des Zeugen: Lukas als Historiker der Paulusreisen*, WUNT 56 (Tübingen: Mohr Siebeck, 1991), 156, points out with terminology that fits our perspective perfectly, "historiography in the spirit of Thucydides aims not so much to *inform* as it does to teach us to *understand the seemingly familiar in a new light*" (italics added; original: "Geschichtsschreibung im Sinne des Thukydides will nicht so sehr informieren als vielmehr das scheinbar Vertraute neu verstehen lehren").

jective in telling a story is not to inform the recipients about certain events that transpired but rather to make them view *known* events from a different perspective, he can reference these events in his narrative in a syntactically less demanding manner.

Such syntactically light and thus pragmatically relieved narrations occur frequently in Paul's letters. To provide just one example, let us revisit our previous discussion of 1 Cor 8:11 (see above, pp. 120–21). Paul uses a modal-instrumental connection to outline a sequence of events. The weak brother is ruined (ἀπόλλυται γὰρ ὁ ἀσθενῶν) by means of the insight of the addressed person (ἐν τῇ σῇ γνώσει). Paul does not need to express these situations in an informing-assertive manner—after all, the sequence is vividly brought to life in verse 10 already. In other words, the events are known; what Paul intends now is to show the Corinthians that these familiar events can be interpreted in a certain way. Essentially, the apostle seeks to encourage a *reevaluation* of a series of events among his readers.

The reference back to the event of Christ dying for that person (ὁ ἀδελφὸς δι' ὃν Χριστὸς ἀπέθανεν) supports this perspective. Although Paul is not sharing new information here, he uses the indicative because even though the death of Christ is known as a historical event among his audience, he seeks to retell it explicitly, framed as an event that occurred in relation to one of the characters involved in the imagined scene. By introducing Christ as a narrative character and associating the other believer with him, the outcome of verse 10—the rather neutral "eating idol meat"—is framed in an entirely different way and takes on a fairly dramatic dimension. Therefore, verse 12 articulates the moral of this "almost story" explicitly: the seemingly harmless action of verse 10 is actually equivalent to "sinning against Christ" (εἰς Χριστὸν ἁμαρτάνετε)!

Of course, the intended reevaluation of a situation familiar to the Corinthians ultimately carries a clearly *directive* dimension. Paul discusses these events not to inform the Corinthians about "what is going on" but rather to open their eyes to "what this really means," thereby encouraging a change in their behavior. Nobody, so Paul's implicit argument goes, should act in a way that a story of such a sort might be told (reliably) about them. Paul relies on his readers being uncomfortable with *certain potential stories* to promote specific behavior.

In line with this, it comes as no surprise that verse 13 explicitly mentions this alternative behavior, when Paul rules out ever eating meat (οὐ μὴ φάγω κρέα εἰς τὸν αἰῶνα) if it might impact a brother or sister in Christ, leading them to stumble. This is precisely the guideline he wants the Corinthian

Stories in Context

Christians to adopt. Note, however, that even here in verse 13 we do not simply have a desiderative clause. What we find is something akin to "predictive narration" with *Paul* as the agent. Perhaps it could be argued that Paul is genuinely informing the addressees of something new here, namely, how drastically he would behave in such a situation. In any case, it is clear that he presents his own (potential) behavior to illustrate an alternative to the course of action in verse 10, which culminates in destruction for one party (verse 11) and sin toward Christ for the other (verse 12). Therefore, Paul offers a (potential) story about himself as a model for the Corinthians, enticing them to adopt behavior that allows them to tell the same story about themselves, possibly with it being especially attractive to emulate the apostle because it would allow them to then share a narrative with this authoritative figure.

In conclusion, when dealing with stories in Paul's letters, we must consider the possibility that he might not tell them in an informing-assertive manner but, rather, with an informing-evaluating or even outright directive intention. Explicit stories with these functions may diverge from what we might expect from a typical storyteller because in our everyday experiences we often encounter people who share stories about their lives to keep us up to date. In fact, our understanding might be influenced by our familiarity with the text sort pattern behind certain letter text sorts characterized by an informing-assertive profile. As a letter writer, Paul is different, but he is still a storyteller.

There is no dichotomy between the use of narration in general, or the particular use of narration in letters, and a text function that focuses on provoking reevaluations or giving directives. Hence, Lukas Bormann's observation, "Paul's letters do not offer narratives *but rather* theologically reflected notes on events," is extraordinarily illuminating, in my view.[62] If we differentiate between the text production strategy on the one hand and the text function of Paul's stories on the other, we can both acknowledge the pivotal role of narrativity in Paul's letters *and* understand how he exhibits a unique profile concerning the pragmatics of his narratives. Therefore, it seems to me that Bormann's concise characterization of Paul's references to events does not contradict the idea of viewing Paul as a storyteller. Instead,

---

62. Lukas Bormann, *Bibelkunde: Altes und Neues Testament*, 4th ed., Uni-Taschenbücher Basics (Göttingen: Vandenhoeck & Ruprecht, 2011), 248: "Die Paulusbriefe liefern keine Erzählungen, sondern theologisch reflektierte Notizen über Ereignisse."

Chapter 3

in my perspective, it accurately captures the pragmatic dimension of text parts that are indeed narrative (or quasi-narrative).

Let us also recognize two implications for this issue of "implicit" stories, which have consistently lingered in the background and occasionally surfaced as a pressing question, despite my earnest efforts to keep them at bay. First, when we do find an informing-assertive communicative function in relation to the portrayal of events in Paul's letters (as perhaps in 1 Cor 8:13; for many examples see chapter 2), it is significant that they often concern decidedly *future* situations. Thus, in Paul's case, we encounter the peculiar circumstance where the communicative intention we more readily associate with the act of narration surfaces particularly in cases that are "merely" instances of predictive narration (i.e., not narration in its traditional sense). Again, this reinforces the idea that we need to allot some space for these phenomena in our narratological analysis of Pauline literature, and we will see in chapter 4 how the notion of "implicit" stories might encapsulate that dimension.

Second, it is notable that the deviation from both the pattern of pragmatically unaffected narration and, underlying this, an informing-assertive function in Paul's narratives stems from the fact that these narratives draw on sequences of events *already familiar* to the recipients. While it is debatable whether 1 Cor 8:10 pertains to a situation bundle that has already occurred or is still completely hypothetical, after verse 10, the basic sequence can be presupposed.[63] In other instances, such as Col 1:6 (see above, pp. 100–101), it is abundantly clear that this basis is not an explicit story within the immediate literary context. Instead, it is the (presumed) shared lived experience of the author and recipients standing in the background. In both configurations,

---

63. This uncertainty of course relates to the question of whether the issue of marketplace food (1 Cor 10:21–11:1) is also in view at the beginning of this section. See Gordon D. Fee, *The First Epistle to the Corinthians*, NICNT (Grand Rapids: Eerdmans, 1987), 395–96, for a forceful argument against that position. I do not understand Wolfgang Schrage, *Der erste Brief an die Korinther*, 4 vols., EKKNT 7 (Neukirchen-Vluyn: Neukirchener, 1995), 2:262, who emphasizes that the connector characterizes the situation in view as a "possible, but not merely hypothetically constructed" case (German: "möglichen, aber nicht bloß als hypothetische konstruierten"), but at the same time he maintains that it shows "that it must have actually occurred in Corinth that Christians have participated in meals in the pagan temple district" ("daß es in Korinth tatsächlich vorgekommen sein muß, daß Christen ... an Mahlen im heidnischen Tempelbezirk teilgenommen haben"). On *private* celebrations that occurred in the context of *local temples*, which seems to me to be the most plausible backdrop for Paul's discourse, see Peter Arzt-Grabner, "Why Did Early Christ Groups Still Attend Idol Meals? Answers from Papyrus Invitations," *EC* 7 (2016): 508–29.

Stories in Context

there is an underlying implied foundation supporting the act of—syntactically light—narration. This foundation might have been a very explicit narrative at the time, but in the current communicative context it is evoked only implicitly. Explicit stories become implicit supporting structures in other places, and scrutinizing these other passages, hence, allows us to make inferences about the original explicit narratives. From their function in passages where they remain implicit, we can learn something about the meaning that they might have had all along. Therefore, to fully comprehend Paul's explicitly told stories—particularly their pragmatic dimension—it actually seems *necessary* to employ the categories of implicit narratives.

Ellipses and the Effect of Context on the Content Side of the Text

This entire conversation on text types, their functions, and production strategies was initiated by our observation that the expression side of Paul's stories indicates a disregard for a syntactically rigid pattern of narration. We have attributed such a storytelling approach to the pragmatics of these narratives and their contextual integration within a wider discourse. As a kind of epilogue to this discussion, I would like to address the phenomenon of "ellipses" in Paul's stories, which in my view can be explained analogously as an alleviation of the demands concerning the *content side* of Paul's letters.

An ellipsis refers to a narrative technique where a time period in the narrated world is "omitted" from the narration.[64] It can be understood as a sub-phenomenon of accelerated narration, one in which the overall narration is expedited by glossing over entire events. Occasionally, it is unclear whether we are dealing with an ellipsis. In 2 Cor 12:8, Paul narrates in the aorist indicative how he pleaded with the Lord three times to remove the "thorn in the flesh" (ὑπὲρ τούτου τρὶς τὸν κύριον παρεκάλεσα ἵνα ἀποστῇ ἀπ' ἐμοῦ). In verse 9, some interpret the indicative perfect in the clause καὶ εἴρηκέν μοι as having an aoristic sense (see above, p. 159) so that it might pertain to the subsequent period after Paul's prayer, best translating the phrase as "And (then) he said to me . . ." Alternatively, we might be dealing with a simple indicative perfect that, according to its typical function, characterizes the apostle's present situation. Paul would then not be recounting what transpired in the past that led him to accept the situation but would instead leap forward to how this presupposed event influences his present attitude. As

---

64. On the whole notion, cf. Heilig, *Paulus*, 463–64.

someone who "has been told" something, he now (cf. the present indicative καυχήσομαι) behaves in a certain way.

There is a way in which "elliptical narration" plays an important role with respect to fictional works that are entirely composed of letters, and this is only of limited relevance with respect to Paul's writings.[65] In said literary works, the narrator—often implicitly framing the narrative about individuals writing letters—is compelled to honor the nature of the medium. Many plot-critical events might transpire between the production of letters. For instance, it would be nonsensical for a lover to detail the prior night's events to their partner.[66] Therefore, the reader is tasked with reconstructing the actual happenings from hints within the text. One could argue that there is a discernible shift in "tone," a common indicator of developments outside of the text world, between Phil 3:1 and 3:2. This is also a factor that has led many to postulate that 2 Cor 1–9 and 10–13 were initially two separate letters. However, unlike in the case of fictional works, it is highly doubtful that the narrator—either Paul or a later compiler—intended to *communicate* (i.e., narrate) the event of, for instance, the arrival of bad news from Philippi.

Regardless, "ellipses" undeniably play a significant role in another respect in the analysis of the narratives in Paul's letters. We have already observed how pragmatic elements can simplify the syntactical level of Paul's narration. But what is crucial to note is that this influence can even extend to what is narrated, that is, to the content level of the text. Just as an event referred to by a nominal verb form can be inferred from the context to be situated in the past and to be actual, not just potential, similarly the occurrence of the event as a whole can be presupposed by a narrator in certain situations.

This can occur on the basis that the narrator presupposes relevant *world knowledge* that aids them in streamlining the narrative by refraining from explicitly noting events that the audience can infer on their own. We particularly find this in purpose-oriented connections.[67] If the means seems suitable for achieving the specified goal, it is, in many contexts, more common than not for the success to be left untold.[68] To be sure, sometimes narrators intentionally put readers in the position where they must decide whether

---

65. Janet Gurkin Altman, *Epistolarity: Approaches to a Form* (Columbus: Ohio State University Press, 1982). Cf. Heilig, *Paulus*, 465–67.

66. Cf. also Heilig, *Paulus*, chapter 8, section 7.2.

67. Heilig, *Paulus*, 471–73.

68. On Gal 2:16–17, see Heilig, *Paulus*, chapter 11, section 6.2. See also above, p. 123, on Gal 1:18.

Stories in Context

they are dealing with an ellipsis or if the goal might still be achieved (or not!) in the future (see above, p. 123, on Gal 1:4).

Another possibility is that *shared experiences* provide the basis for a more succinct narrative. Intriguingly, we also find this in the disputed letters of Paul, where it is questionable whether this implied element is fictive or not (cf. above, pp. 100–101, on Col 1:6 and pp. 106–7, on Col 1:21–22).[69]

Finally, ellipses naturally occur quite frequently in cases of *renarration*, that is, when the narrative in question can build upon previous attempts to communicate the same content—perhaps even to the same recipients, potentially with a new thematic focus, assuming they would recall enough of the original version for mere hints to suffice in reminding them of the events in question.[70]

Note that not everything that appears to us to be an "omission" actually constitutes an ellipsis in the act of narration. We might be prone to such a misjudgment in particular if we are familiar with a previous version of a story and we notice something "lacking." For instance, we can observe how the exodus story is retold in the Wisdom of Solomon in a manner congruent with the author's assumptions concerning the nature of the concept of grace, excluding the episode with the golden calf from Exod 25. However, this omission is likely not an ellipsis in the strict sense because the narrator might have preferred that readers not think about that episode at all.[71]

Similarly, the lines between true ellipses and "summarizing" narration can sometimes be blurry.[72] In the former case, the situation of the narrated world is not represented at all by the situation time of a proposition, while in the latter case the period is covered but only in a very general (non-vivid) way. Often, it is challenging to determine how evident the inference of a situation is and how consciously a narrator might have omitted a more specific reference, assuming that the recipients would understand it anyway (see above, p. 149, on implicatures). The fundamental dilemma in identifying such ellipses is that for there to be an ellipsis, the event must be "absent" from the text. However, for us to know that it transpired in the narrated world, there must still be some indication prompting this recognition.

---

69. Heilig, *Paulus*, 470–71.
70. On modifications in renarration in (modern) Greek, see very fundamentally Alexandra Georgakopoulou, "Same Old Story? On the Interactional Dynamics of Shared Narratives," in *Narrative Interaction*, ed. Uta M. Quasthoff and Tabea Becker, Studies in Narrative 5 (Amsterdam: Benjamins, 2005), 223–41.
71. See John M. G. Barclay, *Paul and the Gift* (Grand Rapids: Eerdmans, 2015), 204.
72. Cf. Heilig, *Paulus*, 464–65, with reference to the transition between Gal 1:21–2:1.

Chapter 3

Narration-Specific Tasks

Now that we have established how pragmatic factors—particularly the *absence of informing-assertive motives*—allow for narratives that are both syntactically simpler and less comprehensive in terms of content, we can explore the means by which communicative intentions may be identified. We have previously alluded to the potential for insights gleaned from the text's illocutionary structure (cf. above, p. 167). We will now delve deeper into the influence of a story's immediate literary context, that is, how Paul's narratives are *integrated* into the overall discourse of his letters.[73]

The fundamental launch pad of this discussion is the recognition that texts are invariably embedded within larger communication frameworks. This is distinctly applicable to the "miniature stories" identified in Paul's letters—paragraphs characterized by a narrative text production strategy. The same principle applies even to literary works like novels.[74] Such works also are associated with "peritexts" (an example would be the term "novel" on the cover) and "epitexts" (something like author interviews), which collectively fall into the category of "paratexts" and provide reader guidance. As an instance, the label "novel" informs the reader that the work at hand is a piece of fiction.

In a similar vein, we can presume that the "peritexts" of the Pauline miniature narratives—the nonnarrative sections surrounding the narrative sections in his letters—provide crucial insights regarding the true substance of the embedded tales, addressing both *content* (i.e., storytelling elements like "plot" and "theme") and the *function* these text portions have within their communication contexts. Narratives, after all, do not materialize spontaneously. They are produced in an act of narration that needs to be identified as such by the recipients *in* the respective act of communication. Unless Paul counts on "epitexts"—such as previous assurances to a community that he would soon tell them a specific story—it is *within* the letter itself that he must signify his shift to narrative if he wants to ensure that his stories are understood as such. Therefore, the choice to adopt this distinct narrative

---

73. For everything that follows, see Heilig, *Paulus*, chapter 8, section 5. I follow in particular the insights by Elisabeth Gülich and Heiko Hausendorf, "Vertextungsmuster Narration," in Antos et al., *Text- und Gesprächslinguistik*, 1:369–85.

74. For what follows, see Gérard Genette, *Palimpsests: Literature in the Second Degree*, trans. Channa Newman and Claude Doubinsky (Lincoln: University of Nebraska Press, 1997); and Gérard Genette, *Paratexts: Thresholds of Interpretation*, trans. Jane E. Lewin (Cambridge: Cambridge University Press, 1997).

text production strategy comes with particular *narration-specific tasks* that Paul, as the storyteller, must fulfill. Given that these duties must be carried through during the act of writing, the manner in which they are executed can, in turn, provide valuable indications of the author's intentions.

In order to narrate in his letters, Paul must complete the following five tasks that are associated with narration:

1. Establishing narration in terms of content and/or form
2. Thematizing
3. Elaborating/Dramatizing
4. Concluding
5. Transitioning

Task number three essentially embodies the actual act of narration, a facet we can aptly capture with narratological categories. Nevertheless, the other steps are equally integral to any effort of storytelling in context—and any *omission* of these tasks becomes quite revealing, permitting conclusions about the communicative context of the narration.

Motivating Narration

"Narratives do not simply fall into one's lap. Rather, they are set up communicatively."[75] In essence, this means that one typically finds an element within the communicative context that provides a backdrop for the narration to organically evolve. There are two primary methods of setting up narration. One method motivates this text production strategy by establishing *content* worthy of narrative examination. The alternative method focuses on the *form* of the text, consequently bringing the choice of text production strategy itself into the spotlight.

Motivating narration by introducing a suitable subject is often more commonplace, even in day-to-day conversations. Occasionally, a matter is broached for some reason, and we, as casual participants in dialogue, often predict—sometimes to our chagrin about the looming discourse—that a winding tale is on its way. Instead, we usually find that we have already arrived at the "topic" that will be narratively expanded in the subsequent

---

75. Gülich and Hausendorf, "Vertextungsmuster Narration," 1:376. German original: "Erzählungen fallen nicht vom Himmel, sondern werden kommunikativ vorbereitet."

183

Chapter 3

discussion. Even though narration may be feasible at this stage, it might still be possible for a speaker or writer to employ a different text production strategy to discuss this issue.

For instance, in Rom 5:5 "hope" (ἐλπίς) is already established as a topic. Paul could have pursued several routes within the text if he wished to delve further into this concept and its significance for Christian believers. For example, he could have proposed an argument as to why they should have hope in the present moment. Indeed, verses 9–10 present such an argument. Nonetheless, this argument relies on a specific historical sequence, depicted in verse 6. Christ died for "us" when "we" were still sinners. The insertion of this miniature narrative plays a vital role in how the topic is unfolded in the text. By enlisting narrative as an aid for argumentation, the topic acquires a much more distinct shape than what a more abstract examination of the concept would have yielded.

Motivating narration with a focus on the level of text production strategy itself is comparatively unusual. A modern instance would be Thomas Mann's short story "The Railway Accident," which opens with, "Tell you a story? But I don't know any. Well, yes, after all, here is something I might tell."[76] We may encounter a similar situation in day-to-day life when we reunite with friends after a significant period and there is a general expectation for us to share intriguing anecdotes from our lives. The content might not be of paramount importance, and heated debates or arguments are not the desired outcomes. It is just about the storytelling as a social activity in itself. At points, we find Paul establishing narration in terms of form in his writings. For instance, in 2 Cor 12:1a, when he remarks that it is "necessary to continue boasting" (Καυχᾶσθαι δεῖ), we may not know what he is about to discuss. However, we can be fairly confident that he will share at least one praiseworthy episode from his past that he can boast about.

Thematization

When we progress to thematization, an act of narration becomes "not only fitting but highly expected."[77] With the decision to tell a story already made

---

76. Thomas Mann, "Railway Accident," in *The Story: A Critical Anthology*, trans. Helen Tracy Lowe-Porter, ed. Mark Schorer (Englewood Cliffs, NJ: Prentice Hall, 1959), 6–16.

77. Gülich and Hausendorf, "Vertextungsmuster Narration," 1:378. German original: "Mit der Thematisierung des fraglichen Ereignisses wird die nachfolgende Erzählung nicht länger nur anschlussfähig, sondern hochgradig erwartbar."

and the recipients having noticed that, anticipation builds. Depending on who is narrating, we might brace ourselves for an elaborate tale unfolding. A good time, perhaps, to refill one's glass of wine.

When Paul states in 2 Cor 12:1b that while it may not hold much benefit, he will nonetheless turn to the subject of "visions and revelations" (οὐ συμφέρον μέν, ἐλεύσομαι δὲ εἰς ὀπτασίας καὶ ἀποκαλύψεις κυρίου), we get a fairly distinct idea of what is to follow. Not only do we understand the topic (visions and revelations), but we also have a sense of how these will be presented—as experiences by Paul meant to showcase him in a commendable light. After all, the narrative form has been motivated not neutrally but as a supporting element for boasting. If Paul does not proceed to share such a story about himself, it would be highly unusual. If he fails to even present a narrative at all, it would seem to outright violate the stage he has already set for the forthcoming discourse, even though Paul has not explicitly stated, "I will tell you a story now."

Thematizations can be quite essential in the interpretation of narratives and the reconstruction of their plots. In this stage, narrators often include an explicit reference to the complete "theme" of the story. For instance, Gal 1:12 prefigures what the ensuing narrative will entail. It is noteworthy that verse 11 merely asserts a character trait of Paul's gospel (its lack of human likeness). This constitutes the topic and the verse's role is to motivate narration. The stark claim in verse 11—and the necessity to substantiate such a foundational statement—invokes the need for a justification and thus becomes the topic of the discourse to follow. In contrast, verse 12 already gives us a concentrated perspective on past events, hypothesizing about what has occurred and what has not. At this juncture, any reader would anticipate that an elaboration, if forthcoming, will almost certainly adopt a narrative form. Moreover, this double thematization of verse 12 already delineates the basic outlines of the ensuing plot by indicating the theses that must be justified in narrative form for the story to maintain a cohesive arc of suspense. Conversely, this implies that every subsequent episode must be interpreted as part of a story that dramatizes this dual theme—a factor often overlooked in analyses that isolate these sections, interpreting Gal 1:15–17 as a "call/conversion" narrative, for example, as if Paul had not just informed us about his intended theme.

As this example illustrates, it is vital for interpreters not to overlook such indications of a narrative's theme in its context. After all, the theme of a story is often something the interpreter discerns with numerous uncertainties after drawing out a plausible plot based on the narrated text. Any assistance in this task of reconstructing the meaning of a story should be appreciated.

Chapter 3

If the author tells us in advance what the story will be "about," what the key point is they wish to convey, it can aid us in recognizing which narrated events are central to the plot and which ones are of peripheral interest in the specific communication context.

However, a word of caution is warranted here. Storytellers sometimes *fall short of expectations* that their audience may have justifiably formed based on thematization. This can occur unintentionally and does not automatically imply that the narrator is deficient. Particularly in oral storytelling, the structure of text production necessitates various adjustments as the narrative unfolds (see also below, pp. 206–8). With respect to Paul's letters, there is some limited evidence suggesting that we have indeed a fairly untouched transcript of how the apostle dictated his stories to a secretary.[78] Certainly, there is also the chance that the storyteller intentionally misleads the audience, possibly for the simple joy of adding complexity.

Therefore, we must approach with caution the quite lavish "heading" in 2 Cor 12:1b. It may imply that verses 7–9 should be read as a second episode, supplementing the experience detailed in verses 2–4. Indeed, some have argued—based on the plural in verse 1b—that as early as verse 3 we are hearing about an event distinct from the one mentioned in verse 2. Nevertheless, one might also ask whether this flamboyant narrative introduction is not just part of a larger, rather whimsical narration strategy behind 2 Cor 12:1–6, deriving pleasure from repeatedly thwarting reader expectations (see also below, pp. 222–24).[79] It is certainly suspicious that Paul's story, after its meticulous introduction in verse 1, never really takes flight.

Initially, verse 2 appears to further specify the theme (an extraordinary experience had by a person that Paul knows). But this already seems at odds with the original thematization, which stimulated the expectation of a story about *Paul's* divine encounters. Moreover, the readers are then left with that appetizer. Rather than satisfying their hunger for exciting events, Paul appears to shy away from *actually telling the story*, thus noticeably disappointing the expectations.

Instead of carrying through the act of dramatization, Paul, as the next step, *repeats* the updated thematization of verse 2 with little variation in

---

78. On this general topic of the Pauline use of secretaries, cf. Heilig, *Paulus*, chapter 4, section 2. For the implications on the hypothesis that stylistic differences in debated Pauline letters might be explained with reference to a secretary, see p. 1007. I will point out at various places throughout this book whenever I think that we see evidence of a rather direct access to the text that Paul dictated.

79. Cf. Heilig, *Paulus*, 487, 653, and 657.

verses 3–4, keeping the Corinthians in suspense. It is as if Paul first uses a heading to introduce a short story, but upon turning the page, the reader encounters ... another heading.

Additionally, in both cases the actual dramatization that would normally follow the thematization is then immediately disrupted again, even at the syntactical level, by Paul's admission that he himself is unsure whether the ascension to the heavens occurred within or outside the body (εἴτε ἐν σώματι οὐκ οἶδα, εἴτε ἐκτὸς τοῦ σώματος οὐκ οἶδα, ὁ θεὸς οἶδεν). Instead of "conveying knowledge" (cf. above, p. 168), Paul underscores with great emphasis what he does *not* know.

Moreover, in verse 4, when he finally comes to the spicy details, even using the quite uncharacteristic (for him) pattern of syntactically strict narration ("he was snatched up into paradise and heard inexpressible words"; ἡρπάγη εἰς τὸν παράδεισον καὶ ἤκουσεν ἄρρητα ῥήματα), thus implying that dramatization is ultimately executed with great deliberation, readers are in for a big disappointment yet again. For once the readers are finally transported to the heavenly place, and they are naturally eager to explore the details further, the most thrilling feature is, unfortunately, "inexpressible" and thus nonnarratable, with the utterance of these words prohibited to humankind (verse 4: ἃ οὐκ ἐξὸν ἀνθρώπῳ λαλῆσαι).

As we will explore further below (p. 225), this emphasis on a lack of knowledge plays a crucial role in subtly suggesting Paul's *unreliable* narration. But concurrently, we can observe that Paul's recurrent revision of the theme not only draws attention to the narrating "I" (by prompting questions about Paul's relationship with the narrated character) but also puts a spotlight onto the act of narration itself. This *repeated implementation of a single narration-specific task* is a technique we recognize from contemporary literature, where authors often bring the act of their narration front and center. Accordingly, what we see in 2 Cor 12 is undoubtedly a quite artful play with the execution of narration-specific tasks.[80] Paul is not merely a storyteller. He is a self-aware storyteller.

Additionally, even though the thematization in 2 Cor 12:1 proves to be misleading, ultimately offering limited aid in reconstructing the narrative's plot, it serves interpretation effectively by illuminating the *text function* of the disappointing story. By ultimately refusing to engage the readers' thirst for information, Paul aims to incite a reassessment of boasting in general,

---

80. On this passage, cf. Heilig, *Paulus*, chapter 8, section 5.5.

Chapter 3

ultimately leading to a change in the Corinthians' behavior toward himself and the super-apostles.

One textual element that routinely helps us associate a narrative's introduction with the category of communicative intention is the connection of the introduction-content type (see above, p. 48). We regularly encounter it right before the commencement of the actual narrative. In fact, it frequently establishes something akin to a frame narrative by either presenting the speaker in relation to the ensuing narrative (Gal 1:6: "I am astonished (to hear) that . . ."; Θαυμάζω ὅτι . . .) or by outlining how the recipients relate to the embedded narrative—whether the story is, for instance, something they are already familiar with or, in the speaker's viewpoint, must become aware of now.

For this reason, this type of connection is crucial in analyzing Pauline miniature narratives. Consider, for instance, 1 Thess 4:13, where the author(s) state, "we do not want you to be uninformed, brothers and sisters, about those who are asleep" (Οὐ θέλομεν δὲ ὑμᾶς ἀγνοεῖν, ἀδελφοί, περὶ τῶν κοιμωμένων). Several things merit attention here. First, this introductory statement provides significant insight into the upcoming narrative. It not only identifies the topic—people who have passed away—but also foreshadows the *theme* by portraying their death as a mere "sleep"—hence, implying a future awakening. Second, the introductory link also prompts us to consider the *text's function* by explicitly commenting on why the forthcoming text segment is incorporated into the letter, namely, for the conveyance of knowledge. In this case, the introduction validates that we are dealing with a typical, though somewhat rare for Paul, informing-assertive function of the following narrative of events.

However, it is crucial to note that even in this instance, the "information" is not an end in itself but ultimately aims to create an emotional impact, thereby serving a systemic function: ". . . so that you will not grieve like the rest, who do not have hope" (ἵνα μὴ λυπῆσθε καθὼς καὶ οἱ λοιποὶ οἱ μὴ ἔχοντες ἐλπίδα). Intriguingly, the imparted information is expected to yield results via an indirect route through acts of consolation within the community: "Therefore comfort each other with these words" (1 Thess 4:18: Ὥστε παρακαλεῖτε ἀλλήλους ἐν τοῖς λόγοις τούτοις). And yet again, "these words"—the "information" that the Thessalonians need to comprehend—do not make up a traditional narrative but are instead the product of predictive narration. Rather than recounting previously unknown past events, Paul and his coworkers discuss future scenarios.

Whether Paul *actually provides new information* in instances where he uses such introductions is sometimes debatable. For instance, I remain skeptical in relation to 2 Cor 1:8, where he employs the same formula to talk "about our affliction that we experienced in Asia" (ὑπὲρ τῆς θλίψεως ἡμῶν τῆς γενομένης ἐν τῇ Ἀσίᾳ). Indeed, the fact that Paul refrains from offering a vivid account of what transpired could imply that the primary intention is to portray the incident there *as* affliction—and, thus, to frame it in the context of the theological interpretation of suffering that he elaborated on in the preceding verses.

In other cases as well, we need to exercise caution when trying to pinpoint the new information that Paul is purportedly imparting. For instance, when utilizing the same formula as in the other two instances in 1 Cor 10:1, Paul references the biblical tradition of the wilderness generation. There is no indication that Paul presumes his audience is encountering the story for the first time. The fact that the rock turns out to be Christ (verse 5) is probably just an Easter egg. However, the implication that the story is about "our" forefathers would likely have astonished the readers. This tidbit of information, therefore, probably drew their attention and might have raised among them the prima facie suspicion that the episode may have been highly pertinent to *their* current situation. And indeed, verse 6 informs them that stories like this one (or, in Paul's words, events like this)—featuring the dreadful fate of even this "spiritual" generation mentioned in verse 5—serve a *directive* function for Christians: "... so that we will not crave evil things" (εἰς τὸ μὴ εἶναι ἡμᾶς ἐπιθυμητὰς κακῶν). What is novel, therefore, is not the story itself. After all, in verse 6, Paul can simply append "as they also craved" (καθὼς κἀκεῖνοι ἐπεθύμησαν) without mentioning in verse 5 this analogous event, which led to the destruction of "most of them." Hence, the informing-assertive function seemingly does not apply to the story itself but rather, on a metalevel, to its *interpretation*, enabling the Corinthians to recognize the hitherto hidden *directive function* of a story already familiar to them.

Indeed, in many cases the introduction-content constructions themselves make it abundantly clear that what follows is "an old story," something that is already fundamentally known and perhaps just needs to be highlighted once more to fulfill a specific role in the current discourse. The Galatians have already "heard" about Paul's former conduct (Gal 1:13: Ἠκούσατε . . .), as have the Philippians regarding Epaphroditus's illness (Phil 2:25). And time and again, Paul at least asserts that the recipients already "know" (οἴδατε) something that he nevertheless puts down in writing (again).[81]

---

81. For references, cf. Heilig, *Paulus*, 488.

Chapter 3

To be sure, just as with debatable assertions that new content is communicated, we also need to approach these introductions with a measure of skepticism. In Eph 4:21, the notion of the audience's prior activity of hearing something is supplemented with a comment about them having learnt about that matter (αὐτὸν ἠκούσατε καὶ ἐν αὐτῷ ἐδιδάχθητε). But even here this detailed scenario is prefaced with the connector εἴ γε ("if indeed"). Hence, the recipients are prompted to reflect on their familiarity with what is said, to consider whether they truly know what they should know and, if not, to swiftly refresh their memory in view of how severe such forgetfulness would be.

Likewise, a little earlier, in Eph 2:11, the readers are urged through an imperative to "remember" something (μνημονεύετε). In 1 Thess 2:9, this memory may either be encouraged or assumed—or both simultaneously, depending on the readers' ability (or willingness) to remember.[82] In 2 Thess 2:5, the construction even appears as a question that anticipates an affirmative response: "Yes, of course we remember that you have already told us these things" (cf. Οὐ μνημονεύετε ὅτι ἔτι ὢν πρὸς ὑμᾶς ταῦτα ἔλεγον ὑμῖν;).

Therefore, while in reality there is undoubtedly a spectrum when it comes to how familiar the recipients are with the events mentioned, the frequent occurrence of these constructions further emphasizes that Paul, at least rhetorically, often does not present his narratives as primarily informing-assertive accounts of past events. Instead, the stories about past or present situations, and quasi-stories about upcoming events, may serve a variety of other functions. Specifically, they may support, along with the context in which they appear, the overriding communicative goal of instigating changes in attitude and behavior.

Concluding Narration and Moving On

All things come to an end, including acts of narration.[83] In some genres of written narratives, this might be signified by the phrase "the end" itself. However, in oral narration there are also means to make it clear *within* the process of narration that the act of storytelling is approaching its conclusion. This aspect is significant for the interpretation of stories, as a speaker or writer might opt to clarify once more what the crux of the story is. After

---

82. On intentional ambiguity and related phenomena, cf. below, p. 270.
83. On what follows, cf. Heilig, *Paulus*, 489–90.

all, it is their final opportunity to ensure that the story is understood by the audience as they intended. If a misunderstanding arises, they might have to wait for their next turn in the conversation to rectify the perception, or they may never get an opportunity to directly tackle misinterpretations about what was told.

Consequently, it is quite typical to find at this juncture of the narrative a statement that somehow correlates with the thematization. This is especially so if there is no opportunity for revisions. In such instances, specifically with oral narration, it is particularly insightful to observe whether the portrayal of the theme has transformed during the narration and to what degree the storyteller seems satisfied with their performance. Giving heed to the *transition between narrative and nonnarrative components* is also significant with respect to the text's linguistic interest in providing an account of the text sort pattern that underlies Paul's letters. After all, we seek to understand how Paul's narratives are incorporated into nonnarrative text sections.

Even in relatively brief narratives, we can sometimes observe that Paul devotes substantial attention to their conclusion. The prooemium of 1 Corinthians, 1 Cor 1:4–9, illustrates this adeptly. We are introduced to the narrative in 1:4 with the thanksgiving setting us up to anticipate a story about the great works of God among the recipients: "I always thank God for you because of the grace that was given to you in Christ Jesus" (Εὐχαριστῶ τῷ θεῷ μου πάντοτε περὶ ὑμῶν ἐπὶ τῇ χάριτι τοῦ θεοῦ τῇ δοθείσῃ ὑμῖν ἐν Χριστῷ Ἰησοῦ). Verse 5 carries this theme further by explaining the gift with a ὅτι clause: "enrichment" has happened through him in every conceivable way in "word" and "knowledge" (ἐν παντὶ ἐπλουτίσθητε ἐν αὐτῷ, ἐν παντὶ λόγῳ καὶ πάσῃ γνώσει). While this may not seem very specific, as the letter later reveals, this already picks up a specific discourse concerning spiritual gifts.

Then, verse 6 is introduced by the connector καθώς, which has been interpreted in numerous ways (καθὼς τὸ μαρτύριον τοῦ Χριστοῦ ἐβεβαιώθη ἐν ὑμῖν). To me, a temporal reading of καθώς ("while"), very common in Modern Greek, makes most sense. Verse 5, with its focus on a diverse array of gifts, suggests a complexive reading of the aorist, thereby forming one constituent of a simultaneous connection. This would mean that Paul narrates the story of spiritual successes in Corinth in a way that would link this growth (highly valued among the recipients) with a deeper understanding of Christ (highly valued by Paul).

Verse 7 then wraps up this miniature narrative. Note that this concluding verse is ushered in by ὥστε. However, rather than presenting another situation from the narrated world that would result from and therefore come

Chapter 3

after the previously told content, the connector appears to display utterance relatedness. This implies that verse 7 essentially recaps the plot of verses 5–6 from a different viewpoint: "In other words, you do not lack any spiritual gift . . ." (ὥστε ὑμᾶς μὴ ὑστερεῖσθαι ἐν μηδενὶ χαρίσματι).

Following this, still within verse 7 Paul supplements a participle construction: ". . . while you are waiting for the revelation of our Lord Jesus Christ" (ἀπεκδεχομένους τὴν ἀποκάλυψιν τοῦ κυρίου ἡμῶν Ἰησοῦ Χριστοῦ). At this point, I would argue, we are already *encountering a shift away from narration*. We have peered into the past and discerned its implications concerning the current state of the Corinthian Christians. Now, we are departing from that temporal horizon with a brief glimpse into the future. To be sure, Paul does not conclude his story without squeezing in something that is quite important to him. The assertion that the current period is still a time of *waiting* is something of which he evidently believes the Corinthians need to be reminded (cf., for example, 1 Cor 4:8). Here, Paul introduces this concept as if it were part of the narration, as a matter of course—in other words, as something that is presupposed in the setting of the story. Note how the impending revelation is simply posited as an action noun, and the act of "waiting" is expressed merely by a participle. In a rhetorically effective manner, Paul finishes his narrative with a twist that already foreshadows much of the later discourse. If the Corinthians take the bait and accept this story about themselves, Paul already has them halfway where he wants them to end up.

In light of 1 Cor 1:4–9, the distinct profiles of other instances that present a similar structure become apparent. In the examples I have in mind, an informing-assertive function transitions to text sections that more directly address the volition of the recipients. Take, for instance, 2 Cor 5:14–15, where Paul initially relates a story involving Christ's death and resurrection and then expounds on the present result—no longer knowing anyone according to the flesh (verse 16: Ὥστε ἡμεῖς ἀπὸ τοῦ νῦν οὐδένα οἴδαμεν κατὰ σάρκα). From a communicative intent standpoint, it appears that verse 16 does something more substantial than just adding another episode to the narrative of verses 14–15 or providing a neutral plot summary. By inserting "us" into the picture and thus reducing the distance from the narrative world, the statement acquires a directive aspect. Clearly, verse 16 is meant to serve as a principle among the Corinthians, and it is presented as the logical outcome of a story with which they are thoroughly familiar.

Then, in verse 17 we can already observe a transition in the discourse to argumentation, as evidenced by the presence of a conditional construction.

Here, we are presented with a summary of the theme of the preceding narrative (note the use of ὥστε once again), which is explained in the form of a general rule. Further, the verb of the matrix clause is not in the (narrating) indicative. In other words, the narrative's conclusion seems to be followed immediately by the narration-specific task of moving away from the narrative. That said, the memory of the narrative remains vibrant. Indeed, the particle ἰδού draws our focus *back* to the story, encouraging us to zoom in by serving as a discourse marker: "That means: if someone is in Christ—new creation! The old has faded away . . . *hey*, something new has occurred!"[84] It could even be argued that ἰδού operates as a focalization signal, inducing us to adopt the astonished perspective of someone witnessing a conversion firsthand.[85] In any event, it is evident that simply reading this story and remaining unaffected is not a viable option for Paul. The narrative deeply involves him and should similarly involve the recipients. While Paul moves on in the discourse, the story is supposed to move the Corinthians.

In other passages, the transition away from a story with a more or less informing communicative function is even more apparent because Paul proceeds with an explicit instruction.[86] We have already observed (see above, p. 189) how in 1 Cor 10 Paul retells the story of the wilderness generation and expressly highlights its directive function for the Corinthians. After this is clarified in verse 6, a sequence of commands follows in verses 7–10 before Paul reiterates the point of verse 6 in different terms in verse 11: "These things occurred to them as examples, and they were written down as lessons for us, in whose time the ends of the ages have come" (ταῦτα δὲ τυπικῶς συνέβαινεν ἐκείνοις, ἐγράφη δὲ πρὸς νουθεσίαν ἡμῶν, εἰς οὓς τὰ τέλη τῶν αἰώνων κατήντηκεν). Then, verse 12 also uses ὥστε as a connector, much like 1 Cor 1:7. But this time, what follows is not another formulation of the theme of the preceding story, but a directive speech act: "Therefore, let the one who thinks they are standing be careful that they do not fall" (Ὥστε ὁ δοκῶν ἑστάναι βλεπέτω μὴ πέσῃ).

When we encounter imperatives, it is usually clear that we have departed from the narrative, which is characterized by assertions about the narrated world. Identifying the boundaries of acts of narration becomes a tad more

---

84. Heilig, *Paulus*, 205.
85. Cf. Heilig, *Paulus*, 659.
86. On the question of how the (quoted) imperative in Gal 4:30 and the subsequent conclusion, introduced by διό, in verse 31 relate to the overall communicative function of the letter, see Heilig, *Paulus*, chapter 8, section 4.4.4.

Chapter 3

challenging when narratives are followed by other assertions, which, although not part of the narrative, are components of argumentation and descriptions.[87] In the upcoming analysis, we will examine the transitions between narrative and argumentation on the one hand and between narrative and description on the other hand.

Regarding *argumentation*, it is widely recognized that narratives often serve to pave the way for specific conclusions (cf. above, pp. 192–93, on 2 Cor 5:17). What I want to highlight here is the inverse relationship: argumentation as a *springboard* for narration. We commonly perceive narratives as effective tools for conveying our core concerns, and I believe that this perspective on the relationship between argument and story generally aligns well with Paul's aims. If Paul tells us about events in the context of an argument, these events and their specific narrative configuration are probably important for his argumentative goals. However, I am sure we all know someone who enjoys presenting a particular argument solely *so that* they might have an opportunity to recount a story from their past (e.g., "The federal government can't effectively handle health insurance because the issue is too intricate. Speaking of which, it reminds me of that time when . . ."). The fact that Paul seems to still be emotionally impacted by his experience in the province of Asia when writing 2 Cor 1:8 perhaps serves as a reminder that Paul occasionally might wish to relay events simply for the solace that comes with being heard.[88] In other words, in rare cases narratives might not just underpin arguments, but arguments may also lead to new narratives.

The shift from narratives to *descriptions* is particularly challenging. This is largely due to the lack of consensus among narratologists as to whether "narrative pauses" are integral components of narratives. The issue is even more pronounced when a descriptive section follows a narrative that is *not* resumed afterward. At times, these descriptive passages seem to be linked to the narrative world in a manner similar to descriptive pauses interspersed within narrative discourse. In other words, the narrative appears to at least influence the ensuing descriptive text production. Even when events are no longer the focus, the previously narrated situations still exert an influence on what is described. A prime example is Gal 3:28, where the discussion

---

87. Cf. Heilig, *Paulus*, chapter 8, section 6.
88. Cf. Heilig, *Apostle*, for the suggestion that the supposedly "coded" criticism of Rome in Paul's letters might at times be better understood with reference to such psychological relief than in the framework of elaborate strategies of communicating hidden messages.

centers on the situation "in Christ," and one might argue that readers are still prompted to consider this, not so much in the concrete terms of the daily communal life of the Galatian believers, but rather within the "story world" of verse 27, where the "putting on" of Christ like clothing that enshrouds all who are baptized has been recounted.[89]

This already provides us with a crucial insight regarding Hays's category of "narrative substructures." Perhaps the notion that *explicit* narratives create ripples in their immediate literary contexts, becoming increasingly *implicit*, can be understood, at least in part, as a result of Paul performing the narration-specific tasks of concluding narration in ambiguous ways and moving on in certain instances. This tendency could be explained by the absence of turn-taking in written discourse, which can complicate the demarcation between different textualization strategies if these changes are not explicitly verbalized. "Narrative substructures" thus might actually be a rather predictable element of the text sort pattern that underlies Paul's letters.

This notion highlights a broader issue. In written form, it is not only challenging to signal the end of a narrative but also more generally to indicate that one communicative act—regardless of employed textualization strategies—has concluded and another is beginning. In other words, we also need to pay attention to the *narrative-to-narrative* transition.

Indeed, a letter in its entirety can be viewed as a long monologue, an extended utterance, despite the fact that the dictation process behind writing might closely resemble a genuine dialogue. This differs from a natural conversation, in which, even if the speaker does not change, it is typically clear when one story has ended and another by the same speaker is beginning. There will normally be a pause followed by a comment such as "Oh, there's another story that comes to mind about that," with that comment also serving automatically as the thematization of the new narrative act. Turn-taking is even more noticeable if conversation partners are prompted to share a story themselves (e.g., "Have you ever experienced something like that?") or to comment on the previous narrative (e.g., "What do you think about that?"). In contrast, Paul's letters provide far fewer such signals, leaving us often in a difficult position to determine whether a narrative has concluded or whether Paul might still continue a larger act of narration, perhaps after a brief interruption.[90]

---

89. For details, cf. Heilig, *Paulus*, 516 and 921–22.

90. This whole issue will become even more pressing once we enter the realm of merely implicit stories. Cf. below, pp. 348–51, and, for more detail, Heilig, *Paulus*, chapter 17, sections 3.2.1 and 4.2.2.

Chapter 3

This question arises both when different situations are presented one after another and when the same nexus of events is depicted repeatedly. In the first case, we need to decide whether we are dealing with two stories about events that happen to occur sequentially in the narrated world or with two subsequent episodes of the same story. In the latter case, we could analogously be encountering either renarration, that is, separate acts of narration of the same events, or an instance of repetitive narration within the same narrative act.[91]

I would like to illustrate this distinction between two distinct acts of narration on the one hand and two phases of a single act of narration on the other hand by means of looking once again at 1 Cor 1:4–9, where it is debatable whether we are dealing with renarration (two acts) or repetitive narration (one act). As previously discussed, the narrative ostensibly concludes in verse 7. And indeed, confirming this impression, upon reaching the prooemium's conclusion in verse 9, we encounter a notably descriptive assertion (πιστὸς ὁ θεός). This statement is further furnished by a brief flashback (δι' οὗ ἐκλήθητε εἰς κοινωνίαν τοῦ υἱοῦ αὐτοῦ Ἰησοῦ Χριστοῦ τοῦ κυρίου ἡμῶν). God is depicted as faithful, having previously acted favorably toward the Corinthians by calling them. This description (with the flashback) further bolsters the prior verse's "predictive narration," where, in verse 8, Jesus Christ's future actions are outlined within a relative clause. It is he who will maintain the Corinthians' steadfastness until the end (ὃς καὶ βεβαιώσει ὑμᾶς ἕως τέλους ἀνεγκλήτους ἐν τῇ ἡμέρᾳ τοῦ κυρίου ἡμῶν Ἰησοῦ [Χριστοῦ]).

In this passage, Paul appears to swiftly segue from one act of narration (in verses 4–7) to another act of (predictive) narration. Or so it seems at first sight. On closer inspection, it is arguable whether Paul truly ever concluded his inaugural narrative. In essence, it seems plausible that the "revelation" from verse 6 is now picked up by means of reference to the "day of our Lord Jesus Christ," that is, the day when he will return and, thus, become fully manifest. This connection is further supported by the fact that we can observe that Paul uses a wordplay that interlaces the divine actions of the past (verse 6: ἐβεβαιώθη) with this prospective sustaining action (verse 8: βεβαιώσει).

This tight-knit relationship between verses 4–7 and verses 8–9 leads to

---

91. Cf. also Vivien Heller, Miriam Morek, and Uta M. Quasthoff, "Mehrfaches Erzählen: Warum wird eine Geschichte im selben Gespräch zweimal erzählt?," in *Wiedererzählen: Formen und Funktionen einer kulturellen Praxis*, ed. Elke Schumann, Elisabeth Gülich, Gabriele Lucius-Hoene, and Stefan Pfänder, Edition Kulturwissenschaft 50 (Bielefeld: Transcript, 2015), 341–67.

speculation concerning the extent to which these events harmonize as a grand quasi-narrative in Paul's consciousness. Did he really dictate a story, highlight its implications, and then proceed to share "another" (predictive) narrative, which is undergirded by a descriptive representation of God (in turn, supported by an account of past happenings)? In other words, it is by no means certain that we are dealing with a case of renarration, where a reference to a current waiting period that extends to a future event of revelation instigates a novel communicative act, an exploration of what the future will hold. Rather, we must at least reckon with the possibility that this entire section is held together by a unified almost-narrative, a narrative in Paul's mind that he gets back to twice, employing reiterative narration to examine the already mentioned waiting period afresh, this time with the focus adjusted to a different narrative figure (not "we" but "Christ")?

Often, a definitive conclusion to this inquiry can remain elusive, partially due to our lack of sufficient evidence, and partially because a letter only provides a partial glimpse into a natural conversation's dynamics. However, the insights we can gain from conversation linguistics regarding turn-taking can significantly enhance our ability to pay keen attention to what is going on, that is, envisioning how Paul *might have* verbalized his text had he been addressing his audience directly. Contemplating this issue could afford considerable insights into the pragmatic aspects of the apostle's storytelling.

In some relatively rare cases, we may even have more direct access to Paul's management of conversational turns. After all, the extent to which a letter discourse deviates from the natural conversation that it is meant to replace varies. At times, Paul even explicitly *simulates dialogue*, allowing a conversation partner to have their turn, as seen in Rom 9:19 and 11:19: "You will say [to me]" ('Ἐρεῖς [μοι] οὖν). In Rom 11:19 it is particularly evident that this verse has the function of *transitioning to a comment by the conversation partner on a Pauline narrative.*[92]

---

92. The conversation partner picks up on the events of breaking off branches and grafting in other branches that are recounted in verse 17—proposing an *interpretation* of the narrative that is diametrically opposed to Paul's interpretation in verse 18. Paul concentrates on the fact that branches are merely parts of the tree that are dependent on the roots. By contrast, the conversation partner in verse 17 perceives the pair of events and integrates them into a purpose-oriented connection, which in the view of this dialogue partner encapsulates the plot succinctly. While Paul focuses on a characteristic of one of the narrative characters (dependency), this interpretation instead draws attention to the gardener's intentions: "The branches were broken off so that I could be grafted in" (ἐξεκλάσθησαν κλάδοι ἵνα ἐγὼ ἐγκεντρισθῶ).

Chapter 3

The Frame Narrative of Paul's Narration

In discussing "events" in the context of Paul's letters, we typically refer to external occurrences that take place in the world and that are represented through verb forms in the writing. Yet, when Paul tells a story in a letter about events in the past, this storytelling activity itself could arguably be designated as an event "in" the letter: "Not all of letter fiction's narrat*ive* events are narrat*ed* events. In the epistolary work, acts of communication (confession, silence, persuasion, and so on) constitute important events; they are enacted rather than reported in discourse."[93] Collectively, these "internal events" of a letter could be understood as composing something like a frame narrative—a story about Paul as the author of a letter.[94] Of course, some of these events will only be a part of *our* narrative pertaining to Paul as a letter writer. However, there are indications suggesting that, at certain times, Paul himself makes the act of authoring his letters the focus of a narrative.

To start, we must acknowledge that Paul can not only construct a vast array of internal events within his letters, but he is of course also capable of making the speech act he is executing explicit. For instance, even the highly condensed phrase in Gal 1:20 "behold, before God, I assure you that . . ." (ἰδοὺ ἐνώπιον τοῦ θεοῦ ὅτι . . .) unmistakably indicates that the event of making an oath is taking place in the act of writing that verse.[95] Consequently, it is not merely us—the exegetes—who make assessments about what Paul is achieving with his letter. Rather, it seems to be Paul himself who either tells a story or at least provides the components for such a story about his letter writing *within* the letter itself. Typically, present tense verb forms are employed for this kind of simultaneous narration with utterance relatedness. However, the "epistolary aorist" can similarly be utilized to refer to the letter writing process itself (see above, p. 158).[96]

On occasion, Paul accentuates the internal act of recounting a story in a similar fashion, even when he does not explicitly state, "I am narrating a story now." First, as previously noted (p. 187), the *repeated execution of the task of introducing narration* in 2 Cor 12 accords greater prominence to the act of narration itself rather than past events being narrated. Thus, the narration becomes "the real story." Second, Paul can direct us even more

---

93. Altman, *Epistolarity*, 207. Italics in the original.
94. See Heilig, *Paulus*, chapter 8, section 7.2.
95. Cf. Heilig, *Paulus*, 520.
96. It can, however, also express events that accompany the process of writing or even look into the future of the completion of the letter (see below, p. 241).

toward the process of narration itself via another kind of internal event: the *metanarrative commentary*.[97] When Paul asserts in Gal 1:20 that the account he has just shared with the Galatians is indeed truthful, he includes this metanarrative commentary as an internal event within the larger internal event of telling a story in which the commentary is integrated.

While it may be overly assertive to proclaim that Paul explicitly tells such a frame narrative in each of his letters, these observations at least allude to a category of "implicit narratives." This idea holds true even though Paul may not provide a coherent, self-conscious chronicle of his letter writing. What cannot be ignored, after all, is his knack for directing readers toward several internal events that can straightforwardly form an interconnected frame narrative. Moreover, often *aspects of the context of utterance* also feature in the apostle's actual miniature narratives, tempting readers to connect the story worlds of these narratives to their own world.

This is of course especially true with respect to Paul himself. On the one hand, he enters the stage as the narrator—the one conveying the story—yet he also frequently emerges as a central narrative character in the episodes he recounts. The frequently encountered interpolated narration type in Paul's letters is indicative of this psychological continuity, prompting us to imagine not just the experiences of the narrated "I" but also the present state of the narrating "I."[98] Similarly, the members of the congregations are not merely recipients of the letter and, by extension, of its narratives; they also often feature in the miniature stories within the letter.

For instance, in Galatians, Paul is the one who is currently astonished (Gal 1:6) and who, as he himself remarks, "writes" (γράφω) in that state, even making comments about this writing process (Gal 1:20) while also being a central figure in numerous references to past events. When the Galatians are explicitly addressed with questions and their responses upon reading the letter are presupposed (Gal 3:1–5 and 3:6), this occurs against the broad context of their prior history having been extensively thematized elsewhere in the letter in narrative form. Consequently, the action of recounting these narratives is part of a larger story, one that is subtly hinted at. Paul hopes he can retrospectively tell this greater story someday, with a happy ending, and with his letter-writing event serving as a positive turning point in the plot.

---

97. Heilig, *Paulus*, chapter 8, section 7.3.
98. Heilig, *Paulus*, chapter 8, section 7.4.

4. Fragments of Implicit Protonarratives

Beyond Explicit Narration

Throughout the preceding chapters, our attention has been devoted explicitly to actual narratives in Paul's letters. Moreover, we have utilized a rather rigid framework to discern which sections of text qualify as stories. However, in our pursuit of miniature narratives—portions of Paul's letters where the apostle employs the text production strategy of narration for various objectives—we have frequently encountered paragraphs that could have been easily interpreted as narratives upon initial observation, even though subsequent detailed analysis revealed that they lacked narrativity according to our definition.

It is noteworthy that despite the primary focus of this work and our calculated omission, so far, of phenomena proposed by scholars such as Hays and Wright, we have consistently found ourselves compelled to apply narratological categories and terminology in our analysis of these text portions—"almost-stories," so to speak. Clearly, the complex array of questions associated with the aspect of implicit stories in Paul's narratives imposes itself on the meticulous reader attuned to narrative dynamics and therefore cannot be avoided in a discussion that consistently applies a narratological perspective.

Defining Implicit Stories

A pragmatic approach might be to simply incorporate these phenomena into our analysis, perhaps using quotation marks around "story" and "narrative" each time we describe them. However, the *demarcation from* explicit narratives is too distinct, and the potential *subdivisions within* this category of implicit stories are too fundamental, making such a practical method ultimately unsatisfactory.

What we, thus, need to propose is a definition of implicit narratives that explains what unifies them and how they differ from explicit stories. This will enable us to classify individual instances of such implicit stories within this framework while also taking into account significant distinctions within this category of implicit narratives.

The Narrative Paradigm of Communication

One approach to associating narrativity with implicit stories could be to simply weave a definition of narrative wide enough to catch the phenomena previously slipping through the net of our understanding of what constitutes a story. Interestingly, in this context we are reminded of how much Hays struggled in his 1983 work to find space for his "narrative substructures" within a dictionary definition of "story."

Shortly thereafter, in two influential articles published in 1984 and 1985, Walter R. Fisher postulated what he called the "narrative paradigm."[1] According to Fisher, this paradigm provides an explanation for *all* human communication, the result being that all texts are considered to exhibit plot and therefore can all be analyzed as narratives: "Hence, works such as Charles Darwin's, *Origin of Species*, and Einstein's, *Relativity* . . . are as usefully interpreted and assessed through the narrative paradigm as the President's last speech or the latest popular film."[2]

Clearly, this concept appears potentially very relevant to Hays's endeavor to establish a framework for analyzing argumentative sections as possessing a narrative substructure. Interestingly, however, it appears that subsequent scholarship on narrative substructures has not embraced this solution. Even Wright, who had the opportunity with his 1992 publication, *The New Testament and the People of God*, to build on Fisher's narrative paradigm, does not seem to be aware of this particular piece of scholarship. For Wright, there does not appear to be a need to further validate the theoretical assumptions

---

1. Walter R. Fisher, "Narration as a Human Communication Paradigm: The Case of Public Moral Argument," *Communication Monographs* 51 (1984): 1–22; and Walter R. Fisher, "The Narrative Paradigm: An Elaboration," *Communication Monographs* 52 (1985): 347–67. For more details on what follows, see Christoph Heilig, *Paulus als Erzähler? Eine narratologische Perspektive auf die Paulusbriefe*, BZNW 237 (Berlin: de Gruyter, 2020), chapter 9, section 3.2.1.

2. Fisher, "Narrative Paradigm," 356.

Chapter 4

underlying the claim that "letters have stories."[3] He presumes this idea is sufficiently justified by Norman R. Petersen's 1985 work *Rediscovering Paul*, which focuses on the events reflected in a letter, even if they are not narrated explicitly (see chapter 5 for more details).[4]

It is not easy to decide whether the lack of prominence given to Fisher's narrative paradigm in discussions on the narrative approach to Paul is indeed regrettable. On the one hand, one could argue that it is a positive outcome, given that Fisher's ideas ultimately failed to convince most of his peers.[5] On the other hand, this also means that the narrative approach has never had to confront the challenges raised against Fisher's narrative paradigm, which could have provided much needed clarity about how to approach the alleged implicit narratives in Paul's letters.

Robert C. Rowland, for instance, contended that expanding the concept of narrativity to include all human communication acts "deprives the term 'narrative' of any clear meaning." After all, "it essentially empties the paradigm of content, as everything is now narrative."[6] To gain any clarity, we would need to define subsets within these "narratives" to still be able to differentiate among them—say, between a political treatise and a novel. In other words, the benefit initially associated with a broad definition of narrativity proves to be fairly superficial. It ultimately blurs the evident differences between stories, as understood in this book, and "stories" in this all-embracing sense. Thus, the supposed theoretical grounding would, in effect, serve mainly as a rhetorical façade obscuring the avoidance of confronting this distinction—and the implications for exegesis—directly.

Protonarratives

For this reason, it appears wise to maintain our rather stringent concept of narrativity and to supplement it with a separate category for our cases

---

3. N. T. Wright, *The New Testament and the People of God*, vol. 1 of *Christian Origins and the Question of God* (Minneapolis: Fortress, 1992), 403.

4. Wright, *New Testament*, 403, takes this assertion directly from Norman R. Petersen, *Rediscovering Paul: Philemon and the Sociology of Paul's Narrative World* (Philadelphia: Fortress, 1985), 43.

5. See Heilig, *Paulus*, chapter 9, section 3.2.2, and chapter 17, section 2.4. Cf. also below, pp. 344–45.

6. Robert C. Rowland, "On Limiting the Narrative Paradigm: Three Case Studies," *Communication Monographs* 56 (1989): 45.

of "almost-narratives." Marie-Laure Ryan, an American narratologist, has acknowledged the need for such a distinction, differentiating between texts that "are" narrative and those that merely "possess" narrativity.[7] According to her, the latter are characterized by a *potential to be narrated*. She provides this illuminating example: "If I observe a fight on the subway, I will construct in my mind the story of the fight, in order to tell it to my family when I get home."

It is important, however, that from this observation we do not simply jump to the conclusion that narrativity is, thus, ultimately an exclusively mental category, which would result in an inflation of narrativity in a way that is analogous to the attempt by Fisher.[8] What Ryan sketches in her example is not simply a "story" that exists as a mental representation of events, totally detached from any "discourse." Rather, her own example demonstrates that the emergence of such a mental story is associated with an act of *construction*.

German narratologists Köppe and Kindt also discuss the "production" of mental narratives. They point out that it occurs whenever we attempt to comprehend another person's behavior: "The various states in which we observe a person are complemented by us through the attribution of opinions and desires, and this makes the states then appear as meaningfully connected."[9] To be sure, this admission that "when we explain the behavior of individuals, we also produce minimal narratives" conflicts with the insistence of these authors that identifying narratives is a task of classifying *texts* (see chapter 1). Köppe and Kindt resolve the tension by turning to simulation theory.[10] Humans are capable of mentally simulating their actions. They can, for example, play the piano or mentally simulate playing the piano. They can cook a dish or mentally simulate cooking the dish. Analogously, they can

---

7. See Marie-Laure Ryan, "Narrative," in *Routledge Encyclopedia of Narrative Theory*, ed. David Herman, Manfred Jahn, and Marie-Laure Ryan (London: Routledge, 2005), 347.

8. For a detailed analysis, see Heilig, *Paulus*, chapter 9, section 3.3.

9. Tilmann Köppe and Tom Kindt, *Erzähltheorie: Eine Einführung*, Reclams Universal-Bibliothek 17683 (Stuttgart: Reclam, 2014), 62: "Auch wenn wir das Verhalten von Personen erklären, produzieren wir minimale Erzählungen: Die verschiedenen Zustände, in denen wir eine Person beobachten, werden von uns durch die Zuschreibung von Meinungen und Wünschen ergänzt, und dies lässt die Zustände dann als sinnhaft verknüpft erscheinen."

10. Cf. Gregory Currie and Ian Ravenscroft, *Recreative Minds: Imagination in Philosophy and Psychology* (Oxford: Clarendon, 2010), who are cited by Köppe and Kindt, *Erzähltheorie*, 76, in a different context.

Chapter 4

both actually narrate stories and mentally simulate the act of storytelling. The outcome of such a *mentally simulated act of narration* is referred to by Köppe and Kindt as a "protonarrative."

In the following discussion, we will adopt this distinction between verbal or written narratives on the one hand (explicit narratives) and mental protonarratives on the other (implicit narratives).[11] To postulate the existence of a protonarrative, one of two prerequisites needs to be met. Either the author must inform us of the thoughts that they had while composing a text, or we must be able to *reconstruct* the protonarrative based on the text itself. For the latter to be feasible, the text must reference at least two events, and we must be able to infer that it is plausible that these events were sequentially and meaningfully linked in the author's mind. Such scattered mentions of events on the text's surface are thus "fragments" of an underlying protonarrative.[12]

Certainly, it is also conceivable that Paul might have contemplated a sequence of events *without* interconnecting them in his mind in a simulated act of narration. In this instance, even on this mental level, we would be dealing with mere fragments of a (proto)narrative that ultimately remains only hypothetical. Therefore, the challenges in determining Paul's *intention* represent a significant hindrance to identifying protonarratives. One might contend that the risk of false positives is exceedingly high. However, I believe that this risk can be managed.

First, even if we cannot definitively attribute a mental narrative to Paul, in certain cases we may be able to determine that specific texts with a narrative potential (to use Ryan's terminology) did indeed prompt acts of mental narration among the recipients (i.e., "So, does Paul really want to tell us that . . . ?"). This is particularly true when larger parts of a correspondence are documented and we have Paul's reactions to the reception of his letters.[13] In such instances, we may not be certain whether, when mentioning specific events in writing, Paul consciously formed a protonarrative. However, this does not mean that we should entirely refrain from applying narratological categories. Indeed, as these events were used as raw material for mental stories in the broader discourse, perhaps even reaching Paul as actual retellings and prompting him to reflect on these narratives, we can safely assume that

---

11. For details, see Heilig, *Paulus*, chapter 9, section 3.4.
12. Cf. Heilig, *Paulus*, 555.
13. Cf. Heilig, *Paulus*, 556.

there were indeed mental narratives that played a role in the conversation between Paul and his congregations.

Second, it should be emphasized that not only is Paul's simulation of narration hard to discern, but his omission of such a mental act is equally difficult to prove, or even to postulate, in many places. In some cases, it might be plausible to assume that the narrative connection of certain events mentioned in the text never occurred to Paul. However, at times it can be demonstrated that the act of constructing a mental narrative (i.e., the act of "protonarration") itself is a topic in the discourse, suggesting that performing acts of mental simulation of narration among the recipients is not only natural but actually anticipated by Paul. At the least, we must thus reckon with a protonarrative that consists of a frame narrative in which the recipients simulate the actual, embedded story!

For instance, in Phil 2:16 Paul anticipates "boasting" on the day of the Lord. This future utterance must also encompass some kind of success story that can be retrospectively told (cf. below, p. 232). Thus, the verse inherently encourages readers to envision Paul actually carrying out this speech act of boasting and, as part of that, narration before Christ—and, by extension, writing that verse must have prompted Paul to contemplate how exactly he would enter the stage as such an eschatological storyteller.

In conclusion, it is crucial to be cautious when discussing "Paul's" protonarratives, considering the possibility that some of the narrative connections that we identify may have only emerged among his recipients or even solely in our own imagination. Nevertheless, Paul's intention of causing protonarration exists on a spectrum, and we must also remain attentive to possible textual hints indicating that the apostle at least considered the possibility that his readers might mentally connect the events he mentioned into a larger mental narrative.

If the extent to which Paul intended to narratively link events mentioned in the text is unclear, this naturally suggests that we must exercise caution to avoid misapplying narratological categories. Yet it is equally critical to acknowledge that this uncertainty does not license researchers to dismiss all narrative considerations. Indeed, even when we confront incomplete protonarratives, which remain mere fragments even on the level of the mind, many narratological categories may remain relevant. We simply must be vigilant not to presume that Paul's mental process of narrativization has reached a definitive conclusion.

Observing explicit narration can indeed sensitize us to the ongoing, process-driven nature of storytelling. We must remember that what we de-

Chapter 4

fine as an "act" of storytelling, whether a verbal or a simulated one, is a complex process rather than a singular event.[14] The term "narrativization" thus encapsulates both the structuring of events into a cohesive narrative and the array of decisions associated with presenting these events.[15] Consequently, when we search for protonarratives we must also consider the possibility that we are encountering only the precursors to fully developed protonarratives. Narratological categories may prove useful in analyzing these "almost-protonarratives," but it is crucial to clearly identify which parameters are in fact applicable.

For instance, the temporal shape of a series of events might be discernible even though there may not yet be sufficient details to extract a "plot." This "almost protonarrative" from Paul's mind could potentially transform into an actual protonarrative in the minds of his readers. From there, it may consequently weave its way into their discourse as various actual stories—differing attempts to funnel this plot into a specific narrative form.

This constellation resembles the predicaments we encounter when dealing with narratives that meet only the "minimal" criteria according to Köppe and Kindt but fail to qualify as "meaningful" stories (cf. above, p. 25 and pp. 165–66). Concepts such as the "arc of suspense" are indeed pertinent to those narratives that satisfy the supplementary requirements of the second definition. In contrast, attempting to trace an arc of suspense in a narrative that merely fulfills these minimal requirements may lead to problematic outcomes—with *us*, ultimately, being the ones who contrive the more elaborate narrative.[16]

That being said, it is essential to underscore that protonarratives are not inherently more "primitive" than the outcomes of verbal narration. Our mental protonarratives can be just as highly developed as a spoken or written narrative. Consequently, the prefix "proto-" should not be interpreted as indicative of inferiority. If it is indeed appropriate to designate the result of narrativization a proto*narrative*, this means that it has met the same criteria we expect from the underlying act of narration, the only distinction being that it is simulated. And just as actual narratives can vary significantly in quality, protonarratives too can range from relatively simple to highly elaborate.

---

14. Therefore, I also do not think that it is advisable to deny the applicability of narratology to movies on the basis that the "act" of narration is somehow punctiliar, which is the argument by Köppe and Kindt, *Erzähltheorie*, 46. Cf. Heilig, *Paulus*, 548.

15. See Heilig, *Paulus*, 555, on this notion of fragments of narratives.

16. Cf. Köppe and Kindt, *Erzähltheorie*, 70.

Fragments of Implicit Protonarratives

Ryan's example of witnessing a fight and subsequently "constructing" a story to relay to family members aptly illustrates this point. As the observer preps for this anticipated disclosure at home, they likely walk through a sequential account of events in their mind—a move that signals the onset of the narrativization process. At this juncture, it may indeed be misleading to invoke fundamental descriptive categories for narratives such as "plot." Nonetheless, narrativization can evolve to its completion and materialize in highly nuanced arrangements. Perhaps the observer commences crafting an impactful narrative opening, searching for elements that convey an eerie and intimidating setting, such as darkness, moonlight, fog, or isolation. Likewise, a child entangled in a schoolyard skirmish that results in a meeting with the principal would be wise to concoct a detailed narrative of the incident that could counteract a less flattering depiction by the adversary.[17] In such instances, even the categories typically useful in dissecting elaborate explicit narratives might prove applicable.

Acknowledging that protonarratives can emerge in highly sophisticated mental configurations does not, however, suggest that explicit narratives are merely physical manifestations of a preceding mental protonarrative. Köppe and Kindt's assertion that we "could" articulate protonarratives, even though we only have them in our minds, is not without its drawbacks.[18] Converting a protonarrative into verbal form is anything but simple, given that text production in general, whether narrative or not, is a complex procedure.[19]

Specifically, we must always consider the strong likelihood that a speaker or author may adjust a preplanned text during the production process.[20] This revision phase necessitates a certain *detachment* from the produced text, a vantage point that can only be simulated to a limited degree, often contingent on individual talent and experience. Even with meticulous planning, the actual act of speaking typically reveals a need for some level of revision. Personally, I frequently discover that a story that "sounded" harmonious during mental rehearsal does not necessarily "emerge" as co-

---

17. We observe a similar spectrum, of course, with respect to other, nonnarrative kinds of speech acts. For example, when preparing a (mostly descriptive) lecture, a scholar might only prepare some general points in advance or even simulate the interaction with the audience down to aspects such as facial expressions and tonality.

18. For this quote from Köppe and Kindt, *Erzähltheorie*, 62, see above, note 9 on p. 203.

19. Gansel and Jürgens, *Textlinguistik*, 137–74. See, in particular, 144–48 on the phases of text production.

20. Gansel and Jürgens, *Textlinguistik*, 147.

herently when spoken.[21] Thus, discussions about "complete" protonarratives should not insinuate that a potential explicit narrative would generate a story with precisely matching elements. Vice versa, it would be equally naive to assume that Paul's explicit stories are always preceded by an exact replica in his mind.

To a substantial extent, Paul's protonarratives, like his thoughts in general, will always remain fundamentally beyond our reach. The verbalization of a protonarrative itself is a form of renarration that unavoidably results in story alterations. Despite these complexities, I firmly believe that protonarratives represent an enchanting and enriching field of study. This focus provides the potential to deepen our understanding of implicit narratives—a phenomenon that has constantly popped up in the periphery of our analysis even when we tried to look elsewhere and to keep a narrow focus on explicit narratives, a phenomenon that, therefore, seems to be of great importance for understanding Paul's letter writing.

Disnarrated Events as Fragments of Protonarratives

Narration is typically understood to necessitate the assertion of events that either had transpired or are occurring at the time of storytelling. However, in our quest for narratives in Paul's letters, we have also encountered many "almost stories" that share two features: on the one hand, they seem to invite narratological analysis, while on the other hand, they fall short of actually asserting the occurrence of events—sometimes even outright denying certain happenings. In the following section, we will scrutinize to what extent this category of nonevents and almost events can be treated as fragments of mental protonarratives.

---

21. More recently, cognitive-linguistic research has taken up many insights from the study of *interaction* among participants in communication. It has become clear that especially in contexts where the participants are in the same physical space, narration is a complex process that is multimodal (involving in particular also gestures) and cooperative, with the feedback of the addressees constantly influencing the act of narration. See Elisabeth Zima, *Einführung in die gebrauchsbasierte Kognitive Linguistik* (Berlin: de Gruyter, 2021), 277–79.

Disnarrated and Virtual Narratives

In an influential essay from 1988, Gerald Price notes that many events mentioned or suggested in narrative works are *not* definitively asserted.[22] First, there are the "unnarratable" or "nonnarratable" events. For instance, the narrative account of a specific event might be impossible due to genre constraints (cf. above, p. 180, regarding novels utilizing the letter form) or because the event is supernatural and thus is beyond human comprehension and ability to narrate (cf. above, p. 187, on 2 Cor 12:4). Second, there are the simply "unnarrated" or "nonnarrated" events, whose occurrence is not explicitly stated but can be inferred by the reader (cf. above, pp. 179–81, on ellipses). Finally, Price introduces the category of "disnarrated" events, which feature in statements that explicitly reject—or at least call into question—the occurrence of events.

> When I speak of [the disnarrated], I am thus referring to alethic expressions of impossibility or unrealized possibility, deontic expressions of observed prohibition, epistemic expressions of ignorance, ontologic expressions of nonexistence, purely imagined worlds, desired worlds, or intended worlds, unfulfilled expectations, unwarranted beliefs, failed attempts, crushed hopes, suppositions and false calculations, errors and lies, and so forth.[23]

Ryan similarly highlights that when we engage with story entities capable of mental processes, we often gain some insight into their projections for the narrative's future—or at least surmise that these projections are taking place.[24] Some of these predictions might align with the actual narrative (for example, when a character's fear is confirmed, or a plan is implemented) while others end up being merely "virtual."

These "virtual embedded narratives" share something with Price's "disnarrations," in that they do not correspond with the story that is actually

---

22. Gerald Prince, "The Disnarrated," *Style* 22 (1988): 1–8. Cf. Heilig, *Paulus*, chapter 10, section 2.

23. Prince, "Disnarrated," 3.

24. Marie-Laure Ryan, "Embedded Narratives and Tellability," *Style* 20 (1986): 319–37. Cf. Heilig, *Paulus*, chapter 10, section 3, for how her conception is used by Sönke Finnern and Jan Rüggemeier, *Methoden der neutestamentlichen Exegese: Ein Lehr- und Arbeitsbuch*, Uni-Taschenbücher 4212 (Tübingen: Francke, 2016), 219–22, and a critique of that appropriation.

Chapter 4

told. Ryan's approach diverges from Price's, however, in that it is more specific when it comes to the source of the virtual narrative, stipulating that it stems from a narrative figure's *mental* act, yet it is simultaneously more general because there is no necessity for the text to *explicitly* inform us about these mental acts. It is enough for them to be inferrable from the character's behavior.

The challenge for narratological analysis is that disnarrated or virtual events cannot form actual elements of a plot.[25] However, even though we cannot assert that "a story is told" in these instances, these expressions undeniably highlight a potential story, one that is ultimately disregarded. This is the case because "every usage of negation presupposes that in the respective context, the affirmed opposite, which is then explicitly rejected by means of the negation, was up for debate."[26] In other words, *each act of disnarration summons protonarratives*—potential narratives, stories that could have been told but that, for whatever reason, the storyteller not only refrained from telling but categorically dismissed.[27]

When considering this negative foil of the actual narrative, it is crucial to make a key distinction at the outset. Most often, disnarration suggests the dismissal of an *entire range of potential narratives*—namely, all those that incorporate the disnarrated event(s) as components of their plot. In some cases, however, the narrator might be contemplating *a particular counter-narrative*, possibly one that has already been articulated and to which they now want to react.

Contrastive Foils

The intimate interplay between disnarration and narration—and, thus, protonarratives and narratives—becomes evident when we examine *"corrective" connections*, where ἀλλά marks propositional negative-positive pairs (on this

---

25. For more details, see Heilig, *Paulus*, chapter 10, section 5.
26. Eva Breindl, "Grundbegriffe der Beschreibung und Prinzipien der Bedeutungskonstitution," in *Semantik der deutschen Satzverknüpfer*, ed. Eva Breindl, Anna Volodina, and Ulrich Hermann Waßner, vol. 2 of *Handbuch der deutschen Konnektoren*, Schriften des Instituts für Deutsche Sprache 13 (Berlin: de Gruyter, 2014), 123. Original: "Mit der Verwendung einer Negation ist immer die Hintergrundannahme gekoppelt, dass im gegebenen Kontext das affirmierte Gegenteil zur Debatte stand, das dann in der Negation explizit zurückgewiesen wird."
27. See Heilig, *Paulus*, chapter 10, section 6.

type of connections, see above, pp. 130–31). Here, we often perceive a miniature story in the positive element while the disnarration in the negative element provides a contrastive foil.[28] Not only is a protonarrative dismissed, but what can or must be assumed instead is also made explicit.

In such instances, the disnarration furnishes additional information about the plot or theme of the narrative, or at the very least about its pragmatic dimension. If we were to consider only the asserted component of these connections, we would frequently run into difficulties deciphering *why* a certain sequence of events is narrated and what potential alternative accounts are excluded by this narration. It is only due to the negative part that we can identify the appropriate context that highlights the key features of the story.

How substantial this contribution of information is can be gauged through a quick test. If we momentarily assume that we only have the positive assertions of these connections, we will immediately realize how challenging it is to infer the precise negative counterpoints that Paul introduces in his letters. In other words, our own guesses of what features he wanted to highlight will probably be off. For there is no one-size-fits-all rule. Even a brief survey of such corrective structures in Paul's writings, which will follow, reveals that the relationship between actual and virtual plots is exceptionally nuanced.[29]

In Rom 8:32 we observe actual symmetry. Both halves of the connection focus on the same point in time—God's decision, which turns out in our favor in the real plot and in favor of his own Son in the counterfactual plot. Similarly, 1 Cor 15:10 appears to focus on the same period on the respective factual and counterfactual timelines. The fact that God acted graciously toward Paul (ἡ χάρις αὐτοῦ ἡ εἰς ἐμέ) "did not turn out in vain" (οὐ κενὴ ἐγενήθη). Thus, what is disnarrated is a storyline in which God's demonstration of grace would have remained without a positive effect. Note that the positive element of the connection does not recount this gracious act itself. That God acted on Paul's behalf is presupposed here as well. The focus remains on the aftermath of this divine encounter: ". . . but I have labored more than all the others" (ἀλλὰ περισσότερον αὐτῶν πάντων ἐκοπίασα).

Note, however, that the aorist aspect in the negated clause might be significant. Unlike, for example, in 1 Thess 2:1 (οὐ κενὴ γέγονεν), we do not have the perfect indicative. In other words, the negative element of 1 Cor 15:10

---

28. For a very detailed assessment, see Heilig, *Paulus*, chapter 12, section 2.
29. Heilig, *Paulus*, chapter 12, sections 2.2 and 2.3.1.

Chapter 4

might have a narrower temporal focus than the positive element. While the latter likewise uses the aorist indicative to summarize the activity during the whole subsequent period after the reception of God's grace, the former takes a counterfactual transition into view. Perhaps Paul indeed scrutinizes the same time period and would have allowed belated effects to still count as contradicting the idea of God's grace having been in vain. However, it is also possible that the actual unfolding of events and his memory of an immediate response to God's grace considers only the immediate aftermath of that divine intervention, presupposing that if nothing would have happened right after that, if there had not been an immediately visible manifestation of that grace in his life, it would have remained without effect also later.

In any case, turning to 2 Thess 3:7b–8 we again encounter "symmetrical disnarration" and, in fact, a rather detailed instance. Upon close examination, the disnarrated element (οὐκ ἠτακτήσαμεν ἐν ὑμῖν οὐδὲ δωρεὰν ἄρτον ἐφάγομεν παρά τινος) seems to outline two sequential counterfactual events—being idle on the one hand and, hence, having to depend on others for sustenance on the other hand—that contrastingly correspond to the affirmed events of working and being able to provide for themselves.[30]

In contrast, there are other cases where the disnarrated element refers to a time that is prior to the event that is actually narrated. Here, the negated event constitutes something that would have made the actual story impossible from the outset. This situation arises in 2 Tim 1:16b–17, where the author includes a brief narrative as a rationalization for their hope that, in the eschaton, the Lord might show mercy to Onesiphorus and his household. First, an event bundle in the complexive aorist is cited: "He used to cheer me up many times" (verse 16b: πολλάκις με ἀνέψυξεν). This is succeeded by καί and a negated component: "and he was not ashamed of my imprisonment" (verse 16c: καὶ τὴν ἅλυσίν μου οὐκ ἐπαισχύνθη). The syntax poses a greater challenge than one might think at first look.

Many versions adhere to the verse division and hypothesize that this second element of verse 16 (verse 16c) is part of a general account about Onesiphorus's behavior. In this view, it either describes an added noble quality or explicates the meaning of "cheering up," with the aorist in the latter scenario also being considered complexive. For instance, the NIV seems to adopt such

---

30. This is rather surprising because usually we would expect οὐδέ to merely imply an additive relationship. The latter is likely what we encounter in Gal 1:16c–17a. See Heilig, *Paulus*, 247–49. For a detailed discussion of the occurrence in 2 Thess 3:7b–8, see Heilig, *Paulus*, chapter 12, section 2.3.2.

Fragments of Implicit Protonarratives

an interpretation of verse 16: "May the Lord show mercy to the household of Onesiphorus, because he often refreshed me and was not ashamed of my chains." Take note of the causal clause with two verbs that are connected by "and," with the subject not even being repeated in the second part.

However, this interpretation encounters the issue that verse 17 commences with ἀλλά, making it difficult for the two situations of verse 16 to collectively form the negative foil for the miniature story that is presented in that next verse: "... when he had come to Rome, he searched for me with great care—and he found me" (... γενόμενος ἐν Ῥώμῃ σπουδαίως ἐζήτησέν με καὶ εὗρεν). To introduce this story with "on the contrary," as the NIV does, seems to presuppose a rather rough narrative transition. For there is, of course, no contrast between the behavior of verse 17 and verse 16b.

Hence, it seems more natural to assume that the adversative connector links the negative foil of what Onesiphorus refrained from doing in verse 16c with the subsequent account of his actions in verse 17. We must, therefore, derive that verse 16b presents the first event bundle of the story, and that the καί that we encounter at the beginning of verse 16c looks forward to the next positive assertion in verse 17. This introduces a plot turn into the narrative with two plausible interpretations. The author either wishes to introduce another commendable characteristic trait—possibly faithfulness, alongside being a source of comfort—or their aim is to detail what "cheering up" meant in one exceptionally challenging circumstance. In summary, it appears most plausible to me that verse 17 serves the function of augmenting the reference to the *frequency* of consolatory acts in verse 16b by emphasizing the *quality* of Onesiphorus's conduct (with verse 16c offering the contrasting narrative), citing his support when Paul had been abandoned by many (cf. 2 Tim 4:10–11a). The disnarrated potential shame for Paul—Onesiphorus's lack of such feelings toward Paul—enables him to seek out Paul.

In this case, disnarration emphasizes the *preconditions* that facilitate the main narrative (similarly in Phil 2:6–7 and arguably in Rom 1:21). If Onesiphorus had felt the same as the others, he would have acted like them, not seeking out Paul and, consequently, not finding him. Stories about his numerous acts of consolation might still hold in that contrafactual scenario. However, this distinctive narrative about his faithfulness, his comforting actions in a particularly daunting situation, becomes feasible only because he perceives the imprisoned apostle differently.

There are other similar instances in Paul's undisputed letters.[31] For in-

---

31. For a detailed discussion, see Heilig, *Paulus*, chapter 12, section 2.2.

Chapter 4

stance, in Rom 4:20 the disnarrated event also precedes the narrated events. Here, we witness a counterfactual plotline marked by negated doubt on one side. Conversely, on the affirmed timeline there does not seem to be an account of the actual act of putting faith in God's promise. Instead, we immediately shift to a mutually reinforcing process of growing faith and glorifying God.[32]

Granted, the syntax in 1 Thess 2:5–7 is somewhat intricate, yet a similar interpretation appears to be the most probable here too. In this passage, the disnarration outlines several associated behavioral patterns, and it is the underlying motivation behind all of them that would have nullified the actual narrative. Galatians 4:14 is also somewhat ambiguous, this time due to uncertainties surrounding its reference. However, Paul's emphasis on how severe the anticipated treatment would have been suggests that the focus is, similarly, on an underlying disposition that would have jeopardized his heartfelt reception.

From this brief overview, it becomes evident that Paul's actual narratives often acquire significant nuances when juxtaposed against the specific nature of the disnarrated events with which they are contrasted. As we will now see, there are even cases where the actual events are not narrated at all because they can be presupposed. Still, there clearly seems to be an implicit, already known, narrative in the background that is *reinforced* by means of pointing to a counterfactual plot.

This is attested by the highly debated and, in my estimation, often misunderstood passage: Rom 10:14–15a.[33] That passage follows a descriptive account in verses 12–13 of the current state where there is "no difference between the Jew and the Greek" (οὐ γάρ ἐστιν διαστολὴ Ἰουδαίου τε καὶ Ἕλληνος). This is attributed to there being only one Lord for all people (ὁ γὰρ αὐτὸς κύριος πάντων). His willingness to show grace "to all who call

---

32. Others, like Benjamin Schliesser, *Zweifel: Phänomene des Zweifels und der Zweiseeligkeit im frühen Christentum*, WUNT 500 (Tübingen: Mohr Siebeck, 2022), 96, emphasize the transformative nature of "empowerment" and deny that Paul "quantifies" faith. But cf. also Acts 9:22, where the imperfect verb form is combined with μᾶλλον and where, accordingly, we have a clear instance of a gradual strengthening. I have not looked in detail into the question of whether the situation that is portrayed in the aorist indeed is a telic change of state from an absolute lack of a quality to its existence. However, due to passages such as Herm. Sim. 78.2 (9.1), I am skeptical. There, being "somewhat weak" (ἀσθενέστερος) is contrasted with a "strengthening" that apparently is gradual indeed, because it results in a strength that now reaches a certain threshold "so that" something could be done (. . . ὥστε δύνασθαί σε καὶ ἄγγελον ἰδεῖν).

33. For a detailed analysis, see Heilig, *Paulus*, 633–38.

upon him" (πλουτῶν εἰς πάντας τοὺς ἐπικαλουμένους αὐτόν) is then, in verse 13, grounded in the quotation from Joel 3:5: "For everyone who calls on the name of the Lord will be saved" (πᾶς γὰρ ὃς ἂν ἐπικαλέσηται τὸ ὄνομα κυρίου σωθήσεται). This is subsequently followed in verses 14-15a by a series of questions in the deliberative subjunctive:

Πῶς οὖν ἐπικαλέσωνται εἰς ὃν οὐκ ἐπίστευσαν;

πῶς δὲ πιστεύσωσιν οὗ οὐκ ἤκουσαν;

πῶς δὲ ἀκούσωσιν[34] χωρὶς κηρύσσοντος;

πῶς δὲ κηρύξωσιν ἐὰν μὴ ἀποσταλῶσιν;

Some scholars believe that Paul is focusing on the situation of the Jews and intends "to show that the Jews have really had full opportunity to call upon the name of the Lord . . . and are therefore without excuse."[35] However, their actual condemnation for disregarding the gospel would seem peculiarly indirect, subtly implied in the subsequent quote from Isa 52:7 in verse 15b, which highlights the "beauty" of the feet of those who bring the good news (ὡς ὡραῖοι οἱ πόδες τῶν εὐαγγελιζομένων [τὰ] ἀγαθά). An interpretation of this nature appears to project the later emphasis on Israel (verse 19: ἀλλὰ λέγω, μὴ Ἰσραὴλ οὐκ ἔγνω;) onto the sketch of a counterfactual plot, which follows the very general statements of verses 12-13. It is much more natural to assume that the questions in verses 14-15a must be in some way connected to the prehistory of the situation that is in view in verses 12-13, which display a universal outlook encompassing both Jews and gentiles.

Regrettably, interpreters who accurately perceive this often fail to pro-

---

34. Note the variant ακουσονται (future indicative). The spelling ακουσωνται in P[46], listed separately in NA[28], does not constitute evidence for an additional variant (a "future subjunctive"). On this topic, see the analogous discussion by Chrys C. Caragounis, *The Development of Greek and the New Testament: Morphology, Syntax, Phonology, and Textual Transmission*, WUNT 167 (Tübingen: Mohr Siebeck, 2004), 547-64, on 1 Cor 13:3, where the textual witnesses for καυχθησωμαι should definitively simply be attributed to the variant καυχθησομαι, and not considered a "grammatical monstrosity," as Bruce M. Metzger, *A Textual Commentary on the Greek New Testament*, 2nd ed. (Stuttgart: Deutsche Bibelgesellschaft, 1994), 564, argues.

35. C. E. B. Cranfield, *The Epistle to the Romans*, 2 vols., ICC (Edinburgh: T&T Clark, 1975 and 1979), 2:533.

vide a detailed explanation of what Paul's actual approach here is, merely emphasizing his concern for "stringency," without making any attempt to clarify the specific scenario that is being outlined.[36] Translations likewise frequently gloss over the nuances of Paul's rhetorical strategy. In contrast, I posit that Paul is making a very specific point here. He is trying to tie the situation of verses 12–13 to his own apostolic ministry. He does this by prompting the readers to contemplate certain critical aspects of a presumed story's plot about the events leading to the current situation depicted in verses 12–13. The posed questions aim to underscore that *Paul's ministry is a necessary element of this narrative* because, as Paul implies, without this component, the story could not have culminated in the happy ending of verses 12–13.

In a first move in verse 14a, Paul asks, "Now, how are they supposed to call on the one in whom they have not believed?" (Πῶς οὖν ἐπικαλέσωνται εἰς ὃν οὐκ ἐπίστευσαν;). Naturally, the answer has to be that this would be completely impossible. As verse 16 explicitly indicates later, this reference to "not believing" indeed pertains to authentic experiences from Paul's mission. Some people do not react positively to Paul's proclamation. Conversely, those individuals in verses 12–13 who actually call upon the Lord have clearly adopted a different attitude toward the Lord.

Most interpreters assume that verse 14b has basically the same scenario in view, the proclamation that immediately precedes the response to the message about Jesus mentioned in verse 14a. However, this understanding is unlikely due to both contextual and syntactical reasons. As verse 18 demonstrates, Paul presumes in this passage that the gospel has indeed reached the entire world. Meaning, when he refers to the disnarrated event of "not hearing" (οὐκ ἤκουσαν), it cannot reference not hearing the apostolic proclamation of the gospel. While not everyone responds positively to the message, everyone has heard it. Furthermore, syntactically it is most natural to assume that the relative pronoun οὗ refers to the one in whom trust is to be placed (cf. εἰς ὃν . . . ἐπίστευσαν in verse 14a and ὁ πιστεύων ἐπ' αὐτῷ in verse 11). Therefore, an accurate translation would be: "But how are they supposed to trust (the one) *whom* they have not heard?" (πῶς δὲ πιστεύσωσιν οὗ οὐκ

---

36. Ulrich Wilckens, *Der Brief an die Römer*, 3 vols., EKKNT 6 (Zurich: Benziger, 1978–1991), 2:228: "The rigor of this chain inference, each part of which refers back to the condition of the preceding segment, gains strong rhetorical impact through the 'how'-questions" (Original: "Die Stringenz dieses jeweils auf die Bedingung des voranstehenden Gliedes zurückführenden Kettenschlusses kommt in den 'Wie'-Fragen zu starker rhetorischer Geltung").

ἤκουσαν;). By contrast, it feels strained to interpret the genitive to mean "how are they to believe in one they have not heard *of*?" (so the NET; emphasis mine). Therefore, it seems that Paul first emphasizes in verse 14a that the act of believing in the Lord is a precondition for calling upon him, and then in verse 14b he refers to the fact that some people have indeed not had the opportunity to hear from the Lord himself.[37]

This observation adds substantial detail to the generic claim about Paul's "stringency." As we can now deduce, the answer to verse 14b, unlike the one implied in verse 14a, is not "Not at all!" but "Through the evangelists!" Interpretations that do not focus on the protonarratives in the background of this passage often overlook this crucial evolution.

Given the proposed reading, the next query in verse 14c makes perfect sense: "But how are they supposed to hear without someone who proclaims?" (πῶς δὲ ἀκούσωσιν χωρὶς κηρύσσοντος;). Note that there is no statement in the indicative about a lack of proclamation. While "not believing" (the gospel) and "not hearing" (the Lord himself) are nonactions that can be ascribed to real individuals in the past, a lack of preachers is only considered as a hypothetical scenario. Thus, χωρὶς κηρύσσοντος should be construed as a condensed form of a *counterfactual* conditional clause akin to εἰ οὐκ ὑπῆρχεν κηρύσσων: "But how could they hear if there were no preacher?" This time, similar to verse 14a, the answer must be again: "Not at all!" If there were no preachers who delivered the good news, then the people who had not had a chance to hear the Lord himself would remain in a state of "not hearing," of spiritual deafness, without ever having the opportunity to listen to the good news either from the Lord himself or through intermediaries.[38]

In summary, verse 14a draws attention to the real scenario of unbelief by some people, and verse 14b indicates that most people would be headed

---

37. As a sidenote, we can observe that Paul is apparently presupposing Jesus's earthly ministry. In my opinion, it is presuppositions like these that call into question some of the more recent treatments about the relationship between Paul and the Gospels. On this whole issue, cf. in particular the influential work by Christine Jacobi, *Jesusüberlieferung bei Paulus? Analogien zwischen den echten Paulusbriefen und den synoptischen Evangelien*, BZNW 213 (Berlin: de Gruyter, 2015).

38. Admittedly, one might argue that the use of the same verb in verse 14c offers contextual support for taking the "hearing" of verse 14b to refer to hearing the gospel *about* Jesus. But note that in verse 14c the verb does not have a direct object at all. What becomes impossible without preachers is "hearing" in general. Of course, the potentially affected people would not become totally deaf; what is in view in this context is, rather, so it seems to me, any kind of "hearing" that is of soteriological relevance.

Chapter 4

down the same path, given their lack of the opportunity to hear the Lord personally. Building on this, verse 14c reconstructs a counterfactual plot: if "the preacher" were absent, then the scenario mentioned in verse 14a would indeed be the necessary outcome of the circumstance admitted in verse 14b. In other words, disbelief would be an inescapable element of a narrative in which the figure of the preacher would not make an appearance after Jesus's ascension. Undoubtedly, the recipients are already aware of the actual events, of how the gospel also made its way to them in Rome. However, what Paul is doing now is emphasizing that the narrative character of "the preacher" is not merely a coincidental part of that story but a crucial component of the plot.

Paul's intent to delve deeper into this narrative character is evident. This is perceptible in verse 15a, where he shifts the focus onto the mediator's role with the generic participle from verse 14c now replaced by the third-person plural subjunctive verb form: "But how are they supposed to proclaim unless they are sent?" (πῶς δὲ κηρύξωσιν ἐὰν μὴ ἀποσταλῶσιν;). Note that here Paul scrutinizes a situation in the past that did not happen. Nevertheless, he uses a prospective conditional clause since the question of verse 14b has taken the readers back in time to the moment of the Lord's ascension. From the position of those who have not yet had personal interaction with Jesus at that point in time, the question of "what now?" arises. What if no preachers will emerge in the future (which is in the counterfactual past of the narrating "I")? What will happen to us? Consequently, verse 15a effectively mirrors the sentiment of verse 14c, but this time the stringency of the plot is not established with an eye on the intermediary figure—a *narrative character*—but by paying attention to a *narrative event*, which is linked with the figure of "the preacher"—the commissioning of preachers. Obviously, the use of ἀποστέλλω in this context is meant to recall κλητὸς ἀπόστολος in Rom 1:1. In a breathtaking narrative maneuver, Paul skillfully *narrates himself into the past of the Roman Christians*. Note that the shift of temporal perspective results in drawing the recipients of the letter into the narrative world. The question posed in verse 15a functions as a focalization signal, suggesting that the Roman Christians—more precisely, their past selves who were yet to become Christians—are part of this story. Their perspective at that time, as individuals who had not had a chance for personal interaction with the Lord, is adopted. The narrative, therefore, brings them (the Christians in Rome, the recipients of the letter) and Paul (the apostle, the letter's author) into close proximity.

To sum up, we can conclude that the questions of Rom 10:14–15a aim to link the presumed grace-filled time depicted in verses 11–13 with Paul's own

Fragments of Implicit Protonarratives

commission (and that of other preachers). This is accomplished by alluding to a counterfactual narrative that, due to the absence of dispatched preachers such as Paul, would never have reached the happy ending.

Moreover, note that in this framework the quotation from Isa 52:7 that follows in verse 15b makes perfect sense: "As it is written: 'How beautiful are the feet of those who proclaim the good news!'" Indeed, the apostles' office deserves commendation since the gracious offer outlined in verses 11–13 can only be imparted to humanity via this avenue. Accordingly, it seems likely that we have still not returned to the temporal position of the narrating "I." Instead, we appear to still perceive the world from the vantage point of those who, following the Lord's departure, face the seemingly bleak prospect of not having access to salvific faith (which includes the not-yet-Christian Romans). For these individuals, the approach of the messengers of the good news must indeed be a most welcome sight.

Different Kinds of Disnarration

I trust that the preceding section has effectively highlighted the crucial significance of disnarration and thus the implied counterfactual protonarratives in interpreting Paul's letters. Having demonstrated the heuristic potential of disnarration, I wish to conclude this segment by highlighting several differentiations that appear valuable for future examinations. We can only shine some spotlights on these phenomena, and readers are encouraged to pursue the provided references for comprehensive treatments of the corresponding subcategories of disnarration.

Partial Disnarration

First, I would like to discuss the concept of *"partial" disnarration*.[39] As we observed previously in relation to 1 Cor 15:10, disnarration often does not influence *every* parameter of the actual narrative. Certain aspects of the affirmed part in a positive-negative connection can be preserved in the disnarrated element. In 1 Cor 15:10, for example, the fact that indeed there was a gracious divine act toward Paul in the past was not challenged; only the consequences were subject to debate.

---

39. For more details, see Heilig, *Paulus*, 638–42.

Chapter 4

Galatians 1:16 provides an exemplary illustration of disnarration with a limited temporal scope. Only with respect to the immediate aftermath of God's decision to reveal his Son to Paul is a trip to Jerusalem denied. Importantly, this does not preclude the possibility that he journeyed there afterward (verses 18–19).

In other instances, the time frame remains consistent between the narration and disnarration, but other parameters of actual and counterfactual situations are contrasted, such as the subject of the verb (the second disnarration case in 1 Cor 15:10; cf. also 1 Cor 7:10; and similarly, with οὐκέτι, in Rom 7:18–20 and Gal 2:20) or the direct object (Rom 8:15; 2 Cor 7:9; 8:5 offer enlightening examples in this regard).

Supplementary Disnarration

Second, we need to briefly consider *"supplementary" disnarration*.[40] It is typically characterized by an extension of the negative-positive pattern, often with μόνον added to the negation and καί following the ἀλλά (οὐ μόνον ... ἀλλὰ καί...). This could also be viewed as a supplemental form of actual narration, as the negative part here represents an actual event. However, it can also be categorized as a form of disnarration, since with this modification the connection communicates that the first proposition does not yet constitute a *complete* account of what happened.

For instance, Rom 1:32 indicates that a narrative about "them" committing death-worthy acts would not do justice to the actual events since it must be underscored, according to Paul, that they also, even worse, applaud such behaviors (οὐ μόνον αὐτὰ ποιοῦσιν ἀλλὰ καὶ συνευδοκοῦσιν τοῖς πράσσουσιν). Here, disnarration distinctly adopts a metanarrative character as certain theoretically possible narratives are assessed. While these purportedly reductionistic narratives do not necessarily appear in the immediate context (or elsewhere), they are considered potential interpretations of the events in question, which are then deliberately reframed by the author.

Other examples from Paul include 2 Cor 9:12 and Phil 1:29. The latter verse clearly illustrates how the supplemented narrative diverges from the rejected implicit protonarrative by encompassing a greater temporal scope. From Paul's perspective, a reliable narrative regarding the Philippians must surpass the initial grace of their salvation and also underscore how they have

---

40. For more details, see Heilig, *Paulus*, 642–47.

equally participated in the suffering that Paul underwent (cf. also verse 30). Although the syntax in 2 Cor 8:10 is similar, here the same time spans are covered. However, the motivation behind the recounted action is emphasized in this instance, thus becoming integral to the narrative about that period.

Just as with partial disnarration, Paul's letters exhibit a wide variety of emphases regarding the syntactical element under the spotlight. Examples include the causal adjunct in Rom 4:23–24 and 13:5, the spatial adjunct in 2 Cor 8:21 (but not in the similarly looking verse 1 Thess 1:8), the instrumental adjunct in 2 Cor 7:7 and 1 Thess 1:5, and even a complement that specifies properties of the subject in 1 Tim 5:13.

Corrective Disnarration

Third, when dealing with *"corrective" disnarration*, the metanarrative dimension becomes even more discernible.[41] While in the case of supplementary disnarration the issue is with the supposed completeness of a potential protonarrative in the background (though, certainly, even the inclusion of this single aspect might be deemed critical to the account's reliability in the narrator's opinion), in this context we are dealing with actual narratives that are marked as in need of modification. Therefore, we are indisputably grappling with utterance relatedness in the relevant connections.

Often, exceptive conditional clauses lie on the cusp of representing such a phenomenon yet do not entirely cross that threshold. The associated connectors allow for the articulation of a qualification in the second part without making the utterance in the first part seem inappropriate. When Paul asserts in 1 Cor 1:14 that he has baptized none of the recipients (οὐδένα ὑμῶν ἐβάπτισα), he can still follow up this statement with the exception of Crispus and Gaius (εἰ μὴ Κρίσπον καὶ Γάϊον) without casting aspersions on the initial assertion. A genuine correction does not occur until verse 16, when Paul adds in an adversative connection that he also baptized the household of Stephanas (ἐβάπτισα δὲ καὶ τὸν Στεφανᾶ οἶκον, λοιπὸν οὐκ οἶδα εἴ τινα ἄλλον ἐβάπτισα).

Exceptive conditional clauses have greater significance for correcting disnarration when they form *restrictive connections* or, in other words, display utterance relatedness (cf. above, pp. 132–33). The most prominent example with εἰ μή in Paul's letters is found in Gal 1:7. In my opinion, μᾶλλον δέ can also operate as a restrictive connector, and this function can also be seen

---

41. For details on what follows, see Heilig, *Paulus*, 647–54.

Chapter 4

in Paul's letters, for instance, in Rom 8:34 (cf. also Gal 4:9). There, a nominalized participle characterizing Christ as "the one who died" (Χριστὸς ['Ιησοῦς] ὁ ἀποθανών) receives an explanatory remark asserting that he is, in fact, also "the one who was raised" (μᾶλλον δὲ ἐγερθείς). The point is that this addition is essential for understanding the events that are then narrated in two relative clauses—being situated at God's right hand and interceding on our behalf (ὅς καὶ ἔστιν ἐν δεξιᾷ τοῦ θεοῦ, ὅς καὶ ἐντυγχάνει ὑπὲρ ἡμῶν). In this case, the continuation of the story necessitates supplementation of a narrative figure's backstory.

The question of why the storyteller does not simply discard the original narration attempt in such cases warrants careful scrutiny in each individual instance. For instance, Paul might choose to employ this disnarrating strategy to first present one version of the story—possibly as it has been recounted by others—in order to explicitly address its deficiencies. Alternatively, it might merely reflect Paul's self-correction during the act of narration, thereby documenting a close correlation between his dictation and what the scribe noted down.[42]

The requirement for some form of corrective disnarration is not exclusively associated with certain connections, but it also becomes apparent when within the broader context *indications of unreliable narration* emerge. For instance, following his suspiciously hesitant narration (cf. above, p. 186) of a story concerning the visionary experience of "a man in Christ," Paul alludes in 2 Cor 12:6 to the fact that the said man is, contrary to initial portrayal, not a separate individual but rather himself. This factor often escapes the notice of commentators as they tend not to consider the narratological concept of unreliable narration. Similarly, when I ask students about the reasons for their conviction that Paul is the man under discussion—a presumption they invariably endorse—they are often taken aback, realizing they have taken this identification for granted, unable to pinpoint its explicit disclosure.

I attribute part of this confusion to seemingly unnecessary complications in the academic literature surrounding the type of conditional construction involved.[43] Paul does not articulate in verse 6a–b: "If I *wished* to boast,

---

42. This also has implications for the secretary hypothesis that is sometimes adduced to explain differences in style when it comes to the disputed Pauline letters.

43. Cf. the detailed discussion in Heilig, *Paulus*, 820–24. I discuss this passage again below, pp. 300–304, in the context of conditional clauses with future reference. There is significant overlap between these two sections, with the latter one being more detailed,

Fragments of Implicit Protonarratives

I would not be a fool" (which in Greek would be Εἰ *ἤθελον* καυχήσασθαι, οὐκ ἄν ἤμην ἄφρον), but rather, "If I *wish* to boast, I will not be a fool" ('Ἐὰν ... *θελήσω* καυχήσασθαι, οὐκ ἔσομαι ἄφρων). The crucial question then is, What form of boasting is Paul contemplating? It has to be a type of boasting that is a *real possibility* at that point in discourse.

It definitely cannot be an instance of boasting about his weaknesses (cf. verse 5b: ὑπὲρ δὲ ἐμαυτοῦ οὐ καυχήσομαι εἰ μὴ ἐν ταῖς ἀσθενείαις) given that he clearly follows through with this boast in 11:30 and 12:10, contradicting verse 6c, where he claims to "refrain" from such boasting (cf. φείδομαι δέ). The only instance of considered but ultimately foregone boasting is that about the anonymous man indicated in verse 5a (ὑπὲρ τοῦ τοιούτου καυχήσομαι). Hence, the conditional construction in verse 6a–b could be reworded as 'Ἐὰν γὰρ θελήσω καυχήσασθαι ὑπὲρ τοῦ τοιούτου... In other words, Paul initially presents himself as entertaining the idea of boasting about the anonymous man only to reject this real possibility later.

He explains this shift by referencing his desire not to influence the Corinthians to think any more highly of him than is warranted by what they see and hear (verse 6e–f: μή τις εἰς ἐμὲ λογίσηται ὑπὲρ ὃ βλέπει με ἢ ἀκούει [τι] ἐξ ἐμοῦ). How does praising the *anonymous man* inadvertently elevate appreciation for *Paul himself*? This becomes plausible only if the two characters are indeed the same. While the recurring emphasis on the uncertainty of the bodily involvement in the visionary experience is already suggestive (cf. above, p. 187), it is not until this point that Paul finally—and still only subtly—discloses the narration so far to have been unreliable.

This interpretation of the conditional construction is also the only one that makes sense of verse 6d, where Paul rationalizes that any prospective boasting about the anonymous man would not render him a fool because the assertion would be truthful (ἀλήθειαν γὰρ ἐρῶ). The only requirement when boasting about another person is that the statement be truthful. However, Paul requires more stringent criteria for self-boasting, permitting only boasting about weaknesses (verse 5b). Commentators who misinterpret the conditional clause in verse 6a do not have a place for verse 6d in their framework, leading them to unfairly suggest that Paul is extremely inconsistent. They assert that while the apostle initially implies that self-boasting about divine visions is vainglorious (cf., e.g., 11:16), he later claims that he could engage in such boasting if he so desired, as it would be grounded in reality.

---

but I think it is an important passage for understanding Paul's protonarration. Readers may thus forgive me the repetition.

Chapter 4

This supposed Pauline argument invites an obvious objection: "Then the super-apostles are not foolish in their boasting either, provided they are not outright lying?" My interpretation dispenses with this contradiction entirely. Yet again, we perceive how the concept of disnarration—in this case, "corrective disnarration," the negation of something previously suggested by the narrative—sheds light on Paul's letters.

Gradual Disnarration

Fourth, I want to examine what I have termed *"gradual" disnarration*, which could be equally well described as "potential/tendential narration."[44] This refers to declarations that are presented as authentic possibilities but ultimately fall shy of explicit claims about actual events. The certainty behind these statements can range from mere suppositions to marginally qualified assertions. Accordingly, there is a wide variety of linguistic means to refer to events of that kind. The situation is further complicated by the fact that the modality of these instances often intertwines with an evaluative component, whereby the expectation (held with varying degrees of certainty) is presented as, for example, a hope or a fear.

Interestingly, the *potential optative* used by speakers and writers "to present a 'situation' as something they consider possible in the present,"[45] and which, consequently, seems an apparent choice for narrating events that are—or might be—happening at the time of utterance, is not central in Paul's letters. The "potential of the past"—vital for subsequent gradual disnarration, or whatever one chooses to call it—is even restricted to classical Greek altogether.[46]

There are, however, many *lexical means* that can yield a very similar effect. In relation to (a) independent declarative clauses, we can mention, for instance, Rom 5:7, where Paul utilizes both μόλις and τάχα to attenuate the probability of two events (or, more accurately, event bundles) to varying degrees; while one will "scarcely" give their life for a merely righteous person, this might "perhaps" be conceivable in the case of an especially good individual (μόλις γὰρ ὑπὲρ δικαίου τις ἀποθανεῖται· ὑπὲρ γὰρ τοῦ ἀγαθοῦ τάχα τις καὶ τολμᾷ ἀποθανεῖν).

---

44. For more details, cf. Heilig, *Paulus*, 654–63.
45. *AGG* 357.
46. *AGG* 208i.

Fragments of Implicit Protonarratives

More frequently, we find that (b) a dependent declarative clause is nuanced by an expression in the governing clause, weakening the assertion of the situation in the dependent clause (and sometimes also contributing an evaluation). We have already seen (above, p. 187) how in 2 Cor 12:2 and 3, Paul thrice introduces situations with "I do not know" (οὐκ οἶδα) when he conspicuously abstains from actual narration, asserting that the events in question are nonnarratable for him, a claim that raises the question of his connection to these events and, therefore, his relationship to the narrative character of the anonymous man. In other instances, epistemic expressions are employed alongside assertions that seem more confident but nevertheless allow for the possibility of the story being inaccurate. Such expressions, marking what follows as speculation or at minimum conjecture, can thus serve as indicators of open unreliable narration.

To give just one such example, I will highlight δοκέω (from the semantic domain 'suppose, think possible').[47] Paul employs this term in a nuanced manner to scale the epistemic mode of the dependent statements along with varying pragmatic effects. In 1 Cor 4:9, for instance, we encounter a protonarrative that nearly takes the form of a complete story but is ultimately presented only under the caveat of being Paul's subjective impression. Here, Paul speaks metaphorically about the event of the apostles being made a "spectacle" and the resulting perception of them as "last of all, as men condemned to death" (δοκῶ γάρ, ὁ θεὸς ἡμᾶς τοὺς ἀποστόλους ἐσχάτους ἀπέδειξεν ὡς ἐπιθανατίους, ὅτι θέατρον ἐγενήθημεν τῷ κόσμῳ καὶ ἀγγέλοις καὶ ἀνθρώποις).

There are also entire categories of clauses that typically, as part of their prototypical usage, carry an epistemic mode (cf. above, p. 225) that to some extent leaves it ambiguous as to whether the proposition's situation actually occurred or is occurring. We can address *fear clauses introduced by* μή πως very briefly, since they do not appear often in the Pauline letters.[48] It is sufficient to mention 1 Thess 3:5 as an example of this phenomenon. Here, the act of sending Timotheus is recounted (διὰ τοῦτο κἀγὼ μηκέτι στέγων ἔπεμψα εἰς τὸ γνῶναι τὴν πίστιν ὑμῶν) and associated with Paul's fear that

---

47. L&N 31.29–34. For a detailed discussion of occurrences in Paul's letters, see Heilig, *Paulus*, 726–29.

48. On Gal 2:2, cf. also Heilig, *Paulus*, chapter 11, section 6.3. The fear clause in Gal 4:11 plays a crucial role in unveiling the purpose of the whole letter. Cf. Heilig, *Paulus*, chapter 9, section 5.4.3. Note that *CGCG* 43.5 assumes that such clauses presuppose regret. Accordingly, one would in fact have to discuss these fear clauses as means of presuppositional disnarration, which we will discuss next.

Chapter 4

"the tempter somehow tempted you and our effort might have been in vain" (μή πως ἐπείρασεν ὑμᾶς ὁ πειράζων καὶ εἰς κενὸν γένηται ὁ κόπος ἡμῶν). It is not until verse 6 that these events are unmistakably disnarrated.

Arguably, questions hold the greatest significance when it comes to independent clauses.[49] Interrogative clauses can introduce a scenario into the discourse without necessitating the speaker to make claims about its actual occurrence. More precisely, *open interrogative clauses* are generally marked by interrogative words (typically corresponding to English "wh-words") and elicit further information from the recipient.[50] Consequently, they are less a tool of disnarration and more a means of prompting the listener to construct their own (proto)narratives (cf. with more detail below, pp. 266–67, in the context of future events). *Closed interrogative clauses*, which demand either affirmation or negation, are, by contrast, particularly well suited to focus on a particular situation, or aspects of it, and to modulate the certainty of the occurrence of the event.[51] This is especially the case since in Koine Greek particles may clarify which answer the speaker or writer expects, thus providing options for expressing different degrees of disnarration.[52] Sometimes, Paul even gives the answer himself (e.g., Rom 10:18).

The epistemic mode connected with all types of questions and, consequently, the communicative function can vary a lot. On one end of the spectrum, the speaker is genuinely unsure and wants to elicit a response in order to gain information, thus formulating the question with a directive illocutionary force. On the other end of the spectrum, we find *rhetorical questions*, which as such do not expect an actual answer.[53] They are usually treated as "(strong) assertion[s]."[54] Despite the sentence type, it thus seems reasonable to treat *rhetorical closed interrogative clauses* as constituents of actual narration if they presuppose a positive answer, and as unambiguous disnarration if they assume a negative answer.

However, it is also important to note that rhetorical questions usually occur in communicative contexts in which the author disagrees with the audience and "intends to move the addressee to adopt a particular view

---

49. Cf. Heilig, *Paulus*, 657–58.
50. On open interrogative clauses, cf. *AGG* 269a. For syntactical details, cf. Heilig, *Paulus*, 707.
51. On closed interrogative clauses, cf. *AGG* 269a.
52. For details, cf. Heilig, *Paulus*, 703–7.
53. Cf. *AGG* 269a and Heilig, *Paulus*, 707–8.
54. *CGCG* 38.19.

Fragments of Implicit Protonarratives

on the state of affairs concerned."[55] Therefore, I would argue that there is an important pragmatic feature associated with events that are disnarrated by means of rhetorical closed question clauses—they might be especially emphatic in what they assert or deny but they do so against the backdrop of the recognition of a *special need to convince the audience*—and, thus, in an utterance context in which the occurrence of events is, actually, in question. They try to accomplish this not simply by challenging opinions directly but by encouraging the recipients more specifically to question their presupposed protonarratives by considering the disnarration of certain events that they so far had presupposed as part of their plots. Disnarration by means of rhetorical questions can thus be understood as a directive speech act that stipulates the creation of new protonarratives.

First Corinthians 1:10–15 offers a compelling example of how the technique of gradual disnarration can be woven seamlessly into larger (proto)narratives through the use of closed interrogative clauses.[56] Additionally, this examination will show that the shift to rhetorical questions can be quite fluid, with the likelihood of an actual response serving as a plausible next turn in the discussion differing only in degree.

In examining our selected passage, the first element we encounter is a command to display unity in verse 10.[57] Verse 11 then articulates, with utterance relatedness, why Paul feels compelled to issue such a directive, namely, because he has heard a story about the current state of the church in Corinth (ἐδηλώθη γάρ μοι περὶ ὑμῶν, ἀδελφοί μου, ὑπὸ τῶν Χλόης).

This embedded narrative is initially renarrated very economically: "... that there are quarrels among you" (ὅτι ἔριδες ἐν ὑμῖν εἰσιν). However, in verse 12, Paul elaborates on the issue that is on his mind (λέγω δὲ τοῦτο ὅτι . . .). This clarification takes the form of what might either be a quote from the narrative, as he had been told it, or his own formulation on the basis of the general sentiment of that story, direct speech that he assigns to different factions within the Corinthian church: "Each one of you is saying: 'I am of Paul,' 'But I am of Apollo,' 'But I am of Kephas,' 'But I am of Christ'"

---

55. Correctly noted in *AGG* 269a. Cf., e.g., Xin Wang, "A Cognitive Pragmatic Study of Rhetorical Questions," *English Language and Literature Studies* 4 (2014): 42–47.

56. For some earlier comments on this passage, cf. Heilig, *Paulus*, 658.

57. We will later (pp. 267–73) delve into the issue of how commands—with their emphasis on future actions yet to be executed—contribute pieces toward the reconstruction of protonarratives.

Chapter 4

(... ἕκαστος ὑμῶν λέγει· ἐγὼ μέν εἰμι Παύλου, ἐγὼ δὲ Ἀπολλῶ, ἐγὼ δὲ Κηφᾶ, ἐγὼ δὲ Χριστοῦ).[58]

With verse 13, we finally come to the subject matter of the present discussion. Paul leaves the embedded narrative by posing a series of *questions*, which, however, are clearly related to the events that have been in view in the simultaneous narration leading up to that verse. First, he employs the indicative perfect to maintain the focus on the current situation, which was also the subject of the quoted statements. Paul inquires: "Is Christ divided?" (μεμέρισται ὁ Χριστός;). Despite the absence of an interrogative particle that might suggest the anticipated response, it is evidently Paul's belief that the only acceptable response would be "no." Yet, the query is not entirely "rhetorical." For Paul's point is precisely that the depicted state of the Corinthian church could be justified only if the question were answered affirmatively. Accordingly, the Corinthians are compelled—provided they accept this assumption—to either abandon their actions and the ensuing narrative or to advance a theologically objectionable assertion.

Intriguingly, Paul then shifts his focus toward the past, delving into the prehistory of the current situation. He queries: "Paul was not crucified for you, was he?" and "You were not baptized in the name of Paul, were you?" (μὴ Παῦλος ἐσταυρώθη ὑπὲρ ὑμῶν, ἢ εἰς τὸ ὄνομα Παύλου ἐβαπτίσθητε;). (Paul's utilization of the third person to refer to himself enables the continuation of the protonarrative with the Corinthians as the focalizers.) Notably, in the first instance the particle μή anticipates a negative response. Paul's objective is to demonstrate that preserving the current situation would require a story about their past that would include counterfactual, and indeed grotesquely absurd, components.

Interestingly, the response to the second question is not as clear-cut, and it seems plausible that Paul intentionally adds the counterfactual event of a baptism in his name to the more outlandish idea of his own crucifixion.[59]

---

58. I admit that the μέν makes more sense as part of the perspective of the narrator, since the Paul fraction in their utterance would not have anticipated the other turns in that way during their own utterance. But shifts between direct and indirect speech in Koine Greek are sometimes fuzzy and taking the δέ as part of the quoted speech results in a more vivid representation of the dispute, which is a more natural reading in my view. Bible translations usually do not opt for this solution. However, Menge also translates along these lines: "... ich meine damit nämlich den Übelstand, dass jeder von euch [als seine Losung] ausspricht: 'Ich halte zu Paulus,' 'Ich dagegen zu Apollos,' 'Ich aber zu Kephas [dh. Petrus],' 'Ich aber zu Christus.'"

59. On the accentuation of η and the question of whether this might be a interrogative particle, see Heilig, *Paulus*, 705–7.

Fragments of Implicit Protonarratives

It appears Paul assumes that such a narrative about being baptized in his name is being circulated. It remains uncertain whether he was informed about actual claims of this nature or if he merely anticipates these ideas to exist as mental protonarratives among his audience. In any case, his intention is to counter a narrative in which the character of the baptizing agent is cast in such a light that it suggests such a close correlation between the baptist and the one baptized that subsequent divisions in the community might be justified. This understanding is supported by verse 14, where Paul introduces an explicit disnarration of his baptizing activity (on which, see above, p. 221), and by verse 15, where he highlights the implication that, due to the lack of baptisms performed by himself, the misunderstanding that underlies the evaluated protonarrative becomes impossible (ἵνα μή τις εἴπῃ ὅτι εἰς τὸ ἐμὸν ὄνομα ἐβαπτίσθητε).

The fact that the disnarration has this function in the discourse also explains why Paul includes it in verse 14 as a part of his thanksgiving to God, who in divine providence has not permitted Paul to baptize more individuals. The point is that this circumstance would otherwise lend more credibility to the counterfactual protonarrative advocated by "his" faction in the prevailing situation (εὐχαριστῶ [τῷ θεῷ] ὅτι οὐδένα ὑμῶν ἐβάπτισα εἰ μὴ Κρίσπον καὶ Γάϊον).

To summarize, in this passage Paul uses interrogative clauses in a very subtle way to demonstrate that a certain somewhat descriptive account of the present, which he introduces via an embedded narrative, would require a story that is practically unnarratable if one is genuinely interested in factual accuracy.

Another option for introducing an event from the past into the discourse without asserting its actual occurrence is through *indefinite conditional clauses*.[60] The use of past tenses in the "if" clause, or protasis, is not reserved for this type of conditional clauses. However, when the "then" clause, or apodosis, refers to the present or future, the identification of indefinite constructions becomes straightforward.[61] In these instances, an event from the past

---

60. For more details on this, see Heilig, *Paulus*, 658–63. We skip present situations here. Cf. Heilig, *Paulus*, 658, with reference to Gal 2:14.

61. Apodosis with reference to the present: Rom 4:2; 15:27; 2 Cor 5:17; 7:8. In Rom 6:8 (see Heilig, *Paulus*, 660), the apodosis refers to the present but is followed by a dependent reference to the future. Sometimes the potential event in the present is additionally part of an interrogative clause: Rom 3:7; 1 Cor 4:7, 9, 11; 15:32; Gal 2:17; Col 2:20. On these passages, see Heilig, *Paulus*, 659. Apodosis with reference to the future: Rom 5:10, 17; 11:21, 24; 2 Tim 2:11; cf. perhaps also Rom 9:22–30, on which see below, pp. 234–39. In

Chapter 4

of uncertain ontological status is presented as a prerequisite for something that might be happening in the present or might transpire in the future from the speaker or writer's standpoint. Since the fulfillment of the condition remains grammatically ambiguous, the same degree of uncertainty, naturally, extends to the dependent event. Even if the consequential occurrence, the event of the apodosis, is also positioned in the past, it is typically feasible to distinguish this type of conditional clause from the counterfactual conditional construction (on which, see below, pp. 234–39).[62]

Romans 5:15 serves as an illustration of this configuration (see also 2 Cor 7:14; Eph 4:20–21; Gal 3:4; possibly Gal 2:21 too). Here, we encounter two events from the past, putting us in proximity to what some might categorize as a prototypical narrative, with the singular distinction being that these circumstances are not confirmed but instead contemplated as possibilities. However, the context clearly indicates that one *could* justifiably generate an authentic story based on these two events. This potential narrative would depict the demise of many due to one character, Adam (εἰ γὰρ τῷ τοῦ ἑνὸς παραπτώματι οἱ πολλοὶ ἀπέθανον), and the consequent bountiful grace extended to the same individuals through another figure, Christ (πολλῷ μᾶλλον ἡ χάρις τοῦ θεοῦ καὶ ἡ δωρεὰ ἐν χάριτι τῇ τοῦ ἑνὸς ἀνθρώπου Ἰησοῦ Χριστοῦ εἰς τοὺς πολλοὺς ἐπερίσσευσεν).[63]

To be sure, Paul probably would not have had any problems actually narrating this story, and perhaps he did so on various occasions. Even so, for the purpose of narratological analysis it is essential to underline the substantial difference between conditional and causal connections. The indefinite conditional clause is *not* a "real case," and its connector should

---

this context, too, we encounter interrogative clauses (Rom 3:3 and 2 Cor 3:7–8). Sometimes, the future element is a command (Phlm 18; Rom 11:17–18; Col 3:1; 1 Tim 5:9–10). Cf. Heilig, *Paulus*, 659–60, on these passages.

62. The particle ἄν might be missing. However, it is still usually clear what is meant. For example, Paul in Gal 4:15 hardly wants to entertain the event of the Galatians giving him their own eyes as a realistic possibility. On the differentiation between indefinite and counterfactual conditional clauses, see also Heilig, *Paulus*, 747, arguing against Thomas Schmeller, *Der zweite Brief an die Korinther*, EKKNT 8, 2 vols. (Neukirchen-Vluyn: Neukirchener, 2010, 2015), 2:203, that we are clearly dealing with an indefinite conditional clause in 2 Cor 11:4.

63. Note that by means of the talk about the "transgression of the one" and the "grace of the one" or "the gift in grace of the one man Jesus Christ," two more events are likely added to that plot—events that apparently can be presupposed in the present communicative context.

Fragments of Implicit Protonarratives

not be translated as "since" (see above, p. 112).[64] Even when in context the epistemic mode is the same, the communicative function varies. If we can ascertain that the situation of the protasis is a shared presupposition of the writer and readers, it centers the attention on what precisely follows from this assumption.[65] Hence, the result is an argumentative text, with the coherence of the protonarrative in the backdrop providing the persuasive power. If the audience can envisage narrating the implied story and if the plot appears plausible to them, this will assist the author in modifying their opinion. Occurrences like these have Hays's "narrative substructures" written all over them.

Less consequential are the *exceptive conditional clauses*, which also mark conditional connections. However, in these instances, the conditional connector expresses "a condition that alone would be able to overturn the nucleus proposition connected with it."[66] Paul employs this as a means of introducing a very faint element of disnarration to what initially appears to be a standard story in 1 Cor 15:2.[67]

Before that, in 1 Cor 15:1, we begin by looking back at Paul's proclamation among the Corinthians and their acceptance of the gospel. Then we pivot to their current adherence to this message (cf. Γνωρίζω δὲ ὑμῖν, ἀδελφοί, τὸ εὐαγγέλιον ὃ εὐηγγελισάμην ὑμῖν, ὃ καὶ παρελάβετε, ἐν ᾧ καὶ ἑστήκατε).[68] In verse 2a the simultaneous narration type is maintained by referencing the presently occurring process of being "saved" through the gospel (δι' οὗ καὶ σῴζεσθε). Following, we see a brief flashback in verse 2b, which reinforces the continuous connection between said gospel—the agent of salvation—and the gospel initially accepted by the Corinthians (τίνι λόγῳ εὐηγγελισάμην ὑμῖν).

Now, nearly all translations associate this latter phrase with the conditional clause that follows in verse 2c: "if you hold on [to it]" (εἰ κατέχετε).

---

64. So the misleading nomenclature by BDF 371 and 372 ("often closely bordering to causal 'since'"). But see Heilig, *Paulus*, 799–800, and *AGG* 281. Daniel B. Wallace, *Greek Grammar beyond the Basics: An Exegetical Syntax of the New Testament* (Grand Rapids: Zondervan, 1996), 694, gets the balance right, pointing out the pragmatic implications of using the indefinite conditional clause in 1 Thess 4:14.

65. See, e.g., Heilig, *Paulus*, 801–3, on Rom 5:10 (where we have the future tense in the apodosis).

66. See *AGG* 331g.

67. On this passage, cf. Heilig, *Paulus*, 661–62.

68. Note that the καί here is used in a temporal connection that expresses sequence. Cf. above, p. 59.

For instance, the NIV translates: "[verse 2a:] By this gospel you are saved, [verse 2c:] if you hold firmly [verse 2b:] to the word I preached to you." However, there is no compelling syntactical reason to adopt this solution. The sequence of the text makes perfect sense as it stands, that is, with verse 2b (τίνι λόγῳ εὐηγγελισάμην ὑμῖν) as a specification of the gospel in verse 2a: "[verse 2a:] You are saved through the gospel, [verse 2b:] in the form in which I preached it to you..."

Therefore, it seems more plausible that the flashback in verse 2b is an initial, very subtle, indication that the story of 1 Cor 15:1–2a cannot be narrated entirely without modifications. Instead, the circumstance that the diachronic identity of the narrative character of the gospel, the saving agent, is preserved turns out to be essential for the integrity and narratability of that story. Otherwise, one could too easily convince oneself of still being a part of that narrative when one has actually already embarked on a different plot.

When we then reach the conditional clause in verse 2c, this possibility is made more explicit, so that the conditional clause "if you prevail/hold fast" *intensifies the disnarration*—a dynamic that gets overlooked if we adopt the unnecessary syntactical solution discussed above.[69]

Against this backdrop, the exceptive conditional clause in verse 2d, "unless you believed in vain" (ἐκτὸς εἰ μὴ εἰκῇ ἐπιστεύσατε), actually serves as an encouragement, contrary to what the continuation in the NIV—"Otherwise, you have believed in vain"—might suggest. Sure, the success story is not yet cut and dried. From a future viewpoint (cf. above, p. 205, on Phil 2:16), there remains the possibility of needing to disnarrate the Corinthians' continuous adherence to the gospel (though not the first two events in verse 1, which would remain unaffected) with the process of salvation failing to reach its conclusion. However, the exceptive conditional clause also underscores that this is the *sole* circumstance that could jeopardize the story's happy ending. We can see here that even the seemingly slight difference in understanding the syntax of these two verses leads to protonarratives that differ significantly in their respective plot and arc of suspense.

A similar dynamic of introducing a trace amount of uncertainty to galvanize the readers can be observed in the exceptive conditional clause with εἰ μήτι in 2 Cor 13:5.[70] The interrogative clause preceding this (see above,

---

69. κατέχω being understood intransitively; as in, for example, Thucydides, *History of the Peloponnesian War* 1.10.1, with λόγος as the subject.

70. See Heilig, *Paulus*, 662.

p. 226) has already established the likelihood of the Corinthians concluding a self-examination with the affirmation that Jesus Christ is indeed within them (ἢ οὐκ ἐπιγινώσκετε ἑαυτοὺς ὅτι Ἰησοῦς Χριστὸς ἐν ὑμῖν;). The only obstacle to this positive outcome would be if they were found to be "unworthy" (εἰ μήτι ἀδόκιμοί ἐστε).[71]

As we draw this discussion to a close, it is important to mention in passing that the conditional connector εἴπερ performs an almost identical function in Rom 3:30, 8:9, and 2 Thess 1:6. When compared particularly to εἴ γε, it becomes evident that this connector is "almost causal," suggesting that the story can be relayed largely free of reservations.[72]

Presuppositional Disnarration

Finally, I wish to comment on a phenomenon I have labeled *"presuppositional" disnarration*. In contrast to the previous subcategory we examined, which differed from standard disnarration with respect to the certainty with which an assertion regarding an event's nonoccurrence is made, here it is not the "dis-" in "disnarration" that takes center stage. Rather, the assertion itself appears in the discourse in a significantly reduced form, emerging merely as an implicature (cf. above, p. 149). Although the act of disnarration itself is not at the heart of the communicative goals in such instances, presuppositional disnarration remains highly relevant to our specific inquiry. This is because it highlights the narrative elements in the backdrop of the discourse—protonarratives and actual stories that are considered counterfactual by both Paul and his readers.

Clearly, the *imperfect of expressions that denote necessity* "may indicate that something is or was necessary, but in fact does not or did not take place."[73] It therefore merits consideration in this context. However, only a handful of passages in Paul's letters utilize this distinct strategy to imply something "should have" or "could have" occurred.[74] Slightly more relevant are *desid-*

---

71. Whatever the complement to the subject means, translations of the clause as "unless, indeed, you fail the test" are misleading because they suggest that Paul has made an entirely tautological statement: You will have a positive result unless you have a negative result. He certainly has something more substantive in view.
72. *AGG* 252.19.
73. *AGG* 209k.
74. On 1 Cor 5:10; 2 Cor 2:3; and 12:11, see Heilig, *Paulus*, 643–46.

Chapter 4

erative clauses that express unattainable wishes.[75] They "serve as a regretful or resigned comment on a situation which can no longer be altered."[76]

For presuppositional disnarration in Paul's letters, *remote conditional constructions* bear much more significance.[77] In these constructions, "the speaker/writer presents the 'situation' referred to by the *if*-clause as counterfactual (epistemic modality), the conclusion, however, as (logically) necessary."[78] Hence, this particular conditional construction type represents a highly efficient manner of disnarrating a two-event sequence.

A notable aspectual tendency presents itself in these constructions: the indicative aorist often refers to counterfactual situations in the speaker's or writer's past ("subsequent presuppositional disnarration"; cf. Rom 9:29 and Gal 4:15), while the imperfect is typically employed for situations that differ from what is actually occurring at the time of speaking or writing ("simultaneous presuppositional disnarration"; cf. Gal 1:10).[79] Naturally, there are also instances where a past nonevent is associated with its present consequence (cf. Gal 3:21).[80]

In the upcoming section, I intend to delve into a discussion of Rom 9:22 as an example to illustrate what we have established about remote conditional clauses thus far.[81] Personally, I find this example particularly compelling because the category of the remote conditional clause is generally not mentioned in the secondary literature on this verse.

Although the syntax indeed poses certain challenges, identifying the conditional clause εἰ δὲ ... ὁ θεὸς ... ἤνεγκεν ... σκεύη ὀργῆς ... is comparatively straightforward. Regardless of our ultimate translation, it is evident that the situation under consideration pertains to God's "bearing of the vessels of anger."

Before we can break down this protasis, we need to ascertain how the participle construction "wanting to show his anger and to make known his power" (θέλων ... ἐνδείξασθαι τὴν ὀργὴν καὶ γνωρίσαι τὸ δυνατὸν αὐτοῦ) ties in with the conditional clause. Some posit that the connection is *causal*.

---

75. Cf. the detailed discussion in Heilig, *Paulus*, 673–75.
76. *CGCG* 38.39. *CGCG* 43.5 would describe fear clauses (cf. above, p. 225) along similar lines so that they should actually be discussed as means of presuppositional disnarration. Cf. Heilig, *Paulus*, 654.
77. For a detailed discussion, see Heilig, *Paulus*, 664–73.
78. *AGG* 284a.
79. On this verse, see Heilig, *Paulus*, 492–94 and 667.
80. Cf. Heilig, *Paulus*, 665.
81. For a detailed discussion of this verse, see Heilig, *Paulus*, 667–73.

Fragments of Implicit Protonarratives

If that interpretation is valid, then God would have tolerated the vessels of anger, primarily "due to" his intent to utilize them for manifesting his wrath in the final judgment. At the same time, it would also be "in order" (cf. verse 23: καὶ ἵνα) to highlight his glory pertaining to the "vessels of mercy." As such, the causal participle of verse 22 and the purpose clause of verse 23 would be on the same syntactical level. They would both supplement the act of bearing in the conditional clause. Thus, this reading presupposes that the act of bearing is not ultimately for the benefit of the vessels of anger, akin to Rom 2:4, but rather reserves them solely as subjects for judgment in the eschatological court.

Despite some supportive arguments, this interpretation is unlikely. It is worth noting that, in contrast to, for example, 1 Thess 2:16, here in Rom 9:22 God's hesitation to act swiftly is expressed much more positively, even supplemented with the phrase "with great patience" (ἐν πολλῇ μακροθυμίᾳ). Therefore, it is most fitting to conclude that the governing finite verb ἤνεγκεν is intended to convey an activity that is *in tension* with what is expressed by the participle. Despite the behavior of the individuals in question provoking anger, they are not yet subjected to God's wrath. As such, the participle is most likely to be interpreted as a *concession*. It means that "even though" God desires to demonstrate his anger and make known his power, he temporarily holds back.

So how do we interpret verse 23 against that backdrop? The most plausible reconstruction of the syntax links καὶ ἵνα with the two infinitives, which depend on the participle (cf., e.g., Rev 6:4 and 1 Cor 14:5).[82] All the positive content about the vessels of mercy is therefore *also* part of the event that God would wish to happen but that is in contrast with the activity of the conditional clause. The real exegetical question, then, is how this threefold wish relates to the bearing with great patience.

To resolve this puzzle, we need to appropriately consider the tense of φέρω. An astounding number of translations and commentators treat the indicative aorist as if it were part of a declarative clause. For instance, Schreiner makes the astonishing claim that "the main clause [!] says that 'he bore with much patience vessels of wrath.'"[83] This is especially surprising given that he correctly notes the "complex syntax" and that we are dealing with a

---

82. Cf. Heilig, *Paulus*, 669–70, on the alternative assumption that verse 23 somehow offers the goal of the wish of verse 22.

83. Thomas R. Schreiner, *Romans*, BECNT (Grand Rapids: Baker Academic, 1998), 519–20. The quote is from p. 520.

Chapter 4

conditional construction with a missing apodosis (the *main clause* on which the subordinate protasis depends), commonly referred to as an "aposiopesis," immediately before making his claim.[84]

Commentators appear to have little interest in determining what kind of apodosis Paul might have intended. This is unfortunate because it implies that their statements concerning the nature of the protasis either remain unnecessarily ambiguous or alternatively lack support. Theoretically, it would be possible to classify the protasis as an *indefinite* type of conditional construction (i.e., "If God *bore* with great patience . . ."). However, it is important to remember that, in the immediate context, the readers have just read about the opposing case where God does *not* endure one of his adversaries. Furthermore, the phrase ἐνδείξασθαι τὴν ὀργήν reminds readers of the fate that Pharaoh in verse 17 undergoes (ὅπως ἐνδείξωμαι ἐν σοὶ τὴν δύναμίν μου). Similarly, καὶ γνωρίσαι τὸ δυνατὸν αὐτοῦ in verse 22 has a clear parallel in καὶ ὅπως διαγγελῇ τὸ ὄνομά μου ἐν πάσῃ τῇ γῇ in verse 17. Consequently, it seems very plausible that Paul is creating a counterfactual scenario here, deviating from the specific example in verse 17 while maintaining a retrospective perspective as the tense suggests. We should therefore probably classify verse 22 as a *remote* conditional construction with reference to the past and paraphrase it something like this: "What if God *had borne* with great patience the vessels of anger (such as Pharaoh) . . . ?"

This type of aposiopesis makes perfect sense when we look back at the fictive dialogue in verses 19–21 that precedes this section. The "you" dares to challenge the validity of God's reproach, considering it seems to be his mercy or hardening that ultimately determines outcomes, rendering human desires and actions irrelevant (cf. verses 16–18). Paul forcefully counters such an objection by attributing to the "you" the role of the crafted artwork (verse 20) or vessel (verse 21). The incomplete conditional construction can be understood as a continuation of this thought experiment, which is then not completed because the answer would simply mirror those already given in verses 19–20. Even if the protasis were true, the matter would still belong solely to the potter. Just as the molded item cannot make demands of the one forming it, it has no say in how the potter might act relative to other products. Just as the potter can decide what he forms and for what purpose (verse 21), *it would also be entirely up to him if, in the end, he chose not to use his products in line with his initial plan.*

In a way, the exegetes who suggest that there is an insinuation here of the

---

84. *AGG* 293f.

possibility that the σκεύη ὀργῆς, "objects of anger," might ultimately become σκεύη ἐλέους, "objects of mercy," are indeed correct.[85] To be sure, we have not yet read anything about the possibility that God might in fact act toward Israel in a manner that is parallel to the behavior that is considered here as a counterfactual alternative to the actual judgment. Nonetheless, the notion that the initial intention of a positive verdict for one group of vessels and a corresponding negative one for the others is brought into contrast with the conceivability of God also showing patience to the second group.

I wish to conclude this section with an elucidating example of a remote type of conditional construction where *both protasis and apodosis refer to situations in the present*: 1 Cor 11:31.[86] This portion on the Eucharist, commencing in 1 Cor 11:17, contains references to a multitude of diverse events (cf. below, pp. 283–86, on the dependent desiderative clauses in this passage). Paul "hears" about the prevailing conditions (verse 18 and verses 20–21) and has "received" something directly from the Lord (verses 23–25). In addition to these embedded narratives, we encounter merely potential events, such as the command that introduces the section in verse 17 and, to some extent, the questions in verse 22. Verses 26, 27, and 29 utilize a variety of mechanisms to express whole event bundles and their interconnections.

Subsequently, in verse 30 we are finally introduced to an actual narrative—one of weakness, sickness, and death in Corinth (διὰ τοῦτο ἐν ὑμῖν πολλοὶ ἀσθενεῖς καὶ ἄρρωστοι καὶ κοιμῶνται ἱκανοί). The consecutive connector διὰ τοῦτο clarifies that the overarching network of events previously articulated is indeed manifested in the Corinthian community. In essence, what has been conveyed in terms of general truths indeed corresponds to the plot of a story that can genuinely be narrated about the Corinthians. We must bear in mind that when Paul then advances to a remote conditional construction in verse 31, he does so with this very narrative context in mind: "But i̲f̲ we examined ourselves, we would not be judged" (εἰ δὲ ἑαυτοὺς διεκρίνομεν, οὐκ ἂν ἐκρινόμεθα).[87]

In the secondary literature, it is often claimed that the use of the first-person plural somewhat softens the implicit reprimand that such self-examination has evidently not occurred, as implied by the remote condi-

---

85. Cranfield, *Epistle*, 2:497.
86. For more details, see Heilig, *Paulus*, 666.
87. The Greek wordplay is much easier mimicked in German: "Wenn wir uns aber selbst kritisch *be*urteilen würden, dann würden wir von Gott nicht *ver*urteilt werden." Cf. Heilig, *Paulus*, 666.

tional clause.[88] However, what seems primarily striking to me is that Paul does not continue his subsequent narration from verse 30. Evidently, he has little interest in elaborating upon the fate of the individuals mentioned. Instead, the brief narrative note in verse 30 serves merely to firmly link the more abstract discourse at this single point to the realities in Corinth, so the readers can then apply the network of related events to their situation on their own. With the conditional construction, Paul therefore reverts back to the level of "regularities," which explains why he employs the first-person plural or, more accurately, why he cannot proceed with the third-person plural with a specific reference. Consequently, verse 32 resumes discussion of God's judging activity, but only by means of a conditional participle (κρινόμενοι δὲ ὑπὸ [τοῦ] κυρίου . . .).

This example is revealing in several respects. First of all, it showcases the intricate intertwining of explicit narration and implicit disnarration in Paul's letters. However, it is also an exemplary illustration of a fascinating dynamic that can transpire with remote conditional constructions in particular. Normally, if both the protasis and apodosis are nonnegated, we find ourselves dealing with the presupposition of a disnarrated event and a likewise counterfactual consequence of that event. But here the *apodosis is negated*. "We would *not* be judged," if only a particular counterfactual condition were met. Thus, what is disnarrated in the apodosis is itself a nonevent. It is presupposed that the "non-judging" is not the reality, indicating, then, that judgment is in fact happening.

In other words, what is evoked here is a counterfactual protonarrative from which the *actual* present situation of judgment is missing. Paul's terse reference in verse 30 to what may seem shocking to modern readers is possible in this context because, evidently, the Corinthians do not require a careful persuasion process. Paul presumes either that they would find this a natural deduction or that they had already suspected it themselves. Therefore, Paul takes the apparently unequivocal situation of judgment as the basis to argue that the event of self-examination, which is presupposed as counterfactual in the conditional clause, has indeed not transpired. This means that verse 31, in other words, presents an *argument against the appropriateness of certain narratives*. The Corinthians cannot maintain that they have conducted an adequate self-examination—because, if they had, things would not have unfolded as they did.

---

88. E.g., Wolfgang Schrage, *Der erste Brief an die Korinther*, 4 vols., EKKNT 7 (Neukirchen-Vluyn: Neukirchener, 1995), 3:55.

We can therefore make a broader observation with respect to the constellation of *remote* conditional constructions with a *negated apodosis*. Usually, remote conditional clauses are interesting from a narratological perspective because they point us to protonarratives, whose nonnarratability is presupposed. Normally, the counterfactual nature of the protasis is uncontroversial and the speaker or writer draws attention to what follows from that. Here, however, the perspective is inverted. The counterfactual character of the event mentioned in the protasis (in this case the notion that self-examination has not taken place) apparently needs to be initially established and cannot be taken as a given. On the contrary, what we can infer from the protasis is the presence of certain *actual (affirmatively told) narratives* within the communicative contexts. These narratives, so Paul lets shine through in such instances, require disnarration in his opinion.

Interestingly, this communicative goal is accomplished against the backdrop of *another* narrative, whose truthfulness is, by contrast, collectively maintained by both the narrator and the audience (in this case constituted by verse 30). This narrative ultimately centers around the event of the apodosis, which is established as real by renarrating a story in a way that already known events appear in new light (sickness and death as symptoms of judgment). The key point here is that if one wants to preserve the narratability of that more uncontroversial story (sickness and death), it follows that the alleged nonevent of the apodosis is indeed reality. Accordingly, one must concur with the idea that the event of the protasis (self-examination) is indeed unreal (because otherwise the nonevent could indeed be disnarrated) and that previous narratives asserting the reality of that situation were in fact told unreliably.[89]

---

89. We see a very similar dynamic in the remote conditional construction that refers to the past (for another example with reference to the present, see Gal 1:10) in 1 Cor 2:8. Cf. Heilig, *Paulus*, 667. Paul wants to demonstrate that God's wisdom cannot be judged according to human standards (cf. verse 5). To make this point, he first employs explicit disnarration in verse 7. The rulers of this age have not recognized the wisdom of God (ἣν οὐδεὶς τῶν ἀρχόντων τοῦ αἰῶνος τούτου ἔγνωκεν). If they had recognized that wisdom (εἰ γὰρ ἔγνωσαν), they would not have crucified the Lord (οὐκ ἂν τὸν κύριον τῆς δόξης ἐσταύρωσαν), as verse 8 explains. Obviously, the crucifixion *did* happen. This means that any narrative that incorporates insight into God's wisdom on the side of the rulers of this age is impossible, thus weakening the case for a compatibility of God's wisdom and human standards for what is wise.

Chapter 4

Future Events as Fragments of Protonarratives

Events that have not yet transpired at the time of utterance cannot be referred to as a part of a text (part) that constitutes a "story" in the narrow sense that we previously defined (see chapter 1), since it is impossible to reflect on them as though they have definitively happened. Simultaneously, it is evident that many speakers under specific circumstances do not differentiate the certainty with which they make claims about events that are located at different points on the timeline. Furthermore, just as we can observe disnarration of the past and present, we can also observe in Paul's letters many references to the future that vary with respect to how certain the happening of these events is predicted to be. Accordingly, we can expect these protonarratives to exhibit a similarly variegated profile when it comes to their pragmatics.

Future Acts of Subsequent Narration

We begin this discussion by considering how events in *future acts of narration* can come into view implicitly, thus emphasizing the need to consider these (at the time of writing or speaking) merely potential narratives. In Greek, as in many languages, this concept is reflected even at the grammatical level. It is feasible in Greek, just as in English, to employ verb forms that suggest a "secondary deictic center." In other words, these forms introduce an additional point of temporal orientation in addition to the time of utterance.[90] In Modern Greek, constructions such as Θα έχω φάει, "I will have eaten," are quite common. They are frequently paired with temporal specifications to clarify when a certain action will have taken place (for example, σε μία ώρα, "in one hour"). The periphrastic version of the future perfect also appears in Koine Greek, albeit rarely.[91]

Distinct from that phenomenon is when said future point in time actually *supplants* the time of utterance as the primary deictic center. Most notably, we encounter such a deictic shift in the Greek epistolary aorist. In this case, the writer adopts the temporal perspective of the recipients instead of the time of utterance. From that standpoint, when the recipients read the letter that has been dispatched to them, the writing process itself

---

90. Heilig, *Paulus*, chapter 6, section 3.2.2.
91. Cf. *CGCG* 33.46 on the future perfect indicative in Classical Greek. Cf. *AGG* 201d and 203a on the periphrastic conjugation of these verb forms.

Fragments of Implicit Protonarratives

is located in the past. Therefore, the epistolary aorist indicative provides a fascinating opportunity for introducing an aspectual nuance into the writing that deviates from the present indicative as the default tense of *simultaneous* narration.[92]

But the epistolary indicative aorist extends to *predictive* "narration" as well. Events that occur between the completion of the writing process and the reading of the letter are also past from the perspective of the recipients. As such, these events can also be "narrated" in the aorist indicative, even though they are still in the future at the time of writing. This phenomenon is often seen when the "sending" of coworkers is cast in the aorist indicative, as Paul regularly does with the usage of ἔπεμψα (for instance, Phil 2:28; Phlm 12; cf. Eph 6:22; Col 4:8 in the disputed letters).[93]

The category of the epistolary perfect, despite strong denials from some factions, is also well documented in Koine Greek.[94] While it appears in the New Testament in Acts 15:27 (ἀπεστάλκαμεν), it is likely absent in Paul's letters. Nevertheless, I wish to mention it in this context because, like the epistolary aorist, it too can be used to refer to anticipated events as completed from the perspective of the recipients.

These epistolary verb forms thus highlight how closely discussions of future events can align, on a grammatical level, with actual simultaneous narration (in which the indicative perfect can feature) or subsequent narration (in which the indicative aorist is employed as the default tense).

Another phenomenon in Koine Greek that underscores how blurred the boundaries between "predictive" and "real" narration can be at the grammatical level involves cases of *reported speech*, which also brings about a deictic shift.[95] This accounts for why the tense in the subordinate clause mirrors the one used or (in cases of merely potential, future speech acts) the ones that would be used by a narrated speaker. In other words, the time of utterance of the narrator of the frame narrative is supplanted by the time of speaking of a narrative character who narrates an embedded story. This causes the lines between quoted (direct) speech and reported (indirect) speech to become quite ambiguous.[96] By contrast, in English the distinction is much

---

92. See above, pp. 158–59, and Heilig, *Paulus*, chapter 6, section 3.4.2.1.
93. Heilig, *Paulus*, 580.
94. The argument by Trevor V. Evans, "Another Ghost: The Greek Epistolary Perfect," *Glotta* 75 (1999): 194–221, that the epistolary perfect does not exist is not convincing. See Heilig, *Paulus*, 310–13.
95. On which, cf. *AGG* 206b and 274c.
96. Cf. Heilig, *Paulus*, 309.

Chapter 4

more straightforward because in reported speech the simple past tense, for example, is replaced by the past perfect. For instance, "I ate lunch at noon" becomes "He will say that he had eaten lunch at noon." This of course does not happen if an utterance is quoted: "He will say: 'I ate lunch at noon.'" For Koine Greek texts, this means that a narrative that is only potential at the time of speaking often appears in the text in the same configuration as it would be in if it would indeed be told in the future.

I would argue that while in the New Testament we have some explicit announcements of such future, often eschatological, storytelling (cf. Matt 25:25–46), this concept of a future act of looking back at past events—and thus being able to narrate a specific story about them—also subtly permeates passages that do not explicitly speak about future acts of narration.[97]

Philippians 2:16 strikes me as particularly notable in this context.[98] In verse 14, Paul endorses a certain lifestyle. Subsequently, in verse 15 he elucidates in a purpose-oriented clause what such behavior on the Philippians' part would yield. Following this, verse 16a details how all of this should be executed, namely, "by holding on to the word of life" (λόγον ζωῆς ἐπέχοντες). Now, in verse 16b Paul concisely adds what the outcome of such a (yet only potentially evolving) scenario would be for *him*: εἰς καύχημα ἐμοὶ εἰς ἡμέραν Χριστοῦ. Most English translations acknowledge the idea that Paul here anticipates a future speech act and thus translate this rather loosely as, "And then I will be able to boast on the day of Christ" (NIV). To make things even clearer, one could also employ the future perfect: "... so that my glory will be that I will not have run or labored in vain." By contrast, note that Paul simply articulates this in the same way he would do in that future narration of the success story, namely, in the indicative aorist: ὅτι οὐκ εἰς κενὸν ἔδραμον οὐδὲ εἰς κενὸν ἐκοπίασα. The text thus offers us an intimate glimpse into the narrative that Paul hopes to recount on the day of the Lord, should the Philippians indeed continue to comply with his instructions.

Prolepses, Predictive Narration, and Foreshadowings

How, then, can we discuss these almost-narratives in a meaningful way from a narratological standpoint? Regrettably, the terminology associated with future events in narratological literature is somewhat confusing. We partic-

---

97. Heilig, *Paulus*, 580.
98. Cf. Heilig, *Paulus*, 580.

ularly encounter Genette's term "prolepsis" and, especially in the German sphere, Lämmert's "foreshadowing" ("Vorausdeutung" in the original) used in various and often contradictory relations.[99]

In the ensuing discussion, I operate under the assumption that narrators can speak in a manner that anticipates events as yet to materialize both with respect to events that happened in their past (namely from the standpoint of an even earlier point in time) and in relation to events located in their actual future (from the perspective of the time of utterance). For the past, they can provide commentary from their own perspective with a "future in the past," typically manifested in English by "would" constructions, as in: "I would learn only later what she was thinking back then."[100] Moreover, they can portray a narrative character making a prediction. Since individuals can occasionally exhibit as much certainty regarding future events as they do with respect to past events that they narrate (or even more so), we can distinguish between *certain* and *uncertain foreshadowings*, where "certainty" in this context pertains to the level of assertiveness in a statement.

Note that both certain and uncertain foreshadowings to the past of the narrator, whether from the narrator himself or herself or from narrative figures, are important tools for traditional retrospective narration.[101] For our current focus, however, we restrict ourselves to events that are indeed in the *future from the perspective of the narrator of the frame narrative*. Here too, mentions of future events can be made by narrative characters, including the narrated "I"—for instance, when an adult recalls their childhood comments about their future as a senior—or the narrator of the frame narrative. Both uncertain and certain foreshadowings to the future of the narrator of the frame narrative can occur. This gives us a total of eight narratologically relevant forms of foreshadowing.

Note also that I reserve Genette's term "prolepsis" for certain foreshad-

---

99. Gérard Genette, *Narrative Discourse: An Essay in Method*, trans. Jane E. Lewin (Ithaca: Cornell University Press, 1980), 67–79; Eberhard Lämmert, *Bauformen des Erzählens*, 7th ed. (Stuttgart: Metzler, 1980). For a detailed discussion, see Heilig, *Paulus*, chapter 11, sections 3–7. If we just look at how Genette and Lämmert use their terminology, one could associate the uncertain foreshadowing of narrative figures with predictive narration in an embedded narrative on the one hand and certain foreshadowing with the prolepsis, the latter being a phenomenon of the frame narrative. Cf. Heilig, *Paulus*, chapter 11, section 3.2. However, Lämmert's account does not seem complete. Cf. Heilig, *Paulus*, chapter 11, section 5.

100. Cf. *AGG* 203d.

101. For a detailed discussion of Gal 2:16–17, see Heilig, *Paulus*, chapter 11, section 6.2; for a detailed discussion of Gal 2:2 and 2:4–5, see Heilig, *Paulus*, chapter 11, section 6.3.

Chapter 4

owings that stem from narrators themselves, usually referring to their narrated past.[102] Similarly, one could further connect Genette's terminology with Lämmert's concepts by arguing that "predictive" or "prior" narration exists in cases of foreshadowings that look forward to the future from the perspective of the respective narrator. If the factor of assertiveness is considered crucial to narrativity, this designation could also be restricted more specifically to the certain foreshadowings of that kind. From the perspective of the speaker, these could constitute narratives just as real as their narrations of the past.

Due to the significance of prophecy in biblical literature, this subcategory—*certain foreshadowing of the actual future of the respective narrator*—holds considerable importance for exegesis.[103] However, it is also pivotal to recognize that we also utilize such statements in our day-to-day lives, especially when dealing with imminent situations such as an object rolling toward the edge of a table or unavoidable events such as climate change or pandemics.

To be sure, not every time we mention a future event, even with great certainty, do we ponder the possibility of one day recounting that story retrospectively. Nonetheless, certain foreshadowings of the narrator's future indeed provide us with *fixed points in the plots of potential protonarratives*. While they may not suggest comprehensive stories in and of themselves, they do *exclude* entire classes of narratives. In other words, they rule out the possibility of any future narrative that includes the foretold event as part of its plotline, provided reliability is maintained.[104]

Interestingly, when it comes to *uncertain foreshadowing of the narrator's future*, the dynamic changes somewhat. Here, readers face the task of predicting how the story will continue and constantly juxtaposing their own anticipations against the actual narrative progression. Thus, uncertain foreshadowings do not provide readers with fixed points for the plot. Instead,

---

102. Some would restrict the use of this term only to cases in which there is no repetitive narration, i.e., where the certain foreshadowing is associated with a later ellipsis. But Genette, *Narrative Discourse*, 73, allows for "repeating prolepses."

103. This had already been recognized by Harald Weinrich, "Narrative Theologie," *Concilium* 9 (1973): 332, who speaks of "hypothetical" narration and comments: "The prophecies in the biblical corpus can be seen as narrative drafts of actions not yet occurred, thus as a pre-telling" (German: "Die Prophetien des biblischen Corpus können als erzählende Entwürfe noch nicht geschehener Handlungen angesehen werden, als ein Vor-Erzählen also").

104. See Heilig, *Paulus*, chapter 11, section 5.1.

they serve as triggers, pushing the readers to move beyond the narrated present and to think ahead. Therefore, once they reach a later point in the narrative, they can evaluate the actual story against the backdrop of alternate narratives that never manifested. In using Ryan's terminology (cf. above, pp. 209–10), these remain "virtual."

At times, this distinction between the two phenomena can become blurred. Note that in the context of addressing the pragmatic relief of syntax (in chapter 3), we have already mentioned, referencing 2 Cor 2:13, that purpose clauses express intentions that in context can often be presupposed to have successfully reached their goals (cf. chapter 2, on purpose-oriented connections, where I cite the example of Gal 1:18). Especially in the case of purpose-oriented connections (on which see below, pp. 304–9), we must therefore reckon with the possibility that what appears to be uncertain foreshadowing at the grammatical level (which is why we will discuss these phenomena under this heading) may, in fact, constitute a fragment of a protonarrative that, to the speaker or author and the recipients, will undoubtedly turn out to be true. In other words, uncertain and certain foreshadowings exist on a spectrum, and the associated functions they serve in protonarration can, accordingly, blend into each other.

A Case Study

In the following analysis, my aim is to offer a comprehensive overview of the diverse linguistic tools Paul uses to create both certain and uncertain foreshadowings, detailing the capacity of each to invoke various types of protonarratives. However, before we delve into this examination, during which we will need to restrict the attention we can assign to individual passages that illustrate the different (proto)narrative devices to adequately cover the full spectrum of possibilities, I want to dedicate a few paragraphs to a single passage: Rom 15:18–32.[105] This will allow us the chance to meticulously trace the dynamics of Paul's foreshadowings at least in this one instance. We will pay particular attention to how the reference to future events is woven into a tapestry of past and present situations and how Paul manipulates this network of events to yield a very specific effect among his readers.

At first glance, Rom 15:18–32 does not seem especially conducive to a narratological analysis. The majority of verb forms in this passage are nonindic-

---

105. For a detailed exegesis of the passage, cf. Heilig, *Paulus*, chapter 11, section 8.

Chapter 4

ative. Among the indicative ones, the past tense verbs (one imperfect and six aorist indicative verbs) do not dominate when compared with present tense forms (five indicative present and three indicative perfect) and those in the future indicative (five). Also, the occurrence of these verbs within the text does not overtly correspond to a transition from past to present to future events.[106] This passage hardly seems a prime candidate for a story Paul is telling. Indeed, if we narrow our focus to past verb forms in the first-person singular, Paul "autobiographically" recounts something he experienced only in verse 22. Ironically, there the matter at hand is what he was *not* able to do due to obstacles (ἐνεκοπτόμην). Still, if we closely scrutinize how these diverse references to events interrelate, we find a *complex and coherent protonarrative with a very specific communicative function*.

The passage begins in verses 18–19 with a flashback. In verse 18, Christ emerges as the protagonist. With the help of Paul ("through word and deed"; λόγῳ καὶ ἔργῳ) he was active (κατειργάσατο Χριστός) with a specific purpose, namely, "to bring about the obedience of the gentiles" (εἰς ὑπακοὴν ἐθνῶν). Here we encounter our first foreshadowing, as the success of this endeavor is not explicitly narrated at this point, even though the readers are well aware that Paul can indeed attest to significant accomplishments in this regard. The emphasis here is more on the divine agency driving this known narrative.[107]

This comes after the initial announcement in verse 18, which establishes the foundation for the subsequent discussion. There, Paul declares that he would not dare to speak about events from his missionary past in which Christ himself is not the agent (οὐ γὰρ τολμήσω τι λαλεῖν ὧν οὐ . . .). In other words, we are already aware that what Paul will discuss will follow a unique plot. We are, hence, dealing with a foreshadowing with utterance relatedness on the level of the frame narrative. Indeed, the story that he could be telling must possess a plot that is interpretable in a way that glorifies Christ in order for the story to offer supportive evidence (cf. γάρ) for the claim in verses 16–17. According to these verses, Paul is truly a servant (λειτουργός) of Christ and, as such, has a valid reason to boast about his service expressly "in Christ" (verse 17: ἔχω οὖν [τὴν] καύχησιν ἐν Χριστῷ Ἰησοῦ τὰ πρὸς τὸν θεόν).

---

106. But see above, pp. 38–39, on how one can perhaps eventually discern a base narrative here, which can serve as the backdrop for identifying departures from the typical narrative order.

107. Cf. above, p. 168, on the evaluative function of stories.

Verse 19a elaborates on the divine power, and verse 19b illustrates the outcome (ὥστε with perfect infinitive; cf. above, p. 115) in the *writer's present day*. The proclamation of the gospel of Christ is completed (πεπληρωκέναι τὸ εὐαγγέλιον τοῦ Χριστοῦ), from Jerusalem and its surrounding areas to Illyrium. Although Paul has mainly addressed what readers will not find in the remainder of the letter—namely, the type of narrative he deems nonnarratable and, thus, what no one else is permitted to suggest—he has already subtly incorporated a sketch of his version of past events and their influence on the present situation.[108]

What follows in verses 20–22, in my opinion, further develops the self-understanding that Paul, so he claims now, adhered to during that period. I believe this still forms part of the flashback begun in verse 18 and whose right boundary—the now of the narrating "I"—was specified in verse 19. In other words, contrary to what many translations suggest, verse 20 clarifies the manner in which Paul, the supporting character of verse 19 (the participle picks up the με from verse 19), acted within the mentioned timeframe.[109] He does so intriguingly through disnarration; he says that something was significant to him ("it has been my ambition"; φιλοτιμούμενον) but explicates this principle negatively as evangelizing "not where Christ had been named" already (cf. εὐαγγελίζεσθαι οὐχ ὅπου ὠνομάσθη Χριστός). Simultaneously, this indicative aorist in this context offers a flashback into a potentially more distant and yet also overlapping past during which other figures were or have been proclaiming the gospel of Christ. The telic clause (ἵνα μὴ ἐπ' ἀλλότριον θεμέλιον οἰκοδομῶ) sketches out a hypothetical plot for that period. Using figurative language, it presents a situation where Paul would not have stuck to that principle but instead would have preached the gospel in regions where communities of Christ followers already existed. These actual and hypothetical plots are primarily differentiated by geography, each presupposing a distinct prehistory.

Verse 21 then introduces a quotation from Isa 52:15, which explicitly contrasts (ἀλλὰ καθὼς γέγραπται) with the principle underlying the counterfactual plot. Unlike in Gal 3:8, where "scripture" through the indicative aorist appears as a narrative character performing actions in the past and

---

108. Cf. above, p. 209, on nonnarratable events.
109. The KJV seems particularly at a loss about how to connect verse 20 to what precedes: "Yea, so have I strived to preach the gospel . . ." The NIV simply continues in an asyndetic way: "It has always been my ambition to preach the gospel . . ." The NET gets the modal-instrumental connection right but confuses the semantic roles by attributing the manner-role to verse 19: "And *in this way* I desire to preach . . ."

Chapter 4

thereby utters certain foreshadowing to the present of the narrating "I," the historical prophetic act is simply assumed here. We are still in the present of the narrated "I." In other words, the quote elaborates on the preconditions under which Paul's recounted actions took place. Hence, we are dealing with a certain (being prophetic) foreshadowing toward the past of the narrating Paul. From the perspective of the newly called apostle, it is the case that in the past "he [i.e., Christ] was not proclaimed" (οὐκ ἀνηγγέλη περὶ αὐτοῦ). Similarly, it is in the present of the narrated "I" that Paul is surrounded by "unreached" people (as one could paraphrase the difficult indicative perfect in καὶ οἳ οὐκ ἀκηκόασιν). It is in this situation that the prophecy offers the apostle the promise that, in the future (of the narrated "I"), people will see (ὄψονται) and understand (συνήσουσιν). What is ardently expected here has already been stated as fact in verses 15–19. Therefore, the quotation from verse 21 provides a flashback into the mental narrative of the newly called apostle Paul, who is yet to fulfill his mission but has already been promised its success.

Certainly, this promise pertains to the future of the narrating "I" as well. Potential future converts (in Spain) could also be part of the reference of the promised hearers of Paul's message. But to claim that the Isaiah citation is something like a charter for Paul's upcoming visit to Rome seems unfounded.[110] After all, when Paul connects this nexus of events with the subject of visiting Rome in verse 22, he clarifies that what has been outlined so far explains why, until now, he has *not* had the chance to come to Rome, namely, because he was simply too preoccupied where he already was (Διὸ καὶ ἐνεκοπτόμην τὰ πολλὰ τοῦ ἐλθεῖν πρὸς ὑμᾶς).[111] While it is plausible that Paul will follow the same principle in the future, he has detailed it to illuminate the future period of the narrated "I" that now, from his current perspective, is his past and circumscribed by the "completion" of verse 19. Consequently, the quote in verse 21 sketches a missionary plan that, for now and in a certain sense, has been fulfilled.

In verse 23, Paul shifts to the "now" (νυνί) of the narrating "I" and, thus, to simultaneous narration. Given that the foreshadowings to his past naturally bring up the question of their continued relevance for his future, readers can

---

110. So Florian Wilk, *Die Bedeutung des Jesajabuches für Paulus*, FRLANT 179 (Göttingen: Vandenhoeck & Ruprecht, 1998), 82, who sees this function in addition to the quotation specifying the norm and goal of Paul's missionary activity. Cf. Heilig, *Paulus*, 605.

111. Note that the medio-passive allows Paul to formulate here very vaguely, i.e., without introducing a narrative figure explicitly for this bundle of events; cf. above, pp. 156–57, on voice.

anticipate that he will also address his present plans. True to this expectation, the participles in verse 23 seem to define the present starting point for a future missionary journey. The reference to lack of room (μηκέτι τόπον ἔχων ἐν τοῖς κλίμασιν τούτοις) aligns well with the completion specified in verse 19, which was also portrayed in geographical terms. Similarly, the assurance that Paul had long wished to visit the Roman Christians (ἐπιποθίαν δὲ ἔχων τοῦ ἐλθεῖν πρὸς ὑμᾶς ἀπὸ πολλῶν ἐτῶν) corresponds with the suggestive notion of having been impeded in verse 22.

After that, verse 24a delivers a temporal clause that anticipates future happenings (ὡς ἂν with the prospective subjunctive πορεύωμαι). It is best regarded as an elaboration on the second participle in verse 23 and should not be associated with the following section as, for example, the ESV suggests: "I hope to see you in passing as I go to Spain." What Paul communicates in verse 23 is that he has harbored a desire to visit Rome for quite some time and, in verse 24, that in these plans the visit was tied to a journey to Spain.

In essence, verses 23–24 signal a shift to simultaneous narration followed by a flashback allowing insight into a longstanding plan of the narrated "I." Following this, we discover in verse 24b that the narrating "I" still harbors the hope of executing this plan in the future.

Paul must then clarify this plan in more detail, which explains why the sentence that he had begun is interrupted here (and not, as some presume, directly after verse 23). He proceeds to provide further details about the connection he perceives between his planned trip to Spain and his visit to Rome. Specifically, his current hope (ἐλπίζω) is that during his transit (διαπορευόμενος) he will have the opportunity to get to know the Christians in Rome (θεάσασθαι ὑμᾶς), and that he will get to "enjoy" their company for some time (ἐὰν ὑμῶν πρῶτον ἀπὸ μέρους ἐμπλησθῶ) before then proceeding to Spain with their assistance (καὶ ὑφ' ὑμῶν προπεμφθῆναι ἐκεῖ).

Paul will restate his purpose somewhat redundantly in verse 28 (ἀπελεύσομαι δι' ὑμῶν εἰς Σπανίαν). The reason for that is that at this point, in verse 25, he must first address a different kind of "now" (νυνί) and a different kind of journey (πορεύομαι), namely, the impending trip to Jerusalem with the purpose of serving the "saints." To illustrate his point, he provides a flashback in verses 26–27, recounting the previous collection for the poor. Interestingly, in this flashback the narrated "I" does not take center stage. Instead, these events seem to be part of a different storyline, which is linked to the narrative "characters" Μακεδονία καὶ Ἀχαΐα.

The two storylines then *converge* in verse 28a, where Paul refers (with

Chapter 4

τοῦτο) not just to the general act of "serving" from verse 25 but also to his aim to ensure the completion of the gentile Christians' endeavors in Jerusalem (... οὖν ἐπιτελέσας), bringing *his* own sealing action and *their* fruit into alignment (καὶ σφραγισάμενος αὐτοῖς τὸν καρπὸν τοῦτον).

Given this context, it is not at all, as some say, "surprising" that Paul mentions his journey to Jerusalem in verse 25.[112] From the standpoint of Paul's (proto)narrative, this is perfectly logical. For in order to shape the protonarrative that he outlined in verse 24b—the journey to Spain via Rome—into a success story, he must first successfully navigate his current task.

Therefore, when Paul uses the term ἀπελεύσομαι, "I will go," in verse 28b to announce his impending departure to Rome (and, ultimately, Spain), it is evident from the context that this usage of future tense is "modal"—that is, it communicates his intentions but does not constitute "predictive narration" in the strictest sense (see below, pp. 257–60, on the modal future).

Intriguingly, in verse 29 Paul seems to abandon this qualifier and, at least rhetorically, operates under the presumption of his upcoming visit. He "knows" (οἶδα) something, namely, that he will arrive filled with the blessing of Christ (ἐν πληρώματι εὐλογίας Χριστοῦ ἐλεύσομαι). The emphasis here is on the manner in which he will come—or intends to come—so the choice of verb does not come under too much scrutiny within the discourse. This depiction of future conditions is simply associated with a participle, which is likely best interpreted temporally: "when I come to you" (ἐρχόμενος πρὸς ὑμᾶς).

The fact that Paul, immediately following this in verse 30, implores the Romans to pray for him leads some interpreters to perceive another potential setback to the apostle's optimism.[113] However, once again, the structure of Paul's text becomes perfectly logical when viewed through the lens of how he manipulates the protonarrative that underpins the entire section. He intends to reveal to the Roman Christians his long-held plan (verses 22–23) so that they can *find their own place in this still only potential narrative*. After this orientation reached its climax in verse 29, here comes the perfect juncture to introduce the means by which this plot point can be successfully realized.

In essence, the Romans are guided from the predictively narrated visit of Paul—the "happy ending" of the story—back to the present, where *their*

---

112. Against, e.g., Heinrich Schlier, *Der Römerbrief*, HThKNT 6 (Freiburg: Herder, 1977), 435, who thinks the move is "überraschend."

113. Schlier, *Römerbrief*, 437, for example, claims: "Aber der Gedanke an Jerusalem läßt ihn noch nicht los."

Fragments of Implicit Protonarratives

prayers can aid in ensuring the success of Paul's imminent visit to Jerusalem (verse 31).[114] This, in turn, has the purpose of subsequently allowing Paul to find some measure of "rest" among the Christians in Rome (verse 32: ἵνα ... συναναπαύσωμαι ὑμῖν).[115] At this juncture, Paul no longer needs to address his even more future intentions because his hopes, which he anticipates will now be shared by the Roman Christians, have already been sufficiently foreshadowed in verse 24b.[116] The use of the verb συναναπαύσομαι ushers not only Paul but also his "narration" into a state of rest.

To summarize the broad outline of narrative dynamics in Rom 15:18–32, it can be said that Paul recounts past events and pairs them with foreshadowings that, in turn, cultivate expectations of a story about the narrator's present situation. He accomplishes this by incorporating mental events—such as desires and plans—into his explicit narrative. The implicit protonarrative that evolves from this thus ties to circumstances that date to a later time—sometimes the present moment of the writing or, at other times, the future of the narrating "I."

The outcome is a complex network of interconnected events that simultaneously form a cohesive storyline with multiple potential twists at varying plot points. The plot(s) that Paul wants to see actualized are supported meticulously and from several angles, such as through the flashback in verse 27, and even via argumentative textualization within that flashback. Alternative narratives are invoked, prompted, for instance, by the motif of fear, which along with the vivid depiction of yet future events, suggest a very specific future trajectory for the plot.

Note that the *function* underpinning this complex protonarrative appears to be that Paul wants the Roman Christians to *adopt* this narrative. Therefore, it would be misguided to assume a merely informing-assertive communicative function (cf. chapter 3), as if Paul, out of pure politeness perhaps, just wished to "announce" his forthcoming visit.[117] In fact, it would even

---

114. On the details of this verse, see Heilig, *Paulus*, 609.

115. Paul adds the phrase ἐν χαρᾷ ἐλθὼν πρὸς ὑμᾶς to this telic clause. It could be related in a modal way to the activity of resting. However, I think it is more plausible that he refers once more to the preceding event of *arrival* because in that scenario the "by God's will" (διὰ θελήματος θεοῦ) contributes more to what is said.

116. Because this foreshadowing is combined with an ellipsis, some might call this a prolepsis. Note, however, that we are not discussing a future that is located in the narrated past.

117. I see such a tendency in, for example, the following comment by Michael F. Bird, *Romans*, The Story of God Bible Commentary (Grand Rapids: Zondervan, 2016), 502:

Chapter 4

be shortsighted to consider the achievement of a specific *evaluation* as the ultimate communicative goal, though that might partially be relevant with respect to his account of past missionary efforts.

Rather, the section seems to more directly target the psychological realm of "volition." If we properly consider the protonarrative underlying the text and the *central role that the event (bundle) of Roman prayer plays within it*, it becomes clear that Paul's primary objective is to inspire the Roman Christians to participate in his mission (verse 30: συναγωνίσασθαί μοι ἐν ταῖς προσευχαῖς ὑπὲρ ἐμοῦ πρὸς τὸν θεόν). Assigning such importance to the prayers of believers is not at all uncommon for Paul (cf., e.g., 1 Thess 5:25; Col 4:3; 2 Thess 3:1).

Also, we can likely identify something akin to an *implicit epilogue* here. If the Roman Christians decide to support him in prayer for his current assignment, then they are accepting a protocol that is part of a broader strategy in which they are woven into the narrative as figures helping Paul achieve the ultimate state of his plan. After all, Paul's readiness "to come" (verse 32: ἐλθὼν πρὸς ὑμᾶς), toward which they work with their prayer, naturally implies their willingness to receive him. This has been associated by Paul in a passing remark in verse 24 (ἐλπίζω ... ὑφ᾽ ὑμῶν προπεμφθῆναι ἐκεῖ) with the readiness to also support his future actions. Therefore, the protonarrative communicated through Rom 15:18–32 not only encourages prayer but also, indirectly, more "tangible" support in the more distant future.

I hope this example effectively illustrates that the notion of future events acting as textual fragments of mental protonarratives is indeed a heuristically fruitful concept. Of course, there can always be debate about the degree to which Paul did indeed envision himself telling a story, from a future perspective, looking back at what led him to Spain, and to what extent such a story would exhibit the kind of plot that we sketched here. Ultimately, we cannot simply *presuppose* from the outset of our analysis that Paul simulated such a narrative.

However, I think we can indeed construe an *argument* that comes to that conclusion.[118] If we presume that authors usually create a text with a

---

"Paul's goal is to inform the Romans of his missionary work to date and how it relates to his plans to travel to Jerusalem, Rome, and Spain." Others, such as Wilckens, *Der Brief an die Römer*, 3:128, recognize correctly what is most important to Paul in this section. Wilckens too, however, is not able to demonstrate this on the basis of the text since he does not focus on the narrative dimension of the textual structure.

118. On the question of how such a move can be justified with reference to confirmation theory, cf. Theresa Heilig and Christoph Heilig, "Historical Methodology," in *God and the Faithfulness of Paul: A Critical Examination of the Pauline Theology of N. T. Wright*,

high degree of coherence, and if we agree this analysis has indeed offered a plausible explanation for the text's structure (making sense of, for example, verse 25, which appears as a rather unusual digression in other frameworks), we can confidently assume that a rather advanced degree of narrativization underlies this text (cf. above, pp. 205–6).

This process involves Paul selecting specific events from the yet potential future, meticulously connecting them in a temporal and meaningful way and relating them to particular past and present event sequences. At the point of writing his letter, Paul already has this web of events mentally at hand, incorporating the different narrative figures, associated storylines, desired and undesired continuations, and key events that constitute plot points. This enables him to navigate according to his rhetorical strategy within this web of events and selectively access individual sequences to present them in the text in appropriate ways, thereby guiding his readers in line with his intentions.

In the subsequent section, I aim to provide a comprehensive yet concise summary of the myriad linguistic methods Paul could utilize to create foreshadowings and, consequently, fragments of larger protonarratives. Considering that this section builds upon two chapters from my German monograph that comprise over 60,000 words, a concise summary will inevitably lack depth. Demonstrating in detail how the category of mental protonarratives elucidates the included passages, as I have attempted with regards to the example of Rom 15:18–32, cannot be the objective. Instead, my goal is to present as thorough an overview of the breadth of possibilities as possible, merely suggesting the potential exegetical payoff on occasion. With the following overview, I hope to convey the vast spectrum of relevant linguistic phenomena and, accordingly, how prevalent future events are in Paul's letters. By doing so, I aim to promote the recognition of at least the potential significance of mental protonarratives for the exegesis of the Pauline writings.

Linguistic Means for Expressing Certain Foreshadowings to Paul's Future

We initiate our analysis with *certain* foreshadowings.[119] Naturally, a *future indicative verb form in independent (main) declarative clauses* is the most

---

ed. Christoph Heilig, J. Thomas Hewitt, and Michael F. Bird, WUNT 2.413 (Tübingen: Mohr Siebeck, 2016), 115–50.

119. On everything that follows, see chapter 13 of Heilig, *Paulus*, with much more detail.

Chapter 4

straightforward choice for such "announcements."[120] However, even at a grammatical level it is evident that the future indicative is not exclusively utilized for "predictive narration" but can also serve nonassertive functions.[121]

Hence, just to get a certain sense of the options available, it is insightful to scrutinize the future indicative verb forms in Romans more closely, which account for nearly one-third of all such occurrences within the Pauline corpus.[122] At times, it has been argued that many of the future indicative verb forms in Romans are not standard. However, the category of a seemingly atemporal, "logical" future, frequently encountered in secondary literature, appears to be a creation of exegetes, especially those studying Romans.[123]

Nevertheless, it is indeed intriguing to see that, of the ninety-eight future indicative verb forms, only a handful occur "normally," that is, in independent declarative clauses articulated by Paul himself (discounting quotations from Scripture).[124] There are a few references to the eschatological future (Rom 5:9; 11:26; 14:10, 12; 16:20). There are also two instances (Rom 5:19 and 14:4) of event bundles, whose situation times probably include Paul's future. However, they also, more generally, seem to refer to the timeline between crucifixion or conversion and parousia.

When one also considers the multitude of occurrences of the future indicative in Old Testament quotations, prophetic declarations concerning the future from Paul's temporal viewpoint, similarly, emerge as only one among several possibilities. There are prophecies narrated as already fulfilled even within the source texts Paul engages (Gen 18:10, 14 in Rom 9:9; Gen 25:23 in Rom 9:12; and, at least partially, Gen 15:5 in Rom 4:18) and others that are at least deemed to have become reality in the period between the narrated time of these texts and Paul's present (Deut 32:12 in Rom 10:19; the sequence of Hos 2:25, Hos 2:1, and Isa 10:22–23 in Rom 9:25–28).[125] However, certain foreshadowings of future events (from Paul's perspective) through the use of future indicative in Old Testament quotations occur only in a few references to the eschaton (Rom 2:6; 11:26; 12:19; and 14:11).[126]

---

120. Cf. *AGG* 267.
121. Cf. *AGG* 202.
122. Heilig, *Paulus*, 677–78.
123. See Heilig, *Paulus*, 678–81, for a discussion of this untenable classification of the indicative future forms in Romans.
124. See Heilig, *Paulus*, chapter 13, section 2.1.
125. See Heilig, *Paulus*, chapter 13, sections 2.2.2 and 2.2.3.
126. See Heilig, *Paulus*, chapter 13, section 2.2.4. There is also predictive disnarration in Rom 3:20 (at least partially future) and 10:11.

Fragments of Implicit Protonarratives

As this brief overview demonstrates, though the future indicative in independent declarative clauses may appear to be a quintessential tool for creating certain foreshadowings, most of these verb forms indeed serve a different function. This finding subsequently raises the question of what other, less apparent linguistic instruments could potentially be utilized to create certain foreshadowings.

Another mechanism for generating such announcements is through the employment of dependent structures after expressions that categorize the ensuing future events as "known," "foretold," "necessary," or the like. In what follows, we will confine our discussion to the *constructions that follow terms of knowing*.[127]

In some circumstances, the known event is situated in the past (cf. Rom 6:6). Under such conditions, we encounter classical subsequent narration albeit with a pragmatic twist, where the story is presented as known to either the narrator, the recipients, or both. However, in other Pauline examples the known event dates to the future, particularly after the use of οἶδα (see particularly Phil 1:25; Col 3:24; Phlm 21).

The impersonal construct δῆλον [ἐστίν] ὅτι... similarly underscores that what is narrated is "obvious," not just to one of the parties but universally. Ironically, in Gal 3:11 where this construct is used, the meaning itself seems far from clear. There is considerable debate over whether Paul assumes as a matter of course that no one receives justification in the law before God (simultaneous narration?) or the certain foreshadowing that "the righteous one will live by faith" (cf. Hab 2:4).[128]

When Paul employs expressions of assertion ("as surely as I live," etc.), the dynamics notably shift. The story is no longer presupposed as a given for all, but rather he, as the narrator, is deeply engaged in an act of *emphatic predictive narration* (cf. Rom 14:11; 2 Cor 11:10). Cases in which Paul uses a term of knowing, which we just analyzed, in the imperative—thus instructing his audience to know something—exhibit a similar dynamic. This implies that the story conveys new information, or at least is intended to remind them of something they might have forgotten. Such a dynamic can be observed, for example, in 2 Tim 3:1, where what Tim-

---

127. Cf. Heilig, *Paulus*, chapter 13, section 3.1. On verbs of foretelling, see Heilig, *Paulus*, chapter 13, section 3.2; on necessary future events, cf. Heilig, *Paulus*, chapter 13, section 3.3.

128. For more details, cf. Heilig, *Paulus*, 698–99. Cf. also 1 Cor 15:27, where we clearly have the future oriented perspective.

Chapter 4

othy is instructed to "know" is situated in the future, specifically "that in the last days there will come difficult times" (ὅτι ἐν ἐσχάταις ἡμέραις ἐνστήσονται καιροὶ χαλεποί).

Of particular interest is 1 Cor 6:2, 3, and 9a, where the verb οἶδα appears within question clauses (cf. above, p. 226).[129] As they imply a positive response, the Corinthians are thus inclined to answer: "Indeed! We certainly know that the holy ones will judge the world, that we will judge angels, and that unjust people will not inherit the kingdom of God." Paul undoubtedly overstates the extent of this shared knowledge because immediately afterward, in verse 9b, he admonishes the Corinthians not to be "deceived" (μὴ πλανᾶσθε). Additionally, verse 10 then enumerates a series of subjects who will not "inherit the kingdom of God" (βασιλείαν θεοῦ κληρονομήσουσιν), thus providing further detail on the ἄδικοι, ensuring the Corinthians comprehend what this familiar predictive narrative truly entails by clarifying the narrative figures involved in the plot they thought they understood.

Linguistic Means for Expressing Uncertain Foreshadowings to Paul's Future

As we move on to *uncertain* foreshadowings, we step into exceedingly intricate subject matter. As previously pointed out, the role of such uncertain foreshadowings is not to propose fixed building blocks for what might later, retrospectively, shape into subsequent narration. Instead, they conjure potential narratives whose, truthful, subsequent narration remains somewhat at stake. Within Paul's letters, we identify a range of different linguistic tools that he uses to indicate events that are yet to occur without explicitly asserting their inevitability. Additionally, dependent on the exact phrasing, both the degree of uncertainty and the intended impact of such protonarratives can vary significantly.

---

129. For the foreshadowing in Eph 5:5, which is similar in content but very different in the way it is construed linguistically, cf. Heilig, *Paulus*, 695–96. Generally, one can note that a look at constructions with οἶδα offer slightly better results than in the case of γινώσκω. With the former verb, we do have several dependent ὅτι clauses with future indicative verb forms (Phil 1:25; Col 3:24; and Phlm 21).

Independent Declarative Clauses

It remains worthwhile to explore *future indicative verb forms in independent (main) declarative clauses* in this context as well.[130] We can attribute the ability of such sentences to form both certain and uncertain foreshadowings to the fact that the tense may be used in circumstances where only mere intentions are at play. The boundary between these two usages can indeed be rather blurry, and Paul's letters thus hold several occurrences that could constitute either certain or uncertain foreshadowings.

In Romans, which we previously discussed in our brief case study, potential examples of modal future are the questions τί [οὖν] ἐροῦμεν . . . ; ("What [then] shall we say?"; Rom 3:5; 4:1; 6:1; 7:7; 8:31; 9:14, 30). Possible uses of the modal future appear with remarkable frequency in the Corinthian correspondence (1 Cor 6:5, 12; 9:15; 2 Cor 10:13; 11:9, 18; 12:1, 5, 14, 15) and less frequently in other letters (cf. Phil 4:4 and Eph 6:16). There are instances where lexical indications in the immediate context suggest a modal understanding of the future. For example, in 1 Cor 15:35, a very general "someone" who might raise a question is mentioned (Ἀλλὰ ἐρεῖ τις . . .).[131]

When English or German speakers read these passages, they often remain oblivious to the fact that quite different assertions might be made in each case. This is because in these languages the future tense can be used with similar flexibility.[132] As a result, Bible versions can also be somewhat inconsistent when it comes to elucidating the degree of assertiveness, sometimes incorporating modal verbs such as "may," and other times not.[133] For speakers of Koine Greek as well, the distinction might have been both intricate and crucial at times.

This is mirrored in the unsuccessful communication between Paul and the Corinthians, as it shines through in 2 Cor 1:18–22. There, Paul is compelled to defend the clarity of his speech in a theological digression because he was unable to adhere to the travel plan outlined in 2 Cor 1:15–16. Consequently, the Corinthians assert that his "Yes (I will come)" also implies a "No."[134] Since he did not visit the Corinthians twice, as he had announced he would, they infer from this that he makes such promises "lightheartedly"

---

130. Cf. Heilig, *Paulus*, chapter 14, section 3.
131. Cf. Heilig, *Paulus*, chapter 14, section 3.2.1.
132. Cf. *AGG* 202b and *GGNT* 202b.
133. Heilig, *Paulus*, 713–14.
134. On the syntax, cf. Heilig, *Paulus*, 715 n. 72.

Chapter 4

(verse 17: τῇ ἐλαφρίᾳ).[135] The Corinthians seem less troubled by this repeated display of Paul's inability to stick to his plan than by the contrast between his resolute announcement and his subsequent decision to act differently.[136] We are unaware of how Paul communicated his plan concerning the double visit to Corinth during the interim visit or in the "letter of tears." However, it is plausible to surmise that part of the problem with the unmet expectations has to do with the openness of the future indicative forms to modal interpretation.

Interestingly, in 1 Cor 16:5–8, we gain insight into an earlier version of Paul's plan, which he, too, seemingly was unable to realize. It is quite enlightening to observe the extent to which Paul there differentiates varying degrees of certainty with respect to future events.

Initially, Paul's forthcoming visit is merely mentioned parenthetically in two temporal clauses with ὅταν and the subjunctive (verse 2: ὅταν ἔλθω ... ; verse 3a: ὅταν δὲ παραγένωμαι ...). The main clause expresses the sending of trusted individuals, using the future indicative (πέμψω). The aim of that commission remains indefinite with respect to mood because it is presented as an infinitive (ἀπενεγκεῖν τὴν χάριν ὑμῶν εἰς Ἰερουσαλήμ). In verse 4, Paul elaborates on their journey, specifying by means of a future indicative verb form that it will be a journey "with me" (verse 4b: ... σὺν ἐμοὶ πορεύσονται). Yet, this time the announcement is explicitly tied to the fulfillment of a condition: "If it seems worthy for me to go too ..." (verse 4a: ἐὰν ... ἄξιον ᾖ τοῦ κἀμὲ πορεύεσθαι ...). It is not until verse 5a that the "coming to you" is predictively narrated in the future indicative (Ἐλεύσομαι δὲ πρὸς ὑμᾶς). While in verses 2–3a this arrival has served as a temporal point of reference for another event, here it is itself viewed in relation to another, preceding event (verse 5b): "... after I will have traveled through Macedonia" (ὅταν Μακεδονίαν διέλθω). This journey is explicitly characterized as merely a transit, that is, something that will not much delay his arrival (verse 5c: Μακεδονίαν γὰρ διέρχομαι).[137]

Thus, the visit to Corinth is temporally connected with two other events—one earlier and one later—which themselves are not progressively disnarrated in the text. It is only the accompanying event of Paul also travel-

---

135. Cf. Christoph Heilig, *Paul's Triumph: Reassessing 2 Corinthians 2:14 in Its Literary and Historical Context*, BTS 27 (Leuven: Peeters, 2017), 156–61.
136. On the assumptions concerning Paul's interaction with the Corinthians that stand behind this interpretation, cf. Heilig, *Paulus*, 715.
137. On the present indicative in 1 Cor 16:5c, see Heilig, *Paulus*, 718.

Fragments of Implicit Protonarratives

ing to Jerusalem that is linked to a condition in verse 4. Likewise, in verse 8 Paul announces without apparent reservations that he will remain in Ephesus until Pentecost (ἐπιμενῶ δὲ ἐν Ἐφέσῳ ἕως τῆς πεντηκοστῆς). However, embedded in verses 6b–7 are several textual signals that subtly modulate the predictive narration of the visit from verse 5a retrospectively.

To start, we can discern some uncertainty concerning the *duration* of the planned visit. Paul does not intend to visit the Corinthians while journeying through the area, as is his plan with the communities in Macedonia (cf. verse 5b). While a quick visit would be possible if he departed immediately (as suggested in verse 7a: οὐ θέλω γὰρ ὑμᾶς ἄρτι ἐν παρόδῳ ἰδεῖν), this is not his preference.[138] Rather, he aspires to "spend some time with you" (verse 7c: χρόνον τινὰ ἐπιμεῖναι πρὸς ὑμᾶς). He further specifies this in 16:6a (παραμενῶ ἢ καὶ παραχειμάσω). While these are not strictly speaking alternatives, with "staying for the winter" also being a form of "staying," the phrasing reflects the fact that Paul has not yet fully decided and is still examining options. The text closely follows his reasoning, to the degree that the first verb only makes sense if we acknowledge that it was chosen before the second one arrived on the horizon.[139] Thus, it may be more appropriate to translate this along the lines of Paul planning to "stay for a while—or even the whole winter."[140]

However, the uncertainty evident in the text does not end there. In verse 6a, the plan to stay (potentially for the entire winter) is qualified by the addition of the adverb/participle τυχόν ("perhaps"). Moreover, the infinitive of "staying" in verse 7c (ἐπιμεῖναι) is explicitly delineated by the governing verb as a mere *hope* (verse 7b: ἐλπίζω) and further hinges on the fulfillment of a condition: ". . . *if* the Lord allows" (16:7d: . . . ἐὰν ὁ κύριος ἐπιτρέψῃ). It is evident that, at least regarding the duration of his visit and subsequent actions, Paul is indeed quite cautious not to make overly precise predictions.

To be sure, we cannot infer from this that Paul had no reservations whatsoever about his forthcoming visit in general. All we can know is that Paul

---

138. The ἄρτι does not contrast "this time" with an earlier visit but refers to the time of speaking and the visit that *would* be possible. It should be noted that we are dealing here with quite a complex move, with a protonarrative—a visit right now—being evoked and immediately rejected again within just a couple of words. Cf. Heilig, *Paulus*, 767.

139. Again, this seems to be a very relevant piece of evidence for our understanding of Paul's use of secretaries.

140. Some translations (NIV in English; Menge and NGÜ in German) resolve this well.

did not ultimately execute this plan.[141] It is conceivable that the Corinthians might have chastised him for making false promises—partially justified indeed. While we can never infer without qualification that an author perceives no circumstances under which the announcement might need to be rescinded merely because they use an indicative future verb form, it is certainly worth noting that, in this section, Paul does explicitly demarcate the uncertainty of some sequences of events. This could potentially give rise to the *perception that the other announcements are certain foreshadowings*, with their subsequent nonfulfilment, understandably, evoking disappointment.

Dependent Constructions after Epistemic Expressions

In our exploration of 1 Cor 16:5–8, we have already observed how an adverb (τυχόν) functions as an indicator of mere possibility. This specific adverb, actually the neuter participle of τυγχάνω, straddles the spectrum between the weaker connotation of ἴσως ("perhaps") and the more assertive implications of εἰ τύχοι or τάχα ("probably").[142]

However, what holds more relevance in relation to the analysis of protonarratives in Paul's letters is the phenomenon we encounter in 1 Cor 16:7b. There, a situation expressed by an infinitive is contingent upon a governing verb that articulates an epistemic state (in that case, hope). Consequently,

---

141. Cf. Schmeller, *Der zweite Brief an die Korinther*, 1:94–98, for the most convincing discussion of options of a very complicated matter. Instead of visiting them for a long time, he merely and hastily visited the Corinthians for what turned out to be an embarrassing "interim visit." It was perhaps during this visit that he presented the Corinthians with the plan of a double visit—visiting them both on his way to Macedonia and on the way back (2 Cor 1:15–17). He later gives up this second plan in favor of writing the "tearful letter." Because he does not hear soon enough from Titus, he moves to Macedonia (2:13) and finally gets good news (7:5–6). His new idea about an upcoming visit is then presented in 2 Cor 13:2 and framed there as being in line (in tone) with the first part of the earlier intended double visit.

142. Functionally quite similar to ἴσως is what syntactically has to count as a fear clause without expression of fear in 2 Tim 2:25, introduced by μήποτε. Unlike in other cases of fear clauses with future reference (cf. the next section), the event in question—God granting repentance—does not seem to be evaluated negatively. Against Ernest D. Burton, *Syntax of the Moods and Tenses in New Testament Greek*, 3rd ed. (Chicago: University of Chicago Press, 1898), §225. Cf. Heilig, *Paulus*, chapter 14, section 3.5.2. On εἰ τύχοι and τάχα, cf. Heilig, *Paulus*, chapter 14, section 3.2.3. There are also some other formulations, which have a similar function and are discussed there.

we also need to examine the utilization of *dependent constructions* following expressions that categorize the ensuing future events as potentialities, whose occurrence remains uncertain at the moment of speaking. Within this subcategory, we can discern further distinctions based on the *semantics of the governing expression*.

First, we can distinguish *"expectations" in a neutral sense*—which merely encompass the belief that something will happen—from a more nuanced understanding of the verb "to expect," which veers toward the concept of 'hope.'[143] The semantic domains of Louw and Nida provide an invaluable resource for a systematic examination of Paul's letters through this lens. For instance, we can unearth fragments of protonarratives by orienting our attention toward the concept of 'trust, rely' (L&N 31.82–101). There are pertinent instances where πέπεισμαι, "to be convinced," is followed by a reference to future events in Rom 8:38–39 and 2 Tim 1:12.[144] With πιστεύω, "to believe," we encounter similar convictions about the future in Rom 6:8 (with an ὅτι clause) and Rom 14:2 (with an infinitive).[145]

The domain 'suppose, think possible' (L&N 31.29–34) is similarly highly relevant for obvious reasons.[146] The verbs οἶμα, νομίζω, δοκέω, and ὑπολαμβάνω are defined as 'to regard something as presumably true, but without particular certainty' (L&N 31.29). This epitomizes the notion of generating a merely "potential narrative"! Indeed, Paul utilizes such verbs to construct uncertain protonarratives that serve a range of rhetorical functions.

In 1 Cor 7:40, he employs δοκέω to introduce an understatement—he is quite confident that he possesses the Spirit of God, which means he is not merely expressing his personal opinion, κατὰ τὴν ἐμὴν γνώμην. Elsewhere (1 Cor 3:18; 8:2; 14:37; Gal 6:3) he invokes the same verb to introduce others' opinions, which he explicitly or implicitly rejects (or, at the very least, has reservations about as in 1 Cor 7:36).

Against this backdrop, it is noteworthy that Paul never applies such verbs to present his own protonarratives about the future. Apparently, in his remarks about the future, he is either more confident or desires to distinguish them explicitly in additional ways and therefore abstains from this type of tentative predictive narration. The absence of clear examples of uncertain

---

143. On the problem of the polysemy of both German "erwarten" and English "to expect," cf. Heilig, *Paulus*, chapter 14, section 3.3.1.
144. Heilig, *Paulus*, chapter 14, section 3.3.2.
145. Heilig, *Paulus*, chapter 14, section 3.3.3. See there also for a discussion of slightly less but still interesting constructions with the noun πίστις.
146. Heilig, *Paulus*, chapter 14, section 3.3.4.

Chapter 4

foreshadowings based on verbs from the semantic domain 'have an opinion, hold a view' (L&N 31.1–7)—such as λογίζομαι, which is used for others' erroneous opinions in Rom 2:3—reinforces this impression.[147]

Further supporting this point, we encounter quite a few pertinent passages when we switch to *"expectations" in a positive sense*.[148] The "desired" or "hoped-for" events can be flagged as such by governing expressions from a variety of semantic domains. These fragments of protonarratives are characterized not only by a positive depiction of what is envisioned, but also by the fact that the expectation is justified and transcends mere wishful thinking. From the semantic domain 'hope, look forward to' (L&N 25.59–64), the lexemes ἐλπίς and ἐλπίζω bear obvious relevance and will be examined here as representatives of the entire semantic domain.[149]

For instance, I would argue that the ὅτι clause in Rom 8:21 is not causally connected to verse 20 (which would render the clause a *certain* foreshadowing), but rather it elucidates what the hope of creation consists of, namely, "that the creation itself will also be liberated from the bondage of decay into the freedom that is part of God's glory" (ὅτι καὶ αὐτὴ ἡ κτίσις ἐλευθερωθήσεται ἀπὸ τῆς δουλείας τῆς φθορᾶς εἰς τὴν ἐλευθερίαν τῆς δόξης τῶν τέκνων τοῦ θεοῦ). Note that creation emerges here as a narrative figure through whose perspective we peer into the future.[150] In Phil 1:20, we encounter a near-identical construction but this time with Paul as focalizer. The verb ἐλπίζω supplies such fragments of protonarratives, both in the form of an

---

147. On λογίζομαι κτλ., see Heilig, *Paulus*, chapter 14, section 3.3.5.

148. Heilig, *Paulus*, chapter 14, section 3.4.

149. On other constructions that occur less frequently with ἐλπίς than the options that we discuss here, cf. Heilig, *Paulus*, 734. Moreover, Rom 1:10 and 11:14, where these lexemes do not feature at all, demonstrate just how variegated the linguistic means are that can be employed towards the communication of hopes. On these two verses, see Heilig, *Paulus*, 730–31. On constructions with ἀπεκδέχομαι, followed in Paul's letters by nouns, see Heilig, *Paulus*, chapter 14, section 3.4.2.

150. I think that this adds a further layer of nuance to the reading of Rom 8:19–23 with sensitivities to narrative concerns, as offered by Cherryl Hunt, David G. Horrell, and Christopher Southgate, "An Environmental Mantra? Ecological Interest in Romans 8:19–23 and a Modest Proposal for its Narrative Interpretation," *JTS* 59 (2008): 546–79. For example, it is not just the case that Paul "envisages" a certain future situation (p. 568). Rather, he portrays the situation in a way as nature herself envisages it. This has also hermeneutical implications. This becomes apparent even from the way the authors themselves frame the apparent anthropocentrism of this passage as a potential obstacle for an approach that aims for "a renewed ecological engagement with Scripture by 'reading from the perspective of Earth.'" After all, the "perspective" of creation features even in the text itself.

Fragments of Implicit Protonarratives

ὅτι clause and future indicative verb form (2 Cor 1:10, 13; 13:6; Phlm 21) and with an infinitive (cf. above, pp. 260–61, on 1 Cor 16:7; see also Phil 2:19, 23; and 1 Tim 3:14). The last mentioned verse is particularly intriguing because, in that instance, Paul expresses the hope (ἐλπίζων) "to come to you soon" (ἐλθεῖν πρὸς σὲ ἐν τάχει). Verse 15 then expressly mentions the possibility that this hope might not actually materialize, namely, by means of a prospective conditional clause—"If, however, I am delayed . . ." (ἐὰν δὲ βραδύνω)—thereby heightening the uncertainty of the foreshadowing.[151]

Less obvious than the semantic domain 'hope, look forward to' (L&N 25.59–64) but equally significant for identifying hoped-for events as fragments of potential narratives are the instances of πέποιθα ("I am confident"), part of the semantic domain 'trust, rely' (L&N 31.82–101).[152] This term appears in conjunction with future events in Gal 5:10; Phil 1:6; 2:24; and 2 Thess 3:4. Also noteworthy are the terms ἐπιποθέω, ἐπιθυμία, and ἐπιθυμέω from the semantic domain 'desire strongly' (L&N 25.12–32) with Rom 1:11; 2 Cor 5:2; 9:14; Phil 1:8, 23; 2:26; 1 Thess 2:17; 3:6; and 2 Tim 1:4 being the most pertinent passages in this context.[153]

Finally, the verbs προτίθημι, βουλεύομαι, and βούλομαι from the semantic domain 'to intend, to purpose, to plan' (L&N 30.56–74) should be considered.[154] Sometimes, the gloss "to wish" appears in occurrences of these verbs. However, note that when I speak of "wishes" in this book, I often have something more specific in mind, namely, a specific type of independent desiderative clauses. We will turn to that phenomenon shortly. Here, we are simply grappling with plans, with the active prognoses of narrative characters, which are marked as such by the governing lexemes. An instructive example is Paul's discourse on his long-held and still entertained plan to visit the Roman Christians, as articulated in Rom 1:13, 15 and 15:24. In this case, we are likely dealing with a single unified protonarrative in the background, not an earlier plan for an evangelistic visit and a new plan for an "inner-church" visit, as some propose. However, this protonarrative only emerges fragmentarily in the text, with the focus shifting among various involved narrative figures.[155]

---

151. On these clauses, see pp. 290–304 below.
152. Heilig, *Paulus*, chapter 14, section 3.4.3. Cf. above, p. 261, on πέπεισμαι.
153. Heilig, *Paulus*, chapter 14, section 3.4.4–3.4.5.
154. Heilig, *Paulus*, chapter 14, section 3.4.6.
155. Cf. Heilig, *Paulus*, 740–43. Cf. also above, pp. 257–58, on 2 Cor 1:15–17, which is also discussed in Heilig, *Paulus*, 743.

Chapter 4

Fear Clauses

Having addressed neutrally "expected" and then positively marked "hoped-for" events, we now turn to future events that may vary with respect to the certainty with which they are anticipated but share a negative evaluation as "feared" events.[156] Unlike in the case of the desired events, here we encounter a specific clause type: *fear clauses*.[157] These are subordinate clauses in the subjunctive that are introduced by μή and dependent on a verb that articulates such a mental state.[158] In Paul's letters, the only such term attested is φοβέομαι.[159] In most of the nine occurrences of the verb, it is followed by a noun, so a potential reference to a future event remains ambiguous (cf. Rom 13:3, 4; Gal 2:12).

In 2 Cor 11:3, however, the situation is different. In verse 2, Paul gazes back into the past, reflecting on the event where he pledged the congregation to its future spouse, Christ (ἡρμοσάμην γὰρ ὑμᾶς ἑνὶ ἀνδρί). Concurrently, he peers into the yet uncertain future, using a telic infinitive to elucidate the objective of that past action as "in order to present you as a pure virgin to Christ" (verse 2: παρθένον ἁγνὴν παραστῆσαι τῷ Χριστῷ). Amid these two temporal poles, Paul in the present ardently labors to ensure the realization of this goal (verse 2: ζηλῶ γὰρ ὑμᾶς θεοῦ ζήλῳ). This endeavor is accompanied, and possibly motivated, by his apprehension (verse 3: φοβοῦμαι) that an occurrence could arise to obstruct the happy ending—specifically, the prospect of their thoughts being led astray from sincere and untainted devotion to Christ (φθαρῇ τὰ νοήματα ὑμῶν ἀπὸ τῆς ἁπλότητος [καὶ τῆς ἁγνότητος] τῆς εἰς τὸν Χριστόν). It is noteworthy that in this fear clause, Paul abstains from using the indicative mood (in contrast to the examples discussed earlier, pp. 225–26). The significance of employing the subjunctive mood is sometimes overlooked by exegetes because Paul likens the feared

---

156. On what follows, cf. Heilig, *Paulus*, chapter 14, section 3.5.
157. Cf. *CGCG* 43 and *AGG* 271e.
158. For fear clauses with reference to the past, cf. above, pp. 225–26.
159. Cf. Heilig, *Paulus*, chapter 14, section 3.5.1. See there also for the suggestion that βλέπετε may introduce fear clauses in some cases (e.g., 1 Cor 8:9). It is more probable, however, that in such instances we are dealing with an asyndetic continuation in the "prohibitive subjunctive." Cf. *AGG* 210e. Therefore, this phenomenon belongs to the discussion of desiderative clauses later in this chapter. Another possibility that one needs to take into account is that the expression of fear is dropped (cf. Heilig, *Paulus*, chapter 14, section 3.5.2). Since negated telic clauses can be introduced by μή alone (instead of ἵνα μή), classification is sometimes difficult. On μήποτε in 2 Tim 2:25, cf. above, p. 260, note 142.

occurrence to the past event of Eve's deception (verse 3: ὡς ὁ ὄφις ἐξηπάτησεν Εὕαν ἐν τῇ πανουργίᾳ αὐτοῦ). However, this does not imply that Paul is, analogously, concerned about something that might have already transpired in Corinth.[160]

In 2 Cor 2:20, we encounter a similar apprehension pertaining to a future moment, specifically "when I come" (ἐλθών). Paul hopes that he will not find the Corinthians to be in an undesirable condition, yet acknowledges the potential for this to be the case (μή πως . . . οὐχ οἵους θέλω εὕρω ὑμᾶς κἀγὼ εὑρεθῶ ὑμῖν οἷον οὐ θέλετε). More precisely, he wants to avoid encountering traits such as "quarreling, jealousy, anger, selfish ambition, slander, gossip, arrogance, and disorder" (cf. μή πως [add. ὦσιν] ἔρις, ζῆλος, θυμοί, ἐριθεῖαι, καταλαλιαί, ψιθυρισμοί, φυσιώσεις, ἀκαταστασίαι). Verse 21 continues this topic of fears, reiterating the temporal reference point (ἐλθόντος μου) and this time focusing on the storyline of Paul. The initial scenario appears to reframe (employing repetitive narration with a shift of focalizer) the entire experience from Paul's perspective, as a humbling before the Corinthians by God (μὴ πάλιν . . . ταπεινώσῃ με ὁ θεός μου πρὸς ὑμᾶς). And the second one seems to proceed to the repercussions, specifically Paul's profound sorrow (καὶ πενθήσω πολλοὺς τῶν προημαρτηκότων καὶ μὴ μετανοησάντων ἐπὶ τῇ ἀκαθαρσίᾳ καὶ πορνείᾳ καὶ ἀσελγείᾳ ᾗ ἔπραξαν). Interestingly, this apprehended future occurrence is portrayed here as a potential recurrence of a past experience. Paul is concerned about the possibility of history repeating itself, and there are several possible interpretations for what he precisely has in mind when referring to "those who have sinned previously but have not repented."[161]

Interrogative Clauses

In our discussion of disnarration, we have already observed how different types of *questions* yield various disnarrating effects concerning events in the past and present (see pp. 226–29). Consequently, it is not surprising that these sentence structures are also pertinent when seeking uncertain foreshadowings.[162] Look-

---

160. Many exegetes think that verse 4 encourages such a reading. But that presupposes a misunderstanding of the conditional construction. Cf. Heilig, *Paulus*, 746–47.
161. On the complex question, cf. Heilig, *Paulus*, 748–49.
162. On what follows, cf. Heilig, *Paulus*, chapter 14, section 2.

Chapter 4

ing once again at indicative future verb forms in Romans provides us with a representative picture.[163]

In Rom 2:26, the particle that introduces the question makes clear that we anticipate with reasonable confidence the paradoxical occurrence of uncircumcision being regarded as circumcision (οὐχ ἡ ἀκροβυστία αὐτοῦ εἰς περιτομὴν λογισθήσεται;). Nonetheless, this implied affirmative response remains contingent upon the fulfillment of a condition, which is also optimistically formulated, namely, in a prospective conditional clause (ἐὰν οὖν ἡ ἀκροβυστία τὰ δικαιώματα τοῦ νόμου φυλάσσῃ; cf. below, pp. 290–304, for further discussion on such conditional clauses). Romans 3:3 bears a similar structure but diverges from the aforementioned passage in two aspects. First, the condition of some having been unfaithful (εἰ ἠπίστησάν τινες) emerges as an indefinite conditional clause (which will likewise be discussed in more detail below). Second, the nature of "predictive *dis*narration" is now more pronounced as the question implies a negative answer—that unfaithfulness *will not* render void God's faithfulness (μὴ ἡ ἀπιστία αὐτῶν τὴν πίστιν τοῦ θεοῦ καταργήσει;).[164]

We also encounter future indicative verb forms in *open* interrogative clauses within the context of Romans. Employing τίς, Paul prompts his readers to devise a range of predictive narratives in response to his own vague outline of a forthcoming storyline.[165] Depending on one's interpretation of Rom 7 as a whole, distinct readings emerge for the desperate query in verse 24: "Who will rescue me from this body of death?" (τίς με ῥύσεται ἐκ τοῦ σώματος τοῦ θανάτου τούτου;). This question may either find its

---

163. For a discussion of interrogative clauses with the future indicative, see Heilig, *Paulus*, chapter 14, section 2.2. Likewise relevant are questions with *deliberative subjunctive*. On Rom 3:8; 6:2, 15, see Heilig, *Paulus*, 711–12. On Rom 10:14–15, cf. above, pp. 214–19. I am focusing here on direct questions. On indirect questions, see Heilig, *Paulus*, 707. The dependent constructions are not as important in this context as they are with respect to declarative and directive constructions, which we likewise discuss in this chapter.

164. Cf. also Rom 9:20, where a negative answer is also implied. The future event in question is a speech act. More precisely, it is, ironically, itself a question (μὴ ἐρεῖ τὸ πλάσμα τῷ πλάσαντι· τί με ἐποίησας οὕτως). Cf. also above, pp. 257–60, on the modal future. Note also that the relationship of the narrative world to Paul's real world in this story is somewhat uncertain, and it is, thus, for ontological reasons, questionable whether this can be classified as a true foreshadowing to the future of the narrator.

165. On the open interrogative clauses with τί in Rom 3:5; 4:1; 6:1; 7:7; 8:31; 9:14, 30, see Heilig, *Paulus*, 710. On the open interrogative clauses with πῶς in Rom 6:2 and 8:32, see Heilig, *Paulus*, 711.

Fragments of Implicit Protonarratives

answer in verse 25 (i.e., "God!") or within verses 7–23 (i.e., "No one!"). In the latter scenario, the implicit response itself becomes a markedly emphatic disnarration of future events. In Rom 8:33, it is highly evident that such an implication is indeed at play—a negation that *anyone* will bring accusations against God's chosen ones (cf. τίς ἐγκαλέσει κατὰ ἐκλεκτῶν θεοῦ;).[166] Similarly, in the subsequent two verses we discover that no one stands capable of condemning them (verse 34) and that no one will sever "us" from the love of Christ (verse 35) even though, in the latter instance, some potential narrative elements—including trouble, distress, persecution, famine, nakedness, danger, and sword—that could potentially play such a role are mentioned, thereby conjuring counterfactual protonarratives.

Independent Desiderative Clauses

Until now, we have examined declarative and interrogative clauses and their diverse ways of constructing foreshadowings by portraying events as neutral expectations, hopes, or fears. The final major category of clauses that demands our attention is *desiderative clauses*.[167] Admittedly, they are not the only choice for expressing directive speech acts. For instance, the declarative clause "It is loud in here" may often function as an indirect directive speech act in specific contexts. Still, desiderative clauses are the main source for a quest for directive speech acts in Paul's letters.

We will first discuss *independent desiderative clauses*.[168] Considering their function, we can distinguish between "directives" and "wishes" within this category.[169] They bear similarities to the hoped-for events, yet with the distinction that this time we encounter not only an epistemic mode (reflecting the speaker's stance toward the event) but also a communicative function (involving the question of how the recipient[s] relate to the event in question).

Commencing our exploration with *directives* that are aimed at a party

---

166. For details on the syntax, cf. Heilig, *Paulus*, 709–10.
167. On this huge category with many subdivisions, cf. Heilig, *Paulus*, chapter 14, section 4.
168. For the differentiation between clause types and communicative functions, cf. Heilig, *Paulus*, chapter 14, section 4.1. Cf. also already above, pp. 161–62, in our discussion of clause types. See also *CGCG* 31.31–37 for a variety of expressions that are used as directives.
169. Cf. *AGG* 268a.

Chapter 4

distinct from the speaker, the imperative mode is typically employed.[170] In instances where speakers intend to issue commands to themselves or when speakers and addressees are to take action collectively, the voluntative subjunctive (referred to as "hortatory" in this context) is utilized. The voluntative subjunctive (referred to as "adhortative" in this context) can also function as an alternative to the imperative in negated directives, encompassing what can be broadly termed as "prohibitions."[171] In the subsequent discussion of this section, I will provide an example of a protonarrative associated with an imperative form followed by an instance of a voluntative subjunctive. Both examples are extracted from Romans, as were the examples we considered for future verb forms.

In Rom 6:13b, the first aorist imperative within the entire letter is encountered.[172] Paul issues a command to the recipients, directing them to present themselves to God (παραστήσατε ἑαυτοὺς τῷ θεῷ) in a specific manner. The same form of the verb παρίστημι appears again a few verses later, in verse 19c, where it is associated with "your members" (τὰ μέλη ὑμῶν). The same verb is also found in the aorist indicative in verse 19b, where it plays a role within an account that introduces a past event as a precursor to the "desired" event. What Paul commands is depicted as akin to what has already occurred. Thus, the protonarrative takes on a nuanced shape by being explicitly linked to an actual narrative. The Roman Christians are instructed to serve righteousness that leads to holiness.[173] What is intended to transpire in the "now" (νῦν) is portrayed as structurally analogous to their previous act of presenting their members "as slaves of impurity and lawlessness leading to further lawlessness" (cf. verse 19b: ὥσπερ γὰρ παρεστήσατε τὰ μέλη ὑμῶν δοῦλα τῇ ἀκαθαρσίᾳ καὶ τῇ ἀνομίᾳ εἰς τὴν ἀνομίαν, οὕτως ...).

Up until now, we have observed the interplay of a desirable protonarrative, contingent upon the collaboration of the addressees, interwoven with a narrative of their past. However, this is not the sole form of narrative integration that takes place here. Paul also interlinks the anticipated protonarrative he aspires to witness with an alternate plot he hopes will remain counterfactual. To achieve this, he contrasts the unmarked aorist

---

170. There are a couple of alternative constructions attested in Paul's letters and that are discussed in Heilig, *Paulus*, chapter 14, section 4.2.1.

171. Cf. *AGG* 268b for the different constructions. In the second person, verbs in the perfective stem always appear in the subjunctive. Cf. *AGG* 212.

172. For a detailed exegesis of Rom 6:13–19, cf. Heilig, *Paulus*, chapter 14, section 4.2.2.

173. Unlike in verse 13b, in verse 19c there is no dative construction, but rather an object complement: δοῦλα τῇ δικαιοσύνῃ εἰς ἁγιασμόν.

imperative in verse 13b with a *negated present imperative* in verse 13a. The act of making themselves available for God stands in stark opposition to the action of presenting their members (notably, the same object that appears later in verse 19) to sin as instruments of unrighteousness (μηδὲ παριστάνετε τὰ μέλη ὑμῶν ὅπλα ἀδικίας τῇ ἁμαρτίᾳ).

How exactly does this negated imperative of the durative stem establish a link between the regrettable past events on the one hand and the anticipated future events on the other hand? As I will elaborate on further in the context of our discussion of conditional clauses (pp. 289–90), it becomes evident that the entire passage in Rom 6 is characterized by the addressees being encouraged to compare the plots of different protonarratives with each other. Paul hopes that in that process the readers will "update" their respective biographies as Christians by making the right choices of storylines that are available. In my view, the utilization of the negated durative imperative further emphasizes this direction.

To begin with, it is noteworthy that the choice of the aorist indicative in verse 19b does not offer insight into when the sinful conduct ceased, or even if it has ceased at all. Instead, what is explicitly presented as a completed event in the past is merely the transition toward such behavior, the change of state. Whether and when this state actually ended is not the topic of the narration. While Paul aspires for each individual to experience baptism as a rupture from these kinds of sinful activities (see Rom 6:4, 6; for further elaboration, cf. below, p. 289), the wording in verse 19 acknowledges the potential divergence in the "faith narratives" of individual believers. It allows for the possibility that the unfolding story of these believers "in Christ" might not differ dramatically from what could have been anticipated, from, in Ryan's terms (see pp. 209–10 above), the "passive prognosis" regarding the future of the addressees immediately prior to their conversion.

It is fascinating to observe that among the recipients, those who experience a sense of moral unease and perceive the narrative in verse 19b extending beyond their baptism and into the present are likely to interpret the negative command in verse 13a differently from those for whom verse 19b is more of a distant memory. For the former group, μηδὲ παριστάνετε and following would be understood as an instruction to *cease* such behavior. To them, the perfective imperatives in verses 13b and 19c would signify a call to take a positive step after addressing this more fundamental issue. Admittedly, my interpretation presupposes that these readers would have needed to reinterpret παρίστημι in a telic manner in instances where the perfective

Chapter 4

stem is utilized.[174] However, allowing for such a reinterpretation seems well within the realm of reasonable expectations for cooperative readers and appears quite plausible, considering how their lived experiences would have shaped their engagement with the text.

Conversely, the negated imperative in verse 13a would also have made (different!) sense to the more confident readers. They would have likely interpreted it as a *general prohibition* of such behavior. Such an openness of the negated present imperative is possible if we understand the "presentation" that is expressed by παρίστημι as an activity.[175] Assuming such a meaning, these Christians would have read the positive perfective imperatives in verse 13a and 19c simply as a command to continue what they were already doing anyway.

The insight this provides into Paul's role as a narrator is truly remarkable. In the realm of typical communication assumptions, authors are presumed to convey a singular meaning and to do so with clarity.[176] Therefore, one might raise doubts about the validity of my interpretation, as it might appear, at a glance, to imply that Paul intentionally employs vagueness. However, it is crucial to note that my proposition does not strictly constitute an "amphibole."[177] Paul is not employing imperatives in an "ambiguous" manner. Rather, his intent is precisely to convey multiple possible readings that arise within different contexts of utterance, with different parities among the recipients causing this differentiation. It is crucial to note that in each context the independent desiderative clauses are disambiguated at the level of utterance, each carrying only one meaning.[178] The events expressed in these independent desiderative clauses can therefore be seen as fragments of two distinct protonarratives. Paul does not just communicate the "material" from which the Romans can construct these protonarratives. These fragments also come with distinct sets of instructions, varying for different segments of the congregation, regarding how to appropriately narrativize them. Although their retrospective narrations might significantly differ, provided they be-

---

174. For παρίστημι with telic situation type, cf. BDAG, s.v. "παρίστημι," 1a.

175. Cf. Michael G. Aubrey, "Greek Prohibitions," in *The Greek Verb Revisited: A Fresh Approach for Biblical Exegesis*, ed. Steven E. Runge and Christopher J. Fresch (Bellingham, WA: Lexham, 2016), 506–7, on the requirement of this situation type.

176. Cf. *AGG* 314.

177. *AGG* 296g.

178. Cf. generally on different levels of meaning above, pp. 145–52. On contextual ambiguity, cf. Sebastian Löbner, *Understanding Semantics*, 2nd ed., Understanding Language Series (New York: Routledge, 2013), 49.

come narratable in the future (which the Romans first must ensure), the plots of both stories are united by the same happy ending that Paul envisions for all readers.

As previously mentioned, subjunctive verb forms within independent desiderative clauses can also convey future events that play a role within broader protonarratives. This is exemplified aptly by the three hortatory subjunctives found in Rom 13:11–14. These subjunctives seamlessly integrate into a cohesive protonarrative alongside indicative (verses 11–12) and imperative (verse 14) verb forms.[179]

As a first observation, we can note that the metaphorical self-command for adopting a transformed way of living in verse 12c ("let us cast off the works of darkness"; ἀποθώμεθα . . . τὰ ἔργα τοῦ σκότους) and verse 12d ("let us put on the armor of light"; ἐνδυσώμεθα . . . τὰ ὅπλα τοῦ φωτός), is introduced by the conjunction οὖν. This marks the entire macroproposition in verses 12c–d as being part of a consequential connection, one that displays utterance relatedness. Thus, the connector indicates that what precedes provides legitimization for why Paul feels so comfortable with formulating two directive speech acts.

This basis for Paul's directives is a *miniature story* that begins in Rom 13:11. The Roman Christians are supposed to follow the command to love (verse 9) because they "know the time" (verse 11a: εἰδότες τὸν καιρόν) and, more specifically, know that the hour of "our waking up from sleep" has already arrived (verse 11b–c: ὅτι ὥρα ἤδη ὑμᾶς ἐξ ὕπνου ἐγερθῆναι). When we then turn to verse 11d, this imagery is connected with the idea of approaching salvation (νῦν γὰρ ἐγγύτερον ἡμῶν ἡ σωτηρία ἢ ὅτε ἐπιστεύσαμεν), and it initially seems as if the figurative language retreats into the background.

However, verse 12a then continues asyndetically, obviously taking up again the image of daybreak, by claiming that "the night is nearly over" (NIV; ἡ νὺξ προέκοψεν) or, again making use of a moving-world conceptualization (not a moving-observer conceptualization), that "the day has approached" (verse 12b: ἡ δὲ ἡμέρα ἤγγικεν). It is against the backdrop of this temporal setting, established by verses 11a–c and 12a–b, that the two self-directives of 12c–d follow, exploring the light-dark dualism. It is time to engage in the tasks of the day, and the appropriate "outfit" must be selected accordingly. Quite obviously, the miniature narrative is presupposed here, even though it is not continued, with the narration not making any progress.

---

179. For more details on this passage, cf. the detailed exegesis in Heilig, *Paulus*, chapter 14, section 4.2.3.

Chapter 4

Most commentators lose sight of this nexus of events by the time they reach the directives in verse 14. In this verse, a perfective imperative verb encourages readers to "put on the Lord Jesus Christ" (verse 14a: ἀλλὰ ἐνδύσασθε τὸν κύριον Ἰησοῦν Χριστόν), while a negated imperfective imperative verb discourages tending to the desires of the flesh (verse 14b: καὶ τῆς σαρκὸς πρόνοιαν μὴ ποιεῖσθε εἰς ἐπιθυμίας). In contrast, I believe that throughout the passage, *we remain immersed within the same "narrated world," following the perspective of a narrative character who awaits the arrival of dawn.* This interpretation is especially suggested by the fact that in verse 13a, where we encounter a third hortatory subjunctive, the self-command is modified by a formulation that directly alludes to daytime: "Let us walk properly, *as during the day*" (. . . ὡς ἐν ἡμέρᾳ). In this context, it seems highly suspicious that the action encouraged in verse 12d (ἐνδυσώμεθα) reappears in verse 14a (ἐνδύσασθε). Both instances involve the concept of "putting on," a notion inherently associated with the morning hours.

Even the negated imperative in verse 14b can be seamlessly integrated into this overarching scene. To be sure, the exhortation appears to be crafted with a consideration of the Christian life's reality. It is noteworthy that certain translations may actually inject *too much* of the imagery into the discourse at this point. For instance, the NET translation mentions "arousing" desire, and the Elberfelder version even suggests their "awakening" ("wach werden" in the German original). This could stem from a valid recognition of the underlying protonarrative and the aim to maintain its visibility throughout the passage. However, this approach proves counterproductive, as the subsequent verses meticulously center around the narrative character who is about to encounter the new day. For them, the event of "awakening" comes with a positive plot turn. Therefore, introducing it at this point casts a negative light on this event, which does not align well with the carefully constructed scene in the rest of these verses. It is thus better to understand the behavior that is rejected in verse 14b and that is explicated in the modal datives in verse 13b (μὴ κώμοις καὶ μέθαις, μὴ κοίταις καὶ ἀσελγείαις, μὴ ἔριδι καὶ ζήλῳ) as relating in a different way to the temporal framework that we have sketched so far. Due to their disgracefulness, these acts are not usually performed in the open, in daylight—they are, in other words, "works of the darkness" (ἔργα τοῦ σκότους). The use of the article, which presupposes that this darkness has already been introduced in the discourse, probably builds on the nighttime that has been evoked as a backdrop throughout. Accordingly, the negated imperfective imperative of ποιέω in verse 14b also finds its place in this temporal framework. Just as verse 12b in a self-command

Fragments of Implicit Protonarratives

speaks of "putting off" these works, here we have a command to stop with a corresponding behavior—that is, now that daytime is arriving.[180]

The second subcategory of independent desiderative clauses, besides directives, involves those that embody *wishes*. These wishes hold a somewhat ambiguous position from a speech act perspective. They seem to exist in a space between directives on the one side and exclamations—expressing the speaker's attitude—on the other.[181] We have already examined unattainable wishes as a method of disnarration (pp. 233–34). Now, we are delving into wishes that are portrayed as achievable in principle.[182] While English generally employs the modal "may" for such wishes, the prevailing approach in Koine Greek is the use of the "optative of wish."[183]

In the writings of Paul, the use of the optative of wish is particularly noteworthy, owing to the apostle's distinctive employment of the formula μὴ γένοιτο, which is especially prominent in his letter to the Romans. Through this construction, Paul effectively rebuts certain notions he has previously introduced via preceding questions. At times, this usage involves matters of classification (cf. Rom 7:7: "Is the law sin?"; ὁ νόμος ἁμαρτία;). However, in verses such as Rom 6:2 (and also 6:15), Paul responds to questions that introduce potential future events into the discourse. Essentially, in these instances, Paul engages with a protonarrative—for instance, one about the persistence in sin to magnify grace (verse 1: ἐπιμένωμεν τῇ ἁμαρτίᾳ, ἵνα ἡ χάρις πλεονάσῃ;).[184] In such cases, we thus encounter the gradual disnarration of

---

180. On the stop-doing-X constructions, cf. above, pp. 269–70.

181. On exclamations, cf. *CGCG* 38.43–51. Cf. *AGG* 266a on the categorization of clause types and communicative functions.

182. On what follows, cf. Heilig, *Paulus*, chapter 14, section 4.3.

183. *AGG* 211c. Moreover, we need to take into account augment indicatives without ἄν. Note that in classical Greek there is a distinction between βούλομαι in the optative with ἄν for attainable wishes and augment indicatives with ἄν for unattainable wishes. In the New Testament, the imperfect verb forms ἐβουλόμην (without ἄν) and ἤθελον followed by infinitives constitute a class of wish clauses where the wished event seems to be at least sometimes attainable. Cf. Heilig, *Paulus*, chapter 14, section 4.3.2. A potential occurrence might be Phlm 13. However, it is more probable that there we are dealing simply with a statement about a mental state—a desire—in the past. See Heilig, *Paulus*, chapter 14, section 5.3.2.4. Cf. generally Heilig, *Paulus*, chapter 12, section 8.4, on unattainable wishes. By contrast, the imperfect verb form ηὐχόμην in Rom 9:3 seems indeed to introduce a desire concerning which Paul apparently thinks that it would at least be possible to utter an attainable wish. See Heilig, *Paulus*, 762.

184. In Rom 7:13; 11:1, 11, Paul has *past* situation times in view. Hence, we are dealing here with a means of subsequent disnarration, covered in detail above. He is disnarrating events that have already been presented as dubious by means of the question.

Chapter 4

future events. While the exclamation "By no means!" effectively captures Paul's attitude, it is crucial to discern the distinction between the optative of wish and the usage of οὐ μὴ γένηται (cf., e.g., Deut 28:65 and Ezek 21:32[37]). The latter definitively precludes the possibility of the protonarratives ever being recounted in retrospect. In contrast, the former does not assume the certain fulfillment of the wish, thereby keeping open the possibility of the horror story materializing after all. Moreover, unlike the strongly negated future indicative, the negated optative of wish conveys an evaluative facet, explicitly encoding the narrator's stance toward the potential event.

When it comes to the affirmative usage of the optative of wish—that is, when we are not dealing with the rejection of protonarratives but with their postulation—we can first observe its broad application in blessings (see, for instance, Rom 15:3, 13). However, this grammatical structure is also employed with respect to more specific situations. Take, for instance, 1 Thess 3:11, where the wish is expressed that God the Father and the Lord Jesus "may direct our way to you" (κατευθύναι τὴν ὁδὸν ἡμῶν πρὸς ὑμᾶς). Notably, this use of the optative of wish maintains the language of prayer from verse 10, where in reported speech we learn about Paul and his coworkers expressing such a wish directly to God: "we ask [him] to see you in person..." (δεόμενοι εἰς τὸ ἰδεῖν ὑμῶν τὸ πρόσωπον...).

Dependent Desiderative Clauses

The last example directs our attention to the next area of consideration: *dependent* desiderative constructions. What appears as a directly expressed wish in 1 Thess 3:11 is also indirectly reflected in verse 10. This pattern can be extrapolated. Dependent desiderative constructions, taking the form of ἵνα clauses or infinitives serving as direct objects of verbs denoting actions like wishing or instructing, can be understood as *derivations* from independent desiderative clauses.[185]

For instance, in Luke 9:3 a statement attributed to Jesus begins with the neutral verb λέγω ("to speak"), followed by an actual quotation of his directive presented in the imperative form: "And he spoke to them: 'Take nothing with you on your journey'" (καὶ εἶπεν πρὸς αὐτούς·μηδὲν αἴρετε εἰς τὴν ὁδόν). In contrast, Mark 6:8 conveys the same directive function by using the semantically explicit verb παραγγέλλω ("to command"; we will discuss

---

185. *AGG* 272b. The following example is taken from there.

Fragments of Implicit Protonarratives

Paul's usage of this verb shortly), which introduces reported speech: "And he instructed them not to take anything with them on their journey..." (καὶ παρήγγειλεν αὐτοῖς ἵνα μηδὲν αἴρωσιν εἰς ὁδὸν εἰ μὴ ῥάβδον μόνον).

When attempting to reconstruct such directives in the form of independent desiderative clauses behind the text, two caveats are in order.[186] First, here too, just as in the case of independent desiderative clauses themselves, we must account for the possibility that the actual communicative function might differ from the way the utterance is framed in the text. For example, what is introduced as a wish could, of course, have been an outright command, even if the supposed original followed the syntactical patterns of a wish clause.

Second, and this is a problem unique to dependent desiderative constructions, the semantics of the governing verbs are more nuanced than the options available for various independent desiderative clause patterns. For instance, if a reported speech act is specified as a "request" by the governing verb (e.g., in English, "I requested him to come"), the corresponding independent desiderative clause will usually employ a simple imperative (e.g., "Come!"), just as it would in explicitly labeled commands (e.g., "I commanded him to come"). In other words, in the case of dependent constructions, there are more options for modulating the specific relationship between the speaker or writer and the addressees.[187] In what follows, we will not undertake the additional effort of discussing the communicative functions of corresponding direct utterances in the background. Instead, we will focus on the classification of the governing verbs according to their semantics, differentiating between verbs of wishing on the one hand and verbs of requesting and commanding on the other.

The verb θέλω ("to want") is the most frequently attested one in Paul's letters from the first category and, thus, is an obvious candidate for the search for fragments of narratives in that corpus.[188] To be sure, Paul some-

---

186. See Heilig, *Paulus*, chapter 14, section 4.4.1.
187. There are some linguistic means for similarly nuancing main clauses. Perhaps παρακαλέω followed asyndetically by an imperative (cf. Rom 16:17; 1 Cor 4:16; Heb 13:22) might be similar to modern "please." The addition of δέομαι in Gal 4:12 seems to come very close to this: "Become like me... brothers and sisters, please!" (Γίνεσθε ὡς ἐγώ, ὅτι κἀγὼ ὡς ὑμεῖς, ἀδελφοί, δέομαι ὑμῶν).
188. On what follows, cf. Heilig, *Paulus*, chapter 14, section 4.4.2.1. On βούλομαι (L&N 25.3: 'to desire to have or experience something, with the implication of some reasoned planning or will to accomplish the goal') in 1 Cor 12:11; 2 Cor 1:15, 17; Phil 1:12; 1 Tim 2:8; 5:14; 6:9; Titus 3:8; and Phlm 13; cf. Heilig, *Paulus*, chapter 14, section 4.4.2.2. The use

Chapter 4

times uses it to express the wish that something may *not* happen (cf. Rom 13:3 and Phlm 14), thereby creating a stronger degree of disnarration. Similarly, the verb itself might be negated, resulting not merely in a statement about a neutral lack of desire but, much like in German or English, in an outright refusal to accept the situation in question. For example, when Paul states that he does "not want" someone "to be ignorant of something," this certainly does not imply that he merely denies such a desire; rather, it means that the addressees should be knowledgeable about something (cf. Rom 1:13; 11:25; 1 Cor 10:1; 12:1; 2 Cor 1:8; 1 Thess 4:13). At times, negated θέλω is also employed concerning specific future events, thus marking them as unfavorable. For instance, Paul opposes the Corinthians becoming "partners with demons" (οὐ θέλω δὲ ὑμᾶς κοινωνοὺς τῶν δαιμονίων γίνεσθαι). In 1 Cor 16:7 and 2 Cor 5:4, Paul similarly employs such a construction to sketch protonarratives about future events and to qualify them as undesirable.[189]

However, in the majority of instances where θέλω is paired with an infinitive, the verb is not negated, and Paul is indeed expressing a positive desire.[190] Sometimes, these wishes are quite general (Rom 7:21 and 16:19). Nonetheless, passages like 1 Cor 7:7 and 7:32, which appear very similar on the surface, serve as a helpful reminder that the vividness of what is narrated in concrete contexts only loosely corresponds to the degree of specificity ("vividness") in the narration. When Paul tells the Corinthians that he harbors the wish that all people might be like him (7:7: θέλω δὲ πάντας ἀνθρώπους εἶναι ὡς καὶ ἐμαυτόν) and free of concern (7:32: Θέλω δὲ ὑμᾶς ἀμερίμνους εἶναι), what he desires concerning the issue of marriage is actually quite concrete, and the Corinthians would have had no difficulty discerning the details of the implied protonarratives. Relatively speaking, the narrative distance appears smaller in passages like 1 Cor 14:19; 1 Thess 2:18; 1 Tim 2:4; and 5:11, where more aspects are explicitly mentioned to guide the readers' imagination. In Galatians, this usage of θέλω frames the entire letter (1:7 and 6:13). Here it is the desire of the opponents that is depicted quite vividly—and Paul's letter, written in the context of this unfolding pro-

---

in 1 Tim 6:9 and the wider context there is particularly interesting for a narratological analysis.

189. For details, see Heilig, *Paulus*, 767–68. On the related phenomenon of θέλω in the protasis of a conditional construction (1 Cor 10:27; 14:35; 2 Cor 12:6; 2 Thess 3:10), cf. Heilig, *Paulus*, 768–69. See also Heilig, *Paulus*, 770, on 1 Tim 1:7.

190. In 1 Cor 14:5, we also have an ἵνα clause. Interestingly it occurs parallel to an infinitive.

tonarrative, serves as the means through which Paul intends to ensure that it can never be narrated as an actual story.[191]

After focusing on mental states and desires, we now turn to verbs that possess an explicitly directive meaning.[192] Within this category, we can further differentiate between verbs that express requesting speech acts and others that convey outright commands—again, always keeping in mind that the pragmatics of the real-world utterance, which might be conveyed through these dependent desiderative clauses, may not adhere to this semantic division.

Louw and Nida list the following verbs for the semantic domain 'ask for, request': ἐρωτάω, αἰτέω (etc.), ζητέω, ἐντυγχάνω, δέομαι, προσαντίθεμαι, and ἐπικαλέομαι (L&N 33.161–77). Our focus here will be on constructions with παρακαλέω.[193] This verb is used to express the speech act of 'ask[ing] for something earnestly and with propriety' (L&N 33.168). In Paul's letters, it is used in conjunction with the infinitive in 1 Thess 2:12 and 1 Tim 1:3 to create foreshadowings referring to the past of the narrator.[194] In most cases, however, the earnest request does indeed pertain to situations in the future of the narrator.[195]

Against that backdrop, 2 Cor 2:8 is a remarkable exception, in that here we are not dealing with a rather vague future scenario but with the request for a concrete and singular event, a communal decision (κυρῶσαι).[196] Moreover, we have a syntactically elaborate—and, thus, quite vivid—protonarrative in 1 Cor 1:10, where "speaking in unity" (cf. ἵνα τὸ αὐτὸ λέγητε πάντες) is elucidated in both a negative (no divisions; cf. καὶ μὴ ᾖ ἐν ὑμῖν σχίσματα)

---

191. See Heilig, *Paulus*, 773–74.
192. Cf. Heilig, *Paulus*, chapter 14, section 4.4.3.
193. Cf. Heilig, *Paulus*, chapter 14, section 4.4.3.1.
194. On the use of the verb with ἵνα clause for past requests (e.g., 1 Cor 16:12; cf. 2 Cor 8:6), cf. Heilig, *Paulus*, 777.
195. The infinitive considers the following, still only potential, situations: "to present your bodies" (Rom 12:1: παραστῆσαι τὰ σώματα), "to fight together with me" (Rom 15:30: συναγωνίσασθαί μοι; see above, p. 252), "to watch out" (Rom 16:17: σκοπεῖν), "to receive" (the grace of God, namely not in vain; 2 Cor 6:1: μὴ εἰς κενὸν τὴν χάριν τοῦ θεοῦ δέξασθαι), "to walk" (in a manner worthy of the calling; Eph 4:1: ἀξίως περιπατῆσαι τῆς κλήσεως ἧς ἐκλήθητε), "to be of one mind" (in the Lord; Phil 4:2: τὸ αὐτὸ φρονεῖν ἐν κυρίῳ), "to do so even more" (1 Thess 4:10: περισσεύειν μᾶλλον), "to make" (requests, prayers, intercessions, and thanks on behalf of all people; 1 Tim 2:1: ποιεῖσθαι δεήσεις προσευχὰς ἐντεύξεις εὐχαριστίας ὑπὲρ πάντων ἀνθρώπων), and "to be self-controlled" (Titus 2:6: σωφρονεῖν).
196. On the situation type and grammatical aspect, cf. Heilig, *Paulus*, 777 n. 373.

Chapter 4

and a positive (state of agreement; cf. ἦτε δὲ κατηρτισμένοι ἐν τῷ αὐτῷ νοῒ καὶ ἐν τῇ αὐτῇ γνώμῃ) way.[197]

There are two other constructions with an ἵνα clause, in 1 Thess 4:1 and 2 Thess 3:12, where the verb παρακαλέω is coordinated with another verb of utterance. In the latter passage, παρακαλοῦμεν is combined with παραγγέλλομεν, whose directive nature is stronger (see, thus, below, p. 282).[198] In the former passage, we have the elaborate construction ἐρωτῶμεν ὑμᾶς καὶ παρακαλοῦμεν.[199] The content, too, not just the introduction, of this request is remarkable. Right after the connector ἵνα, Paul introduces a comparative clause: "as you received from us" (καθὼς παρελάβετε παρ᾽ ἡμῶν). Just as the future-oriented protonarrative is beginning to take shape, an analepsis takes us back to the time of the foundation of the community. The content of that past speech act is expressed by an indirect question clause: "how you should walk and please God" (τὸ πῶς δεῖ ὑμᾶς περιπατεῖν καὶ ἀρέσκειν θεῷ).[200] At this point, we would expect the correlating piece to this past comparison. In other words, there is a current speech act (i.e., "we ask you") and a past analogy to what is requested (i.e., "as you received from us"), and what is still lacking is the actual content of the request (something like ". . . to continue walking like that"). Instead, we get another comparative clause with καθὼς: "as you indeed walk" (καθὼς καὶ περιπατεῖτε). The simultaneous narration is thus first strengthened before, finally, we get the anticipated foreshadowing. What Paul requests is "that you do so more and more" (ἵνα περισσεύητε μᾶλλον).

For a more complete picture of fragments of protonarratives behind dependent desiderative clauses, one must also consider lexemes like προσεύχο-

---

197. On this passage, cf. Heilig, *Paulus*, 777.
198. For details, see Heilig, *Paulus*, 777–78.
199. The verb ἐρωτάω (L&N 33.161: 'to ask for, usually with the implication of an underlying question') appears also in Phil 4:3; 1 Thess 5:12; 2 Thess 2:1. Cf. Heilig, *Paulus*, 778 n. 377. The consideration of papyrological evidence is important in that regard because it highlights that ἐρωτάω in the papyri is a quite specific verb that is mostly used in letters of personal interest, either in letters that deal with a specific interpersonal relationship or in business or legal letters that deal with issues with a clear impact on the personal life of the letter writers. Cf. Christina M. Kreinecker, *2. Thessaloniker*, Papyrologischer Kommentar zum Neuen Testament 3 (Göttingen: Vandenhoeck & Ruprecht, 2010), 77–84. However, I am skeptical whether this can count as an argument for the pseudepigraphic nature of 2 Thessalonians. First and foremost, it seems to be one of many indications that within the Pauline letter corpus, across the boundary between undisputed and disputed letters, we find a very nuanced use of such terms that modulate the pragmatic dimension of the text.
200. *AGG* 273b. Cf. above, p. 266, note 163, on indirect question clauses.

μαι ("to pray"), where, at least in some cases, the focus is not so much on the speech act—the address to God—per se; instead, quite frequently we gain insight into the actual request that is presented to God, and thus into events that might happen in the future if God grants the request.[201]

Even though some of the above utterances, if addressed directly to the readers (i.e., "I ask you to . . ."), might actually constitute outright commands in their respective contexts, it is important to note that they are introduced within a rhetorical framework that differs from the phenomenon that we will discuss in what follows. These are cases in which the employed verbs themselves express this idea of commanding. While they might also contribute to this picture, we will disregard mere "recommendations" (cf. L&N 33.343–46 'recommend, propose') and verbs that focus on the utterance itself in a rather neutral way (such as λέγω) and that are followed by constructions that correspond to desiderative clauses.[202] The same applies to verbs that focus on an aspect that might sometimes be associated with commands but is not inherent to that concept (such as διαμαρτύρομαι in 1 Tim 5:21).[203] The verbs that are listed by Louw and Nida under the subdomain 'command, order' (L&N 33.323–32) are:

κελεύω, διαστέλλομαι = 'to state with force and/or authority what others must do'

τάσσω (also with prefix: συν-, προσ-, ἐπι-, δια-) = 'to give detailed instructions as to what must be done'

---

201. Cf. Heilig, *Paulus*, chapter 14, section 4.4.3.2. See, for example, Col 1:9; Phil 1:9; and 2 Thess 1:11. For cases in which the act of praying is itself still future, cf. 1 Cor 14:13; 2 Thess 3:1; and Eph 6:19.

202. Cf. *AGG* 218f. There are also two other related phenomena that we cannot discuss here. The first has to do with the negation of "verbs indicating an obligation" (cf. *AGG* 218e). While in German "Du musst nicht" does not imply a directive function, English "you must not" is to be understood as a negative command, a prohibition. Interestingly, for ὀφείλω in Paul we seem to have attestation of both inner negation (cf. 1 Cor 11:7; there is an obligation not to do something) and outer negation (cf. 2 Cor 12:14; the existence of an obligation itself is denied). Cf. Heilig, *Paulus*, chapter 14, section 4.4.3.7. A related phenomenon is the negation of verbs of allowing, specifically the use of ἐπιτρέπω in 1 Tim 2:12 and 1 Cor 14:34. In that case, it is not the question of the scope of negation itself that is of relevance. However, the information structure of 1 Tim 2:12 determines what kind of protonarrative is in view here. Cf. Heilig, *Paulus*, chapter 14, section 4.4.3.8.

203. Cf. Heilig, *Paulus*, 781 n. 391.

Chapter 4

ἀπαγγέλλω, παραγγέλλω = 'to announce what must be done'

ἐντέλλομαι = 'to give definite orders, implying authority or official sanction'

ἐπιτιμάω = 'to command, with the implication of a threat'

Interestingly, despite good attestation in the New Testament generally, only ἐπιτάσσω, διατάσσω, and παραγγέλω are of relevance for our analysis.[204]

The first of these three verbs occurs in a single Pauline verse, Phlm 8.[205] Moreover, even in that passage Paul actually *refrains* from commanding. First, Paul emphasizes that he would, of course, be in the position (πολλὴν ἐν Χριστῷ παρρησίαν ἔχων) to "*command* you what is appropriate" (*ἐπιτάσσειν* σοι τὸ ἀνῆκον). Even though (cf. the concessive participle) Paul thinks that the relationship between him, the apostle, and Philemon would allow for such a command, Paul prefers, as verse 9 says, merely "to *request* through love" (διὰ τὴν ἀγάπην μᾶλλον *παρακαλῶ*). This explicit contrast shows clearly that what is focal in verse 8 is the speech act itself, that the focus is on how precisely Paul tries to get Philemon to act in a specific manner.

Note that the content of the (potential but ultimately rejected) command in verse 8 remains quite vague and is not, as one might expect, expressed by an infinitive. It is such a "matter of course" that it does not even require explication. Similarly, the verb παρακαλέω (cf. above) is used intransitively in verse 9. Instead of specifying the content of the request, the verse offers a detailed description of the supplicant.[206] In verse 10, we encounter παρακαλέω yet again, but there is still no mention of the requested action. All we learn is who would be the beneficiary if the request were fulfilled (παρακαλῶ σε περὶ τοῦ ἐμοῦ τέκνου . . .).

It is not until verse 13 that Paul's desire eventually surfaces in the form of an analepsis that talks about a past wish of the apostle to "keep" Onesimus (see above, p. 273, on ὃν ἐγὼ ἐβουλόμην πρὸς ἐμαυτὸν κατέχειν). The goal of this act would have been that Onesimus could have served Paul in his imprisonment in place of Philemon (ἵνα ὑπὲρ σοῦ μοι διακονῇ ἐν τοῖς δεσμοῖς

---

204. For references, see Heilig, *Paulus*, chapter 14, section 4.4.3.3.
205. For a detailed exegesis of this verse, see Heilig, *Paulus*, chapter 14, section 4.4.3.4.
206. Cf. Peter Arzt-Grabner, *Philemon*, Papyrologische Kommentare zum Neuen Testament 1 (Göttingen: Vandenhoeck & Ruprecht, 2003), 201, on the function of this element in ancient letters.

τοῦ εὐαγγελίου). Note that this goal would pertain to the future of the letter writer because, until now, Paul, in fact, has had Onesimus at his disposal.[207] However, this whole nexus of events, from the past decision to keep Onesimus to his continuous support in the future (at least until the end of Paul's imprisonment), becomes a counterfactual protonarrative because Paul does not carry through with his desire but instead sends him back (verse 12 with epistolary aorist).

The reason for Paul favoring παρακαλέω over ἐπιτάσσω—or at least the reason for why he prefers the former framing of his action—is then explicated in more detail in verse 14. He wants Philemon's "good deed" (τὸ ἀγαθὸν σου) not to occur under force (κατὰ ἀνάγκην ᾖ) but to be based on his free decision (ἀλλὰ κατὰ ἑκούσιον). The content of the request-not-demand is not specified until verse 17, where it occurs as an explicit imperative! Paul wants Philemon to "accept him as [you would] me" (προσλαβοῦ αὐτὸν ὡς ἐμέ). It is by adding the conditional clause "if you consider me a partner" (εἰ... με ἔχεις κοινωνόν) that Paul, at least superficially, adds a certain restriction, which allows his claim that no "commanding of what is proper" (verse 8: ἐπιτάσσειν τοῦ ἀνήκοντος) is taking place to seem justifiable, at least superficially.

The protonarrative of a theoretically possible but not implemented command serves two functions in this passage. First, it ensures that Onesimus will be motivated to fulfill the request of verses 10–14. It is better for him simply to comply with Paul's wishes rather than risk explicit orders. After all, if Paul refrains from issuing a command for now solely because he wants to give Philemon an opportunity to do the right thing freely, the prospect of the apostle exercising his authority in the future remains a possibility. Additionally, accepting Onesimus specifically as a "beloved brother" (ἀδελφὸν ἀγαπητόν) may be more difficult if perceived as a forced action. Therefore, the challenges in maintaining such an alternative narrative further suggest that it might be easier for Philemon simply to adhere to the protonarrative that Paul obviously favors.

Second, it is important to note that from verse 13 onward, the counterfactual protonarrative in the background is marked by a desire of the apostle that has a much larger scope than the (non)command of verse 17, further emphasizing how reasonable it would be to fulfill this smaller request. To be sure, this larger desire itself also remains intact and is something with

---

207. Cf. Heilig, *Paulus*, 835–36. Cf., more generally, the discussion on telic clauses at the end of this chapter.

Chapter 4

which Philemon must contend. We will discuss this below (pp. 304–9) in our analysis of telic clauses.

The verb διατάσσω is used in Titus 1:5 for commands from Paul to his coworker Titus: "... as I had commanded you" (ὡς ἐγώ σοι διεταξάμην). In Gal 3:19, it is employed for the decree of the law "through angels, by the hand of a mediator" (διαταγεὶς δι' ἀγγέλων ἐν χειρὶ μεσίτου). Moo considers it an "unusual verb" in this context simply because it is "never used elsewhere in Biblical Greek to refer to the giving of the law."[208] This assessment is surprising. After all, the verb is quite common in Greek literature in legal contexts, including in the works of Philo and Josephus.[209] What actually appears to be "unusual" is, by contrast, the frequency with which διατάσσω occurs in 1 Corinthians (7:17; 9:14; 11:34; 16:1), especially when compared to the general rarity of verbs of commanding across Paul's letters.[210]

In contrast to the two previously discussed verbs, παραγγέλλω occurs quite frequently in Paul (and Acts), especially when compared to the Gospels.[211] Moreover, while other -αγγέλλω verbs oscillate between the semantics of commanding and merely announcing, the directive aspect here is quite clear.[212] In the disputed letters, we find a notable accumulation in 2 Thess 3 (in verses 4, 6, 10, 12) and 1 Timothy (1:3; 4:11; 5:7; 6:13, 17).[213] By contrast, only three of the twelve occurrences in the Pauline corpus belong to undisputed letters (1 Cor 7:10; 11:17; 1 Thess 4:11).

Of those, 1 Cor 7:10 and 1 Thess 4:11 are of particular interest to us because of the way the act of commanding—and thus the commanded event—is related to other directive speech activities. In 1 Thess 4:11, a discussion about a command is preceded by a request in verse 10, namely, "to do so more and more" (cf. above, p. 278, on Παρακαλοῦμεν δὲ ὑμᾶς, ἀδελφοί, περισσεύειν μᾶλλον καὶ φιλοτιμεῖσθαι). This future storyline is continued in verse 12 with

---

208. Douglas J. Moo, *Galatians*, BECNT (Grand Rapids: Baker, 2013), 235.

209. Cf., e.g., Philo, *On the Special Laws* 2.79; and Josephus, *Jewish War* 4.249. Cf. Hesiod, *Works and Days* 277; and Diodorus Siculus, *Library of History* 13.34.6. Cf. also Acts 23:31 and 24:23 for commands in a military/political context. The decree of Claudius in Acts 18:2 likewise is referred to by means of this verb: διὰ τὸ διατετατχέναι Κλαύδιον χωρίζεσθαι πάντας τοὺς Ἰουδαίους ἀπὸ τῆς Ῥώμης.

210. On these passages, cf. Heilig, *Paulus*, 787–88.

211. For details on the passages that are adduced in what follows, see Heilig, *Paulus*, chapter 14, section 4.4.3.6.

212. Cf. also BDAG, s.v. "παραγγέλλω": 'to make an announcement about someth. that must be done.'

213. For a detailed discussion of the occurrences in 2 Thess 3, see Heilig, *Paulus*, 792–94; on the attestations in 1 Timothy, see Heilig, *Paulus*, 794–96.

an ἵνα clause that explicates the goal, and thus the prospect, of such potential behavior, namely, behaving properly toward outsiders and not being in any need. Within this protonarrative fragment, Paul embeds an analepsis to past commanding in verse 11: "as we have commanded you" (καθὼς ὑμῖν παρηγγείλαμεν). In other words, the protonarrative that emerges on the basis of the request is presented as a continuation of the initial instruction. Accordingly, the terminological distinction between παρακαλέω and παραγγέλλω points to the progress that has occurred in the meantime, with the result being that *gentler* forms of motivation are now sufficient. In 1 Cor 7:10, by contrast, the commanding nature of the speech act is not nuanced itself. However, the verse is similar in that here we encounter correcting disnarration (cf. above, pp. 221–24) with respect to the person who commands: "I command—not I, but the Lord . . ." (παραγγέλλω οὐκ ἐγὼ ἀλλ' ὁ κύριος) and thus, indirectly, a *strengthening* of the directive nature owing to the Lord's superior authority.

Even though these two passages already reveal interesting dynamics when analyzed from a narratological perspective, the usage in 1 Cor 11:17 is even more fascinating. The entire passage must be read against the backdrop of the praise in 1 Cor 11:2. There, Paul acknowledges that the Corinthians remember him in everything and maintain the traditions just as he had passed them on to them. Then, in verse 17 Paul states that he cannot praise them again in light of an upcoming instruction that he, according to the subtext, apparently believes should be unnecessary (Τοῦτο δὲ παραγγέλλων οὐκ ἐπαινῶ . . .).[214] Clearly, Paul would have preferred to tell a glorious story about them instead.

Even though Paul explicitly announces a directive speech act, what follows is not quite what one would expect. Instead, ὅτι introduces an explanation of what Paul perceives as misbehavior. We are presented with a story, but one whose plot Paul finds objectionable. This analepsis continues until verse 21. For Paul, this entire narrative is evidently quite anomalous, one that should be "unnarratable" because the underlying sequence of events ought never to have taken place. This is why, in verse 22, Paul employs a question clause to outline an alternative storyline, one that would actually make sense. He asks, "Do you not have houses in which to eat and drink?" (verse 22a: μὴ . . . οἰκίας οὐκ ἔχετε εἰς τὸ ἐσθίειν καὶ πίνειν). The issue is that the Corinthians, of course, cannot negate this question. Thus, the story of verses 18–21 remains absurd.

---

214. On the syntax, cf. Heilig, *Paulus*, 790.

Chapter 4

This raises the possibility that perhaps something is missing in the account of verses 17–22, that Paul may have told this story in an unreliable manner. As Paul sees it, the only modification to that narrative that could be made would further exacerbate the Corinthians' situation, introducing the very negative element of ill intent: "Or do you despise the church of God and shame those who do not possess anything?" (verse 22b: ἢ τῆς ἐκκλησίας τοῦ θεοῦ καταφρονεῖτε, καὶ καταισχύνετε τοὺς μὴ ἔχοντας;).[215] Paul does not directly insinuate such an attitude, but the concluding questions indicate that he is at a loss as to how one could otherwise make sense of the bizarre occurrences in Corinth (verse 22c: "What shall I say? Shall I praise you?"; τί εἴπω ὑμῖν; ἐπαινέσω ὑμᾶς;). For him, there does not seem to be a way to construct a coherent narrative about what has transpired without that story implying a plot that includes such a deplorable attitude from the church in Corinth.

It is for this reason that he says in verse 22d—in a repetition of the litotes of verse 17—that he does not "praise" them (ἐν τούτῳ οὐκ ἐπαινῶ).[216] This resumption raises the expectation that in what follows we will finally encounter the announced command of an alternative, better behavior. By contrast, an actual directive—encouraging self-examination—does not appear until verse 28. Before we get there, Paul offers in an analepsis a renarration of Jesus's institution at the Last Supper (verses 23–25) and, against that backdrop, an interpretation of eucharistic practice (verses 26–27). It is not accurate to say that this explicit story serves as a "corrective and norm."[217] Rather, the narrative bolsters the directive of verse 28—the actual "corrective"—by highlighting its necessity.

The continuation of this passage is also constructed with the aim of reinforcing verse 28. In verse 29, a conditional participle creates a protonarrative, which offers a counterfactual plot and, therefore, specifies what would transpire if one does *not* heed the command of verse 28 (cf. below on conditional participles). A narrative figure who fails to discern the body of the Lord appropriately (μὴ διακρίνων τὸ σῶμα) is evidently someone who does not fully grasp the implications of verses 26–27 and thus ignores verse 28. For such an individual, the "profane" act of eating and drinking constitutes

---

215. On the question of whether there should be an "or," see Heilig, *Paulus*, 705–6. While Caragounis, *Development*, 209, makes a valid point regarding, for example, 1 Thess 2:19 (which he expresses in rather stark terms: "the disjunctive significance … is grammatically impossible"), in this context the use of "or" does indeed seem appropriate.

216. See *AGG* 296h on the litotes.

217. Schrage, *Der erste Brief*, 3:29: "Korrektiv und Norm."

Fragments of Implicit Protonarratives

an action that leads to judgment (verse 29: "For the one who eats and drinks eats and drinks judgment against themselves [if they . . .]"; ὁ γὰρ ἐσθίων καὶ πίνων κρίμα ἑαυτῷ ἐσθίει καὶ πίνει).

Against this backdrop, verse 30, which offers an interpretation of past events, is quite startling: "<u>For this reason</u>, many among you are weak and ill, and a good number have died" (διὰ τοῦτο ἐν ὑμῖν πολλοὶ ἀσθενεῖς καὶ ἄρρωστοι καὶ κοιμῶνται ἱκανοί). The implication of this consequential connection is that the protonarrative of verse 29 is *not* purely hypothetical. Likewise, the devastating analysis of verse 22, which had been introduced there merely in the form of questions, is now retrospectively confirmed to be, in fact, accurate.

Accordingly, we find in verse 31 a construction with a remote conditional clause, in which—ironically—it is now the situation of *not* being judged that appears as the merely hypothetical event in an alternative storyline (cf. above, pp. 237–39, on this verse and how it relates to presuppositional disnarration). Quite a dramatic twist! Against that backdrop, the condition contained in the participle κρινόμενοι in verse 32 must be considered to be fulfilled: yes, "we" indeed experience judgment, for the protonarrative of verse 29, including the κρίμα that had been mentioned there, corresponds to the actual occurrences in Corinth.

Now, this could be the end of the whole story with no happy ending in sight. But Paul proceeds differently. While the protonarrative of the unworthy Corinthians has turned out to be factual, the alternative salvific plot can still be partially realized in the future. Indeed, the divine judgment is not to be understood as the sudden end of the story but rather as a momentum that has the potential to advance it. After all, the judgment is ultimately a "lesson" from the Lord (verse 32: κρινόμενοι δὲ ὑπὸ [τοῦ] κυρίου παιδευόμεθα) with the pedagogical goal of bringing the Christians in the future back on the right track, on a storyline that does *not* contain condemnation in the last judgment (ἵνα μὴ σὺν τῷ κόσμῳ κατακριθῶμεν).

Paul has made it easier for the Corinthians to adopt the suggested continuation of the plot in that the suggestion of a despicable attitude in verse 22 is only one of two options. If the Corinthians identify with that condescending perspective, they indeed need to repent and discard that narrative. However, they can also choose to admit that their prior practice just did not make any sense, remaining unnarratable not due to horrific moral implications but because of a lack of any coherence. In any case, Paul offers them a way out of this misery in verse 33, an opportunity to finally become storytellers of an acceptable narrative, a narrative in which they would again figure as praiseworthy characters.

Chapter 4

As already in verse 27, ὥστε introduces an independent clause that draws an inference from what has been said before. It is only now that the prospect of παραγγέλλειν is fulfilled. The third-person imperative of verse 28 (δοκιμαζέτω) is supplemented by a quite specific command to the brothers and sisters (ἀδελφοί μου). Whenever they meet for meals (συνερχόμενοι εἰς τὸ φαγεῖν)—that is, in future instantiations of the event bundle that had been so problematic in the past—they must "wait for each other" (ἀλλήλους ἐκδέχεσθε). This quite specific command is now no longer supported simply by a rather vague discontent (verse 17). Rather, Paul has embedded it into a complex narrative framework in order to heighten the chances of this positive protonarrative becoming reality, that is, becoming narratable.

Conditional Clauses

We are now in a position to turn to the last two important textual phenomena that we need to consider in our search for potential future events that might constitute fragments of protonarratives. To introduce them, we must take a step back to gain a bird's-eye perspective on what we have considered so far.[218] Until now, our analysis has been guided by certain types of clauses, which we have differentiated according to their communicative functions: declarative, interrogative, and desiderative.[219] Moreover, we have adhered to a syntactical subdivision of independent clauses on the one hand, and dependent clauses on the other hand, also discussing alternative syntactical phenomena such as infinitives within the latter category.

If we wanted to classify those latter dependent clauses according to their syntactical function (which we did not have any reason to do until now), we would say that they are "sentence constituents" (i.e., not attributive modifiers).[220] More specifically, we can say that they function as complement clauses of the subtype object clause (cf. "What do you command?"—"I command that you do X"). From a text-grammatical perspective, such object clauses contribute the content of an introduction-content relationship (cf. above, p. 48).

---

218. On these different perspectives of classifying the textual phenomena in question, see Heilig, *Paulus*, chapter 14, section 5.1. I simplify in what follows. For considerations that complicate matters, see in particular Heilig, *Paulus*, 798–99, n. 459.
219. Cf. *AGG* 266a.
220. *AGG* 270a.

Fragments of Implicit Protonarratives

In what follows, we will focus on another kind of complement clause: the adverbial (adjunct) clause. More specifically, we will discuss adjunct clauses that express a condition ("conditional" clauses) or indicate purpose ("final" or "telic" clauses). We will also, again, mention a few other constructions that, on the content level of the text, result in analogous connections, that is, in propositional pairs of the type condition-result on the one hand and means-purpose on the other. As discussed above (when introducing them in chapter 2), they do not constitute miniature stories. Nonetheless, as we will see, they are of significant importance when it comes to evoking protonarratives.

When we speak about future events that are dependent on the fulfillment of a condition, conditional conjunctions are the most obvious connectors to consider. Other relevant linguistic phenomena include the conditional use of the adverbial participle, the generic use of nominalized participle phrases, relative clauses with additional conditional force, and nouns with merely potential referents in the real world.[221]

Among the conditional clauses, we can first turn to the *indefinite conditional clauses*, which we have already introduced above (pp. 229–31) as a means of gradual disnarration of past events, namely, when the protasis (the "if" clause) employs a past tense for its verb. Now, we focus specifically on instances where we find future indicative verb forms in (at least) the apodosis (the "then" clause) of the conditional construction.[222] Whether or not we can envision this future event as actually taking place, as ultimately becoming subject to real narration, depends on whether or not the event mentioned in the protasis (the "if" clause) occurs. In some cases, the entire storyline—as constituted by the condition mentioned in the protasis and the consequence that occurs in the apodosis—is set in the future.[223] More commonly, however, a future event is connected to a situation in the past or present, with the status of that situation being somewhat ambiguous (here we encounter overlap with subsequent or simultaneous gradual disnarration).

---

221. On conditional participles, see Heilig, *Paulus*, chapter 14, section 5.2.3.1. There, I comment on Rom 2:27; Gal 6:9; 1 Tim 4:6, 16; 6:8. On the generic use of nominalized participles, see Heilig, *Paulus*, chapter 14, section 5.2.3.2. The focus is on Rom 13:2–4. On relative clauses with an additional conditional force, see Heilig, *Paulus*, chapter 14, section 5.2.3.3. The phenomenon is illustrated with reference to Rom 2:12. On nouns with only a potential referent, see Heilig, *Paulus*, chapter 14, section 5.2.3.4. Here, Rom 2:13 serves as an example.

222. For more details, cf. Heilig, *Paulus*, chapter 14, section 5.2.1.1.

223. On 1 Cor 3:14–15 and 2 Tim 2:11–13, see Heilig, *Paulus*, chapter 14, section 5.2.1.3.

Chapter 4

If we once again consider the future indicative verb forms in Romans, which have served as a point of reference throughout our discussion of various forms of foreshadowings, we see that the protonarratives emerging from such references to the future in the apodosis are an important means by which Paul advances his argumentation.[224]

This is evident, for example, in Rom 5:10. The condition—the reconciliation with God (εἰ ... κατηλλάγημεν τῷ θεῷ)—is clearly fulfilled. That it happened "when we were (still) enemies" (ἐχθροὶ ὄντες) is explicitly narrated in verse 8, with reference to Jesus's death and the phrase "still being sinners" (ἔτι ἁμαρτωλῶν ὄντων) alluding to an analogous time interval. Verse 9 links this past event of recent justification (πολλῷ οὖν μᾶλλον δικαιωθέντες νῦν ἐν τῷ αἵματι αὐτοῦ) with predictive narration: "... we will be saved from the wrath through him" (... σωθησόμεθα δι' αὐτοῦ ἀπὸ τῆς ὀργῆς). This is one of the rather rare unambiguous references to the future in the future indicative that we mentioned above (p. 254). What, then, does the conditional construction in verse 10 contribute?

First, "we" are put into focus as narrative characters (contrast this with the love of God in verse 8a, Christ in verse 8b, and his blood in verse 9). To be sure, the already promised salvation is not directly made dependent on human behavior in the present. However, Paul emphasizes that there is a connection between said future event and the present lived reality. Thus, there is at least a hint at the possibility that the future situation might look different or might have looked different, if the transition from sinners to justified people had not occurred.

Second, and this is often overlooked in the exegetical literature, the conditional construction in verse 10 does not merely "repeat" the conclusion of verse 9.[225] Rather, the connector γάρ in verse 10 merits serious consideration.[226] Verse 10 provides, with utterance relatedness, the reason why the conclusion contained in verses 8–9 (Paul's interpretation of the story of Jesus's death, so to speak) is justified. In Paul's view, the guarantee of safety from God's wrath through Jesus's death is made even more compelling because this does not yet take into account the believers' participation in his

---

224. On everything that follows with respect to these conditional constructions in Romans with future indicative in the apodosis, see Heilig, *Paulus*, chapter 14, section 5.2.1.2. For the specific case that we have a future indicative in the protasis as well, see chapter 14, section 5.2.1.3.

225. Wilckens, *Der Brief an die Römer*, 1:298.

226. Against, e.g., Schlier, *Römerbrief*, 155.

life (cf. the contrast between διὰ τοῦ θανάτου τοῦ υἱοῦ αὐτοῦ, which picks up the metonymic αἷμα of verse 9, and ἐν τῇ ζωῇ αὐτοῦ).

Third, we can note that verse 10 supplements verses 8–9 by referring to the future event of salvation in a different manner. In verses 8–9, the loving action of Christ in the past is narrated in the indicative and then revisited through the use of a participle. By contrast, the inference concerning the future in verse 9 remains a postulate, inferred in a rather subjective manner from the experience of divine love at different stages of worthiness. Verse 10 strengthens this conclusion. The past events that have already been narrated are only introduced as a condition, with the future salvation in the apodosis, however, emerging as a *logical necessity*.

We find very similar rhetorical dynamics also in Rom 6:5 (cf. also 5:17). Note, in particular, how in that verse "our" assimilation to Jesus in baptism (... σύμφυτοι γεγόναμεν τῷ ὁμοιώματι τοῦ θανάτου αὐτοῦ) has already been established in verses 3–4. However, what appears as merely a telic adjunct (cf. the next section on how they create protonarratives) in verse 4, namely, walking in newness of life (<u>οὕτως</u> καὶ ἡμεῖς ἐν καινότητι ζωῆς περιπατήσωμεν), is expressed emphatically in the apodosis of verse 5 as a logical necessity: "we will certainly also be united with him with respect to his resurrection" (ἀλλὰ καὶ τῆς ἀναστάσεως ἐσόμεθα).

The conditional connection thus serves a dual purpose. On the one hand, it indeed *advances the plot* by strengthening a connection that has so far only been hinted at. On the other hand, it provides contours to the plot by setting it against the backdrop of an *alternative storyline*, in which the event associated with βαπτίζω in verse 3 cannot be presupposed. The implied contrast is probably not with nonbelievers. Rather, readers are encouraged to imagine the counterfactual continuation of their own biographies without this radical break.

What follows from verses 3–4, therefore, appears in constant contrast with that protonarrative. While the plot of the protonarrative that Paul clearly considers to be narratable as an actual story in the future—although it is not yet wholly narratable—is outlined again in verses 8–10, this counterfactual protonarrative never completely vanishes from sight. To be sure, the imperative in verse 11 ("Consider yourselves dead to sin and alive to God in Christ Jesus"; ... λογίζεσθε ἑαυτοὺς [εἶναι] νεκροὺς μὲν τῇ ἁμαρτίᾳ ζῶντας δὲ τῷ θεῷ ἐν Χριστῷ Ἰησοῦ) puts the future of the addressees, the yet-to-be-realized part of the protonarrative, into focus. However, the precise temporal reference of the apodosis in verse 5 and the apodosis in verse 8 remains somewhat vague. The fact that Paul encourages his readers, through

Chapter 4

the conditional construction, to constantly compare his sketch of the plot with an alternative story, whose plot would consist of a linear continuation of the circumstances before the conversion of the addressees (a "passive prognosis," in Ryan's terminology), also reminds the readers of the *future that lies ahead for the baptizands*. Even the concluding predictive disnarration in verse 14—"sin will not rule over you" (ἁμαρτία γὰρ ὑμῶν οὐ κυριεύσει)—is ultimately rooted in the grace that applies to everyone who comes to faith (οὐ γάρ ἐστε ὑπὸ νόμον ἀλλ᾽ ὑπὸ χάριν).

In other words, Paul does not simply "report" what has happened and will happen (cf. chapter 3 on text function). The conditional constructions and the introduction of the plot point of baptism encourage a comparison of individual spiritual biographies with the counterfactual plot in the background. Of course, Paul hopes that such a comparison will reveal that the protonarrative of the passive prognosis is indeed solely and decisively "virtual," to use Ryan's terminology again, and that the two storylines diverge significantly. This gap is intended to encourage the addressees in their future commitment to the directives of verses 11–13. At the same time, the contrasting protonarrative also serves to support those who are not able to identify the divergence to the extent that Paul considers desirable, allowing them to readjust their lives and ultimately align their individual biographies with the kind of plot that Paul believes is the only appropriate one for a baptized person. Accordingly, the imperative in the imperfective aspect in verse 13 can be integrated in various ways by the readers into their individual biographies (cf. above, pp. 268–71).

We find a similar dynamic involving the evocation of alternative protonarratives that reinforce a specific plot in Rom 8:9–13, which we will not discuss here.[227] Instead, I would like to move directly to Rom 11:17–24, which adds another dimension to our observations.[228] This passage also affords us the opportunity to consider the second important type of conditional clauses relevant to the analysis we are undertaking here: the *prospective conditional clause*. Introduced by ἐάν, this type differs from the indefinite conditional clause in that the situation it describes is more closely related to the real world; specifically, it refers to "something one can or must expect."[229]

---

227. See Heilig, *Paulus*, 806–8.
228. For details, see Heilig, *Paulus*, 808–12.
229. *AGG* 282a. For an introduction to the phenomenon with an eye to the differentiation between the specific and the general prospective case in Romans, see Heilig, *Paulus*, chapter 14, section 5.2.2.1. For a detailed discussion of the various passages from that letter, see Heilig, *Paulus*, chapter 14, section 5.2.2.2.

Fragments of Implicit Protonarratives

Embedded in Rom 11:17–24, which addresses the question of God's dealings with Jews and gentiles, we encounter an indefinite conditional clause in verse 21a immediately following a command to avoid hubris and to instead fear God in verse 20b (μὴ ὑψηλὰ φρόνει ἀλλὰ φοβοῦ). As the γάρ in the protasis of verse 21a indicates, the entire conditional construction serves as a justification for the command in verse 20b (i.e., we are dealing once again with utterance relatedness). According to the most plausible syntactical reconstruction, the apodosis is located in verse 21b: the attitude commanded in verse 20b is justified "for . . . he will not spare you either" (γὰρ . . . οὐδὲ σοῦ φείσεται).[230] This announcement builds on the presupposition that God has also not spared the natural branches (cf. verse 21a: εἰ γὰρ ὁ θεὸς τῶν κατὰ φύσιν κλάδων οὐκ ἐφείσατο).

The protonarrative evoked by this connection in the broader context appears quite clear. In this passage, Paul engages with a fictive dialogue partner. In verse 20a, the apostle acknowledges as part of this fictional dialogue that God has indeed broken off the "natural branches" (καλῶς τῇ ἀπιστίᾳ ἐξεκλάσθησαν). Importantly, he adds the reason for God's decision: "unbelief." In other words, the party that experienced God's stringent treatment brought about that behavior through their own attitude. What Paul disputes—and there can be little debate given the obvious information structure of his response—is that the past event should be explained primarily with reference to God's *positive intention* toward the gentile Christians, the new branches. The dialogue partner in verse 19b claims that God broke off the natural branches specifically *in order to* make room for them (ἵνα ἐγὼ ἐγκεντρισθῶ). Paul accepts the story of his counterpart but stresses that it is only reliably narrated if this element of God's motivation for his action is correctly characterized.

In Paul's view, narrating the story *in this particular way* automatically implies a call to action—hence the asyndetically attached command in verse 20b. The rationale (γάρ) for this is that the God who acted so severely against the natural branches—the Jews—will undoubtedly not "spare" the unnatural branches either. Note that the condition for this unambiguous announcement is clearly met: "if . . . God did not spare the natural branches" (εἰ . . . ὁ θεὸς τῶν κατὰ φύσιν κλάδων οὐκ ἐφείσατο). After all, we have just learned in verses 19–20a that there is agreement on the fact that this has indeed occurred.

This interpretation—and the resulting protonarrative, which inevitably includes some form of "trouble," likely in the sense of facing critical scru-

---

230. For a detailed justification of why verse 21b must constitute the apodosis, cf. Heilig, *Paulus*, 809–10.

Chapter 4

tiny at the last judgment—presupposes that φείδομαι has a rather general meaning.[231] It seems that this issue caused concern for some ancient readers, who, based on common usage, deduced that the verb signified a more active form of intervention, a "saving" act. Accordingly, in their reading the negated occurrence here implies that Paul announces—under the caveat of the fulfilment of a condition, to be sure, but after all a condition that is clearly met—future *destruction* to the dialogue partner![232]

Several contextual factors would facilitate such a reading. First, it is easy to read the referent of God not "sparing" the natural branches behind the indicative aorist in verse 20a (οὐκ ἐφείσατο)—namely, the very destructive action of removing them from the tree (verses 19–20a)—into the discourse meaning of the negated future indicative οὐδὲ σοῦ φείσεται. If God will, to phrase it positively, treat the ingrafted branches the same way he did the natural branches, this suggests that he will break them off as well. Second, verse 22, which we will address shortly, also seems to make it problematic to assume that mere "strictness" is the issue in verse 21b.

This entire dynamic is likely the reason for the insertion of μή πως before verse 21b, seemingly transforming it into a *fear clause*. For a fear directed toward the future, one would usually expect the subjunctive φείσηται (cf. above, pp. 264–65). However, to some ancient readers the implications of the text apparently seemed so unacceptable that the scribe responsible probably did not worry very much about this minor grammatical inconsistency (assuming that the subjunctive is indeed original).[233]

Perhaps the scribe intended for the fear clause to serve as (part of) the apodosis, with the main clause being omitted. While this is not the most natural reading—especially if other independent clauses could be construed

---

231. Cf. L&N 22.28: 'to cause someone not to be troubled.'

232. Cf. LSJ, s.v. "φείδομαι": '*spare* persons and things, e.g. in war, i.e. *not destroy*' (I). BDAG, s.v. "φείδομαι" likewise explicates the gloss "to spare" with the rather broad definition 'to save fr. loss or discomfort' (1). It would be worthwhile to investigate to what extent the usage is indeed constrained by the degree of severity of what is avoided. In any case, it is easily imaginable how in this particular context the negated verb might have been read as implying looming disaster.

233. It is not uncommon in Koine Greek for the aorist subjunctive to replace future indicative, even if the two forms do not resemble each other. Cf. Caragounis, *Development*, 547–64. Cf. above, p. 215, note 34, on Rom 10:14. Still, it is unfortunate that NA[28] gives an incomplete picture of the evidence here. The combination of μή πως with the future indicative, such as in the base text of Codex Boernerianus, seems to be rather rare. Contrast this with the church fathers who have μή πως but have this followed by the subjunctive.

Fragments of Implicit Protonarratives

as the apodosis—it is not grammatically impossible.[234] How would such a textual alteration and syntactical understanding improve the apparently problematic Pauline protonarrative? The meaning would be: "For if God did not spare the natural branches but rather broke them off, you should fear that he will not spare you from destruction either." In this case, Paul's *certain yet only potentially devastating event* would be replaced by an *uncertain but definitely threatening* (after all, feared!) prospect.

This significantly alters the plot of the protonarrative. While in Paul's view, as I reconstruct it, the directive in verse 20b serves a positive function with respect to the inevitable scrutiny on the day of judgment, now an ambiguous threat of unsalvation motivates the command against arrogance. The underlying notion would be that looking down on the natural branches is unwise when there remains the possibility of also being cut off, for whatever reason.

Whether this disimprovement truly results in a compelling protonarrative is debatable.[235] I posit that we should consider the likelihood that the scribe who inserted μή πως aimed for a more extensive modification—one that attributes the role of the apodosis to a different textual element.

Yet, identifying a suitable candidate for the apodosis becomes challenging when we exclude verse 20b. By converting verse 21b into a fear clause—a dependent declarative clause—we encounter the issue that no clear independent clause remains in the immediate context to assume the role of the apodosis. One theoretical option would be to interpret verse 21b not as a dependent fear clause but as an independent interrogative sentence. However, this does not appear to be grammatically feasible.[236] Consequently, we are

---

234. It seems to me that we would have to assume an aposiopesis, with the omitted expression of fear constituting the independent clause. This is how the KJV translates Rom 11:21: "For if God spared not the natural branches, *take heed* lest he also spare not thee." Cf. above, p. 264, on fear clauses without governing expressions of fear. Cf. also above, p. 236, on the aposiopesis in Rom 9:21–23.

235. John Chrysostom, *Homilies on Romans* 19, apparently thought so. He explicitly states that it is significant that Paul used the aorist subjunctive and not the future indicative: "'For if God spared not the natural branches,' and then he does not say, 'neither will He spare thee,' but 'take heed, lest He also spare not thee.' So paring ... away the distasteful from his statement, representing the believer as in the struggle, he at once draws the others to him, and humbles these also" (translation from *NPNF¹* 9). The Greek is: "εἰ γὰρ ὁ Θεὸς τῶν κατὰ φύσιν κλάδων οὐκ ἐφείσατο," καὶ οὐκ εἶπεν, οὐδὲ σοῦ φείσεται. ἀλλὰ "μήπως οὐδὲ σοῦ φείσηται." ὑποτεμνόμενος τοῦ λόγου τὸ φορτικὸν τῇ ἀμφιβολίᾳ, καὶ ποιῶν ἐναγώνιον εἶναι τὸν πιστόν. κἀκείνους ἐφελκόμενος, καὶ τοῦτον καταστέλλων.

236. Cf. the CEV, which translates: "If God cut away those natural branches, couldn't

Chapter 4

left with only the independent directive clause in verse 20b as an immediate contextual candidate, and I believe this is precisely what the individual who added μή πως intended to convey with this amendment. The fear expressed in verse 21b now stands autonomously and follows a directive in verse 20a that hinges on the fulfilled condition stipulated in verse 21a.

To be sure, in this scenario also we must assume that the scribe accepted some grammatical irregularities at the expense of transforming the protonarrative. In particular, accommodating the γάρ in verse 21a is challenging.[237] The main reason I still believe an ancient scribe might have devised this purported connection between verse 20b (as the apodosis) and verse 21a (as the protasis) is that the resulting conditional construction would then nicely mimic verses 17–18. In those verses, we also encounter a fulfilled condition (verse 17: Εἰ δέ τινες τῶν κλάδων ἐξεκλάσθησαν, σὺ δὲ ἀγριέλαιος ὢν ἐνεκεντρίσθης ἐν αὐτοῖς καὶ συγκοινωνὸς τῆς ῥίζης τῆς πιότητος τῆς ἐλαίας ἐγένου) and, as a consequence, a directive that closely corresponds to verse 20b (verse 18: μὴ κατακαυχῶ τῶν κλάδων). The order of the two constituents would just be reversed this time.

---

he do the same to you?" If the variant were only an additional μή, such translations would make more sense. Then we could have an interrogative clause with the expected answer "no." But I do not see how we can have this interrogative particle and at the same time an open interrogative clause that requires an answer to the question "how?" (πῶς). Note that the German NGÜ translates with an open "why" question: "Denn wenn Gott die natürlichen Zweige nicht verschont hat, warum sollte er dann dich verschonen?" That, by contrast, ignores the μή. I have not found an example of μή as an interrogative particle followed by πώς in the sense of "somehow" and a future indicative. If evidence for such a cautious question relating to the future existed, this would of course make the translation of the CEV much more plausible. Note that in Modern Greek μήπως, "perhaps," is indeed used with the same sense as ίσως (on whose usage in Koine see above, p. 260) but with an association with questions. Note how the TGV translates verse 21: Πρόσεξε, μήπως ο Θεός, που δε λυπήθηκε τα φυσικά κλαδιά, δε λυπηθεί ούτε εσένα. Cf. also NET: "For if God did not spare the natural branches, perhaps he will not spare you." I have not looked in any detail into the diachronic development of μήπως.

237. In German, "wenn" is the standard gloss for the conditional connector εἰ, and "denn" is the standard gloss for the causal connector γάρ. However, in the translation "wenn denn" (unlike in "denn wenn") the "denn" appears as an adverb and the whole construction means something like "if in fact." Interestingly, the NIV translates the identical construction in Rom 4:2 (εἰ γὰρ Ἀβραὰμ ἐξ ἔργων ἐδικαιώθη) precisely along these lines, as "If, in fact, Abraham was justified by works." BDAG s.v. "γάρ" (2) seems to leave some room for such an understanding. In any case, one could argue that a scribe who did not care about the indicative future in verse 21b instead of the subjunctive in rendering it as a fear clause probably also would not be hindered by γάρ in connecting verse 21a as the protasis to the apodosis in verse 20b.

Fragments of Implicit Protonarratives

How does this understanding of the textual change affect the implied protonarrative? As in the version that interprets the reworked text of verse 21b as a fear clause and treats it as the apodosis of the conditional construction, the future event of "destruction" to which Paul is purportedly alluding is merely potential—and very explicitly so. After all, in this reading the fear clause would not be syntactically connected to the protasis in verse 21a but rather would be loosely dependent on φοβοῦ in verse 20b. It would function as a justification (add: "For you should fear that . . .") for the conditional construction, reinforcing the idea that heeding the command of verse 20b is indeed wise, given what God did to the natural branches as per the fulfilled condition in verse 21b. The sense would be: "Assuming that God has not spared the natural branches (verse 20a), you should avoid arrogance and instead fear God (verse 21b)! After all, he could do the very same to you (if you do *not* obey my commands)."

This threat thus looms over the branch that has been grafted into the tree. It is something that Paul fears might happen and that the conversation partner should also fear. It is this threat—*more specific but at the same time less certain* than in the case of the protonarrative that I reconstructed—that hangs over the narrator of verse 19. There may be some flexibility concerning how one narrates the breaking off of one narrative character, the natural branches. However, an acceptable account must also include the possibility that a similarly destructive event might be part of the future storyline concerning the other character, the unnatural branch. Note that the condition remains fulfilled in this scenario, too, but what now follows is not the imminent destruction that one might otherwise assume Paul to be foreshadowing in verse 21b, that is, if one takes it as a standard independent declarative clause and assumes that absence of the action denoted by φείδομαι signifies refraining from a crucial, salvific activity. Rather, this future event of destruction is implied to remain counterfactual as long as the conversation partner adheres to the directive of verse 20b. This, of course, results in a significantly less provocative protonarrative for non-Jewish Christians: "Don't act like a jerk and you won't find the same bad end as the Jews."

This protonarrative might ultimately share a similar plot to what, I think, Paul originally said, but the narration—the presentation of the relevant narrative fragments—still differs markedly.[238] I maintain that Paul indeed

---

238. I do not think it is possible that μή πως is original. The protonarrative that emerges from weakening the apodosis so that it becomes a mere fear and the motivating factor for adherence to the command could have been expressed so much more clearly

Chapter 4

formulates a *certain* foreshadowing in verse 21b, and it is this *fixed* future plot point, only rhetorically made dependent on a condition that everyone knows is fulfilled, which in his mind should motivate compliance with the command of verse 20b. For if one does not adopt that storyline, if the unnatural branch behaves arrogantly and does not fear God, this will result in an alternative storyline in the future, namely, after the plot point of God's eschatological judgment. In my interpretation, the focus in verse 21b is on *God's attitude, which remains constant with respect to the different narrative figures.* The new branches will not receive special treatment. In a protonarrative that is not marked by the hubris of an ingrafted branch—at least not after it has read Paul's letter—this expected strictness will not be problematic. A protonarrative that continues to be marked by arrogance, however, will inevitably lead to disaster.

Note that in verse 22, the potentially devastating future event is finally mentioned explicitly. There is a prospect of the unnatural branch being "cut off" again (the verb used this time is ἐκκόπτω). However, it is equally important to note that while God's "not sparing" equates to "being strict with" the unnatural branch, as foreshadowed in verse 21b, Paul now clearly seems to focus on the continuation of the plot that he obviously favors and encourages through the directives in verse 20b. After all, remaining in God's benevolence, which certainly involves obeying the commands of verse 20b, is now presented as a future development that is indeed to be expected, as made clear by the use of a *prospective* conditional clause (ἐὰν ἐπιμένῃς τῇ χρηστότητι).[239]

Likewise, the alternative plot of not following the directives, stepping out of grace, and thus ultimately being cut off is now presented as something that is *not* actually expected (ἐπεὶ καὶ σὺ ἐκκοπήσῃ). Interestingly, Paul now introduces the aspect of "strictness," which we have identified behind the "not sparing" in verse 21b, explicitly with the lexeme ἀποτομία, "harshness." Hence, a certain tension with our understanding of verse 21b

---

by Paul in many different ways. If Paul had really used φείδομαι with the implication of its negation having destructive consequences, and if he had wanted to present the directives of verse 20b as a way of avoiding this destruction, he could, for example, simply have announced the destruction in the future indicative (as he actually did!) and then added an exception, namely, the adherence to the behavior that is encouraged in verse 20b. Cf., e.g., how Demosthenes, *4 Philippic* 62, uses εἴπερ to announce future destruction but makes it dependent on a condition: "For that reason he will not spare you, if he gets you in his power" (διὰ ταῦθ᾽ ὑμῶν οὐχὶ φείσεται, εἴπερ ἐγκρατὴς γενήσεται). Cf. Rom 8:9.

239. For more details on Rom 11:22, see Heilig, *Paulus*, 819–20.

is created that likely contributed to the textual variant. While "strictness" is indeed associated with God's treatment of those "who have fallen" (ἐπὶ μὲν τοὺς πεσόντας ἀποτομία), the "you" does not seem to be facing such an attitude. To the contrary, God deals with them in "kindness" (ἐπὶ δὲ σὲ χρηστότης).

This tension can be resolved, however, if we adequately consider how much Paul now focuses on the storyline that he favors. On the one hand, he looks back to the ingrafting of the unnatural branch. When he associates this event in verse 20a with "faith" (σὺ δὲ τῇ πίστει ἕστηκας), this already implies, against the backdrop of his larger thought world, that this event is due to God's grace. But it is only now that the past situation is explicitly connected with a relational idea, which, as such, also has implications for the present and future. It thus replaces the egocentric motive that the "you" alleges by means of a telic clause in verse 19b. On the other hand, Paul now apparently presupposes, at least for rhetorical reasons, that the unnatural branch has not yet adopted a narrative portrayal of the past that places them outside the boundaries of God's grace, which is demarcated by humility. Moreover, he assumes that the commands of verse 21b will indeed be followed; that is, the "you" will *continue to follow this salvific storyline*. To be sure, God remains "strict" in the sense that in the final judgment he will not make an exception for the unnatural branch if it does not appreciate God's grace. At the same time, this quality of strictness is ultimately, of course, compatible with a favorable attitude toward the unnatural branch at present, as long as the salvific story continues to unfold. In other words, we can observe here a shift in focalization, following different temporal standpoints of the narrative character of the ingrafted branch.

In what follows, the future portion of the protonarrative that Paul sketches takes another optimistic turn. In verse 23, Paul switches back again to the storyline of the cut-off branches. Because God has the general ability to graft them back into the tree (δυνατὸς γάρ ἐστιν ὁ θεὸς πάλιν ἐγκεντρίσαι αὐτούς), all that is necessary for this happy ending to occur is that they do not continue in the unbelief that resulted in their removal in the first place (κἀκεῖνοι δέ, ἐὰν μὴ ἐπιμένωσιν τῇ ἀπιστίᾳ, ἐγκεντρισθήσονται). Notably, this future possibility is introduced again by a *prospective* conditional clause, bringing the two storylines associated with the two kinds of branches closer to each other.

In fact, in verse 24 Paul lays all his cards on the table: "They will be grafted in" now appears in an apodosis (ἐγκεντρισθήσονται) whose condition is clearly fulfilled. The past event of the surprising experience of kindness that the unnatural branch underwent is connected with the far less surprising, much more natural event of the natural branches receiving that treatment in the future (εἰ γὰρ σὺ ἐκ τῆς κατὰ φύσιν ἐξεκόπης ἀγριελαίου καὶ παρὰ φύσιν ἐνεκεντρίσθης εἰς καλλιέλαιον, πόσῳ μᾶλλον . . .). Of course, this implies that Paul presupposes that the condition of the protasis in verse 23 will indeed be met. However, he apparently wants this to be regarded as a matter of course, something that barely needs to be narrated at all, as it is such an obvious part of the story. Hence, in verse 24 the only condition that he mentions is one that he has made the conversation partner already utter himself or herself in verse 19; he does not mention the natural branches' return to belief. Once again, just like in verse 20a, Paul simply accepts the story of the conversation partner but supplements it—there with an appropriate understanding of God's motivation, here with the emphasis on the "natural" and "unnatural" character of the respective branches.

In conclusion, I want to draw attention to two inferences that we can glean from this analysis. The first concerns what Paul chooses to articulate, and the second focuses on what he decidedly omits. First, while the story of the conversation partner in verse 19 relies on the sufficiency of God's past action, Paul emphasizes that the actions of cutting off and engrafting come with two parallel storylines that have the potential to intersect eventually. Behavior in the present and future can still influence the trajectory of the narrative. In other words, Paul offers an *interpretation of the story presented in verse 19*, pointing out that if interpreted correctly—taking into account both God's disposition and the essence of the branches—this should motivate the unnatural branch to adopt a certain attitude. This attitude, in turn, can assure the positive continuation of the narrative.[240]

Second, note that in this emphasis on the optimistic conclusion of the story and how present behavior can contribute to it, Paul also fundamentally defines what can be considered "positive" in the first place. If the unnatural branch could ultimately craft a success narrative that derives its significance from contrasting with the unfortunate fate of the natural branches, such a story would be unnarratable in Paul's view. Indeed, even harboring the intention of one day recounting such a narrative is self-defeating, according to the apostle. Having a value system that renders such a story desirable would create conditions that would make the narrative impossible to tell! Sure, the story in verse 19 can be told. It is a fine story. Yet, when analyzed with the appropriate attitude (verse 20), it reveals a plot that encourages the narrator

---

240. See Heilig, *Paulus*, 820.

to hope that they themselves may stay on track and to hope for the regrafting of the natural branches. For Paul, the act of narrating—and envisioning future narratives—is not solely about completeness or the events themselves. It is a deeply *ethical* matter. Appropriate storytelling presupposes the correct value system to be already in place.

This also sheds light on what Paul chooses *not* to articulate or at least not to tell emphatically. Observe how the sequence of events, although clearly reconstructable, remains somewhat vague in its relationship to reality. The closest we come to an assertion about the topic of "branches" appears just before the passage in question, in verse 16, where the holiness of the branches is deduced from the holiness of the roots (side by side with a similar argument about the first part of the dough and the dough as a whole; εἰ δὲ ἡ ἀπαρχὴ ἁγία, καὶ τὸ φύραμα·καὶ εἰ ἡ ῥίζα ἁγία, καὶ οἱ κλάδοι). Contrastingly, Paul seems hesitant to narrate the event of natural branches *actually* being broken off. Initially, this scenario appears only as part of the conditional clause in verse 17 (Εἰ δέ τινες τῶν κλάδων ἐξεκλάσθησαν . . .). Only in his response to the conversation partner in verse 20 does Paul concede that this event has apparently transpired, immediately shifting focus to the inappropriate arrogance of the unnatural branch. It is striking that even though the sequence of events is vividly outlined, Paul is not eager to explicitly narrate what, in his view, is a lamentable development. As far as he is concerned, the protonarrative hinted at in verse 17 should have remained a merely potential story. The act of explicitly narrating it seems to presuppose the arrogant mindset of verse 20, for which reason the story should actually remain unnarratable.

Note that the significantly optimistic turn that the narrative takes in verse 24 for the natural branches revisits the conditional clause of verse 17. The entire section from verses 18–23 can thus be understood as an interpretive and critical discussion of the protonarrative alluded to in verse 17. According to what seems to be Paul's final provocative verdict, if one wishes to narrate this story at all, a meticulous analysis of its plot demonstrates that it can only be considered complete (or narratable) when the conclusion from verse 24 is integrated. This is because only the full story would justify the act of narrating it in the first place. Needless to say, such a narratologically motivated analysis stands in stark contrast to approaches that merely utilize Rom 11:17–24 to discern "Paul's stance on Israel." The very manner in which Paul presents his protonarrative suggests that he would have significant comments on the motives behind such an inquiry.

As we have observed throughout our exploration of Rom 11:17–24, appreciating how indefinite and prospective conditional clauses relate events

Chapter 4

to reality is crucial for a comprehensive grasp of the protonarrative or, more precisely, the degree of protonarration in Paul's epistles.

An examination of the rest of the prospective conditional clauses in Romans confirms that Paul employs this tool of creating narrative fragments very consistently.[241] To conclude our discussion, let us turn to 2 Cor 12:6, an example that vividly underscores the significance of meticulously considering Paul's selection of conditional constructions.[242]

We have already seen above that 2 Cor 12:1–6 is a peculiar story in many ways. Initially, Paul leads us to anticipate a comprehensive narrative about someone else's visions, but he ultimately underscores his lack of knowledge and the unnarratability of the events.[243] Moreover, within the course of the story it becomes evident that Paul is, in fact, referring to himself. This revelation subverts the reliability of the initial suggestion that he was discussing another individual.[244]

Notably, while scholarly consensus supports this latter observation, a question that rarely surfaces overtly pertains to *how* we come to understand that Paul was, in fact, describing himself through the consistent use of third-person singular references. In my perspective, the prospective conditional clause in verse 6a holds pivotal significance in addressing this matter. Here, Paul contemplates the potential for boasting through a conditional construction: "For if I want to boast . . ." (Ἐὰν γὰρ θελήσω καυχήσασθαι . . .). Immediately before this, in verse 5, Paul assures his readers that his boasting is reserved solely for the narrative character presented in verses 1–4, excluding any self-promotion except when discussing his weaknesses (ὑπὲρ δὲ ἐμαυτοῦ οὐ καυχήσομαι εἰ μὴ ἐν ταῖς ἀσθενείαις). Given this context, many commentators find verse 6a to be perplexing. How does Paul first disavow boasting only to reevaluate the possibility immediately thereafter?

---

241. On Rom 2:25–26; 7:2–3, 5; 10:9; 12:20 (cf. Prov 25:21–22); 14:8; 15:24, see Heilig, *Paulus*, chapter 14, section 5.2.2.1 and 5.2.2.2. The same attestations also show that one must be more careful when it comes to the differentiation between the general and specific subtypes of the prospective conditional construction, with the present indicative typically expressing general statements, and the future indicative being used for expectations of specific events.

242. For a detailed exegesis of the passage, see Heilig, *Paulus*, chapter 14, section 5.2.2.3.

243. See above, pp. 184–88, on the introduction of the story. On unnarratability, cf. above, p. 209.

244. Cf. above, pp. 222–24, for a shorter discussion of the unreliability of this passage along similar lines.

Fragments of Implicit Protonarratives

The prevailing viewpoint among commentators proposes that the solution to this lies in recognizing that the apodosis in verse 6b pertains to a counterfactual scenario. According to this interpretation, although Paul explicitly chooses not to boast, he aims to convey to the Corinthians that he would indeed have the capability to do so. His intention is to highlight that, hypothetically, if he were to boast, he *would not be a fool* (οὐκ ἔσομαι ἄφρων).[245] The CEV, for instance, translates verse 6a–c in this manner: "Yet even if I did brag, I would not be foolish. I would simply be speaking the truth."

Note that in this interpretation the justification in verse 6c (ἀλήθειαν γὰρ ἐρῶ) becomes highly problematic. One has to assume that Paul is very inconsistent. Initially, Paul seems unequivocal about the folly of boasting regarding spiritual experiences (e.g., 11:16). Yet suddenly, so this interpretation alleges, Paul endorses counterfactual self-praise as acceptable as long as it is grounded in reality. The logical follow-up question that he would have had to anticipate from the Corinthians is, of course: What about the boasting of the super-apostles—is it fine unless they are outright lying? Given how carefully Paul thinks about such potential objections elsewhere, I find it highly implausible that he would make himself so vulnerable here.[246] Moreover, this interpretive position is untenable on syntactical grounds anyway. Had Paul indeed wanted to express what the CEV above communicates, he would have used a remote conditional clause: Εἰ ἤθελον καυχήσασθαι, οὐκ ἄν ἤμην ἄφρον . . .[247]

---

245. Cf. NGÜ: "Wenn ich wollte, könnte ich mich sehr wohl auch mit anderen Dingen [d. h. nicht nur mit Schwachheiten] rühmen, ohne mich deshalb zum Narren zu machen; denn was ich sagen würde, währe die Wahrheit."

246. On Paul's reaction to an implicit accusation in 2 Cor 2:14, which demonstrates great sensitivity for the perception of his conversation partners, see Heilig, *Paul's Triumph*, 156–61. On this, see also below, p. 315. Cf. also above, p. 257, on his fictional dialogues in Romans.

247. For such conditional clauses with θέλω, cf. Ps 50:18 LXX: ὅτι εἰ ἠθέλησας θυσίαν ἔδωκα ἄν ὁλοκαυτώματα οὐκ εὐδοκήσεις. Cf. also Judg 13:23: εἰ ἤθελεν ὁ κύριος θανατῶσαι ἡμᾶς οὐκ ἄν ἔλαβεν ἐκ χειρὸς ἡμῶν ὁλοκαύτωμα καὶ θυσίαν καὶ οὐκ ἄν ἔδειξεν ἡμῖν ταῦτα πάντα καὶ καθὼς καιρὸς οὐκ ἄν ἠκούτισεν ἡμᾶς ταῦτα. See above, pp. 234–39, on remote conditional clauses and presuppositional disnarration. The attestations in Gal 1:10 (εἰ ἔτι ἀνθρώποις ἤρεσκον, Χριστοῦ δοῦλος οὐκ ἄν ἤμην) and 1 Cor 11:31 (εἰ δὲ ἑαυτοὺς διεκρίνομεν, οὐκ ἄν ἐκρινόμεθα) offer two examples that are completely analogous to how many exegetes understand 2 Cor 12:6a–b. In the immediate literary contexts, a specific situation is first ruled out and the conditional clause then refers to this counterfactual situation in order to point to the likewise counterfactual consequence.

Chapter 4

Given Paul's decision not to use that formulation, we must explore the context for a type of boasting that is *not categorically disnarrated*. One possibility could be that in verse 6a, Paul picks up on the exception he mentioned just prior in verse 5, resulting in the meaning: "If I desire to boast *about my weaknesses* . . ." However, even this interpretation faces a significant challenge in verse 6c. It appears that, in this case, Paul would be implying that other forms of boasting, specifically those about evident demonstrations of God's power in his life, would be untruthful. Furthermore, the subsequent content in verse 6d seems to dismiss this option entirely. In that verse, Paul explicitly declares his intention to "refrain" from the particular boasting in question (φείδομαι δέ). This contrasts with the clear impression that Paul seems to have already begun explicit boasting about his weaknesses in 11:30 and will do so again in summary in 12:10.

Which kind of boasting is considered in the context but not actually carried out? It seems that there is only one plausible option available in the context. Rather than referring to verse 5b, where Paul entertains the possibility of boasting in his weaknesses (ὑπὲρ δὲ ἐμαυτοῦ οὐ καυχήσομαι εἰ μὴ ἐν ταῖς ἀσθενείαις), he must be referring to the statement immediately preceding it in verse 5a, where Paul says: "*About him* I will boast" (ὑπὲρ τοῦ τοιούτου καυχήσομαι). The sense of verse 6a must thus be: "For if I want to boast *about him* . . ." ('Ἐὰν γὰρ θελήσω καυχήσασθαι ὑπὲρ τοῦ τοιούτου . . .).[248]

The whole section makes perfect sense if we make this assumption. After all, Paul has just told a story about this narrative figure in verses 2–4, which clearly has potential for constituting the *basis* for subsequent acts of praise. The narration of the events themselves arguably stops short of constituting such a speech act. Now that the story about the anonymous man is complete, Paul adds the general announcement that he will indeed make this man the object of his boasting. So far, the irony of Paul's response to the Corinthians' demand to hear about visions and revelations (verse 1) lies in the fact that Paul agrees to offer something on the *subject* but insists on selecting a different "hero" than himself.

In this framework, verse 6c can finally be integrated as well. While choosing a person different from oneself is a *necessary* condition for acceptable boasting, it is not a *sufficient* condition for that verdict. Therefore, if the boasting occurs in favor of a different person and the first criterion is, thus,

---

248. See, e.g., Herm. Sim. 86.2: καὶ ἐὰν αὐτοὺς θελήσω τετραγώνους ποιῆσαι, πολὺ δεῖ ἀπ' αὐτῶν ἀποκοπῆναι.

Fragments of Implicit Protonarratives

met, another test is needed to differentiate between foolish and nonfoolish boasting of that kind—namely, that it is indeed rooted in reality.

Now we can also integrate verse 6d. Even though Paul generally plans to boast about the anonymous narrative figure (verse 5a), and even though in that case he would not be a fool because he would do so for the benefit of another person and would speak the truth (cf. verse 6b–c), he still refrains from doing so, at least for now (verse 6d).

Given that the understanding of verse 6a suggested here seems to be the only option that allows for a coherent interpretation of the passage, and considering the syntactic intuitiveness of the prospective conditional clause picking up on the indicative future of verse 5a, it is astonishing that the exegetical discussion routinely overlooks it.

One potential reason for this oversight could be the tendency for exegetes to assume the identity of the anonymous man and Paul in verses 2–4 even before delving into verse 6a. As a result, they assume that Paul must be talking about boasting concerning himself. When teaching about this passage, I usually ask students how they know that Paul is discussing himself—a presupposition they consider self-evident. They are often surprised when they realize that they cannot attribute this understanding to a specific feature of the text; they simply "know" it. Professional commentators, likewise, often appear to approach this text with the preconceived notion that it is clear Paul must be talking about himself. This tendency is likely influenced, at least in part, by the reception history of this passage, exemplified by the famous painting by Nicolas Poussin.[249] Accordingly, they do not attend to the textual signals as rigorously as they should.

By contrast, if we approach the text from the perspective of its first readers, we must acknowledge that while Paul has already given some indications that his relationship with the anonymous man might actually be closer than initially implied (cf. above, pp. 184–88), the narrator and the narrative figure have not yet been identified as one and the same. In fact, Paul never does so explicitly. He only indicates indirectly that he himself is indeed the recipient of the vision. It is not until the explanation of the omission of boasting in verse 6d, which occurs in verse 6e (μή τις εἰς ἐμὲ λογίσηται ὑπὲρ ὃ βλέπει

---

249. James Clifton, "The Limits of 'Mute Theology': Charles Le Brun's Lecture on Nicolas Poussin's *Ecstasy of Saint Paul* Revisited," in *Quid est sacramentum? Visual Representation of Sacred Mysteries in Early Modern Europe, 1400–1700*, ed. Walter Melion, Elizabeth Carson Pastan, and Lee Palmer Wandel, Intersections 65.1 (Leiden: Brill, 2020), 580–605.

Chapter 4

με ἢ ἀκούει [τι] ἐξ ἐμοῦ), that this shift to a more open form of unreliable narration happens. There, Paul states that he will refrain from boasting about *the other person* so that the Corinthians do not think too highly of *him*. This would only be a concern if that person is indeed identical with him. Otherwise, boasting about the anonymous figure should not lead the Corinthians to form an overly elevated view of Paul.

In other words, not even in retrospect does Paul clearly admit that he has just related a story about his divine encounter, an encounter worthy of boasting. Nevertheless, he has managed to convey the type of story he could tell—indeed, by somehow telling it after all, or has he not?—while also addressing the unnarratability of such experiences and the ethics surrounding their narration. In doing so, he highlights the lack of such necessary humility among his opponents, who have no such scruples.

Taking into account what the prospective conditional clause contributes specifically as a fragment of a larger protonarrative proves to be heuristically extremely fruitful for our understanding of 2 Cor 12:1–6. Once again, a narratological perspective on Paul's letters illuminates an important Pauline passage, shedding light on aspects of the text that are crucial for its correct interpretation.

Purpose Clauses

Having delved deep into the nuances of conditional connections, we can now afford to provide a merely high-level overview of situations that serve as the goal in purpose-oriented connections, even though "intended events" are certainly just as crucial for a narratological analysis.[250]

When it comes to relevant telic connectors, dependent clauses with ἵνα—or, less frequently, ὅπως—are most important.[251] If the matrix clause refers

---

250. On everything that follows, cf. Heilig, *Paulus*, chapter 14, section 5.3. On allegedly *consecutive* ἵνα, see Heilig, *Paulus*, chapter 14, section 5.3.2.3.

251. For other purpose-oriented connectors, see Heilig, *Paulus*, chapter 14, section 5.3.1. In the papyri, we can observe, on the one hand, a shift in frequency in favor of ἵνα from Ptolemaic to Roman times (with the ratio being roughly equal in the former period) and, on the other hand, a continuous difference in register, with ὅπως being preferred in more official documents. Cf. Giuseppina di Bartolo, *Studien zur griechischen Syntax der dokumentarischen Papyri*, Sonderreihe der Abhandlungen Papyrologica Coloniensia 44 (Leiden: Brill, 2020), 58. One phenomenon in Koine texts that deserves special attention is the occurrence of future indicative verb forms after telic clauses with subjunc-

Fragments of Implicit Protonarratives

to the *future* from the perspective of the narrator, it is naturally most obvious that the situation in the telic clause is likewise only a potential one and, thus, a fragment of what is still only a protonarrative and not a real story yet. Above (p. 82), we have already discussed how ὅταν is used in 1 Cor 15:28 to sketch a series of events that follow each other immediately: "As soon as" everything is subjected to the son (ὅταν δὲ ὑποταγῇ αὐτῷ τὰ πάντα), he himself will be subjected to the one who has subjected everything to him (τότε [καὶ] αὐτὸς ὁ υἱὸς ὑποταγήσεται τῷ ὑποτάξαντι αὐτῷ τὰ πάντα). The purpose of that last mentioned situation is that God may be "all in all" (ἵνα ᾖ ὁ θεὸς [τὰ] πάντα ἐν πᾶσιν).

Even more frequent in Paul's letters is the related constellation where a purpose clause is dependent not on an announcement but on a *command*.[252] However, here we encounter the difficulty that often these narrative fragments cannot easily be integrated into *embedded mental narratives*, the "active prognoses" (to use Ryan's terminology) of narrative characters.

For example, in 1 Cor 11:34 we encounter the future scene, presented to us

---

tive verb forms. In such cases, exegetes often postulate that—to use our terminology—a certain foreshadowing follows the uncertain foreshadowing of the goal proposition. For example, in Phil 2:9–11 we would then have a narrated past event (Jesus's exaltation by God in verse 9: διὸ καὶ ὁ θεὸς αὐτὸν ὑπερύψωσεν καὶ ἐχαρίσατο αὐτῷ τὸ ὄνομα τὸ ὑπὲρ πᾶν ὄνομα) in the means proposition, then a still future, eschatological, situation in the goal proposition (verse 10: ἵνα ἐν τῷ ὀνόματι Ἰησοῦ πᾶν γόνυ κάμψῃ ἐπουρανίων καὶ ἐπιγείων καὶ καταχθονίων), followed by an announcement, a certain foreshadowing, of precisely this situation or, in an alternative interpretation, a subsequent event (which would imply the realization of the goal) in the next verse (verse 11: καὶ πᾶσα γλῶσσα ἐξομολογήσηται ὅτι κύριος Ἰησοῦς Χριστὸς εἰς δόξαν θεοῦ πατρός). However, it is much more likely that verse 1 should be understood as being coordinated with verse 10, that is, as expressing yet another goal, with the future indicative replacing the aorist subjunctive. For a detailed justification, see Heilig, *Paulus*, chapter 14, section 5.3.3. Note that this does *not* necessarily mean that Paul deems the eschatological confession—still—"unnarratable" as a certain foreshadowing (cf. Rom 14:11). The purpose-oriented connector, after all, also gives Paul the opportunity to add an *additional* element (intention!) to the connection. For the same reason, it is misguided to deduce, as Ernst Käsemann, *Exegetische Versuche und Besinnungen*, 5th ed. (Göttingen: Vandenhoeck & Ruprecht, 1967), 85, does, from the transformation of the formulation from Isa 45:22 (where the first verb occurs likewise in the future indicative, κάμψει) that the future character itself is dropped (implying a past, cosmic proskynesis at Christ's enthronement).

252. On telic clauses after imperatives, such as in 1 Cor 9:24, see Heilig, *Paulus*, chapter 14, section 5.3.2.3. Of course, the adhortative subjunctive is also relevant here. In Rom 3:8, what is in view in the telic clause is indeed the motivation of the narrative figures. The same is true for the deliberative subjunctive in Rom 6:1. On ἵνα clauses after other uses of the subjunctive in 1 Cor 8:13 and 13:3, cf. Heilig, *Paulus*, 834–35.

Chapter 4

in a conditional connection with a command in the main clause, of the Corinthian Christians being hungry before they gather and thus eating at home (εἴ τις πεινᾷ, ἐν οἴκῳ ἐσθιέτω).²⁵³ This is followed by a purpose clause, "so that you will not come together for judgment" (ἵνα μὴ εἰς κρίμα συνέρχησθε). It seems unlikely that Paul encourages a sequence of events in which the hungry members of the congregation are motivated to act in this manner before they all come together *because they fear* that otherwise God might judge them. By contrast, the way Paul analyzes the current situation in verse 22 (see above, pp. 283–86) shows that he sees a lack of love in the community and wants *a loving attitude* to be the driving factor in their interaction.

It should be noted that such a constellation does not imply, as many in the literature suggest, that we are dealing with a "consecutive ἵνα" in such cases, which would render the situation in the subordinate clause the "actual results" of the potential event of the fulfillment of the command.²⁵⁴ The explanation for why this mental state does not fit well into the plot of the reconstructed protonarrative is much simpler. It is due to the fact that we are dealing with utterance relatedness. In other words, the situation of the telic clause must be integrated as part of the *frame narrative* of the (proto)narrator, as a reference to Paul's hope for the future. It offers his justification for suggesting an event in the directive that, in his view, will lead to that happy ending, namely, that the Corinthians will not be judged, which would be Paul's "passive prognosis" for them. Judgment would be the end result of the wealthy Corinthians satisfying their hunger for excessive meals at the assembly of the whole community, thereby putting to shame the poor members (cf. verse 22).

It is usually also possible to establish the future reference of the telic clause if the matrix clause—which underlies the means proposition—makes use of the *present indicative*.²⁵⁵ One example would be 1 Cor 11:32, right before the verse that we just discussed (and analyzed above, p. 237). There,

---

253. On the protonarrative, in which this future narrative fragment is embedded, cf. above, pp. 237–39 and pp. 283–86.

254. Against, e.g., Schrage, *Der erste Brief*, 3:57 on 1 Cor 11:34: "'Ἵνα also indicates here ... the actual consequence" (German: "'Ἵνα bezeichnet auch hier ... die tatsächliche Folge"). Albrecht Oepke, "εἰς," *TWNT* 2:427, is similarly off-target: "Likewise, in 11:34 ... the idea is not that the Corinthians may be aiming for judgment; rather, that their behavior may have the actual consequence of judgment" (German: "Ebenso ist in 11,34 ... die Meinung nicht, die Korinther könnten es auf Gericht abgesehen haben, vielmehr, ihr Verhalten könne die tatsächliche Folge des Gerichts haben").

255. For such cases, see Heilig, *Paulus*, chapter 14, section 5.3.2.1.

a conditional participle entertains the possibility of being "judged by the Lord" (κρινόμενοι δὲ ὑπὸ [τοῦ] κυρίου). The result part of this conditional connection consists of two propositions, which form a telic connection. If the condition is fulfilled, this means that we can speak about that particular present experience (i.e., renarrate it) as a "lesson" (cf. παιδευόμεθα), which has the goal of making sure that "we may not be condemned together with the world" (ἵνα μὴ σὺν τῷ κόσμῳ κατακριθῶμεν). Hence, it is the (potential) present activity of the Lord that is explained with respect to an aim for the future, rendering a certain story with a tragic end *un*narratable.

Even if the means proposition has a situation in view that has been *completed in the past*, the situation in the goal proposition might be relevant for the reconstruction of future-oriented protonarratives.[256] To be sure, we might also be dealing with a certain foreshadowing related to the *past* of the narrator, namely when it is clear from the context that the intention has either reached its goal or been definitively thwarted (cf. above, p. 123, on ἱστορῆσαι Κηφᾶν in Gal 1:18). But in 2 Cor 11:2, for example, it is clear that Paul is talking about his past intention with a situation in view that is eschatological and, therefore, still future. He had promised the Corinthians to one husband, Jesus (ἡρμοσάμην γὰρ ὑμᾶς ἑνὶ ἀνδρί), while already thinking about their spotless status as pure virgins at the time of their eschatological marriage (παρθένον ἁγνὴν παραστῆσαι τῷ Χριστῷ)—a happy end that he sees currently in danger (cf. above, pp. 264–65, on the fear clause in verse 3).

Sometimes the question of whether a past intention has already been dealt with conclusively or whether it corresponds to an *ongoing* mental state, and thus has to count as an uncertain foreshadowing of future events, remains quite open in Paul's letters, creating significant rhetorical potential.[257] For example, we have already seen how Paul in Phlm 13 talks about his past desire to keep Onesimus (cf. above, p. 273, on ὃν ἐγὼ ἐβουλόμην πρὸς ἐμαυτὸν κατέχειν). A telic clause offers us insight into Paul's past motivation for such a wish: "in order that he might serve me in your place in my imprisonment for the gospel" (ἵνα ὑπὲρ σοῦ μοι διακονῇ ἐν τοῖς δεσμοῖς τοῦ εὐαγγελίου).

Note that *until now*, Paul indeed had Onesimus at his disposal. Therefore, when Paul in verse 14 continues with explicit disnarration about the option

---

256. For such cases, cf. Heilig, *Paulus*, chapter 14, section 5.3.2.4.
257. For a detailed discussion of Gal 1:4 and the implications for the whole letter, cf. Heilig, *Paulus*, chapter 14, section 5.3.2.6.

Chapter 4

he did not take (just keeping Onesimus without Philemon's consent; cf. verse 14a: χωρὶς δὲ τῆς σῆς γνώμης οὐδὲν ἠθέλησα ποιῆσαι), he actually points to a counterfactual plot that affects *his future*. His previous intention, in other words, is not a matter of the past. The protonarrative that includes the goal of Onesimus serving Paul in his imprisonment remains unnarratable at the moment, but there is still a storyline that involves Onesimus as a narrative character that might lead to the same result. After all, Paul now sends Onesimus back with the explicit goal of avoiding that "your good deed may be as due to force" (ἵνα μὴ ὡς κατὰ ἀνάγκην τὸ ἀγαθόν σου ᾖ). Note that if the situation of having Onesimus at his disposal—even though it is not possible in the short term after his decision to send him back—remains "good" after all, this of course means that nothing has changed about Paul's intention for the long term. To make things crystal clear, Paul even adds "but of free will" (ἀλλὰ κατὰ ἑκούσιον). With Philemon's future motivation being focal, the deed itself remains presupposed.

To be sure, in verses 15–16 Paul admits the possibility that the divine plan behind all that has unfolded might consist in God's intention of having Onesimus close to Philemon again, but now as a beloved brother in Christ. And at least for the moment, Paul wants to ensure this situation of community by means of a (non)command (verse 17; on the directive function in the whole passage, cf. above, pp. 280–82). But there can be little doubt that the "knowledge" in verse 21 introduced a certain foreshadowing to the event of Philemon not just following Paul's immediate intentions but also making sure that Onesimus returns, that is, of Philemon doing "more than what I tell you to do" (αἳ ὑπὲρ ἃ λέγω ποιήσεις), which, I think, must be the good deed of verse 14b.

Note that there is not necessarily a tension between Onesimus returning to serve Paul *in his imprisonment* (verse 13: ἵνα ὑπὲρ σοῦ μοι διακονῇ ἐν τοῖς δεσμοῖς τοῦ εὐαγγελίου) and the idea in verse 15 of him being united with Philemon, ultimately (i.e., after that period) "forever."[258] In my view, we are thus most likely dealing with three stages: the reception of Onesimus as a brother, his return to Paul, and his eventual return to Philemon's household. This naturally has implications for the date and location of Paul's imprison-

---

258. Alternatively, if one assumed Paul to be less stringent, one could argue that Paul's wish of having Onesimus around him during his imprisonment will merge into a desire to have him at his disposal even as a free man once that becomes a real option. However, the tone of verse 22, which, at least rhetorically, entertains the visit at Philemon's house as a realistic prospect, suggests that Paul is conscious of his wording in verse 13.

Fragments of Implicit Protonarratives

ment, as it means that Paul can reasonably expect Onesimus to return before a verdict is reached. Note that verse 22 adds more events to the plot of this protonarrative: Paul's present hope (ἐλπίζω γὰρ ὅτι . . .) to eventually be released and visit Philemon (. . . χαρισθήσομαι ὑμῖν). At that point in time, Onesimus might return to the company of Philemon, who will have already accepted him as a brother by then. And that happy ending, featuring the convergence of storylines, will be brought to pass, just as in Rom 15:30 (cf. above, pp. 250–52), through the prayers of the letter's recipients (. . . διὰ τῶν προσευχῶν ὑμῶν . . .).

5. Of Narrative Substructures and Worldview Narratives

Narrative Substructures and Worldview Narratives as Protonarratives

Having addressed the intricate details of various kinds of protonarrative fragments in Paul's letters, we can now turn to the fundamental proposals made by both Hays and Wright. Hopefully, the presentation in the last chapter has made a convincing case for the relevance and prevalence of implicit narratives in Paul's letters. As I see it, there can be no doubt that a narratological perspective on this corpus is incredibly fruitful heuristically. Likewise, I am confident that the evidence I have assembled so far strongly supports the inclusion of both explicit and mental stories as categories in the analysis of these writings. However, even though the emphasis on narrativity in Pauline studies has generally been vindicated by the discussion thus far, we have not yet considered whether this also applies to some of the most central theses of the "narrative approach." To this task we now turn.

We have already taken a quick look at how both Richard B. Hays and N. T. Wright incorporate the idea of implicit narratives into their respective interpretive frameworks (see chapter 1). However, doing full justice to their conceptions of story actually requires extensive analysis. This necessity arises from, among other factors, the fact that narrativity features prominently in a wide range of their works and occasionally assumes different roles. It is relevant not only in terms of the concepts most frequently associated with these two authors, namely, narrative substructures and worldview narratives. From epistemic to dogmatic concerns, narrative is *everywhere*.

Moreover, diachronic analysis reveals *mutual influences* with these conceptions evolving over time.[1] Wright even goes so far as to present Hays

---

1. Cf. Christoph Heilig, *Paulus als Erzähler? Eine narratologische Perspektive auf die*

as the missing link between E. P. Sanders and his own version of the New Perspective on Paul, thereby making Hays a key witness against James D. G. Dunn's version of this approach. One might be tempted to say that Wright has "hermeneutically reconfigured" an account of the history of scholarship to serve his purpose. Describing it as having been "put to death and brought through to new life" might also be an apt characterization.[2]

We will not delve into the details of the diverse use of the category 'story' in the oeuvres of Hays and Wright here. Interested readers may consult my German work on narratives in Paul's letters, where an entire chapter is devoted to examining how the approaches of these two scholars relate to each other.[3]

For the present purpose, the following generalization suffices: Hays is primarily interested in *elucidating specific texts*. His concept of "narrative substructures" serves as a tool for interpreting particular formulations that would otherwise remain inexplicable.[4] In contrast, the general thrust of Wright's approach moves from individual texts toward the *synthesis of a unified narrative, which he considers central to the worldview of the respective individual*.[5] The contribution that I want to make to this debate consists in the crucial thesis that what unites both conceptions is that they can be *explicated in terms of protonarratives*.[6]

Wright's worldview narrative emerges from a creative act of mental narrativization. It is a story that, in principle, could be told but, in actuality, remains "normally out of sight," being merely "occasionally summoned into

---

Paulusbriefe, BZNW 237 (Berlin: de Gruyter, 2020), chapter 15, section 4, on how Hays and Wright relate to each other in their respective use of the category of 'story' in a variety of discourses.

2. I am echoing here a formulation from N. T. Wright, *Paul and His Recent Interpreters: Some Contemporary Debates* (London: SPCK, 2015), 101. Wright's account of "Life after Sanders" can be found in chapter 4 of his book. I critically discuss his account in Heilig, *Paulus*, chapter 15, section 4.5.1.

3. See Heilig, *Paulus*, chapter 15. I will not offer specific references to the many aspects that are covered there, as this would take up too much space. If you are looking for explications of concepts associated with the approaches by Hays and Wright, such as "worldview," there is a good chance that you will find more information there.

4. For details on how Hays makes use of the category of narrativity in his research, cf. Heilig, *Paulus*, chapter 15, section 2.

5. As already mentioned, I do not differentiate terminologically between "mindset" for a single person and "worldview" for a group of people. For details on the more general question of how Wright makes use of the category of narrativity in his research, see Heilig, *Paulus*, chapter 15, section 3.

6. For a detailed discussion, see Heilig, *Paulus*, chapter 15, section 5.

Chapter 5

view" through narrative fragments.[7] Sources for synthesizing such a unified mental narrative could be explicit stories, but reconstructed protonarratives could also be considered here. The latter might be posited on the basis of "almost-narrations," as is the case with disnarrated events and foreshadowings (cf. chapter 4). The extraction of narrative substructures from argumentative passages might similarly be understood as one piece of a larger narrative puzzle. To be sure, it is also possible that in a search for narrative substructures, we encounter elements that are not part of Wright's presupposed worldview narrative (or only as part of an insignificant subplot) and are therefore not pertinent to his undertaking, even though they may still be highly relevant for determining the passage's meaning.

Conversely, various kinds of stories—whether implicit or explicit—can be in an intertextual relationship with an argumentative (or, even though Hays does not delve into this in detail, narrative) passage. Both explicitly articulated and merely mentally simulated narratives can influence the production of arguments (and other stories). And Wright's larger implicit narrative, if it indeed exists as such, can of course be one of these protonarratives that shape the discourse of Paul's letters.

Narrative Substructures

In what follows, we will scrutinize both concepts, narrative substructures and worldview narratives, against the backdrop of what has been established so far. We begin with Hays's proposal. As will become apparent, it indeed holds the potential to illuminate numerous Pauline passages. Still, if we reconceptualize narrative substructures in terms of mental protonarratives, this will also sensitize us to the caveats that need to be kept in mind when applying this category.

Hypertextuality

The influence of a narrative or protonarrative on a Pauline passage can aptly be described using Gérard Genette's concept of "hypertextuality."[8] A hy-

---

7. N. T. Wright, *Paul and the Faithfulness of God*, vol. 4 of *Christian Origins and the Question of God* (London: SPCK, 2013), 128.

8. Gérard Genette, *Palimpsests: Literature in the Second Degree*, trans. Channa New-

pertext is derived from a preexisting hypotext (whether written/spoken, or merely virtual) through a process Genette terms "transformation," or—if the process is more indirect and complex—"imitation."[9]

Genette's focus lies on the transformation of one narrative text into another.[10] By contrast, Hays's focus is explicitly on the influence of implicit narratives on argumentative passages. However, one could argue that the very passages he takes as points of departure—Gal 3:13-14 and 4:3-6—could be seen as parallel (narrative) transformations of the same implicit (narrative) hypotext. The plot of this hypotext would presumably resemble that of the story Paul narrates in Phil 2:6-11, assuming we accept Hays's general assumptions about the centrality of Jesus's faithfulness as a narrative element for Paul.

Note that while the influence of a hypotext could, in principle, be located solely at the stylistic level (i.e., affecting only the narration of the story), what Hays envisions clearly also involves semantic elements—namely, aspects of that which is narrated, such as theme, plot, figures, and implications concerning the story world.

Sometimes, the story serving as the narrative substructure of a passage can be found in the immediate literary context. For example, one might point to Gal 4:1-2 as a hypotext for verses 3-7.[11] In the following section, however, I will focus on the alternative scenario: a passage that "we know or suspect to be hypertextual" even when its "hypotext is missing."[12]

---

man and Claude Doubinsky (Lincoln: University of Nebraska Press, 1997). Note that Genette uses the term "intertextuality" more broadly, as a subcategory—on the same level as "hypertextuality"—of what he calls "transtextuality."

9. The first subcategory covers cases like the usage of Homer's *Odyssey* in James Joyce's *Ulysses* (with the action being transposed to twentieth-century Dublin). The second includes cases where the hypertext builds on the intermediate step of an abstraction from a hypotext (as in the case of the movement from the *Odyssey* to Vergil's *Aeneid*).

10. He addresses "intermodal changes" in general and "narrativization" in particular (cf. Genette, *Palimpsests*, 239, 277-78). But he limits his analysis mostly to the interplay between narrative and "dramatic" mode. On his understanding of "description," in the context of summarizing transformations in the widest sense, see 241-42. On the relationship between "description" (in a more everyday sense) and "narrative," see 463.

11. For a detailed analysis, see Heilig, *Paulus*, chapter 16, section 3.

12. Genette, *Palimpsests*, 381. For such a constellation, see chapter 78.

Chapter 5

A Narrative Hypertext

Paul's choice of the verb θριαμβεύω in 2 Cor 2:14 has long puzzled exegetes. In my view, the evidence strongly supports the hypothesis that Paul is employing the metaphor of the Roman triumphal procession. Such usage presupposes as its hypotext one or several accounts, quite possibly even from eyewitnesses, of Emperor Claudius's triumphal procession in 44 CE.[13] Both this specific proposal and even the more general acknowledgment that a narratological perspective is appropriate for analyzing 2 Cor 2:14 are commonly overlooked in the secondary literature.

The latter is particularly surprising, given that the context of 2 Cor 2:14 is manifestly narrative. In verse 12, Paul narrates his journey to Troas (Ἐλθὼν δὲ εἰς τὴν Τρῳάδα εἰς τὸ εὐαγγέλιον τοῦ Χριστοῦ) and the missionary success he experiences there (καὶ θύρας μοι ἀνεῳγμένης ἐν κυρίῳ). Immediately following this, verse 13 offers a surprising continuation of the narrative. Owing to the absence of Titus, whom Paul had evidently expected to encounter (... τῷ μὴ εὑρεῖν με Τίτον τὸν ἀδελφόν μου), Paul becomes so concerned about the situation in Corinth that he discontinues his evangelistic activities and departs for Macedonia, apparently in the hope of meeting his coworker sooner (ἀλλὰ ἀποταξάμενος αὐτοῖς ἐξῆλθον εἰς Μακεδονίαν).

The outcome of this renewed travel is not immediately disclosed. It is only in 2 Cor 7:5–7 (Καὶ γὰρ ἐλθόντων ἡμῶν εἰς Μακεδονίαν . . .) that readers learn Paul did indeed encounter Titus in Macedonia and received favorable news from him about developments in Corinth. Instead of giving this information in 2 Cor 2, Paul there transitions to a doxology in verse 14 (Τῷ δὲ θεῷ χάρις τῷ . . .). While some exegetes have considered 2:14–7:4 to be a temporary digression, others contend that this passage should be seen as a letter fragment later inserted by a compiler. These scholars argue that the transition from 2:13 to 2:14 is rather abrupt and that 2:12–13 flows smoothly into 7:5. Hence, if anything, narratological considerations have previously been employed to assert a literary break.

However, a meticulous analysis of the narrative in 2:12–13, considered against earlier statements in the correspondence, actually points toward

---

13. I have offered a narratological assessment of 2 Cor 2:14 in its literary context in Heilig, *Paulus*, chapter 16, section 4.2. On the lexical-semantic and historical considerations that influence my interpretation, see Christoph Heilig, *Paul's Triumph: Reassessing 2 Corinthians 2:14 in Its Literary and Historical Context*, BTS 27 (Leuven: Peeters, 2017). Cf. also Christoph Heilig, *The Apostle and the Empire: Paul's Implicit and Explicit Criticism of Rome* (Grand Rapids: Eerdmans, 2022), for a more focused presentation of the argument.

Of Narrative Substructures and Worldview Narratives

literary unity. When Macedonia is mentioned for the first time, in 2 Cor 1:16, Paul already finds himself needing to defend against the charge of "vacillation" (1:17). There as well, the issue centers on Paul's actual travel movements compared to his initial plan (discussed above, pp. 257–60). Now, following 2:13, Paul can anticipate similar skepticism from the Corinthians, given that he ultimately does not continue his evangelistic efforts in Troas. Paul addresses this anticipated reaction by employing the metaphor of the Roman triumphal procession.

The thanksgiving is directed to God, "who always presents us in Christ as captives in his triumphal procession(s)" (Τῷ δὲ θεῷ χάρις τῷ πάντοτε θριαμβεύοντι ἡμᾶς ἐν τῷ Χριστῷ).[14] On the one hand, the metaphor allows Paul to depict himself and his coworkers in a manner that engages the Corinthians' perception; in the metaphor, they correspond to the implied audience that would witness this spectacle on the streets of Rome.[15] On the other hand, the metaphor enables Paul to challenge and transform this perception in several interconnected ways.

First, it is noteworthy that in Paul's metaphor the triumphator is none other than *God*. The implication, of course, is that if someone takes issue with Paul's travels, they are ultimately criticizing God, who orchestrates all travel movements. Furthermore, Paul appears to engage with the ambiguity surrounding ancient discourses about prisoners of war who were featured in triumphal processions. Our sources provide a more nuanced picture than the caricature of pitiful figures, which most modern exegetes presuppose. Indeed, many triumphators ensured that the *nobility* of their captives was visible (for example, through luxurious clothing) to the onlooking crowd,

---

14. On the question of whether a single, permanent procession is in view or whether Paul, rather, wants us to imagine a multitude of processions, see now Heilig, *Apostle*, 86–93. This is a question that arises due to Paul's choice of the imperfective aspect. Cf. Heilig, *Apostle*, 125–27, on Col 2:15, where the perfective aspect is employed with the same verb.

15. It is instructive what Tilmann Köppe and Tom Kindt, *Erzähltheorie: Eine Einführung*, Reclams Universal-Bibliothek 17683 (Stuttgart: Reclam, 2014), 124, write with respect to the analysis of narrative figures (from an "internal" point of view): "Readers have always recognized their own problems in the concerns and issues of characters. In this sense, literary character portrayals are sometimes viewed as a simulation or experimental field in which universal human possibilities are represented and explored" (German: "Leser haben zu allen Zeiten in den Anliegen und Problemen von Figuren ihre eigenen Probleme wiedererkannt. Literarische Figurendarstellungen werden in diesem Sinne bisweilen als ein Simulations- oder Experimentierfeld angesehen, in dem allgemeinmenschliche Möglichkeiten dargestellt und ausprobiert werden").

Chapter 5

as this reflected favorably upon the one presenting them.[16] As a result, Paul can acknowledge a positive aspect to his role in the triumphal procession, allowing him to introduce this metaphor through a thanksgiving. This positive dimension is further elucidated by the coordinated participial phrase "... and who spreads the scent of the knowledge of him through us in every place."

To sum up, a careful narratological analysis of 2 Cor 2:12–13, which takes into account the broader communicative context of the Corinthian correspondence, actually affirms the literary *unity* of 2 Cor 1–7. Concurrently, the precision with which Paul crafts the figurative language of 2 Cor 2:14 (also through the use of adjuncts) to engage and modify the Corinthians' attitudes illustrates his *deliberateness* as a narrator and his sensitivity to the impact of his narratives on his audience.

More specifically, the passage appears to *validate the heuristic utility of Hays's concept of narrative substructures*. Narrative(s) about Claudius's triumph, not explicitly documented but still plausibly reconstructable, serve as a hypotext. From this, Paul extracts essential insights concerning the plot and the arrangement of characters. This, in turn, enables him to reframe a different hypotext—namely, one that is known to us through 2 Cor 2:12–13— in a corresponding manner in 2 Cor 2:14.[17]

Argumentative and Descriptive Hypertexts

Especially in our analysis of conditional connections (cf. chapter 4), we have observed that protonarratives can indeed serve as what might aptly be termed "narrative substructures" for passages that are textualized using an *argumentative* strategy. For example, note that in Gal 3:29 it is not only the case that the protasis, "... if you belong to Christ" (εἰ ... ὑμεῖς Χριστοῦ) is

---

16. Fundamental for this is the seminal work of Mary Beard, *The Roman Triumph* (Cambridge: Harvard University Press, 2007).

17. In fact, we can even see here a reciprocal dynamic: Paul obviously wants his readers to revisit the narrative of 2 Cor 2:12–13 against the backdrop of the hypertext that he has created in 2 Cor 2:14, with the hope that they will now (mentally) retell these events in such a way that these protonarratives will lend themselves to a different kind of interpretation. In other words, 2 Cor 2:14 also serves as the hypotext for the protonarratives that are occasioned by this verse and that build on the events from verses 12–13. In any case, the readers now have enough time to make such reevaluations, while Paul continues his excursus until 7:4.

rooted clearly in the narrative of Gal 3:26-28.[18] Rather, on top of that, the if-then relationship itself—in other words, the question of *why* the apodosis "... then you are Abraham's offspring, heirs according to the promise" (ἄρα τοῦ Ἀβραὰμ σπέρμα ἐστέ, κατ' ἐπαγγελίαν κληρονόμοι) follows from the protasis—is also substantiated by a narrative, namely, in the protonarrative that emerges fragmentarily throughout Gal 3.[19]

Often, the potency of the argument stems from Paul's ability to presuppose a certain narrative relationship. This occasionally influences the surface structure of the text. In fact, in some of Paul's arguments the narrative substructure becomes so prominent that the connectors typically employed in arguments—conditional and causal connectors—recede into the background.

For example, note how in Rom 13:11-12 the preceding directives in verses 3, 7, and 8 are grounded in the knowledge of "what time it is" (cf. 13:11: Καὶ τοῦτο εἰδότες τὸν καιρόν, ὅτι ὥρα ἤδη ὑμᾶς ἐξ ὕπνου ἐγερθῆναι). A causal connector (γάρ) then occurs within that figurative language concerning the progress of time in terms of the advance of the night. Then, in verse 12 a consequential οὖν introduces yet another directive (ἀποθώμεθα οὖν τὰ ἔργα τοῦ σκότους). Strictly speaking, it is only here that Paul actually "argues." Even though on the surface of the text Rom 13:11-14 as a whole looks like a quite loose collection of phrases, we find here a high degree of coherence, which is constituted by the underlying protonarrative (cf. above, pp. 271-73, on this passage). Description, argumentation, and narration seem to blend into each other.

With *descriptive* passages as well, we can often identify relevant narrative substructures—that is, when they appear to be embedded in presupposed narrative hypotexts (cf., e.g., above, pp. 194-95, on Gal 3:28). Modal-instrumental connections in particular lend themselves to being read as reflecting denarrativized constellations of characters (cf. above, pp. 120-22, on 1 Cor 8:11).

The Limits of Narrative Substructures

In our analysis of the Pauline letters, we have encountered numerous cases where passages that initially do not seem to display narrativity ultimately

---

18. On whether Gal 3:28 is part of the narrative, cf. above, pp. 194-95.
19. Cf. Heilig, *Paulus*, 922-23.

Chapter 5

permit the reconstruction of protonarratives. This vindicates Hays's intuition that narrative substructures are essential for understanding the apostle's discourse. However, given that these protonarratives are merely reconstructions based on what we interpret as narrative fragments in the text, we must exercise caution so as not to overinterpret Paul's letters in relation to this category.

The metaphor of the Roman triumphal procession in 2 Cor 2:14 emphasizes not only the value of approaching Paul narratologically but also the importance of exercising restraint in postulating implicit narrative dynamics.[20] For example, some exegetes have suggested that the second half of 2 Cor 2:14 (verse 14b: καὶ τὴν ὀσμὴν τῆς γνώσεως αὐτοῦ φανεροῦντι δι' ἡμῶν ἐν παντὶ τόπῳ) continues to presuppose the setting of a Roman triumphal procession, with Paul participating joyfully in the parade as an incense carrier.[21] Not only do such proposals conflict with the semantics of θριαμβεύω in verse 14a (where Paul and his coworkers are invoked, after all, in the role of prisoners of war), but additional reasons also exist for concluding that Paul does not elaborate on a larger "fictional story" about himself and his coworkers in a victory celebration by God in Rome. For example, the prepositional phrase ἐν τῷ Χριστῷ in verse 14a presents difficulties when one attempts to integrate it within the imagery of the triumphal procession. This suggests that Paul shifts his focus already within verse 14a to the target domain of the metaphor, namely, the missionary journeys and Christ's pivotal role in them. Then, in verse 14b, evidence accumulates that Paul has moved beyond the imagery of the Roman triumph, possibly taking the element of burnt incense as a point of departure but developing this olfactory imagery independently in light of more general ancient assumptions concerning scent and in parallel to his understanding of his own proclamation.

Similarly implausible is the hypothesis that the fate of the captives from verse 14b remains the focus throughout verses 15–16. Those who attempt to associate the σῳζόμενοι of verse 15 with captives who receive a pardon at the end of the procession, and the ἀπολλύμενοι with captives who are executed, encounter the insurmountable problem that the discussion about "scent from death to death" and "scent from life to life" (ὀσμὴ ἐκ θανάτου

---

20. On what follows, cf. Heilig, *Paulus*, chapter 16, section 4.2.2.

21. Cilliers Breytenbach, "Paul's Proclamation and God's 'Thriambos': Notes on 2 Corinthians 2:14–16b," *Neot* 24 (1990): 257–71; and George H. Guthrie, "Paul's Triumphal Procession Imagery (2 Cor 2.14–16a): Neglected Points of Background," *NTS* 61 (2015): 79–91, who, however, differ with respect to how they ground this in the supposed semantics of θριαμβεύω in verse 14a.

Of Narrative Substructures and Worldview Narratives

εἰς θάνατον and ὀσμὴ ἐκ ζωῆς εἰς ζωήν) cannot be integrated into such a narrative. The same is true for a purported dichotomy between victorious (σῳζόμενοι) and defeated (ἀπολλύμενοι) parties. While assuming a Roman hypotext for verse 14a sheds considerable light on that construction, the same does not hold true for the continuation of the text.

A similar critique must be leveled against those who reverse the direction of argumentation and attempt to illuminate verse 14, especially the imagery of the triumphal procession in verse 14a, against the backdrop of clues that appear later in the text and are interpreted to suggest an entirely different, Jewish, hypotext. For example, Scott has built such a case in several argumentative steps. First, he postulates that Ps 67:18–19 LXX provides evidence of a connection between the idea of God's throne chariot (ἅρμα) and the revelation at Sinai.[22] With respect to 2 Cor 2:14, he acknowledges that the verb θριαμβεύω certainly evokes a Roman context and, thus, the Roman *quadriga*. However, he then argues that for Paul, the psalm serves as the "missing link" that allows the apostle to evoke the entire tradition of merkabah mysticism, drawing on Ezek 1, through the implied vehicle. Scott goes even further by claiming that, in doing so, Paul implicitly contrasts himself with Moses.

Similarly, Webb argues that Paul employs the Roman institution merely to convey a genuinely Jewish conception of the return from exile, as evidenced by the adaptation of the exodus narrative in the prophetic writings of the Old Testament.[23] Therefore, Webb also believes that verse 14a merely "introduce[s] the section on [Paul's] new covenant ministry (in contrast to Moses' old covenant ministry)."[24]

Admittedly, both scholars can point to the fact that, in the immediate literary context, the character of Moses indeed plays a significant role. This is arguably the case not only later in 2 Cor 3 but perhaps even in the question in 2 Cor 2:16 because the formulation "Who is adequate for such things?" (καὶ πρὸς ταῦτα τίς ἱκανός;) may allude to Exod 4:10.

Nonetheless, this does not change the fact that the hypothesis suggesting a protonarrative where Paul emerges as a second Moses in a "new exodus" is highly implausible. This protonarrative, allegedly stretching back from verse 16 and undergirding even verse 14a as a narrative substructure, appears

---

22. James M. Scott, "The Triumph of God in 2 Cor 2.14: Additional Evidence of Merkabah Mysticism in Paul," *NTS* 42 (1996): 268–70.
23. William J. Webb, *Returning Home: New Covenant and Second Exodus as the Context for 2 Corinthians 6.14–7.1*, JSNTSup 85 (Sheffield: Sheffield Academic Press, 1993), 72–84.
24. Webb, *Returning Home*, 82.

Chapter 5

far-fetched. If Paul had truly intended to make such a connection, he would have had many linguistic means at his disposal to make this explicit, or at least to leave the possibility open—for instance, by using the more general verb πομπεύω in verse 14a. By contrast, Paul's *actual* word choice is not an obvious selection at all if he intended to express the idea that Scott and Webb posit at the core of his communicative intentions.

What these proposals share is that although they may seem intuitively convincing, they offer *poor explanations of the text* when viewed through the lens of the philosophy of science.[25] In other words, if these hypotheses were accurate (and there is indeed some contextual justification for considering this possibility), we would *anticipate different phrasing* rather than Paul's actual word choice. These hypotheses are therefore characterized by low "explanatory potential" or "predictive power."

Bayesian confirmation theory instructs us that when we assess the "probability" of a hypothesis (for example, concerning the existence of a narrative substructure) in light of the evidence (in this case, the phrasing encountered in a text), we must consider this aspect—often confusingly called "likelihood"—as one of two essential characteristics of the hypothesis. Equally important (and I mean *exactly* as important, as it is not possible to privilege one over the other) is what I term the "background plausibility" of the hypothesis, or "prior probability" in more technical language. This factor considers how probable the hypothesis is before incorporating the new evidence (hence the term "prior" probability).

When we analyze the hypotheses concerning 2 Cor 2:14–16 that were dismissed earlier, it is evident that the publications in which they appear almost exclusively concentrate on tradition-historical matters. They attempt to establish that Paul *could have* been in contact with certain institutions and ideas, thus naturally increasing the probability that we may encounter statements about these topics somewhere in his letters (prior probability). However, they consistently fail to demonstrate that the text's surface structure is what we would anticipate if these hypotheses were correct (likelihood).[26]

Note that in determining the probability of a hypothesis, it is the interac-

---

25. On what follows, cf. Heilig, *Paulus*, chapter 16, section 4. There, I reference several publications relevant to different aspects of applying Bayes's theorem to exegetical questions.

26. This is even truer for hypotheses that try to get rid of the imagery of the Roman triumph in 2 Cor 2:14a altogether. Cf. Heilig, *Apostle*, 55–60, with further references to Heilig, *Triumph*.

tion between prior probability and likelihood that shapes the conclusion.[27] The same principle applies when we reframe the question to *compare two specific hypotheses* instead of asking for a single probability in isolation. This latter approach is often more useful in exegetical discussions. For instance, we may encounter a "strange" formulation in Paul's letters that seems to demand a sophisticated explanation.[28] In such situations, some scholars might propose a narrative substructure to "shed light" on the passage, while others may assert that the wording can be adequately explained by assuming that the apostle incorporated nonnarrative material, such as theological claims from opponents. It is crucial to understand that it is not sufficient for one of these two hypotheses to merely explain Paul's word choice "better" for it to also be the more probable explanation overall.[29] *How* good the predictive power of a hypothesis needs to be to ultimately tip the scale in its favor depends on the background plausibility that we assign to, for example, the idea of narrative substructures in Paul's letters in the first place.[30]

To be sure, calculating specific numbers is often not a realistic goal when applying this so-called Bayes's theorem to historical matters. However, this does not mean that a quantitative approach is entirely out of the question. One can often employ a rule of thumb sufficiently valid to at least ensure the logical consistency of one's arguments, even if it might not be precise enough to allow for intersubjectively shared conclusions. Namely, I would suggest that an exegete pondering the question of whether or not to assume

---

27. The advantage of comparing two specific hypotheses is that it not only mimics what we usually do in biblical studies but also gets rid of the difficult question of how probable an event is in general on the basis of all possible explanations.

28. On the process of abduction that leads to new hypotheses, see Theresa Heilig and Christoph Heilig. "Historical Methodology," in *God and the Faithfulness of Paul: A Critical Examination of the Pauline Theology of N. T. Wright*, ed. Christoph Heilig, J. Thomas Hewitt, and Michael F. Bird, WUNT 2.413 (Tübingen: Mohr Siebeck, 2016), 115–50. For a defense of a more far-reaching scope of this "inference to the best explanation," see Matthew B. Joss, *Weighing Interpretations in Science, Biblical Studies, and Life: The Quest for the Best Explanation* (Lanham, MD: Lexington, 2023).

29. I.e., to already use terminology that will be introduced later in the text, to have the higher "posterior probability."

30. I assume that in this context the question of the appropriate *choice of hypotheses* is equivalent to establishing *which hypothesis is more probable* in light of the evidence. It is not a matter of course that the two questions can be conflated in such a manner. Specifically, this equivalence presumes that the "appropriateness" of a hypothesis is solely determined by its posterior probability, a presumption that may not hold true in all epistemological or methodological frameworks. See Heilig and Heilig, "Historical Methodology," for details.

Chapter 5

a narrative substructure behind a specific Pauline verse should pause and contemplate the general frequency of such narrative substructures.

If they judge this to be a feature in, let's say, roughly half of the verses in the Pauline corpus, it means that whenever they approach a new verse, they should presuppose that there is approximately a 50 percent chance that a narrative substructure underlies it. In such cases, it may suffice for the hypothesis of a narrative substructure to explain the text just slightly better than the alternative, to make what we actually find in the text a little more predictable than if we assume that protonarratives did not influence Paul's choice of words.

However, if an exegete assumes that the category of narrative substructures is relevant to Paul's letters only in very few, select cases, it will not be enough for the hypothesis to shed some light on an otherwise slightly "obscure" passage. Instead, a rather dramatic explanatory advantage would be needed to conclude that this is the most plausible explanation for the text. Differences in the assessment of the prior probability of the narrative-subtext hypothesis among different scholars explain why focusing solely on whether or not a certain hypothesis makes sense of the text in question cannot ultimately advance the discussion on its own.

Two more points must be made concerning this estimation of the prior probability. First, every successful inference regarding the existence of a narrative substructure in Paul's letters naturally results in a new prior probability for the next verse under examination. The old "posterior probability" (the probability *after* accounting for new evidence) provides us with a new prior probability for the next piece of evidence we wish to evaluate. Therefore, it is entirely logical (indeed, a hallmark of logically consistent research) that our conclusions about the presence of narrative substructures behind certain Pauline texts will evolve over time, as the narrative approach itself develops. Initially, we may identify these phenomena only in very conspicuous places. At that stage, even a slight advantage in terms of the explanatory potential of the narrative-substructure hypothesis may not suffice to tip the balance in many other verses. However, upon revisiting these more difficult constellations later, we may establish more nuanced hypertextual relationships informed by our *updated* priors.[31]

---

31. Cf. also Heilig, *Apostle*, 103–16, using Rom 13:1–7 as a test case on how to enter and proceed in a hermeneutical spiral that allows us to conclude more and more subtle forms of intertextual references.

I hope that my preceding analyses have convinced you, the reader, of at least one thing: regardless of your initial level of skepticism toward Hays's thesis, there are indeed instances where the existence of narrative substructures is more probable than not. My aspiration is that this realization will inspire you to further explore the extent to which this category is applicable in Pauline exegesis.

Second, the quantitative estimate that I advocate here is, of course, merely a rough approximation of our actual prior expectation regarding the existence of a discernible narrative substructure in any specific Pauline text under examination.[32] We typically do not select a Pauline verse at random when considering this hypothesis. Instead, we are usually guided by contextual factors that have already influenced our direction. In essence, our prior probability has likely already been shaped by other pieces of textual evidence, elevating it to a level where even a minor predictive advantage of the narrative-substructure hypothesis may be sufficient to confirm it.

This resembles the dynamics in a medical setting. Owing to the COVID-19 pandemic, most people have become much more conversant with the dynamics of testing than they were in earlier times. They may even understand that a test with, for example, a "mere" 5 percent false positive rate—meaning that only 5 percent of healthy individuals still receive a positive result—can nevertheless be misleading in specific contexts. This can occur when the disease in question is rare within a population. Under such circumstances, the proportion of individuals who test positive but are actually healthy among all positively tested individuals could be significantly high. After all, the 5 percent of the healthy population might be a huge group in absolute numbers. Indeed, when the disease prevalence in a community is low, a positive test result alone may not suffice to make it more probable than not that a person who tests positive is actually sick![33]

---

32. It was originally presented as a challenge to N. T. Wright by Heilig and Heilig, "Historical Methodology," 141–42. There, the issue was intertextual echoes, another category introduced by Richard B. Hays into biblical studies. See Richard B. Hays, *Echoes of Scripture in the Letters of Paul* (New Haven: Yale University Press, 1989). Unfortunately, N. T. Wright, "The Challenge of Dialogue: A Partial and Preliminary Response," in Heilig, Hewitt, and Bird, *God and the Faithfulness of Paul*, 719–21, did not directly address this question in his response at the end of the volume.

33. This also depends on the question of how many false negative results the test produces (i.e., how many persons who are sick may believe that they are healthy). This latter constellation might under many circumstances be the bigger problem for the health situation of a society because it means that potentially contagious people might not distance themselves from others. However, once the prevalence of the sickness becomes very low,

Chapter 5

Research indicates that even medical professionals often struggle to interpret these numbers accurately.[34] They are frequently led astray by the compelling explanatory power of the sickness hypothesis. Their reasoning typically goes as follows. A positive test emerges. *If* the person is indeed sick, then there is very high probability for the test to turn out positive. Conversely, *if* the person is healthy, this circumstance does not explain the new evidence (the positive test result) well; we would expect a negative result instead. However, without taking prior probabilities into account, it is impossible to confidently give a diagnosis. This also implies that a test may be useful in contexts where a particular sickness is prevalent but may be virtually useless in others, where it would only marginally alter the prior probability of the disease being present.

This reaffirms the importance of considering priors. More significantly, it underscores that we generally consider a broad range of evidence when making diagnoses. While there are cases where population-wide screening is advisable, most medical tests are conducted following the observation of

---

people who falsely believe that they are sick and, hence, cannot do their jobs, can indeed become the bigger problem for society. For purposes of illustrating these dynamics, let us assume we are testing 10,000 people. With a disease prevalence of 5 percent, there will be 500 people (5 percent of 10,000) who actually have the disease and 9,500 who do not. If the test has a sensitivity of 95 percent (i.e., it assigns false-negative results to 5 percent of actually sick people), then it will correctly identify 475 (95 percent of 500) people as having the disease (true positives). However, it will also falsely identify 5 percent of the healthy people as having the disease. Since there are 9,500 healthy people, this means that 475 (5 percent of 9,500) healthy people will also test positive (false positives). So, with a disease prevalence of 5 percent and a test with a false positive rate of 5 percent and a false negative rate of 5 percent, the total number of people testing positive will be made up of an equal number of people who actually have the disease (true positives) and people who do not (false positives). If the prevalence were to fall below 5 percent, the number of false positives would exceed the number of true positives.

34. The classical study on this is Ward Casscells, Arno Schoenberger, and Thomas B. Graboys, "Interpretation by Physicians of Clinical Laboratory Results," *New England Journal of Medicine* 299 (1978): 999–1000. They asked twenty house officers, twenty fourth-year medical students, and twenty attending physicians at Harvard Medical School: "If a test to detect a disease whose prevalence is 1/1000 has a false positive rate of 5 percent, what is the chance that a person found to have a positive result actually has the disease, assuming you know nothing about the person's symptoms or signs?" Despite the hints that the question contains concerning the direct procedure for figuring out the correct result, only eleven respondents gave the right answer (ca. 2 percent). The most frequent incorrect answer, given by almost half the participants in the study, was the (from the perspective of the hypothetical patient) absurdly pessimistic number of 95 percent!

specific symptoms typical of the disease under consideration.[35] The physician who opts for this diagnostic method has likely already concluded that they are working with a higher prior probability than if they had selected a patient at random from the general population because, once again, the symptoms are better explained by the assumption of the sickness than on other grounds.

Similarly, we often approach Pauline passages with preexisting "symptoms" in mind that suggest the verse in question might be a strong candidate for the presence of narrative substructures. One such clue might be that the broader section of text deals with a particular *topic* that is commonly explored narratively elsewhere.

Additionally, regardless of the subject matter, there may be *structural indicators* that heighten our awareness of potential protonarratives underlying the discourse. For instance, when we encounter the narration-specific task of "motivating narration," even if it is solely in terms of form, the absence of a subsequent narrative might prompt us to search for traces of an originally intended story (cf. above, pp. 183–84).

However, the most significant factors that elevate the prior probability of the narrative-substructure hypothesis are, of course, *explicit narratives found in the context* of the passage. This is particularly the case if we observe that Paul is configuring these narratives in such a way that their inherent narrativity becomes increasingly elusive as the discourse progresses. This can dramatically increase our prior expectation that a narrative substructure is present, even if we are generally reluctant to rely heavily on this explanatory framework. Conversely, this means that the hypothesis of a narrative substructure underlying a nonnarrative (or, adopting a prototypical approach, "less narrative") segment becomes increasingly speculative the more remote the supposed hypotext is from the alleged hypertext—a principle that, of course, holds even more firmly when the hypothesized hypotext lacks any attestation and is merely a reconstruction.

To be sure, while the presence of an explicit narrative in the immediate context does boost the prior probability of the substructure hypothesis, ascertaining whether it serves as a template for an underlying protonarrative often hinges on intricate questions related to the interpretation of the story itself.

---

35. Whether or not random screening is advisable depends on a variety of factors, such as the false positive and false negative rates of the test, the seriousness of the sickness, its prevalence, and consequences in case of misdiagnosis.

Chapter 5

For example, in Phil 2:12 Paul appears to argue (cf. the beginning with the connector Ὥστε . . .) for specific behavior. It seems reasonable to suspect that he bases this conclusion on the narrative of the Christ hymn presented in Phil 2:6–11. Yet, the secondary literature is divided over the question of whether the command in verse 12b to "work out your salvation with fear and trembling" (μετὰ φόβου καὶ τρόμου τὴν ἑαυτῶν σωτηρίαν κατεργάζεσθε) truly aligns with any discernible pattern of the Christ story.[36]

The situation becomes somewhat more straightforward concerning the directives in Phil 2:2–4. The entire hymn exists in an item-description relationship with "Jesus Christ," who is mentioned in verse 5 and subsequently elucidated in the narrative (cf. above, pp. 134–35, on this type of connection).[37] When Paul states in verse 5 that the readers should maintain "such" an attitude among themselves (Τοῦτο φρονεῖτε ἐν ὑμῖν ὃ καὶ ἐν Χριστῷ Ἰησοῦ), this could either anticipate the hymn or simply refer back to the attitude encouraged in verses 2–4. In any case, the actions of Jesus in verses 6–8 provide fairly obvious parallels to the behavior that Paul has just prescribed—with the protonarrative of the commanded actions even guiding the interpretation of the actual narrative.

With verse 12, however, many exegetes remain skeptical about the notion of "imitation" of Christ being encouraged here. They contend that it is not valid to equate the obedience of the believers (cf. verse 12a: καθὼς πάντοτε ὑπηκούσατε . . .) with Christ's obedience in verse 8b (γενόμενος ὑπήκοος μέχρι θανάτου, θανάτου δὲ σταυροῦ). Similarly, they argue that the goal of "salvation" (σωτηρία in verse 12b) can scarcely be equated with Christ's exaltation in verses 9–11.

The situation is indeed complex. What makes the attempt to map the situation of the Christians onto the Jesus story so enticing is that the plot of Phil 2:6–11 seems to offer itself as a template for a protonarrative. This protonarrative concerns a party other than God taking action on the one hand and God responding to that action on the other. After all, even though resolving the propositional structure of verses 6–11 at a microlevel is quite complicated, the basic macropropositional structure appears straightforward. Verses 6–8

---

36. Various other external connects have been suggested, such as verse 2. However, if ὥστε does not connect verse 12 with the hymn, it seems to me that it is probably best to assume that it does not function as a connector at all but connects elements of the text on a speech act level, as a *discourse marker*. See above, p. 152. Cf., for example, how the MSG translates it as a kind of *reformulation marker*: "*What I'm getting at*, friends, is . . ." On reformulation markers, see Heilig, *Paulus*, 205.

37. Cf. *AGG* 319a.

Of Narrative Substructures and Worldview Narratives

form one nexus of propositions that, as a macroproposition, serve as the reason-element in a consequential connection with verses 9–11. In this first part, Jesus is the agent, while in the second God takes on that role, with Jesus now assuming the position of the patient. This might well be interpreted as indicating a clear *plot*: Jesus carried out an action, and as a result God undertook another. This pattern aligns well with the notion of believers taking specific actions and subsequently experiencing a favorable response from God. The parallels between verse 12 and verses 6–11 are suggestive and convince me that the narrative indeed offers the substructure for the command. Note, for example, that the rationale provided in verse 13 for the command in verse 12 also focuses on God as the agent, much like verses 9–11 do (θεὸς γάρ ἐστιν ὁ ἐνεργῶν ἐν ὑμῖν καὶ τὸ θέλειν καὶ τὸ ἐνεργεῖν ὑπὲρ τῆς εὐδοκίας).[38] Furthermore, verse 16, which concludes the entire line of reasoning, explicitly takes into account the "day of Christ" and considers what kind of

---

38. This presupposes that verse 13 does not simply justify the "fear and trembling" part of verse 12b. To be fair, it seems possible to me that μετὰ φόβου καὶ τρόμου is focal and verse 13 explains why the working out of salvation has to occur in precisely this mode, namely, because the one who is associated with the wishes and actions of the Philippians is none other than *God*. There is another reason why such a reading might be attractive. If the demonstrative pronoun in verse 5 does not refer back to verses 2–4 but points forward in the text, it arguably has in view Jesus's attitude in verse 6. Note that there the famous "story" about Jesus actually begins with *dis*narration. It is controversial what exactly Paul denies to have happened or to have been the case. Is the point that Jesus did not—unlike Adam—seize equality with God (verse 6b: οὐχ ἁρπαγμὸν ἡγήσατο τὸ εἶναι ἴσα θεῷ), even though he was in the "form of God" (verse 6a: ἐν μορφῇ θεοῦ ὑπάρχων), which then must denote something lesser than divinity? Or did he already possess this equality with God—with the "form of God" then indicating this very status—but decided not to hold on to it? Both options seem to overlook that the narrative figure of Jesus is characterized here more directly, not simply with reference to what he abstained from doing. It seems to me that verse 6b actually makes a statement about Jesus's attitude in a more direct way, giving us insight into his mental inner life and the value he attaches to divinity. And here the directives of verses 2–4 come into play, with the *protonarrative perhaps giving important indications for how to read the actual narrative.* It is only against the backdrop of verse 4—with the emphasis on the distinction between one's own matters and those of other persons—that one might see in the actual disnarration in verse 6b a model for the disnarrated protonarrative in verse 4, with the implication that Jesus did not show an interest in what belongs to God. Verse 6a might still mean that he had "access" to what is in view here, but read in context verse 6b seems indeed to presuppose an ethical maxim of not pursuing τὸ εἶναι ἴσα θεῷ, even for Christ. Now, if we assume that Paul adds the Christ hymn because verse 6 offers him a justification for his directives in verses 2–4, in particular in the last of these verses, the question remains what the rest of the passage is actually good for communicatively. Against that backdrop, one might consider the option

Chapter 5

story Paul might be able to tell about the Philippians in this context, that is, in a setting where everyone is giving praise to Christ (verses 10–11).[39]

At the same time, critics who dispute the notion of a narrative substructure behind verse 12 also have points in their favor. It seems to me that much of their discomfort can be traced back to the *manner* in which Phil 2:6–11 is narrated. Note that while we gain insight into Jesus's mental inner life in verse 6, specifically how he assesses equality with God, once the action starts the story is rather devoid of markers that indicate that Jesus could be the focalizer. He is characterized as having been "obedient" (verse 8b), but the narrative does not provide insights into his motives for "emptying" himself (verse 7a) and "humbling" himself (verse 8a), the two events recounted through indicative verb forms. One might argue that this configuration of the narration is compatible with classifying the text as externally focalized in relation to Jesus, thus perhaps suggesting a more general, Christian perspective on the story. However, I would at least point out that the framing of the situation seems to point more to a perspective that is not yet aware of the developments in verses 9–11. Incarnation and cross are not, in other words, portrayed as a stepping stone to something that undoubtedly will come later and relativize the suffering.

But I will gladly admit that there is a certain disbalance between, on the one hand, Paul explicitly bringing into focus the believers' attitudes, exemplified by the mention of their "fear and trembling" in verse 12b and the explicit reference to their volitional power in verse 13 (τὸ θέλειν), as well the fact that *they* are provided with a potential motive for their encouraged behavior in verse 15,[40] whereas, on the other hand, in the so-called *Christ* hymn, we gain a rather detailed insight not into his but into *God's* intentions in verses 9–10. And it is, thus, not Christ's mental life that is presented as a model, but rather Paul presents *himself* as a model for the Philippians to imitate, placing much emphasis on his own thought processes during the period of the current struggle.

The tension that exists between the observations (1) that the protonarrative of verse 12 seems to mimic the plot of verses 6–11 but (2) that, at the

---

of whether verse 13 is added as an attempt to flesh out how *God's* part in this story should affect Christian behavior.

39. On Phil 2:10–11, cf. above, p. 305. On Phil 2:16, cf. above, p. 232.

40. On the extent to which such purpose-oriented clauses after directives reflect the agents' motives, cf. the discussion above, pp. 305–6, of a supposedly consecutive ἵνα in 1 Cor 11:34.

same time, Paul does not go down the rather obvious route of giving us insights *into* Christ's thinking might thus be taken as confirmation of the view that we are here indeed dealing with a *piece of tradition*. Paul does not focus on its narrative configuration—something he is fully capable of doing in other instances—but concentrates on its content and builds upon his interpretation of the story without touching the original parameters of the narration. To be sure, Christ's motives are not explicated in verses 7–8, but as we have previously noted (see chapter 1), what a story "is about" can depend on quite subjective judgments. Paul recognizes a structural similarity to his protonarrative about the believers and leverages a certain feature of the narrated world that likely was not central in the original context.[41]

In other words, verse 12 (the hypertext) allows us to reconstruct how Paul understood verses 7–8 (the hypotext). Note that the macropropositional structure there is quite uncertain. What, after all, did Jesus do precisely? Observe that both the encouraged future actions and the consequent prospect of God's salvific vindication in verse 12 (μετὰ φόβου καὶ τρόμου τὴν ἑαυτῶν σωτηρίαν κατεργάζεσθε) are explicitly connected to the believers' previous behavior, which adhered to the same standard and is explicated in detail (καθὼς πάντοτε ὑπηκούσατε, μὴ ὡς ἐν τῇ παρουσίᾳ μου μόνον ἀλλὰ νῦν πολλῷ μᾶλλον ἐν τῇ ἀπουσίᾳ μου). As I have explained, it seems to me that we can observe a similar bifurcation within verses 7–8, with the text detailing two subsequent situations in Jesus's biography united by a common motivation yet differentiating two steps with the second one requiring an additional conscious decision to follow that pattern of behavior:

7a: ἀλλὰ ἑαυτὸν ἐκένωσεν
7b: μορφὴν δούλου λαβών,
7c: ἐν ὁμοιώματι ἀνθρώπων γενόμενος·

7d: καὶ σχήματι εὑρεθεὶς ὡς ἄνθρωπος
8a: ἐταπείνωσεν ἑαυτὸν
8b: γενόμενος ὑπήκοος μέχρι θανάτου, θανάτου δὲ σταυροῦ.

---

41. This would be an illustration of how substantial differences can be in renarrations of "the same story." We will come to that issue shortly in the context of Wright's hypothesis of a unified Pauline worldview narrative. See below, pp. 356–59.

Chapter 5

I believe it is most likely that the καί in verse 7d introduces the main clause of verse 8a. Accordingly, verse 7d, with its reference to Jesus's appearance in "human shape" (σχήματι εὑρεθεὶς ὡς ἄνθρωπος), would pick up the endpoint of the previous narrative block in verses 6–7c (cf. above, pp. 62–64, on information structure). After all, this block had concluded with verse 7c discussing Jesus becoming "in human likeness" (ἐν ὁμοιώματι ἀνθρώπων γενόμενος). We can thus envision that in the narrative world of verse 8a, the narrative character Jesus finds himself at a point in time when he had already "emptied" himself (verse 7a: ἀλλὰ ἑαυτὸν ἐκένωσεν)—something that had been accompanied by the associated phenomena of verse 7b–c—and was still looking forward to "humbling" himself (verse 8a: καὶ ... ἐταπείνωσεν ἑαυτόν). This act would then lead ultimately to his crucifixion, which, although not narrated explicitly, is clearly implied by the reference to the cross in verse 8b (γενόμενος ὑπήκοος μέχρι θανάτου, θανάτου δὲ σταυροῦ).

Alternatively, one could reject the idea that καί introduces the main clause of verse 8a, with verse 7d picking up verse 7c for orientation. In that case, verse 7d (καὶ σχήματι εὑρεθεὶς ὡς ἄνθρωπος) is actually coordinated with verse 7c (ἐν ὁμοιώματι ἀνθρώπων γενόμενος). In this scenario, verse 8 would connect asyndetically to verses 6–7 as a whole.

Note that with this latter syntactical construal and the resulting macro-propositional structure, it is still possible to extract the same plot. However, it seems to me that if the Christ hymn does indeed offer the narrative substructure for verse 12, it is more likely to assume that Paul read verses 7–8 in the first manner. In this interpretation, the narrated past and future (i.e., future in the past, when Jesus still could decide whether or not he would go to the cross) of Christ exist in a balanced proportion, triggering a similar bifurcation with respect to the believers' behavior.

I want to conclude this discussion by emphasizing what should be clear anyway: Bayes's theorem does not automatically provide us with all the answers, certainly not with mathematical precision. However, it is a highly valuable tool for posing the right questions, especially when grappling with complex matters such as narrative substructures. With sufficient experience and keen intuition, we might approach the issue appropriately, even without the help of this tool. Yet there is also the risk that we, as researchers of narratives, succumb to the allure of what seems to be a "good story"—an explanatory narrative about phenomena in the text—without critically examining its crucial plot points, the significant argumentative steps that must be considered for a thorough and sound inference. I wish to illustrate this point by briefly examining Wright's influential thesis that the exodus

Of Narrative Substructures and Worldview Narratives

story underpins Rom 6–8 as a narrative substructure, as one might term it following Hays.[42]

First, Bayes's theorem allows us to consider the basic necessary conditions that must be met for this hypothesis to possess sound background plausibility. Did Paul know the biblical exodus narrative? Certainly. Had this story, with its motif of deliverance from slavery, already become an established hypotext for prophetic discourse about the return from exile? Undoubtedly. Did Jews during Paul's era perceive themselves as living in a continuing exile due to the Holy Land being under Roman rule? Arguably so, though here the prior probability, in the eyes of many, already takes a hit. Had Paul integrated the story of Jesus as a plot point into this larger narrative so that we can generally expect him to speak about salvation in terms of a return from exile? Many would say perhaps. Those more confident in this regard, likely swayed by Wright's argumentation concerning *other* evidence (other passages), will naturally be inclined to detect traces of these convictions also in Rom 6–8, even if the explanatory advantage of this hypothesis turns out to be minimal.

Others will, by contrast, require quite specific evidence to conclude that Paul—at least in these chapters—allows such ideas to shine through. It is entirely possible that Rom 6–8 itself serves as the crucial evidence for Wright's reconstruction of Paul's worldview narrative rather than the reverse. Bayes's theorem does not resolve this debate, but it elucidates why different scholars might actually engage in disparate debates even though they refer to the same passage.

Next, Bayes's theorem encourages us to critically examine the precise value of the evidence in question. It prompts us to ascertain whether the text of Rom 6–8 is genuinely well explained under the assumption of a new exodus/return from exile protonarrative as its hypotext, and whether the passage indeed remains relatively opaque without such a backdrop. In Wright's view, Rom 6:17–18 appears to serve as such a "smoking gun." There, he contends, baptism is clearly linked with the deliverance from slavery experienced by the Jewish people in their exodus from Egypt.

> There is no question that in Judaism in general any story about slaves and how they come to be free must be seen at once as an allusion to the events

---

42. N. T. Wright, *Pauline Perspectives: Essays on Paul 1978–2013* (London: SPCK, 2013), see chapter 11: "New Exodus, New Inheritance: The Narrative Substructure of Romans 3–8 [1999]." For a short summary, see Wright, *Faithfulness*, 659. On my hints at how to evaluate this proposal by Wright, see Heilig, *Paulus*, 904–9 and 929.

Chapter 5

of the Exodus. When, in that context, we discover that the critical event in the story of the great liberation, the new exodus, is when the Christian passes through the water of baptism, we have (I suggest) a prima facie reason for making the same connection. "Sin," conceived here as an independent power takes of course the role of Egypt and/or Pharaoh; "righteousness," suggestively, seems to be almost a periphrasis for God.[43]

From this, Wright extrapolates: "If [Rom] 6 tells the story of the Exodus, or at least the crossing of the Red Sea, the next thing we should expect is the arrival at Sinai and the giving of the Torah."[44] According to Wright, this is "exactly the topic" of Rom 7:1–8:11.[45] Similarly, Rom 8:12–17 is said to fit into this "narrative sequence," as Paul considers the Christians here to be "God's new Exodus-people," on their way to their inheritance—not a piece of land, but "nothing less than the renewed, restored creation."[46]

Note that the crucial issue in Wright's view is the "*coherence*" of the passage in light of the assumed hypotext.[47] That is, he focuses on the question of whether the Pauline text is explicable if we assume his explanation about its genesis to be true. To be fair, Wright intuitively seems to understand that for an actual confirmation of his hypothesis, more may be needed, namely, an *explanatory advantage*. He also writes that when Paul composes Rom 6–8 with the story of the exodus in mind, "both in the large-scale shape of his presentation and in many details of actual arguments this emerges into the light of day, making fresh sense of passages which otherwise remain opaque, and holding together the different sections of the argument."[48]

Bayes's theorem helps us to unpack this claim. In order to properly evaluate it, one would need to closely examine which elements of the text are allegedly "opaque"—that is, difficult to explain or not well predicted—under *alternative hypotheses*. For example, is the sequence of baptism, law and sin, and Spirit really something that only makes sense against the backdrop of such a hypotext, or does this train of thought follow quite naturally from the subject matter itself? Additionally, is a reference to slavery truly explainable only with recourse to the exodus story as a hypotext, or might alternative contexts, such as everyday experiences with the institution of slavery, also

43. Wright, *Pauline Perspectives*, 166.
44. Wright, *Pauline Perspectives*, 162–63.
45. Wright, *Pauline Perspectives*, 163.
46. Wright, *Pauline Perspectives*, 163.
47. Wright, *Pauline Perspectives*, 163. Italics added.
48. Wright, *Pauline Perspectives*, 161.

serve as satisfactory explanations for the reference?[49] In fact, what about the idea that Paul directly employs the scriptural hypotext without first transforming it into a revised protonarrative? After all, Wright himself only states that "an allusion to the events of the Exodus" (not a *new* exodus as a return from exile, retold around Jesus and the Spirit) is what allegedly provides such an obvious explanation for the wording.

Moreover, the question is not just whether the competing explanatory potentials are as lacking as Wright implies; it also seems to me that he might be *overstating the predictive potential of his own approach*. Is the text of Rom 6–8 really what we would *expect* if his hypothesis were true? To choose just one example, why does Paul not portray baptism more explicitly in terms of crossing the Red Sea? Note that in 1 Cor 10:2 he explicitly makes a similar connection, in a reversed way, talking about the deliverance from Egypt in terms of baptism (καὶ πάντες εἰς τὸν Μωϋσῆν ἐβαπτίσθησαν ἐν τῇ νεφέλῃ καὶ ἐν τῇ θαλάσσῃ). While this may raise the prior probability of Paul connecting these two motifs also in Rom 6, it also points us, in terms of the likelihood factor, to the fact that in the Corinthian passage Paul uses much clearer terminology.[50] In Rom 6, by contrast, Christians do not pass through the sea with Christ's help; rather, burial is the dominant imagery. Hence, we can conclude that there are certainly many ways to discuss the Christian experience that draw on a mentally revised exodus story as a hypotext and that perhaps Rom 6–8 is one of them—but it is not clear to me that it is, in fact, the most likely product of such a process, and certainly not the only one that is conceivable.

---

49. Note that when Wright says that "in Judaism in general any story about slaves and how they come to be free *must* be seen at once as an allusion to the events of the Exodus" (emphasis mine) he seems to suggest that it is not imaginable that someone might refer to slavery with a different tradition-historical background in place. That seems clearly way too confident. Cf. the older work by Samuel Vollenweider, *Freiheit als neue Schöpfung: Eine Untersuchung zu Eleutheria bei Paulus und in seiner Umwelt*, FRLANT 147 (Göttingen: Vandenhoeck & Ruprecht, 1989), 325–30; and the critique of Wright by Oda Wischmeyer, "N. T. Wright's Biblical Hermeneutics: Considered from a German Exegetical Perspective," trans. Wayne Coppins and Christoph Heilig, in Heilig, Hewitt, and Bird, *God and the Faithfulness of Paul*, 82.

50. This is a typical problem when scholars deal with "parallels." They often do not notice that while the evidence that they adduce might raise the background probability of their hypothesis, it also points to specific possible formulations to express a certain idea—options that often differ from the passage that is now to be explained. Frequently, such "parallels" are thus a zero-sum game in terms of confirming the hypothesis.

Chapter 5

Remember that Bayes's theorem requires us to consider not only whether the hypotheses in question explain the text at stake—that is, whether they offer compelling causal narratives for its emergence—but also how well they would explain alternative, *counterfactual* textual products. This is a line of reasoning that is not intuitive to many biblical scholars, but it is important. The hypothesis of a narrative substructure might make sense of the text. However, if this assumption allows for a myriad of other creative choices on Paul's part, the explanatory potential of this theory will still be relatively weak.

Worldview Narrative

Having discussed the heuristic value of Hays's "narrative substructures" for Pauline exegesis, we now shift our focus to Wright's attempt to reconstruct Paul's "worldview narrative."[51] Wright's proposal is complex and analyzing it in terms of protonarratives, as I aim to do here, is further complicated by the fact that Wright's use of narrative terminology sometimes appears imprecise or at least confusing from a narratological perspective. This is, of course, due to Wright never having framed his approach in such terms, although he does employ some structuralist methods of narratological analysis, specifically Greimas's actantial model.

In what follows, I will not detail at each turn the considerations that lead me to specific decisions on how I ultimately integrate aspects of Wright's work into such a narratological framework, or which alternatives I reject.[52] Instead, I will provide a sketch of what, in my opinion, constitutes a charitable reading of Wright while remaining consistent with narratological conceptions. Whether this narratologically framed reconstruction of Paul's thought processes aligns with historical reality is another question altogether, one that we can only partially address in this work. In any case, we first need to clarify what it is that we are evaluating.

---

51. What follows summarizes some of the key points of Heilig, *Paulus*, chapter 17. Many more details and whole additional arguments can be found there.

52. On that, cf., for example, Heilig, *Paulus*, chapter 17, section 5.1–5.3, where I discuss how to interpret Wright's sometimes muddled talk about there being different stories that interlock.

The Original Act of Mentally Simulated Narration

It all begins, in my estimation, with what I have termed a *guiding act of narration* (German: "Leiterzählakt"), albeit only a mentally simulated one.[53] After all, if we aim to attribute a large implicit worldview narrative to Paul, we must assume that it originated at some point.

As far as I can see, Wright is not very explicit about this aspect, but it appears that what he has written in one of his articles about the "lost years" of the apostle—the time between his encounter with Christ near Damascus and his return to that city (Gal 1:17b–c: ἀλλὰ ἀπῆλθον εἰς Ἀραβίαν καὶ πάλιν ὑπέστρεψα εἰς Δαμασκόν)—may offer a fitting context for such a contemplative, narratively creative phase in Paul's life.[54]

According to Wright, Paul did not go to "Arabia" to evangelize (on Paul's thinking behind his account of these travel movements, cf. above, pp. 142–44). Rather, this move was an expression of his perception of himself as a zealous Elijah, as portrayed in 1 Kgs 19 (cf. ζηλωτής in Gal 1:14), with him going there in order to develop a better understanding of his new "job description" (cf. the mention of Mount Horeb in 1 Kgs 19:8 with Gal 4:25: τὸ δὲ Ἁγὰρ Σινᾶ ὄρος ἐστὶν ἐν τῇ Ἀραβίᾳ).[55]

If this is indeed when and where Paul's message took shape, one must assume that such contemplation would not have occurred in a vacuum but would also have involved making sense of the "ancestral traditions" (Gal 1:14), not least the stories about God's history with his people against the backdrop of the revelation of the Son of God (Gal 1:16).

---

53. Heilig, *Paulus*, chapter 17, section 5.6.

54. Wright, *Pauline Perspectives*, chapter 10: "Paul, Arabia and Elijah [Galatians 1.17] [1996]." I find it interesting that N. T. Wright, *Paul: A Biography* (San Francisco: HarperOne, 2018), 41–47, uses the approach to Damascus to introduce the treasure trove of Israel's stories that "Saul" would have brought with him on that journey. However, the goal of the stay in Arabia is then recounted in not so vivid terms, namely, "to hand in his former commission and to acquire a new one" (66). Wright is more explicit in his discussion of the subsequent years, as involving a lot of rereading of Scriptures (71), having found Jesus "as the infinite point where the parallel lines of Israel's long narrative would eventually meet." On what follows, cf. Heilig, *Paulus*, chapter 17, section 5.6.1. Designating these years as "lost," which occurs frequently in the secondary literature, is misleading in my view. We do not have a true ellipsis here but rather a summarizing narration. Cf. above, p. 181.

55. Wright, *Pauline Perspectives*, 156.

Chapter 5

Paul's Original Protonarrative and Its Various Storylines

What is characteristic of Wright's worldview-narrative hypothesis is not only that, according to him, a *unified* protonarrative underlies all of Paul's letters, but also that it has a quite specific shape. In Wright's writings, these assumptions are expressed through a somewhat confusing oscillation between talk of a coherent worldview narrative *in the singular* on the one hand and a *multitude* of stories on the other: "There are, after all, several 'stories' which are commonly thus detected within the implicit worldview of the apostle Paul. . . . I shall now suggest that these various stories do actually have a coherent interlocking shape, nesting within one another like the sub-plots in a play."[56]

What is meant here is difficult to decipher. Negatively, we can first note that these "stories" do not simply constitute three subsequent *episodes* of a single story.[57] Moreover, the fact that Wright seems to suggest that these narrative elements might relate to different narrative *levels*—indicated by his extensive talk about a "play within a play" for the story of Jesus as "the small, close-up story in which the others are resolved"—is not particularly helpful either.[58] Clearly, none of the narrative entities he has in mind are embedded within each other in such a manner. Consequently, readers may find themselves misled early in their efforts to understand Wright's objectives.

One helpful clue to understanding Wright's approach comes from recognizing how he *oscillates between the terms "plot" and "story"* when attempting to differentiate the various narrative elements within the overarching worldview narrative. First, Wright reconstructs the "overall story of the creator God and the cosmos."[59] He believes this narrative possesses a plot that "frames all the sub-plots that constitute the more obvious and immediate subject-matter of Paul's writing."[60] He refers to this narrative as both the "overarching narrative" and the "main plot," into which a "main subplot" and a "second but vital subplot" are integrated.[61] The first subplot concerns "the story of the human creatures through whom the creator

---

56. Wright, *Faithfulness*, 474.
57. Cf. Heilig, *Paulus*, 981–84.
58. Wright, *Faithfulness*, 519. On the whole issue, cf. Heilig, *Paulus*, 981–84.
59. Wright, *Faithfulness*, 475.
60. Wright, *Faithfulness*, 476.
61. Wright, *Faithfulness*, 477, 516.

intended to bring order to his world," while the second subplot focuses on the story of Israel.[62]

This language directs us to an important observation: Wright is *not describing the worldview narrative itself, but rather its plot*.[63] There exists a *single story* featuring various narrative figures, including God, creation, humanity, Israel, and Jesus. Examining all the significant events in this story allows us, as Wright seems to suggest, to extract *one coherent plot*. In this plot, God creates the world and installs humans as his representatives. However, they fail in this role, prompting God to choose Israel to restore humanity's role. Israel also fails, leading Jesus, as the "true Israelite," to fulfill Israel's purpose and, thereby, bring humanity and the whole of creation back into communion with God.[64] More specifically, Wright appears to assert that within this overarching action, we can identify *three distinct storylines*, each associated with different narrative figures.

Reading Wright's claim in this manner renders his hypotheses narratologically accessible, lending at least an initial semblance of plausibility to his endeavor. However, it is crucial to remember that our classification of the object(s) under his scrutiny carries immediate and far-reaching implications. The fact that we are discussing plot(s) here is significant. A story is not synonymous with a plot, nor does it merely "have" a plot that can be straightforwardly extracted (cf. chapter 1). Plots lack properties that narratives possess—such as the various dimensions of narration, the specific manner in which the story is told—and vice versa. Therefore, it is essential to stress that what we encounter in Wright's work is *not a reconstruction of Paul's protonarrative*. Instead, it is an *account of Wright's interpretation of said protonarrative*—presented to us in narrative form.

Note that the same observation applies to the analogy that Wright em-

62. Wright, *Faithfulness*, 516, 495.
63. For a detailed analysis, see Heilig, *Paulus*, chapter 17, section 5.1–5.4.
64. Wright, *Faithfulness*, 521, summarizes this as follows: "When we understand the triple narrative which forms the basis of Paul's worldview, we can see the way in which, bewildering though it often seems to us, Jesus the Messiah functions for him in relation to all three stories simultaneously. As Israel's Messiah, he has accomplished Israel's rescue from its own plight, passing judgment on the evil that has infiltrated even his own people. As Israel-in-person, which is one of the things a Messiah is . . . , he has completed Israel's own vocation, to bring rescue and restoration to the human race, passing judgment on human wickedness in order to establish true humanness instead. And as the truly human one (Psalm 8, blended with Psalm 110, as in 1 Corinthians 15) he has re-established God's rule over the cosmos, defeating the enemies that had threatened to destroy the work of the creator in order to bring about new creation."

ploys. When Wright asserts that the play within the play (Shakespeare's *A Midsummer Night's Dream*) is the climax of the entire performance, this reflects his interpretation of the events that transpire on stage.[65] Importantly, the play itself is *not a story* that can be simply transcribed onto paper.[66] While the text that Shakespeare produced—the "foul papers," followed by the first quarto edition published in 1600—refers to specific events, narration primarily takes place in the monologues of the actors. Beyond that, events appear only as stage directions; they must be enacted rather than recounted. The very first line, "*Enter* Theseus . . . ," serves as an example. In contrast, many of the events that Wright recounts in great detail, as well as the meaningful connections between them, are not present in the text itself.[67]

For our attempt to evaluate Wright's proposal—or at least to offer some suggestions for future discussions of this proposal—it is imperative that we differentiate between the reconstruction of the protonarrative on the one hand and the abstracting description of its content in terms of plot on the other. Failing to do so puts us at risk of conflating categories belonging to the level of narration with parameters related to the semantics of the story.

Take, for instance, how Wright speaks of the story or the plot that concerns creation as the "larger framework," warning of catastrophic theological consequences if one mistakes the narrative about humanity as the "main story."[68] While it is true that, according to the events Wright identifies as part of Paul's worldview narrative, creation and new creation chronologically "frame" the entire story, this does not necessarily mean that they are the most significant storyline.[69] Note that in Wright's analogy as well, the events

---

65. Wright, *Faithfulness*, 473. On the important role of the play-within-play, see 472.

66. On the whole topic, see Alexander Weber, *Episierung und Drama: Ein Beitrag zur transgenerischen Narratologie*, Deutsche Literatur: Studien und Quellen 24 (Berlin: de Gruyter, 2017). Note that even though this no longer can count as a very recent contribution, I unfortunately still have not had the time to engage with it in detail.

67. In movie scripts we usually have a far greater number of such directions. Therefore, it might be more intuitive to talk about them as actual narratives. Cf. Köppe and Kindt, *Erzähltheorie*, 46.

68. Cf. Wright, *Faithfulness*, 494: "This narrative, told in a hundred different hints and fuller passages in Paul's writings, is the element that most western readers over the last half millennium or so assume is the main story: humans sin, God rescues them, humans are saved. I hope it is becoming clear that though this is indeed one way (a somewhat truncated way) of pointing to the subplot in question it is by itself inadequate, and that when we explore this subplot we see the sin/salvation dynamic within its larger framework."

69. I want to be careful not to insinuate that Wright assumes the plot about creation to be the main plot specifically on the basis of its core events framing the other events in

Of Narrative Substructures and Worldview Narratives

concerning the wedding of Theseus and Hippolyta do indeed provide the context within which other storylines develop. However, it seems clear to me that the dominant theme of love is primarily developed in the storylines associated with the four young people from Athens.[70]

Moreover, it is not even clear that the initial and last situations in the plot appeared in that order in Paul's worldview narrative, even if it has the plot that Wright suggests. It is, for example, entirely possible that the cosmic storyline corresponds only to a series of flashbacks and foreshadowings— perhaps even inserted by Paul for the sole purpose of consistency, without actually being highly invested in that plotline.[71] With similar arguments, one could question Wright's claim that the Jesus story is central to Paul's worldview narrative. After all, one might question whether the "play within the play" truly constitutes the "climax" in Shakespeare's *A Midsummer Night's Dream* or, more precisely, in the plot of the mental narrative that the poet had told himself. Keep in mind that one could easily omit the events related to the performance without significantly impacting the other storylines

---

a chronological matter. After all, Wright, *Faithfulness*, 484, explicitly mentions the possibility that the "framing plot of creator and creation" *could* be connected with the subplots in a looser way, even though he does not think that this is the case in Paul's thinking. Still, it seems noteworthy to me that he introduces the subject matter by speaking, on the one hand, about this plot as the "larger framework" and then, on the other hand, continues with attributing a particular *significance* to the plot: "This 'cosmic' story . . . is not often found explicitly within Paul's writings, but when it does show up we should realize that it is crucial and foundational for everything else. We would be correct to suppose that it is in principle present to his heart and imagination, as a shaping influence on all else, even when it remains unstated" (475).

70. Cf. Wright, *Faithfulness*, 475, who explicitly connects the storyline of Theseus and Hippolyta with the storyline of creation. Moreover, he seems to suggest later (485) that the "framing" events indeed constitute an emphasis in terms of content: "As with Shakespeare, so with Paul: it is when we get to the first subplot that we feel the story is really starting. Indeed, just as some theatregoers may leave the play thinking only of Lysander and Hermia, Demetrius and Helena, and perhaps the strange story of Bottom the Ass by which their problems are first intensified and then resolved, so some readers of Paul come away with the impression that his sole concern is the human plight and the strange means of its resolution. It is important, however, to see that, for Paul, the human plight is related directly to the overarching plot."

71. Flashbacks and foreshadowings of course do not necessarily imply that we are dealing with merely supporting material. We would need to take a look at the whole narrative in order to come to an interpretation from which such a conclusion could be drawn. I use this as an illustration here because it is obvious that flashbacks or foreshadowings can function in such a supportive way with respect to a main plot.

(only the narrative concerning the theater personnel would remain incomplete; plus, the "tellability" of the entire story would be reduced).

I put forward these considerations not to offer a counterargument concerning the plot(s) of Paul's supposed worldview narrative, but rather to draw attention to the fact that what Wright communicates about this story pertains not to the narrative itself but to its plot. His own analogy illustrates this perfectly. What Wright conveys about Shakespeare's play represents the *action* as he understands it, likely based on having attended multiple performances and having consulted the script.

The *Shakespearean* "story" in this context is the protonarrative that the English playwright told himself. Similarly, Wright takes fragmented accounts of series of events from Paul's letters, reconstructs a *Pauline* protonarrative, and then interprets it, ultimately presenting his interpretation in narrative form. In my view, there is no shortcut from individual narrative fragments to discussions about storylines. Even if we are ultimately compelled to make such a significant leap because we cannot definitively reconstruct the thoughts of Paul or Shakespeare, we must strive to get as close as possible to the protonarrative itself. Furthermore, under such conditions, we are obligated to clearly indicate where we are speculating about the content of a story without having been able to establish the parameters of its original narration.

In what follows, we will first consider how the mental protonarrative, Paul's actual worldview story, can be reconstructed to the best of our abilities. Subsequently, we will address the question of whether and how Wright's hypotheses concerning the plot(s) of this narrative can be confirmed.

Finding Paul's Own Story

First of all, we must note that if we aim to transform the narrative approach into a narratological perspective, as advocated in this book, we must sever ties with Petersen's theses concerning the stories behind Paul's letters.[72] For Petersen, the most crucial step in reconstructing the "stories of letters" involves gathering *all* the events mentioned in these writings and arranging

---

72. On the methodology by Norman R. Petersen, *Rediscovering Paul: Philemon and the Sociology of Paul's Narrative World* (Philadelphia: Fortress, 1985), cf. Heilig, *Paulus*, chapter 17, section 2.1. For the critique that is offered here, see the more detailed discussion in Heilig, *Paulus*, chapter 17, section 2.4.

them in chronological order.⁷³ Subsequently, we are instructed to augment this "referential sequence" with events that are either implied by the letter or necessitated by the referential sequence.⁷⁴ For instance, *every* story reconstructed from a letter using Petersen's methodology will include the event of the letter's future arrival.⁷⁵

What we have stated above (pp. 201–2) concerning the inadequacy of a weak understanding of narrativity, as evident in Fisher's work, automatically implies that Petersen's methodology is also ultimately unsuitable for our aims. To be sure, we can analyze Paul's letters much like we would movies or plays, discussing the events that can be inferred from them. However, in this scenario, it is only the product that *we* create that constitutes an actual story.⁷⁶ To make this more concrete, we can indeed affirm that if we take Petersen's referential sequence of the letter to Philemon and read it as a coherent text, *this text* unquestionably constitutes a narrative:

> Philemon incurs a debt to Paul. Paul is imprisoned. Onesimus runs away and incurs a debt to Philemon. Onesimus is converted by an imprisoned Paul. Paul hears of Philemon's love and faith. Paul sends Onesimus back to Philemon. Paul sends a letter of appeal to Philemon and offers to repay Onesimus's debt. Onesimus and the letter arrive. Philemon responds to Paul's appeal. Paul's anticipated visit to Philemon [happens].⁷⁷

But this is *Petersen's* story. By contrast, Petersen illegitimately associates the stories that he has in mind with the *sender* of the letter. He acknowledges that the list of events that one might extract from a letter could be narrated from various perspectives.⁷⁸ However, he then continues with the assertion that the "selection and arrangement of actions in our story" are determined by the author of the letter.⁷⁹ That is why, in Petersen's view, the narrative

---

73. Petersen, *Rediscovering*, 47–48, see also 45: "All actions referred to are equally actions in the letter's story."

74. Petersen, *Rediscovering*, 49: "It will be recalled that the implied actions are referential actions implied in the letter or logically required by the referential sequence."

75. Petersen, *Rediscovering*, 50.

76. Köppe and Kindt, *Erzähltheorie*, 46. On this topic, cf. also their comment on p. 102: "We take what is communicated as the material for a concise narrative" (German: "Wir nehmen das Dargestellte als den Stoff einer konzisen Erzählung"). Cf. Heilig, *Paulus*, chapter 17, section 2.3.

77. Cf. Petersen, *Rediscovering*, 70.

78. Petersen, *Rediscovering*, 47.

79. Petersen, *Rediscovering*, 47.

that we reconstruct primarily belongs to the sender of the letter: "The story we construct from a letter is Paul's fiction, but the one we construct from that story is ours."[80]

This distinction rests on a faulty understanding of how narrative voice and narrative perspective relate to each other. While it is correct that every reference to an event by linguistic means is viewpointed to some extent, Petersen wrongly assumes that in a story told by a first-person narrator, "everything he tells us is told from his perspective."[81] A narrator can make use of different focalizers in their portrayal of any given situation. Just because we take an event from Paul's letter, this does not mean that the conceptualization of this situation corresponds to his own perspective. Moreover, it is naive to think that the bare list of events from the Letter to Philemon bears any close similarity to how Paul conceptualizes these events in question. Petersen not only overestimates our ability to directly access Paul's perspective; he also misunderstands the nature of Paul's narration in general.

If the letter itself does not constitute a narrative text, the only Pauline story that we can meaningfully discuss is a mental protonarrative. This is the level where issues of arrangement, temporal order, and meaningful relationships—alongside parameters such as distance and perspective—are dealt with. That there is no simple way of extracting such a story from the letter, based on the events that occur in the letter, becomes evident from the fact that Petersen himself gives the following definition for the term "fiction": 'the construction, the making, of an order.'[82] Nowhere does he offer any reason for the assumption that the construction of the order, carried out by the *exegete*, actually constitutes a reconstruction of what *Paul* had originally constructed in his mind. Petersen has to remove the entire process of Paul's simulation of narration for the text, as it stands, to offer immediate access to Paul's fiction—but if that were the case, the fiction that we would focus on then would no longer constitute a story "of Paul." There is simply no way around this dilemma that Petersen's approach faces, and Pauline

---

80. Petersen, *Rediscovering*, 14. Cf. also Petersen, *Rediscovering*, 47, with reference to *BGU* 1.37, a letter by a certain Mystarion to a priest named Stotoetis: "Because our outline of actions is derived from Mystarion, there are actually only two possible narrative voices, Mystarion's and ours, and if ours, we would be telling *Mystarion's story*. Thus the story is in the first instance his and only derivatively ours."

81. Petersen, *Rediscovering*, 80. On viewpoint in linguistics, see Barbara Dancygier and Eve Sweetser, eds., *Viewpoint in Language: A Multimodal Perspective* (Cambridge: Cambridge University Press, 2012).

82. Petersen, *Rediscovering*, 10.

scholars have unfortunately too often overlooked this fundamental problem because they were unaware of how flawed Petersen's notion of narrative perspective is.[83]

For Wright's approach, this conclusion appears devastating at first glance. After all, Petersen is crucial for him because his framework allows Wright to transition from *our* act of narrative construction to language that seems to imply that *Paul himself* had such a narrative in mind:

> It would be possible to *construct* from the Pauline corpus a narrative world of Paul's own life and experience. . . . That, we may safely say, was the narrative world *upon which Paul drew* to make sense of his day-to-day experience. . . . Within all his letters . . . , *we* discover a larger implicit narrative. . . . *Paul* presupposes this story even when he does not expound it directly.[84]

There is nothing wrong in principle with Petersen's methodology as long as we recognize that it is not a means of reconstructing Paul's worldview narrative but rather a tool for using his letters to create our own narratives.[85] There might be real value in such an endeavor, perhaps as part

---

83. Cf. Joel R. White, "N. T. Wright's Narrative Approach," in *God and the Faithfulness of Paul: A Critical Examination of the Pauline Theology of N. T. Wright*, ed. Christoph Heilig, J. Thomas Hewitt, and Michael F. Bird, WUNT 2.413 (Tübingen: Mohr Siebeck, 2016), 181–204, who shows no awareness of narratological debates about the distinction between narrative voice and narrative perspective. Scholars of the Gospels have been more attentive to this problem at times. For example, Jan Rüggemeier, *Poetik der markinischen Christologie: Eine kognitiv-narratologische Exegese*, WUNT 2.458 (Tübingen: Mohr Siebeck, 2017), 33, correctly calls out Petersen for conflating the identity of the narrator with the choice of focalizers.

84. Wright, *New Testament*, 404–5.

85. Cf. Köppe and Kindt, *Erzähltheorie*, 56, with respect to the question of how to deal with the situation of a lack of meaningful connections: "Firstly, we can leave open whether the text is intended as a narrative. Its status is thereby *indeterminate*; it is a classificatory borderline case. Secondly, we can read the text as if it *were* a narrative. In this case, we set aside the fact that the narrative is a concrete communicative artifact dependent on the specific intentions of a speaker and consider what assumptions we can meaningfully read into the text. *Strictly speaking, we are thus using the text to create a new narrative from it*" (German: "Wir können erstens offenlassen, ob der Text als Erzählung gemeint ist. Sein Status ist damit *unbestimmt*, es handelt sich um einen klassifikatorischen Grenzfall. . . . Zweitens können wir den Text lesen, als *handele* es sich um eine Erzählung. Wir sehen in diesem Fall davon ab, dass die Erzählung ein konkretes kommunikatives Artefakt ist, das von den bestimmten Intentionen eines Sprechers abhängig ist, und überlegen uns,

Chapter 5

of a program of "narrative theology."[86] However, what must be avoided at all costs is adopting Petersen's facile procedure and combining it with implicit or explicit claims about the mental life of the author, that is, with their protonarratives.

Unfortunately, the use of Petersen's methodology for the reconstruction of Paul's worldview narrative has largely remained unchallenged.[87] Once again (cf. already above, pp. 201-2), we must note how problematic it is that Fisher's "narrative paradigm" *and its critique* have largely gone unnoticed by biblical scholars. Note how Rowland, already in 1989, reacts to Fisher. First, he concedes that it would indeed be possible to analyze nonnarrative texts within Fisher's framework, that is, by focusing on "narrative probability" and "narrative fidelity."

> Even if the form of a work cannot be treated from a narrative perspective, this does not necessarily deny the value of the narrative paradigm. It is possible that a work lacking an explicit narrative structure still can be treated from a narrative perspective, just as a dramatistic method (the pentad for example) could be applied to works that are not theater. The work could be viewed as containing or drawing upon an implicit story.[88]

---

welche Annahmen wir sinnvollerweise in den Text hineinlesen können. *Strenggenommen benutzen wir damit den Text, um aus ihm eine neue Erzählung zu machen*"). Italicization of the last sentence is mine.

86. See, e.g., Timo Eskola, *A Narrative Theology of the New Testament: Exploring the Metanarrative of Exile and Restoration*, WUNT 350 (Tübingen: Mohr Siebeck, 2015). Generally, it is noticeable in the recently rekindled debate on "narrative theology" in the English-speaking world that the initial contribution of the German linguist Harald Weinrich, "Narrative Theologie," *Concilium* 9 (1973): 329-34, is not taken into account. See from a German-speaking perspective the well-informed piece by Andreas Mauz, "Theologie und Narration: Beobachtungen zur 'Narrative Theologie'-Debatte—und über sie hinaus," in *Textwelt—Lebenswelt*, ed. Brigitte Boothe, Pierre Bühler, Paul Michel, and Philipp Stoellger, Interpretation Interdisziplinär 10 (Wurzburg: Königshausen & Neumann, 2012), 41-66. On Weinrich's text-linguistic work and its potential relevance for discussions about the information structure of biblical texts, see Heilig, *Paulus*, chapter 6, section 3.3.4.

87. For example, White, "Narrative Approach," 190, is critical of Wright's methodology but explicitly emphasizes how promising Petersen's work is for the future of the narrative approach.

88. Robert C. Rowland, "On Limiting the Narrative Paradigm: Three Case Studies," *Communication Monographs* 56 (1989): 42.

He then illustrates this by an analysis of *Liberty and Justice for Some* by David Bollier along these lines:

> *Liberty and Justice for Some* could be interpreted as part of what Fisher calls "an episode in the story of life." . . . In this view, the radical right might be treated as mythic villains, representing the power of darkness itself. Censorship and book bans could be seen as representing a return to the dark ages. By contrast, liberals and the People For in particular might be treated as the heroes who are fighting for all the values represented by the American Revolution. A full scale application of the narrative paradigm could flesh out this story by deriving an overall plot outline from the organization of the book. The various chapters then could be treated as incidents building to a climax and the appendices interpreted as an epilogue. Characterization might be developed out of the quotations in each chapter.

The objection that Rowland then formulates can also be read as a damning critique of the use of Petersen's methodology within the narrative approach to Paul, which is why I quote it here in full:

> While such an interpretation could be developed, I suggest that treating *Liberty and Justice For Some* as an episode in a larger story points more to the potential for critical creativity than it does to the power of the narrative paradigm. To treat *Liberty and Justice For Some* as a narrative, a critic would have to create his or her own story out of the arguments in the work. Such an interpretation would be virtually impossible to test, since the critic is inventing a story out of what otherwise would be considered discursive material. If one critic did not see the story, another could say simply that he or she did. Textual proof would lose its importance. Moreover, such a process blurs the distinction between works that explicitly tell a story and works for which the critic must discover the story. With enough work, any text could be interpreted as a story, but that critical "work" may obscure the basic appeal of the text. In this case a narrative interpretation both ignores a far simpler explanation and also has the potential to deny the difference between *Liberty and Justice For Some* and novels or films that explicitly rely on plot development to make their point.[89]

89. Rowland, "Limiting the Narrative Paradigm," 43–44.

Chapter 5

Narrative Figures as Crystallization Points for Pauline Protonarratives?

To be fair, it is important to note at this point that it is not only Wright and his followers who are misled by Petersen's methodology. To the contrary, it seems that at least implicitly, such a methodology has deep roots in exegetical discussions.[90] I want to illustrate this by means of one example.[91]

John M. G. Barclay is very critical of Wright's claims concerning a Pauline worldview narrative.[92] As we have seen above (in chapter 1), he objects to the "all-encompassing" usage of the word "story" and prefers to limit himself to explicit narratives: "Whatever other 'stories' Paul may, or may not, relate in his letters, my brief here is, in one respect, relatively uncontroversial: Paul manifestly tells some stories about himself in the course of his letters.... In fact, Galatians 1–2 is a quintessential narrative, containing sequential episodes of a single story, complete with time indicators."[93]

For Paul's "story ... of his churches" and his "story of Israel," Barclay likewise can point to continuous sections of text, namely, Gal 4:12–19 and Rom 9–11.[94] A critical reader might object that even in these latter passages the narrative mode is broken up at points, for example by means of the questions in Gal 4:15–16. Accordingly, one might raise the heretical suspicion that Barclay's "stories" are, in fact, themselves protonarratives. But we may grant that he at least focuses on individual paragraphs in these cases for each alleged story.

By contrast, a couple of pages later, when Barclay turns to the structural correspondence between "Paul's story (as a Jew) and the story of his 'people' (fellow Jews), as outlined in this letter [Galatians]," the situation is entirely different.[95] The story "of" Israel is cobbled together from statements found in a variety of verses, which appear at different places in the text, even in a different order. Accordingly, what Barclay retells is not first explicitly narrated by the apostle himself anywhere within the extant text of his writings. It

---

90. On everything that follows, cf. Heilig, *Paulus*, chapter 17, section 3.

91. Cf. Heilig, *Paulus*, chapter 17, section 3.1.

92. John M. G. Barclay, "Paul's Story," in *Narrative Dynamics in Paul: A Critical Assessment*, ed. Bruce W. Longenecker (Louisville: Westminster John Knox, 2002), 134 n. 7. See also John M. G. Barclay, review of *Paul and the Faithfulness of God*, by N. T. Wright, *SJT* 68 (2015): 235–43.

93. Barclay, "Paul's Story," 135.

94. Barclay, "Paul's Story," 135.

95. Barclay, "Paul's Story," 144.

is only in *Barclay's* act of narration that this narrative emerges—with Barclay at the same time, however, implying that he is reconstructing the apostle's own story about Israel in Galatians. Therefore, even Barclay, the fierce critic of Wright's allegedly speculative worldview narrative, operates under the presumption that he can reconstruct a narrative, based on Paul's letter, that Paul himself *could have* explicitly articulated.[96]

Against this backdrop, I have sympathy for Wright's frustration when responding to his opponents. He emphasizes that his procedure is actually not different from the practices of "Geertz, Berger and Luckman, Petersen and the thousand writers who have made this and similar points (and with whom the real quarrel should take place if the dissenters want to pick one)":

> I insist that it is possible in principle, and not actually difficult in practice, to discover within the larger worldview and mindset, to which we have remarkably good access, what implicit story Paul is telling, behind, above, underneath, in and through (whatever spatial metaphor you like) the particular things he says in this or that letter. Discerning this is not arcane, not dependent on some fancy French philosophy, not particularly difficult.[97]

I would maintain, against Wright, that what he has in view when talking about reconstructing worldview narratives—if we understand these stories as something substantial, as actual protonarratives—is indeed a quite difficult task. But I would agree that he is not alone in these ambitions but rather united with "the thousand writers" who follow similar goals, and some of his fiercest critics are among them.

In fact, it seems to be one of the most frequent rationales behind collected volumes that scholars meet to discuss specific "topics" in biblical writings, which usually equates to selecting a specific entity—such as "Israel"—as the object of study and then collecting all the statements that refer to it, implying

---

96. It would look something like this: [3:8:] Προϊδοῦσα δὲ ἡ γραφὴ ὅτι ἐκ πίστεως δικαιοῖ τὰ ἔθνη ὁ θεός, προευηγγελίσατο τῷ Ἀβραὰμ ὅτι ἐνευλογηθήσονται ἐν σοὶ πάντα τὰ ἔθνη. [Cf. 3:24a:] Ἀλλὰ τότε ὁ νόμος παιδαγωγὸς ἡμῶν γέγονεν [cf. 3:22:] καὶ συνέκλεισεν ἡ γραφὴ τὰ πάντα ὑπὸ ἁμαρτίαν [cf. 3:23b:] ὥστε ὑπὸ νόμον ἐφρουρούμεθα συγκλειόμενοι. [Cf. 3:23a + 3:23c + 3:25a:] Τότε ἦλθεν ἡ πίστις. [Cf. 3:25b:] Νῦν δὲ οὐκέτι ὑπὸ παιδαγωγόν ἐσμεν [cf. 3:16:] καὶ κατανοοῦμε τὴν γραφήν. Τῷ δὲ Ἀβραὰμ ἐρρέθησαν αἱ ἐπαγγελίαι καὶ τῷ σπέρματι αὐτοῦ. οὐ λέγει· καὶ τοῖς σπέρμασιν, ὡς ἐπὶ πολλῶν ἀλλ' ὡς ἐφ' ἑνός· καὶ τῷ σπέρματί σου, ὅς ἐστιν Χριστός. [Cf. 6:16:] Ὥστε καὶ ὁ Ἰσραὴλ τοῦ θεοῦ ἤλλακται. [Cf. 3:28a:] Τοιγαροῦν οὐκ ἔνι Ἰουδαῖος οὐδὲ Ἕλλην.

97. Wright, *Faithfulness*, 466.

Chapter 5

that we thus somehow learn something about Paul's view on these matters. This is usually presented as some kind of paraphrase and, thus, at least partially in narrative form.[98] Indeed, the classic study by C. K. Barrett, which orients itself toward the figures of Adam, Abraham, Moses, and Christ, is emblematic of the view that such a procedure will indeed bring to light the apostle's own conceptions: "Paul sees history gathering at nodal points, and *crystallizing upon outstanding figures.*"[99]

To be sure, while many have suggested analyzing Pauline theology by focusing on specific narrative figures—the world, Israel, Jesus, the Church, Paul, etc.—Wright goes beyond these more modest claims. He assumes that all these elements can be combined into *a single coherent whole*.[100]

In this respect, Barclay is indeed more reluctant. He views the connection between the different stories he identifies as merely consisting in a shared relation to the Christ event. The result is that the story of Paul as the "paradigm Jew" becomes the "microcosm of the story of his people," and there is a "striking, though subtle, homology" between the story of Paul and the story of his congregation.[101] In other words, Barclay seems to assume the existence of several independent protonarratives, which are held together not by one original governing act of narration but by a common theme or conviction. We will address this additional layer of Wright's specific proposal later.

That being said, in my view, what is most problematic about Wright's approach—or, perhaps more precisely, what constitutes the first fundamental obstacle to it—is indeed this widespread idea that we can reconstruct Paul's stories by following his statements about specific narrative figures. Such a conviction will more or less automatically lead to a synthesis of statements from different parts of a Pauline letter or even the Pauline corpus as a whole, and the difference between Wright and his critics thus seems to be one of quantity only.

What complicates such an analysis tremendously is that it is by no means clear that every time Paul mentions creation, humanity, Israel, or Jesus, he is providing insight into a single, unified story about such an entity. After all,

---

98. In this respect, cf. Predrag Dragutinović, Tobias Nicklas, Kelsie G. Rodenbiker, and Vladan Tatalović, eds. *Christ of the Sacred Stories*, WUNT 2.453 (Tübingen: Mohr Siebeck, 2017), a volume that shares a focus with Hays in that it concentrates on "Christ stories."

99. C. K. Barrett, *From First Adam to Last: A Study in Pauline Theology* (London: Black, 1962), 5. Emphasis mine.

100. For references, cf. Heilig, *Paulus*, chapter 17, section 3.2.

101. Barclay, "Paul's Story," 144 and 145.

there is a great variety of ways in which events featured at different places in Paul's letters might be connected.[102] Admittedly, some of these options will rarely be relevant in the task of synthesizing a large Pauline protonarrative. Ironically, the option that Wright himself highlights by discussing the "play within the play" may be the least useful one, as I do not see much evidence of narrative fragments that should be integrated into a narrative whole by designating one as an *embedded* narrative and another as its frame narrative.[103]

To me, a more critical distinction lies between events that constitute *sequential phases of a single narrative* and instances where we are dealing with a *series of distinct acts of narration*, each describing events that coincidentally occur or have occurred sequentially in the real world.[104] For example, even if we accept Wright's interpretation of Rom 6–8 as reflecting the "new exodus" portion of Paul's worldview narrative, we could still question whether in Rom 4, with his references to Abraham, Paul is indeed hinting at an "earlier episode," or whether we are simply dealing here with two (proto)narratives about sets of events that just happen to follow each other in (Paul's understanding of) the real world. The fact that in Rom 5 Adam seems to disturb this chronology might lead one to suspect the latter—an argument that is, admittedly, itself of limited value because protonarratives, just like explicit narratives, can of course contain flashbacks.

We can thus conclude that at times the question of whether or not a mental act of narration has ended or is taken up again later can be very difficult to determine. However, at least sometimes we receive some indications in the text as to whether a new act of narration begins or an old act of narration is continued. This is mostly true for oral narration but also occurs, though to a lesser extent, in written narratives. For example, in the case of the narration that is dropped after 2 Cor 2:13, we can see in 7:5 that Paul makes it clear he is continuing with the same story (cf. above, pp. 314–16).[105] The study of "turn-keeping" discourse markers in written Koine texts will

---

102. On what follows, cf. with much more detail Heilig, *Paulus*, chapter 17, section 4.2.
103. For details, cf. Heilig, *Paulus*, chapter 17, section 4.2.5.
104. Heilig, *Paulus*, chapter 17, section 4.2.2.
105. Generally, an informing communicative intention seems to make the identification of such a resumed act of narration easier. Cf. Heilig, *Paulus*, 489, where I use the letter in Queneau's *Exercises in Style* as an example for a text that is explicitly written with the intention to inform about new developments. Later, the author explicitly tells the recipient of the letter that the story is not yet finished. Cf. Heilig, *Paulus*, 966–67.

undoubtedly further improve our ability to detect such resumptions of acts of narration.[106]

The decision to assume a new act of narration is naturally somewhat dependent on whether we can indeed identify a prior implementation of the *narration-specific task of concluding the narrative* (cf. above, pp. 190–97). In collections of written short stories, we often find a lexical indication, such as "the end."[107] But in oral narration, we also employ several means that mimic literary closure.[108] By contrast, with respect to merely mental narration, which occurs in the background of text production, all of this can be applied only to a very limited extent, that is, mostly when the fragments with which we are dealing are larger stories with a discernible implementation of narration-specific tasks. Here we might have enough indications from the prior thematization to know what kind of *arc of suspense* we should expect, though it is, of course, possible that a narrative remains incomplete.

One additional insight we can glean from the study of oral narration is that the shift from the narrative world to the communication situation typically comes with a clear contrast, such that the resumption of the narrative mode usually *requires a renewed act of thematization*.[109] Accordingly, if the shift back to narration, following a direct address to the readers, occurs without this change being explicitly marked, it may indicate that, in the mind of the author, we are still dealing with (another episode of) *the same story*.[110]

So far, we have discussed the constellation where we are confronted with narrative fragments that refer to situations that occur sequentially in a single narrative world, underscoring the possibility that we might be dealing with separate acts of narration. However, this option—of distinct acts of narration—should arguably be taken even more seriously if the fragments, in fact, pertain to the *same* event.[111] After all, one might argue that in such cases,

---

106. On discourse markers in general, cf. above, p. 152. On "turn-keeping" discourse markers, see Heilig, *Paulus*, 205–6.

107. Elisabeth Gülich and Heiko Hausendorf, "Vertextungsmuster Narration," in *Text- und Gesprächslinguistik / Linguistics of Text and Conversation*, ed. Gerd Antos, Klaus Bringer, Wolfgang Heinemann, and Sven F. Sager, Handbücher zur Sprach und Kommunikationswissenschaft / Handbooks of Linguistics and Communication Science 16 (Berlin: de Gruyter, 2000–2001), 1:380.

108. Gülich and Hausendorf, "Vertextungsmuster Narration," 1:380.

109. Gülich and Hausendorf, "Vertextungsmuster Narration," 1:381. On thematization, see 1:378–79.

110. Cf. Heilig, *Paulus*, 966, where I discuss Gal 4:8 as an example.

111. On what follows, cf. Heilig, *Paulus*, chapter 17, section 4.2.3.

Paul simply "tells the same story" again but in a different context or, to put it more precisely, discusses the same events in narrative form once more.

However, those who wish to combine such statements into a single narrative also have a valid point. After all, especially when dealing with a single writing, and thus a single (macro)utterance, we must also consider the possibility that Paul indeed refers to the same nexus of events in the real world multiple times *within a single act of narration*.[112] This means that the repetition of thematization or dramatization does not necessarily indicate a new act of narration but may simply be due to *repetitive* (mental) narration.

While this consideration does not imply that Wright's approach is universally valid, it does suggest that the synthesis of different narrative fragments into a single mental protonarrative must indeed be taken seriously. However, it must also be stressed that for the reconstruction of Paul's single worldview narrative, such repetitions are not very important. After all, no new episodes are added to the plot in such cases. As has already been noted in the discussion of the repeated processing of narration-specific tasks (cf. above, p. 187), such narrative techniques do not so much contribute to what is narrated but rather put the act of narration itself into focus.

Things are, admittedly, somewhat different if the renewed reference to an event is connected with the revision or addition of information, thereby giving us access to previously "overlooked" aspects or a version that supersedes a prior "unreliable" presentation. An example of the first case is Gal 4:9a, where μᾶλλον δέ introduces a reformulation, indicating that the event of getting to know God is more accurately portrayed as an event of being recognized by him (νῦν δὲ γνόντες θεόν, μᾶλλον δὲ γνωσθέντες ὑπὸ θεοῦ . . .).[113] An example of the second situation appears right after that in Gal 4:9b–11, where Paul uses questions to cast doubt on the story as he had presented it so far.[114]

---

112. On the topic of repeated explicit narrations within the same conversation, see Vivien Heller, Miriam Morek, and Uta M. Quasthoff, "Mehrfaches Erzählen: Warum wird eine Geschichte im selben Gespräch zweimal erzählt?," in *Wiedererzählen: Formen und Funktionen einer kulturellen Praxis*, ed. Elke Schumann, Elisabeth Gülich, Gabriele Lucius-Hoene, and Stefan Pfänder, Edition Kulturwissenschaft 50 (Bielefeld: Transcript, 2015), 341–67, who offer a nuanced answer to the question: "Why is a story told twice in the same conversation?" (German: "Warum wird eine Geschichte im selben Gespräch zweimal erzählt?"). Cf. also generally Heilig, *Paulus*, chapter 3, section 4.2, on the distinction between renarration and repetitive narration. Cf. also Heilig, *Paulus*, chapter 9, section 5.4.1, and chapter 16, section 3, on the relationship between Gal 4:3–6 and Gal 4:8–9.

113. On μᾶλλον δέ, see above, pp. 221–22.

114. For a detailed analysis of the complex protonarrative behind Gal 4:8–12, see Heilig, *Paulus*, chapter 9, section 5.4.

Chapter 5

Finally, we must note that the option of repetitive narration can also occur with a modification, presenting us with a choice among three possible explanations for how the mention of the same event at different locations in Paul's letters might relate to Paul's (mentally simulated) storytelling activity. Specifically, I am referring to the possibility that Paul might discuss the same time frame multiple times because his (mental) story portrays an action that can be differentiated into a *multitude of relatively independent storylines* that follow different figures, who just happen to experience different things at the same time or to partake in the same larger event. In other words, different conceptualizations of roughly the same happening at various points in Paul's letters may indeed point to a protonarrative in the background whose plot may necessitate a description in terms of several distinct storylines to accurately capture its complex action.[115]

Given these considerations, it becomes clear that the quest for Pauline protonarratives is indeed an intricate undertaking. To facilitate such research, I would like to propose two guiding principles. First, it seems prudent to step back from a focus on specific narrative figures and to orient the analysis initially toward the *textual order*. In other words, the first step should involve noting the events as they appear in the text and then considering to what extent they could represent a protonarrative in the background.[116] Only subsequently should we investigate the *roles* played by specific narrative figures featured in such a story.[117]

Second, I believe more attention must be directed toward the *connections* between events as they manifest within individual fragments. These connections offer valuable clues regarding how Paul conceived of the relationships between certain events, thereby shedding light on the kind of plot he aimed to convey. After all, to evaluate, for instance, the plausibility of Wright's specific proposal of three storylines as a representation of the content of Paul's worldview narrative, merely identifying the *events* that fea-

---

115. Cf. Heilig, *Paulus*, chapter 17, section 4.2.4.

116. In other words, there is a place for Petersen's "poetic sequence"—the issue is only that it should not immediately be transformed into a referential sequence that gets rid of the element of the order of narration. Plus, neither of these two sequences can simply be equated directly with "Paul's story." Moreover, we may ultimately decide that there are *several* independent poetic or referential sequences within a single letter, each being part of a distinct act of (proto)narration.

117. Cf. Heilig, *Paulus*, chapter 17, section 4.1.

ture in Wright's plot description is insufficient.[118] The adversaries with whom Paul engages in Gal 3 arguably also discuss the same events in their narrative, yet their communicated plot appears to be remarkably different in shape. Consequently, future contributions to the discussion that seek to evaluate Wright's proposal must focus on the narrative relationships between events that Wright attributes to different storylines. Are there narrative fragments in which humanity is depicted as part of creation as a whole, fulfilling the role that Wright ascribes to humans in Paul's cosmic vision? Do we encounter clusters of events concerning Israel where God's people are said to have the alleged role with respect to humanity as a whole? And do references to Jesus's actions suggest that he is part of such a story of Israel (and, therefore, of humanity and, by extension, of all creation)?

A Dynamically Evolving Master Narrative?

All that has been discussed thus far could be interpreted as suggesting that Wright's entire endeavor has minimal prospects for success, given the numerous hurdles that must be cleared to construct a convincing argument and to negate alternative interpretations. Nevertheless, I wish to conclude this chapter by introducing one factor that could eventually serve to vindicate Wright—although it would necessitate refining our understanding of what it means for Paul's theology to originate from a single guiding act of narration and, consequently, one cohesive worldview narrative. We must concede, in favor of Wright's general hypothesis, that the mere identification of two narrative fragments as originating from different acts of narration is not, in itself, a counterpoint against the supposition that these narratives can ultimately be *traced back* to a singular worldview narrative that underlies Paul's theological thought.

After all, the notion that Paul consistently had his original protonarrative in mind every time he composed one of the narrative fragments we encounter in his letters is just one possibility that aligns well with Wright's general framework. There could also be other less apparent, organic ties between the initial guiding act of narration and subsequent narrative acts. In the following discussion, I will explore two possibilities: the first serves as an alternative to Wright's conceptualization of this original guiding act of narration, while the second simply introduces an additional layer to the sce-

---

118. On this first critical consideration, cf. Heilig, *Paulus*, chapter 17, section 5.7.

Chapter 5

nario we have outlined thus far in our narratological elaboration of Wright's proposal.

First, we should remain open to the idea that the process leading to the formation of Paul's presumably unified worldview narrative may have taken some time, possibly evolving in tandem with his missionary activities.[119] After all, even if we assume that Paul's worldview remained relatively stable throughout his life—at least in terms of its narrative shape, thereby rejecting various theses about supposed shifts in his thinking (e.g., regarding eschatology and the role of Israel)[120]—it does not necessarily follow that each narrative fragment we later find in Paul's letters can be traced back to an original, fully formed protonarrative that existed prior to his gospel proclamation.

On the contrary, it appears highly plausible that, due to specific circumstances, Paul may have revisited and revised his worldview narrative at a later stage, irrespective of how comprehensively he might have initially formulated it, perhaps during his time in the wilderness. While conceding that the apostle did not fundamentally alter the plot of this story, we might still anticipate that he would increasingly emphasize certain episodes as time progressed, elaborating on them in greater detail (cf. perhaps Rom 9–11). Alternatively, he might indeed have concluded that some sequences of events needed to be articulated differently (cf. perhaps the chronological argument in Gal 3:15–17, which appears to be more nuanced in Rom 4:9–12).[121]

Interestingly, an article by Richard B. Hays, which at first glance does indeed seem to confirm that in his later writings Hays closely aligns with Wright's approach, takes this idea a step further.[122] It proposes an *alternative* understanding of Paul's guiding act of mental narration, accentuating the influence of Paul's specific mission circumstances and, consequently, diminishing the role of any foundational guiding narrative.[123]

When Paul in 1 Cor 10:1 refers to the exodus generation as "our fathers," even though he is addressing a largely gentile audience (οἱ πατέρες ἡμῶν

---

119. Cf. Heilig, *Paulus*, chapter 17, section 5.6.2.

120. Cf., e.g., Udo Schnelle, *Wandlungen im paulinischen Denken*, SBS 137 (Stuttgart: Katholisches Bibelwerk, 1989).

121. On this, cf. James D. G. Dunn, *A Commentary on the Epistle to the Galatians*, BNTC (London: Continuum, 1993), 182–83.

122. Richard B. Hays, "The Conversion of the Imagination: Scripture and Eschatology in 1 Corinthians," *NTS* 45 (1999): 391–412. It is reprinted as the first chapter in Richard B. Hays, *The Conversion of the Imagination: Paul as Interpreter of Israel's Scripture* (Grand Rapids: Eerdmans, 2005).

123. For a detailed analysis, see Heilig, *Paulus*, chapter 15, section 4.5.1.

πάντες ὑπὸ τὴν νεφέλην ἦσαν καὶ πάντες διὰ τῆς θαλάσσης διῆλθον), he indeed incorporates his readers as narrative characters into this Jewish story. Up to this point, we are still in Wrightian territory. However, it seems to me that Hays does not view this as an indicator of prior awareness of living within a unified narrative that links Jewish ancestors and gentile converts. Instead, what is fundamental in Hays's perspective is Paul's conviction about the eschatological place of the church, "within an apocalyptic narrative that locates present existence in the interval between cross and parousia."[124] It is on this basis that "*all* the scriptural narratives and promises must be understood to point forward to the crucial eschatological moment in which he and his churches now find themselves."[125] Whether or not Paul has already (mentally) retold the explicit stories of Scripture with a focus on the church is thus an entirely secondary question. What is pivotal is that he has adopted a hermeneutical lens that holds the potential to allow him to reread Scripture in a manner that aligns with his current circumstances. Accordingly, in Hays's view, the way Paul links the Corinthians to the exodus generation is not so much indicative of an underlying worldview narrative. Instead, the emphasis is on the pragmatics of this connection, on a "metaphorical leap" that Paul encourages. In other words, what is central is the invitation extended *to the readers*—to embark on a journey of "an imaginative projection of their lives into the framework of the Pentateuchal narrative."[126]

Extrapolating from this case study, we might conclude that when considering Paul's theological reimagination of reality in terms of protonarratives, it may be more fruitful not to approach this subject through the lens of a supposedly monolithic guiding narrative. Even if he does approach individual situations with such a narrative in mind, we must entertain the possibility that it could exhibit significant flexibility. The apostle may have no qualms about modifying this narrative based on new experiences, thereby allowing for unexpected additions, fresh interpretations of Scripture, and extensions to the story. If Hays is correct, the essence of Paul's thinking does not lie in a rigid worldview narrative.[127] Instead, the interpretation of Scripture as

---

124. Hays, "Scripture," 21, with reference to 1 Cor 11:26.
125. Hays, "Scripture," 11. Italics added.
126. Hays, "Scripture," 10.
127. Wright's method seems to presuppose that the category of "story" is always equally important for worldviews. Given that the different symptoms on whose basis one might reconstruct a worldview are not always equally accessible, one might raise the question of whether this might not be due to, for example, "story" sometimes indeed playing a less central role than "practice" or "questions and answers." In other words,

Chapter 5

well as engagement with "ancestral traditions" in general would *themselves* constitute "particular circumstances," which Paul brings into dialogue with this core.[128] This process would not differ fundamentally from how this core functions as a hermeneutic framework for integrating other facets of Paul's missionary experiences.

Renarrations of Story lines of the Original Worldview Narrative

Second, if we are inclined toward the idea that Paul's entire mission is built on a solid narrative foundation, there is still room for reconciling the primacy of this original guiding act of narration with the possibility that Paul in his letters appears to begin anew several times with his storytelling, without merely reproducing snippets from a preexisting story.[129]

Particularly in cases where he addresses the same situation multiple times in different parts of his letters, it is difficult to see how these could simply reflect various facets of a single story. One would need to argue that an all-encompassing narrative exists in the background, and that while different elements are omitted on various occasions, they are nevertheless always presupposed—a presupposition that many are unlikely to accept.[130]

However, what may come to Wright's rescue is that we should certainly not deny Paul the abilities that we claim to possess ourselves.[131] If *we* find it possible to extract plots from Pauline narratives and protonarratives, this abstracting operation was naturally also available to *Paul himself*. And indeed, as we have observed, for instance, in relation to Rom 11:17–24, Paul demonstrates a propensity for such interpretative assessments of his own stories (cf. above, pp. 290–300). Similarly, if we consider ourselves capable of presenting reconstructed plots in narrative form—a capability I have

---

Wright seems to assume an irreducibly narrative character of worldviews, and this might cause him to prioritize this aspect in the analysis of specific texts unduly. Cf. Heilig and Heilig, "Historical Methodology," 142–44.

128. On the quest for the "core" of Paul's theology, see Richard B. Hays, *The Faith of Jesus Christ: The Narrative Substructure of Galatians 3:1–4:11*, SBLDS 56 (Atlanta: Society of Biblical Literature, 1983), 1–9. Cf. p. 1 on the phrase "particular circumstances."

129. On the rather brief suggestions that follow, cf. also the quite fundamental contributions in Elke Schumann, Elisabeth Gülich, Gabriele Lucius-Hoene, and Stefan Pfänder, eds., *Wiedererzählen: Formen und Funktionen einer kulturellen Praxis*, Edition Kulturwissenschaft 50 (Bielefeld: Transcript, 2015).

130. See Heilig, *Paulus*, chapter 17, section 5.8.2.

131. On what follows, cf. Heilig, *Paulus*, chapter 17, section 5.8.4.

assumed at various points throughout this book—why should we not also attribute to Paul the ability to renarrativize the convictions that emerged in his mind from contemplating the implications of his own protonarrative?

In other words, we are by no means forced to assume that what seem to be quite independent miniature stories necessarily replaced the original guiding protonarrative, eradicating it completely. Paul might, for example, have chosen at times to focus on one of the three subplots that Wright has postulated, *transforming it into a narrative of its own*, without, however, this detracting in any way from the validity of the larger story as such.

To illustrate this dynamic, it is worth taking a closer look at Gal 1:4.[132] According to Wright, the overall plot of Paul's worldview narrative encompasses the following series of events:

The creation of the world
The creation of humanity
The problem of Sin
The promise to Abraham
Israel's inability to fulfill her mission
The deeds and fate of Jesus
The restoration of Israel and salvation of humanity
The glorification of the world

Given this schema, can we consider Gal 1:4 as a fragment of a larger protonarrative that encompasses these events? Furthermore, can we discern the intricate relationships among these events that Wright presumes—relationships that enable him to identify several subplots within the comprehensive narrative?

At first glance, Gal 1:4 seems to directly address the problem of sin, the deeds and fate of Jesus, and the salvation of humanity. It is plausible to assert that the outermost events—creation and new creation—are implicitly present in this verse. However, the connection between Jesus and the human storyline, pivotal in Wright's interpretation, is not so readily apparent. There is no evident role for Abraham and Israel in this verse, which casts doubt on whether Jesus, in this context, is portrayed as the faithful Israelite.

However, proponents of Wright's view might justifiably point to the possibility of "retelling the same story" or, more accurately, repeatedly referencing a larger protonarrative in fresh narrative utterances. In support of

---

132. On what follows, cf. Heilig, *Paulus*, 984–85.

Chapter 5

this view, one might note that Jesus is introduced in Gal 1:3 as "the Lord Jesus Christ" (κύριος Ἰησοῦς Χριστός). If we interpret Χριστός as "Messiah" (as Wright does) and conceive of the concept of people's representation as central to Paul's messianism (also a view Wright holds), it could be argued that Israel's storyline is indeed presupposed when Paul writes Gal 1:4.[133]

Alternatively, diverging slightly from Wright's conception but still upholding the centrality of a guiding act of narration for Paul's theology, we might posit that this verse exemplifies Paul's tendency to condense his all-encompassing protonarrative into a main plot, with the extent to which the omission of certain elements implies lesser importance for the plot of the original worldview narrative remaining debatable.

Note that this does not mean we need to supply the rest of this expansive story for the interpretation of each of these smaller, condensed renarrations. In fact, we might distort what Paul is saying by including aspects that Paul explicitly wanted to exclude at that point.[134] The situation is similar to a modern author who writes a cover text for one of their books and, for this purpose, focuses on the main storyline. Here too, this smaller narrative needs to be read on its own. Still, the larger narrative might retain its primacy to some extent.

From the perspective of a *historian*, it is, of course, of interest to determine which preconditions gave rise to the smaller narrative. Especially if we try to locate Paul tradition-historically, this might be a valuable line of inquiry—though, I would argue, we then move beyond exegesis proper (cf. the comments on interpretation in chapter 1). Likewise, a *systematic theologian* might wish to inquire to what extent the shorter version is theologically coherent only when read against the backdrop of the larger framework. For the enterprise of "narrative theology," such considerations might thus also be of value.

Where do we stand at the end of this chapter with respect to Wright's bold proposal about Paul's worldview narrative? I do not think he has success-

---

133. For a work on the interpretation of Χριστός that is largely supportive of Wright's understanding, cf. Matthew V. Novenson, *Christ among the Messiahs: Christ Language in Paul and Messiah Language in Ancient Judaism* (Oxford: Oxford University Press, 2012). On the debate, see also Aquila H. I. Lee, "Messianism and Messiah in Paul: Christ as Jesus?," in Heilig, Hewitt, and Bird, *God and the Faithfulness of Paul*, 375–92. On the latter point, see the evaluation by J. Thomas Hewitt and Matthew V. Novenson, "Participationism and Messiah Christology in Paul," 393–415 in the same volume.

134. On the possibility that parts of the original story are omitted even though the narrator is well aware of them at the time of the new utterance, cf. also Heilig, *Paulus*, chapter 17, section 5.8.3.

fully demonstrated that we can discern a single unified worldview narrative behind all of the apostle's letters. Properly understood, such a task is indeed daunting; we would first need to analyze the narratives and protonarratives of individual letters, assessing to what extent a synthesis is even possible on such a limited basis. The narratological commentary on Galatians on which I am currently working is produced with the intention in mind of trying to offer a first building block toward such a task.[135] Moreover, my suspicion is that in pursuing this elusive unified worldview narrative, we will have to make some concessions regarding its genesis and accessibility. These concessions may ultimately prevent us from speaking as definitively about its contours as Wright prefers.

Still, it seems highly likely to me that Paul made new sense of his world by integrating his experience of Christ and the Spirit, along with his various encounters with people and the traditions he had grown up with, into a mental protonarrative. Likewise, we must account for the very real possibility that he continued to reflect upon this story, offering us at least fleeting glimpses of how it evolved over time. Therefore, in my opinion, Wright's proposal, much like Hays's, has the potential to exert a significant heuristic influence on our field. The story of the narrative—pardon me, narratological—approach has only just begun.

---

135. For now, readers may consult Heilig, *Paulus*, 1013 n. 1, where I assemble the most important discussions of passages from Galatians in textual order.

Bibliography

Adams, Edward. "Paul's Story of God and Creation: The Story of How God Fulfils His Purposes in Creation." Pages 19–43 in *Narrative Dynamics in Paul: A Critical Assessment*. Edited by Bruce W. Longenecker. Louisville: Westminster John Knox, 2002.
Altman, Janet Gurkin. *Epistolarity: Approaches to a Form*. Columbus: Ohio State University Press, 1982.
Arzt-Grabner, Peter. *Philemon*. Papyrologische Kommentare zum Neuen Testament 1. Göttingen: Vandenhoeck & Ruprecht, 2003.
———. "Why Did Early Christ Groups Still Attend Idol Meals? Answers from Papyrus Invitations." *EC* 7 (2016): 508–29.
Aubrey, Michael G. "Greek Prohibitions." Pages 486–538 in *The Greek Verb Revisited: A Fresh Approach for Biblical Exegesis*. Edited by Steven E. Runge and Christopher J. Fresch. Bellingham, WA: Lexham, 2016.
———. "Linguistic Issues in Biblical Greek." Pages 161–89 in *Linguistic and Biblical Exegesis*. Edited by Douglas Mangum and Josh Westbury. Lexham Methods Series 2. Bellingham, WA: Lexham, 2017.
Aubrey, Rachel. "Motivated Categories, Middle Voice, and Passive Morphology." Pages 563–625 in *The Greek Verb Revisited: A Fresh Approach for Biblical Exegesis*. Edited by Steven E. Runge and Christopher J. Fresch. Bellingham, WA: Lexham, 2016.
Aumüller, Matthias. "Text Types." The Living Handbook of Narratology, March 6, 2014. https://www-archiv.fdm.uni-hamburg.de/lhn/node/121.html.
Bache, Carl. "Aspect and Aktionsart: Towards a Semantic Distinction." *Journal of Linguistics* 18 (1982): 57–72.
Barclay, John M. G. *Paul and the Gift*. Grand Rapids: Eerdmans, 2015.
———. "Paul's Story." Pages 133–56 in *Narrative Dynamics in Paul: A Critical Assessment*. Edited by Bruce W. Longenecker. Louisville: Westminster John Knox, 2002.

Bibliography

———. Review of *Paul and the Faithfulness of God*, by N. T. Wright. *SJT* 68 (2015): 235–43.

Barrett, C. K. *From First Adam to Last: A Study in Pauline Theology*. London: Black, 1962.

Bartolo, Giuseppina di. *Studien zur griechischen Syntax der dokumentarischen Papyri*. Sonderreihe der Abhandlungen Papyrologica Coloniensia 44. Leiden: Brill, 2020.

Beard, Mary. *The Roman Triumph*. Cambridge: Harvard University Press, 2007.

Berger, Klaus. *Formen und Gattungen im Neuen Testament*. Uni-Taschenbücher 2532. Tübingen: Francke, 2005.

Betz, Hans Dieter. *Galatians: A Commentary on Paul's Letter to the Churches in Galatia*. Hermeneia. Philadelphia: Fortress, 1979.

Bird, Michael F. *Romans*. The Story of God Bible Commentary. Grand Rapids: Zondervan, 2016.

Bollier, David. *Liberty and Justice for Some: Defending a Free Society from the Radical Right's Holy War on Democracy*. Washington, DC: People for the American Way, 1982.

Bormann, Lukas. *Bibelkunde: Altes und Neues Testament*. 4th ed. Uni-Taschenbücher Basics. Göttingen: Vandenhoeck & Ruprecht, 2011.

Breindl, Eva. "Additiv basierte Konnektoren." Pages 393–588 in *Semantik der deutschen Satzverknüpfer*. Edited by Eva Breindl, Anna Volodina, and Ulrich Hermann Waßner. Vol. 2 of *Handbuch der deutschen Konnektoren*. Schriften des Instituts für Deutsche Sprache 13. Berlin: de Gruyter, 2014.

———. "Die semantische Klassifikation der Konnektoren des Deutschen." Pages 239–51 in *Semantik der deutschen Satzverknüpfer*. Edited by Eva Breindl, Anna Volodina, and Ulrich Hermann Waßner. Vol. 2 of *Handbuch der deutschen Konnektoren*. Schriften des Instituts für Deutsche Sprache 13. Berlin: de Gruyter, 2014.

———. "Das Zusammenspiel von syntaktischer und semantischer Struktur in Konnektorkonstruktionen." Pages 53–78 in *Semantik der deutschen Satzverknüpfer*. Edited by Eva Breindl, Anna Volodina, and Ulrich Hermann Waßner. Vol. 2 of *Handbuch der deutschen Konnektoren*. Schriften des Instituts für Deutsche Sprache 13. Berlin: de Gruyter, 2014.

———. "Grundbegriffe der Beschreibung und Prinzipien der Bedeutungskonstitution." Pages 120–36 in *Semantik der deutschen Satzverknüpfer*. Edited by Eva Breindl, Anna Volodina, and Ulrich Hermann Waßner. Vol. 2 of *Handbuch der deutschen Konnektoren*. Schriften des Instituts für Deutsche Sprache 13. Berlin: de Gruyter, 2014.

———. "Temporale Konnektoren." Pages 274–389 in *Semantik der deutschen*

Bibliography

Satzverknüpfer. Edited by Eva Breindl, Anna Volodina, and Ulrich Hermann Waßner. Vol. 2 of *Handbuch der deutschen Konnektoren*. Schriften des Instituts für Deutsche Sprache 13. Berlin: de Gruyter, 2014.

Breindl, Eva, Anna Volodina, and Ulrich Hermann Waßner, eds. *Semantik der deutschen Satzverknüpfer*. Volume 2 of *Handbuch der deutschen Konnektoren*. Schriften des Instituts für Deutsche Sprache 13. Berlin: de Gruyter, 2014.

Breytenbach, Cilliers. "Paul's Proclamation and God's 'Thriambos': Notes on 2 Corinthians 2:14–16b." *Neot* 24 (1990): 257–71.

Brinker, Klaus. *Linguistische Textanalyse: Eine Einführung in die Grundbegriffe und Methoden*. 3rd ed. Grundlagen der Germanistik 29. Berlin: Schmidt, 1992.

Burton, Ernest D. *Syntax of the Moods and Tenses in New Testament Greek*. 3rd ed. Chicago: University of Chicago Press, 1898.

Buth, Randall. "Participles as a Pragmatic Choice: Where Semantics Meets Pragmatics." Pages 273–306 in *The Greek Verb Revisited: A Fresh Approach for Biblical Exegesis*. Edited by Steven E. Runge and Christopher J. Fresch. Bellingham, WA: Lexham, 2016.

Campbell, Douglas A. "The Story of Jesus in Romans and Galatians." Pages 97–124 in *Narrative Dynamics in Paul: A Critical Assessment*. Edited by Bruce W. Longenecker. Louisville: Westminster John Knox, 2002.

Caragounis, Chrys C. *The Development of Greek and the New Testament: Morphology, Syntax, Phonology, and Textual Transmission*. WUNT 167. Tübingen: Mohr Siebeck, 2004.

Carroll, Noël. *Beyond Aesthetics: Philosophical Essays*. Cambridge: Cambridge University Press, 2001.

Casscells, Ward, Arno Schoenberger, and Thomas B. Graboys. "Interpretation by Physicians of Clinical Laboratory Results." *New England Journal of Medicine* 299 (1978): 999–1000.

Clifton, James. "The Limits of 'Mute Theology': Charles Le Brun's Lecture on Nicolas Poussin's *Ecstasy of Saint Paul* Revisited." Pages 580–605 in *Quid est sacramentum? Visual Representation of Sacred Mysteries in Early Modern Europe, 1400–1700*. Edited by Walter Melion, Elizabeth Carson Pastan, and Lee Palmer Wandel. Intersections 65.1. Leiden: Brill, 2020.

Cranfield, C. E. B. *The Epistle to the Romans*. 2 vols. ICC. Edinburgh: T&T Clark, 1975, 1979.

Currie, Gregory, and Ian Ravenscroft. *Recreative Minds: Imagination in Philosophy and Psychology*. Oxford: Clarendon, 2010.

Dancygier, Barbara, and Eve Sweetser, eds. *Viewpoint in Language: A Multimodal Perspective*. Cambridge: Cambridge University Press, 2012.

Bibliography

Dinkler, Michal Beth. "Influence: On Rhetoric and Biblical Interpretation." *Brill Research Perspectives in Biblical Interpretation* 4 (2001): 1–105.

———. *Literary Theory and the New Testament*. Anchor Bible Research Library. New Haven: Yale University Press, 2019.

———. "New Testament Rhetorical Narratology: An Invitation Toward Integration." *BibInt* 24 (2016): 203–28.

Dragutinović, Predrag, Tobias Nicklas, Kelsie G. Rodenbiker, and Vladan Tatalović, eds. *Christ of the Sacred Stories*. WUNT 2.453. Tübingen: Mohr Siebeck, 2017.

Dunn, James D. G. *A Commentary on the Epistle to the Galatians*. BNTC. London: Continuum, 1993.

Ensor, Jonathan B. *Paul and the Corinthians: Leadership, Ordeals, and the Politics of Displacement*. LNTS 652. London: Bloomsbury, 2022.

Eskola, Timo. *A Narrative Theology of the New Testament: Exploring the Metanarrative of Exile and Restoration*. WUNT 350. Tübingen: Mohr Siebeck, 2015.

Evans, Trevor V. "Another Ghost: The Greek Epistolary Perfect." *Glotta* 75 (1999): 194–221.

Fee, Gordon D. *The First Epistle to the Corinthians*. NICNT. Grand Rapids: Eerdmans, 1987.

Finnern, Sönke. *Narratologie und biblische Exegese: Eine integrative Methode der Erzählanalyse und ihr Ertrag am Beispiel von Matthäus 28*. WUNT 2.285. Tübingen: Mohr Siebeck, 2010.

Finnern, Sönke, and Jan Rüggemeier. *Methoden der neutestamentlichen Exegese: Ein Lehr- und Arbeitsbuch*. Uni-Taschenbücher 4212. Tübingen: Francke, 2016.

Fisher, Walter R. "Narration as a Human Communication Paradigm: The Case of Public Moral Argument." *Communication Monographs* 51 (1984): 1–22.

———. "The Narrative Paradigm: An Elaboration." *Communication Monographs* 52 (1985): 347–67.

Fresch, Christopher J. *Discourse Markers in Early Koine Greek: Cognitive-Functional Analysis and LXX Translation Technique*. Septuagint and Cognate Studies 77. Atlanta: SBL Press, 2023.

———. "Discourse Markers in the Septuagint and Early Koine Greek with Special Reference to the Twelve." PhD diss., University of Cambridge, 2015.

Gansel, Christina, and Frank Jürgens. *Textlinguistik und Textgrammatik*. 3rd ed. Uni-Taschenbücher 3265. Göttingen: Vandenhoeck & Ruprecht, 2009.

Genette, Gérard. *Narrative Discourse: An Essay in Method*. Translated by Jane E. Lewin. Foreword by Jonathan Culler. Ithaca: Cornell University Press, 1980.

Bibliography

———. *Palimpsests: Literature in the Second Degree*. Translated by Channa Newman and Claude Doubinsky. Foreword by Gerald Prince. Lincoln: University of Nebraska Press, 1997.

———. *Paratexts: Thresholds of Interpretation*. Translated by Jane E. Lewin. Cambridge: Cambridge University Press, 1997.

Georgakopoulou, Alexandra. "Same Old Story? On the Interactional Dynamics of Shared Narratives." Pages 223–41 in *Narrative Interaction*. Edited by Uta M. Quasthoff and Tabea Becker. Studies in Narrative 5. Amsterdam: Benjamins, 2005.

Gülich, Elisabeth, and Heiko Hausendorf. "Vertextungsmuster Narration." Pages 369–85 in vol. 1 of *Text- und Gesprächslinguistik / Linguistics of Text and Conversation*. Edited by Gerd Antos, Klaus Bringer, Wolfgang Heinemann, and Sven F. Sager. Handbücher zur Sprach und Kommunikationswissenschaft / Handbooks of Linguistics and Communication Science 16. Berlin: de Gruyter, 2000–2001.

Guthrie, George H. "Paul's Triumphal Procession Imagery (2 Cor 2.14–16a): Neglected Points of Background." *NTS* 61 (2015): 79–91.

Hays, Richard B. *The Conversion of the Imagination: Paul as Interpreter of Israel's Scripture*. Grand Rapids: Eerdmans, 2005.

———. "The Conversion of the Imagination: Scripture and Eschatology in 1 Corinthians." *NTS* 45 (1999): 391–412.

———. *Echoes of Scripture in the Letters of Paul*. New Haven: Yale University Press: 1989.

———. *The Faith of Jesus Christ: The Narrative Substructure of Galatians 3:1–4:11*. SBLDS 56. Atlanta: Society of Biblical Literature, 1983. Repr., Grand Rapids: Eerdmans, 2002.

———. "Introduction to the Second Edition." Pages xxi–lii in Richard B. Hays, *The Faith of Jesus Christ: The Narrative Substructure of Galatians 3:1–4:11*. Foreword by Luke Timothy Johnson. 2nd ed. The Biblical Resource Series. Grand Rapids: Eerdmans, 2002.

Heilig, Christoph. *The Apostle and the Empire: Paul's Implicit and Explicit Criticism of Rome*. Grand Rapids: Eerdmans, 2022.

———. "Counter-Narratives in Galatians." Pages 171–90 in *Scripture, Texts, and Tracings in Galatians and 1 Thessalonians*. Edited by A. Andrew Das and B. J. Oropeza. Lanham, MD: Lexington, 2023.

———. *Hidden Criticism? The Methodology and Plausibility of the Search for a Counter-Imperial Subtext in Paul*. 2nd ed. Minneapolis: Fortress, 2017.

———. "The New Perspective (on Paul) on Peter: How the Philosophy of Historiography Can Help in Understanding Earliest Christianity." Pages 459–

Bibliography

595 in *Christian Origins and the Establishment of the Early Jesus Movement*. Edited by Stanley E. Porter and Andrew W. Pitts. Christian Origins and Greco-Roman Culture 4. Leiden: Brill, 2018.

———. *Paul's Triumph: Reassessing 2 Corinthians 2:14 in Its Literary and Historical Context*. BTS 27. Leuven: Peeters, 2017.

———. *Paulus als Erzähler? Eine narratologische Perspektive auf die Paulusbriefe*. BZNW 237. Berlin: de Gruyter, 2020.

———. "Zeit im Verhältnis: Narratologische und linguistische Perspektiven." In *Zeit und Ewigkeit: Ein Lehrbuch*. Edited by Benjamin Schliesser, Jan Rüggemeier, and Michael Jost. Uni-Taschenbücher. Tübingen: Mohr Siebeck, in press.

Heilig, Theresa, and Christoph Heilig. "Historical Methodology." Pages 115–50 in *God and the Faithfulness of Paul: A Critical Examination of the Pauline Theology of N. T. Wright*. Edited by Christoph Heilig, J. Thomas Hewitt, and Michael F. Bird. WUNT 2.413. Tübingen: Mohr Siebeck, 2016.

———. "Teaching Biblical Exegesis: The Distinction between Methods of Description and Interpretation." Forthcoming from *Didaktikos*.

Heller, Vivien, Miriam Morek, and Uta M. Quasthoff. "Mehrfaches Erzählen: Warum wird eine Geschichte im selben Gespräch zweimal erzählt?" Pages 341–67 in *Wiedererzählen: Formen und Funktionen einer kulturellen Praxis*. Edited by Elke Schumann, Elisabeth Gülich, Gabriele Lucius-Hoene, and Stefan Pfänder. Edition Kulturwissenschaft 50. Bielefeld: Transcript, 2015.

Hewitt, J. Thomas, and Matthew V. Novenson. "Participationism and Messiah Christology in Paul." Pages 393–415 in *God and the Faithfulness of Paul: A Critical Examination of the Pauline Theology of N. T. Wright*. Edited by Christoph Heilig, J. Thomas Hewitt, and Michael F. Bird. WUNT 2.413. Tübingen: Mohr Siebeck, 2016.

Horrell, David G. "Paul's Narratives or Narrative Substructure? The Significance of 'Paul's Story.'" Pages 157–71 in *Narrative Dynamics in Paul: A Critical Assessment*. Edited by Bruce W. Longenecker. Louisville: Westminster John Knox, 2002.

Hunt, Cherryl, David G. Horrell, and Christopher Southgate. "An Environmental Mantra? Ecological Interest in Romans 8:19–23 and a Modest Proposal for Its Narrative Interpretation." *JTS* 59 (2008): 546–79.

Jacobi, Christine. *Jesusüberlieferung bei Paulus? Analogien zwischen den echten Paulusbriefen und den synoptischen Evangelien*. BZNW 213. Berlin: de Gruyter, 2015.

Bibliography

Jong, Irene J. F. de. *Narratology and Classics: A Practical Guide*. Oxford: Oxford University Press, 2014.

Joss, Matthew B. *Weighing Interpretations in Science, Biblical Studies, and Life: The Quest for the Best Explanation*. Lanham, MD: Lexington, 2023.

Käsemann, Ernst. *Exegetische Versuche und Besinnungen*. 5th ed. Göttingen: Vandenhoeck & Ruprecht, 1967.

Kindt, Tom, and Hans-Harald Müller. "Narrative Theory and/or/as Theory of Interpretation." Pages 205–19 in *What Is Narratology? Questions and Answers Regarding the Status of a Theory*. Edited by Tom Kindt and Hans-Harald Müller. Narratologia 1. Berlin: de Gruyter, 2003.

―――. "Wieviel Interpretation enthalten Beschreibungen? Überlegungen zu einer umstrittenen Unterscheidung am Beispiel der Narratologie." Pages 286–304 in *Regeln der Bedeutung: Zur Theorie der Bedeutung literarischer Texte*. Edited by Fotis Jannidis, Gerhard Lauer, Matías Martínez, and Simone Winko. Revisionen 1. Berlin: de Gruyter, 2003.

Köppe, Tilmann, and Tom Kindt. *Erzähltheorie: Eine Einführung*. Reclams Universal-Bibliothek 17683. Stuttgart: Reclam, 2014.

―――. *Erzähltheorie: Eine Einführung*. 2nd ed. Reclams Studienbuch: Germanistik. Stuttgart: Reclam, 2022.

Kreinecker, Christina M. *2. Thessaloniker. Mit einem Beitrag von Günther Schwab*. Papyrologischer Kommentar zum Neuen Testament 3. Göttingen: Vandenhoeck & Ruprecht, 2010.

Lämmert, Eberhard. *Bauformen des Erzählens*. 7th ed. Stuttgart: Metzler, 1980.

Lee, Aquila, H. I. "Messianism and Messiah in Paul: Christ as Jesus?" Pages 375–92 in *God and the Faithfulness of Paul: A Critical Examination of the Pauline Theology of N. T. Wright*. Edited by Christoph Heilig, J. Thomas Hewitt, and Michael F. Bird. WUNT 2.413. Tübingen: Mohr Siebeck, 2016.

Lee, Jae Hyun. "Richard B. Hays and a Narrative Approach to the Pauline Letters." Pages 2:421–40 in *Pillars in the History of Biblical Interpretation*. Edited by Stanley E. Porter and Sean A. Adams. McMaster Biblical Studies Series 2. Eugene, OR: Wipf & Stock, 2016.

Löbner, Sebastian. *Understanding Semantics*. 2nd ed. Understanding Language Series. New York: Routledge, 2013.

Longacre, Robert E., and Shin Ja J. Hwang. *Holistic Discourse Analysis*. 2nd ed. Dallas: SIL International, 2012.

Longenecker, Bruce. "Narrative Interest in the Study of Paul: Retrospective and Prospective." Pages 3–16 in *Narrative Dynamics in Paul: A Critical*

Bibliography

Assessment. Edited by Bruce W. Longenecker. Louisville: Westminster John Knox, 2002.

Mann, Thomas. "Railway Accident." Pages 6–16 in *The Story: A Critical Anthology*. Translated by Helen Tracy Lowe-Porter. Edited by Mark Schorer. Englewood Cliffs: Prentice Hall, 1950.

Mauz, Andreas. "Theologie und Narration: Beobachtungen zur 'Narrative Theologie'-Debatte—und über sie hinaus." Pages 41–66 in *Textwelt—Lebenswelt*. Edited by Brigitte Boothe, Pierre Bühler, Paul Michel, and Philipp Stoellger. Interpretation Interdisziplinär 10. Wurzburg: Königshausen & Neumann, 2012.

Mayordomo, Moisés. *Argumentiert Paulus logisch? Eine Analyse vor dem Hintergrund antiker Logik*. WUNT 188. Tübingen: Mohr Siebeck, 2005.

———. *Den Anfang hören: Leseorientierte Evangelienexegese am Beispiel von Matthäus 1–2*. FRLANT 180. Göttingen: Vandenhoeck & Ruprecht, 1998.

———. "Exegese zwischen Geschichte, Text und Rezeption: Literaturwissenschaftliche Zugänge zum Neuen Testament." *VF* 55 (2010): 19–37.

———. "Rezeptionsästhetische Analyse." Pages 417–39 in *Das Studium des Neuen Testaments*. Edited by Heinz-Werner Neudorfer and Eckhard J. Schnabel. Rev. ed. Wuppertal: Brockhaus, 2006.

Metzger, Bruce M. *A Textual Commentary on the Greek New Testament*. 2nd ed. Stuttgart: Deutsche Bibelgesellschaft, 1994.

Moo, Douglas J. *Galatians*. BECNT. Grand Rapids: Baker, 2013.

Motsch, Wolfgang. "Handlungsstrukturen von Texten." Pages 414–21 in vol. 1 of *Text- und Gesprächslinguistik / Linguistics of Text and Conversation*. Edited by Gerd Antos, Klaus Bringer, Wolfgang Heinemann, and Sven F. Sager. Handbücher zur Sprach und Kommunikationswissenschaft / Handbooks of Linguistics and Communication Science 16. Berlin: de Gruyter, 2000–2001.

Novenson, Matthew V. *Christ among the Messiahs: Christ Language in Paul and Messiah Language in Ancient Judaism*. Oxford: Oxford University Press, 2012.

Oepke, Albrecht. "εἰς." Pages 418–32 in vol. 2 of *Theologisches Wörterbuch zum Neuen Testament*. Edited by Gerhard Kittel and Gerhard Friedrich. 10 volumes. Stuttgart: Kohlhammer, 1932–1979.

Pasch, Renate, Ursula Brauße, Eva Breindl, and Ulrich Hermann Waßner, eds. *Linguistische Grundlagen der Beschreibung und syntaktische Merkmale der deutschen Satzverknüpfer (Konjunktionen, Satzadverbien und Partikeln)*. Vol. 1 of *Handbuch der deutschen Konnektoren*. Schriften des Instituts für Deutsche Sprache 9. Berlin: de Gruyter, 2003.

Petersen, Norman R. *Rediscovering Paul: Philemon and the Sociology of Paul's Narrative World*. Philadelphia: Fortress, 1985.

Powell, Padgett. *The Interrogative Mood: A Novel?* New York: Ecco, 2009.
Prince, Gerald. "The Disnarrated." *Style* 22 (1988): 1–8.
———. *Narratology: The Form and Function of Narrative.* Janua Linguarum: Series Maior 108. Berlin: Mouton, 1982.
Queneau, Raymond. *Exercises in Style.* Translated by Barbara Wright. New York: New Directions, 2013.
Robbe-Grillet, Alain. *Jealousy.* Translated by Richard Howard. New York: Grove, 1957.
Robertson, Archibald T. *A Grammar of the Greek New Testament in the Light of Historical Research.* 3rd ed. London: Hodder & Stoughton, 1919.
Rowland, Robert C. "On Limiting the Narrative Paradigm: Three Case Studies." *Communication Monographs* 56 (1989): 39–54.
Rüggemeier, Jan. *Poetik der markinischen Christologie: Eine kognitiv-narratologische Exegese.* WUNT 2.458. Tübingen: Mohr Siebeck, 2017.
Rüggemeier, Jan, and Elizabeth E. Shively, eds. "Cognitive Linguistics and New Testament Narrative: Investigating Methodology through Characterization." Special issue, *BibInt* 29 (2021).
Ryan, Marie-Laure. "Embedded Narratives and Tellability." *Style* 20 (1986): 319–37.
———. "Narrative." Pages 344–48 in *Routledge Encyclopedia of Narrative Theory.* Edited by David Herman, Manfred Jahn, and Marie-Laure Ryan. London: Routledge, 2005.
———. "Toward a Definition of Narrative." Pages 22–35 in *The Cambridge Companion to Narrative.* Edited by David Herman. Cambridge: Cambridge University Press, 2007.
Schlier, Heinrich. *Der Römerbrief.* HThKNT 6. Freiburg: Herder, 1977.
Schliesser, Benjamin. *Zweifel: Phänomene des Zweifels und der Zweiseeligkeit im frühen Christentum.* WUNT 500. Tübingen: Mohr Siebeck, 2022.
Schmeller, Thomas. *Der zweite Brief an die Korinther.* 2 vols. EKKNT 8. Neukirchen-Vluyn: Neukirchener, 2010, 2015.
Schmidt, Karl Matthias. "Ein Anklang wohnt dem Anfang inne: Die relative Datierung neutestamentlicher Pseudepigraphen im Lichte eines dynamisch veränderten Briefformulars." Pages 79–119 in *Die Datierung neutestamentlicher Pseudepigraphen: Herausforderungen und neuere Lösungsansätze.* Edited by Wolfgang Grünstäudl and Karl Matthias Schmidt. WUNT 470. Tübingen: Mohr Siebeck, 2021.
Schnelle, Udo. *Wandlungen im paulinischen Denken.* SBS 137. Stuttgart: Katholisches Bibelwerk, 1989.
Schrage, Wolfgang. *Der erste Brief an die Korinther.* 4 vols. EKKNT 7. Neukirchen-Vluyn: Neukirchener, 1991–2001.

Bibliography

Schreiner, Thomas R. *Romans*. BECNT. Grand Rapids: Baker Academic, 1998.
Schumann, Elke, Elisabeth Gülich, Gabriele Lucius-Hoene, and Stefan Pfänder, eds. *Wiedererzählen: Formen und Funktionen einer kulturellen Praxis*. Edition Kulturwissenschaft 50. Bielefeld: Transcript, 2015.
Scott, James M. "The Triumph of God in 2 Cor 2.14: Additional Evidence of Merkabah Mysticism in Paul." *NTS* 42 (1996): 260–81.
Smith, Carlota S. *The Parameter of Aspect*. 2nd ed. Studies in Linguistics and Philosophy 43. Dordrecht: Kluwer Academic, 1997.
Talmy, Leonard. *Concept Structuring Systems*. Vol. 1 of *Towards a Cognitive Semantics*. Cambridge: MIT Press, 2000.
Thornton, Claus-Jürgen. *Der Zeuge des Zeugen: Lukas als Historiker der Paulusreisen*. WUNT 56. Tübingen: Mohr Siebeck, 1991.
Vollenweider, Samuel. *Freiheit als neue Schöpfung: Eine Untersuchung zu Eleutheria bei Paulus und in seiner Umwelt*. FRLANT 147. Göttingen: Vandenhoeck & Ruprecht, 1989.
Wallace, Daniel B. *Greek Grammar beyond the Basics: An Exegetical Syntax of the New Testament*. Grand Rapids: Zondervan, 1996.
Wang, Xin. "A Cognitive Pragmatic Study of Rhetorical Questions." *English Language and Literature Studies* 4 (2014): 42–47.
Waßner, Ulrich Hermann. "Faktivität." Pages 137–48 in *Semantik der deutschen Satzverknüpfer*. Edited by Eva Breindl, Anna Volodina, and Ulrich Hermann Waßner. Vol. 2 of *Handbuch der deutschen Konnektoren*. Schriften des Instituts für Deutsche Sprache 13. Berlin: de Gruyter, 2014.
———. "Finale und instrumentale Konnektoren." Pages 1013–60 in *Semantik der deutschen Satzverknüpfer*. Edited by Eva Breindl, Anna Volodina, and Ulrich Hermann Waßner. Vol. 2 of *Handbuch der deutschen Konnektoren*. Schriften des Instituts für Deutsche Sprache 13. Berlin: de Gruyter, 2014.
Watson, Francis C. "Is There a Story in These Texts?" Pages 231–39 in *Narrative Dynamics in Paul: A Critical Assessment*. Edited by Bruce W. Longenecker. Louisville: Westminster John Knox, 2002.
Webb, William J. *Returning Home: New Covenant and Second Exodus as the Context for 2 Corinthians 6.14–7.1*. JSNTSup 85. Sheffield: Sheffield Academic, 1993.
Weber, Alexander. *Episierung und Drama: Ein Beitrag zur transgenerischen Narratologie*. Deutsche Literatur: Studien und Quellen 24. Berlin: de Gruyter, 2017.
Weinrich, Harald. "Narrative Theologie." *Concilium* 9 (1973): 329–34.
Weiser, Alfons. *Der zweite Brief an Timotheus*. EKKNT 16.1. Zurich: Benziger, 2003.
White, Joel R. "N. T. Wright's Narrative Approach." Pages 181–204 in *God and

the Faithfulness of Paul: A Critical Examination of the Pauline Theology of N. T. Wright. Edited by Christoph Heilig, J. Thomas Hewitt, and Michael F. Bird. WUNT 2.413. Tübingen: Mohr Siebeck, 2016.

———. Review of *Paulus als Erzähler?*, by Christoph Heilig. *Jahrbuch für evangelikale Theologie.* April 25, 2021. https://rezensionen.afet.de/?p=1208.

Wilckens, Ulrich. *Der Brief an die Römer.* 3 vols. EKKNT 6. Zurich: Benziger, 1978–1991.

Wilk, Florian. *Die Bedeutung des Jesajabuches für Paulus.* FRLANT 179. Göttingen: Vandenhoeck & Ruprecht, 1998.

Wischmeyer, Oda. "N. T. Wright's Biblical Hermeneutics: Considered from a German Exegetical Perspective." Translated by Wayne Coppins and Christoph Heilig. Pages 73–100 in *God and the Faithfulness of Paul: A Critical Examination of the Pauline Theology of N. T. Wright.* Edited by Christoph Heilig, J. Thomas Hewitt, and Michael F. Bird. WUNT 2.413. Tübingen: Mohr Siebeck, 2016.

Witherington, Ben, III. *Paul's Narrative Thought World: The Tapestry of Tragedy and Triumph.* Louisville: John Knox, 1994.

Wong, Eric Kun Chun. *Evangelien im Dialog mit Paulus: Eine intertextuelle Studie zu den Synoptikern.* SUNT 89. Göttingen: Vandenhoeck & Ruprecht, 2012.

Wright, N. T. "The Challenge of Dialogue: A Partial and Preliminary Response." Pages 711–68 in *God and the Faithfulness of Paul: A Critical Examination of the Pauline Theology of N. T. Wright.* Edited by Christoph Heilig, J. Thomas Hewitt, and Michael F. Bird. WUNT 2.413. Tübingen: Mohr Siebeck, 2016.

———. *The Climax of the Covenant: Christ and the Law in Pauline Theology.* London: T&T Clark, 1991.

———. *Paul: A Biography.* San Francisco: HarperOne, 2018.

———. *Paul and His Recent Interpreters: Some Contemporary Debates.* London: SPCK, 2015.

———. *Paul and the Faithfulness of God.* Vol. 4 of *Christian Origins and the Question of God.* London: SPCK, 2013.

———. *Pauline Perspectives: Essays on Paul 1978–2013.* London: SPCK, 2013.

———. *The New Testament and the People of God.* Vol. 1 of *Christian Origins and the Question of God.* Minneapolis: Fortress, 1992.

Yoon, David I. "Prominence and Markedness in New Testament Discourse: Galatians 1,11–2,10 as a Test Case." *Filología Neotestamentaria* 26 (2013): 3–26.

Zima, Elisabeth. *Einführung in die gebrauchsbasierte Kognitive Linguistik.* Berlin: de Gruyter, 2021.

Index of Authors

Adams, Edward, 4, 8
Allen, Woody, 28
Altman, Janet Gurkin, 180, 198
Arndt, William F., 65–67, 270, 282, 292, 294
Arzt-Grabner, Peter, 178, 280
Aubrey, Michael G., 18, 270
Aubrey, Rachel, 156
Aumüller, Matthias, 173
Austen, Jane, 12

Bache, Carl, 192
Bakker, Mathieu de, 115, 118, 151, 162–63, 225–26, 234, 240, 264, 267, 273
Barclay, John M. G., 8–9, 181, 346–48
Barrett, C. K., 348
Bartolo, Giuseppina di, 304
Bauer, Walter, 65–67, 270, 282, 292, 294
Beard, Mary, 316
Beardslee, William, 6
Berger, Klaus, 172
Berger, Peter, 347
Betz, Hans Dieter, 11
Bird, Michael F., 251–52
Blass, Friedrich, 231
Bollier, David, 345
Bormann, Lukas, 177
Brauße, Ursula, 49
Breindl, Eva, 49, 58, 61, 67, 72, 81, 84, 88, 90, 98, 101–2, 111, 116–17, 128, 135, 210
Breytenbach, Cilliers, 318
Brinker, Klaus, 46

Burton, Ernest D., 260
Buth, Randall, 165

Campbell, Douglas A., 8, 20
Caragounis, Chrys C., 215, 284, 292
Carroll, Noël, 27
Casscells, Ward, 324
Clifton, James, 303
Cranfield, C. E. B., 215, 237
Crites, Stephen, 6
Cullmann, Oscar, 6
Currie, Gregory, 203

Dancygier, Barbara, 342
Danker, Frederick W., 65–67, 270, 282, 292, 294
Darwin, Charles, 201
Debrunner, Albert, 231
Dinkler, Michael Beth, 45, 173
Dodd, C. H., 6
Dragutinović, Predrag, 348
Dunn, James D. G., 75, 311, 354

Einstein, Albert, 201
Emde Boas, Evert van, 115, 118, 151, 162–63, 225–26, 234, 240, 264, 267, 273
Ensor, Jonathan B., 160
Eskola, Timo, 344
Evans, Trevor V., 241

Fee, Gordon D., 95, 178
Finnern, Sönke, 32, 41–42, 209
Fisher, Walter R., 201–3, 341, 344–45
Fresch, Christopher J., 152

373

Index of Authors

Frey, Jörg, ix
Frye, Northrop, 6
Funk, Robert W., 6, 231
Gansel, Christina, 45–46, 166–68, 170, 174, 207
Geertz, Clifford, 347
Genette, Gérard, 34, 36–37, 58, 76, 160–61, 182, 243–44, 312
Georgakopoulou, Alexandra, 181
Gingrich, F. Wilbur, 65–67, 270, 282, 292, 294
Graboys, Thomas B., 324
Greimas, Algirdas Julien, 11, 17, 334
Gülich, Elisabeth, 82–84, 350, 356
Guthrie, George H., 318

Hausendorf, Heiko, 182–84, 350
Hays, Richard B., ix, xiii, 2–11, 14–16, 19, 21, 28, 37, 173, 195, 200–201, 231, 310–13, 316, 318, 323, 331, 334, 348, 354–56, 359
Heilig, Christoph, ix–xii, 2–5, 7, 15, 17–20, 22, 25, 34–35, 37–40, 45, 47–53, 58, 62, 65–66, 68, 70, 73, 79, 82, 84–85, 92–93, 98, 102, 104, 106, 109, 111–12, 115–16, 120, 123, 129, 135, 138, 142, 144, 150–62, 165, 167–69, 172, 174–75, 179–82, 186–87, 189–90, 193–95, 198–99, 201–4, 206, 209–14, 219–22, 224–27, 229–35, 237–48, 251–68, 271, 273, 275–84, 286–88, 290–91, 296, 298, 300–301, 304–7, 310–11, 313–15, 317–18, 320–23, 326, 331, 333–37, 340–41, 343–44, 346, 348–59
Heilig, Theresa, 3, 40, 252, 321
Heller, Vivien, 196, 351
Hemingway, Ernest, 28
Hewitt, J. Thomas, 358
Horrell, David G., 8, 92, 262
Howard, Ellen, xiv
Huitink, Luuk, 115, 118, 151, 162–63, 225–26, 234, 240, 264, 267, 273
Hunt, Cherryl, 92, 262
Hwang, Shin Ja J., 35

Jacobi, Christine, 217
Jones, H. S., 292
Jong, Irene J. F. de, 41

Joss, Matthew B., 44, 321
Joyce, James, 313
Jürgens, Frank, 45–46, 166–68, 170, 174, 207
Kantartzis, Triantafillos, xiv
Käsemann, Ernst, 6, 305
Kindt, Tom, 21–27, 30, 32, 35–37, 40, 112–13, 164–65, 203–7, 210, 315, 338, 341, 343
Köppe, Tilmann, 21–27, 30, 32, 35–37, 40, 112–13, 164–65, 203–7, 210, 315, 338, 341, 343
Kreinecker, Christina M., 278

Lämmert, Eberhard, 243
Lee, Aquila H. I., 358
Lee, Jae Hyun, 173–74
Liddell, Henry G., 292
Löbner, Sebastian, 148–50, 270
Longacre, Robert E., 35
Longenecker, Bruce, 2
Louw, Johannes P., 18–19, 225, 261–63, 275, 277–79, 292
Lucius-Hoene, Gabriele, 356
Luckmann, Thomas, 347

Mann, Thomas, 184
Mauz, Andreas, 344
Mayordomo, Moisés, xiv, 15, 42, 175
Menge, Hermann, 228, 259
Metzger, Bruce M., 215
Moo, Douglas J., 282
Morek, Miriam, 196, 351
Motsch, Wolfgang, 168
Müller, Hans-Harald, 40

Nicklas, Tobias, 348
Nida, Eugene A., 18–19, 225, 261–63, 275, 277–79, 292
Novenson, Matthew V., 358

Oepke, Albrecht, 306

Pasch, Renate, 49
Petersen, Norman R., 6, 202, 340–47, 352
Pfänder, Stefan, 356
Poussin, Nicolas, 303

Index of Authors

Powell, Padgett, 27
Prince, Gerald, 34, 209

Quasthoff, Uta M., 196, 351
Queneau, Raymond, 29, 349

Ravenscroft, Ian, 203
Ricoeur, Paul, 6
Rijksbaron, Albert, 115, 118, 151, 162–63, 225–26, 234, 240, 264, 267, 273
Robbe-Grillet, Alain, 27
Robertson, Archibald T., 159
Rodenbiker, Kelsie G., 348
Rowland, Robert C., 202, 344–45
Rüggemeier, Jan, 32, 42–43, 209, 343
Ryan, Marie-Laure, 20, 203, 209–11, 245, 269, 290, 305

Sanders, E. P., 311
Sanders, James A., 6
Schlier, Heinrich, 250, 288
Schliesser, Benjamin, 214
Schmeller, Thomas, 98, 230, 260
Schmidt, Karl Matthias, 174
Schnelle, Udo, 354
Schoenberger, Arno, 324
Schrage, Wolfgang, 127, 178, 238, 284, 306
Schreiner, Thomas R., 235
Schumann, Elke, 356
Scott, James M., 319–20
Scott, Robert, 292
Shakespeare, William, 338–40
Shively, Elizabeth E., 43
Siebenthal, Heinrich von, 45–49, 52–53, 56, 58, 61–62, 70–73, 77, 81–87, 89–91, 93–95, 98–99, 101–2, 112–19, 121, 123, 125, 128–30, 132–35, 138, 140–41, 152–54, 162, 167–68, 224, 226–27, 231, 233–34, 236, 240–41, 243, 254, 257, 262, 264, 267–68, 270, 273–74, 278–79, 284, 286, 290, 326
Smith, Carlota S., 47, 156
Southgate, Christopher, 92, 262
Sweetser, Eve, 342

Talmy, Leonard, 90
Tatalović, Vladan, 348
Thornton, Claus-Jürgen, 175

Via, Dan, 6
Vollenweider, Samuel, 333
Volodina, Anna, 49

Wallace, Daniel B., 116, 119, 231
Wang, Xin, 227
Waßner, Ulrich Hermann, 49, 111, 117, 119
Watson, Francis C., 12
Webb, William J., 319–20
Weber, Alexander, 338
Weinrich, Harald, 244, 344
Weiser, Alfons, 136
White, Joel R., 15–16, 343–44
Wilckens, Ulrich, 216, 252, 288
Wilder, Amos, 6
Wilk, Florian, 248
Wischmeyer, Oda, 333
Witherington, Ben, III, 8
Wöllstein, Angelika, 71, 116, 124, 128
Wong, Eric Kun Chun, 169
Wright, N. T., ix, xiii, 2–3, 5–9, 11–16, 21, 200–202, 252, 310–12, 321, 323, 329–40, 343–44, 346–49, 351–59

Yoon, David I., 51

Zima, Elisabeth, 208

Index of Subjects

abduction, 321
Abraham, 11, 71, 137, 294, 317, 348–49, 357
action. *See* plot
Adam, 230, 327, 348–49
adverbs. *See* connections
Aktionsart. See situation types
analepsis, 38–39, 57, 100, 109–10, 120, 134, 196, 231–32, 246–51, 278, 280, 283–84, 339, 349
arc of suspense, 25, 37, 185, 190–97, 206, 232, 250, 338–39, 345, 350. *See also* epilogue
argumentation, 10–11, 53, 169–75, 194, 313, 316–17
artificial intelligence, xiv–xv
aspect, 38, 54, 65–68, 72, 87–91, 92–94, 97, 106, 156–60, 268–72, 277, 290, 315
assertion. *See* communicative function
authorial intention, 23, 40, 45, 147, 202–8, 340–45, 352
autobiography, 106, 346. *See also* narrating/narrated "I"

baptism, 86, 119, 132, 195, 221, 228–29, 269, 289–90, 331–33
base narrative, 38–39, 246. *See also* analepsis; prolepsis
Bayesian confirmation theory, 320–34

canon, xiv, 169–75
chiasm, 110
Christ. *See* messiah
churches, 95, 110, 198–99, 227–29, 263, 283–86, 346–48, 355. *See also* pragmatics
clause types
    declarative, 161–62, 224–26, 253–64. *See also* fear clause
    definitions, 161–62, 286–87
    desiderative, 161–62, 227, 233–40, 235, 263, 267–86
    interrogative, 161–62, 226–29, 257, 265–67, 293–300
close reading, 41
cognitive linguistics, 52, 148, 208. *See also* cognitive narratology; conceptualization; information structure; viewpoint
cognitive narratology, 41–44, 52
comedy. *See* movies; plays, literature
communicative function, 46–47, 95, 113, 150–52, 162, 173, 178, 193, 226, 231, 246, 251, 267, 273, 275, 286. *See also* pragmatics
communicative weight. *See* information structure
conceptualization, 32, 156. *See also* focalization
connections
    additive, 128–32
    adversative, 48, 105–7, 109, 128–32, 210–14
    causal, 47, 50, 107–8, 112–14, 138–42
    concessive, 106, 124–28, 134
    conditional, 98, 111–12, 217, 222–24, 229–39, 286–304
    consequential, 114, 85

Index of Subjects

definition, 47
explanatory, 133–35
modal-instrumental, 107, 115–22
purpose-oriented, 50, 107–8, 116, 122–24, 304–9
restrictive, 132–33, 221–22
sequential, 55–80
simultaneous, 50, 58, 80–111
connector. *See* connections
conversation, 182–97, 208, 236, 291–92, 349–50, 301
creation, 71, 77, 92, 100, 183, 262, 332, 336–40, 348, 353, 357–58

definitions, 8–9, 17–54, 163–66, 200–208
deictic center, 34–35, 159–60, 240–42
description, 23, 27, 40–45, 51, 85, 94, 110, 134–35, 171–72, 194–96, 280, 313, 316–17, 326, 338, 352–53. *See also* narrative pause
discourse, 28, 54, 203
discourse markers, 129–30, 141, 152, 193, 326, 349–50
disnarration
corrective, 221–24
definition, 208–10
gradual, 224–33
partial, 219–20
presuppositional, 233–39
and protonarratives, 210–18
supplementary, 220–21
distance. *See* vividness
directive. *See* clause types: desiderative; communicative function
drama. *See* plays, literature

ellipsis, 37, 39, 179–81, 209, 244, 251, 335
embedded narratives. *See* narrative levels
epilogue, 142, 252, 345
epistemic mode, 47, 113–14, 150–51, 167, 173, 225–26, 231, 234, 267
epistolary aorist, 158, 198, 240–41, 281
epistolary perfect, 241
epitexts, 182–83
eschatology. *See* foreshadowing; narration types: predictive/prior narration; prolepsis

ethics of narration, 299, 304
Eucharist, 59, 74, 95, 237, 284
evaluation. *See* communicative function
event, 22. *See also* situation types
event bundle, 38, 85, 90–98, 117–18, 212–13, 224, 237, 252, 254, 286
eventfulness, 25, 155–56
exegesis, 39–45
exodus, 59, 114, 181, 189, 193, 319–20, 330–34, 349, 354–55
explication, 171

factuality, 12, 30–32, 112, 163, 211, 229, 285. *See also* disnarration
fear clause, 225, 234, 260, 264, 292–95, 307
fictionality, 12, 28, 30–32, 101, 180, 182, 198, 291, 301, 318, 342
figure/ground. *See* information structure
flashback. *See* analepsis
flash fiction, 28
focalization, xiv, 32–34, 36–37, 108, 110, 114, 126–27, 157–59, 193, 218, 228, 262, 265, 272, 297, 328, 342–43
focus/background. *See* information structure
foreshadowing, 39, 242–309, 339
frame narrative. *See* narrative levels
frequency, 37
function. *See* communicative function
future. *See* foreshadowing; narration types: predictive/prior narration; prolepsis; tense

genre, 1, 14, 31, 166, 169–75, 190, 209. *See also* Gospels
gospel, 3–4, 13, 100–101, 107–10, 118, 132–33, 144, 185, 215–18, 231–32, 247, 307, 354
Gospels, xiv, 1, 20, 58, 77, 94, 169–75, 282, 343. *See also* genre
Greek terms and phrases
ἀλλά, 128–32, 210–14
ἅμα, 85–86
ἀπό, 100
ἀφ' ἧς, 100
ἀφ' οὗ, 100

377

Index of Subjects

ἄχρι[ς], 74–76, 102, 104–11, 161
βουλεύομαι, 263
βούλομαι, 263, 273, 275
γάρ, 112–14
γινώσκω, 256
δέ, 130, 141, 152
δῆλον, 255
διὰ τοῦτο, 285
διά, 107
διατάσσω, 282
δοκέω, 225
ἐὰν καί, 125
ἐάν, 112, 222–24, 258–59, 263, 300–304
εἰ καί, 125
εἰ μήτι, 233
εἰ, 112, 229–31, 234–39, 286–301
εἰς, 75, 78
εἶτα, 59
ἐκτός, 232
ἐλπίς/ἐλπίζω, 262–63
ἐν, 86–87, 120
ἐξ οὗ, 100
ἐπεί, 296
ἔπειτα, 59
ἐπιθυμία, 263
ἐπιποθέω, 263
ἐπιτάσσω, 280–82
ἐφ᾽ ὅσον, 102–4
ἕως, 69–73, 97, 102
η, 284
ἡνίκα, 95–98
θέλω, 275–77
θριαμβεύω, 314–16, 317–26
ἵνα, 122–24, 161, 304–9
καθώς, 135–37, 278
καί τότε, 58
καί, 48–49, 128–29, 133, 138–40, 142
καίτοιγε, 132
λογίζομαι, 262
μᾶλλον δέ, 222, 351
μετά, 69
μέχρι[ς], 74
μή (πως). *See* fear clause
μόλις, 224
μόνον, 220

νῦν/νυνί, 104–11
οἶδα, 256
οἷον, 135
ὃν τρόπον, 136
ὅπως, 122–24, 304–9
ὅς, ἥ, ὅ, 110, 133–35
ὅταν, 68–69, 74, 82–83, 87–91, 94–95, 258
ὅτε, 65–68, 78–79, 87, 94, 106
ὅτι, 112–14
οὐδέ/οὔτε, 212
οὕτως, 135–37
πάντοτε, 91
παραγγέλλω, 274–75, 278, 282–86
παρακαλέω, 277–83
πέπεισμαι, 261
πεποίθα, 263
πιστεύω, 261
πότε, 104–11
πρίν, 69–73
πρό, 69–73, 77–88
προσεύχομαι, 278–79
προτίθημι, 263
τάχα, 224
τότε, 58, 80
φοβέομαι. *See* fear clause
ὥστε, 115

hermeneutical spiral, 322
historical-critical method, 45
historical perfect, 159–60
historical present, 34–35, 158–59
hypertextuality, 312–17
hypotheses. *See* Bayesian confirmation theory

iconicity, 56–57, 61, 64, 67–69, 76, 79, 84, 104–10, 115
illocution, 150, 152, 162, 167–68, 182, 226. *See also* communicative function
imperative, 69, 85, 109, 146, 161, 190, 193, 255, 268–72, 274–75, 281, 286, 289–90, 305, 317. *See also* clause types: desiderative
infinitive, 47, 60, 72, 77, 79, 86–87, 97,

Index of Subjects

107, 115, 123, 160, 162–66, 247, 258–64, 273–77, 280, 286
information. *See* communicative function
information structure, 49–51, 62–65, 77–79, 84, 102, 127–28, 279, 291, 330, 344
interpretation. *See* exegesis; plot; theme; topic
intertextuality, 7, 254, 312–13, 322–23. *See also* hypertextuality
Israel, 8, 96–98, 107, 114, 215, 237, 299, 337, 346–48, 353–54, 357–58
iterative narration, 38. *See also* event bundle

law. *See* Torah
letter, 31, 169–75, 179–81
linearization, 64, 67–69, 84, 86–87, 90
literariness, 27–28, 45, 165, 170, 180, 187
literary unity, 31, 180, 314–16

macroproposition, 49–50, 145–52. *See also* connections
markedness, 51, 71, 76–78, 81, 84, 91, 100, 155, 264, 268
meaning, 145–52. *See also* proposition
messiah, 74–75, 106, 120–21, 132, 176–78, 184, 189, 191–97, 205, 222, 227–33, 242, 246–50, 264, 267, 269, 272, 288–89, 308, 315–17, 326–30, 335, 337–40, 348, 353, 357–58, 359
metanarrative comments, 128, 132–33, 146, 199, 220–21. *See also* utterance relatedness
methodology, 3. *See also* exegesis; narratology; text grammar
middle. *See* voice
mindset, 6, 311
modern Greek, 90, 181, 191, 240, 294
mood, 36, 47, 157, 160–62, 258, 264. *See also* subjunctive
Moses, 96–97, 136, 319, 348
movies, 24, 28, 206, 338, 341

narrating/narrated "I," 33–34, 187, 199, 218, 243, 247–49

narration. *See* narrating/narrated "I"; narration types; unreliable narration
narration-specific tasks, 182–97
 predictive/prior narration, 35–36, 39, 58, 68, 69, 73–74, 83, 196, 242–56. *See also* foreshadowing
 simultaneous narration, 34–35, 158–59
 subsequent narration, 34–35, 58, 158
 thematization, 143–44, 184–90, 350–51. *See also* theme
narration types
 concluding narration and moving on, 143–44, 190–97, 350
 in general, 182–83, 351
 interpolated narration, 34, 159–70, 199
 motivating narration, 13, 183–84, 325
narrative approach, xiii–xiv, 1–17. *See also* narrative substructures; worldview narratives
narrative characters/figures, 29–31, 33, 43, 48, 110, 114, 120–21, 127, 136, 143, 158–59, 176–77, 187, 197, 199, 209–10, 218, 222–23, 225, 229–30, 232, 241, 243, 247–49, 253, 256, 262–63, 272, 284–85, 288, 296–300, 305, 308, 313, 315–17, 319, 326–337, 348–52, 355
narrative levels, 31–32, 110, 132, 136, 188, 198–99, 205, 209–10, 227–29, 241, 243, 246, 259, 305–6, 336–39, 349. *See also* virtual narratives
narrative paradigm, 201–2, 341, 344–45
narrative pause, 27, 37, 194. *See also* description
narrative perspective. *See* focalization
narrative substructures, 3–5, 7, 10–11, 195, 201–2, 231, 310–34
narrative theology, 244, 343–44, 358
narrative theory. *See* narratology
narrative world, 6, 30, 32, 39, 78, 101, 120, 146, 192–95, 199, 218, 266, 313, 330, 343, 350
narrativity, 21–28
narratologies, 17
narratology, 8–9, 15, 17–54
narrator, 31

379

Index of Subjects

negation, 161. *See also* disnarration
new perspective, 75, 79, 311

one-liner, 28
optative, 93, 161, 224, 273–74
order, 23, 38–39, 55–111

parallels, 333
participles, 47–48, 60, 67–68, 85, 94, 100, 103, 106, 110–11, 116–20, 126–27, 141, 159, 162–66, 192, 218, 222, 234, 235, 238, 247–50, 259–60, 280, 284–89, 307
passive. *See* voice
peritexts, 182
plays, literature, 12, 313, 336–40
plot, 22, 29–30, 40, 45, 96, 107–8, 110, 116, 121, 132, 137–39, 142–43, 148, 180, 182, 185–87, 192, 197, 199, 201, 206–7, 210–18, 227, 230–33, 237, 244, 246–47, 249–53, 256, 265–66, 268–72, 282–99, 306–9, 312–13, 316, 326–31, 336–40, 345, 351–58
pragmatics, 46, 95, 107–8, 144–52, 162–99, 227, 290, 315–16. *See also* communicative function
prepositions, 48, 60, 64, 69, 74–75, 77–79, 84, 86–87, 94, 100, 318
probability. *See* Bayesian confirmation theory
prognosis. *See* foreshadowing; prophecy; virtual narratives
prolepsis, 38–39, 242–53
prophecy, 35, 244, 248, 254, 319, 331
proposition, 47–48, 145–52. *See also* connections
protonarratives, 202–8. *See also* disnarration; foreshadowing; narrative substructures; worldview narratives
pseudepigraphy, 30–31, 101, 136, 174, 278. *See also* secretary

questions, 27, 65. *See also* clause types: interrogative

reader-response criticism, 42, 147, 168, 204–5, 303

reception. *See* reader-response criticism
renarration, 37, 59, 119, 181, 196–97, 208, 227, 239, 284, 307, 329, 349–59
repetitive narration, 37–39, 79, 109–10, 116, 121, 196, 244, 265, 349–59
reported speech, 31, 228, 241–42, 274–75
rhetorical narratology, 173

secretary, 89, 186, 222, 259
semantics. *See* meaning
simulation, 203–4, 315. *See also* protonarratives
sin, 87, 106, 177, 269, 273, 289–90, 332, 338, 357–58
situation. *See* event
situation types, 70–73, 80, 83, 88, 92, 99, 118, 154–56, 158, 269–71, 277
slavery. *See* exodus; secretary
speech act, 4, 31, 47, 113, 130, 151, 162, 167–78, 193, 198, 205, 207, 227, 241, 242, 266–67, 271, 273, 275, 277, 278–80, 282–83, 302, 326. *See also* communicative function; utterance relatedness
speed, 37, 78. *See also* summary
Spirit, 359
story, 18, 28
storyline. *See* plot
storyteller, 31
story world. *See* narrative world
structuralism, xiii, 11, 17–18, 41–42, 173, 334
subjunctive, 51, 82–83, 87–90, 94, 103, 160–61, 163, 215, 218, 249, 258, 264–73, 292–94, 305
summary, 37, 121, 158, 181, 192–93, 212, 302, 335

telicity. *See* connections: purpose-oriented; situation types
tellability, 25, 340
tense, 34, 157–60, 253–65. *See also* mood; narration types
text function, 172–75. *See also* communicative function
text grammar, 45–54, 144–52

Index of Subjects

text linguistics, 45–54
text production strategy, 172–75. *See also* argumentation; description; explication
text sort, 170–77, 191, 195
text type, 171–73, 179
textuality, 4–8, 24, 26, 45–54, 203
theme, 30, 143–44, 171, 182, 185–88, 191, 193, 211, 339, 348. *See also* narration types: thematization
theory, 3, 40–45
topic, 29–30, 51, 137, 143, 171, 183–85, 188, 205, 265, 299, 325, 332, 347
Torah, 11, 75–78, 103, 105, 174, 255, 273, 282, 332, 332
traditions, 59, 217, 284, 329, 335, 356. *See also* Eucharist; exodus

unreliable narration, xi, 32, 68, 92, 124–25, 128, 132, 176, 187, 220–25, 239, 244, 284, 291, 300–304, 351
utterance relatedness, 113, 130, 132–33, 135, 146, 150, 152, 191–92, 198, 221, 227, 246, 271, 288, 291, 306

viewpoint, 342. *See also* focalization
virtual narratives, 209–11, 245, 263, 269, 290, 305–6, 313
vividness, 36–37, 78, 105, 131–32, 158, 176, 181, 189, 228, 251, 276–78, 299, 335
voice, 100, 156–57, 248

wishes. *See* clause types: desiderative
world knowledge, 62, 127, 141, 180–81
worldview narratives, 5–7, 12–17, 201–2, 310–12, 334–59

Index of Scripture and Other Ancient Sources

Old Testament

Genesis
15:6	137
18:10	254
18:14	254
25:23	254

Exodus
4:10	319
7:11	136
12–24	333–34, 354–55
25	181, 354–55
34:24	97
34:34	96–97
34:35	97

Leviticus
10:9	97
22:16	87

Deuteronomy
28:65	274

Judges
13:23	301

1 Kings
19	335
19:8	335

2 Kings
4:40	87

Psalms
8	338
50:18 LXX	301
57:10 LXX	72
67:18–19 LXX	319
109 LXX	337

Proverbs
25:21–22	300

Isaiah
10:22–23	254
23:8	71
45:22	305
52:7	215, 219
52:15	247

Ezekiel
1	319
21:32(37)	274

Hosea
2:1	254
2:25	254

Joel
3:5	215

Habakkuk
2:4	255

Haggai
2:16	93

Deutero-canonical Books

Wisdom of Solomon 181

Ancient Jewish Writers

Josephus

Jewish War
4.249	282

Philo

On the Special Laws 2.79

New Testament

Matthew 58–59, 77, 80, 94, 145, 169–70, 282
6:8	79
6:16	94
9:25	65–67
13:10–11	65
13:45–46	138–42
25:25–46	242
27:12	86

Mark 58, 77, 94, 169–70, 282
3:11	94
6:8	274–75

Index of Scripture and Other Ancient Sources

11:19	94	**Romans**	290, 301	6:3–13	289–98
14:30	71	1:1	218	6:4	159, 269
16:6	159	1:4	100	6:6	255, 269
16:11	159	1:10	262	6:8	229, 261
16:14	159	1:11	263	6:13–19	268–71
		1:13	263, 276	6:15	266, 273–74
Luke	31, 58, 77, 86, 94,	1:15	263	6:17–18	331
	169–70, 282	1:20	99, 156	6:20	87
1:1–4	31	1:21	213	7:1–2	103–4
2:21	79	1:27	117	7:1–8:11	12, 332
2:27	86	1:32	125–26, 220	7:2	104
3:21	86	2:4	235	7:2–3	300
7:29–30	119	2:6	254	7:5	87, 300
7:47	114	2:12	287	7:7	257, 266, 273
9:3	274	2:13	287	7:7–25	266–67
9:34	86	2:14	94–95	7:9	105–6
15:13	119	2:16	87	7:13	273
22:15	79	2:25–26	300	7:21	276
22:20	69	2:26	266	8:3–4	11
		2:27	287	8:9	233, 296
		3:3	230, 266	8:9–13	290
John	58, 77, 94, 169–70,	3:5	257, 266	8:12–17	332
	282	3:7	229	8:15	220
1:3	71	3:8	266, 305	8:19–23	262
1:14	71	3:20	254	8:22	92
4:1–3	132	3:30	233	8:23	92–93
4:49	79	4	349	8:31	257, 266
8:58	71	4:1	257, 266	8:32	211, 266
16:30	123	4:2	229, 294	8:33–35	267
17:5	71–72, 79	4:9–12	354	8:34	221–22
		4:18	254	8:38–39	261
		4:20	213–14	9–11	346, 354
Acts	31, 58, 77, 86,	4:23–24	221	9:3	273
	169–70, 282	5	349	9:6–10:21	12
8:40	97	5:5–10	184	9:9	254
9:22	214	5:7	224	9:11–12	68
10	79	5:8–10	289	9:12	254
11:4–17	31	5:9	254	9:14	257, 266
15:27	35, 241	5:10	229–31	9:16–22	234–37
18:2	282	5:15	230	9:17–19	197
20:7	48–50, 149–50	5:17	229–30, 289	9:20	266
23:31	282	5:19	254	9:21–23	293
24:23	282	5:20	161	9:22–30	229
27:20	97	6	269, 333	9:25–28	254
27:40	97	6–8	330–34, 349	9:29	234
27:41	117	6:1	257, 266, 305	9:30	257, 266
		6:2	266, 273–74	10:9	300

383

Index of Scripture and Other Ancient Sources

10:10–19	214–19	**1 Corinthians**	82, 191, 282	11:2	283
10:11	254	1:4–9	191–93, 196–97	11:7	279
10:14	292	1:10	277–78	11:17–33	237–39, 283–86
10:14–15	266	1:10–15	227–29	11:21	86–87
10:18	226	1:14–16	221	11:22	306
11:1	273	2:5–8	239	11:24	59, 67–68
11:11	108, 273	2:8	157	11:25	69, 95
11:14	262	3:4	94–95	11:26	74, 95
11:16	299	3:14–15	287	11:31	301
11:17–18	230	3:18	261	11:32	306–7
11:17–24	290–300, 356	4:5	74	11:34	95, 282, 305–6
11:19	197	4:7	229	12:1	276
11:21	229	4:9	225, 229	12:2	87, 94
11:22	296	4:11	229	12:11	275
11:24	229	4:16	275	13:3	215, 305
11:25	74, 276	5:10	233	13:10	82
11:26	254	6:2	256	13:11	87
11:30–37	106–9	6:3	256	13:35	257
12:1	277	6:5	257	14:5	235, 276
12:19	254	6:9–10	256	14:13	279
12:20	300	6:12	257	14:19	276
13:1–7	322	7:7	276	14:26	95
13:2–4	287	7:10	220, 282–83	14:34	279
13:3	264, 275–76	7:17	282	14:35	276
13:3–14	317	7:18–20	220	14:37	261
13:4	264	7:32	276	15	74, 159, 337
13:5	221	7:36	261	15:1–2	231–32
13:9	271	7:39	104	15:4	74
13:11–14	271–73, 317	7:40	261	15:5–7	59
14:2	261	8:2	261	15:10	211–12, 219–20
14:4	254	8:9	264	15:20	74
14:8	300	8:10–11	120–22	15:23–24	59
14:10	254	8:10–13	176–79	15:24	74, 82, 88–91
14:11	254–55, 305	8:11	317	15:25	74
14:12	254	8:13	305	15:27	82, 255
15:3	274	9:14	282	15:28	82, 305
15:13	274	9:15	257	15:32	229
15:16–17	246	9:19	126–27	15:54	82
15:18–32	38–39, 245–53	9:24	305	16:1	282
15:24	263, 300	10:1	276, 354–55	16:2–8	258–62
15:27	229	10:1–6	189	16:3	82
15:30	277, 309	10:2	333	16:5	68–69, 82
16:17	275, 277	10:5	114	16:7	262–63, 276
16:19	276	10:6–12	193	16:12	82, 277
16:20	254	10:8–10	59		
		10:21–11:1	178	**2 Corinthians**	314–16
		10:27	276	1–7	316

Index of Scripture and Other Ancient Sources

1–9	180	11:9	257	1:16	51, 180, 335
1:8	115, 189, 276	11:10	255	1:16–17	212
1:8–9	33–34, 159–60, 194	11:16	223, 301	1:16–19	220
1:9	159–60	11:18	257	1:17	83, 129, 335
1:10	262–63	11:25	159	1:18	59, 123, 180, 245, 307
1:13	262–63	11:30	223	1:19–21	133–34
1:15	275	11:33	59	1:20	198–99
1:15–17	260, 263	12:1	257	1:21	37, 59, 181
1:15–22	257–58	12:1–6	31, 59, 184–88, 198, 300–304	1:21–23	110
1:16	315			1:21–2:1	181
1:17	275, 315	12:2	225	1:23	134–35
2:3	233	12:3	225	2:1	59, 181
2:8	277	12:4	59, 209	2:1–10	144
2:12–14	314–16	12:5	257	2:2	243
2:13	67–68, 159, 163–64, 245, 260, 349	12:5–6	222–24	2:3	125
		12:6	276, 300	2:4–5	243
2:13–7:5	37	12:7–9	186	2:11	67
2:14	301	12:8	179	2:12	67, 77–79, 264
2:14–17	318–20	12:9	159	2:13	115
2:14–7:4	314, 316	12:10	94–95, 223, 302	2:14	67, 158, 229
2:20	265	12:11	233	2:16–17	180, 243
3	319	12:14	257, 279	2:17	229
3:7–8	230	12:15	257	2:20	220
3:15–16	95–98	12:17	35	2:21	230
5:2	92, 263	12:19	158–59	3	317, 353
5:4	276	13:2	260	3–4	10, 11
5:14–17	192–93	13:5	232–33	3:1–5	11, 137, 144, 199
5:17	194, 229	13:6	262–63	3:1–4:11	3
6:1	277	13:9	94–95	3:4	230
7:5	159, 162, 349			3:6	137, 199
7:5–6	260	**Galatians**	121–22, 144, 157, 199, 276, 307	3:6–14	11
7:5–7	314			3:8	247–48, 347
7:7	221	1–2	12, 346	3:11	255
7:8	229	1:3	357–58	3:13–14	10, 37, 313
7:9	220	1:4	123, 181, 307, 357–59	3:15–17	354
7:14	230	1:6	133, 188, 199	3:15–18	11
8:5	220	1:7	121–22, 132–33, 221, 276–77	3:16	75, 347
8:6	277			3:19	75–76, 161, 282
8:21	221	1:10	234, 239, 301	3:21	234
9:12	220	1:10–12	144	3:22	347
9:14	263	1:12	144, 185	3:23	75, 77–78, 134, 347
10–13	180	1:13	110, 134, 189	3:24	75, 347
10:3	125, 127–28	1:13–17	130, 142–44	3:25	68, 78, 347
10:6	83	1:13–2:21	59, 67, 143–44	3:26–29	316–17
10:13	257	1:14	134, 335	3:26–4:11	11
11:2–3	264–65, 307	1:15	100	3:27–28	194–95
11:4	230	1:15–17	185	3:28	347

385

Index of Scripture and Other Ancient Sources

4:1–2	313	5:2	136–37	3:4	82
4:1–7	104	5:3	256	3:6–8	109
4:3	87	5:8	109	3:7	68, 87
4:3–6	10, 37, 313, 451	6:19	279	3:10	75
4:3–7	313	6:22	35, 241	3:24	255–56
4:4	67			4:2–3	85
4:8	350	**Philippians**		4:3	252
4:8–9	451	1:6	263	4:8	35, 241
4:8–12	351	1:7	135	4:16	30, 82
4:9	121–22, 221–22, 351	1:8	263		
4:9–11	351	1:9	279	**1 Thessalonians**	
4:11	225	1:12	275	1:5	221
4:12	275	1:15	67	1:8	221
4:12–14	132	1:20	262	1:10	82
4:12–19	346	1:23	263	2:1	211–12
4:12–20	11	1:25	255–56	2:5–7	126–27, 214
4:13	102	1:29–30	220–21	2:9	117, 190
4:14	214	1:30	135	2:12	277
4:15	117, 230, 234	2:2–13	326–30	2:13	276
4:15–16	346	2:6–7	213	2:16	235
4:17	121–22	2:6–11	4, 10, 12, 313, 326–30	2:17	263
4:18	86			2:19	284
4:19	74	2:9–11	305	3:4	87
4:21	121–22	2:14–16	242	3:5–6	225–26
4:21–31	11, 174	2:16	232, 328	3:6	263
4:25	335	2:19	262–63	3:11	274
4:30–31	193	2:23	262–63	4:1	278
5:10	263	2:24	263	4:10	277
5:17	161	2:25	189	4:11–12	282–83
6:3	261	2:26	263	4:13	276
6:9	287	2:28	35, 241	4:13–18	188
6:10	104	3:1–2	180	4:14	231
6:12–13	121–22	3:2–11	12	4:15	75
6:13	276–77	4:2	277	5:3	87–88, 94
6:16	347	4:3	278	5:12	278
		4:15	67	5:25	252
Ephesians	174–75				
1:4	77	**Colossians**	30, 174–75	**2 Thessalonians**	174–75
1:11–13	106	1:6–9	100–101, 178–79, 181	1:6	233
2:1–5	109			1:11	279
2:11–13	110–11	1:9	279	2:1	289
4:1	277	1:20–22	106–7, 181	2:5	190
4:13	74	2:15	315	2:7	73–74
4:20–21	230	2:20	229	2:8	58
4:21	190	3:1	230	3	282

386

3:1	252, 279	4:10–11	213	Shepherd of Hermas, Similitudes	
3:4	263, 282	4:17	83	78.2 (9.1)	214
3:6	282			86.2 (9.9)	302
3:7–8	212	**Titus**	174–75		
3:8	117–19	1:5	282	**GRECO-ROMAN LITERATURE**	
3:10	87, 276, 282	2:6	277		
3:12	278, 282	3:3–5	105–6		
		3:4	67	**Demosthenes**	
1 Timothy	174–75, 282	3:8	275	*4 Philippic*	
1:3	277, 282	3:10	69	62	296
1:7	276	3:12	82–83		
2:1	277			**Diodorus Siculus**	
2:4	276	**Philemon**	341–43	*Library of History*	
2:8	275	4	93	13.34.6	282
2:12	279	8	85		
3:14–15	262–63	8–17	280–82	**Hesiod**	
4:6	287	12	35, 241	*Works and Days*	
4:11	282	13	85, 273, 275	277	282
4:13	103	13–17	307–9		
4:16	287	14	275–76	**Homer**	
5:7	282	18	230	*Odyssey*	313
5:9–10	230	21	255–56, 262–63		
5:10–13	85	21–22	85–86	**Thucydides**	
5:11	83, 276			*History of the Peloponnesian War*	175
5:13	221	**Hebrews**		1.10.1	232
5:14	275	13:22	275		
5:21	279			**Vergil**	
6:8	287	**Revelation**		*Aeneid*	313
6:9	275–76	6:4	235		
6:13	282	11:6	95	**OTHER ANCIENT SOURCES**	
6:13–14	74–75				
6:17	282	**EARLY CHRISTIAN LITERATURE**			
				BGU	
2 Timothy	174–75			1.37	342
1:3	95	**Gospel of Nicodemus**	xiv		
1:4	263			**Codex Boernerianus**	292
1:12	261	**John Chrysostom**			
1:16–17	212–13	*Homilies on Romans*		P[46]	215
2:11	229	19	293		
2:11–13	287				
2:25	260, 264				
3:1	255–56				
3:8	135–37				
4:3	87				